Praise for Shakespeare and the Stars

"The truth is now obvious: Shakespeare's worldview was essentially identical with the occult philosophy of the Renaissance. Anyone who doubts this fact should read this exciting, revelatory, and authoritative new book. It will help you understand Shakespeare in a totally fresh and insightful way."

> —Richard Smoley, author of *Inner Christianity: A Guide to the Esoteric Tradition*

A book that will carry you beyond the stars into the heart of the cosmos. In *Shakespeare and the Stars*, Priscilla Costello recreates the ancient cosmological view of the heavens, infuses it with elements of the western mystery tradition that pose the interconnectedness of above and below where the mythic attributes of planetary deities are the archetypes for human personality.

Then through this profound philosophical lens, she looks at six of Shakespeare's plays with meticulous precision, offering the secret key to unlock the deeper significance of his work.

This book is much more than a new analysis of Shakespeare's work; it is an illumination of the cosmic vision that informed his creative outpouring.

> —Demetra George, M.A., author of *Astrology for Yourself*

In this extraordinary book Priscilla Costello brings a new and surprising perspective to our reading of Shakespeare. We discover the eternal symbols and archetypes in his characters and plays seen through the lens of astrological signs and planets. In turn, astrology is similarly enriched by the master of Western literature where his creative genius gives life, story and character to the planets and signs.

> —Ami Ronnberg, Director and Head Curator, Archive for Research in Archetypal Symbolism (ARAS) at the C. G. Jung Center in New York City

This wonderful book brings together everything I have ever held dear in life. Priscilla Costello's profound study is a substantial, scholarly work that is also completely accessible. The author knows her subject inside out and—even more importantly—she has the ability to convey her knowledge in a way that is constantly stimulating for her readers. We are both educated and entertained.

This book inspires me to re-visit the plays, especially the ones she has analysed in depth. Having absorbed this superb study of Shakespeare's world, I feel armed with fresh insights, and will experience his plays in an entirely new way. Riches lie in store. Four hundred years on, Shakespeare himself would be applauding.

> —Lindsay Radermacher, MA Oxon (English), MPhil, professional astrologer (DFAstrol S.), Trustee of the Sophia and Urania Trusts

Priscilla Costello's groundbreaking book *Shakespeare and the Stars* will finally put to rest the question as to whether the greatest playwright who ever lived consciously alluded to astrology throughout his writings. The detailed and thoroughly researched examples that Costello provides will leave no doubt that the Bard utilized astrology to show how the fate of humankind is left less to chance than we would like to believe.

Costello's knowledge and love of both astrology and Shakespeare make this book a classic which, like the Bard's plays, will be read and re-read for years to come.

> —Ronnie Gale Dreyer, M.A., author of *Vedic Astrology and Venus*

Shakespeare and the Stars

*The Hidden Astrological Keys to
Understanding the World's
Greatest Playwright*

LINES FROM THE BARD

... a good heart, Kate, is the *sun* and the *moon*; or rather the *sun* and not *moon*; for it shines bright and never changes, but keeps his course truly.
— Henry V to Princess Katharine of France (*Henry V*: V, ii, 156–9)

It is the very error of the *moon*:
She comes more nearer earth than she was wont,
And makes men mad. — (*Othello*: V, ii, 118–20)

I know thy *constellation* is right apt
For this affair. — (*Twelfth Night*: I, iv, 34–5)

It is the *stars*,
The *stars* above us, govern our conditions;
Else one self mate and make could not beget
Such different issues. — (*King Lear*: IV, iii, 31–4)

... there was a *star* danced, and under that was I born.
— (*Much Ado About Nothing*: II, i, 293–4)

Comets, importing change of times and states,
Brandish your crystal tresses in the sky ...
— (*I Henry VI*: I, i, 2–3)

But when the *planets*
In evil mixture to disorder wander,
What plagues and what portents, what mutiny?
What raging of the sea! shaking of earth?
— (*Troilus and Cressida*: I, iii, 94–7)

There is a tide in the affairs of men
Which, taken at the flood, leads on to fortune;
Omitted, all the voyage of their life
Is bound in shallows and in miseries.
On such a full sea are we now afloat,
And we must take the current when it serves
Or lose our ventures. — (*Julius Caesar*: IV, ii, 270–6)

Shakespeare and the Stars

The Hidden Astrological Keys to Understanding the World's Greatest Playwright

PRISCILLA COSTELLO, M.A.

Great works of literature arc like stars; they stay put,
even as we draw them into new constellations.

—Adam Kirsch[1]

IBIS PRESS
Lake Worth, FL

Published in 2016 by Ibis Press
A division of Nicolas-Hays, Inc.
P. O. Box 540206
Lake Worth, FL 33454-0206
www.ibispress.net

Distributed to the trade by
Red Wheel/Weiser, LLC
65 Parker St. • Ste. 7
Newburyport, MA 01950
www.redwheelweiser.com

ISBN 978-0-89254-216-1
Ebook: ISBN 978-0-89254-631-2

Library of Congress Cataloging-in-Publication Data
Available upon request

Book design and production by STUDIO 31
www.studio31.com

Cover painting: the Cobbe portrait, ca. 1610
Smile retouch by Mimi Alonzo
Cover design by STUDIO 31

Printed in the United States of America
[MG]

Table of Contents:

INTRODUCTION

> ... by my prescience
> I find my zenith doth depend upon
> A *most auspicious star*, whose influence
> If now I court not, but omit, my fortunes
> Will ever after droop.
> —Prospero (*The Tempest*: I, ii, 181–5)

[NOTE: Italics in quotations are in all cases added for emphasis unless otherwise noted.]

In Shakespeare's time, this speech had a meaning entirely missed by modern audiences: they knew that Prospero's "most auspicious star" had to be Jupiter, "the greater benefic," considered throughout western cultural history to be the bringer of success and prosperity. These lines signal that the play is a comedy since it implies that the hero's fortunes are on the rise. Knowing that Jupiter has a twelve-year cycle (it takes twelve years to circle the Sun as viewed from Earth), the spectators of Shakespeare's time also got the significance of Prospero's twelve-year exile on the island: with one revolution of Jupiter completed and another beginning, his luck is about to change.

This is only one of dozens of references to the astrological language in Shakespeare's works. Modern audiences may be surprised at the frequency of such allusions since astrology has been marginalized in our day, but the audiences of Shakespeare's time were steeped in its language, partly because the people of his time were more aware of and attuned to the skies than ours: "Poets wrote of the wonder of the heavens, mariners steered by the stars, shepherds found their clock in the skies, farmers worked by the weather portents. All and sundry were astronomers in a greater or less degree ..."[2] Since only very wealthy Elizabethans would have owned clocks—and they were known to be unreliable—if you wanted to know the time of day, you might listen for church bells, or find a sundial, or just look outside to check the angle of the Sun.

Consequently Shakespeare's audience, the uneducated as well as the educated, would have been familiar with astrological symbols and their meanings. For those who were illiterate (the majority of the population), oral traditions passed down for many generations made the astrological language commonplace. In rural areas gardening and farming were often practiced according to lunar cycles, and herbalists learned their lore with reference to astrological signatures. Everyone, learned and unlearned, would have been familiar with the various meanings of the signs of the zodiac and the planets linked to them because personality classification (an elementary form of psychology) and medical practice were based on types related to "temperament" and thus to the stars. Both the administration of medicines and the timing of treatments were correlated with astrological cycles.

Educated Elizabethans would probably have gotten the more obscure references and would also have grasped astrology's more profound implications, partly due to its frequent appearance in religious writings (especially in debates about fate versus free will). They might also have understood a deeper dimension of astrology since it is part of an elegant, sophisticated and intelligently-thought-out spiritual philosophy (explored in Chapter 3) whose language and symbolism had been transmitted through classical literature originating in ancient Greece and Rome and were part of lively discussion well into the seventeenth century and are still vital today.[3] Unlike some Elizabethan poets and playwrights, Shakespeare does not provide precise data about the horoscopes of his characters,[4] nor does he need to. Details of their physical appearance and behavior would immediately have revealed to all the members of his audience the astrological principles that inspired their creation.

For a modern audience, these clues are largely lost. Unlike Shakespeare's era when the astrological language was commonly known, astrology in our time is an "esoteric" language, that is, a somewhat private or secret language understood by a self-selected few. A small percentage of this language—usually only related to Sun signs—is current in newspapers, magazines, or e-zines, but the richer vocabulary is no longer part of common discourse. Our culture does not know these references any more. What is most familiar to us are the plot patterns and character types basic to twentieth and twenty-first century books, films, television shows, video games, and other forms of popular culture. We may instantly understand allusions to *The Hobbit* or "Mad Men" or "Star Wars" or various reality television shows because they have established the conventions of contemporary storytelling. In contrast, Shakespeare relies on his audience's familiarity with the astrological alphabet to create characters whose personalities reflect astrological types and to shape stories that "unpack" the deeper meanings of the planets and signs.

The Unique and Elusive Shakespeare: Poet and Playwright
Shakespeare is everyone and no one. —Jorge Luis Borges

Born in Stratford-upon-Avon, England in April, 1564, William Shakespeare is credited with producing what is arguably the greatest body of work in the history of Western literature. Writing both poetry (two long narrative poems and one hundred and fifty-four sonnets) and a combination of prose and poetry (in the thirty-seven or so plays attributed to him), his collected writings reveal a uniquely gifted creative artist. But why focus on Shakespeare in particular? What is so unique about the works attributed to him that he is routinely put first on the list of outstanding contributors to Western culture? Why are *his* works still performed when others' works have been sidelined or completely forgotten?

Shakespeare's extraordinary reputation rests on a broad spectrum of accomplishments. Literary critics believe that he helped to create modern English, coining numerous phrases that have become part of the language (like "Double, double, toil and trouble" from *Macbeth* and jealousy as "the green-eyed monster" from *Othello*); that he was the first to introduce "modern" human beings (according to literary critic Harold Bloom),[5] characters who are thoughtful, self-aware, and deeply questioning; and that he was a brilliant psychologist, who makes diverse and differently motivated characters (like the vengeful Shylock or the love-struck Romeo) come to life. These characters are so vivid, sometime seeming more vital than people we know in our everyday lives, that we feel that they could indeed exist. In part this derives from their complexities, having weaknesses as well as strengths. This memorable dynamism is the first clue that his characters are based on ideas that are universal and therefore captivating to people of any era.

And so his works continue to fascinate whether on the page or in performance, making his dramas endlessly appealing to audiences over time and in varied cultures. The plays are more popular now, over four hundred years after they were written, than they were in Shakespeare's own day. Our ongoing engagement with them is due to their visual spectacle, the rhythm of their poetry, the vividness of their language, the timeless situations and common concerns, and most especially to the compelling nature of the characters. The tormented Hamlet, the enraged Lear, the jealous Othello all suffer titanic emotions in the midst of unbearable crises and all act in ways that we struggle to understand. Again and again we question their behavior, analyze their psychological motivations, ponder the appropriateness of their fates—and relate them to our own.

The heroes obviously engage our attention, but often the secondary characters are just as—sometimes even more—memorable. The gleefully mischievous Puck, Juliet's garrulous Nurse, the unabashedly gluttonous and life-affirming Falstaff all establish their personalities in an economy of lines and with a vividness of portraiture that etches them in our memories and vivifies them in our imaginations.

The personality that is missing in the plays, ironically, is Shakespeare's. While we have some but not much data on Shakespeare's exterior life, we have even less evidence to establish his personal opinions.[6] For instance, from his plays and poems it is unclear what his religious beliefs were, despite the fact that he was living in a time of extraordinary religious tension in England between the crown's recent rejection of Roman Catholicism and the establishment of the newly created Anglican Church, whose head was not the Pope but the King.[7] Though we can recognize Shakespeare as a man of his time, scholars cannot establish with certainty his attitudes and beliefs about important issues of his era.[8]

Every opinion, even the most opposite, on every significant human issue—love, marriage, the law, morality, religion, death—is voiced by his characters. Essential themes appear and reappear in his works, each time explored from different perspectives so that they always seem fresh and entertaining. Whether it is kingship and its legitimacy, or identity and its construction, or love in all its permutations, Shakespeare's concerns are constant. Though he "endlessly recycles ideas," he never repeats himself.[9] It is as though Shakespeare transcended his own personality, sacrificing singularity in favor of universality, so that he was able to imagine and create every possible human type. This is a supremely important point about Shakespeare's uniqueness as a creative artist and another clue that his work is grounded in an expansive worldview that this book posits includes astrology.

Shakespeare's plays are unusual also in that the entire spectrum of human life, from the lowest to the highest, is represented in the worlds he creates. We meet bawds and drunkards in a London tavern frequented by the lusty Falstaff and the young Prince of Wales. We are party to the plots and plans of nobles and royalty, as we witness Claudius' schemes to get rid of Hamlet or accompany King Henry V to the battlefields of France. We become acquainted with people of such purity and goodness, like King Lear's daughter Cordelia, that they seem more like saints or angels. We are even taken into spiritual or supernatural worlds, where Puck can magically put ass's ears on the unsuspecting Bottom or the ghost of the murdered Banquo can return to haunt his killer Macbeth. Only a "capacious consciousness"—a sign of genius according to Bloom—could contain all these levels and worlds. And only an artist working with the expansive worldview transmitted from ancient times could logically and easily reproduce such an infinite variety of the universe in his works.

Besides the astonishing range of human life depicted in his works, another remarkable point is that Shakespeare is skilled in writing both poetry and plays. For an author to be talented in both is unusual since the different forms demand contrasting skills and mindsets. Poems are more likely to be narrower in focus, more personal and subjective in attitude, and reliant on more concentrated language. Plays demand the imaginative capacity to vivify numerous characters who act and react dramatically with each other mainly through dialogue (with no authorial commentary), in a series of sequenced scenes and acts. While staged dramas appeal to our enjoyment in seeing a story acted out before us, poetry encourages a feeling response and an intuitive leap. It appeals not to the rational part of us but to our emotional and spiritual selves. Consequently poetry is most often enjoyed in private while plays are performed in public. To add to the magnitude of Shakespeare's accomplishment, writing verse in English is extremely difficult since English, unlike Italian, French, or Spanish, is a rhyme-poor language.[10]

Just as remarkable is the fact that Shakespeare is equally adept in creating both comedies and tragedies. As a general rule, playwrights tend to concentrate on and be more skilled in one or the other of these dramatic forms.

Another clue that Shakespeare's works are based on core or archetypal ideas transcending the time and place of their creation is that his plays are unusually—suspiciously—elastic. Over the centuries they have been drastically cut (especially the lengthy *Hamlet*), endings have been changed, and settings have been moved. David Garrick, the famous mid-eighteenth-century actor at London's Drury Lane Theatre, freely adapted Shakespeare's works, saying of *Hamlet* "... I rescued that noble play from all the rubbish of the fifth act. I have brought it forth without the grave-digger's trick, Osrick, & the fencing match"—which shocks us today.[11] From the Restoration period in England through the nineteenth century, audiences were so distraught by Cordelia's death at the end of *King Lear* that the play was staged with her saved from hanging and married to the honorable Edgar.

In the twentieth century directors have creatively (or disastrously) moved the action of the plays to alternate times and places. Some plays have rather nebulous locales (like *The Tempest*, set on an unidentified island) that are easily adapted, but even those that have a specified setting can work rather well when re-located or updated, consequently challenging our assumptions and perceptions. In 1936, Orson Welles staged *Macbeth* in New York's Harlem district with an all African-American cast. The most unusual relocation is undoubtedly the 1956 science-fiction film *Forbidden Planet*, which sets *The Tempest* on the planet Altair IV, many light-years distant from Earth.

The most famous and most successful adaptation of a Shakespearean play is the mid-twentieth century reworking of *Romeo and Juliet*. The story is transported from Renaissance Verona to the gang-fighting streets of modern New York City, with hostilities between the Jets and the Sharks replacing the enmity between the Montagues and the Capulets. The play becomes a musical, and the ending is changed, with Maria (a modern Juliet) surviving in the last scene.

Artistic directors like to twist the plays in other ways too. Staging and sets have been altered. In 1911 Gordon Craig used Cubist-inspired sets for a run of *Hamlet*, with flexible monochrome flats manipulated to create abstract settings. Costumes have varied widely as well. We are now accustomed to seeing characters in modern dress, a trend that started in the twentieth century with Barry Vincent Jackson's notable 1923 production of *Cymbeline*. Directors have occasionally toyed with casting in unconventional ways. Shakespeare's plays work equally well with males playing female parts (as they did in his time) or with flipping the gender of the hero. Famously, the nineteenth-century actress Sarah Bernhardt played the role of Hamlet in a French production in 1899, to great acclaim. Julie Taymor's film of *The Tempest* (2010) changed the gender of the magician-hero from male Prospero to female Prospera, played by Dame Helen Mirren.

Is there another playwright whose works have been so freely and so successfully adapted? What is both intriguing and mystifying is this very "elasticity," the ability of something to return to its original length or shape after being stretched or twisted. No matter what you do to or with Shakespeare's plays, they resiliently remain whole. This is extremely unusual, and not characteristic of the creative output of any other playwright. How to account for this?

Such flexibility implies an underlying and essential core in these works that allows for this extreme adaptability and yet always enables them to remain what they essentially are; in other words, all of Shakespeare's works have an "archetypal" basis. While this idea will be explored in more depth in Chapter 5, suffice it to say here that an "archetype" is a prototype, an original pattern or model from which all things of the same kind are copied or on which they are based. To survive despite— or even flourish with—all these changes, Shakespeare's plays must be attuned to fundamental ideas that have endured over time—and these include astrological symbols that are themselves archetypal. Understanding the worldview that underlies Shakespeare's works enables not only a deeper understanding of the plays, but also accounts for some of their extraordinary qualities: their visionary power, their mysterious elasticity, and the infinite variety of human and supernatural entities that animate his stage.

Astrology ...

Is astrology really so intrinsic to Shakespeare's works? We should not be surprised at its prominence in his plays since astrology has been an integral part of every major civilization on our planet, both Eastern and Western: from the Sumerian and Babylonian cultures to the Persian Empire and Dynastic Egypt, into Greek and Roman times, as well as in the Chinese, Indian, and Meso-American civilizations. It is a nearly universal language describing the interaction between humanity and the cosmos, its language crossing cultures and enduring over time. In the West it has flourished particularly in times of heightened creative and intellectual ferment—classical Greek and Roman times; the

Hellenistic era in Alexandria, Egypt; the High Middle Ages—and in particular during the Renaissance, when Shakespeare was writing.[12] While the public attitude to astrology in our time is one of skepticism, privately most people have a more favorable attitude toward it. Astrology in the twentieth and twenty-first centuries is having a renaissance of its own, and has become especially popular in the psychological and financial communities.

Yet most people do not have a clear grasp of what "astrology" is. What is actually meant by the term? A useful working definition might be that *astrology consists of the calculation and meaningful interpretation of the positions and motions of the heavenly bodies and their correlation with all aspects of earthly experience.*

From ancient times through the Renaissance, astrology and astronomy were one, but they were divided in the West beginning in the seventeenth century. The difference between astrology and astronomy is that astronomy limits itself to analyzing only the *physical* aspects of the heavenly bodies: their material constituents and movements. It omits the "meaningful interpretation" and "the correlation with earthly experience." Astrology takes the point of view that we have a relationship with our environment—not just our local environment, or even our global environment, but to the *total* environment. It is the original holistic philosophy.

Put concisely, astrology is the language that connects humanity with both nature and the cosmos.[13]

While the term "astrology" comes from the Greek "astron" for "star" plus "logos," meaning "the study of" or "the words about," it is more than just the study of the stars. It embraces a larger philosophical or spiritual perspective that incorporates ideas about what constitutes a human being. Whether influenced by religion or philosophy, most people in Shakespeare's time believed that human beings had both a body and a soul. The body is mortal and corruptible while the soul is the indwelling immortal essence surviving bodily death and subject to an after-death assessment. Othello takes this for granted when bemoaning the wife he has just murdered.

> [To Desdemona] Now, how dost thou look now? O *ill-starred* wench,

Pale as thy smock! When we shall meet at count [Judg-
   ment Day]
This look of thine will hurl my *soul* from heaven,
And fiends will snatch at it.

(V, ii, 279–82)

As an ensouled physical creature, you are born into a dimension constrained by space and time. In line with this, your horoscope is calculated
for the precise *place* of your birth on the Earth's surface and at the exact
time that you first breathe—which many believe is the moment that the
soul establishes its link with the body. The coordinates for your birth
chart are thus space and time. Both of these—geographical place and
moment of time—are often experienced as having a unique quality. The
wise depth psychologist C. G. Jung noticed this and observed, "Whatever is born or done at [a] particular moment of time has the quality of
[that] moment of time."[14]

Since your physical body is of earth, at death the elements that constitute it go back to the earth. But your soul, being eternal, comes from
the heavens and so returns there. The heavens envisioned by many Elizabethans are multiple ("heavens," not just one Heaven) through which
the soul descends before incarnating on Earth. These levels were equated
with the spheres of the planets—and thus astrology was originally an
integral part of a religious or spiritual worldview.

Encountering the dimension of astrology within Shakespeare's work
can open your mind to a different way of thinking, a way that is not
customary in our modern materially-oriented culture. You might start
to notice coincidences, synchronicities, events that seem on the surface
to be unrelated but are deeply meaningful. You begin to see the world in
terms of analogies, comparisons between one type of thing and another,
between different levels of existence. This perspective is common to
poets, who use comparisons frequently in the images they create. Like
Robert Burns who penned, "O my love is like a red, red rose" or John
Keats who wrote "Bright star! Would I were steadfast as thou art," poets
throughout history have found inspiration in seeing the connectedness
of all created things. This way of looking at the world was familiar to the
people of Shakespeare's time.

Astrology and Shakespeare:
His Attitude to and Knowledge of Astrology

Astrology permeated Elizabethan culture. Queen Elizabeth I herself had her coronation date selected ("elected") by Dr. John Dee, a philosopher, mathematician, geographer, and astrologer (and apparently her personal astrologer). So, we should not be surprised at Shakespeare's knowledge of it and at the many astrological allusions in his works. As Noga Arikha remarks,

> Astrology was inherent in the interrelation of the heavens with the elements and the human realm; it was a rather ordinary practice in the Renaissance, not just an abstruse, occult tradition for the initiated. The stars were signs that helped direct and regulate one's life … Astrology was therefore not a mere predictive tool … it was used much more imaginatively then … It was not only a playful, but also a serious, scholarly, activity that many people during the Renaissance believed crucial to self-understanding—an ingredient in the "high" culture of the sixteenth century.[15]

So how to verify Shakespeare's familiarity with the astrological language? What evidence should be considered first? A good place to start is looking for references to specific planets because they are the most obvious. If you are just counting the numbers, Cumberland Clark has done that: he records that Mercury is mentioned 15 times, that Venus is mentioned 21 times, Mars 36 times, Jupiter 30 times, and Saturn a mere 5 times.[16]

But the number should be much higher since Shakespeare is steeped in classical learning and often refers to the planets (the Sun and Moon in particular) by their mythological names. Instead of saying "the Moon" directly, for instance, he may refer to Phoebe, Luna, Cynthia, or Diana—or use poetic phrases like "the governess of floods" (*A Midsummer Night's Dream*: II, i, 103), "goddess of the night" (*Much Ado About Nothing*: V, iii, 12), or "thrice-crowned queen of night" (*As You Like It*: III, ii, 2).

These references are not just decorative. They fulfill an important dramatic purpose: to establish the status and qualities of the characters. When Caesar is called by the admiring Enobarbus "the Jupiter of men," for instance, Shakespeare's audience would have appreciated both Caesar's nobility and his excess ambition, qualities associated with Jupiter.

A client consults an astrologer, who points to the positions of the planets in the sky. (woodcut, ca. 1500)

(*Antony and Cleopatra*: III, ii, 9) But Jupiter has other meanings as well. As Parr remarks,

> Several of Shakespeare's characters are governed by particular stars, and Shakespeare is always consistent in assigning the planet which would endow the appropriate qualities. Posthumus was born under the benevolent planet Jupiter, and consequently has a favorable destiny at the end of the play [*Cymbeline*].[17]

Parr adds, referring to other planets, "Monsieur Parolles would be born under Mars because he would be known as a soldier. [*All's Well That Ends Well*: I, i, 177–90] Elizabeth, who weeps throughout *Richard III* is indeed "governed by the watery moon." [*Richard III*: II, ii, 69][18] Other direct references to the planets in the plays are equally revealing. In *Titus Andronicus*, Aaron the Moor responds to Tamora's inquiry "… wherefore look'st thou sad …?" by saying, "Madam, though *Venus* govern your desires, / *Saturn* is dominator over mine." (II, iii, 30–1) This is a short-hand method of immediately revealing the character of both: Tamora is a seductress (as Venus was sometimes characterized) and Aaron is not only melancholic but also hard-hearted and cruel (qualities often associated with Saturn)—all of which is borne out in the play as Tamora infatuates Rome's ruler and Aaron contrives the rape and mutilation of Titus' daughter.[19]

But there are numerous references to astrological symbols other than the planets in Shakespeare's works. Just as members of his audience could instantly recognize and speak the wider language of astrology (not just the planets), so do his characters.

> His *dramatis personae* speak of stars, planets, comets, meteors, eclipses, planetary aspects, predominance, conjunction, opposition, retrogradation, and all sorts of astro-meteorology. They know that the Dragon's Tail exerts an evil influence, that Mercury governs lying and thievery, that Luna [the Moon] rules vagabonds and idle fellows, that Saturn is malignant and Jupiter benevolent, that the signs of the zodiac rule the limbs and organs of the body, that planets influence cities and nations, that each trigon or triplicity pertains to one of the four elements, that stars rule immediately as well as at birth, that one with a strong constitution might avert the influence of his stars, and so on. Although they do not go into details regarding the technical workings of the science, his characters on the whole seem to possess a general knowledge of stellar influence on human destiny.[20]

Shakespeare's references to astrological/astronomical events such as eclipses or the appearance of comets are particularly telling. In *Antony and Cleopatra*, Antony foresees his downfall with reference to the heavens: "Alack, our terrene [earthly] *moon/ Is now eclipsed*, and it portends alone/ The fall of Antony." (III, xiii, 156–8) In *Julius Caesar*, when Calpurnia warns her husband not to go to the Senate, she avows, "When beggars die there are no *comets* seen;/ The heavens themselves blaze forth the death of princes." (II, ii, 30–1) Both eclipses and comets are still believed by many to be portents of doom, especially for great men or a country's king.

If you include all the references to the daily cycles of the Sun and Moon, to seasonal cycles based on the apparent revolution of the Sun around the Earth, and to the astrologically-derived personality theory related to the four elements, the number of references to astrology in Shakespeare's plays is much higher. Since astrology is based on the daily cycle of night and day and the yearly cycle of the four seasons, even allusions to sunrise and morning, to sunset and dark night, to spring, summer, autumn, or winter, are astrological as well as astronomical in nature.

Both types of allusions to astrology, direct and indirect, appear in all the different forms of Shakespeare's writing: sonnets, longer poems, histories, comedies, and tragedies. His interest is constant, for there are as many references to astrology in the later plays as in the early ones.

One of the main reasons that we do not catch these references is that we are no longer familiar with the larger worldview that was fundamental to Elizabethan thinking, one that included astrology and one that S. K. Heninger, Jr. calls "the most forceful orthodox determinant of renaissance thought."[21] We are conditioned in our time by the dominant beliefs of physical science: that only physical things are real and that the only way to know a thing is through five-sense perception. Because of this, we do not grasp ideas that were fundamental in Shakespeare's time. Our modern beliefs would have shocked most Renaissance thinkers, who had inherited the idea that the universe was a Totality unfolded from Divinity in an orderly progression of hierarchical levels that included the seven classical planets.

> The notion of a divinely ordered universe is one of our most ancient propositions, having emanated from the school of Pythagoras as early as the sixth century B.C. It was assimilated by Plato and thence by the Church Fathers, and after that it was a basic premise, stated or unstated, in most Western philosophy, religion, and science until the seventeenth century. The early renaissance humanists, and later the scientists, enthusiastically reaffirmed it.[22]

We can only understand many Renaissance literary creations—Shakespeare's among them—by understanding this worldview.

So Shakespeare, like everyone in his audience, is familiar with the astrological language. In our time, influenced by materialistic science, people wonder if Shakespeare's familiarity with astrology means that he "believes" in it. To determine this, critics often focus on characters' speeches that either support or refute the astrological worldview as a whole. The speeches that get the most attention in our skeptical age are the few that reject the influence of the stars, like Cassius' observation in *Julius Caesar* that "Men at some time are masters of their fates;/ The fault, dear Brutus, is not in our stars,/ But in ourselves, that we are underlings." (I, ii, 139–41) Cassius is at that moment trying to persuade Brutus to join the conspiracy to overthrow Caesar, protesting that the ambitious Caesar is no better than they are and that they should take action to prevent him becoming sole ruler. But what is overlooked is that Cassius' optimistic assertion of control over his own and others' destiny rings hollow since, despite the fact that the conspirators succeed in murdering Caesar, the battle against Caesar's heir Octavius is lost and both Cassius and Brutus commit suicide.

If we look closely at the many references to astrology in Shakespeare's plays, the overwhelming majority of them *do* support the astrological perspective. This is no surprise in an era in which astrology was pervasive and commonly accepted. In about four hundred lines of the most obvious astrological allusions, almost every character affirms astral influence: "only four characters—two villains, the Papal legate, and a 'hothead' ... deride it ..."[23] Perhaps the most famous rejection is voiced by the villainous Edmund the bastard in *King Lear*, who argues passionately for his independence from nature and the cosmos. When his father Gloucester laments that "These late eclipses in the sun and moon portend no good" (since they were believed to coincide with discord, treason and disruptions between family members and in the state), Edmund dismisses these notions with

> This is the excellent foppery of the world, that, when
> we are sick in fortune,—often the surfeit of our own
> behavior,—we make guilty of our disasters the sun, the
> moon, and stars; as if we were villains by necessity; fools
> by heavenly compulsion; knaves, thieves, and treachers
> [traitors] by spherical predominance; drunkards, liars, and
> adulterers, by an enforced obedience of planetary influ-
> ence; and all that we are evil in, by a divine thrusting on.
> An admirable evasion of whoremaster man, to lay his
> goatish disposition to the charge of a star!
>
>   (I, ii, 109–17)

Of course, the irony is that what unfolds in the play *is* precisely the disruption to the kingdom and the breaking of the bond between father and son that Gloucester fears. And Edmund *is* exactly the kind of person whom the stars portend. His comment that "My father compounded with my mother under the dragon's tail, and my nativity was under Ursa Major, so that it follows, I am rough and lecherous" accurately reveals his character. (I, ii, 117–20) He *is* a devious plotter who instigates some of the terrible tragedy of the play by maligning his brother, betraying his father, and enjoying dalliances with both of Lear's older daughters. Even though Edmund rejects any synchronicity between his character and the cosmos, Shakespeare creates his personality and intentions very much in accord with the astrological pattern.

Shakespeare writes consistently and eloquently in support of the view that the heavens and humanity are intimately connected. Characters frequently declare that they are born under either positive or negative astrological configurations, or that their efforts might be supported or obstructed by the stars, or that some celestial phenomenon forebodes either favor or disaster for themselves or for others. In every case the unfolding action of the play confirms the characters' statements.

A famous example of this is Romeo's premonition on the way to crashing the Capulets' party that "some consequence yet hanging in the *stars*/ Shall bitterly begin his fearful date/ With this night's revels, and expire the term/ Of a despised life, clos'd in my breast,/ By some vile forfeit of untimely death." (*Romeo and Juliet*: I, iv, 107–11) His fearful intuition comes too dreadfully true. But there are many other instances of this. In justifying the deaths of the sons of Queen Elizabeth (widow to Edward IV), Richard III declares, "Lo, at their births good *stars* were opposite." (*Richard III*: IV, iv, 216) Antony, aware that Caesar is taking advantage of his current weakness, regrets his falling fortunes: "…[M]y good *stars* that were my former guides,/ Have empty left their orbs, and shot their fires/ Into th' abyss of hell." (*Antony and Cleopatra*: III, xiii, 147–9) Hermione, unjustly accused of adultery by her jealous husband Leontes, acquiesces to her fate: "There's some ill *planet* reigns./ I must be patient till the heavens look/ With an *aspect* more favourable." (*The Winter's Tale*: II, i, 107–9)]

What is surprising is how much Shakespeare leans toward the view that astrology is not just *de*scriptive but *pre*scriptive. While his characters in theory have free will—Macbeth or Hamlet or Timon of Athens could have chosen to act differently in their respective situations—they act entirely in line with their temperaments and the astrological portents. Shakespeare has Hamlet voice this view: "… There's a divinity that shapes our ends,/ Rough-hew them how we will—" (V, ii, 10–11).[24]

Shakespeare's familiarity with even some rather obscure astrological terminology certainly implies a deeper engagement with it. Here's Puck's description of the hostility between the fairy king and queen in *A Midsummer Night's Dream*:

> And now they never meet in grove, or green,
> By fountain clear, or spangled starlight sheen,
> But they do *square*, that all their elves for fear
> Creep into acorn-cups, and hide them there.
>
> (II, i, 28–31)

"Square" is an astrological term referring to the most conflict-ridden mathematical aspect (90° or a quarter of the circle) between two planets or other bodies. This "aspect" (a specialized astrological term that Shakespeare has Hermione employ in the quotation just cited above) describes two factors that are working at cross-purposes, with each jostling for dominance and creating discord—a perfect way of picturing the enmity between Oberon and Titania.

Here is another specific astrological term, this one from *Hamlet*. The usurper Claudius has killed his brother in part so that he can marry his brother's wife. He tells Laertes how important Gertrude is to him by saying, "She's so *conjunctive* to my life and soul/ That, as the *star* moves not but in his sphere, / I could not but by her." (IV, vii, 14–16) A conjunction between two planets occurs when they appear to be very close together in the sky as observed from Earth—so close, in fact, that they appear to be one entity. This is a beautifully poetic way of the villainous Claudius describing his passionate need for his now-wife.

Not only is Shakespeare familiar with the astrological language, not only is he in sympathy with the astrological worldview, but he is also so confident of his audience's awareness of astrological correspondences that he can make jokes about them. In *Twelfth Night*, the heavy-drinking Sir Toby Belch and Sir Andrew Aguecheek, who is described by Olivia's waiting-woman as "a very fool, and a prodigal" (I, iii, 20), plan more dancing and carousing:

> SIR TOBY BELCH: I did think, by the excellent constitu-
> tion of thy leg, it was formed under the star of a
> galliard.
> SIR ANDREW AGUECHEEK: Ay, 'tis strong, and it does
> indifferent well in a divers-coloured stock[ing]. Shall
> we set about some revels?
> SIR TOBY BELCH: What shall we do else—were we not
> born under Taurus?
> SIR ANDREW AGUECHEEK: Taurus? That's sides and heart.
> SIR TOBY BELCH: No, sir, it is legs and thighs: let me see
> thee caper.
> [SIR ANDREW capers]
> Ha, higher! Ha, ha, excellent.
>
> (I, iii, 110–19)

Of course, being foolish ignoramuses, Sir Toby and Sir Andrew have got it wrong both times. Taurus rules neither the "sides and heart" nor "the legs and thighs." It rules the throat in the human body. (As Parr ruefully comments, "... the most ignorant Elizabethan theatre-goer probably knew it. Such humor is wasted on modern audiences."[25]) Shakespeare's audience would immediately have understood the comic effect of the characters' mistake.

Two other references in Shakespeare's works suggest that the play-wright was even aware of astronomical discoveries in his own time and may have alluded to them in his plays. In 1572 a supernova was observed by Danish astronomer Tycho Brahe. Some modern astronomers specu-late that the star mentioned in *Hamlet* "that's westward from the pole" refers to that supernova.[26] More recently, Peter D. Usher of the Depart-ment of Astronomy and Astrophysics at Pennsylvania State University has published a paper in which he argues that the "bright particular star" spoken of by Helena in the opening scene of *All's Well That Ends Well* refers to yet another supernova, one observed by Johannes Kepler in 1604.[27] (I, i, 81) Usher also remarks on other speeches in the play that allude to a Mars retrograde cycle in 1604 occurring in the sign Virgo, which might establish a date for the writing of the play.

So ... Shakespeare obviously knows the astrological vocabulary and perhaps some contemporary astronomy too.[28] How might he have learned the astrological alphabet? Everyone, educated or not, would have known of or read the almanacs published in English each year that described astrological portents and gave agricultural recommendations for the year (much like the still-published Farmers' Almanacs). Popular with those who were literate but preferred simple material, these "almanacks" or pamphlets (called "Prognostications") also listed unusual celestial events like comets or eclipses. Shakespeare has Prince Hal from *Henry IV* refer to one such event: "Saturn and Venus this year in conjunction! What says th' *almanac* to that?" (*2 Henry IV*: II, iv, 236–7). Saturn governed old age and Venus ruled youth and love; since Hal is watching old Falstaff kiss young Doll Tearsheet, he is in effect watching Saturn conjoin with Venus and making a joke about it, one that must be explained to audiences today.

The pervasiveness of astrology was also due in part to the advent of the moveable-type printing press into Europe, developed in Germany in the mid-1400s by Johannes Gutenberg. Printers immediately began to publish and republish many of the classical and medieval astrological texts as well as newly-written treatises by fifteenth and sixteenth century writers. Probably the most widely disseminated work was still Claudius Ptolemy's famous *Tetrabiblos* (second century CE), but a more practical and comprehensive text for learning how to delineate horoscopes was Julius Firmicus Maternus' *Matheseos* (fourth century CE).[29]

There were other easily available books on astrology besides these two. The most popular and complete text from the medieval period was Guido Bonatti's *Liber astronomicus*. Bonatti cites not only Ptolemy but also other classical writers on astrology as well as many of the famous Arabic astrologers that flourished in the Middle East between the eighth and twelfth centuries CE.[30] John Ganivet's *Amicus medicorum* ("The Friend of Physicians") concentrated on using astrology to maintain health, overcome disease, and concoct medicinal preparations.[31] These four works "are chiefly the source-books, so to speak, for the hundreds of other treatises published in the sixteenth century. Material in them was rehashed again and again in the copious printings" of other astrological writings.[32]

In the century after the invention of the printing press in Europe, especially by the mid-to-late 1500s, more and more writings about astrology appear in English. In 1558 Dr. John Dee—apparently Queen Elizabeth I's personal astrologer—issued a book of astrological aphorisms. The average literate sixteenth-century middle-class Englishman might have encountered an astrological encyclopedia like Bartholomaeus Anglicus' *De proprietatibus rerum*, which cribbed from famous earlier astrologers, and was available in English in an edition of 1582. Or he might have read *The Kalender of Shepherdes*, an encyclopedic handbook translated into English from French. Being tremendously popular, it circulated in sixteen editions throughout the 1500's.

For the more literate and the nobility, a variety of writings were available, many based on the four works mentioned above. Some of these were in-depth treatises written in Latin, many brought from the Continent and found in scholars' or nobles' libraries. A slew of translations of other foreign books appear in the late 1500s, among them two of better quality: Claudius Dariot's *A Briefe Introduction to the Astrologicall Judgement of the Starres* (1583, 1591, 1598, 1653), and Augier Ferrier's popular *A Learned Astronomical Discourse of the Judgement of Nativities* (1593, 1642). (Though there were many others, I have simplified the list; interested readers can consult Parr's thorough eighteen-page survey.) So Shakespeare would have had easy access to information about astrology.

Since Shakespeare alludes to astrology so frequently, we might return to speculating about his personal beliefs on the subject. It is impossible to say definitively what Shakespeare believed about this (or any other subject) because he puts into the mouths of his characters statements that suit *their* attitudes and personalities (like Prospero or Edmund or Romeo). But it is clear that whatever Shakespeare's personal beliefs, the vast majority of his characters' statements are overwhelmingly in line with a Renaissance astrological worldview. This perspective was so accepted in his age that astrological symbols were used as a kind of shorthand in both philosophical and literary works. Shakespeare obviously draws on this common symbolism as creative inspiration for his art.

So how does Shakespeare use astrology in his plays? For various purposes: to establish time and its passage; to link characters with planets considered indicators of personality traits (through the "theory of the humours"); and to allude to themes and philosophical ideas embedded in astrological symbolism. But there is another much more subtle way in which astrology is fundamental to Shakespeare's creations. Not only are there direct and indirect references to astrology, not only are characters based on astrological types, but *many of his works are also entirely "keyed" to specific zodiacal signs and their ruling planet(s).*

Consequently particular plays explore profound ideas that are consistent with the related signs and planets. In this way, astrological ideas inspire the shaping of the stories and are the basis for plots, characters, and central symbols in the plays. Like an accomplished musician, Shakespeare is performing extended "riffs" on astrological symbols in creating each work. *A Midsummer Night's Dream,* for example, is "in the key" of the Moon. References to the Moon abound in the play, and the Moon even comes on stage as a character in the skit that the Athenian workmen present to the court in the last act. (See Chapter 7 for a full discussion.)

The Many Lenses for Viewing Shakespeare's Works—and This One

Shakespeare draws on the symbolism of astrological factors in part because he was living in a milieu that was flooded with astrological materials. The plays reveal that he was familiar with the language of astrology and that he used it consciously in creating them.

While this is the approach taken in this book, it is, of course, not the only perspective on Shakespeare's works. His poems and plays are so rich, varied, and all-encompassing that there are many lenses through which you can view them and every lens seems to "work." You can examine Shakespeare from different literary perspectives. You can look at clusters of images and symbols in his overall oeuvre or within a specific drama, as Caroline Spurgeon does; you can focus on larger-than-life characters like Hamlet or Falstaff as forerunners to the "modern human," as Harold Bloom does; you can explore the discrepancies of awareness between groups of characters, and characters and the audience, as Bertrand Evans does; you can even look for Elizabethan slang for the "naughty bits" to catch frequent—and often astonishingly gross—sexual jokes, as in Eric Partridge's *Shakespeare's Bawdy.*[33]

There is a plethora of other "lenses" as well. You can poke around in the plays looking for references to historical events like Elizabethan sailors' voyages to the Caribbean, possibly an inspiration for Ariel's speech about the "still-vex'd Bermoothes" (ever-stormy Bermudas) in *The Tempest*. Or you can trace the sources of his plots as, for example, in Jonathan Bate's *Shakespeare and Ovid*.[34] Or you can approach Shakespeare's works from the perspective of other disciplines: you can search for evidence of his religious beliefs and references in his works to the Bible[35]; you can relate his works to fundamental philosophical issues like identity and consciousness[36]; you can even extract advice from the plays for contemporary businesspeople.[37]

Or you can, as this book does, explore resonances with the now-esoteric worldview both to illuminate the plays and to account for their numinosity and vitality. *This book views Shakespeare's works through the lens of astrological symbolism within the larger context of the cosmological model of which it is a part.* This tradition derives so significantly from ancient Greek and Roman mythology and philosophy that I have given them great emphasis in the book, including many allusions to ideas and stories from those times. The thought and culture of the Renaissance, the exciting time during which Shakespeare was writing, was invigorated by the recovery of materials from these ancient cultures, especially lost works of Plato and those attributed to an ancient Egyptian sage, Hermes Trismegistus.

If you are wondering why no one has looked through this particular lens at Shakespeare's work before, the short answer is bias. As David Wiles remarks, "Modern literary scholarship has consistently neglected the importance of astrology in renaissance thinking.... It would seem that critics close their eyes to an aspect of renaissance thinking that they are unwilling to palate because of their distaste for astrology in the twentieth century.... They have not wanted to confront the possibility that Shakespeare accepted or used the popular astrological beliefs of his period."[38]

To make it easy to see the pervasiveness of astrology in Shakespeare's writings, this book is divided into two sections. Section I: Decoding Shakespeare considers general references to cycles of the Sun and Moon (that establish time and mood) and to the planets (that convey a character's personality) in a number of the plays. Then it places astrology within the greater worldview of which it is a part and which was generally accepted both before and during the Elizabethan era. Understanding this cosmology puts the plays into a larger context and opens a window that reveals how most Elizabethans saw the world.

SECTION II: THE PLAYS probes six of Shakespeare's plays to elucidate specific references to astrology in each and to show that astrological symbolism provides their conceptual foundation. Without question, individual plays are keyed to a particular zodiacal sign and its ruling planet. This is revealed by the titles of the plays, the characters and their types, the settings for the plays, the direction of the plot, and multiple overarching themes.

Astrology thus illuminates some of Shakespeare's best-known plays in unexpected ways to provide fresh and exciting insights into these works. The six plays are *A Midsummer Night's Dream, Romeo and Juliet, The Merchant of Venice, Macbeth, The Tempest, and King Lear.* They are presented in a sequence that introduces readers to the planets in the order that they appear as we gaze out into the heavens: the Moon, Mercury, Venus, Mars, Jupiter, and Saturn. (Although the Moon is technically a satellite of the Earth and the Sun is a star, for convenience they are often referred to as "planets.") This sequence omits the Sun, which should appear between Venus and Mars. (For a discussion of "The Sun in Shakespeare's Plays," see Chapter 1.)

Given the rich associations of astrological symbolism and their many connections to other studies, I have included much that is relevant and illuminating from a variety of disciplines. If you are knowledgeable about these (like the ubiquity of the number seven or the basics of poetic rhyme and rhythm), you can certainly skip the familiar and concentrate on the unfamiliar. Although it is tempting to turn immediately to the section on the plays, I have structured Section I in thoughtful and deliberate steps to introduce ideas that lay the groundwork for Section II.

The resulting wide-ranging book is intended most especially for perceptive play-goers and eager readers of Shakespeare's works who wish to explore their hidden depths. It presents a readable synthesis that will appeal to a wide and intelligent public audience, one willing to open-mindedly revisit a worldview fundamental to western thought up to the modern period. In doing so, it brings together astrology, classical and Renaissance philosophy, Greek and Roman mythology, esoteric wisdom, modern psychology (especially that of Jung), and great literature.

Drawing on many streams of thought, this work is intended to be introductory and thought-provoking. No commentary on Shakespeare can be exhaustive. My intention is to excite by approaching his works from a fresh angle, and to encourage deeper reflection and further exploration. To that end (and also because a book of this broad scope must of necessity oversimplify in places), for those who would like to pursue these ideas in greater depth, copious endnotes and an extensive bibliography may lead you to other intriguing and substantial works. The endnotes expand points discussed in the body of the book, give more supportive proofs and quotations, and add some fascinating relevant facts and comments.

I am grateful to the many scholars who have come before me and have done so much of the groundwork that enables a work like this to take shape. As a synthesizer, I appreciate the work of the many specialists cited in this book. If you are as intrigued as I am by this perspective on these wonderful works, I hope you will explore further the richness and complexity of many of the subjects introduced here.

I now invite you to accompany me on a mind-bending and hopefully mind-opening journey into the hidden and cosmic Shakespeare.

NOTE: Quotations from Shakespeare's plays are from *The Norton Shakespeare*, based on the Oxford Edition, 2nd ed., New York: W.W. Norton & Company, 2008. Where words or phrases in quotations are italicized, emphasis has been added unless otherwise noted. Although the Norton edition uses Arabic numbers, I have chosen to keep the traditional Roman numerals to indicate acts, scenes, and line numbers.

Quotations from *Pericles* only are from *The Complete Plays and Poems of William Shakespeare*, ed. William Allan Neilson and Charles Jarvis Hill, Cambridge, Mass., Houghton Mifflin Company, 1942.

SECTION I
DECODING SHAKESPEARE

CHAPTER I

Shakespeare's Use of
Daily and Seasonal Cycles:
Astrology in Essence

The Sun in Shakespeare's Plays

For the ancients, for contemporary indigenous peoples, and for anyone living outside today's artificially-lit urban centers, the daily rising of the Sun and the ever-changing phases of the Moon are dramatic events. We have lost sight of the fact that "The daily movement of the [S]un, its rising at dawn and setting at dusk, is the fundamental feature of human existence...."[39] But Shakespeare has not. He often writes eloquently in celebration of the rising Sun, as in *Romeo and Juliet:* "Night's candles are burnt out, and jocund day / Stands tiptoe on the misty mountain tops" (III, v, 9–10).

As the most conspicuous, elevated, and magnificent celestial object in the sky, the glorious Sun inspires awe and praise. While no one play of Shakespeare's is keyed to the Sun, *all* of the history plays in particular resonate to this celestial body and its associated zodiacal sign of Leo.

One meaning of the Sun in astrology relates to kingship or leadership. This is an extremely old association. As early as some four thousand years ago in ancient Mesopotamia, gods and goddesses were believed to exert influence through the person of the ruler who was considered the son of the Sun.[40] In the West this tradition continued through the classical Greek and Roman periods, and into medieval and Renaissance times. [41] Some elaborate court entertainments put on for Elizabeth I and James I reflected this view: "the court masque centers about the king, equating him symbolically with the mythological gods as well as the sun."[42] In line with this, all of Shakespeare's history plays explore the legitimacy and suitability of a monarch for his position—in other words, how "sunlike" is he?

The most dramatic of these is the trilogy of plays about Henry V, which tracks his behavior in *Henry IV, Parts 1 and 2* before he becomes king. To assume the role of King, Prince Hal must reject the boisterous

Falstaff, as lively and endearing a character as he is, for he symbolizes irresponsibility, cowardice, and licentiousness, all qualities inappropriate for the ideal king. The Sun in its most exalted and positive expression incorporates majesty, liberality, and the charisma of the leader who (ideally) is beyond influence and temptation because he is disciplined in his life and uses reason to control his passions. Hal tells us early in *I Henry IV* that he intends to leave drinking and riotous living behind:

> Yet herein will I imitate the *sun*,
> Who doth permit the base contagious clouds
> To smother up his beauty from the world,
> That when he please again to be himself,
> Being wanted he may be more wonder'd at
> By breaking through the foul and ugly mists
> Of vapours that did seem to strangle him.
>
> (I, ii, 175–82)

The King was considered by most to be the center and soul of a country, his position with its attendant charisma making him the focus of attention for those who orbit his sphere of influence:

> [Yon King's] to me like to my father's picture,
> Which tells [me] in that glory once he was;
> Had princes sit like *stars* about his throne,
> And he the *sun* for them to reverence.
> (*Pericles, Prince of Tyre*: II, iii, 37–40)[43]

Aside from leadership many other meanings are associated with the Sun, coming from various traditions:

> The king is like the sun in his physical aspects of brilliance and power, and he sits in the midst of his courtiers as the sun sits in the middle of the planets. But this comparison is effective also because of its conceptual significance, because the sun represents the concepts of goodness, beauty, and truth in the Platonic tradition, the concepts of divinity and providence in the Christian tradition, and the concept of beneficent cosmic control in the Aristotelian tradition.[44]

Though dressed in kingly splendor, Richard III has behaved in an unking-like or "un-SUNlike" manner since he manipulated and murdered his way to the throne. (Mark Rylance as Richard III in the Shakespeare Globe Theatre production, 2013–04. Photo: Geraint Lewis)

But the Sun exists in the heavenly or ideal realm, and all too often human kings fail to rule in accord with the highest possibilities inherent in meanings attributed to the Sun. Shakespeare frequently shows the darker side of Sun symbolism. Instead of dramatizing kings ennobled by qualities of courage, generosity, and a humility born of awareness of the distinction between their inner identity and outer role, he sometimes presents kings whose power and position have allowed their egos to run rampant—like Richard III who blatantly conspires against members of his own royal family to get the throne, plotting and murdering initially without remorse. Leontes, king of Sicilia in *The Winter's Tale,* allows jealousy and resentment to overcome reason, accusing his queen Hermione of an affair with his best friend and imprisoning her. According to astrologer and author Stephen Arroyo, "the solar principle always tries to concentrate authority in itself and to shine as brightly as possible by polishing its ego through amassing social power and prestige...."[45] Shakespeare's allusions, though, generally emphasize the more positive and more desirable interpretations of the Sun.

While the history plays are particularly keyed to the Sun, *all* of Shakespeare's plays contain references to the Sun either explicitly or by synonym. Some equivalents for the Sun are drawn from Greek and Roman mythology. Whether he refers to the sun directly or as Sol (the Latin word for Sun) or as Phoebus (meaning "bright" in Greek and depicted as a figure riding a wheeled chariot driven by fiery steeds across the heavens), for Shakespeare the Sun is most often the emblem of *Good,* equivalent to the most noble and desirable of qualities, and a source of blessings:

> For 'tis the mind that makes the body rich,
> And as the *sun* breaks through the darkest clouds,
> So honour peereth in the meanest habit.
>
> (*Taming of the Shrew*: IV iii, 166–8)

Poetic Use of the Sun and Moon

Since the Sun is the source of life and light upon which our very existence and Earth's wellbeing depends, it is a perfect source for poetic comparisons. For a poet like Shakespeare, living before the age of wristwatches and electric lights, it is natural to compare characters directly

The Sun and Moon are the lights of day and night, and symbolize the fundamental principles of Being and Becoming as well as the polarities of male and female. (Michael Maier, *Atalanta Fugiens*, Frankfort, 1617)

to the Sun or Moon. In one of Shakespeare's most affecting tragedies, *Romeo and Juliet*, Romeo first sees Juliet emerge on her balcony late at night after the masked ball at her parents' house, and rhapsodizes on her glorious beauty:

> But soft! What light through yonder window breaks?
> It is the east, and *Juliet is the sun.*
> Arise, *fair sun*, and kill the *envious moon....*
>
> (II, ii, 2–4)

Of course Juliet is not literally the Sun, but associating Juliet with this celestial body expresses Romeo's blossoming love: she has become the "light," the center, of his life. Since Juliet is his "Sun," Romeo's very life now depends upon her person, just as life on this planet depends upon the Sun's light and warmth. It is a dramatic comparison, too, since if she is like the Sun she is shining in the middle of the night! This new birth of love within him, as dramatic as a sunrise, chases away his previous dark mood and dries up his former infatuation with Rosaline, who is equated with the lesser light, the Moon.

The Moon, with its ghostly light and ever-changing phases, has less exalted associations. In *King Lear* when the disguised Edgar fools his blinded father Gloucester into thinking that he has leapt off the cliffs of Dover and survived, he describes the "fiend" that parted with his aged parent: "he had a thousand noses, / Horns whelk'd and waved like the [enridged] sea.... Methought his eyes / Were two *full moons* ..." (*King Lear*: IV, vi, 70–1, 69). As the ghostly light of night, a time when the darkest fears emerge, the Moon is easily associated with such a horror. At the very least—because it is a heavenly body that constantly changes shape—it is untrustworthy.

For centuries writers have used references to the Sun, Moon and other astrological factors for purposes other than poetic comparisons between heavenly and earthly bodies. One is purely practical. Like other poets, Shakespeare frequently refers to the Sun's daily cycle to indicate the time of day—morning, noon, or evening—or the passage of time. In *Cymbeline*, the doltish Cloten desires Imogen for his wife and hires musicians to serenade her as she wakes: they begin, "Hark, hark, the lark at heaven['s] gate sings, / And Phoebus [the Sun] gins arise ..." (II, iii, 17–8). Similarly, in *All's Well That Ends Well*, when the ailing King of France agrees to take medicine prepared by the virtuous and youthful Helen, whose father was a physician, he asks how soon it will take effect. Helen's reply is: "Ere twice the horses of the sun shall bring / Their fiery coacher his diurnal ring ..." (II, i, 160–1). In other words, a mere two days! At the end of *Love's Labour's Lost*, when King Ferdinand and his lords are exposed as secret wooers of the lovely French ladies visiting the court, their suits are rejected and a penance is imposed: the French princess declares that the sincerity of their love must be tested for a specified period of time, a whole year as marked by the Sun's journey through the twelve signs of the zodiac:

> [G]o with speed
> To some forlorn and naked hermitage

Remote from all the pleasures of the world.
There stay until *the twelve celestial signs*
Have brought about the annual reckoning.

(V, ii, 776–80)

Poets also employ allusions to the time of day or part of the year to conjure an atmosphere and generate emotional resonses in the audience. These daily and seasonal cycles are the basis of astrology and are frequently imaginatively used by Shakespeare. Days are calculated as twenty-four hour periods during which the Sun rises, culminates, sets, and disappears until it emerges again at the next dawn. Traditionally the year begins with spring, progresses through summer into autumn, and finally winter, when in the northern hemisphere nature seems to die, to be reborn the following spring. Both of these cycles are open, because the apparent ending of one full sequence leads to the beginning of a new one.

They are also analogous: each part of the day is like a season of the year as well as a "season" or stage of a human life, and each of them correlates with emotions likely to be felt at these times. "The seasons are identified with particular human emotions—spring with hope, summer with joy, autumn with sadness, winter with pain—and often the time of year … emphasize[s] certain traits of character or aspects of the dramatized story."[46] Shakespeare frequently makes these comparisons explicit: "See how the morning opes her golden gates / And takes her farewell of the glorious sun. / How well resembles it the prime of youth, / Trimmed [dressed up] like a younker [young man] prancing to his love!" (*3 Henry VI*: II, i, 21–4) We are more deeply sensitized to these rhythms, a staple in poetic writing, than we may consciously realize and we respond feelingly to the most delicate and subtle allusions to these cycles.

Such comparisons are especially obvious in *Romeo and Juliet*. After the two young lovers speak and exchange vows of love, she bids him good night by saying: "This bud of love by *summer*'s ripening breath / May prove a beauteous flower when next we meet" (II, i, 163–4). Between one meeting and the next, time has leapt forward, moving from the joyous spring of their first encounter to the expansive summer of its growing strength. Events move very quickly in this play about youthful, impatient, and passionate love.

Season of the Year	Time of Day	Part of Life Cycle	Human Emotions
Spring	Dawn	Birth	Hope, joy, excitement
Summer	Noon	Growth	Happiness, satisfaction, fulfillment
	Late Afternoon	Maturity	Melancholy, sadness
Autumn	Evening	Old Age	Anger OR calm acceptance
Winter	Night	Death	Despair, pain
Spring	Dawn	Rebirth	Hope, joy, excitement

At a different stage of life altogether, King Lear, in a play about an aging monarch, rages against loss of position and power as he moves through the autumn or evening stage of life towards the winter of death. Lear explicitly announces the downward trajectory of his life—and the play—the very first time he speaks:

> Know that we have divided
> In three our kingdom; and 'tis our fast intent
> To shake all cares and business from our age,
> Conferring them on younger strengths, while we
> Unburthened *crawl toward death.*
>
> (*King Lear*, I, i, 35–9)

While Lear cannot avoid death, at least one of Shakespeare's charismatic kings is so powerful that he is (in poetic terms) able to alter the seasons and consequently change peoples' emotions. *Richard III* opens with these famous lines, as the scheming and envious Richard reflects on the power of his brother, King Edward IV and son to York, to convert a dark time of recent conflict to one more pleasing and temperate:

> Now is the *winter* of our discontent
> Made glorious *summer* by this son of York;
> And all the clouds that loured upon our house
> In the deep bosom of the ocean buried.
> Now are our brows bound with victorious wreaths,

Our bruised arms hung up for monuments,
Our stern alarums changed to merry meetings,
Our dreadful marches to delightful measures.

(I, i, 1–8)

Sensitive to the rhythm of the seasons, Shakespeare occasionally entitles plays with specific references to times of the year. These titles signal their type and tone, whether comic or tragic. The comic *A Midsummer Night's Dream* is set in the most joyous season and ends with the main couples all happily mated. Conversely, the first half of *The Winter's Tale* has an appropriately grim atmosphere, as King Leontes succumbs to jealousy, accuses his Queen of adultery, and imprisons her. Their son, the kingdom's sole heir, suffers in sympathetic rapport with her:

Conceiving the dishonour of his mother,
He straight declined, drooped, took it deeply,
Fastened and fixed the shame on't in himself;
Threw off his spirit, his appetite, his sleep,
And downright languished.

(II, iii, 13–17)

Soon he is dead, and the Queen apparently dies also. The tone of the story *declines* and *droops*, as the King, now penitent, inhabits a sterile and lonely land. Yet Shakespeare does something radical in this play, turning the wheel of time sixteen years into the future where we discover that the King's daughter has survived, to be married to a King's son, and the seemingly dead Queen is brought back to life. The cycle of life—and the seasons—has progressed and the somber tone has turned to one of celebration. The "Winter's Tale" has been transformed to one of summer.

Shakespeare's plays thus reveal a consciousness acutely aware of the poetic potential of comparisons to the Sun and Moon, of their role in creating calendar time, and especially of the emotional effect of their daily and monthly cycles of rising, culmination, and setting and the seasonal cycles of spring, summer, autumn, and winter. These daily, monthly, and seasonal cycles are the basis of astrology and are frequently and imaginatively used by Shakespeare.

CHAPTER 2

THE PLANETS, THE ELEMENTS, AND THE HUMORS: WHY SHAKESPEARE'S CHARACTERS ARE THE WAY THEY ARE

The Players and the Planets: How Shakespeare Uses Astrology to Create Character(s)

While Shakespeare often compares his characters to the Sun and Moon, he also frequently connects them to other heavenly bodies. In some of his plays characters are explicitly linked to a particular planet by what others say about them, providing keys to their personality types and consequently their attitudes and actions.

Sometimes the characters *themselves* announce their attunement to a particular planet. As an example, in *Much Ado About Nothing*, Don John the Bastard describes both himself and his companion Conrade as being "born under *Saturn* ... I cannot hide what I am: I must be sad when I have cause, and smile at no man's jests ..." (I, iii, 9–11). Saturn has the reputation in astrological circles of having a serious and sober demeanor and being disinclined to enjoy the pleasures of life. Don John is a particularly stubborn and resentful Saturn type, announcing plans to do mischief to his legitimate brother:

> I had rather be a canker in a hedge than a rose in his
> grace, and it better fits my blood to be disdained of all
> than to fashion a carriage to rob love from any. In this,
> though I cannot be said to be a flattering honest man, it
> must not be denied but I am a plain-dealing villain.
>
> (I, iii, 21–5)

In another play, *The Winter's Tale*, Autolycus (a thief) says of himself: "My father named me Autolycus, who being, as I am, littered under *Mercury*, was likewise a snapper-up of unconsidered trifles" (IV, iii, 24–6).[47] Mercury is a sly fellow—in Greek mythology his first act after being born was to steal Apollo's cattle! Thought of as an abstract idea—the principle of quick movement and physical agility—Mercury is associated with a cleverness that can succumb "to trickery and deceit—and at an extreme, to lying and outright thievery. Mercury is the archetypical *Trickster*, a god who plays games with human beings, sometimes for sheer sport (like Puck in *A Midsummer-Night's Dream*, another Mercurial figure) and sometimes to shatter their self-generated illusions."[48]

Sometimes it is the characters' names that reveal their astrological attunement. Hotspur, the very incarnation of the battle-god Mars, describes himself after warfare as "dry with rage and extreme toil" (I *Henry IV*: I, iii, 31). The two parts of his name reveal his connection with Mars, which was thought to have a "ho*t* and dry" nature, and to be associated with anything that goads or incites (like a spur used to prick a horse's flank). These are typical associations with the principle of Mars. Hotspur speaks like the warrior he is, anticipating the final battle with these Mars-related words (all italicized) and relishing the coming conflict:

> Let them come!
> They come like sacrifices in their trim,
> And to the *fire-eyed* maid of *smoky war*
> All *hot and bleeding* will we offer them.
> The *mailed Mars* shall on his altar sit
> Up to the ears in *blood*. I am on *fire*
> To hear this rich reprisal is so nigh
> And yet not ours! Come, let me taste my horse,
> Who is to bear me like a thunderbolt
> Against the bosom of the Prince of Wales.
> Harry to Harry shall, *hot* horse to horse,
> Meet and ne'er part till one drop down a *corpse*.
> (I *Henry IV*: IV, i, 112–23)

In other instances it is not characters' names that reveal the astrological link but their language and behavior. Another typical Mars-like character is "the fiery" Tybalt (as Benvolio dubs him—I, i, 102) who is always picking fights every time he appears in *Romeo and Juliet*. During the opening skirmish between the Montagues and Capulets, Tybalt furiously resists Benvolio's attempts to stop the bloodletting, saying, "What, drawn, and talk of peace? I hate the word / As I hate hell, all Montagues, and thee. / Have at thee, coward!" (I. i, 63–5). When he spies the masked Romeo at the Capulets' ball, he immediately urges his servant, "Fetch me my rapier, boy … To strike him dead I hold it not a sin" (I, v, 52, 56). Capulet restrains him, admonishing him to "be patient, take no note of him. / It is my will, the which if thou respect, / Show a fair presence and put off these frowns, /An ill-beseeming semblance for a feast" (I, v, 68–71)—a perfect instance of cautious old Saturn trying to rein in unruly youthful Mars whose actions are inappropriate at a Venusian party. Tybalt complies, but with great resentment (another Mars-correlated emotion), muttering: "Patience perforce with wilful *choler* [anger] meeting / Makes my flesh tremble in their different greeting. / I will withdraw, but this intrusion shall, / Now seeming sweet, convert to bitt'rest *gall*" (I, v, 86–9), and stomps off. (Bitter substances, like gall, and hot and spicy ones, like red hot peppers, were assigned to Mars.)

Both Hotspur and Tybalt are consistently angry and aggressive throughout the plays, showing Mars' passion for direct engagement in physical combat. But the activity of Mars can shift to its opposite—cowardice—if Mars is poorly placed or poorly aspected in the horoscope. This is true for Mars in Parolles' horoscope, according to Helena in *All's Well That Ends Well*:

> HELENA: Monsieur Parolles, you were born under a charitable star.
> PAROLLES: Under Mars, I.
> HELENA: I especially think, *under* Mars.
> PAROLLES: Why '*under* Mars'?
> HELENA: The wars hath so kept you under that you must needs be born under Mars.
> PAROLLES: When he was predominant.
> HELENA: When he was retrograde, I think rather.
> PAROLLES: Why think you so?
> HELENA: You go so much backward when you fight.
> (I, i, 177–86. Emphasis in the original.)

Every two years in its cycle around the Sun, Mars appears to go backwards ("retrograde") for several months, an optical illusion caused by the different orbital speeds of Earth and Mars. Astrological tradition suggests that such a Mars placement might correlate with a lack of energy, displaced aggression, and an unwillingness to fight either physically or verbally in defense of one's honor and goals. Helena sees through Parolles early in the story as a braggart, liar, and coward, as he is revealed to be later. When he is tricked by his fellow soldiers into thinking that he has been captured by the enemy, he immediately blabs "all the secrets of our camp ... Their force, their purposes ..." (IV, i, 79, 80). Since his Mars is retrograde—meaning contrary or reversed—it is entirely appropriate that instead of being courageous in battle, he would retreat or capitulate to the enemy. For Shakespeare to have known this term and its meaning is another indication of his familiarity with the more sophisticated language of astrology.

The 'Humours': Using Astrology to Discover a Person's "Temperament"

O, you are sick of self-love, Malvolio, and taste with a *distemper'd* appetite. —Olivia *(Twelfth Night*: I, v, 97–8)

Shakespeare does not randomly allude to planets, like the just-mentioned Saturn, Mercury, and Mars. Rather, his work indicates that he knows that they are part of a complex and sophisticated theory of personality relating human beings to the four elements (and to four of the planets in particular: Saturn, the Moon, Jupiter, and Mars). So pervasive and so accepted was this theory that Shakespeare has Sir Toby Belch and Sir Andrew Aguecheek joke about it:

> SIR TOBY: Does not our lives consist of the *four elements?*
> SIR ANDREW: Faith, so they say, but I think it rather consists of eating and drinking.
> *(Twelfth Night*: II, iii, 7–10)

Sir Toby and Sir Andrew are not philosophical by temperament; they would rather indulge their appetites than speculate on more profound subjects. A more serious reference occurs when Pericles speculates on the nativity of his daughter, born during a storm at sea with her mother apparently dead in childbirth. "Now, mild may be thy life!/ ... Thou hast as chiding a nativity / As *fire, air, water, earth*, and heaven can make / To herald thee from the womb." (*Pericles, Prince of Tyre*: Scene 11, 27, 32–4 in the Norton edition; III, i, 27, 32–4 in the Houghton Mifflin edition)

These four elements are an integral part of astrological classification. Each sign of the zodiac is associated with one of them as well as with an assigned planet. As an example, the first sign of the zodiac, Aries, is linked to fire and to the planet Mars. Whenever Shakespeare's characters speak of the elements or one of these four planets, his Renaissance audience would immediately associate them with the astrological theory of personality dubbed the "theory of the humours."

Over the centuries many fine philosophical minds contributed to the development of this humoral theory. Though the history of the theory's evolution is long and convoluted, it is simplified in the following section. It is essential to understand this theory since it is fundamental to understanding Shakespeare's creation of character.

The Origin and Development of the Theory of the "Humours"

The theory of four elements as constituents of both human beings and the cosmos began to coalesce in ancient Greece, though the ideas that came together to form this theory may be much older. Long before Shakespeare's time philosophers in the Western world speculated about the origins and nature of both the universe and human beings. The ancient Greeks, being a practical people who appreciated the physical world, looked first to the elements that obviously constituted it:

- We stand on solid ground, EARTH
- We breathe the AIR that blankets the Earth
- We drink, swim in, and sail on WATER, and
- Occasionally and dramatically FIRE descends from heaven to Earth when lightning strikes flammable tinder or flames out when two pieces of wood are rubbed together. Fire is also present in the blazing Sun that illuminates the day and in the twinkling stars (imagined as fires shining through holes in the dome of heaven).[49]

Four elements may feature in this theory due to their importance for Pythagoras (sixth century BCE) and his school of mystical philosophers, who emphasized both music and mathematics in their thinking. The number four was special to Pythagoreans for several reasons: for one, it was the first number formed by the addition and multiplication of equals (4 = 2 + 2 and 4 = 2 x 2). Michael S. Schneider ruminates on the symbolism of the number four in relation to life on Earth:

> The planet earth below us, solid ground, terra firma, is the supreme symbol for substance, mass, volume, strength, and stability. We organize space on the ground by the four cardinal directions of the compass and our body, dividing the circle of the horizon around us into four quarters in front and back of us, to the left and right. The four-cornered cross in a circle has long been the astronomical symbol for planet Earth. The four traditional winds blow across the four corners of the globe. We quarter not only space but time, naturally dividing the year into four seasons based on the relationship of the sun with the earth around the two equinoxes and two solstices.[50]

But of the four, which element was the most important one? The earliest pre-Socratic thinkers argued about the original or primal "stuff" out of which the world was created. Water? Or fire?[51] Whichever one dominated, the supreme ancient Greek philosopher Plato (fifth century BCE) was the first to call earth, water, air, and fire "elements" in his dialogue *Timaeus*, in which he also said that diseases resulted from an excess or deficiency of each. Aristotle (384–322 BCE), Plato's most famous student, linked the qualities of hot-dry, cold-dry, hot-wet, and cold-wet with the four fluids in the body and the elements, pulling all the categories together.

Not until the second century CE was a coherent theory of human personality developed related to these ideas. It was Galen, the Roman physician to Emperor Marcus Aurelius, who coined the phrase "theory of the humours." ("Humor" is the Latin word for "moisture," from which our word "humidity" derives; the reference was to the four principal bodily fluids.[52]) Galen believed that the fluid balances in the body were influenced by the foods you ate (warm foods tended to produce yellow bile, while cold foods produced phlegm), geographic location, time of year, stage of life, and occupation, so that the ratio of the fluids could change. Thus the theory reflected a connection between personality and place as well as an interdependence of mind and body. It was the first truly *holistic* theory of health.

Up to this point in history these theories are being developed by philosophers and physicians. The astrology comes in with Claudius Ptolemy (late first and early second century CE), the most famous transmitter of astrological ideas for the next fifteen hundred years. Ptolemy was not a practicing astrologer but a writer and compiler whose treatises on astronomy, mathematics, and geography were as influential as his astrological works. Ptolemy does not refer to humors or four bodily fluids, but he does assign qualities to the signs of the zodiac, partly based on their order in the seasonal cycle and partly on their planetary rulers:

> In Book I of the *Tetrabiblos*, Ptolemy sets forth his contribution to the idea that the astrological mixtures in a birth chart can be useful in understanding a person. Here is temperament applied by the astrologer, working with the criteria supplied by the philosopher (and used by the physician for the body). Ptolemy firmly believes that the "co-mixtures" in a person's birth chart describe that person's body and soul—in this we can see the application of "temperament" to soul as well as to body—the beginnings of its psychological application.[53]

Ptolemy even sets out a method of determining an individual's characteristics by analyzing the horoscope—the first writer to do so.

With the decline of the Roman Empire and the fading of the classical traditions, only a few additions and contributions are made to this theory over the ensuing centuries. Vettius Valens, who lived during Ptolemy's time, was the earliest astrologer to connect the elements to the triplicities of fire, earth, air, and water (so that Aries, Leo and Sagittarius, for example, are all fire signs). The only important additional piece was to link the humors to the planets and the zodiacal signs they rule. This was added by the Arabs, when learning flourished in the Middle East (eighth to twelfth centuries CE), particularly by astrologer Abu Mashar (787–866 CE). As an example, for the sign Aries, Mashar writes, "Its nature is hot, dry, fiery, yellow bile, its taste is bitter, and it is masculine."[54] Arabic astrologers kept alive not only the astrology of the Greeks but also their philosophical works.

Now we have a fully developed theory of both health and personality whose connections are shown in the accompanying table. Your "temperament" (from the Latin word "to blend") or disposition depends on the balance of the four fluids. Though amounts of these fluids could fluctuate over time, people did tend to be predominantly one type or perhaps two combined. In *Antony and Cleopatra*, for example, Cleopatra claims to be attuned to more than one element: "I am *fire and air*, my other elements / I give to baser life" (V, ii, 280–1).[55] An emphasis on one particular element gives rise to very obvious and recognizable personality traits as well as tendencies to certain diseases, (also shown in the accompanying table, drawn from a variety of sources).[56] Since the elements are associated with qualities, seasons of the year, and most especially the planets, your temperament can be determined from your horoscope and its planetary placements.

Even from the beginning of the theory's development, though, philosophers think that you are not completely at the mercy of your humoral balance or temperament type: "The Galenic-Hippocratic system allowed … for the conjunction of physical with moral health, and for the possibility of channeling passions and correcting excesses through the use of reason and will…."[57] The exaltation of reason in the philosophical worldview that underpins Shakespeare's works implies that you can influence your temperament by controlling your attitudes and thoughts as well as regulating your emotions and behavior.

The table on the following page illustrates these qualities.

During the period of the Arabic flowering, this system is transmitted back into Europe and can be found in its entirety in the works of an important medieval astrologer, Guido Bonatti (thirteenth century CE). Bonatti writes an eight-hundred-page encyclopedic textbook, the *Liber Astronomiae*, which draws on Greek and Arab sources. Like his predecessors, he clusters qualities, elements, polarities, and descriptors together with the signs. By this time the types are also associated with certain physical characteristics (sanguine types were thought to be typically red-faced, while phlegmatics were pale of complexion—Shakespeare frequently mentions such physical details, giving his audience clues to the character's type) and with a tendency to certain illnesses.

Bonatti was famous, so much so that in his *Inferno*, the famous Italian poet Dante Aligheri placed Bonatti in the eighth circle of hell with his head turned backwards as a punishment for trying to look into the future. Bonatti's work was circulated long after his death and was an important source of information about astrology through the Renaissance. Since understanding the associations between signs, their ruling planets, and their qualities and characteristics is essential for our pur-

The Elements, the Planets, and the Temperamental Types

ELEMENT	FIRE	WATER	AIR	EARTH
Associated Planet:	Mars	Moon	Jupiter	Saturn
Nature:	hot	cold	wet	dry
Qualities:	hot and dry	cold and wet	hot and wet	cold and dry
Humor or Fluid	yellow bile (gall, choler)	phlegm	blood	black bile
Temperament:	choleric	phlegmatic	sanguine	melancholic
Character Traits:	enthusiastic	patient	agreeable	reserved
	excitable	shy	optimistic, cheerful	pessimistic, gloomy
	impulsive, rash	cautious	passionate	moody
	energetic	easy-going	generous	studious
	quick-tempered	tranquil	simple, naive	introspective, pensive
	violent	sluggish, lazy	impulsive	depressive, sad
	impatient	steady	hopeful	thoughtful
	lively	dull	communicative	obstinate
	bold	cowardly	amorous, loving	pragmatic
	assertive/aggressive	calm, relaxed	sociable, friendly	cynical
	ambitious	placid	fun-loving	unenterprising
	proud	conservative	talkative	loyal
	irritable, angry	apathetic, passive	lively	philosophical
	boisterous	self-contained	even-tempered	analytical
	vengeful	inactive	happy	serious, sober
Season of the Year	summer	winter	spring	autumn

poses in probing Shakespeare's plays, here is a bit of Bonatti's commentary on the twelve signs of the zodiac, grouped in threes according to their associated elements. The important point in the following is the clustering together of elements (fire, etc.), the zodiacal signs, and the consequent personality types (choleric, etc.):

> Aries, Leo and Sagittarius make up the first triplicity.... This triplicity is called hot and dry because each of the three signs is *fiery*, hot, dry, masculine, oriental, diurnal, *choleric*, and bitter with respect to taste.... Taurus, Virgo and Capricorn make up the second triplicity because each one of these signs is *earthy*, cold and dry, feminine, nocturnal, *melancholic*, southern, and sharp or acid with respect to taste.... Gemini, Libra and Aquarius make up the third triplicity because each of these signs is *airy*, hot and moist, masculine, diurnal, *sanguine*, occidental and sweet with respect to taste.... Cancer, Scorpio and Pisces make up the fourth triplicity because each of these signs is *watery*, cold and moist, feminine, nocturnal, *phlegmatic* and salty with respect to taste, though some say insipid [emphasis added].[58]

This theory was popular and much discussed and developed through the medieval period and into the Renaissance. It was the basis of classical, medieval, and Islamic medicine, persisting into the nineteenth century and even the modern day. The idea of an internal balance is still fundamental to Ayurvedic medicine in India and in the traditional medicine of China. Although this theory is no longer part of common discourse in the West, we still speak of people being "even-tempered" or "good-humored" and say that on an off-day someone is "out of humor" or "bad-tempered." We also continue to use some of the humoral remedies despite the fact the model upon which they are based has fallen out of favor:

> It still seems reasonable to eat root vegetables and "warming" spices like mustard, ginger, pepper, and cloves in the winter and "cooling" foods like green vegetables and lemons in the summer ... [since] one needed to counteract the heat and dryness of summer weather with cold and moist substances.[59]

Introduction to
Shakespeare's Use of the Humoral Types

In Shakespeare's era most people still believed in this theory of the humors, still believed that everything in the visible or "sublunary" world ("beneath the Moon") derived its nature from some combination of these four elements: earth, water, air, and fire. Since the system correlating the four elements and four planets with personality profiles was still in common use, Shakespeare quite naturally uses the four types as templates to create characters and reveal their qualities, though through his art he transforms them from stereotypes to vital and memorable personalities.

The theory offered a number of ways to convey personality. The model was a comprehensive one that correlated many aspects of human and cosmic experience—the planets, hours of the day, seasons of the year, stages of a human life, the appearance of the physical body, organs within the body, and even predispositions to certain diseases and associations with particular professions. A humoral type might be revealed through physiognomy—features of the face or shape and size of the body. Phlegmatics, for instance, were described as having pale complexions, the lack of color resulting from a lack of "blood" or courage—explaining their easy-going or even cowardly nature. When Sir Toby comments on Sir Andrew Aguecheek's hair, describing it as hanging "like flax on a distaff" (*Twelfth Night*: I, iii, 85) in long, thin yellowish strings, the implication is that since even his hair lacks strength, he is the cowardly type of phlegmatic—a small detail but one the audience would have noted.

As for cholerics, any number of details might identify them, among them the overaction of a particular organ in the body. In *Julius Caesar* Brutus chastises Cassius for taking bribes, and when Cassius protests, Brutus admonishes him to swallow his anger with reference to a part of the body with which it was associated: "By the gods,/ You shall digest the venom of your *spleen*,/ Though it do split you." (IV, ii, 100–2) Since choler was also synchronous with the summer season, it is entirely appropriate that Benvolio begs Mercutio to go indoors rather than walk about the streets of Verona in mid-day (the choleric time of day), for "The day is hot, the Capels are abroad,/ And if we meet we shall not scape a brawl,/ For now, these hot days, is the mad blood stirring." (*Romeo and Juliet*: III, i, 2–4)

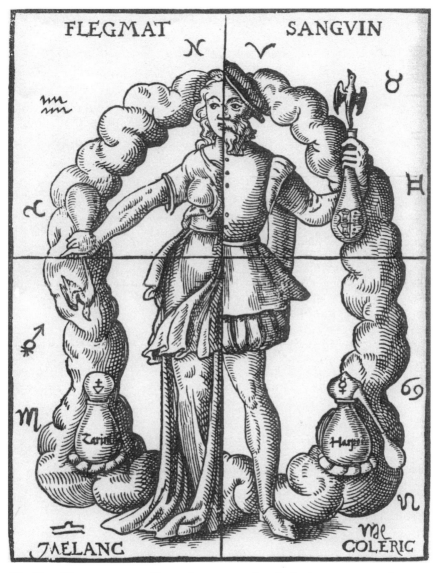

The Four Temperaments. From the upper right, clockwise: sanguine, choleric, melancholic, and phlegmatic types depicted in one person. The sanguine opposes the melancholic as the phlegmatic opposes the choleric. (Thurneysser, Quinta essentia, 1574)

Some of these associations are explored in the sections below, though writers on the humoral system are often inconsistent in the connections they make between all these categories. Shakespeare, though, is on the whole consistent in *his* use of them. To make a character's type clear to the audience, he often gives more than one clue. For dramatic purposes, he often emphasizes the more negative qualities, even taking them to extremes, to make it easy to identify the type. Using the theory of the humors allows him to explore the consequences of imbalances in personality, whether for comic or tragic effect. The scheme not only provides a shorthand method of conveying character, but it is also useful to a creative artist since it lends itself to more subtle revelation of character type through poetic description.

This theory is also pertinent to the plays themselves. Since each is keyed to a sign associated with one of the four elements—and thus one of the four humors—at least one character in each play is an outstanding example of the type associated with that element. This will be obvious from the discussion of various characters in the following sections, as well as in the chapters on each of the six plays to be considered. Since *Romeo and Juliet*, for instance, is keyed to Gemini (an air sign), we would expect to find a sterling example of the sanguine type (related to air) in the play. Friar Laurence is an obvious choice, "cheerful" and "optimistic" that a marriage between the two lovers will resolve the enmity between the two families. The young lovers, of course, are sanguine too: "amorous" as well as "lively" and "impulsive."

The Melancholic Type: Keyed to Earth and Saturn

JAQUES: I prithee, pretty youth, let me be better
    acquainted with thee.
ROSALIND: They say you are a *melancholy* fellow.
JAQUES: I am so. I do love it better than laughing.
ROSALIND: Those that are in extremity of either are
    abominable fellows ...

                         (*As You Like It*: IV, i, 1–6)

Of the four types, the melancholic is one of the most complex and fascinating, Hamlet being an outstanding example. This tragic hero reveals his type in the very first scene in which he appears, when his mother

Gertrude inquires about his health and he describes his own appearance in a number of significant physical details:

> 'Tis not alone my *inky cloak*, good-mother,
> Nor customary *suits of solemn black*,
> Nor *windy suspiration of forced breath*,
> No, nor the *fruitful river in the eye*,
> Nor the *dejected haviour of the visage*,
> Together with all forms, moods, *shows of grief*
> That can denote me truly.
>
> (I, ii, 77–83)

Every single line in this speech contains details that disclose his type. Although Hamlet insists that these are but "the trappings and the suits of woe," they accurately reveal his temperament. Shakespeare's audience would instantly recognize him as a melancholic. This means that he has a dominance of the earth element, with a personality likely to be depressed, gloomy in outlook, and disinclined to take action. Because earth is the heaviest element, melancholics are "heavy," with low spirits and little energy. Fittingly, they are also thought to be profound or "deep" thinkers, much given to philosophical speculations on the distressing but inevitable experiences of human life (pain, illness, poverty, injustice, and—most of all—one's inevitable mortality). Hamlet perfectly expresses these qualities.

Another pure melancholic type (this one comic rather than tragic) is Jaques in *As You Like It*, who jests with Rosalind in the quotation cited at the beginning of this section. Though Rosalind cautions against being either too pessimistic (melancholic) or too optimistic (sanguine), Jaques actually relishes being the former. The lord Amiens, who along with Jaques attends the banished Duke in the Forest of Arden, sings the lovely song "Under the greenwood tree." When Jaques asks to hear more, Amiens demurs, saying, "It will make you *melancholy*, Monsieur Jaques." He responds, "I thank it. More, I prithee, more. I can suck *melancholy* out of a song as a weasel sucks eggs" (II, v, 10–12). Jaques' attitude toward life, like that of some melancholics, is distinctly negative: he enjoys the observation of a fool he meets in the forest, that "from hour to hour we ripe and ripe, / And then from hour to hour we rot and rot ..." (II, vii, 26–7).

Shakespeare is poking fun at the self-pitying melancholic who uses his personality type to get attention and enjoys wallowing in a superficial depression. Other characters in the play easily and independently recognize his type and continue to make direct references to it. One of the lords attending on the banished Duke refers to him as "melancholy Jaques," recounting Jaques' diatribes against hunting in the forest and his weeping over a wounded deer (II, i). It is Jaques who delivers the drily melancholic speech beginning, "All the world's a stage...."[60] This speech mocks every phase of life, ending in the extreme reductionism of "second childishness and more oblivion, / Sans teeth, sans eyes, sans taste, sans everything"—sad thoughts that would indeed delight the comic melancholic (II, vii, 164–5).

But melancholics could be serious threats, not only to others' psychological health but also to the health of the state. Another recognizable melancholic is "that spare Cassius" whom Julius Caesar (rightly) distrusts. Shakespeare uses the same technique he used for Hamlet, providing physical details of physiognomy and appearance to establish Cassius' type and personality. Caesar draws attention to these to justify his discomfort around Cassius:

> He reads much,
> He is a great observer, and he looks
> Quite through the deeds of men. He loves no plays
> As thou dost, Antony; he hears no music.
> Seldom he smiles, and smiles in such a sort
> As if he mocked himself, and scorned his spirit
> That could be moved to smile at anything.
> Such men as he be never at heart's ease
> Whiles they behold a greater than themselves,
> And therefore are they very dangerous.
>
> (I, ii, 202–11)

Since melancholics were thought to be intelligent and observant, their enhanced critical faculties often made them profoundly dissatisfied with other human beings and the general state of the world. Caesar obviously prefers a different type: "Let me have men about me that are fat, / Sleek-headed men and such as sleep a-nights. / Yon Cassius has a lean and hungry look. / He thinks too much. Such men are dangerous" (I, ii, 192–5). Caesar obviously prefers an entourage of phlegmatics! He would be more comfortable with men around him who are likely to be easy-going, placid, and even dull. Although Caesar disdains the melancholic type, the Elizabethans, like the ancients, were fascinated by melancholia because it often correlated with creative genius as well as depression, "frenzy," and even madness. This will be explored further in Chapter 12 on *King Lear*—a play that features a melancholic.[61]

Melancholy was so pervasive and recognizable a humor that it could describe not only a personality but also a place or situation. In *I Henry IV*, when the dissolute Falstaff and the Prince are joking together and deciding what pleasures to engage in next, the Prince suggests, "What sayest thou to a hare, or the *melancholy* of Moor-ditch?" (I, ii, 68–9) Hares were thought to be chronically sad so that eating their flesh could produce a melancholic state. Moor-ditch was a swampy area just outside the London city walls and was more like a sewer—certainly a place to inspire morose thoughts.

Since melancholy resonates more with tragedies, such a mood is inappropriate for occasions of festivity and feasting. At the opening of *A Midsummer Night's Dream* Theseus instructs Philostrate, the master of his revels (and so in charge of organizing the entertainment for Theseus' coming wedding),

> Go, Philostrate,
> Stir up the Athenian youth to merriments.
> Awake the pert and nimble spirit of mirth.
> Turn *melancholy* forth to funerals—
> The pale companion is not for our pomp.
>
> (I, i, 11–5)

The Choleric Type: Keyed to Fire and Mars

> Do you find some occasion to anger Cassio ...
> he's rash and very sudden in *choler*, and haply may
> strike at you. —Iago to Roderigo (*Othello*: II, i, 256, 261–2)

Of the four temperaments, the choleric, keyed to the fire element and Mars, is the easiest to recognize, particularly because Shakespeare so often exaggerates the traits typical of the type. Extremely choleric characters appear frequently in his plays. Being at the very least energetic and excitable, they generate interest—and being at an extreme angry and violent, they provoke conflict and drive the plots. Shakespeare scholar John W. Draper notes that:

> Shakespeare's plays mention *chole*r and *choleric* some forty times, and provide ... more than thirty bona fide examples: some of these are blunt, honest soldiers, men of a word and a blow, like Tybalt, Capulet, Hotspur, Glendower, Fluellen, Fortinbras, Othello, Cassio, Macduff, Enobarbus, and Coriolanus; some are rulers or courtiers like Longaville and Biron in *Love's Labour's*, or Valentine in *Two Gentlemen*, who "hunts" for "honor," or the Bastard of Faulconbridge, Henry V, Claudio in *Much Ado*, Laertes, Bertram, Brabantio, and the jealous Leontes.... These choleric characters are active and dynamic; they make events and keep the plot in motion. They are the very stuff of drama and especially of tragedy with its catastrophic clash of wills.[62]

So this type is particularly useful in generating conflict in the tragedies—and in some cases humor in the comedies. Katherine, the vitriolic shrew in the comic *The Taming of the Shrew*, is overwhelmingly choleric. Petruccio, determined to make her more patient and amenable, deprives her of food upon their arrival at his house after the wedding.

> PETRUCCIO: What's this—mutton? ...
>   'Tis burnt, and so is all the meat.
>   What dogs are these? Where is the rascal cook?
>   How durst you villains bring it from the dresser
>   And serve it thus to me that love it not?
>   There, [throwing food] take it to you, trenchers, cups,
>   and all,
>   You heedless jolt-heads and unmannered slaves.
>   What, do you grumble? I'll be with you straight.
>   [He chases the servants away]
> KATHERINE: I pray you, husband, be not so disquiet.
>   The meat was well, if you were so contented.
> PETRUCCIO: I tell thee, Kate, 'twas burnt and dried away,
>   And I expressly am forbid to touch it,
>   For it engenders *chole*r, planteth anger,

And better 'twere that both of us did fast,
Since of ourselves are *choleric*,
Than feed it with such overroasted flesh.

(IV, i, 140, 141–55)

One of Petruccio's servants perceives his plan: "He kills her in her own humour" (IV, i, 160). In other words, he will outdo her in displaying bad temper. But by the end of the play her angry temper has subsided into gracious acquiescence as she even agrees with her husband that the Sun is the Moon in order to keep him in good "temper." She illustrates the Elizabethan belief that it is possible—though not always easy or without suffering—to modify your temperament and consequently alter the balance of your bodily fluids.

In line with the theory of the humors, characters not normally choleric can become choleric not only because of the food they eat (like meat, especially burnt meat) but also because of frustrating circumstances. Witness the dialogue between the disillusioned Brutus accusing Cassius, his fellow conspirator in the assassination of Julius Caesar, of selling offices for gold. Brutus' criticism of Cassius' actions incites anger:

CASSIUS: Brutus, bay not me;
    I'll not endure it. You forget yourself
    To hedge me in. I am a soldier, I ...
    Urge me no more, I shall forget myself.
    Have mind upon your health. Tempt me no
        farther....
BRUTUS: Hear me, for I will speak.
    Must I give way and room to your rash *choler*?
    I be frighted when a madman stares?
CASSIUS: O ye gods, ye gods! Must I endure all this?
BRUTUS: All this? Ay, more. Fret till your proud heart
    break.
    Go show your slaves how *choleric* you are,
    And make your bondmen tremble.

(*Julius Caesar*: IV, ii, 80–2, 88–9, 92–8)

Similarly, in *Hamlet* Guildenstern informs Hamlet of his uncle Claudius' aroused anger at Hamlet's disturbed behavior: "The King, sir, ... [i]s in his retirement marvelous *distempered*." When Hamlet sarcastically responds, "With drink, sir?," Guildenstern's reply is, "No, my lord, rather with *choler*" (III, ii, 274, 276–8). Claudius is so fearfully wrathful of Hamlet that he plots to have his nephew murdered when sent shipbound for England.

Even when a play is not attuned to a fire sign, choleric characters may be introduced to spark the action, as Hotspur and Tybalt do—the hot-tempered types mentioned earlier. In *As You Like It* the resentful Oliver deprives his younger brother Orlando of the education appropriate to a gentleman and maliciously urges Charles the wrestler to do him serious injury: "I had as lief thou didst break his neck as his finger" (I, i, 124–5). When that plan fails, Oliver intends to burn down Orlando's lodging while he sleeps—a dastardly use of the very element that corresponds to his type (a detail the Elizabethan audience would doubtless have caught). In a parallel plot the usurping Duke Frederick, who has already banished his older brother and legitimate ruler, suddenly threatens his niece Rosaline. As the courtier Le Beau warns Orlando,

> [O]f late this Duke
> Hath ta'en displeasure 'gainst his gentle niece,
> Grounded upon no other argument
> But that the people praise her for her virtues
> And pity her for her good father's sake.
> And, on my life, his malice 'gainst the lady
> Will suddenly break forth.
>
> (I, ii, 244–50)

Being "humorous," the Duke has changed his opinion of Orlando as a "gallant youth" who overthrew Charles the wrestler. Now he also doubts the wisdom of allowing Rosaline to stay at court as a companion to his daughter Celia. Due to his choleric threats, Orlando and the two women flee for their lives to the Forest of Arden where the tone of the play changes to romantic comedy.

Choleric characters are highly useful additions to a drama (as they are to furthering the plot of a comedy like *As You Like It*), but their temperaments make them dangerous to be around and provoke others to try and restrain them. In *I Henry IV* Henry Percy, son of the Earl of Northumberland and dubbed "Hotspur," is relentlessly caustic and aggressive in his speech, especially in a scene in which he repeatedly verbally abuses the Welsh wizard Glendower. (This seems extremely unwise if Glendower has the magical abilities he says he has.) Hotspur's fellow rebels chastise him for his contemptuous disrespect and try to moderate his speech, drawing attention to Glendower's self-command in contrast to Hotspur's rashness:

> MORTIMER: Fie, cousin Percy, how you cross my father[-
> in-law]!
> HOTSPUR: I cannot choose. Sometimes he *angers* me ...
> MORTIMER: He holds your *temper* in a high respect
> And curbs himself even of his natural scope
> When you come 'cross his *humour;* faith, he does....
> WORCESTER: [to Hotspur]. In faith, my lord, you are too
> willful-blame,
> And since your coming hither have done enough
> To put him quite besides his patience.
> You must needs learn, lord, to amend this fault.
> Though sometimes it show *greatness, courage, blood*—
> And that's the dearest grace it renders you—
> Yet oftentimes it doth present *harsh rage,*
> Defect of manners, want of government,
> Pride, haughtiness, opinion, and disdain,
> The least of which haunting a nobleman
> Loseth men's hearts, and leaves behind a stain
> Upon the beauty of all parts besides ...
> (III, i, 143–4, 166–8, 173–84)

This is an especially revealing speech about the dangers of extreme choler: while spurring courage and honor, in excess it alienates others and spoils one's best qualities. Though Hotspur agrees with Worcester, admitting "Well, I am schooled," implying that he will rein in his temper, Glendower sees that, "hot Lord Percy is on *fire* to go" to war against Henry IV and his son Prince Hal (III, i, 259). On the battlefield Hotspur courts "brave death," demands to hear "all the lofty instruments of war, / And by that music let us all embrace" (V, ii, 86, 97–8), and dies by Prince Hal's sword. Though he has to defeat Hotspur to protect the throne, the young Prince praises Hotspur's "great heart" and large spirit (V, iv, 86). Still, for choleric types, like the rebel Hotspur in *I Henry IV* and the rebellious Macdonwald in *Macbeth*, Martian energy is liable to overwhelm their personalities so that their actions threaten others and even the state. In the end, they most threaten themselves: they are all dead by the conclusion of the plays.[63]

The Phlegmatic Type: Keyed to Water and the Moon

PETO: Falstaff!—Fast asleep behind the arras, and snort-
     ing like a horse.
PRINCE HARRY: Hark how hard he fetches breath.
                              (I Henry IV: II, iv, 482–3)

Phlegmatic types, with too much water, are likely to be passive and easily intimidated—almost literally "water-logged." Gentle Ophelia, Hamlet's former love, is revealed to have a phlegmatic temperament by other characters' sad remarks about her poignant death. Attempting to hang garlands of flowers and weeds on a willow branch overhanging a brook, Ophelia falls into the water and drowns. The Queen's comment to Ophelia's brother Laertes is that she seemed, "As one incapable of her own distress, / *Or like a creature native and indued / Unto that element.*" Laertes can only add, "*Too much of water* hast thou, poor Ophelia" (IV, vii, 149–51, 157). It is ironically apt that she, a watery type, died in the water element. Gertrude's comments would have carried a profound significance to the Elizabethan audience familiar with the types. Though women in general—as well as children—were thought to be "moist" and consequently phlegmatic, Ophelia is phlegmatic to the extreme: so easily manipulated by her father Polonius and the King and so wounded by Hamlet's rejection of her that her sensitivity and passivity lead to her tragic end.

Phlegmatics turn up in plays that are attuned to one of the three water signs of the zodiac. Bottom the Weaver in *A Midsummer Night's Dream* is a typical phlegmatic in a play keyed to one of them, Cancer. Unlike the shy and easily dominated Ophelia, Bottom fits some of the other descriptors for a phlegmatic by being "easy-going," "steady," and "calm," even when ass-headed and loved by a faery queen. Unlike Ophelia, he exhibits the more positive qualities of this temperament.

BOTTOM: I see their knavery. This is to make an ass of me, to fright me, if they could; but I will not stir from this place, do what they

can. I will walk up and down here, and I will sing, that they shall
hear I am not afraid.

(III, I, 106–9)

Phlegmatics are completely opposite in character to the cholerics. Lacking the energy and courage of the choleric, they are typically
averse to action and effort or are downright cowardly. In *Twelfth Night*,
the foolish knight Sir Andrew Aguecheek is manipulated into dueling
with the disguised Viola (whom other characters rightly judge to be an
unlikely fighter). Sir Andrew is encouraged by Sir Toby, Olivia's uncle, to
sue for Olivia's hand in marriage, but he spends more time drinking and
carousing with Sir Toby than in courting her. When Sir Andrew protests
Olivia's attentions to Viola instead of him, he is persuaded that Olivia
only wants to make him jealous, "to exasperate you, to awake your dor-
mouse valour, to put *fire* in your heart, and brimstone in your liver" (III,
ii, 16–17). But when Sir Andrew exits to write a challenge "in a *martial*
hand," Sir Toby vows that if Sir Andrew "were opened and you find so
much *blood* in his liver as will clog the foot of a flea, I'll eat the rest of th'
anatomy" (III, ii, 52–3). True to his type, Sir Andrew regrets the challenge
and wants to avoid fighting by bribing his perceived rival:

> SIR TOBY: They say he [Viola] has been fencer to the
> Sophy [the Shah of Persia].
> SIR ANDREW: Pox on't, I'll not meddle with him.
> SIR TOBY: Ay, but he will not now be pacified, Fabian can
> scarce hold him yonder.
> SIR ANDREW: Plague on't, an I thought he had been
> valiant and so cunning in fence I'd have seen him
> damned ere I'd have challenged him. Let him let the
> matter slip and I'll give him my horse, grey Capulet.

(III, iv, 247–55)

In another water-keyed play, *Macbeth*, the tipsy Porter is a phlegmatic type. Even while inebriated, he calmly imagines himself as the
"porter of hell-gate" and makes witty jokes about professions notorious
for defrauding the public and about alcohol's effect on sexual desire. It is
apt that he philosophizes about the effect of drink since he observes that
it increases urine and urination is often referred to as "making water."

Somewhat "dull"—or with his senses dulled by wine—he seems entirely unaware of and unfazed by the castle's atmosphere.

Inebriates in Shakespeare's plays—Sir Andrew, Sir Toby, and the Porter, among them—all are phlegmatics. Since wine was the drink of choice in Elizabethan times (with water not always available or safe to drink), it substitutes for water and becomes the key to a character's temperament. In *The Tempest*, the drunken butler Stephano escapes from the wrecked ship and arrives safely on shore by riding the waves on a butt of sack (a cask of Spanish white wine). Linking up with the jester Trinculo and the resentful Caliban, soon they are all drunk and end up mired in a "filthy-mantled *pool* ... dancing up to th' chins, that the foul *lake* / O'er-stunk their feet." Appropriately, like Ophelia, they are mired in water. Even their precious bottles of wine sink into the water and are lost, returning to their native element. (IV, i, 182–4, 207)

The most notable phlegmatic in all of Shakespeare's plays— and equally notably a drunkard—is Falstaff. "Easy-going," "lazy," and "cowardly" to the extreme, like the other drunken phlegmatics in Shakespeare's works he is a comic figure. Upon his first entrance, Prince Hal jocularly describes him as "fat-witted with drinking of old sack, and unbuttoning thee after supper, and sleeping upon benches after noon …." (I, ii, 2–4)

Falstaff and his comrades are thieves by night, and the Prince pulls a trick on them to expose Falstaff's timidity and cowardice. After Falstaff and his confederates have snatched three hundred pounds destined for the King's exchequer from some night travelers, the disguised Prince and Poins surprise them. They run away, leaving the booty behind. When everyone gathers the next day at the Boar's Head Tavern in Eastcheap, Falstaff protests that they were set upon by a dozen—no, sixteen—no, fifty—men and that he fought valiantly against the attackers: "I have scaped by miracle. I am eight times thrust through the doublet, four through the hose, my buckler cut through and through, my sword hack'd like a hand-saw.... I never dealt better since I was a man ..." (II, v, 151–5). That this fantasy fight took place only in Falstaff's imagination is exposed by the Prince, who declares that only two of them set on Falstaff and his friends, that he has the money here in the tavern to prove his story, and that Falstaff "carried [his] guts away as nimbly, with as quick dexterity, and roared for mercy, and still run and roared, as ever I heard bull-calf" (II, v, 239–41).

Falstaff is unfazed and continues to be incorrigibly himself, even on the battlefield. When the desperate Prince begs Falstaff to lend him his sword and Falstaff balks, the Prince sticks his hand into the sheath to draw it out—and finds a bottle of sack instead of a sword! (Not the weapon of a choleric type but as a liquid more suitable for a phlegmatic.) In line with his temperament being most opposite to that of a fighter, when Falstaff is conscripted by Hal to lead a regiment into the battle, Falstaff meditates on the word "honor" and decides that it is meaningless to him: "What is honour? A word." (V, i, 133) Since it applies not to the living but to the dead, he will have none of it. When attacked by the enemy Douglas, Falstaff's tactic is to fall down and play dead. To add to his blatant effrontery, when Falstaff leaps up and discovers that he is alone on the field with the dead Hotspur (killed by the Prince), he boasts that *he* killed Hotspur—and the Prince graciously allows him to get away with the lie. Sluggish, lazy, and disinclined to fight, Falstaff is phlegmatic to the end.[64]

The Sanguine Type: Keyed to Air and Jupiter

Yet who would have thought the old man to have had so much *blood* in him?
—Lady Macbeth about King Duncan (Macbeth: V, i, 33–4)

The sanguine type comes closest to being perfectly balanced, though of course for a human being to be perfectly balanced is almost impossible. Even if you achieve equilibrium for a brief moment, emotional states and environmental conditions change and can upset this delicate state. The sanguine type was certainly the ideal. It is still defined very positively: "of buoyant disposition; hopeful, confident; cheerful. Ruddy and robust." Just the type of person you would like to have around! Sanguines are thought to exhibit mental stability and robust health since each of the four humors is found in equal proportions in both body and psyche. The implication is that the original perfect human being was of this type. The other three temperaments represent devolutions from this first "edenic" state, that of being warm and moist ("hot and wet" in the Table).[65]

The sanguine type was actually added to the Greek scheme by the Romans. There is no word in Greek for "sanguine." In Latin "sanguine" means "blood."[66] (If you bleed to death, you have died by "exsanguination.") The reference to blood likely arose because sanguines were typically thought to have rosy (that is, healthful) complexions. One of the highly praised sanguine types in Shakespeare's works is the honorable Brutus in *Julius Caesar*. At the end of the play Mark Antony delivers an elegiac tribute to the dead Brutus, praised as the perfectly balanced man:

> This was the noblest Roman of them all.
> All the conspirators save only he,
> Did that they did in envy of great Caesar.
> He only in a general honest thought
> And common good to all made one of them.
> His life was gentle, and *the elements*
> *So mixed in him* that Nature might stand up
> And say to all the world "This was a man."
>
> (V, v, 67–74)

Given that sanguinity was most desirable and few dubious traits were associated with it (except possibly naïveté like King Duncan's in *Macbeth*), sanguine characters in Shakespeare are consistently presented as admirable.

Another sanguine type, this one female, is Rosalind, who counters Jacques' invitation to indulge in melancholy by protesting that those who overindulge in either laughing or crying are "abominable fellows" (*As You Like It*: IV, i, 1–6, cited before the section on melancholy). With these lines, she reveals the balance of her temperament. While the love-struck Orlando dashes about the Forest of Arden penning bad verses and posting them on trees, the disguised Rosalind attempts to reason him out of his fantasy of her and into genuine love—in other words, to make him temperamentally more balanced like her.

Rosalind is not the only sanguine type in this play. Her father, Duke Senior, maintains an optimistic view of life despite having been banished by his younger brother from the court and into the wilds of the forest. There he determines to make the best of it and to appreciate even the "icy fang / And churlish chiding of the winter's wind" (II, i, 6–7), which feelingly persuade him of the vulnerable human condition. Surely, he avows, this honest life is better than the falsities and hypocrises of courtly life:

> Now my co-mates and brothers in exile,
> Hath not old custom made this life more sweet

Than that of painted pomp? Are not these woods
More free from peril than the envious court?

(II, i, 1–4)

He champions a philosophical approach to life's altering circumstances in these famous lines that follow the ones above:

Sweet are the uses of adversity,
Which, like the toad, ugly and venomous,
Wears yet a precious jewel in his head;
And this our life, exempt from public haunt,
Find tongues in trees, books in the running brooks,
Sermons in stones, and good in everything.

(II, i, 12–17)

No wonder the noble Amiens, who has accompanied the Duke into exile, can chime in, "Happy is your Grace, / That can translate the stubbornness of fortune / Into so quiet and so sweet a style." (I, i, 18–20) Duke Senior is a classic sanguine.

So too is Viola in *Twelfth Night*, another heroine who meets with adversity and makes the best of it. Shipwrecked on the coast of Illyria, she determines to disguise herself as a man (as Rosaline does when banished from court) and take service with Duke Orsino, reputed to be as noble in nature as in name. Resourceful and adaptable, once she commits herself to this plan, she resolves to trust to the fortunate unfolding of events: "What else may hap, to time I will commit" (I, ii, 56). Of course the situation, as is characteristic of comedies, becomes more complicated: she falls in love with Orsino, who is in love with Olivia, who falls for Viola disguised as a man—but she calmly and patiently trusts in something greater than herself to sort things out:

How will this fadge [turn out]? My master loves her
    dearly,
And I, poor monster, fond as much on him;
And she, mistaken, seems to dote on me.
What will become of this? As I am man,
My state is desperate for my master's love.
As I am woman, now alas the day,

What thriftless sighs shall poor Olivia breathe!
O time! Thou must untangle this, not I.
It is too hard a knot for me t' untie.

(II, ii, 31–9)

  Shakespeare often introduces a sanguine personality to provide strong contrast to the dominant temperament foregrounded in a given play. Amid a plethora of choleric types in *Macbeth*, King Duncan stands out as sanguine. Approaching Glamis castle he cheerfully remarks, "This castle hath a pleasant seat. The air / Nimbly and sweetly recommends itself / Unto our gentle senses" (I, vi, 1–3). Consistently positive, generous, and appreciative of everything done for him, Duncan rewards Macbeth with new titles and properties, gifts his wife with a rich diamond (II, i, 14), and speaks frequently with loving concern for the well-being of his followers and supporters. On first seeing the brave captains Macbeth and Banquo after the double battle, Duncan greets Macbeth specifically with a self-deprecating regret that his generosity cannot match Macbeth's worth:

     O worthiest cousin,
  The sin of my ingratitude even now
  Was heavy on me! Thou art so far before
  That swiftest wing of recompense is slow
  To overtake thee. Would thou hadst less deserved,
  That the proportion both of thanks and payment
  Might have been mine. Only I have left to say,
  "More is thy due than more than all can pay."

(I, iv, 14–21)

  Banquo is included too: "Noble Banquo, / That hast no less deserved, nor must be known / No less to have done so, let me enfold thee / And hold thee to my heart" (I, iv, 29–32). All these behaviors reveal Duncan's characteristic temperament to readers or playgoers. This is supported by a physical detail Lady Macbeth reveals while sleepwalking: that Duncan had "so much *blood* in him." Every Elizabethan playgoer would have caught this reference and made the connection between the fluid associated with this humor and Duncan's psychological type.[67]

We can find vestiges of this personality classification system in current language or modern slang. We still describe people as "airheads" or "windbags" (equivalent to air signs), or "crybabies" (obviously related to water signs), "fireballs" or "hotheads" (undoubtedly fire sign types), or "couch potatoes" (settled in place like the earth signs). We categorize people as hot-tempered or emotionally cold. You might still hear the words "choleric" or "phlegmatic" as character descriptors. Even popular culture sometimes recognizes these categories, as in "Come to me, my *melancholy* baby"![68]

CHAPTER 3

The "Elizabethan World Picture": The Framework for Shakespeare's Plays

By contemplating the forms existing in the heavens we come to understand
time and its changing demands. Through contemplation of the forms
existing in human society it becomes possible to shape the world.

—*I Ching* (the Chinese Book of Changes), Hexagram 22, "Grace"[69]

H ow did Shakespeare and his contemporaries view the world and
their place in it?

Before examining the Elizabethan scheme, consider what a contemporary model of the universe might look like and how it might be
mapped. If you were asked to draw one, you would probably draw a
picture of the *physical* universe only, featuring Earth, the other planets,
and the stars and galaxies beyond our solar system, out into deep and
unfathomable space. Suppose now that you were asked to draw a map
of the cosmos that depicts the entire universe, one with the *invisible* as
well as the *visible* dimensions. What would you draw? I invite you to
stop reading at this point and do just that: draw a representation of the
cosmos as you understand it, including both visible and invisible levels
in your picture.

* * * * *

Most of us will likely discover that we do not have a clear and comprehensive picture that incorporates both of these dimensions, in part
because our secular, day-to-day culture is dominated by a mechanist-
materialist paradigm assuming that the only reality is physical. Such a
worldview dismisses and disallows discussion of levels of being other
than the one perceived by the five senses. The difference between the
materialistic perspective of the modern scientific worldview and the one
current in Shakespeare's time is that the latter incorporates dimensions
that are omitted today: spheres or levels not perceptible to the five senses
but considered nonetheless *real*.

For some in the West, orthodox religion may offer a general idea of a three-part universe: hell below, Earth in the middle, and Heaven above. Even so, our ideas of Heaven and hell are rather vague, drawing on conventional representations of haloed angels playing harps or sadistic devils roasting sinners over a blazing fire.

While there was not one worldview accepted by everyone who lived in Shakespeare's time, many believed in a universe that had common elements: various levels of being, all originating in a Divinity (however envisioned and described), culminating in the manifest world filled with an astonishing variety of life forms. For the orthodoxly religious, the levels between God and humanity were filled with archangels and angels, and with human beings who had been elevated to the rank of saints and sages. For those familiar with philosophical and esoteric traditions, those levels also included the spheres of the planets. This worldview thus incorporates astrology. Understanding this perspective sheds light on every aspect of Shakespeare's works: characters and their actions, aspects of the plots and subplots, and themes and images unique to particular plays or consistent in all of them.[70]

In the West this philosophical and mystical worldview emerges in ancient Greece in the teachings of Pythagoras (sixth century BCE) and in Plato's dialogue *Timaeus* (fifth and fourth centuries BCE). The seed ideas migrate to Alexandria, Egypt and inspire Neo-Platonists in the early centuries of the current era. Ideas about the planetary spheres become an accepted commonplace through the Middle Ages and into the Renaissance.[71] But they assume a new importance in the century before Shakespeare when ancient philosophical writings (those of Plato and others attributed to an Egyptian sage called Hermes Trismegistus ["thrice-great"]) are translated by priest-physican-astrologer Marsilio Ficino in Florence, Italy in the late 1400's.

Ficino is a brilliant thinker—according to Nicholas Campion "the greatest intellect of the fifteenth-century Renaissance."[72] Ficino's translations are circulated throughout Europe in the sixteenth and seventeenth centuries. Lost to the West for many hundreds of years, these rediscovered works convey an exciting view of humanity's dignity and potential, outline a version of creation different from the orthodox one, and describe a sophisticated model of the universe that includes the spheres of the planets. With the rediscovery of Plato's works in particular, the planets in their spheres assume a new importance. There they are described as governors or "administrators," transmitters of Divine Will or Intention between the higher and lower levels.[73] The recovery of these books—and especially of ideas about the planets and their place in creation—helped catalyze the great artistic, architectural, and literary flowering that began in Italy as the "Italian Renaissance" and spread through Europe and into England.

These texts describe the planets as revolving in perfect concentric circles contained within shimmering crystalline spheres. Shakespeare is familiar with this idea and refers to it in several places. He has the love-besotted Demetrius celebrate the beauty of Hermia by saying that she "look[s] as bright, as clear / As yonder Venus in her *glimmering sphere*" (*A Midsummer Night's Dream*: III, ii, 60–1). In the same play Oberon tells Puck of a mermaid singing so harmoniously that "the rude sea grew civil at her song / And certain stars shot madly from their *spheres* / To hear the sea-maid's music" (II, i, 152–4).

But how did these various levels or dimensions, including the planetary spheres, originate? Classical thinkers, like scientists and theologians today, debated theories about creation. How did the universe come into being? Gradually, in stages ("days"), or in one abrupt and explosive blast? Or a combination of both? And what are the various components of the universe and their relationships to each other? The last question belongs to that aspect of speculative thought called "cosmology," a branch of philosophy that deals with the origin and general structure of the universe. While astrology in itself does not offer a story about how the universe came into being, it does offer a picture of its organization and the dynamic interrelationships of various parts based partly on mathematics. Given its history as originally a facet of spiritual philosophy, astrology is in fact part of a grander "cosmological model."

Every culture, every civilization, in every time period has a characteristic description of ingredients that make up the universe and their relationship to each other—that is, a cosmology.

> By cosmology [is meant] the composition of the universe, how our world is put together. It comprises our beliefs about the fundamental constituents of the environment ...
>
> Many different things have at one time or another been urged as the elemental components of reality. A few of the better known include atoms (both in classical times and in our own), the sense data

of humans, the mental impressions of humans, bundles of energy, electronic fields, ideas in the Platonic sense, numbers as defined by the Pythagoreans, and basic qualities (such as hot, cold, moist, and dry). Cosmology consists in designating the intrinsic ingredients of reality and defining the interrelations between them.[74]

Elizabethan cosmology delineated a multitude of levels, from Divinity at the top of the scale to rocks and stones at the bottom. This worldview was dominant in Western culture from ancient times until the end of the seventeenth century. According to this view, the universe unfolds from the invisible into the visible dimensions in a great linked chain called "the Great Chain of Being," each link being a different (and lower) level of creation. E. M. W. Tillyard, author of the seminal book *The Elizabethan World Picture*, speculates that this idea originates in Homer's account of the chief Greek god Zeus letting down a golden chain from heaven.

Proceeding from the One or Godhead or Mind (different names were given to the instigating creative force), the action is that of a flow (or overflow) downwards that creates sequentially the realm of the fixed stars and then the spheres of the planets. Eventually the creative "stuff" (variously described then and now as "thought" or "energy") crystallizes as the visible world, which derives its variety and characteristics from mixtures of the four elements: fire, air, water, and earth. (These elements, introduced in the previous section, are not the ones you can see and touch, but represent more abstract qualities of being.) The bulk of the universe is actually non-physical and non-perceptible through human senses. This theory is called the "emanationist" theory of creation.[75]

So creation begins with the invisible and insubstantial, and goes through many stages, intermediate levels, or "planes" before devolving into the visible and material.

From the priests of the Egyptian temples to today's secret societies, from Pythagoras to Rudolf Steiner, the great Austrian initiate of the late nineteenth to early twentieth century, this model has always been conceived of as a series of thoughts emanating from the cosmic mind. Pure mind to begin with, these thought-emanations later became a sort of proto-matter, energy that became increasingly dense, then became matter so ethereal that it was finer

One Version of the Elizabethan Worldview:

The Great Chain of Being or the Ladder of Heaven and Earth
A Pattern of Order Fundamental to Shakespeare's Plays

(THE UNFATHOMABLE)

GOD/DIVINITY/THE ONE/MIND (NOUS)/LOVE

ARCHANGELIC/ANGELIC SPHERE

9 levels altogether   —Archangels
                             —Angels   pure intelligence (no body)

REALM OF THE FIXED STARS

SPHERE OF THE ZODIAC (THE 7 PLANETS)

Saturn
Jupiter
Mars
Sun
Venus
Mercury
Moon

THE MUNDANE or physical WORLD:
created from admixtures of the 4 elements:

HUMANITY   have REASON
—King   have being
—nobility   grow
—commoners   have five senses
                                  have power of movement

ANIMAL KINGDOM   have being
—lion ...   grow
                                  have five senses
                                  have power of movement

PLANT KINGDOM   have being
—oak ...   grow

MINERAL KINGDOM   have being
—diamond/gold, silver ...

than gas, without particles of any kind. Eventually the emanations became gas, then liquid and finally solids.[76]

The important point for our purposes is that the planets, revolving in their perfect spheres and interpreted according to astrological tradition, are an integral part of this hierarchy. On the facing page is a diagram that represents the unfolded cosmos pictured vertically, one that includes all of the envisioned levels from the highest down through the intermediate spheres to Earth and all of its inhabitants.[77]

With each lower level, some qualities are lost until we arrive at the totally inanimate mineral realm.[78]

Each level contains hierarchies within itself: kings are at the top rank of humanity just as the lion is the "king of the jungle" at the animal level; the oak is the largest and grandest of trees; the diamond is the most indestructible of gems; and gold the most valuable of minerals. So it carries a particular significance when Thaisa in *Pericles, Prince of Tyre*, says admiringly of a handsome gentleman, "To me he seems like diamond to glass" (II, iii, 36 in Houghton Mifflin edition).

An important point about these correspondences is that one from a particular level of the hierarchy can be substituted for another at a similar position but on a different level, making them comparable. This sets up many series of analogies, so that king = oak = gold = heart within the body, and so on. Shakespeare uses these associations frequently in his plays. Here is an example from *Richard II*, mentioned by Tillyard:

> See, see, King Richard doth himself appear,
> As doth the blushing discontented *sun*
> From out the *fiery* portal of the east....

York adds:

> Yet looks he like a *king*! Behold, his eye,
> As bright as is the *eagle*'s, lightens forth
> Controlling majesty.
>
> (*Richard II*: III, iii, 62–4, 68–70)

Tillyard comments, "There in short space we have four of the traditional primacies: fire among the elements, the sun among the planets,

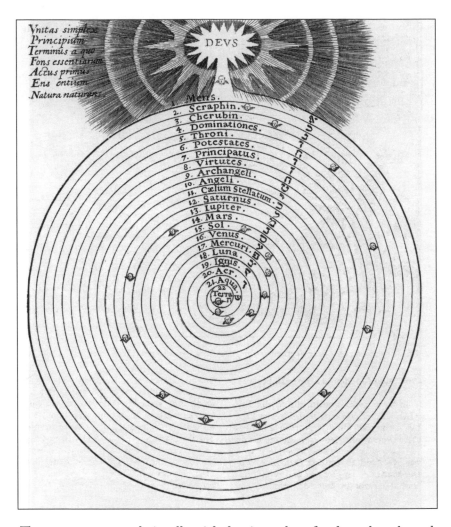

The cosmos represented visually with the nine orders of archangels and angels (#s 2-10), the realm of the fixed stars (Caelum Stellatum, #11), and the seven spheres of the planets (#s 12-18). Below the Moon ("Luna"), all things are admixtures of the four elements (#'s 19-22). Everything issues from God ("Deus" at the top) in a maze-like series of concentric circles creating a spiral downward vortex. The intelligences or archetypes governing each sphere are symbolized by the 22 Hebrew letters and by winged heads. (Robert Fludd, Ultiusque Cosmi Maioris ... ca. 1618)

the king among men, the eagle among the birds. Again at the beginning of act five, Richard is first a rose and then a lion."[79]

A particularly fascinating dimension is the space between the invisible and visible worlds: the area below the Moon, between the Moon and Earth. Since creation had to be "full" on every level, beings had to exist there. As early as Plato's time, in fifth century Greece, philosophers

The Sun in the sky is symbolically equivalent to the King in the human realm (represented by the crown) and the lion or "king of the jungle" in the animal realm. (Musaeum Hermeticum Reformatum et Amplicatum, Frankfort, 1678)

suggested that various spirits inhabited this liminal space. In the *Symposium*, Socrates recounts a conversation he had with a wise woman named Diotima, who assured Socrates that spirits "are halfway between god and man."

> What powers have they, then, [Socrates] asked?
> They are the envoys and interpreters that ply between heaven and earth [answers Diotima], flying upward with our worship and our prayers, and descending with the heavenly answers and commandments, and since they are between the two estates they weld both sides together and merge them into one great whole. They form the medium of the prophetic arts, of the priestly rites of sacrifice, initiation, and incantation, of divination and of sorcery, for *the divine will not mingle directly with the human, and it is only through the mediation of the spirit world that man can have any intercourse, whether waking or sleeping, with the gods.... There are many spirits and many kinds of spirits, too, and Love is one of them.*[80]

With this worldview being multi-leveled and multi-faceted, including all the levels of creation from the highest to the lowest, it is not surprising that Shakespeare features in his works a variety of beings who normally reside at different levels: gods and goddesses (Diana in *Pericles, Prince of Tyre*, Jupiter in *Cymbeline*, Juno and Ceres in *The Tempest)* who correlate with the planets and their spheres; faeries and witches, who are supernatural beings living in the space between the Earth and the Moon; and an astonishing spectrum of human beings, as individual as the mixtures of the elements in them, who inhabit the earthly realm. This may be one reason that we intuitively feel the greatness of Shakespeare's works, that he may have the "capacious consciousness" that Bloom notes partly because, in line with the dominant cosmological model of his time, Shakespeare includes in his plays beings that exist in all the different dimensions and at different levels. This worldview underlies Shakespeare's work and accounts for the exuberant vitality and variety of his characters.

The realm of the fixed stars (*Caelum Stellatum* in Fludd's diagram on page 80), at almost the top, has special significance.

> The eighth sphere ... is analogous to the divine world because of its relatively unchanging nature. The seven levels below, realms of the

planets (literally "wanderers"), whose orbits vary and whose movement is now forwards and now backwards, represent the mutable world. To look up at the star-scattered heavens through which the planets wander is to see the changeable imposed upon the unchanging, a dramatic experience of the paradoxical nature of existence.[81]

The important idea intrinsic to this model and relevant to Shakespeare's works is one that is fundamental to astrology: interconnectedness or correspondence. The entire universe is envisioned as a single conscious and intelligent entity, with each of the unfolded parts corresponding in design to levels above it and in sympathetic resonance with *all* levels both above and below it. That means that everything has a secret sympathy with everything else, and every level is connected to every other level. This is a particularly useful perspective for poets, since they so often use comparisons between human beings and nature or human beings and the heavens for artistic effect.

Because human beings are miniature universes and reflect the cosmic structure, all aspects of our physical and psychic selves have similarities to the cosmos. This idea inspired a branch of astrology that focuses on physical health and on medical diagnosis and treatment, based on the connections between parts of the body, vegetable and animal substances, and specific planets. These connections were frequently represented in images of the "zodiacal man," showing the association between the twelve signs of the zodiac and specific parts of the body. Shakespeare often alludes to various body parts that were thought to have a particular significance within this model, especially the liver, spleen, and heart.

Not only do individual human beings contain the universe within them analogously, but also the entire human realm (the section labeled "Humanity," in the diagram on page 78) constitutes a single entity, a "body politic," which may be healthy or unhealthy. Shakespeare often characterizes the situation in a kingdom by using images of health or disease—so something may indeed be "rotten" in the state of Denmark.

While Shakespeare sometimes treats humanity collectively, as an entire "body" in itself, he more often individualizes human beings. They are more special than is obvious from the diagram. Existing at the point where the invisible becomes the visible, human beings contain the universe within them analogously in that they are imaged as an amalgam of the angelic realm above them and the animal one below. This makes them unique in the entire hierarchy. It means that they are capable of the most noble and loving actions, which exalt them, as well as the most despicable, which lower them to the level of the beasts. The remarkable potential of humanity is celebrated by Hamlet:

> What a piece of work is a man! How noble in reason, how infinite in faculty, in form and moving how express and admirable, in action how like an angel, in apprehension how like a god—the beauty of the world, the paragon of animals!
>
> (II, ii, 293–7)

But the opposite exists simultaneously: we are material creatures, "the quintessence of dust."

Spiritual philosophers also speak of connections between the various levels by saying that the *microcosm* (the familiar world in which we live) is intimately linked to the *macrocosm* (the greater cosmos). Literally, our earthly experience is reflected in the heavenly realm—and vice versa. Materialistic science bases its worldview on the reality of only the physical dimension and takes the position that astrology is a projection of the human onto the screen of the heavens. But for thousands of years, philosophers thought of the cosmos in just the reverse way: as a "top-down" not a "bottom-up" model. Everything unfolds out of Divinity, however conceptualized. It does not start with a physical human body with a brain that somehow generates consciousness out of flesh. It begins with the invisible and works downwards. Some Creative Power projects an image of Itself into the visible world and into the human psyche and even into the physical body. For the Elizabethans, the nobility of a human being that Hamlet rhapsodizes about is largely due to an affirmation of an indwelling spiritual element.

For people before and during Shakespeare's time, all of creation was unified by subtle and hidden affinities or resonant bonds of sympathy between these many levels. This is the conceptual basis for astrology, as expressed in the Hermetic maxim "as above, so below." These sympathetic links, or connections between parts analogous to each other, can sometimes be recognized because entities or objects may have the same color, or the same function, or be the recognized expression of a fundamental principle. For example, the planet Jupiter, the largest body in the solar system, is associated with a variety of ideas, beings, or objects at

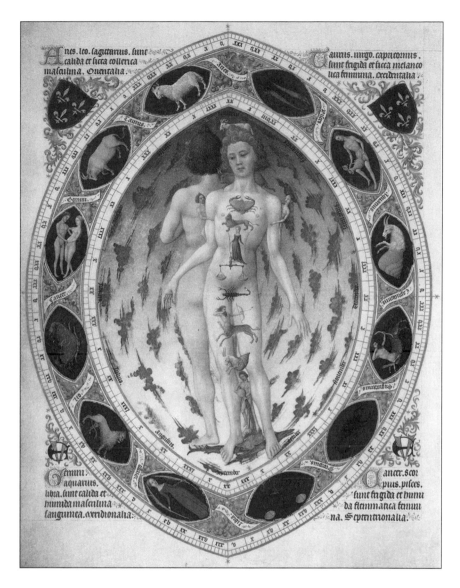

The human being imaged as a microcosm, replicating in its structure the design of the cosmos. The twelve signs of the zodiac correlate with parts of the human body, starting with the first sign Aries ruling the head and ending with the last sign Pisces ruling the feet. (Les Très Riches Heures du Duc de Berry, French, early 15th c.)

various levels of creation, all resonating with its essence—as a principle: mercy, generosity, and enlightened rulership; as a god or goddess: Zeus and Athena; as an image: a crowned and throned king; as a bird: the owl (symbol of wisdom); as trees: the oak and cedar; as a metal: tin; as a gemstone: the sapphire; in the human body: the liver (since it is the largest organ in the body); as a color: royal blue.[82]

So interlinked are the various levels of creation that levels can influence each other. Shakespeare's plays harmonize with this worldview because very often disturbances in the human world synchronize with disturbances in nature. An outstanding example of this occurs after Macbeth's vicious murder of King Duncan, when Ross and an Old Man are disturbed by numerous disruptions in the natural world:

> ROSS: Thou seest the heavens, as troubled with man's act,
>   Threatens his bloody stage. *By th' clock 'tis day,*
>   *And yet dark night strangles the travelling lamp* ...
> OLD MAN: 'Tis unnatural,
>   Even like the deed that's done. On Tuesday last,
>   *A falcon, tow'ring in her pride of place,*
>   *Was by a mousing owl hawked at and kill'd.*
> ROSS: And *Duncan's horses*—a thing most strange and
>   certain—
>   Beauteous and swift, the minions of their race,
>   Turned wild in nature, broke their stalls, flung out,
>   Contending 'gainst obedience, as they would
>   *Make war with mankind.*
> OLD MAN: 'Tis said *they ate each other.*
> ROSS: They did so, to th' amazement of mine eyes
>   That looked upon't.
>   (*Macbeth*: II, iv, 5–7, 10–20)

Such a powerful sympathetic resonance exists between the various levels of creation that disturbances can occur even *before* people act in ways that violate the established order. While the conspirators are only *planning* the assassination of Julius Caesar the heavenly, human, and animal worlds evidence upheavals. It is as if the very thoughts of the plotters influence the world they live in:

CASCA: Are you not moved, when *all the sway of earth*
    Shakes like a thing unfirm?
    ... never till tonight, never till now,
    Did I go through a *tempest dropping fire....*
CICERO: Why, saw you anything more wonderful?
CASCA: A common slave—you know him well by sight—
    Held up his left hand, which did flame and burn
    Like twenty torches joined; and yet *his hand,*
    Not sensible of fire, remained unscorch'd ....
    And yesterday *the bird of night did sit*
    Even at noonday upon the market-place,
    Hooting and shrieking....
    For I believe they are portentous things
    Unto the climate that they point upon.
        (*Julius Caesar*: I, iii, 3–4, 9–10, 14–19, 26–8, 31–2)

This worldview thus posits a continuum between the heavens, humanity, and nature. Things that exist on one level, though, are not *equal* to those on other levels. Although somehow (in a way that defies rational explanation) they share the same fundamental essence, they differ in expression, so they are not precisely equivalent. But this worldview makes it possible—even logical—for events in the natural world to reflect either harmonies or disturbances within the human realm because they are mutually interconnected. Only this worldview allows for sympathetic resonances between various levels of creation. So Shakespeare can write of tempests both external to Lear and within his mind, of eclipses that portend the fall of kings, of horses that eat each other when a king is murdered, and of comets foretelling disastrous events in human life. Events on one level of being can reflect events on another.

Climbing the "Ladder" of Heaven

Besides the "Great Chain of Being," another metaphor describing this hierarchical structure is a "ladder of lights," with the various rungs suggesting different levels of creation from the most ethereal to the most solid. This recalls the story of Jacob's Ladder in the Old Testament, an account of his vision of angels ascending and descending one. Later

Christian writers use this same image: St. Augustine, for instance, interprets the seven gifts of the Holy Spirit as a ladder, with the highest rung being wisdom.[83] "Ladder" is an apt metaphor because it was believed by some that the soul not only descended from the heavens through the planetary spheres to be born, but could ascend back up through them while still embodied. The ascent could be facilitated by intense spiritual practices and philosophical study. This point disturbed the orthodox because you did not need the intervention of a divine being or the intermediary of a church to make the ascent; you could rise through your own efforts.

Both mystics and magicians use various techniques—prayers, meditation, and rituals among them—to engage the imagination and catalyze an ascent. The key is entering an altered state that opens the door to an inner vision of the higher dimensions. Philosophers, though, use thought and perception to move upward from rung to rung. In Plato's dialogue the *Symposium*, Socrates delivers the final speech about the nature of Love in which he recounts a conversation he had with a wise woman named Diotima. Diotima's teaching is that you can move progressively from a focus on earthly forms (the lowest level of the ladder) to the ultimate perception of the divine Form: the abstract Principle of Beauty itself. Here's a condensed version of the sequence:

The candidate for this initiation first falls in love with the beauty of one individual body.

Next he must consider how nearly related the beauty of any one body is to the beauty of any other, and so set himself to be the lover of *every* lovely body.

Next he must grasp that the beauties of the body are as nothing to the beauties of the soul, so that wherever he meets with spiritual loveliness, even in the husk of an unlovely body, he will find it beautiful enough to fall in love with and to cherish.

And from this he will be led to contemplate the beauty of laws and institutions.

Next, his attention should be diverted from institutions to the sciences, so that he may know the beauty of every kind of knowledge.

And turning his eyes toward the open sea of beauty, he experiences a wondrous vision which is the very soul of beauty. It is an everlasting loveliness that neither comes nor goes, that neither

Jacob's Ladder: Angels descending and ascending the ladder of heaven connect the celestial and terrestrial realms. They blow a trumpet to wake Jacob from the sleep of the senses. (frontispiece to alchemical text, 18th c.)

flowers nor fades, but subsists of itself and by itself in an eternal oneness. Every lovely thing participates in it and yet it remains the same inviolable whole. At this point universal beauty dawns upon his inward sight.

The final revelation is the experience of the sanctuary of Love: beauty's very self—unsullied, unalloyed, and freed from the mortal taint that haunts the frailer loveliness of flesh and blood. It's the heavenly beauty face to face.[84]

If you count the steps that Diotima outlines here, you will see that there are seven. Undoubtedly this number corresponds to the seven planetary spheres, the intermediate levels of heaven or the seven "rungs" making up the ladder.

If the soul did not have the experience of ascension while in material form, it would inevitably ascend after dying—though not necessarily to the "seventh heaven." How far "up the ladder" you went after death had much to do with your level of spiritual attainment and your preparation for the experience of dying. Texts like *The Egyptian Book of the Dead* and *The Tibetan Book of the Dead* were designed specifically to enable souls to reach the highest level possible for them after bodily death and to recognize the level they were on when they got there.

The Number Seven—as in the Seven Classical Planets

The number seven is good.—Saint Ambrose (ca 340–397 CE)[85]

Seven are the planets which not only adorn the world but exert their influence on things below, an influence transmitted to them by the highest nature, which is God. —Alexander Neckam[86]

The seven classical planets have a very important role within the system just described. (The Sun and Moon are technically "lights" but they are frequently and loosely called "planets.") They are consistently described as "administrators" or handmaidens of Divinity, deputized to function as middle managers and transmitting (as Neckam asserts above) its influence to the realms below.

But why seven? The number seven has had special significance in many cultures for thousand of years. In Sumer, probably the oldest known civilization of the Middle East,[87] ziggurats or stepped pyramids had many levels, each stacked on top of the one below and smaller in size, reaching dramatically to the skies. In Babylon (as at Borsippa), the ziggurat dedicated to Marduk had *seven* levels. (This was likely the Tower of Babel mentioned in the Old Testament of the Bible; "Babel" is Babylon, a word meaning "Gate of the Gods.")[88]

One purpose for these structures was as an astronomical observatory. Priests or other functionaries climbed laboriously to the very top in order to follow and record the movements of the planets and the drift of the stars. Since the skies were thought to be the abode of the immortals, it is plausible that the Babylonians built these structures with seven levels to replicate on earth the seven levels of heaven (the spheres of the seven visible planets). Peter Levenda reflects on the emphasis given to this number:

> The number seven has importance in Sumerian and Babylonian culture as much as it does in the Egyptian, and consistent with the Egyptian version "seven" is related to astronomical phenomena and to the gods. While the Sumerian number system is a sixty-base system, from which we derive our 360-degree circle, seven has special significance for Sumerian ascent and descent myths and rituals. This might be seen as odd, since seven is the one number between one and ten that cannot divide a circle of 360 degrees evenly. Thus, it does not "fit" into the sixty-base system but is still the structure of the Underworld and of the astral gods, seven seeming to represent transcendence: i.e. a number that stands outside the created world of 360 degrees. The Tower of Babel itself had seven levels as the Sumerians reached for the heavens.[89]

Levenda recounts the story of the Sumerian goddess Inanna who not only descended from the heavens to Earth to mate with the King of Babylon, but also descended further, down through the seven levels of the Underworld.[90] The seven levels of the heavens have parallels in the seven levels of "hell" since the two were thought in many systems to be mirror images of one another. The Sumerian scripture telling of the journey of Inanna, goddess of love and the Queen of Heaven, into the underworld to visit her sister Queen Ereshkigal, the Queen of Death, records that she must pass through seven gates, manned by seven gatekeepers. At each she must shed an article of clothing (a spiritual version of Salome's seductive "dance of the seven veils")[91] which she puts on again as she ascends after her adventures in the underworld.[92]

In Egypt, Pyramid Texts (hieroglyphs discovered on the four walls of a fifth-dynasty tomb for the pharaoh Unas) illustrate the same theme of navigating seven levels. These writings were intended to guide his soul through the various stages of the afterlife on an ascent to the "imperishable" stars (ones that never set below the horizon but endlessly circle the Pole Star, a pointer to true north). Undiscovered until the late nineteenth century, these texts are perhaps the most ancient written scripture in existence. One of the "utterances" in them encourages a flight "to the seven houses of the Red Crown," possibly a reference to the seven stars of the Great Bear constellation (which we now call the "Big Dipper").[93] His ascent completed, the pharaoh would join the immortal gods among the stars.

Pervasive in Middle Eastern cultures, the number seven occurs frequently in Jewish and Christian scriptures, most especially in the first book of the Bible, Genesis, where creation is described as unfolding in seven days. Seven thus denotes completeness or perfection. The seventh day, being the day that God presumably rested, was dubbed the Sabbath and set apart as a day for human beings to rest and reflect in imitation of the Creator. The last book of the Bible, Revelation, features the mysterious seven seals, seven angels, and seven last plagues. In between these books are many references to seven: the seven fat and lean cows of Pharaoh's dream, which Joseph interprets as seven years of abundance and seven years of famine (Genesis 41); the seven circuits around the walls of Jericho by Joshua, accompanied by seven priests carrying seven trumpets (Joshua 6); the seven devils that Jesus casts out of Mary of Magdala (Luke 8:2), among others.[94]

In the classical period of ancient Greece and Rome, commentators drew up lists of the seven seas and the seven wonders of the world. Certain constellations seem to have had special importance to these ancient civilizations, particularly the Pleiades, whose principal stars are called "The Seven Sisters," and the already mentioned Big Dipper with its very bright seven stars. Their luminosity in a cloudless sky made them markers by which to navigate or orient. In *I Henry IV* Falstaff assures Hal that he and his thieving accomplices "go by the moon and the seven stars ... " (I, ii, 12).

Seven is still an important number in our lives. In part, we structure time on the principle of seven, in the seven days of the week, named after the planets or the gods and goddesses associated with them.[95]

Seven is not just an arbitrary number for dividing up the calendar; seven days are roughly one-quarter of the lunar monthly cycle. So our month ("moonth") too is based in part on our relationship with the heavens. The number seven is significant for the cosmos, nature, and culture. There are seven colors in the rainbow and seven notes in the musical scale. Seven has long been central to Eastern philosophy; Hindus believe that the human body has seven "chakras" or energy centers that accord with seven levels of human beings and may resonate with the seven levels of the cosmos.

Sevens still are relevant in Shakespeare's time. The seven liberal arts, studies grounded in classical languages (Latin and Greek) and literature, were considered necessary to educate a man for intelligent participation in public life. One of the main sources for Shakespeare's plots is Ovid's *Metamorphoses*, which would have been part of such a curriculum.[96] The seven vices and virtues, developed from the original four (cardinal) virtues set forth by Plato and Aristotle with additions by Christian writers, were still popular concepts in the Elizabethan era. Some of the vices are clearly displayed by certain of Shakespeare's characters: Falstaff is gluttony personified (along with a good dose of sloth and lust); both King Lear and Timon of Athens are studies in wrath taken to an extreme. Christian thinkers also correlated the seven gifts of the Holy Spirit and the seven virtues with the seven heavenly spheres and the planets that coursed through them.[97]

The number seven shows up in Shakespeare's oeuvre several times. In *Twelfth Night* the love-sick Duke Orsino seeks the hand of Olivia, a rich Countess, but since Olivia's brother has just died, the Countess has determined that she will remain in seclusion for seven years (I, i, 25–6). A much more famous instance of Shakespeare playing with the number seven occurs in *As You Like It*, when Jaques riffs on the Seven Ages of Man, a commonplace of Elizabethan thought that originated with Ptolemy in ancient Alexandria.[98]

> All the world's a stage,
> And all the men and women merely players.
> They have their exits and their entrances,
> And one man in his time plays many parts,
> His acts being *seven* ages.
>
> (II, vii, 138–42)

In Jacques' speech Shakespeare is explicitly alluding to astrology. Each of the "seven ages" accords with descriptions and associations with the planets in their apparent order from Earth out to Saturn both in Shakespeare's time and our own. The associations of each of these ages with the various stages of human life—from birth through growth to maturity, decline, and death—are very clear. In actuality, since the last two "scenes," old age and death, are both in Saturn's domain, Shakespeare is actually describing six stages with their associated planetary rulers. He omits a stage equivalent to the Sun.

> At first the infant,
> Mewling and puking in the nurse's arms.
> [The Moon phase of life]

> Then the whining schoolboy, with his satchel
> And shining morning face, creeping like snail
> Unwillingly to school.
> [The Mercury phase of life]

> And then the lover,
> Sighing like furnace, with a woeful ballad
> Made to his mistress' eyebrow.
> [The Venus phase of life]

> Then, a soldier,
> Full of strange oaths, and bearded like the pard [leopard],
> Jealous in honour, sudden, and quick in quarrel,
> Seeking the bubble reputation
> Even in the cannon's mouth.
> [The Mars phase of life]

> And then the justice,
> In fair round belly with good capon lined,
> With eyes severe and beard of formal cut,
> Full of wise saws and modern instances;
> And so he plays his part.
> [The Jupiter phase of life]

> The sixth age shifts
> Into the lean and slippered pantaloon,
> With spectacles on nose and pouch on side,
> His youthful hose, well saved, a world too wide
> For his shrunk shank, and his big, manly voice,
> Turning again toward childish treble, pipes
> And whistles in his sound. Last scene of all,
> That ends this strange, eventful history,
> Is second childishness and mere oblivion,
> Sans teeth, sans eyes, sans taste, sans everything.
> [THE SATURN PHASE OF LIFE AS WELL AS DEATH]
>
> (II, vii, 138–65)

The idea of seven ages/stages of human life was well known in Shakespeare's time, but as voiced by the melancholic Jaques, it has a particularly comic edge. This is really an elaboration of the theory of the humors, expanding it to include all the planets and not just four. The Moon correlates with childhood, Mercury with early youth, and so on, through to Saturn ruling old age and death.

The order of the planets in Jaques' speech is precisely the order followed in considering six of Shakespeare's plays in Section II: it is the order of the planets in increasing apparent distance from Earth: the Moon, Mercury, Venus, Mars, Jupiter, and Saturn.

The "Music of the Spheres"

> [U]ndertake another suit,
> I had rather hear you to solicit that
> Than *music from the spheres.*
>
> (*Twelfth Night*: III, i, 100–102)

The seven planets, as they circle endlessly in their crystalline paths, are not silent; their movement creates sounds, tones that together create a celestial harmony. It was a common belief, both before and during Shakespeare's time, that this "music of the spheres" was an exquisite and unearthly song normally inaudible and only perceivable by pure souls or in rare moments of grace.[99] Thus music had a special place in Elizabethan culture, esteemed in part because of its philosophical, religious, and astrological significance. Appropriately, it also has a special place in Shakespeare's plays.[100]

The idea that the heavens are "making music" apparently originated in the West with Pythagoras (sixth century BCE), who not only discovered the mathematical ratios underlying musical harmony[101] but also theorized that distances between the planets represented tones.[102] So the ratio between the Earth and the Moon, or the Moon and Mercury (and so on), by musical proportion would consequently become a sound, one of seven tones making up a full octave.[103] As Censorinus, a Roman writer (ca 238 BCE), explains:

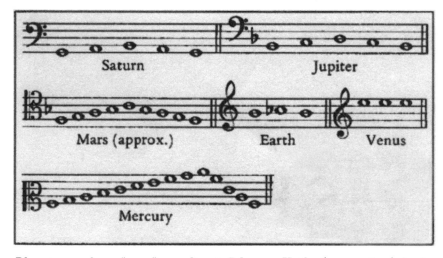

Planetary scales or "songs" according to Johannes Kepler (1571-1630). Jupiter and Saturn sound "bass" lines while Venus is a soprano, though these are inaudible to human ears.

Convinced that the solar system manifested celestial harmony and believing like the ancient Greek philosophers Pythagoras and Plato that number was the key to the cosmos, Kepler discovered harmonies in the ratios of a planet's speed both with regard to its own orbit and in relation to the orbits of its neighbors.

Kepler's ideas have resurfaced in the 20th century and been validated by many researchers, including Joscelyn Godwin and John Martineau (in A Little Book of Coincidence in the Solar System, Wooden Books, rev. ed. 2006).

To these things we may add what Pythagoras taught, namely, that the whole world was constructed according to musical ratio, and that the seven planets ... have a rhythmical motion and distances adapted to musical intervals, and emit sounds, every one different in proportion to its height [Saturn was said to be the highest, as it is the farthest away, and was supposed to give the gravest note of the heavenly Diapason ...], which sounds are so concordant as to produce a most sweet melody, though *inaudible to us by reason of the greatness of the sounds*, which the narrow passages of our ears are not capable of admitting.[104]

This theory had practical value in creating music. The lyre, the stringed instrument reputedly played in classical times by the mythical Orpheus as well as the philosopher Pythagoras, often had seven strings, no doubt to represent the seven classical planets. Music played on it would be more likely to harmonize with the heavens. In Shakespeare's time stringed instruments, especially the viol, were particularly thought to symbolize order and harmony.[105] In *Pericles, Prince of Tyre*, the main character answers a riddle set to him by King Antiochus, king of Antioch, and in an aside remarks that his daughter is "a fair *viol*, and your sense the strings; / Who, finger'd to make man his lawful music, / Would draw heaven down and all the gods to hearken ..." (I, i, 81–3 in the Houghton Mifflin edition).[106]

The diatonic musical scale in the West today still has *seven* principal notes to an octave, the white keys on a piano. The chromatic scale has in total *twelve* notes when the white and back keys are combined. This again points to the importance of mathematics and astrology to music since these obviously correlate with the *seven* classical planets and the *twelve* signs of the zodiac. For many centuries music was thought of as "number made audible."[107]

Shakespeare features music in his plays frequently, sometimes having his characters make comments about music in line with the Elizabethan worldview, sometimes stressing music's ability to affect or reveal a character's inner state, and sometimes cuing the action and tone of a scene through the music accompanying it.

One particularly lovely explication of the philosophical view of the time is Lorenzo's speech to Jessica at the end of *The Merchant of Venice*.

This is an unusually clear statement confirming the connection between the harmony of heaven and the harmony of the individual soul.

> How sweet the moonlight sleeps upon this bank!
> Here will we sit, and let the sounds of *music*
> Creep in our ears. Soft stillness and the night
> Become the touches of sweet harmony.
> Sit, Jessica. Look how the floor of heaven
> Is thick inlaid with patens [disks] of bright gold.
> *There's not the smallest orb which thou behold'st*
> *But in his motion like an angel sings,*
> Still choiring to the young-eyed cherubins;
> Such harmony is in immortal souls,
> But whilst this muddy vesture of decay
> Doth grossly close it in, we cannot hear it.[108]
>
> (V, i, 53–64)

The only character in any of Shakespeare's plays who actually hears the celestial music is Pericles. After he is brought out of a deep depression by a woman's singing, Pericles recognizes the "gallant" singer as his missing daughter Marina. In an ecstasy of joy, he is transported:

> PERICLES: Give me my robes. I am wild in my beholding.
>   O heavens bless my girl! But, hark, what music?...
> HELICANUS: My lord, I hear none.
> PERICLES: None!
>   *The music of the spheres*! List my Marina....
>   *Rarest sounds*! Do ye not hear? ...
>   *Most heavenly music*!
>   It nips me unto listening, and thick slumber
>   Hangs upon mine eyes. Let me rest.
> (V, i, 224–5, 229–31, 233, 235–7 in the Houghton Mifflin edition)

It is obvious that Pericles is still in an altered and transcendent state, for after falling into a restorative sleep he is graced with a vision of a being from a higher sphere. The goddess Diana appears and tells him in a dream to leave for Ephesus—where, even more amazing than his discovery of his presumed-dead daughter, he will be reunited with his deemed-dead wife.

The reunion with his wife Thaisa at the very end of the play can only happen because of music's power. Since music was capable of sounding a harmony that is in essence divine, it can reanimate the soul, thus giving life to the body. Pericles' wife apparently died in childbirth while shipbound with Pericles for Tyre. The mariners encase her body in a chest and throw it into the sea, where it is tossed upon the shores of Ephesus and taken to Cerimon, a lord skilled in herbalism and natural magic. To the accompaniment of music, he resuscitates her:

> Cause it to sound, beseech you.
> The *viol* once more. How thou stirr'st, thou block!
> The *music* there! I pray you, give her air.
> Gentlemen,
> This queen will live. Nature awakes; a warmth
> Breathes out of her. She hath not been entranc'd
> Above five hours. See how she gins to blow
> Into life's flower again!
> (III, ii, 89–96 in the Houghton Mifflin edition)

So music has remarkable restorative properties and accompanies an apparent resurrection several times in Shakespeare's plays.[109] Another instance occurs in *The Winter's Tale.* Queen Hermione is thought to have died sixteen years before due to her jealous husband's accusations of adultery and her son's death. In the appropriate setting of a chapel and to the accompaniment of music, the lady Paulina unveils what appears to be a statue of the dead queen to the repentant king and promises to bring it to life. Though we know Hermione is not really dead, Paulina attributes the Queen's reanimation to the power of music.

> PAULINA: *Music; awake her; strike!*
>   [Music.]
> [To Hermione] 'Tis time. Descend. Be stone no
>   more. Approach.
> Strike all that look upon with marvel. Come,
> I'll fill your grave up. Stir. Nay, come away.
> Bequeath to death your numbness, for from him
> Dear life redeems you.
> [To Leontes]   You perceive she stirs.
>   [Hermione slowly descends.] ...

LEONTES: O, she's warm!
  If this be magic, let it be an art
  Lawful as eating.
    (V, iii, 98–103, 109–11 in the Houghton Mifflin edition)

Music can have almost magical properties because if it is sounded in alignment with the tuneful spheres, close to the creative Source, it can restore life. Such celestial music harmonizes with and revives the soul.[110]

Because music has a regular and repeated beat, it is expressive of divine order and has the power not only to restore life but also influence every part of the manifest world. Just after Lorenzo tells Jessica about heavenly orbs singing to the angels, he assures her that music has the power to calm disturbed animals and to affect the plant and mineral kingdoms as well:

  For do but note a wild and wanton herd
  Or race of youthful and unhandled colts,
  Fetching mad bounds, bellowing and neighing loud,
  Which is the hot condition of their blood,
  If they but hear perchance a trumpet sound,
  Or any air of music touch their ears,
  You shall perceive them make a mutual stand,
  Their savage eyes turned to a modest gaze
  By the sweet power of music. Therefore the poet
  Did feign that Orpheus drew trees, stones, and floods ....
    (*The Merchant of Venice*: V, i, 70–9)

Since human beings are inextricably connected to the natural world through sympathetic resonance, their inner quality may be revealed by their responses to music. Lorenzo continues in Shakespeare's most celebratory paean to music's power to both alter your nature and reveal your inner quality:

  Since naught so stockish, hard, and full of rage
  But music for the time doth change his nature.
  The man that hath no music in himself,
  Nor is not moved with concord of sweet sounds,
  Is fit for treasons, stratagems, and spoils.

The motions of his spirit are dull as night,
And his affections dark as Erebus [hell].
Let no such man be trusted. Mark the music.

(V, i, 80–7)

What a dramatic warning these lines are! A person who "hath no music in himself" is a dark and dangerous character. The villainous Edmund in *King Lear*, who plots against his father and brother, reveals himself in a small, almost throwaway, detail of musical disharmony. After he mentions that the eclipses his father refers to (being disruptions to the natural order) "do portend these divisions" between parent and child, king and counselors, he ends his soliloquy with "*fa, sol, la, mi*" (I, ii, 125). This musical phrase contains an augmented fourth, or *mi contra fa*, which was considered in Shakespeare's time to be discordant; it was described as the "devil's sound." In this simple musical phrase Edmund reveals his hidden and malignant self.

Since it can affect all the elements of nature, music can do the same to all the levels of a human being. It can strongly affect both your temporary moods and your more fixed temperament—the types introduced in Chapter 2 that correspond to four specific planets. Most positively it can bring a disordered spirit into balance. Shakespeare's plays, the romances in particular, contain a multitude of allusions to music's potential to heal the body, mind, and soul.[111]

But music can also intensify an unproductive mood. In *Twelfth Night*, it feeds Duke Orsino's self-indulgent melancholy, as he begs his musicians to continue playing:

If music be the food of love, play on,
Give me excess of it that, surfeiting,
The appetite may sicken and so die.
That strain again, it had a dying fall.
It came o'er my ear like the sweet sound
That breathes upon a bank of violets,
Stealing and giving odour.

(I, i, 1– 8)

The "dying fall" or descending line accords with his melancholic state.

But in *Pericles, Prince of Tyre*, music does the opposite: it helps to relieve Pericles' "distemperature." He is also in a deep melancholic state, but in his case it is a tragic one. Brought on by the news of his daughter's death, Pericles has sworn neither to cut his hair nor to speak. After three months on board a ship, he arrives in Mytilene. In gratitude for Pericles' previous generous provision of gold to the starving city, the governor sends for a young woman, Marina, in hopes "her *sweet harmony* / And other chosen attractions, would allure, / And make a batt'ry through his deafen'd parts" (V, i, 45–7 in the Houghton Mifflin edition). Marina employs her "sacred physic" and sings to Pericles, who is brought out of his deep grief and back into human connection.[112]

Marina is uniquely capable of healing Pericles' psychological imbalance because of the elevated quality of her spirit. Remaining unsullied even when imprisoned in a brothel, she persuades the madam's clients to change their intentions by appealing to their honor and inner worth. Even the governor himself, who has brought "a corrupted mind" to the house of prostitution, finds that Marina's speeches change him (IV, vi, 111–2). Credit is given to Marina's musical studies, for "She sings like one immortal, and she dances / As goddess-like to her admired lays." (V, i, 3–4) Dancing, too, in its rhythmic ordered movements, helps to align the soul with the orderly heavens. Catherine M. Dunn comments "since Marina has never 'disordered' her soul, the study of music has helped to maintain the harmony of her being ... Her ability as performer is just further proof that she is 'in perfect tune' with ... the ideal and ordered perfection of the universe ...." So much so that she, like Imogen in *Cymbeline* "echoes the singing of the angelic intelligences which govern the [planetary] spheres."[113] Another character describes Marina as "goddess-like," the clue for Shakespeare's audience that all three levels of her—body, soul, and spirit—are attuned and aligned with the heavens.

Other exceptional beings besides the females so often celebrated by Shakespeare reflect this heavenly harmony in their character, their action, their very being. Cleopatra extols Antony by saying,

> I dreamt there was an Emperor Antony....
> *His face was as the heav'ns, and therein stuck*
> *A sun and moon*, which kept their course and lighted
> The little O o'th'earth....
> His legs bestrid the ocean; his reared arm

Crested the world; *His voice was propertied*
As all the tuned spheres ...

(*Antony and Cleopatra*: V, ii, 75, 78–83)

In contrast, when characters are emotionally and mentally disturbed, Shakespeare describes them as like discordant or broken music. The distressed Ophelia, after encountering the antic Hamlet, bemoans the change in him: "I ... That suck'd the honey of his *music* vows, / Now see that noble and most sovereign reason / *Like sweet bells jangled, out of tune and harsh ...*" (*Hamlet*: III, i, 154–7). Later in the same play, Ophelia herself is truly mad, and her mental state is reflected in her inability to sing whole songs; she can sing only snatches of them.

According to the worldview of Shakespeare's time, in the same way that music can express the inner condition of a human body, it can reveal the temper of the greater community, the "body politic." So profound is the connection between the music of the heavens and harmony on Earth that the state of a kingdom can be described in musical metaphor. Imprisoned in Pomfret Castle, King Richard II hears music from outside the walls, and meditates on the "sad contrast between his quick 'ear' for 'broken time' in music, and his slowness to hear the 'breaking' of his own 'state and time.'"[114]

Music do I hear.
Ha; ha; keep time! How sour sweet music is
When time is broke and no proportion kept.
So is it in *the music of men's lives.*
And here have I the daintiness of ear
To check time broke in a disordered string;
But for the concord of my state and time
Had not an ear to hear my true time broke.

(V, v, 41–8)

Shakespeare also specifies what type of music should accompany certain scenes or dominate in plays of a certain genre. Comedies are more likely to feature the music of concord while tragedies (and sometimes histories) foreground the music of discord. We might think of this as the music of Venus versus the music of Mars. Martian—or "martial"—music is obviously composed of sounds chosen to accompany human conflict, to stir the blood of its hearers to combat. In Shakespeare's works, drums sound frequently (often as "alarums") in plays where there is civil strife or international war. Louis the Dauphin in *King John*, rejecting the papal legate's petition for peace, orders his men to "Strike up the *drums*, and let the tongue of war / Plead for our interest and our being here" (V, ii, 164–5).

In contrast to Martial music, the Venusian kind is pleasing and calming, more suited to comedies and played on different instruments. Benedick's satiric observation about the change in Claudio, who was in the wars but is now love-struck, is that "I have known when there was *no music with him but the drum and the fife*, and now had he rather hear the *tabor and the pipe*" (*Much Ado About Nothing*: II, iii, 12–4).

These two types of music, the warlike and the peaceable, are the only two that the ancient Greek sage Socrates will allow in his ideal society. Dismissing certain modes of music that are "useless" or too "soft" (even for women!), he will permit "that mode that would fittingly imitate the utterances and the accents of a brave man who is engaged in warfare or in any enforced business, and … in all these conditions confronts fortune with steadfast endurance and repels her strokes." He also sees the value of allowing the opposite type of music, one "for such a man engaged in works of peace, not enforced but voluntary … acting modestly and

Elizabethan musicians play the drums, horn, and fiddle. Drums and trumpets are the music of Mars, background to battles and conflict. (From an engraving in Orchésographie *by Arbeau, 1588)*

moderately and acquiescing in the outcome."[115] Given the influence of Platonic thought on Renaissance culture, it is likely that Shakespeare was familiar with Socrates' opinion.

One literary critic, G. Wilson Knight, builds an entire theory around the opposition in Shakespeare's plays of "music" and "tempests," that is, harmony and discord (or sounds appropriate to either Venus or Mars, though he does not use those categories). Knight creates a grid that juxtaposes harmony or conflict within a human being to harmony or conflict within the social and political spheres, each accompanied by the appropriate sounds or music. Tempests reflect disorder in both spheres. When conflict descends into armed opposition, the sounds heard are alarums and battle sounds. If discord within a human being devolves into despair, nihilism, or madness, it is accompanied by "broken music." In the tragedies, which end in the inevitable death of the protagonist, we hear either death marches or solemn music—or finally, nothing. There is only silence.[116]

"The rest is silence" is in fact the last line delivered by the tragic hero Hamlet. It is fitting that earlier in the play Hamlet delivers one of Shakespeare's most profound speeches comparing a human being to an instrument. Showing his presumed friend Guildenstern a recorder and chiding him for being unable to play it, Hamlet rebukes him:

> Why, look you now how, unworthy a thing you make of
> me! You would play upon me, you would seem to know
> my stops, you would pluck out the heart of my mystery,
> you would sound me from my lowest note to the top of
> my compass; and there is much music, excellent voice in
> this little organ, yet cannot you make it speak. 'Sblood, do
> you think I am easier to be play'd on than a pipe? Call me
> what instrument you will, though you can fret me, you
> cannot play upon me.
>
> (III, ii, 334–41)

The heart of the human mystery may indeed lie in the synchronicity between the harmonious heavens and the beauteous human soul capable of sounding the harmony, proportion, and balance of sweet music.

The Importance of Rhyme and Rhythm to This Worldview

Some poets, like musicians, strive to write such mellifluous lines that their words flow like divine music and transport their listeners to the higher spheres, the spheres of the planets and even beyond. According to Shakespeare's contemporary, the poet Sir Philip Sidney, poetry can facilitate our journey up the "ladder of creation," making us feel immortal. One way that poetry does that is by reflecting the cosmos in the poetic creation; the reader then hears what Sidney referred to as the "Planet-like Music of Poetry" in its very lines, and is transported from an ordinary level of consciousness into an expanded one.[117]

> [This phrase] implies not only that poetry is measured in quantity like music, but also that poetry should echo the cosmic order inherent in the music of the spheres. Just as each planet generates a note contributing to the harmony of the heavens to comprise an all-inclusive diapason which represents the cosmos in musical terms, so must the elements of a poem fit together to comprise a comprehensive whole which reflects the universal order.[118]

Poetry is like music in that it has a measured rhythm or flow. It is music in words. That is part of its appeal to the human ear. In Shakespeare's plays the soliloquies, speeches delivered by characters alone on stage, resemble operatic arias: they are high points in the drama in which characters reveal their deepest thoughts and feelings, and playwrights have golden opportunities to show their art.

Poetry reflects the order of the cosmos particularly when it has an obvious and recurrent beat. This effect is intensified if the poem's lines have similar sounds at the end of each—that is, if they rhyme. Before the modern period, when the majority of poetry ceased to have regular rhythm and rhyme, poetry *was* most often rhymed. In fact, Shakespeare's audience would have expected actors to speak frequently in rhymed verse, especially if they were kings and nobles and especially if the plays were serious in tone, like the histories and tragedies.

Shakespeare does not use rhyme all the time. When he does use it, it is often for emphasis, usually in rhyming couplets with the ending sounds of just two lines matching. Rhymed lines occur in speeches when a character is in a heightened emotional state or when Shakespeare wants to draw attention to particularly significant comments. Frequently he ends a scene with rhymed couplets, to signal the completion of the scene or the interaction between certain characters. For instance, at the end of the scene in which Hamlet has seen his father's ghost and received the injunction to avenge his murder, his last lines, a rhyming couplet, carry tremendous significance: "The time is out of joint. O cursed spite / That ever I was born to set it right!" (I, v, 189–90).

Even when Shakespeare does not use rhyme, his poetic lines have a particular rhythm. His choice of rhythm has a deep significance that fits into the overall scheme of the Elizabethan worldview. Without getting too technical, it is illuminating to know that he uses syllables arranged in a particular pattern of strong and weak stresses. Each possible combination of syllables (STRONG-weak, weak-STRONG, STRONG-weak-weak, or weak-weak-STRONG) has a name. The type that Shakespeare (as well as Chaucer and Milton) typically uses is called an iamb or an iambic foot, and it is the one that has the pattern "weak-STRONG." Whether he is writing rhymed or unrhymed lines, Shakespeare customarily uses five of these "blocks" to a line (called "iambic pentameter"—"penta" means five in Greek), so that the rhythm of his poetic lines looks like this:

WEAK-STRONG, WEAK-STRONG, WEAK-STRONG, WEAK-STRONG, WEAK-STRONG

If you match up Hamlet's well-known lines cited above with this pattern, you can feel the rhythm:

The TIME is OUT of JOINT. o CURsed SPITE
That EVer I was BORN to SET it RIGHT!

In Shakespeare's earlier plays, the rhythm tends to be rather regular. Of course, if every line in every play followed this rhythm exactly, the poetry would be sing-song and soon sound ridiculous. In the later plays to vary the pace Shakespeare sometimes inserts two strong stresses in a foot, or truncates a line, or throws the stress off so that it does not quite match the exact pattern. He also frequently runs a sentence over from one line to the next, masking the basic pattern. But the rhythmic pattern is always there in the background, and when it is altered, the effect is the same as syncopation in music: the overlay of the "off" line is heard against the subliminal background of the regular rhythm, adding variety and interest to the musical effect of the language. What we are hearing in such cases is "discord" overlain on "concord" often reflecting a character's upset or a disruption in the state. (This also reflects the cosmology of Shakespeare's time in that the imperfect mundane world is superimposed on and co-exists with the perfect ideal one.)

Here is the wonderful point about the iambic foot or "weak-STRONG" pattern: *it is the same rhythm as the beat of the human heart.* Surely this is yet another reason why great poetry written in this rhythm has a special appeal. Listeners unconsciously sense it and feel the attunement to their own internal rhythms. Whether Shakespeare employed it consciously or unconsciously, his use of it is entirely in tune with the esoteric truths embedded in the plays. In the symbolic language of astrology, the heart is analogous to the Sun or to the spiritual self, and so this rhythm relates to the most exalted of its symbols. [119]

Not only does Shakespeare's choice of the iambic foot with its heartbeat rhythm have special significance; so does his use of the *five*-foot (pentameter) line. The number five is called "the number of man": human beings have five fingers on each hand, five toes on each foot, and five senses that enable them to perceive and interpret their experience of this world. The famous representation of the "Vitruvian Man," standing in an enclosed circle with his arms and legs outstretched, creates a five-pointed star. Stars—the single word that most represents astrology—are usually drawn with five points. The star has been a magical symbol for protection since ancient times, in Babylon, Egypt, Greece, India, China, Africa, and the Americas, and still is in esoteric groups to this day.

To the ancient followers of Pythagoras, the most sacred of the five Platonic solids was the fifth, the dodecahedron, with twelve faces each having the form of a pentagon with five sides equal in length. For the Pythagoreans the number five may have had special meaning as the midpoint of the sequence from one to nine, being the fulcrum or balance point. Similarly, humanity in the Elizabethan world picture occupies a central position, a place of connection between the above and below worlds, the invisible and visible.

Star-like structures occur in nature too, supporting the idea that the cosmos is reflected in the physical world. A pattern of five occurs frequently in the natural world and appears to carry the power of regeneration. The flowers of every edible fruit have five petals; cut through the center of an apple or a pear and you will see the internal five-pointed star

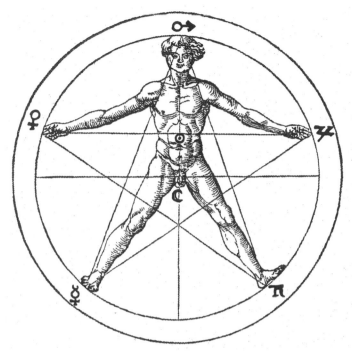

*A version of the "Vitruvian Man." This outstretched human body within a
circle creates a perfect five-pointed star, a pentagram. Symbols for the planets
are placed around the circle to mark each point of contact, with the Sun and
Moon inside. This image represents a balanced human being in harmony
with the cosmos.* (Agrippa, *De occulta philosophia*, 1531)

shape. In sea creatures like starfish, sea cucumbers, and sand dollars, the
pentagonal shape is the basis of its structure.

It is no accident that Hamlet asks, "What is this *quint*essence of
dust?" (II, ii, 298) "Quint" means five in Latin. The visible world is composed of four elements (fire, air, water, and earth, all in various combinations that create the multitudinous forms in the material dimension), but
the ancient worldview also postulated a fifth element, a subtle non-mate-
rial essence or "aether." This is the soul or the spirit of life that imbues
all forms with the energy of being. Without that vivifying energy, they
indeed are "dust." So the number five had a deeper—or higher—spiritual
meaning, something Hamlet may have been seeking in his question.

So Shakespeare's choice of the iambic foot (the two-beat foot reminding us of the human heartbeat) and the pentameter line (with five beats to a line recalling the "number of man") actually has esoteric significance and may have a secret and subtle influence on us as we listen to the plays. By making these poetic choices, Shakespeare perfectly matches the philosophical content of the plays with the most appropriate form to express that content.

Connecting the Levels:
the Imagery of Similes and Metaphors

God is the supreme poet, and the world is His poem.
—Cristoforo Landino[120]

Words…to accompany the music. Because Renaissance thinkers considered that the ability to speak ranked just below reason in the list of God's gifts to humanity, they believed that poetry was the highest of the arts.[121] It unites the rhythmic beats and tones of music, transmitted from the planetary spheres above, with sounds vocalized by human beings below. Like human beings, whose nature is both spiritual and physical, "words have a dual citizenship, belonging to both the physical world and the conceptual world."[122] To be maximally effective and enduring, though, words and the images created by them had to be in accord with the grander cosmological view described earlier in this chapter.

> [T]o insure that his poem is a genuine product of the imagination rather than of the irresponsible fantasy—the poet must necessarily observe the divinely ordained relationship between the physical world and the conceptual world.… the poet should devise an assemblage of analogies with the hope of providing a continuum of meaning from the highest to the lowest. His poem should be a network of active correspondences.…[123]

The extraordinary impact of Shakespeare's work is greatly due to his choice of words, particularly images that link the various levels of being. Poetry's power often derives from the poet's almost magical ability to conjure images in the minds of readers. Our imaginations may fixate on certain pictures in a particular poem; we pick out striking ones just as we might extract cherries or walnuts from a fruitcake, thinking that ones studded with the largest and tastiest morsels must be the best. However, Shakespeare's memorable little pictures—especially comparisons between persons and things or persons and gods/goddesses—have a more profound significance than most because they reflect the Elizabethan worldview.

What exactly is an "image"? It is "a literal and concrete representation of a sensory experience or of an object that can be known by one or more of the senses."[124] We may respond to a work of art—whether a poem, a painting, or a statue—because the artist creates such a realistic representation of something previously experienced or something imagined that the representation, whether verbal or physical, etches itself sharply into our minds. Hamlet's opinion about Denmark and his unhappiness at living there, for instance, is vividly and dramatically conjured when he compares Denmark to "an *unweeded garden* / That grows to seed; things rank and gross in nature / Possess it merely." (I, ii, 135–7)

At other times we delight in a work because it reveals an object in a fresh light or subverts our expectations of what something is or how it operates. Instead of liking a portrait painter's work because he captures the actual lineaments of the sitting subject (as the Dutch realists do), we appreciate the picture because the person is presented with the human outlines utterly scrambled (as in Picasso's works).

Shakespeare's imagery manages to do both of these things: it is both realistic *and* original, the product of acute observation and masterful craft. Here is an extraordinary image from the second scene of *Macbeth*, spoken by the bleeding sergeant describing a battle whose outcome is initially uncertain: "Doubtful it stood, / As two spent swimmers that do cling together / And choke their art." (I, ii, 7–9) In this brilliant image (also "brilliant" in that it enables us to envision the situation with great clarity), the soldiers seem to be fighting in a sea of roiling bodies, with the wave of dominance shifting from one side to the other, threatening to pull both down to die in the ocean's depths.[125]

Here is another original image, a favorite of mine, spoken by Juliet in the balcony scene when the two young people first declare their love for one another: "My bounty is *as boundless as the sea*, / My love as deep. The more I give to thee / The more I have, for both are infinite." (II, i, 175–7) This picture also draws on sea-imagery, but in an entirely different context and with an entirely positive meaning. Opposite to what you might expect—and that is what startles us in the image—the inexhaustible flow of Juliet's love *increases* instead of depletes the more it is offered.

The way in which a writer creates these dynamic images is through comparison, using one of two main techniques. The first is the simile (*similis* means "similar" in Latin), in which the writer describes the object or person *indirectly*, "like" (or "as") something else. Juliet's expression of the breadth and depth of her love, "*as* boundless as the sea," is of this type. The juxtaposition of the two specified things—often quite unexpected because the two items retain their distinctness—jolts us into seeing the first differently, in a richer context.

More than most poets, Shakespeare is a master at conjuring such images. Again from *Romeo and Juliet*, here is a beautiful word-picture, another simile, spoken by the romantic hero newly fallen in love: "O, she doth teach the torches to burn bright! / It seems she hangs upon the cheek of night / *As a rich jewel in an Ethiope's ear*— / Beauty too rich for use, for earth too dear" (I, v, 41–4). Here Shakespeare is even more adept, overlapping and equating *two* images, one of bright torches against the background of dark night and another of a sparkling gem against a dark-skinned African's cheek. What is original about this image is the idea that a human being can glow more brightly than lighted torches.

Not all of his similes are so lovely, though. In another example of Shakespeare's ability to contain opposites, he can write not only comparisons that are enobling and beautifying but also ones that are insulting and demeaning, even disgusting. The angry Hotspur disparages the wizard Glendower by saying, "O, he is as tedious / *As a tired horse, a railing wife / Worse than a smoky house.* I had rather live / With cheese and garlic, in a windmill, far, / Than feed on [deli]cates and have him talk to me / In any summer house in Christendom." (*I Henry IV*: III, i, 155–60) In *Pericles* the main character overhears fishermen philosophizing about the similarities between the natural and human worlds:

> 3RD FISHERMAN: Master, I marvel how the fishes live in
> the sea.
> 1ST FISHERMAN: Why, as men do a-land; the great ones
> eat up the little ones. *I can compare our rich misers*
> *to nothing so fitly as to a whale;* 'a plays and tumbles,
> driving the poor fry before him, and at last devour

them all at a mouthful. Such whales have I heard on
o' th' land, who never leave gaping till they swallow'd
the whole parish, church, steeple, bells, and all.
(II, i, 30–8, in Houghton Mifflin edition)

In the same play, Pericles' daughter Mariana describes the brothel in
which she is imprisoned as a hell; the food served "is such / *As hath been
belch'd on by infected lungs.*" (IV, vi, 178–9) Very disgusting!

The second technique is by *direct* comparison, called a metaphor.
Now the focus of the comparison is not just "like" something else; it
is that other thing, so two apparently discrete and different objects are
linked. Their essences come together in a fusion that is rationally inexplicable but emotionally satisfying. *It is as if the secret sympathy between
the different levels of the cosmos, part of the Elizabethan worldview but only
hinted at in a simile, suddenly reveals fully itself in the inner connection of
the two items.* Despite their apparent twoness, an underlying oneness is
affirmed. Caroline Spurgeon, in *Shakespeare's Imagery and what it tells us*,
speaks of this as a mystery:

> [A]nalogy—likeness between dissimilar things—which is the fact
> underlying the possibility and reality of metaphor, holds within
> itself the secret of the universe. The bare fact that germinating seeds
> or falling leaves are actually another expression of the processes we
> see at work in human life and death, thrills me, as it must others,
> with the sense of being here in the presence of a great mystery,
> which, could we only understand it, would explain life and death
> itself.[126]

Metaphors are consequently especially powerful images, pointing
at an underlying spiritual connection between two apparently separate
things.[127]

Here is a lovely and apt one: right after Romeo's beautiful lines cited
above (in which he used the simile comparing Juliet to a rich jewel),
he continues with a metaphor: "So shows a *snowy dove* trooping with
crows." (I, v, 45) Shakespeare is consistent in opposing brightness and
whiteness to blackness and darkness in both these images, with Juliet
emerging as a gloriously appealing figure, a being of light and a paragon
among women. Adding to our first impression of her beauty is the inti-
mation of a loving and peaceful nature, for the dove is the bird sacred to

the goddess of love herself, Venus, as well as emblematic of the soul.[128] Such an image affirms Juliet's essential spiritual nature since she is sympathetically resonant to a divinity.

Metaphors, like similes, can also be put-downs. Since Shakespeare is celebrated for his inventive invective, we should expect that some of his metaphors are, at the very least, uncomplimentary. Some are mild, like Don Pedro's greeting the morose Benedick with "Why, what's the matter / That you have such *a February face, / So full of frost, of storm and cloudiness?*" (*Much Ado About Nothing*: V, iv, 40–2). Others are more disagreeable, like Biron's rueful admission that he and his fellows have been wooing the disguised princesses with false flattery and exaggerated language:

> O, never will I trust to speeches penned …
> Taffeta phrases, silken terms precise,
>   Three-piled hyperboles, spruce affectation,
> Figures pedantical—*these summer flies*
>   *Have blown me full of maggot ostentation.*
> I do forswear them …
> Henceforth my wooing mind shall be expressed
>   In russet [homespun] yeas and honest kersey
>   [coarse woolen] noes …
>   (*Love's Labour Lost*: V, ii, 402, 406–10, 412–3)

Worse, though, is Falstaff's comparison of Bardolph's face to "*Lucifer's privy-kitchen, where he doth nothing but roast malt-worms* [drunkards]." (*2 Henry IV*: II, iv, 303–4)

Whatever the comparison, whether poets uses similes (something is *like* something else) or metaphors (something *is* something else), the important point is this: no matter which type they use, the image either hints at or unmasks the secret sympathy, testifying to the underlying unity of all visible things. But Shakespeare goes further: he reinforces the implications of the model delineated earlier in this chapter by deliberately linking persons and objects at radically different levels of creation. In line with the idea that human beings are at the center of the spectrum and able either to rise above their level or sink below it, the images that most reveal his characters are ones that make links between these different levels. People can choose to behave in ways that either exalt them or lower them in the hierarchy, either elevating them to the level of the gods and the angels or degrading them to the level of the animals, plants, or even minerals.

Shakespeare commonly raises his comedic and romantic heroines to a higher degree by comparing them to goddesses or to heavenly objects like the Sun, Moon, and stars. To Romeo, Juliet is the Sun. When the love-struck (or more accurately juice-struck) Demetrius in *A Midsummer Night's Dream* wakes and sees Helena, he declares "O Helen, *goddess, nymph*, perfect, divine!" (III. ii, 138) In *As You Like It*, on the occasion of overcoming the usurping Duke's wrestler, Orlando meets and immediately falls in love with the Duke's niece. Being warned that his life is in danger, he vows to leave the court, acknowledging his love for her in the final lines of the scene: "But *heavenly* Rosalind!" (I, ii, 256)

This is a consistent motif in Shakespeare's writings. The men in *Love's Labour's Lost*, who try and fail to live ascetic lives, rhapsodize on their new-found loves, comparing them in letters and speeches to both divinities and celestial objects. Biron's love, like Orlando's, is "the *heavenly* Rosaline"; every eye that looks upon the "*heaven* of her brow" must be "blinded by her majesty" (IV, iii, 217, 223, 224). Longaville's paean celebrates his love with a promise to be faithful: the "*heavenly* rhetoric" of her eyes inspires him to "prove, / Thou being a *goddess*, I forswore not thee. / My vow was earthly, thou a *heavenly* love." (IV, iii, 55, 59–61) The King too writes a letter in which he swears:

> So sweet a kiss the golden *sun* gives not
> To those fresh morning drops upon the rose …
> Nor shines the silver *moon* one-half so bright
> Through the transparent bosom of the deep …
> O Queen of queens, how far dost thou excel,
> No thought can think, nor tongue of mortal tell.
>
> (IV, iii, 22–3, 26–7, 36–7)

Shakespeare usually exalts women more than he does men, but men too may be glorified. Miranda in *The Tempest* has been isolated on an island with her father and the misshapen Caliban for company. When she first glimpses the young and handsome Ferdinand, only the second human male she has ever seen, she is entranced: "I might call him / A thing *divine*, for nothing natural / I ever saw so noble." (I, ii, 422–3) (He is equally charmed by her, thinking her to be "the *goddess* / On whom these airs attend" and "a wonder" [I, ii, 425–6, 430]).

In another play, Julius Caesar, a man whom many in Rome idolize as a god and whose ambition is perceived as a threat by Cassius and the other conspirators, is described as having a vast size and grandeur comparable to one of the immortals:

> Why, man, he doth bestride the narrow world
> Like a *Colossus*, and we petty men
> Walk under his huge legs, and peep about
> To find ourselves dishonourable graves.
>
> (I, ii, 136–9)

The Colossus of Rhodes, one of the Seven Wonders of the Ancient World and straddling the city's harbor, was a statue of the god Apollo. Apollo symbolizes wisdom, among other things, and this simile exalts Caesar as comparable to a god. Caesar seems to believe his own press, though; he trumpets his superiority by comparing himself to a relatively fixed light in the heavens, the Pole Star which mariners relied on to steer their ships:

> But I am constant as the *Northern Star*,
> Of whose true fixed and resting quality
> There is no fellow in the firmament.
> The skies are painted with unnumbered sparks;
> They are all fire, and every one doth shine;
> But there's but one in all doth hold his place.
> So in the world; 'tis furnished well with men,
> And men are flesh and blood, and apprehensive;
> Yet in the number I do know but one
> That unassailable holds on his rank,
> Unshak'd of motion; and that I am he ...
>
> (III, i, 60–70)

Conversely, if you behaved in a manner out of keeping with the superlative potentials of humankind, you descended to the levels below. In *King Lear* the faithful servant Kent blasts the treacherous Oswald in this image: "Such smiling rogues as these, / *Like rats*, oft bite the holy cords [of natural affection] a twain ..." (II, ii, 65–6). Continuing to hurl abuse at the despicable Oswald, Kent adds, "Smile you my speeches, as I were a fool? / *Goose*, if I had you upon Sarum plain / I'ld drive ye cackling home to Camelot." (II, ii, 74–6) In Kent's eyes Oswald is as silly and stupid as a goose (traditionally thought to be exceptionally unintelligent), being easily led to pander to Lear's evil daughter and to follow her commands thoughtlessly.

Even more extreme, you could descend to the level of inanimate minerals, whose only quality is that of simply existing. At the opening of *Julius Caesar* the tribunes chastise the mob gathered to welcome Caesar to Rome and celebrate his victories. The angry Marullus addresses them as "You *blocks*, you *stones*, you worse than senseless things! / O, you hard hearts, you cruel men of Rome" and sends them fleeing, abashed, to their homes (I, i, 34–5). Clearly they are at the absolute bottom of the hierarchy. We can confidently assess the quality of characters in the plays according to the comparisons Shakespeare makes with levels either higher or lower than the human one in the grand hierarchy.

CHAPTER 4

If All Is Order and Harmony,
How Do Disorder and Disharmony (Evil) Enter?

Our lives certainly unfold in an orderly—and irrevocable—sequence, from birth to death. We also experience time as orderly, with the sun rising and setting each day and the seasons following a predictable—and also irrevocable—sequence from spring through winter and renewal in spring again.

Not just from experience but also for political and cultural reasons, the people of Shakespeare's time fixated on the necessity of celestial order being reflected on Earth. In part this was because the majority espoused the worldview just described and in part because of the dramatic disruption in religious history during the sixteenth century: Henry VIII wrenched England away from its Catholic past and subsequent rulers flip-flopped from Protestantism to Roman Catholicism and back again. The result was that the populace held even more tenaciously to an underlying principle of order.

Historians and literary critics have remarked on the importance of the idea of order in the Elizabethan age. Shakespeare, typical of his time, is intensely aware of order on all levels—personal, social, political, spiritual, and cosmic. Tillyard, for one, assures us in *The Elizabethan World Picture* that the "idea of cosmic order was one of the genuine ruling ideas of the age, and perhaps the most characteristic" and that "cosmic order was yet one of the master-themes of Elizabethan poetry."[129] Shakespeare joins other Elizabethan poets in championing the dominant philosophical view of his time, with its emphasis on order and hierarchy. It is most obvious in Ulysses' famous speech on order in *Troilus and Cressida*:

> The heavens themselves, the planets, and this centre
> Observe degree, priority, and place,
> Infixture, course, proportion, season, form,
> Office and custom, in all line of *order*.
> And therefore is the glorious planet *Sol [the Sun]*
> In noble eminence enthroned and sphered

> Amidst the other, whose med'cinable eye
> Corrects the ill aspects of planets evil
> And posts like the commandment of a king,
> Sans check, to good and bad.
>
> (I, iii, 85–94)

Ulysses goes on for many more lines in this vein, elaborating on the importance of order and the dangers of disorder.

The model described earlier certainly depicts a perfect order of the stars and spheres unfolding in a stratified hierarchy, with the more important elements higher or "above" the lower ones. Just as the Sun is superior to other planets (as Ulysses specifically mentions), so each level of creation is imaged as subordinate to the one above and dominant over the one below.

This hierarchical order is reflected in the human world as the stratified social classes of Shakespeare's time. In *Twelfth Night* Malvolio, who is steward (household manager) to the countess Olivia, aspires to marry her although she is above him in social rank. His foolish hopes make him the butt of a joke played upon him by members of Olivia's household. Imitating Olivia's handwriting, her waiting-woman Maria writes a letter that Malvolio is allowed to discover suggesting that Olivia has a romantic interest in him. The pseudo-Olivia of the letter urges Malvolio not to be afraid of greatness, even though "In my *stars* I am above thee" (II, v, 125). His swelling egotism, fed by the instructions in the letter, leads to his humiliation when his intentions are ultimately exposed. Malvolio's ambitions are mocked and he is not allowed to violate the established social order.

But of course there are situations in Shakespeare's works where order *is* challenged and sometimes utterly violated. In fact, the trajectory of Shakespeare's tragedies is one of increasing *dis*order that undermines the health of the state and every person in it. This was possible because only the levels of creation above the Moon were thought to be perfect; everything below it was imperfect and therefore subject to degeneration, decay, and ultimately death. Consequently human beings had to commit themselves diligently to aligning themselves and everything in their world with Divine Order in order to preserve both personal and communal health. Once disorder appeared and increased, the consequences for everything in the material world might be catastrophic. No surprise that G. Wilson Knight observes that,"'Disorder' and 'tragedy' are in Shakespeare practically synonymous."[130]

Disorder threatens in the comedies too, but never seriously since it is often temporary, exists on a small scale, or is contained within one person. In *Twelfth Night*, Maria insists that Olivia's uncle Sir Toby stop his noisy partying and drinking: "By my troth, Sir Toby, you must come in earlier o' nights. Your cousin, my lady, takes great exceptions to your ill hours.... [Y]ou must confine yourself within the modest limits of *order*." (I, iii, 3–4, 6) The irrepressible Sir Toby, like the irrepressible Falstaff, pushes the boundaries of acceptable behavior by continuing to carouse, but is not allowed to disrupt the household completely—in fact he contributes to the re-establishment of order by participating in the joke on Malvolio.

The existence of disharmony, disorder, and even downright evil in the world has been a perplexing problem for philosophers and theologians through the ages.

> The ladder in its idealized form depicts a perfectly unfolding continuum, with successive levels in harmony with the Will of the One and in sympathy with each other. But one has only to look about the world to see that there are aspects of nature ("red in tooth and claw"), types of people (criminals and murderers), and inexplicable events (fires, hurricanes, floods, and famines) that are incompatible with this perfection.[131]

So how does disorder enter into and disrupt this lovely framework? One answer is that this scheme represents the IDEAL. The world frequently does not work in the way that the model suggests that it could... or should.[132]

In the speech cited earlier, Ulysses blames the physical planets.

> But when the *planets*
> *In evil mixture to disorder wander,*
> What plagues and what portents, what mutiny?
> What raging of the sea, shaking of earth?
> Commotion in the winds, frights, changes, horrors
> Divert and crack, rend and deracinate
> The unity and married calm of states
> Quite from their fixture. O when degree is shaked,

Which is the *ladder* to all high designs,
Then enterprise is sick.

(I, iii, 94–103)

From the perspective of this hierarchical model, this makes sense since the realm of the fixed stars beyond the planets is the only one that appears to be just that—relatively fixed. And fixity is associated with the Divine which by definition is perfect and unchanging. But the planets (meaning "wanderers" in Greek—just the word that Ulysses uses to describe their deviation) have orbits of different time periods, and all of them (except the Sun and Moon, of course, which are not technically planets) appear to slow down, come to a stop, and then go backward and forward in the sky. They are not fixed and so their changing positions and movements reflect the changing nature of the visible world.

But since the planets actually have rather regular patterns perceivable by observation over time, their movements cannot be responsible for disorder. Venus, for instance, has a unique and predictable cycle: every eight years within two days, she comes back to nearly the same sign and degree she had eight years previously. At five different times during that eight-year cycle she appears to stop at a certain point, retrograde and then turn direct. If you trace these points on the circle of the zodiac, with the Earth at its center, you create a lovely five-pointed star!

The planets might be blamed not because they all have variable cycles but because two of them in particular, Mars and Saturn, were thought in traditional astrology to be "malefics" (Latin: "to do ill" or, literally "make bad"). While modern astrology tends to view all the planetary factors as having both positive and negative potentials, these two for many hundreds of years had the reputation of being difficult and disruptive. They were the specific causes of disorder and hardship. The darker side of Mars might correlate with aggression, violence, cruelty, and destruction and that of Saturn with inhibitions, limitations, disappointments, pain, suffering, and finally, death. (These interpretations will be explored in greater depth and detail in Chapter 10 on *Macbeth* and Chapter 12 on *King Lear*.)[133]

On the whole, though, since the planets belong to the "above" world, in Shakespeare's plays they are more commonly symbols of harmony rather than disharmony. So Shakespeare employs other symbols of disorder. As one critic notes, "The physical symbol of order is that of the stars in their courses: rebellion is symbolized by comets, thunder and lightning, 'exhalations,' and similar aspects of meteorology unusual enough to be called unnatural, because they interrupt the sense of nature as predictable."[134] Shakespeare focuses more on these anomalies—comets, shooting stars, and eclipses—as violators of the established order, since they are rarer and more dramatic. All of them were thought to be special portents of evil and to coincide with threats to king and kingdom. "When beggars die there are no *comets* seen," warns Caesar's wife, but "The heavens themselves blaze forth the death of princes." (*Julius Caesar*: II, ii, 30–1)

This same belief features in *Richard II*. Richard unwisely confiscates some of his nobles' wealth and leaves England to fight the Irish. When his return is delayed, his superstitious Welsh troops take multiple signs in the heavens as indications that he has been killed.

> WELSH CAPTAIN: 'Tis thought the King is dead. We will
>   not stay.
>   The bay trees in our country are all withered,
>   And *meteors fright the fixed stars of heaven,*
>   The *pale-faced moon looks bloody* on the earth,
>   And lean-looked prophets whisper fearful change....
>   *These signs forerun the death or fall of kings....*
> SALISBURY: Ah, Richard! With the eyes of heavy mind
>   I see thy glory, like a *shooting star,*
>   Fall to the base earth from the firmament.
>   Thy sun sets weeping in the lowly west,
>   Witnessing storms to come, woe, and unrest.
>   Thy friends are fled to wait upon thy foes,
>   And crossly to thy good all fortune goes.
>   (II, iv, 7–11, 15, 18–24)

Eclipses are especially malevolent omens, associated with the fall of great men. The Roman general Antony, besotted with Cleopatra, himself recognizes his falling fortunes: "Alack, our terrene [earthly] moon / Is now eclips'd, and it portends alone / The fall of Antony!" (*Antony and Cleopatra*: III, xiii, 156–8) So horrifying to Othello is his killing the innocent Desdemona that he exclaims,

O insupportable, O heavy hour!
Methinks it should be now a huge *eclipse*
Of sun and moon, and that th'affrighted globe
Should yawn at alteration.

(V, ii, 107–10)

(It is astronomically impossible to have an eclipse of both the Sun and Moon at the same time. An eclipse of the Moon can only happen either two weeks before or two weeks after a solar eclipse. For Othello to imagine that both should happen at the same time accords with the terrible nature of the murder and magnifies it as resonating with cosmic disorder on a grand scale.)

When the Ghost of Hamlet's dead father appears, Horatio is sure his appearance "bodes some strange eruption to our state" and compares the

Halley's Comet is depicted above the tower next to the phrase "Isti Mirant Stella" ("These men wonder at the star") in this section of the Bayeux Tapestry. The tapestry was created to celebrate the victory in 1066 of the Norman French under William the Conqueror. It also marks the fall of the last Anglo-Saxon king of England, Harold II, killed at the Battle of Hastings.

current time to ancient Rome when the "mightiest Julius fell," accompanied by omens of ill fate. (*Hamlet*: I, i, 68, 106.7) Then too the "sheeted dead" walked the streets and shrieked at

> [S]*tars* with trains of fire, and dews of blood,
> Disasters in the sun; and the *moist star [the Moon]*,
> Upon whose influence Neptune's empire stands
> Was sick almost to doomsday with *eclipse*.
>
> (I, i, 106.10–13)

What is not clear in Shakespeare's references to planets, comets, eclipses, and other symbols of disruption is whether they are truly *causes* or merely *signs*—that is, are they responsible for disorder or merely the visible correlates of disorder?

Another explanation for the presence or periodic resurgence of disruption and disorder may just be the inherent nature of the visible world, the world beneath the sphere of the Moon, where elements inevitably mix and mingle in ever-varying combinations. Philosophers and theologians for many centuries saw the mundane world as necessarily imperfect and therefore only occasionally—perhaps only rarely—reflective of the higher and underlying perfection.[135]

Clearly there is something "off" or "wrong" with the material world.

> Plato also recognized in the world's composition an irreducible element of stubborn errancy and irrationality, which he referred to as *ananke*, or Necessity. In the Platonic understanding, the irrational was associated with matter, with the sensible world, and with instinctual desire, while the rational was associated with mind, with the transcendent, and with spiritual desire.... Reason overrules Necessity in the greatest part of the world so that it conforms to good purpose, but on some points Reason cannot overcome the errant cause—hence the existence of evil and disorder in the world. As a finite creation, the world is necessarily imperfect.[136]

Everyone—religious, philosophical, and esoteric thinkers alike—agrees that the physical world has an element of imperfection, or irrationality, or disorder, even periodic chaos.

But to what extent are human beings contributors to or even instigators of disruptions and disasters? In Shakespeare's works, despite many references to the power and influence of the heavens (good or bad stars, comets and eclipses, and so on), there is an equal emphasis on the choices his characters make, putting a great deal of responsibility on human beings. In particular if they go against the established order, especially if they challenge a King, they become the imaginative equivalent in the earthly dimension of a disrupter in the heavenly one, illustrating the secret sympathy between different levels of creation. Henry IV, for example, rebukes the rebellious Worcester, comparing him to a dreaded meteor:

> Will you again unknit
> This churlish knot of all-abhorred war?
> And move in that *obedient orb[it]* again
> Where you did give a fair and natural light,
> And be no more an exhaled *meteor*,
> A prodigy of fear, and a portent
> Of broached mischief to the unborn times?
>
> (*I Henry IV*: V, i, 15–21)

If like Macbeth or Claudius they are so brazen as to actually kill a king in an inappropriate attempt to rise from their ordered place in the social hierarchy to a higher level, they create catastrophe within the kingdom. Each has made the choice to act against the prevailing hierarchical view, and, as is consistently true for the villains and disrupters of order in the plays, their efforts come to nought. At the end of the play, what awaits Macbeth, Claudius, and Edmund is death, and order is—must be—restored with another and wiser, or at least more appropriate, ruler (Malcolm, Fortinbras, and Edgar) replacing them.

But before we get there, there has been terrible collateral damage—upheavals in the state and deaths of the innocent, like Ophelia and Lady Macduff and her son. Do human beings then have a special responsibility to cultivate order, both within society and within themselves? Since all levels of the cosmos, from the highest to the lowest, are connected, if you become disturbed, your inner discord can spread outward to infect others, nature, and even the state. As Shakespeare shows, the way you can most support order on all levels is to exercise the faculty of reason, the higher mind, to control desire.

Mastering the Passions:
The Moral Dimension of Shakespeare's Works

[T]he astrologers themselves say that the wise man commands the stars, in so far as he commands his passions ... —St. Thomas Aquinas[137]

The Elizabethans had inherited centuries of debate about the terrible problem of injustice in the world. Why do the innocent suffer? And why do the guilty often go unpunished? A partial answer was formulated in the image of the Wheel of Fortune. No matter your inner quality or disciplined efforts, the wheel turns inexorably, taking you from the heights of achievement to the depths of despair—and then up again. This is just the "round of life," a cycle that may be relentless and inexplicable. Shakespeare is familiar with this image, for King Lear's loyal adherent, the disguised Earl of Kent, refers to it when he has been disgraced by being put in the stocks: "Fortune, good-night; smile once more; *turn thy wheel.*" (*King Lear*: II, ii, 165).

But the apparent randomness of the turning wheel offended theologians and philosophers alike. While "fickle Fortune" still played a role, from the late classical period (in such influential works as Boethius' *The Consolation of Philosophy*) through the Middle Ages (in popular stories like Chaucer's *The Canterbury Tales* or Dante's *The Divine Comedy*), and into the Renaissance, emphasis fell equally on human beings' role in creating their own difficulties. The way they did this was to let their desires and passions run riot.

In modern North American culture, where businesspeople and politicians are regularly aassumed to be money- and power-hungry and where celebrities regularly get attention for throwing tantrums, posting sex tapes online, or getting arrested for driving drunk or egging neighbors' homes, it may be hard for us to understand the emphasis in Shakespeare's day on a person's ability to master such passions as greed, anger, and lust. Both orthodox religion and the philosophical/spiritual worldview described earlier emphasize restraining these all-too-human drives. Keeping them in their place bestows personal benefits: it strengthens your character and prevents impulses from imbalancing your psyche and messing up your life. As well, maintaining your own psychic balance has a greater consequence: your efforts help restore humanity to its previous glorious position (prior to Adam's fall in the Garden of Eden or the

The Wheel of Fortune, perhaps an allusion to the zodiac or the turning wheel of the seasons, expresses the temporal nature of all earthly things and the changeability of human life. The multi-armed Fortuna (on the right) turns the wheel, taking you from the depths to the heights and down again. The king at the top of this wheel is losing his crown, signaling his downfall. Tragedy focuses on the downward arc, comedy on the upward one. The moral message (represented by the religious figure to the left) was to be philosophical and patient: if you wait, the wheel will inevitably turn again. (John Lydgate, The Fall of Princes, *1494)*

In Henry V *Shakespeare has the disreputable Pistol protest "cruel fate/ And giddy Fortune's furious fickle wheel" (III, vi, 23–5).*

soul's enmeshment in matter) as the fulcrum of creation. Such passion-mastering contributes to righting the balance within creation itself. By doing this you help to maintain or re-establish divine order.[138]

But where do we get these "passions"? Defined as "intense, extreme, or over-powering emotions or feelings," especially "ardent affection or love," "intense sexual desire or lust," and "overwhelming anger or rage," such passions were often thought to arise because human beings have physical bodies. The Neo-Platonists, however, believed that such qualities were attached to the soul even before incarnation. As she descends through the planetary spheres, she takes on the qualities of each, some more desirable and others less so. Whichever ones you borrow, they are handed back later when the soul re-ascends through those spheres.

While ancient theorists do not make this explicit, zodiacal placements of the planets at the time of the soul's descent may account for differing expressions of planetary qualities in human beings. If the soul descends while Mars is journeying through the backdrop of the zodiacal sign of Scorpio, it would assert itself differently than if it were descending while Mars is transiting the sign of Pisces. (The first might be more wily and strategic in taking action while the second might have trouble being assertive at all, with actions perhaps dissipated and misdirected.)

Philosophical thought and astrological tradition connect each of the planets with specific personality traits and vulnerabilities to particular passions or character flaws. (The listed qualities of Mars, the Moon, Jupiter, and Saturn obviously relate to the theory of the humors.) The "passions" are generally identified with the negative qualities.

If you exhibit the negative qualities of the planets, you are encouraged to modify your behavior to convert them to the positive.

Whether you think of vices or sins as associated with a planet's prominence in your psyche (as indicated in your horoscope) or with imbalances in your temperament (linked to four specific planets), Shakespeare's dramas show that there are consequences from being drunk, lustful, wrathful, villainous, or murderous. Actions that certain characters take are meant to be understood as not just undesirable but morally wrong. We associate a moral code—that is, a set of injunctions determining good or "right" behavior and wrong or "bad" behavior—with both religions and the legal system. Morality that is established and reinforced by a religion relies on revelation and commentary on it to set guidelines for human behavior. Morality promulgated and reinforced by

Planet	Positive Qualities	Negative Qualities
Saturn:	discipline, prudence, patience, wisdom, self-control	fear, coldness, hard-heartedness, miserliness, depression, melancholy
Jupiter	faith, optimism, generosity	power-hunger, greed, gluttony, laziness, going to excess
Mars	courage, daring, initiative	irritability, impatience, anger, cruelty, violence
Sun	authentic selfhood, leadership, heroism	arrogance, pride, boastfulness, self-aggrandizement
Venus	love, beauty	lust, wantonness, covetousness, avarice, envy, (sexual) jealousy, vanity
Mercury	intelligence, quickness of thought and action	superficiality, lying, cunning
Moon:	fertility, adaptability	moodiness, instability, sloth

the legal and political system accumulates from decrees and laws that are established, interpreted, and enforced over a long period of time. Some of these derive from what benefits a society and protects its citizens rather than what is presumed to be divine direction.

What is intriguing about Shakespeare's work is that a moral vision certainly pervades it, but it is not explicitly based on a religious framework. Curiously, given the historical period during which the works were created, the framework of Shakespeare's dramas is not obviously Christian. As literary critic Northrop Frye observes,

> The Elizabethans had little place for the gods … which they regarded as personifications of natural forces. This means that social and political situations have a much more important place in Elizabethan than in Greek tragedy. In Greek tragedy catastrophe is referred primarily to the gods: crimes are offences against them … Elizabethan tragedy not only had no gods, but was also a secular form avoiding the explicit use of Christian conceptions of deity. For the Elizabethans, the royal figure or human ruler tended to become

the mythical centre of the action, and the relations of the ruler and his people take the place of the relations of gods and men.[139]

This is not entirely true since Shakespeare's plays do occasionally feature gods and goddesses, but they are the classical divinities of ancient Greece and Rome. These divinities are referred to frequently, and even make appearances in the plays. Juno, Ceres, and Iris (the goddess of the rainbow) are conjured in *The Tempest*, the Moon goddess Diana appears in a vision to Pericles in *Pericles, Prince of Tyre*, and Jupiter makes a sudden and stunning appearance in *Cymbeline*. These gods erupt into the action sometimes spontaneously and sometimes through human agency. While there are many resonances to Biblical sayings and stories in Shakespeare's works, Frye is right that the drama of the time generally avoided explicit references to a Christian dogma. The morality of Shakespeare's plays, though influenced by Christianity, is based on an ethical system relating very much to the worldview discussed in Chapter 3 that goes back to classical times.

The Elizabethans' view of the cosmos is, like the ancient classical view, theocentric and multi-leveled. Humanity is at the fulcrum of creation, midway between the angels above and the animals below. The key concept underlying the system is order: an ordered cosmos, an ordered nature, and an internal order within the human being. What upsets the order of both the human and natural worlds are desires and drives overcoming the proper dominance of the mind: "the conflicts of mature Shakespearean tragedy are those between the passions and reason."[140] This is precisely the crux of so many of Shakespeare's tragedies: the hero succumbs to jealousy (Othello), craves a higher position (Macbeth), or is betrayed by lust (Antony).

That classical worldview was much in evidence in a variety of works published during Shakespeare's lifetime. A popular one was *A Mirror for Magistrates* (1559), reprinted in 1574 with added stories of tragedies by John Higgins, all selected to show that the fall of princes is due not to the capriciousness of the gods but to their own vices. Higgins refers to "that wonderful and excellent [Neo-Platonic] Philosopher" Plotinus (third century CE) who recommends "temperance," one of the four cardinal virtues and defined as "habitual moderation; self-control." "The property of Temperance," paraphrases Higgins, "is to covet nothing which may be repented: not to exceed the bounds of measure, and to keep desire under the yoke of Reason."[141] Using the examples of Alexander the Great, Caesar, Pompey, Cyrus, and Hannibal, Higgins moralizes that all of these men "felt the reward of their immoderate and insatiable lusts ... "[142]

This same recommendation appears in the works of a famous astrologer of Shakespeare's time, Girolamo Cardano (1501–76), whose moral philosophy associated human misery with unrealistic drives spurred by

Queen Elizabeth I presides over the cosmos. Each planetary sphere correlates with a virtue of good government: majesty (Saturn), Prudence (Jupiter), Fortitude (Mars), Religion (Sun), Mercy (Venus), Eloquence (Mercury), and Abundance (Moon), with Immoveable Justice at the center. The Queen thus provides a stabilizing order for all creation. (John Case, *De sphaera civitatis*, 1588)

endless human desires: "Since human nature is driven to the infinite by appetites, it can never be satisfied, for it cannot contain the infinite, indeed, not even a great part of what it desires."[143] (This is very much in line with Buddhist philosophy: the source of human suffering is endless desire.) Consequently people unable to restrain their appetites, no matter their wealth or social status, are doomed to be unhappy. Cardano urged both self-knowledge (from a thoughtful consideration of the human condition) and self-control.

The rewards of self-control are not only social and cosmic; they are personal: not only greater happiness but also calmness in the face of adversity, so that when encountering difficulties in life, you can face them with a quiet mind. (An unquiet mind was considered one of the punishments for evil-doing—as is obvious with Richard III, Macbeth, and Claudius in *Hamlet*.) Self-mastery also strengthened your character, and doubtless spurred your spiritual growth. Even your body benefited, for "Voluntary self-restraint ... was the mark of virtue, and its reward was physical health, the counterpart of moral vigor."[144] Every level of a human being profited.

To overcome the temptation to indulge the passions, you had to know what temptations to avoid. Elizabethan moralists were sure they knew what these were and exhorted readers to

> [A]void the vices which are incident to the weakened mind. As the Pride of life. The Envy of the mind at the prosperity of another. The Wrath which wastes and molests the heart. The Gluttonous excess of ... pampered paunches, in their dainty fare and drunken delights. The lascivious and unlawful desire of the flesh. The Covetous consciences of wealthy worldly misers. And lastly the sluggish Sloth and idle life, enemy to all virtuous actions.[145]

Many of Shakespeare's characters are studies in passions gone to excess: Julius Caesar proud to equate himself to the North Star and aspire to be Emperor; Falstaff both gluttonous and slothful; Shylock miserly and covetous. Lily B. Campbell believes that Shakespeare's tragic heroes enact the typical tragic pattern precisely because each succumbs to a particular passion: Hamlet to grief; Othello to jealousy; Macbeth to fear; and King Lear to wrath. Some vices were dangerous, too, because they could easily and sequentially lead to more serious ones: lust to anger (at not getting the desired object), anger to vengefulness (a desire to hurt), and vengefulness to murder. Iago, for instance, is motivated by both resentment of Othello and a desire for Desdemona: "Now, I do love her too," he says, though he protests that it is "Not out of absolute lust" (II, i, 278–9). Lustful, angry, and vengeful, he provokes Othello to murder Desdemona, as culpable as if he had strangled her himself.

But how exactly to control passion? Moralizing and sermonizing, telling yourself or someone else to be reasonable, to control desires and appetites, is easy, but the actual doing of it is not (as every dieter or addict knows). It is certainly a good idea to start with a reasoned and intelligent consideration of the wisdom of an action and its possible consequences. This belief derived in part from an ancient tradition of moral psychology based on a combination of Aristotle's thought and Stoic philosophy and in part from Elizabethan ideas about the anatomy of both body and soul. Being at the top of the body (literally closest to heaven) and containing the rational and immortal part, the brain was supposed to rule the heart, thought to be the seat of the passions. Being fond of hierarchies, philosophers divided the brain (like the body) into three parts: "The highest contained the supreme human faculty the reason, by which man is separated from the beasts and allied to God and the angels, with its two parts, the understanding (or wit) and the will. It is on these two highest human faculties, understanding and will, that Elizabethan ethics are based."[146]

We witness some of Shakespeare's heroes struggling with moral issues and arguing with themselves in a battle between passion and reason. Macbeth debates in a soliloquy the wisdom and rightness of killing King Duncan: he would do it if only there were no spiritual consequences to assassinating him; if only others would not do the same to him; if only he were not bound by social custom to honor the king as both kinsman and subject; if only Duncan were not such a virtuous man; and if only it was not just "vaulting ambition" that motivated him. By the end of the speech, reason has won. But with Lady Macbeth's needling, prudence gives way and he vows, "I am settled, and bend up / Each corporal agent to this terrible feat." (I, vii, 79–80) His reason recognizes that the murder is a "terrible" act, a sinful one, and his conscious admission of it makes it worse. But for him passion has won the argument.

Elizabethans also took into account your personality type when evaluating your potential to be reasonable. Your temperament might determine your response when desire surged or emotion swelled.

> Those who naturally tended to be carried away by humoural passions were naturally less amenable to self-control; and those whose passions were less bold could ponder their reactions and fully exert free will. Humoural temperament determined how strong free will was in the face of appetite or passion. We ha[ve] no immediate control over the physiology that enable[s] us to exert self-control: we [a]re born with it under a particular zodiac.[147]

Cholerics, for instance, would have a much more difficult time controlling anger than either phlegmatics or melancholics.

Age is also a factor. Older, more temperate men, whose passions have ebbed and whose will has strengthened over time, are less subject to passion. They are frequently depicted in Shakespeare's plays trying to reason with younger and more volatile ones. A good example is Old Capulet trying to restrain Tybalt at his party.

> CAPULET: Why, how now, kinsman? Wherefore storm
>   you so?
> TYBALT: Uncle, this is a Montague, our foe,
>   A villain that is hither come in spite
>   To scorn at our solemnity this night.
> CAPULET: Young Romeo is it?
> TYBALT: 'Tis he, that villain Romeo.
> CAPULET: Content thee, gentle coz, let him alone.
>   A bears him like a portly gentleman,
>   And, to say truth, Verona brags of him
>   To be a virtuous and well-governed youth.
>   I would not for the wealth of all this town
>   Here in my house do him disparagement.
>   Therefore be patient, take no note of him.
>   It is my will, the which if thou respect,
>   Show a fair presence and put off these frowns,
>   An ill-beseeming semblance for a feast.
>   (*Romeo and Juliet*: I, v, 57–71)

Like the extreme choleric, Tybalt will not be reasoned with, saying "I'll not endure him," which only spreads wrath for now Old Capulet begins to be angry too:

CAPULET: He shall be endured.
     What, goodman boy, I say he shall. Go to,
     Am I the master here or you? Go to—
     You'll not endure him! God shall mend my soul.
     You'll make a mutiny among my guests,
     You will set cock-a-hoop! You'll be the man!
TYBALT: Why, uncle, 'tis a shame.
CAPULET: Go to, go to,
     You are a saucy boy. Is't so, indeed …
     You must contrary me.… You are a princox [cheeky
          boy]; go.
     Be quiet, or … for shame,
     I'll make you quiet.

                                             (I, v, 73–80, 82–5)

Ominously, rather than quell his passion Tybalt leaves the party vowing that his anger ("gall" being the physical manifestation of wrath and assigned to Mars) will eventually out:

TYBALT: Patience perforce with willful *choler* meeting
     Makes my flesh tremble in their different greeting.
     I will withdraw, but this intrusion shall,
     Now seeming sweet, convert to bitt'rest *gall*.

                                             (I, v, 86–9)

The same type of interaction occurs in *I Henry IV* when Mortimer and Worcester try to talk some sense into Hotspur.[148] Cholerics in Shakespeare's works, other than the shrew Katharina, do not seem to be able to control their anger, and most end up fighting or at war and ultimately (like both Tybalt and Hotspur) dead.

Since mastering the passions was the key to true free will (which presumably included freedom from celestial influence, as asserted by St. Thomas Aquinas in the quotation at the head of this section), there were many antidotes recommended to mitigate passions and allow reason to reign supreme. The goal was balance, a very laudable aim, one that went back to classical philosophy's ideas of "moderation in all things" and adherence to "the golden mean" in order to approximate the ideal balance of all four humors. Recommendations were many and quite detailed, taking into consideration not only the temperament but also environmental and hygienic factors, like air quality, typical food and drink, and sleeping patterns. This tradition began with Hippocrates (the "father of medicine") in fifth century Greece and Galen (practicing in second century Rome) and evolved through many centuries. Galen believed that you could fight off the more powerful passions and abstain from acting on them but it took work. Stoic-like, he "recommended a long period of self-conscious, systematic efforts, the help of a wise and disinterested friend capable of giving honest criticism, and the cultivation of a sense of shame."[149]

Besides using such tactics encouraging reason to keep passion in check, there were abundant specific suggestions geared to your dominant humor. Many of these recommendations seeped into Renaissance culture through Marsilio Ficino's seminal work, *The Book of Life*. Written, compiled, and circulated in 1489, Ficino's book re-introduced earlier ideas about physical and psychological health into Renaissance culture.[150] Much of Ficino's advice seems reasonable: melancholics, ruled by Saturn, should periodically leave their dark and gloomy studies and take walks in the fresh air and bright sunshine. Phlegmatics should

> Avoid too much cold food, and even moist food, lest black bile become a problem.... It is necessary that eating be moderate, but even more moderate must be your drinking.... The room you live in should be high up, far from heavy mist and air, the humidity driven out of it either by fire or incense. Cold must be kept away from the head, and especially from the neck and the feet, for it is very harmful to thought. A small amount of aromatic spices is useful on colder dishes. Dishes spiced with nutmeg, cinnamon, saffron, and ginger, served on an empty stomach in the morning, are especially good for the senses and for memory.[151]

Ruled by the Moon and therefore subject to rheumy diseases, phlegmatics are logically advised to avoid cold and moist food and live in a warm, dry environment—advice you might receive even today.

Ficino, like many Renaissance thinkers, was most fascinated by the challenges of melancholia, (his own temperament and that of his fellow philosophers in the Florentine Academy).

> Melancholy was in a class of its own, and a matter of some complexity. It presented a large variety of symptoms, and it could be caused either by internal organs or by external factors. External causes included grief, which led the vital heat to die down; the lovesickness diagnosed as a real disease by Hippocrates, Erasistratus, and others; and passionate love itself, in fact a version of this syndrome. Prescriptions for externally caused melancholy included exercise, moist foods, massages, baths, music, poetry, exemplary tales from the lives of sages, and sexual distraction. All sufferers of melancholy, regardless of its source, should seek out light and gardens, calm and rest, purges and laxatives; inhalations and warm baths with moistening plants, such as nenuphar, violets, and lettuce leaves; and a diet of lamb, lettuce, eggs, fish, and ripe fruit. They should avoid acidic foods like vinegar and mustard, as well as garlic, onion, cabbage, lentils, and red meat.[152]

The characters in Shakespeare's plays, though, often do not listen to reason or follow this type of advice, to either comic or tragic effect: cholerics stay angry, phlegmatics drink and party, and melancholics over-indulge in grief, passion, or frenzy. Always assumed—and often explicit—is the audience's awareness of the benefits of exalting reason over passion. *Antony and Cleopatra*, for instance, depicts the fall of a great man overcome by desire. Enobarbus, though he is a loyal friend to Antony, pinpoints Antony's flaw. When Antony flees the sea-battle against Caesar to follow Cleopatra's ships and is consequently disgraced for cowardice, Cleopatra asks Enobarbus, "Is Antony or we in fault for this?" His reply is "Antony only, that would make his will [desire] / Lord of his reason" (III, xiii, 2–4).

Yet despite presenting characters who succumb to their passions, we never get the sense that Shakespeare, like the Puritans of his time, was judging them and their choices harshly. The moral choices they make in every instance are understandable, resulting from who they are in terms of their temperament and situation. With an admirable compassion and an acceptance of their humanity, as mixed creatures with qualities both laudable and condemnable, Shakespeare presents us with a pageant of possibilities. There is an ambiguity in the overall scheme: the basic order of the universe is in place but human beings have the freedom to go against it. We are to some degree fated, but we also have some free will and can influence the outcome of events by focused intention and self-control. Helena in *All's Well that Ends Well* voices the same idea:

> Our remedies oft in ourselves do lie
> Which we ascribe to heaven. The fated sky
> Gives us free scope, only doth backward pull
> Our slow designs when we ourselves are dull.

> (I, i, 199–202)

In line with the mysterious double-sidedness of Shakespeare's work, he provides us with two superimposed perspectives, both of which seem valid. On the one hand, actions taken in the plays unfold apparently inevitably. Whether it is because there is "some consequence yet hanging in the stars" or whether characters are born with horoscopes that make them behave predictably (like Edmund, whose birth occurs "under Ursa Major") or whether their temperaments predispose them to act in certain ways, they seem fated. On the other hand, the characters, both to themselves and to us in the audience, seem absolutely free to make their choices. Shakespeare maintains a dual perspective, much in the way that we live our lives: feeling constrained by the limitations of our personalities and circumstances and at the same time feeling free to make independent and individual choices.

Underlying the action of the plays as well as the unfolding of our lives, like the bass line of a musical piece, is divine order. Above it, the melody plays freely, sometimes in tune with the bass and sometimes wandering away from it. This creates a discord that works against the regular rhythm, like syncopated offbeats or the "off rhythm" of some of Shakespeare's poetic lines. Underlying the action—or perhaps above it—is always the affirmation of harmony and order in the human soul and the greater cosmos, to which the plays return at the cadence of the final scene, when order is restored.

CHAPTER 5

ARCHETYPES AND SYMBOLS:
EXPLORING THE LANGUAGE OF ASTROLOGY

[Archetypes] constitute the veiled essence of things. —Richard Tarnas[153]

The realm of divine order far above the mundane world, the ongoing "bass line of celestial music," is the dimension in which reside "archetypes." Both the numbers underlying the rhythm of Shakespeare's poetry and the images that characterize it can be classed as archetypes. Understanding archetypes and their offshoots, symbols, is crucial because they are fundamental to understanding Shakespeare's creative process and to the approach taken in Section II in analyzing Shakespeare's plays. But they are not easy to grasp. These concepts are unfamiliar partly because education now de-emphasizes the humanities and neglects Western history and philosophy. To make them more comprehensible, this chapter "dances around" the concept, approaching archetypes and symbols from several perspectives and citing different thinkers.

It is helpful to begin by going back to the picture of the cosmos described in Chapter 3, one that most Elizabethans would have understood. Key to this model is the idea that the universe unfolds from the invisible into the visible realms in an orderly sequence, like a series of waterfalls, creating a multitude of interrelated dimensions. In Greek thought, as early as the Homeric epics (eighth century BCE?) and flowering in Athens (in the sixth and fifth centuries BCE), the tendency was to give more weight to the *invisible* dimension as a storehouse of transcendent Ideas or Forms, now more commonly called "archetypes." Only the highest level of the cosmos contains archetypes, which are best thought of as abstract concepts. They are:

[C]ertain primordial essences or transcendent first principles, variously conceived as Forms, Ideas, universals, changeless absolutes, immortal deities, divine *archai*, and archetypes,

[T]he Greek universe was ordered by a plurality of timeless essences which underlay concrete reality, giving it form and meaning.

These archetypal principles included the mathematical forms of geometry and arithmetic; cosmic opposites such as light and dark, male and female, love and hate, unity and multlplicity; the forms of man (*anthropos*) and other living creatures; and the Ideas of the Good, the Beautiful, the Just, and other absolute moral and aesthetic values.[154]

This notion of an "Idea" (capital "I") is very different from our modern definition of an idea (small "i") thought of as a subjective mental construct arising only in one person's mind. To the Greeks—and to many Elizabethans—"Ideas" (capital "I") were expressions of a greater Mind, though capable of being "downloaded" into individual human minds as "ideas" (small "I").

They do not depend on human thought, but exist entirely in their own right. They are perfect patterns embedded in the very nature of things. *The Platonic Idea is, as it were, not merely a human idea but the universe's idea,* an ideal entity that can express itself externally in concrete tangible form or internally as a concept in the human mind. It is a primordial image or formal essence that can manifest in various ways and on various levels, and is the foundation of reality itself.[155]

On the diagram of the cosmos in Chapter 3, the dimension containing the archetypes coincides with the realm of the fixed stars. Like the archetypes themselves, these beautiful points of light were believed to be unmoving and unchanging. But archetypes originate and are generated from the level <u>above</u> that, the one of Divinity/Divine Mind, the mysterious and unknowable realm out of which all Forms unfold. So archetypal principles can be described as Ideas that arise in the Mind of God.

Since this archetypal realm is the repository of templates for all created things, the Ideas existing in it are constant principles behind a variety of forms that all express similar qualities. Willows, pines, and oaks are very different trees in their appearance, but behind each is the Idea of Tree. You may judge a woman to be beautiful, or you can describe a painting in a museum as beautiful, or ooh and aah over a sunset as beautiful, but you can only say that each is *beautiful* because above and beyond these individual expressions exists the Idea of Beauty. The appearance of each differs but the essence is the same.

Archetypes emerge out of chaos at the beginning of Creation. (Marolles, Tableaux du temple des muses, 1655)

Depending on how you perceive the cosmos and what descriptors you tend to use in order to understand it, you might describe these basic principles in different ways. For the followers of the philosopher Pythagoras (or the mathematically minded), these basic principles are the numbers from one to ten. They are like the building blocks of the universe: everything can be related to one of them or to several in combination. Since the number two, for instance, is often interpreted as "opposition" or "conflict" arising from a dramatic polarity, any situation in which two political parties vie for dominance, or two people in a relationship encounter inevitable conflicts, or two families like the Capulets and the Montagues have a running feud, is a stepped-down manifestation of that number. They are all expressions of "twoness."

For many philosophers of Pythagoras' time and after, the four elements were the starting points for the creation of the universe. Whether considered as opposite qualities (hot versus cold or wet versus dry) or physical elements (earth, water, air, and fire), all visible things were characterized according to the proportional balance between them. So you might experience a "hot" summer day or a person with a "dry" sense of humor or someone described as a "cool" customer.

If you are visually oriented, you might be more inclined to imagine these constructive principles as the colors of the spectrum. If you start with the basic three—red, yellow, and blue—you can blend them, combine them with shades of white or black, and eventually develop an entire color wheel that encompasses every color visible to human beings, even the most subtle. Everything we see during our daytime experience in this dimension has color, and those colors suggest qualities. A red stop sign (a warning to halt), a red-headed person (possibly hot-tempered), a red sunset (a "sailor's delight") all convey meaning and are all related to the color "red."

If you are aurally oriented, you might gravitate to a musical interpretation of these building blocks: they are like the seven basic notes of the diatonic scale. An infinite number of musical pieces can be spun out from them, some more harmonious than others. Or if you are in love with language, you might consider the twenty-six letters of the English alphabet analogous to these basic elements.[156] With them you can make endless combinations of words, phrases, and sentences, with meanings and pronunciations altered depending on whether they are capitalized or which letters you put together.[157]

Whichever lens you prefer using to understand archetypes, according to Platonic thinkers the philosopher's task is to see beyond the appearance to the fundamental Idea behind each object or person or experience. To do this you have to rely on a different type of sight: "the archetype is apparent not so much to the limited physical senses, though these can suggest and lead the way, as to the more penetrating eye of the soul, the illuminated intellect. Archetypes reveal themselves more to the inner perception than to the outer."[158]

An important point about archetypes is that they are the structural principles—whether envisioned as a sequence of numbers from 1 to 10 or a series of tones making up a scale—that give the universe meaning and *order* (that favorite word of the Elizabethans): "The human mind and the universe are *ordered* according to the same archetypal structure or essences, because of which, and only because of which, true understanding of things is possible for the human intelligence."[159] Only because these ruling principles are common to both humanity and the cosmos can we hope to comprehend this order, whether you seek to grasp it from the "top down" (considering the Principle first) or the "bottom up" (starting with the experience of a person or thing). This perspective underlies the astrological worldview and justifies the interpretation of the human psyche and human experience in light of the stars (a "top down" approach).

The Modern Psychological Perspective on Archetypes

Philosophical ideas about archetypes may not be familiar to us now but a psychological understanding of them may be because the concept of archetypes re-emerges in twentieth century discourse through the psychology of C. G. Jung. From his own studies and work with patients, building on his classical education in Latin and Greek and his familiarity with Platonic thought and esoteric traditions, Jung makes archetypes a key concept in his psychology. He understood them as

> [F]undamental governing principles of the human psyche. On the basis of his own analyses as well as those of others, not only of a diverse range of clinical phenomena but also of the art, myths, and religions of many eras and cultures, Jung had come to view archetypes as innate symbolic forms and psychological dispositions that unconsciously structure and impel human behavior and experience at both the personal and collective level.[160]

Jung expresses his understanding of archetypes in psychological terms, framing them as part of every individual's inheritance as a human being and thus innate in the human psyche. He includes in the category of archetypes a host of divinities, such as Aphrodite (Venus), Prometheus, and Saturn (in the Western tradition) and Wotan, Sophia, and Kali (in the Norse, Gnostic, and Eastern traditions). So you might see Aphrodite in the image of a Marilyn Monroe or an Angelina Jolie, or meet Saturn if you experience your father as patriarchal and repressive. Or you might play at being one of the gods or goddesses yourself at a Hallowe'en party or a masked ball.

Along with the mathematical principles of number and geometry, Jung also writes voluminously on such archetypal ideas as the Hero, the Great Mother, the Child, the Trickster, and the Shadow as well as on sacred forms like the circle, the cross, and the mandala. Later in his career his thought evolves and he begins to see archetypes as patterns of meaning common to *both* the human psyche *and* the greater cosmos. Thus archetypes become the link between the inner landscape and the outer world, with inner and outer not separate but part of a continuum (as in the astrological worldview.)

From a psychological perspective archetypes may play roles, interact, and conflict entirely within an individual's psyche. So it is possible to interpret not only our own lives but also Shakespeare's plays as "intrapsychic dramas," with the action taking place not only as a series of outer events but also as a representation of an inner drama entirely *within* ourselves or *within* the play's main character.

> In Shakespeare's plays, everything happens first in the soul; and what he shows us on the stage   and the world was a stage in his view—is the embodiment of these psychic events.... Shakespeare's picture of the soul is a kingdom in which rival powers are contending; this kingdom within, when the true self is enthroned, will become 'the kingdom of heaven'; but, in man's tragic phase, it is a kingdom in civil war.[161]

So every character in a Shakespearean play can be understood allegorically, as a representation of an archetypal idea. Iago is not just an envious lieutenant to Othello: he is the tempter, the Devil itself. The gentle Desdemona is not just the beautiful daughter of the senator Brabantio and married to Othello; she is the very incarnation of Love. The tragic heroes in particular fail and fall because they reject Love. This is clear in *Hamlet* when, in a crucial scene near the beginning of the play, Hamlet spurns Ophelia, bidding her go to a nunnery (another meaning of which was "a brothel").

> Ophelia is a dual character of this kind: she is the girl we all know, and she is also an allegorical figure representing a quality in Hamlet's soul. When Hamlet speaks to her, he is sometimes talking to a girl, sometimes to an entity in himself, and often to both. As

an allegorical figure, she is that point of love in Hamlet which is the centre of his true nobility; and therefore she coincides with his highest self.... Everything that happens to Ophelia is an allegory of what is taking place in Hamlet.[162]

An allegory is an extended narrative in which the characters, their actions, and the settings have meanings above and beyond their literal ones. This type of fiction is sometimes disparaged if the imposed structure of ideas dominates the story. It becomes tedious if every element in it has only a single meaning, and the message, whether religious, moral, or political, is so obvious and belabored that the author seems to be clubbing you over the head with it on every page. But this never happens with Shakespeare's work. Even though his plays may be interpreted allegorically, as intra-psychological dramas, his characters have a dual nature: they are fully realized and believable representations of human beings *as well as* embodiments of essential and higher ideas. We are not used to thinking like this, thinking allegorically, since "Our background is the rationalism of the eighteenth and nineteenth centuries, while his was the mysticism of the Middle Ages.... Europe has been sharpening its intellect, but in an earlier age it was much more interested in the exploration of its soul."[163]

Archetypes link not only the inner and outer but also the *above* and *below*. Jung makes this explicit in his psychology, considering early in his career that they originate in what is termed a collective unconscious, a substratum of consciousness common to every human being and a storehouse of primordial images. For him initially the archetypes emerge from below, though later thinkers have equated this collective unconscious with a superconscious. While the archetypes are obvious in myth, fairy tales, and religions, they are most accessible as the symbols in your dreams. For Jung your psychological health thrives if you develop a rapprochement between your conscious and unconscious minds, the above and below within you, with myths and dreams the intermediary and symbols the uniting factor.[164] Perhaps Shakespeare's plays affect us profoundly and foster our psychological health because, like collective dreams or myths, they appeal to and connect both our conscious and unconscious minds: they feature recognizable human types and common human experiences that are aligned with these transcendent archetypes.

Archetypes and their Expression as Symbols

Put out the light, and then put out the light. —Othello (V, ii, 7)

Though they are inherent in the material world as the veiled essences of all created things, archetypes, eternal and immutable, seem hidden and distant, existing on a plane far above us. So they are frequently personified as mythic entities or divine beings, powerful gods and goddesses who interact in cosmic dramas of creation and conflict.

Archetypes also become approachable and comprehensible through their expression as symbols. (While some use "archetype" when they mean a symbol or an archetypal image, there is a definite distinction between the archetype and its symbolic expression.) "The archetype ('arche' means an origin, a cause or beginning, a primordial source, and 'type' implies a copy, imprint or form, usually abstract) ... *is made manifest by symbols*, which bring the abstract (the Platonic Idea) into concrete form as an image, an image which can be shown forth or made in different forms or modes."[165]

Since astrology is a language of symbols and poetic works are suffused with symbols, it is extremely important to understand what they are and what they mean. What is a "symbol"? A symbol conflates a literal meaning, commonly a reference to a physical object, and an abstract meaning, a reference to an idea or perhaps several ideas (thus the root definition, "to throw together"). Manfred Lurker called the symbol "a 'throwing together' of time and eternity."[166] To understand the many rich and varied meanings of a symbol, you consult not a standard reference but a dictionary devoted entirely to symbols and their multitudinous meanings.[167]

Of all the fathers of modern psychology, Jung most stressed the importance of symbols, especially in dream interpretation, an essential component of Jungian analysis. In the wonderfully accessible introduction to his psychology, *Man and His Symbols*, Jung ruminates on the psychological meaning of a symbol. He starts with a basic definition: "What we call a symbol is a term, a name, or even a picture that may be familiar in daily life, yet that possesses specific connotations in addition to its conventional and obvious meaning. It implies something vague, unknown, or hidden from us."[168] He goes on to emphasize the inability of the rational mind to fully grasp it: "[A] word or an image is symbolic when it implies something more than its obvious and immediate meaning. It has a wider 'unconscious' aspect that is never precisely defined or fully explained. Nor can one hope to define or explain it. *As the mind explores the symbol it is led to ideas that lie beyond the grasp of reason.*"[169] He explicitly points to a religious or spiritual dimension of symbols: "Because there are innumerable things beyond the range of human understanding, we constantly use symbolic terms to represent concepts that we cannot define or fully comprehend. This is one reason why all religions employ symbolic language or images."[170]

Symbols may have great power in culture and literature because they are identical in essence to something "higher." Like the personified gods and goddesses, symbols are bridges that take us from the apparent world to a loftier one, from the world of objects to the world of archetypes. The symbol's origin in something "higher" is what makes fixing its meaning so difficult. Something ineffable at the root of the symbol makes it, like liquid mercury, impossible to grasp completely. For many theorizers about symbolism, it has a powerful effect on us because of the "incontrovertible equation macrocosm = microcosm."[171]

One famous writer on symbolism, Rene Guenon, "points out that 'The true basis of symbolism is ... the correspondence linking together all orders of reality, binding them one to another, and consequently extending from the natural order as a whole to the supernatural order.'"[172] This is entirely in line with the world-picture introduced in Chapter 3: a principle of which is the interconnectedness or correspondence of all things to all other things, creating a cosmic unity or synthesis. Symbolism is based on the analogy between the invisible and visible worlds, since "True symbolism depends on the fact that things, which may differ from one another in time, space, material nature, and many other limitative characteristics, can possess and exhibit the same essential quality."[173]

Because of the symbol's often secret link to something greater, it has a dramatic vitality that impresses its vivid image on your mind and often grips you until you probe its meaning. It is this quality that makes the symbol—and poetic works that teem with symbols—so memorable. This is also how you can recognize the presence of the archetype behind or above the symbol: it fixes your attention on itself and kindles an emotional response in you, impressing itself on both your conscious and unconscious minds. So a symbol has "numinosity," that is, an ability to evoke awe or reverence as if you are in the presence of something holy or divine.

So how to approach understanding symbols as a prerequisite to appreciating Shakespeare's use of them? To begin, symbols are generally thought of as one of two types. The first type includes ideas, objects, or animals that are relatively universal in that they feature in many cultures and over many time periods, like the Sun and Moon or the wheel or the snake. Their meanings are often similar despite cultural differences, though some interpretations may be particular to a nation, culture, or part of the world, or may evolve over time. The snake has more negative meanings in the West and more positive meanings in the East, where the snake by itself can signify wisdom and when biting its tail may represent the endless cycle of life. As tends to be true in the West, Hermia's dream of a snake in *A Midsummer Night's Dream* is clearly an omen of impending heartbreak since it is eating away at her heart. She wakes to find that Lysander has abandoned her and transferred his love to Helena. The wheel, though, in both Eastern and Western cultures almost always refers to the passage of time and the sufferings endured while living as a time-bound creature. Lear in *King Lear* images his sufferings as like being "bound / Upon a *wheel* of fire, that mine own tears / Do scald like molten lead" (IV, vii, 46–8). Such a symbol has primarily collective or universal significance.

The second type of symbol includes objects that accrue significance because they are key to a particular artistic work or have personal meaning. In Herman Melville's novel *Moby Dick*, for example, a white whale becomes a numinous object with multiple meanings: it is of course a physical sperm whale that becomes the focus of Captain Ahab's determined revenge, but it also looms large in the reader's imagination as the embodiment of the power of nature or the force of fate or the inscrutability of the universe itself. It is initially a symbol with intense personal meaning for Ahab (and Melville), one that is rarely featured in literary works, but it accrues a range of more impersonal and profound meanings as the story unfolds.

One of the peculiar qualities of a symbol is that it can be both universal and particular at the same time (like the image of the snake in Hermia's dream). This tends to be true of the symbols in Shakespeare's plays; they are both specific to the action *and* universally applicable. This contributes to the power and profundity of Shakespeare's works: his

Three interpretations of snake symbolism:

[LEFT] *In the West the snake inspires both fascination and fear, and most often symbolizes temptation, evil, and death.*

[CENTER] *The ouroboros or snake biting its tail. The circular form represents the unceasing cycle of creation and destruction through time. The snake both devours itself and regenerates itself, also symbolized by its periodic skin shedding. This snake here incorporates both negative and positive meanings.*

[RIGHT] *The snake as entirely beneficent. The caduceus is the emblem of the medical profession with its ability to bring the ill or dying back to life. The serpent's venom now converts from killing to healing. The wings, wand, and upright snakes represent acquired wisdom and accrued spiritual power.*

plays catalyze our emotional responses and impress images in our minds in part because of his deft and sophisticated use of symbolism.

An unusual point about a symbol is not only that it can have multiple meanings, but also that some meanings may be entirely opposite. Since all pairs of opposites are contained within the One, even a symbol with one favored meaning, like the wheel, may hold within itself a contrary interpretation. Time may bind you to physical limitations OR it may heal all wounds. Similarly, an apple can carry a positive overtone of respect and acknowledgement of quality (as in an apple given to a teacher) or a negative association of temptation into sin (as in the apple Eve presumably gave to Adam). Such polarized meanings can be extreme and baffle the intellect. In *A Midsummer Night's Dream*, a play infused with Moon symbolism, characters refer not only to fecundity (a principal symbolic interpretation of the Moon) but also to its opposite meaning of chastity and barrenness ("the cold fruitless moon"—I, i, 73). In Jung's view, symbols are important precisely because they contain contraries: they "are natural attempts to reconcile and reunite opposites within the psyche."[174]

The meaning of a particular symbol may depend on cultural bias, on context, and on your familiarity with a spectrum of possible interpretations, so that the exploration of symbols has to be open-ended. Exploring the almost inexhaustible dimensions of a symbol often involves an "amplification" of it, looking at it from many different perspectives, some of which are mythological and some of which are historical.

> Any one symbol is not a symbol of any one thing in particular but holds rather a number of suggestions. It might be said to have infinite relations: it is both infinite and yet closely defined.... The sea is usually impregnated with tragic power. Often it holds a 'death' suggestion; it is often a formless chaos; and yet it may, if imaged as calm, suggest peace. Again, its infinite expanse may suggest the infinities of either guilt or glory; its raging contest with rocks may indicate either nobility or savagery; its fathomless depths are rich with the piled treasuries they have filched from navigation. And the implications extend indefinitely.[175]

Shakespeare frequently makes poetic use of sea imagery, most often to connote turbulence and upset as in Hamlet's "sea of troubles" (III, i, 61), but Juliet's avowal that "her bounty is as boundless as the sea" is a positive affirmation of her unlimited love for Romeo (II, i, 175).

Shakespeare constantly plays with symbols' multiple meanings and multiple levels of meaning. He does this, for example, in Othello's ominous line quoted at the beginning of this section: "Put out the light, and then put out the light." Othello is about to murder Desdemona, believing that she has been false to him. The first time he uses the word "light" it is obvious he is referring to a physical light, the candle he is carrying into their bedroom where Desdemona sleeps. He wants to blow it out in order to hide his terrible act under the veil of dark night. But the second time he uses the word "light" it has become a symbol, a reference to Desdemona's soul or spirit, the "light" of her being. In case we miss this, Othello goes on to say:

> If I quench thee, thou flaming minister,
> I can again thy former light restore
> Should I repent me; but once put out *thy light*

I know not where is that Promethean heat
That can thy light relume.

(V, ii, 8–10, 12–3)

Shakespeare frequently uses the imagery of light in this way: "When Shakespeare lays special stress on light, he is using it symbolically.... Shakespeare uses light in a way we might call sacramental, as the outward sign of the inward grace.... The defeat of the spirit is often shown as an extinguishing of light."[176] Like Othello, Macbeth seeks to banish light: "*Stars*, hide your fires. / Let not light see my black and deep desires." (I, iv, 50–1) When a tragic event has taken place or is about to take place, light often fades: "The day frowns more and more ... I never saw / The heavens so dim by day" (*The Winter's Tale*: III, iii, 53, 54–6), comments Antigonus ruefully as he abandons the baby Perdita in the deserts of Bohemia. When characters need the clarity of spiritual guidance, they often call for greater illumination: "Give me some light," urges King Claudius, frighted by the Players' performance of a scene disturbingly like the poisoning of his brother, and the courtiers echo, "Lights, lights, lights!" (*Hamlet*: III, ii, 247, 248)

Astrology as a Language of Symbols

Just as Shakespeare's use of symbols reflects their many meanings and many levels of meaning, astrologers interpret their symbols as variable in meaning and resonant on many different levels. This makes the interpretation of a horoscope challenging, as there is no one definitive meaning for a particular symbol. Instead, as Richard Tarnas discovered as his explorations and research into astrology progressed, the key to astrological interpretation was appreciating the "multidimensional and multivalent nature of archetypes" that can generate a multitude of meanings and manifestations conveyed through particular symbols.

> The archetypes associated with specific planetary alignments were equally apt to express themselves in the interior life of the psyche as in the external world of concrete events, and often both at once. In addition, any particular manifestation of a given archetype could be "positive" or "negative," benign or destructive, admirable or ignoble, profound or trivial. Closely linked yet entirely opposite polarities contained in the same archetypal complex could be expressed in

coincidence with the same planetary configuration. Individuals with the same alignment could be on either the acting or the receiving end of the same archetypal gestalt, with altogether different experiential consequences. Which of all these related multivalent possibilities occurred seemed to be determined largely by contingent circumstances and individual response....[177]

Tarnas' ultimate and stunning conclusion is that, "contrary to its traditional reputation and deployment, such an astrology is not concretely predictive but, rather, *archetypically* predictive."[178] The challenge for practicing astrologers in analyzing a horoscope then becomes one of interpretation. They have to be selective: which of the multitude of meanings attributed to one of the symbols is applicable to that person and likely to be active or activated over time? The challenge for researchers is the lack of exact repetition. Not only does no heavenly pattern repeat exactly in toto, but also any piece of it that does might manifest entirely in line with the archetype but in a different way each time. This means that from the materialistic perspective of modern science, astrology stubbornly resists conventional testability.

Astrology is not the only "language" that works with symbols. Mathematics does (with "X" standing for the unknown) and so do sciences like chemistry (with its table of the elements listed with atomic numbers and chemical symbols). But in the case of the sciences, each symbol has only *one* established meaning. Since astrology is an archetypically-based symbol system, the meanings are variable and theoretically infinite. An unusual feature of astrology is that like the Greek thinkers' conflation of Ideas and images, the language of astrology speaks both in terms of mathematics (best understood through logic and reason) and in terms of poetry (best appreciated through the imagination and intuition). The western (or tropical) zodiac is a sequence of 30° segments of space along the Ecliptic (the apparent path of the Sun around the Earth) arranged in an alternating rhythm of two's (masculine and feminine), three's (qualities), and four's (elements) with each segment at the same time representing a constellational image, whether of an animal, artifact, or person. A horoscope is a two-dimensional picture of three-dimensional space mathematically calculated but containing layers of symbolism: of planets, sectors ("houses"), and relationships ("aspects"). Thus the astrological language has elements of both a science and an art.

The planets are particularly rich in meanings partly because they have an archetypal core. From the spiritual/philosophical viewpoint taken in this book and reflected in Shakespeare's work, they are understood to function on at least four different levels, spanning the visible and invisible realms. Using the planet Venus as an illustration,

- there exists a physical planet which we call Venus
- there are symbols that represent Venus
- there is a divine being called Venus who is the goddess (or image) of love
- and there is an archetype of Love which is the originating Idea behind all of these.

Of course philosophers in the classical or esoteric tradition would reverse the order to reflect the "top down" model: the archetype of Love gives rise to its personification as Venus, which gives rise to symbols for her qualities, which then crystallize as the physical orb. Focusing on the archetype and its subsequent symbol does not demean the physical correlative of the archetype—it does just the opposite: it infuses it with meaning and exalts it beyond being merely a dead and meaningless material object. In either case, you can get to the meaning of the symbol either by starting from the bottom or the top.

Though the archetypal essence remains the same, the principle "behind" each of the planets (the fourth level above) may be "stepped down" and expressed as various divinities (at the third level above). Venus is the name for the Roman goddess of love and beauty, the one most familiar in the West, but in other mythologies she has different names and images: among others, Hathor or Bastet in the Egyptian tradition, Inanna in Mesopotamian myth, Aine in Celtic mythology, and Freyja in the Norse and Germanic one. At the next level down, the second one, the physical symbols for Venus are roses and myrtles in the plant kingdom and doves in the realm of the birds. (Shakespeare frequently uses roses and doves as symbolic substitutes for the idea of Love.) Cultures other than the Western may have different symbols for Venus, but they all represent an expression of deep feeling and attraction to something or someone envisioned as Love or lovely.[179]

If you start from the "bottom," the first level, physical details of an object's appearance are clues to its essence. Sunflowers are considered a symbol of the Sun because its center and yellow radiating petals physically resemble the Sun and because their heads turn to follow the Sun's daily path. The fact that the planet Mars has a red color suggests its connection to anger. (We still describe people who are incensed as "seeing red.") Along with details of physical appearance, the many meanings attached to the planets have accrued from mythology as well as from centuries of observing events synchronous with their cycles. These interpretations have been remarkably consistent over several thousand years. No surprise that Shakespeare's use of astrological symbolism is very much in line with interpretations from ancient times right through to today.

The Mystery of Artistic Creation and the Genius of Shakespeare— And Did He Create Consciously?

The brain has as many neurons as there are stars in the Milky Way.
—Nancy C. Andreasen[180]

A great work of art that touches the hearts and minds of its viewers over a long period of time may have long-lasting and universal appeal because it is a concrete expression of abstract archetypes. Archetypes are basic to art, mythologies, and religions spanning many cultures and eras. Just as the Ideas or archetypes are templates from which the Creative Source unfolds all the particulars of this world, ideas and images blooming within the mind or imagination of creative artists give rise to their creations. The deduction, then, is that artists who aspire to create great and lasting works must be responsive to at least the symbolic and—in rare cases—the archetypal level of creation.

Creative artists have one of two ways to connect to these higher levels: either they "invoke the Muse," so to speak, drawing inspiration for the creative work down to them, or they ascend, progressing upward "through the planes" where creative inspiration resides in the form of ideas/Ideas. In either case, the excellence of the final creation also depends on the disciplined and developed technique or craft of the artist, whether a trained hand or knowledgeable mind. Encouraging creativity, though, has several requirements: solitude, since the Muse seems to prefer quiet places consecrated to art, and some kind of preparatory ritual, like organizing your pens or brushes or papers. Though these are by no means guarantees, they help prepare for the reception of inspiration.

If you think of the source of the numinous archetypes psychologically, as residing in the unconscious (or a "superconscious"), then in order to access this, artists have to open themselves to that dimension by unfocusing on the objective world and widening their field of awareness. (We might also describe this as altering your brain waves, moving from beta to the slower alpha, by becoming deeply relaxed, encouraging daydreaming, or meditating. Being in "alpha state" stimulates the imagination and the ability to visualize.) This involves modifying the normal mental state in which you are all too subject to the critical voice of the rational mind. Something that can help encourage the creative moment is listening to music. In Shakespeare's case, the fact that he is often writing in poetry may have helped his creative process since "Rhythm helps [the poet] to restablish communication with the unconscious...."[181]

Shakespeare himself (through the mouth of Theseus in *A Midsummer Night's Dream*) describes the creative process:

> Lovers and madmen have such seething brains,
> Such shaping fantasies, that apprehend
> More than cool reason ever comprehends.
> The lunatic, the lover, and the *poet*
> Are of imagination all compact.
> One sees more devils than vast hell can hold:
> That is the madman. The lover, all as frantic,
> Sees Helen's beauty in a brow of Egypt.
> *The poet's eye, in a fine frenzy rolling,*
> *Doth glance from heaven to earth, from earth to heaven,*
> *And as imagination bodies forth*
> *The forms of things unknown, the poet's pen*
> *Turns them to shapes and gives to airy nothing*
> *A local habitation and a name.*
>
> (V, i, 4–17)[182]

Shakespeare is implying that the poet has to be in an altered state of consciousness, "in a fine frenzy rolling." He leaves it open as to whether you receive inspiration ("from heaven to earth") or ascend to higher levels to access it ("from earth to heaven"). Perhaps he was able to do both. At least he seems aware of both possibilities. Since he is obviously familiar with Platonic and Neo-Platonic philosophy, surely the phrase "*forms of things unknown*" had a special significance for both him and educated members of his audience as a reference to the Platonic Ideas. The poet/dramatist sees in his mind's eye "shapes," symbols that descend from the archetypal plane, and embodies them as the people and places in his plays.

Another key speech in a different play suggests a theory of creativity and may be an important clue as to how Shakespeare viewed his own creating. In *Richard II*, the King has been imprisoned in Pomfret Castle and comforts himself with some imaginative speculation:

> I have been studying how I may compare
> This prison where I live unto the world; ...
> I cannot do it; yet I'll hammer it out.
> *My brain vI'll prove the female to my soul,*
> *My soul the father, and these two beget*
> *A generation of still-breeding thoughts;*
> *And these same thoughts people this little world*
> *In humours like the people of this world....*
>
> (V, v, 1–2, 5–10)

In line with Elizabethan thought, the brain must be receptive (the female) to inspiration from the realm of soul (the male), and both soul and mind together conceive ideas ("still-breeding thoughts") that the artist births as characters in the "little world" of a play, each one modeled on the humoral types and thus on astrological correspondences.

To what extent might Shakespeare have been *consciously* doing this? That is, drawing on the conceptual model of his time and deliberately using archetypal ideas (among them astrological symbols) to animate the characters, themes, and action of his plays? This question is difficult to answer, in part because we have so little historical information about Shakespeare as a literary artist. But his works reveal that the philosophical/spiritual worldview described in Chapter 3 is fundamental to them. This makes it possible that he not only knew but also intentionally used cosmic symbolism as a conscious inspiration for his art.

A clue suggesting a more conscious approach is that the Renaissance had inherited from the classical and medieval periods a technique called "the art of memory." People who wished to increase their ability to remember envisioned an architectural structure and imprinted a series of images on its various rooms. As they imagined themselves moving from room to room, each worked as a trigger for recalling a vast amount of learned material. Very few books about this method survive, but one, a book on rhetoric by the Roman writer Quintillian (first century CE), mentions that a prior practitioner of the system, Metrodorus of Scepsis (second century BCE), used the zodiac as a template on which to pin his images.[183]

In the Renaissance this mnemonic device was adapted by occult philosophers like the Italian Giulio Camillo who chose a theater as the preferred image and even built a "complete wooden theatre for the purpose of illustrating his mnemonic system...." Like the earlier developers of the memory system, he too "associated the parts of the theatre with the zodiac."[184] However, the goal of the Renaissance system (also known to such Elizabethan luminaries as Dr. John Dee and Robert Fludd) was not just to enhance memory:

> Camillo was attempting to develop a memory system that would, in the Hermetic manner, reflect the universe internally through memory. Because based on celestial powers, the memory would be activated magically and would thus inspire the speech of the orator, or poet, with the divine harmony of celestial proportions.... To the Hermeticists, therefore, memory images were paramount forces in activating the psyche....[185]

So the storehouse of images attached to these "memory palaces" could enable a speaker or poet to achieve extraordinary effects and could also, due to its virtually inexhaustible source of images, inspire endless creative invention.

Here is how this may even have a physical connection to Shakespeare's creative process. Although we do not know what the Globe Theatre looked like (it burned down in 1613 and its replacement was destroyed in 1644), we do know that the underside of the canopy covering the stage was painted to represent the heavens. What image best represents "the heavens"?

> In the Adams reconstruction of the Globe the ceiling of the inner stage cover is shown as painted with the signs of the zodiac ... Naturally this is a modern attempt to reconstruct the ceiling; no specimen of these painted theatrical heavens has survived. They would certainly not have shown a vaguely decorative sky indiscriminately sprinkled with stars. *They would have been representations of the zodiac with its twelve signs [and] the spheres of the seven planets within it* ...[186]

Not only would Shakespeare's plays have been performed under the primary image of the cosmos, but Yates also suggests that the whole of the Globe Theatre itself was built according to the principles of sacred geometry—in harmony with and as a deliberate reflection of the heavens. One seventeenth-century observer who lived near the theater tells us that its form was six-sided on the outside and round within. It may be that the interior form was based on interlocking triangles.[187] Both the physical structure of the theater and the image of the heavens above the stage might have aided Shakespeare's imaginative faculty in the creation of his plays.

This approach emphasizes the power of the image and the importance of the imagination. While in our time imagination is associated with the fantastic and unreal, for the Elizabethans the faculty of the imagination (along with intuition) was the only faculty capable of perceiving higher and subtler levels of creation—in other words grasping the Real.

One of the few well-known literary critics who posits the importance of the imagination to Shakespeare's creative process is G. Wilson Knight, who was Professor of English Literature at Leeds University and a prolific writer on Shakespeare's plays. In an essay on "The Prophetic Imagination," Knight theorizes that Shakespeare's approach is not intellectual but imaginative, and so his creative work exists "not in the past from which it arises but in the future to which it points and which it helps to create."[188] In other words, as the artist transcends the mind (apprehending "More than cool reason ever comprehends"), the artist transcends time, and thus the work of art that is created is experienced as time-*less*. So naturally it endures through time.

For Knight, the creative process is analogous to the way in which a chess master envisions a game—not as a logical consideration of step-by-step moves and their results but as a single vision of a total game, a "whole movement simultaneously outrolled and leading to an ideal [check]mate."[189] The artist does something similar: "He does not think in terms of a process but rather visualizes what he names a 'pattern' spread out immediately in space and time, or rather in space-time, and rejects moves that do not fit this pattern. This is clearly an aesthetic and creative, rather than an intellectual and analytic, method."[190]

It is possible—in fact, it is likely—that in creating a play, Shakespeare's process was like this. Inspired by a familiar story taken from one or more of a remarkably wide variety of sources (Greek and Roman writers like Ovid and the playwright Terence, to the Middle Ages' Chaucer and *The Romance of the Rose,* to tales retold from French and Italian sources during the Elizabethan age), he then shaped it to more closely fit an archetypal pattern, a unified picture relating to eternal realities, as well as to create a more dramatically interesting play. The "patterns" he visualized and embodied in the plays are in many cases based on the archetypal symbols of astrology. To fashion a play in line with them, Shakespeare had to do two things. One, recognized by Knight, is that like a sculptor chipping away excess stone to free the perfect statue within, the poet has to eliminate what does not fit the ideal pattern. The creative process

> ... should be considered not as a 'thinking out', but as a conscious rejection of effects incompatible with the creative ideal in the soul, or unconscious mind, or imaginative intuition. The conscious intellect cannot create: it can only reject. Art is largely the rejection of incompatibilities whilst having regard to an ideal recognized first in terms of what it is not and realized after by the expression of what it is.[191]

There is for Shakespeare a second and complementary process, one of accretion and adaptation: adding or developing characters or actions that harmonize with the essential idea. "The creative process, so far as we are able to follow it at all, consists in the unconscious activation of an archetypal image, and *in elaborating and shaping this image into the finished work.* By giving it shape, the artist translates it into the language of the present, and so makes it possible for us to find our way back to the deepest spring of life."[192]

In the case of *Romeo and Juliet,* for instance, the story of young lovers seeking to escape an unwelcome marriage by using a sleeping potion goes back to a fourth century tale recounted by Xenophon of Ephesus. Many versions appear shortly before Shakespeare's, which seems to be largely based on a tedious and pedestrian poem by Arthur Brooke (1562). Shakespeare makes a lot of changes in his rendition. Among others, he increases the importance of Mercutio and the Nurse, making these two witty and wordy talkers the literal incarnations of Mercury in a play keyed to the zodiacal sign Gemini. In line with this archetypal symbol, he heightens the opposition between the two Italian families. Gemini is a sign associated with young people, so it is entirely fitting that Juliet's age is lowered from sixteen to thirteen and that the "The lyric vitality of this play is in accord with the youthful passion it celebrates."[193]

An even better example is *King Lear*. In adapting a story going back to Geoffrey of Monmouth's *History of the British Kings* (ca 1135) and retold in Holinshed's *Chronicles* and Sir Edmund Spenser's *The Faerie Queen* during Shakespeare's lifetime, he transforms it into a narrative more in keeping with the planet Saturn and its zodiacal sign of Capricorn by changing the original happy ending to a sad one. Instead of the combined English and French forces winning, restoring Lear to his throne to rule for two more years, to be followed by the reign of Cordelia and her husband, the play ends in the devastating tragedy of both Lear's and Cordelia's deaths.

> Having resolved upon this fundamental change, Shakespeare directs all his resources to making the catastrophe terrible. He doubles the pity of it by making not only Lear's death but Cordelia's follow the failure of their cause; he adds immeasurable tragic force through the invention of Lear's madness; he augments pathos and irony through the banishment of the loyal Kent and the creation of the faithful Fool. Finally, he enlarges the dimensions of the tragedy and deepens its intensity by introducing the story of [the blinded] Gloucester and his sons.[194]

From a psychological point of view, such an adaptive process is a collaboration between the conscious and unconscious minds. The source of the work of art comes as inspiration, the seeing of the "pattern" that resides in its archetypal perfection, not in the personal unconscious of the poet but in the collective unconscious of humankind. Artists then employ all of what is consciously available to them—their perceptive awareness, their intelligence, their developed skills, and memories of all they have been exposed to through education and life experience—to transfer their vision to the page or the stage.

Of course, this is where imperfection enters. The painter's canvas is not stretched properly or is affected by humidity; the sculptor is suffering from indigestion or the effects of too much indulgence the night before; the writer's pages are destroyed by fire, lost, or eaten by the dog— or the Muse remains stubbornly elusive. Yet if the visionary artist has perceived the archetypal essence, what remains still radiates inspiration and still has the power to affect us.

> The impact of an archetype, whether it takes the form of immediate experience or is expressed through the spoken word, stirs us because it summons up a voice that is stronger than our own. Whoever speaks in primordial images speaks with a thousand voices; he enthralls and overpowers, while at the same time he lifts the idea he is seeking to express out of the occasional and the transitory into the realm of the ever-enduring. He transmutes our personal destiny into the destiny of mankind.... That is the secret of great art, and of its effect upon us. [195]

The gift that the interpreter of such creations offers to the readers and viewers of such great art is to "lift the awareness of poetic truth from the unconscious to the conscious,"[196] in effect removing the veil to reveal the hidden archetypal inspiration and exploring the symbols that express its meaning.

The works of art attributed to Shakespeare are considered some of the greatest ever produced in the Western world precisely because of the unique marriage in them of transcendent inspiration and developed human artistry. This helps to explain why we find his work so unique—characterized as it is by the vitality of his characters and the universality of their types, by the odd lack of a personal presence, and by a suspicious "elasticity" allowing them to be cropped and changed without affecting their core. Such creations that have the power to move us, to imprint themselves on our innermost being, and to catalyze a soulful response, must have their source in the archetypal dimension. And what better archetypal principles to draw on—what could be more awe-inspiring or more universally experienced—than those of the planets and the stars? "The ability to reach a rich vein of such material and to translate it effectively into philosophy, literature, music, or scientific discovery is one of the hallmarks of what is commonly called *genius.*"[197]

Section II

The Plays

Introduction to Section II

The second half of this book probes six of the most famous and familiar plays of Shakespeare to reveal the hidden astrological symbolism that undergirds them. The chapters are arranged to introduce the planets in the order in which they appear as viewed from Earth (the Ptolemaic order)—that is, from the apparently closest to the most distant: Moon, Mercury, Venus, Mars, Jupiter, and Saturn (omitting the Sun, which appears between the orbits of Venus and Mars). Each of the selected plays is exquisitely in tune with one of these. These planets and the signs they "rule" provide keys that unlock the many meanings embedded in each play, showing that the main themes, character descriptions, settings for the action, and arc of the plot all correlate with astrological symbolism.

For readers who have either forgotten or are unfamiliar with the plays' plots, each section begins with a summary of the story. Next comes the revelation of the key to that play, the zodiacal sign and its associated planet, which Shakespeare usually announces in the opening scene or scenes. The main body of each chapter explores the play's astrological symbolism by considering its significance from different perspectives and on different levels. Words that convey the essence of the symbol are capitalized to make it easy for readers to identify core ideas associated with each planet and sign. Some sections concentrate more on associations with the sign; others focus more on the planet. Whichever one is foregrounded is an entry into an appreciation of the astrological key to the play. Each chapter thus "unpacks" the associated archetype and shows its relevance to the play.

In psychological language this discursive approach is called the "circumambulation of the symbol." Since the essence of the symbol, the archetypal idea that underlies its various expressions, is impossible to fully articulate in words and impossible to be fully grasped by the human mind, "walking around" the symbol, seeing it on various levels, exploring many of its possible manifestations and meanings on those levels, prepares the mind for the moment when it makes the leap and intuitively grasps the symbol's essence.

The Multiple Levels of Astrological Interpretation

The Elizabethans envision a world in which the heavens are reflected on Earth and the realm of Earth mirrors the heavens. The glorious Sun dominates the skies just as the King is the focus of court and country. Shimmering moonlight is symbolically reflected in the sheen of silver. Since all life is linked in both more obvious and more subtle ways, astrological principles are reflected on every level in many different manifestations and lend themselves to many different interpretations. So my explorations of astrological correlatives in Shakespeare's plays are multifaceted, looking not only at direct references to astrological factors (such as the planets or epithets for the planets derived from Greek and Roman mythology) but also to physical objects, character traits and types, and philosophical themes associated for millennia with both planets and zodiacal signs. Shakespeare tells us "The poet's eye, in a fine frenzy rolling, / Doth glance from heaven to earth, from earth to heaven" (*A Midsummer Night's Dream*: V, I, 12–3); evidence for Shakespeare's familiarity with and use of astrological language in the creation of his plays is equally wide-ranging.

Modern readers are likely most familiar with the use of the astrological alphabet to describe human personality. Very early in human history, astrological symbolism—especially the prominence of certain planets and the balance of the four elements—was correlated with a person's character and inner psychology. A "theory of the humors" was developed over time and used to determine a dominant temperament. So in looking for astrological symbolism in Shakespeare's plays, it is natural to consider the *psychological* level: that is, how characters are the embodiment of one of these the four temperament types and how their thoughts, motives, and actions are in line with them. Macbeth, for example, is clearly a choleric type, given to taking direct action but also predisposed to irritability and anger if his goals are not easily achieved. In some chapters I include discussions not only of the terminology that Elizabethans used in character analysis but also contemporary terms that synchronize with the earlier terminology.[198] As an archetypically-based language, astrological symbols can be described in the language of any time or place.

Some psychological interpretation of astrological principles derives from mythic stories told about gods and goddesses for whom the planets are named. In the early Sumerian and Babylonian civilizations the planets were linked to divinities whose intentions could be determined by planetary movements and their interrelationships. Mythological stories told about them, revealing their essences and behaviors, gravitated to the Egyptian, Greek, and Roman cultures—and on to us. Consequently, astrological tradition has looked to *mythological* traditions to unfold the nature of planetary symbolism. One such mythic story is that of Mercury's theft of Apollo's cattle, mentioned in Chapter 8 on *Romeo and Juliet*.

Since the heavens and the Earth are interconnected, both divinities and astrological symbols have *literal or mundane* correlatives. Developed through the Hellenistic, Medieval, and Renaissance periods, whole categories of associations with the signs and planets were elaborated. The essences of physical objects in the natural and human worlds—gems and minerals, plants and animals, weather conditions, even the separate parts of the human body—reflect principles that reside in the upper world. The principle of Saturn is correlated to heavy lead (mentioned in *King Lear*); Mars governs red blood, whose imagery saturates *Macbeth*. Such connections were often established because of the physical appearance of a thing or its function. These associations were familiar to the Elizabethans and so they would immediately recognize the symbolic import of mundane objects. Many things—for example, the dove, or the fragrance of roses, or the whorl of a seashell—are embodiments on Earth of the Venus of the skies.

Since astrology is part of a rich *philosophical* tradition, astrological factors correlate with profound themes explored in the plays: knowledge and its validity (Mercury), identity and its basis (the Sun), and the moral determinants of right versus wrong (Jupiter and Saturn). As part of a comprehensive God-centered model that includes the planets in their spheres, it is also appropriate to consider larger issues that belong in the category of the *religious or spiritual*. These include the reality and nature of beings beyond the physical dimension, the question of whether we are fated or free, the problem of determining not only personal but transpersonal purposes for our lives, and debates about where we come from before we are born and where we go after our death. Astrology in the modern era has lost touch with its philosophical and spiritual roots, and is now used mainly as a psychological tool for understanding human personality and as a practical instrument for determining cycles and patterns in an unfolding human life. But in ancient times and into the Renaissance, astrology was an integral part of a more comprehensive spiritual philosophy that evolved from profound and wide-ranging speculations, many of which are touched on in these chapters.

As one of the *esoteric* arts and sciences, astrology is related to a variety of studies that are pertinent to some of the plays: number symbolism that goes back to Pythagorean mathematics (especially the numbers 2, 4, 5, 7, and 12); mystery school initiations; herbalism and plant/flower symbolism; magic (as used positively by Prospero in *The Tempest*) versus witchcraft (as used negatively by the witches in *Macbeth*); and alchemy (or the practical, psychological, and spiritual practices of transmutation both within and without) which may be a key to *King Lear.*

Astrological tradition and symbolism encompass all of these which figure into discussions of the plays in Section II.

The Dominant Key to Shakespeare's Romantic Comedies: Venus

> All tragedies are finish'd by a death,
> All comedies are ended by a marriage.
> —George Gordon, Lord Byron (Don Juan, Canto 3)

Shakespeare wrote three types of plays: comedies, tragedies, and histories. Section II includes three comedies and three tragedies, omitting any of the histories. Although individual plays may be keyed to different zodiacal signs and their ruling planets, *all* of the comedies and *all* of the tragedies have one dominant and consistent symbol: Venus for the former and Mars for the latter.

While the dating of his plays is an ongoing matter of debate, it is fairly well established that Shakespeare's first plays—probably *The Comedy of Errors* and *The Two Gentlemen of Verona*—were comedies. In all his comic plays Shakespeare is clearly drawing on conventions of comedy widely known in his time, due in part to the revival of classical literature in the Renaissance.

From a literary perspective, comedy evolved from ancient Greek performances that in turn evolved from fertility rituals marking the renewal of life after a period of quiescence or apparent death. (Fertility is a prominent theme in *A Midsummer Night's Dream.*) Comedies commonly end with marriages, a pre-eminent symbol of rebirth, announcing a change in the protagonists' identities and promising the eventual birth of new beings. They thus celebrate the triumph of life over death, analogous to warm spring overcoming cold winter.

All of Shakespeare's comedies provide pleasure and feature ROMANCE—especially romantic involvement leading to at least one wedding. The archetypal VENUS is always associated with the comedies, either primarily or secondarily, since she symbolizes the powerful attraction between people that leads to their bonding both privately and publicly and so to the creation of new life. (More will be said about Venus in the chapter on *The Merchant of Venice*.) As the principal symbol for comedy, Venus is on one level the type of love that ideally leads to marriage: the private union of two happy people and the public celebration reassuring society that the family and the social order will continue.

Shakespeare's comedies follow the comic pattern developed in Roman times, featuring plots about various obstacles in the way of such lovers uniting and being allowed to marry. Many literary critics, like the brilliant Northrop Frye, remark on this:

> At the core of most Renaissance comedy including Shakespeare's, is the formula transmitted by the New Comedy pattern of Plautus and Terence. The normal action is the effort of a young man to get possession of a young woman who is kept from him by various social barriers: her low birth, his minority or shortage of funds, parental opposition, the prior claims of a rival. These are eventually circumvented, and the comedy ends at a point when a new society is crystallized, usually by the marriage or betrothal of hero and heroine. The birth of the new society is symbolized by a closing festive scene featuring a wedding, a banquet, or a dance.[199]

Shakespeare knows this tradition. Since "the course of true love never did run smooth," in *A Midsummer Night's Dream* he has Lysander and Hermia deliver a list of all the obstacles that can delay the joining of the young man and the young woman (all useful plot devices to the playmaker of comedies).

> LYSANDER: But either it was different in blood—
> HERMIA: O cross!—too high to be enthralled to low.
> LYSANDER: Or else misgraffed in respect of years—
> HERMIA: O spite!—too old to be engaged to young.
> LYSANDER: Or merit stood upon the choice of friends—

HERMIA: O hell!—to choose love by another's eyes.
LYSANDER: Or if there were a sympathy in choice,
     War, death, or sickness did lay siege to it,
     Making it momentary as a sound,
     Swift as a shadow, short as any dream ...

                                        (I, i, 134–44)

Each of Shakespeare's romantic comedies focuses on a different type of love and in some cases a different obstacle. *A Midsummer Night's Dream* and *Romeo and Juliet* focus on youthful and exuberant love, while *Much Ado About Nothing* features mature lovers. What keeps the older Beatrice and Benedick apart is not an external obstacle but an internal factor: their own cynical and sharpened wit arising from overdeveloped intellects which lead them to attack each other verbally. In other words, they are too much in their heads and not enough in their hearts. (Or too much Mercury and not enough Venus!)

In *A Midsummer Night's Dream*, though, the lovers do face an external obstacle: the parental opposition of Hermia's father. He objects partly because he thinks that Lysander has bewitched the naïve Hermia by the usual ploys of Venus—rhymes, nosegays, and sweetmeats among them. Egeus believes that his daughter is too young and inexperienced to recognize true love. And *A Midsummer Night's Dream* is a certainly about superficial love, typical of youth and particularly subject to fluctuating tides of emotion and changes in circumstances.

The young lovers featured in that play—Hermia and Lysander and Helena and Demetrius—are not especially individualized characters. They could be *any* young lovers. No surprise that their feelings are easily and comically transferred from one object of love to another during their time in the forest. Whether we accept that a flower's juice alters their affections or that it is a symbol of shallow emotional attachments thought to be characteristic of the young, first Lysander and then Demetrius switch the objects of their affections with stunning speed. Venus has a hand in this. Oberon explicitly attributes the power of the flower's juice to her son Cupid (and so indirectly to her) and asserts that whomever the lover sees when he wakes, she will "shine as gloriously / As the Venus of the sky." (III, ii, 106–7)

Obstructive parents lurk in *Romeo and Juliet* and *The Merchant of Venice*, too. Old Capulet insists on Juliet marrying Paris despite her protests and threatens to throw her out onto the streets if she does not comply. Portia's dead father has imposed a strange test on any suitor for her hand: choosing between three caskets of gold, silver, and lead. Although she finds this frustrating, in the end it works to her advantage as only her preferred suitor Bassanio passes the test. But in *The Tempest* a powerful father is not an obstacle but the principal arranger of the happy union of his daughter Miranda with the princely Ferdinand. We can be assured of the attunement of their souls because they (like Romeo and Juliet) recognize and fall in love with each other at first sight.

Despite the erratic trajectory of the lovers' relationships in all of Shakespeare's comedies, we are happy to see that in the end, as Puck promises, "Jack shall have Jill, / Naught shall go ill, / the man shall have his mare again, and all shall be well." (III, iii, 45–7)

The Dominant Key to Shakespeare's Tragedies: Mars

Tragedies are some of the most compelling of all staged enactments, with a history that goes back to the acclaimed dramas of classical Greece and Rome. At the time Greek drama flowered in Athens, many centuries before the Renaissance, the philosopher Aristotle theorized about tragedies and the reasons for their profound impact on the audience. He argued that such plays had to be about persons of significance, that the action had to culminate in a catastrophe which brought down the tragic hero (and often others around him), and that the subjects introduced in the plays had to be treated with dignity and seriousness. Most significantly for our purposes, Aristotle believed that the fall of the tragic hero resulted from choices made by the protagonist that were related to a "tragic flaw" in his character (*hamartia*).[200]

While Shakespeare (and his contemporaries) modified the classical pattern, extending the dramatic action over longer than a single day and adding comic scenes to relieve the serious tone, the emphasis in his heroic tragedies still falls on the person and character of the hero, whose spectacular rise and fall fascinates us. Aristotle emphasized the hero's tragic flaw or personal quality that causes him to make an obvious error of judgment: like Hamlet's tendency to over-rationalize that leads him to spare his uncle's life just at the most opportune time to kill him, or Othello's jealousy that leaves him vulnerable to Iago's poisonous insinuations and schemes and drives him to murder the one he loves best, or

Lear's foolish expectation that he will be treated like royalty after abdicating the throne and entrusting his care to his two flattering daughters.

No figures are more compelling in Shakespeare's works than his tragic heroes—most especially Hamlet, Othello, King Lear, and Macbeth. They are exceptional men whose ascendancy is due to their noble rank, elevated status, unusual talents, or great achievements. While their catastrophic descents into emotional torment, profound misery, spectacular failure, and ultimately death, which the audience witnesses with a fascinated fear and pity, occur for apparently different reasons, they can all be related to one astrological factor. In accord with the theory of the humors introduced in Chapter 2, Shakespeare's tragic heroes struggle because of imbalances in their temperament. To a man, they are either excessively choleric or lacking in choler—in other words, they have an imbalance related to the element of fire and the planet Mars.

Looking at Shakespeare's tragedies through the lens of astrology, in some way all of the tragic heroes in these plays—and that includes Brutus, Coriolanus, and Timon of Athens besides the ones mentioned above—misuse or do not use the qualities attributed to the most masculine of archetypal gods: MARS. They are MEN, and their relationship to this fundamental energy of maleness and their ability to integrate it positively into their lives dictates their success or failure. Mars is the armed god of war, the assertive, even aggressive fighter and extreme opposite to the peace-loving, well-mannered Venus whose realm is the bedroom and not the battlefield. Many of Shakespeare's male heroes are in fact celebrated warriors and leaders. Titus Andronicus, Julius Caesar and Coriolanus are noble Roman generals. Another, the "valiant" Othello who is petitioned by the senators to fight for Venice against the Ottoman, describes himself in distinctly Martian terms: "Rude am I in my speech, / And little blessed with the soft phrase of peace ... / And little of this great world can I speak / More than pertains to feats of broils and battle ..." (I, iii, 81–2, 86–7).

Positive aspects of Mars are many, beyond literally fighting on a physical battlefield. The principle of Mars:

> .... represents strength of will and the desire of an individual to conquer. It stands for stamina, the perseverance and energy that you need to fight the obstacles in life ... straightforwardness of

approach, a high degree of determination, readiness to take on conflict, and enjoyment of risk....[201]

Mars' strengths also include

Strong, goal-oriented action with great staying power. Imposing willpower, great commitment, and considerable willingness to take risks ... The force of aggression [that] finds an appropriate goal which it can conquer, simultaneously discharging itself and spontaneously developing in committed, courageous, decisive, passionate, or persevering ways. Powerful, but controllable drives. Lusty, satisfying sexuality. [202]

Some typically praiseworthy Martian traits are listed in the Table provided in Chapter 2 under the heading of "choleric": "energetic," "bold," "assertive," "courageous," and "ambitious."

Macbeth in particular initially exemplifies many of these laudable qualities of Mars. His tragic flaw is often said to be ambition, yet ambition is a commendable trait; it is simply "a strong desire to achieve something; [the] will to succeed." He exhibits the persistent and passionate commitment to a goal that is so often valued on the battlefield or in the boardroom. But Macbeth misuses the energy and force of Mars by directing it to ignoble purposes. He does concentrate on a single goal, that of becoming king, but he transgresses moral and religious law to achieve that end. The force of aggression that was appropriately directed at rebels and invaders is displaced onto innocent civilians, including women and children. The risks he takes in trying to consolidate his position, like hiring others to commit murder and seeking out the witches, all lead him into greater criminality and to an ignominious death. He also displays specifically *un*desirable Martian traits detailed in astrological literature, such as being impatient, "hot-headed, brutal, unrestrained, sadistic, distracted by vague drives. The force of aggression spreads out destructively, and not infrequently, self destructively."[203]

Hamlet's problem, on the other hand, seems to be the opposite of Macbeth's: it is not that he is displaying the negative side of Mars but that he cannot muster the positive. His assignment to wreak revenge on his murderous and (possibly) adulterous uncle appears to be weakened by doubts and indecision. He avoids the opportunity to dispatch his uncle at prayer. In a displacement of his assertive force, instead of his uncle he kills the nosy but innocent Polonius.

Lear too is in an entirely different situation from Macbeth. His Martian pride, devolved into an egotism that cannot distinguish sincerity from flattery, causes him to denounce the only daughter who truly loves him. His violence is all verbal; an aged and impotent man, he can only rage at the gods and the cosmos. No positive Martian goal presents itself to him, and finally Martian rage overcomes him and he goes mad—berserk not in the sense of battlefield invincibility but collapsing inwardly into ineffective invective and wild behavior.

The arc of a tragedy, despite ending in despair and death, often concludes with the re-establishment of communal and social order, a new order of greater promise. The progression of its action affirms a larger pattern of order—to many of the Elizabethans, a divine order—in which good men tempted to evil or evil men threatening the good are eventually and inevitably punished. Our inner satisfaction with the shape and outcome of the tragedy, with us feeling that the story could not have happened or ended any other way, is in part an appreciation for the dramatist's artistic achievement. It is also in part a confident belief in the power of Good to overcome Evil. We have met this grander order earlier, one that links humanity with both the angelic and animal realms. In line with this,

> If a generalization can be made about so protean a subject as tragedy, it is probably that tragedy treats man in terms of his godlike potential, of his transcendent ideals, of the part of himself that is in rebellion against not only the implacable universe but the frailty of his own flesh and will. In this sense tragedy as the record of man's strivings and aspirations is in contrast to comedy, which is the amusing spectacle of man's limitations and frailties.[204]

This energy—that struggles against human nature and human frailty, that rebels against limitation, that aspires to great achievements, that reflects the potential nobility of the human spirit so often depicted in tragedies—is encompassed in the astrological symbol of Mars.

Together Venus and Mars represent perhaps the fundamental polarity of the cosmos, the tension that fosters conflict but also keeps creation in balance: the energy of attraction opposed to the energy of repulsion, of harmony versus conflict, of receptivity in contrast to activity, and of creation versus destruction. It is apt that these two symbols underlie all of Shakespeare's creative works and are reflected in the two types of music that accompany his plays: sweet viols in contrast to the drums of war. Like the yin-yang diagram in which each half contains a germ of the other, his comedies include elements of threatened tragedy and his tragedies have moments of comedic brilliance. Since Venus and Mars are both opposite and complementary symbols, and despite their opposition are contained within a larger Unity, his plays embrace both.

CHAPTER 7

The Hidden Astrological Key to

A Midsummer Night's Dream

Cancer and its Ruler the Moon

snout: Doth the *moon* shine that night we play our play?
bottom: A calendar, a calendar—look in the almanac,
find out *moonshine*, find out *moonshine*.

(*A Midsummer Night's Dream:* III, i, 44–6)

The Story

In Athens, Duke Theseus will be married to Hippolyta, Queen of the Amazons, in four days at the time of a new moon. One of his subjects, Egeus, complains to Theseus that his daughter Hermia refuses to marry his choice for her, Demetrius, because she loves Lysander, an equally handsome and appropriate suitor. Theseus supports Athenian law: Hermia must marry Demetrius or face death or life in a convent. Hermia and Lysander decide to elope the next evening through a wood near the city. They unwisely tell Hermia's friend Helena, who betrays the plan to Demetrius, whom she loves, hoping to win his favor. Demetrius, who loves Hermia, heads for the same forest and the unhappy Helena follows him.

In the same woods are faeries, whose king (Oberon) and queen (Titania) are quarrelling over a young boy in Titania's care. Witnessing Demetrius' rude rejection of Helena, Oberon instructs his henchman Puck to apply the juice of a magical flower to the young man's eyes as he sleeps. This will induce him to fall irresistibly in love with the first person he sees when he wakes. But Puck mistakenly squeezes the potion into Lysander's eyes, and the first person he sees upon awakening is ... Helena! Now each of the lovers loves someone who loves someone else and none have their love reciprocated.

A group of Athenian workingmen has also come to this same wood to rehearse a play for Theseus' wedding. Puck mischievously puts an ass's head onto their leader, Bottom the weaver. Oberon has anointed Titania's eyes with the love juice as part of a scheme to get the changeling boy from her. The first person she sees—and loves—on waking is the ass-headed Bottom.

Instructed to correct his mistake with the lovers, Puck only further confuses the situation by squeezing the flower's juice into Demetrius's eyes. Although upon awakening he first sees Helena and immediately loves her, she becomes angry, thinking that he is mocking her. With the re-application of the flower's juice into Lysander's eyes once more, the lovers are now magically matched.

Taking compassion on Titania and having obtained the young boy he sought, Oberon instructs Puck to remove the ass's head from Bottom and to see that all the human company return to Athens thinking "no more of this night's accidents / But as the fierce vexation of a dream." He frees Titania from her enchantment and they are reconciled.

With the coming of dawn, Theseus, his fiancée Hippolyta, and Hermia's father arrive in the forest to agree that the mystified pairs may marry each other. Bottom awakes to marvel at his "most rare vision."

In Theseus' palace, all three nuptials are celebrated with a well-intentioned but hilariously incompetent performance by the workingmen of the Greek myth of Pyramus and Thisbe. At midnight, the faeries appear to bless the place and the couples. Finally, Puck begs the audience's indulgence: if these "shadows" have offended, they are to think of what they have seen as but a dream.

The Sign Cancer and its Ruler the Moon

In the case of *A Midsummer Night's Dream* we do not have to look far to deduce the secret key. Although we would normally listen carefully to the language of the first (or second) scene to discover the underlying astrological symbolism, in this case the title itself reveals the sign and planet inspiring the play's action and themes—in fact, every word of the title gives away the secret key! "Summer" begins around June 21st each year, at the time of the summer solstice, when day and night are of equal length, at the beginning of the zodiacal sign of Cancer which is assigned the Moon as its ruler. "Night" is obviously the dark half of the 24-hour day, whose light is the Moon. It is the time when we sleep and "dream."[205]

Supporting the idea that the key to the play is CANCER, a sign ruled by the MOON, *A Midsummer Night's Dream* has more references to the Moon than all of Shakespeare's other plays combined. In Caroline Spurgeon's pioneering study of Shakespeare's imagery, she notes that in this play:

> The word "moon" occurs twenty-eight times, three and a half times more often than in any other play, partly of course owing to the prominence of moonshine, often addressed as "moon," as a character in the comedy of the "homespuns." "Moonlight" naturally also occurs unusually often; indeed Shakespeare only mentions moonlight in his plays eight times altogether, and six of these are in *A Midsummer Night's Dream*, as is also his only reference to moonbeams.[206]

The very first lines of the play mention the Moon. Theseus announces the time of his wedding to Hippolyta and impatiently awaits the nuptial day: "Four happy days bring in / Another *moon*—but O, methinks how slow / This old *moon* wanes!"(I,i, 2–4). Hippolyta assures him that the time will speedily pass:

> Four days will quickly steep themselves in night,
> Four nights will quickly dream away the time;
> And then the *moon*, like to a silver bow
> New bent in heaven, shall behold the night
> Of our solemnities.
>
> (I, I, 7–11)

In Greek myth Hippolyta was Queen of the Amazons, a group of women warriors who invaded Athenian territory and were repulsed by Athenian forces. In some accounts their Queen, captured by Theseus, married him. Robert Graves suggests that "Amazon" is an Armenian word meaning "moon-women" (since the Amazons were an exclusively female society and therefore Moon-ruled), an interpretation that would harmonize with the principal symbolism of the play.[207] This association is reinforced by details about the shape of the Amazons' armor:

> [The Elizabethan poet Edmund] Spenser wrote a description of an Amazon—'She wore a scimitar on her thigh, and hung her shield

from her shoulder. The shield was designed so that 'to the moon it mote be like in each respect.' This crescent-shaped shield is a standard attribute of an Amazon. It appears in Virgil and other Roman authors, and can be seen, surprisingly small in its proportions, in visual representations. It is mentioned in Seneca's *Hippolytus*, one of Shakespeare's known sources for *A Midsummer Night's Dream*: when Phaedra resolves to dress like an Amazon, she plans to equip herself with a crescent-shaped shield. When, therefore, Theseus and Hippolyta begin Shakespeare's play by talking about the new moon, we must assume that an emblem of the moon was displayed to the audience as part of Hippolyta's costume.[208]

Besides appealing to the imagination, such a visual detail would immediately alert the educated in Shakespeare's audience to the play's attunement to the Moon.

You cannot miss the emphasis on this astrological symbol. Each time new groups of characters appear they mention the Moon. This provides a unifying symbolism that helps to harmonize the disparate groups of characters in the play. The nobles, Theseus and Hippolyta, are only the first to reference this light of night. When Hermia and Lysander make their plans to escape from Athens, Lysander reveals all to the unhappy Helena:

> Helen, to you our minds we will unfold.
> To-morrow night, when *Phoebe* [the Greek name for the
>   Moon] doth behold
> Her *silver* visage in the wat'ry glass,
> Decking with liquid *pearl* the bladed grass—
> A time that lovers' sleights doth still conceal—
> Through Athens' gates have we devised to steal.
>
>   (I, i, 208–13)

Shakespeare keeps the symbolism consistent with lunar associations, since PEARLS are the precious "gem" associated with the sign Cancer and the Moon, and SILVER ("her silver visage") is the metal attributed to the Moon. Appropriately, since Cancer is assigned to the WATER element ("the "wat'ry" glass), pearls are generated by a mollusk that lives in water. Moon symbolism encompasses water in all its forms: the water of the womb; the water that falls as rain or appears magically as morning dew (described delightfully as "liquid pearl" in the above speech); and the vast ocean, whose rising and ebbing tides are a result of the Moon's attractive pull.

Several other references to water sprinkled throughout the play also support the connection between this play and the sign Cancer. Titania's long complaint to Oberon about the consequences of their conflict on the natural world refers explicitly to forms and bodies of water, now contaminated by their discord:

> Therefore the winds, piping to us in vain,
> As in revenge have sucked up from the sea
> Contagious fogs which, falling in the land,
> Hath every pelting river made so proud
> That they have overborne their continents.....
> The fold stands empty in the drowned field ...
> Therefore the *moon, the governess of floods*,
> Pale in her anger washes all the air,
> That rheumatic diseases do abound ...
>
> (II, i, 89–92, 96, 103–5)

Titania later speaks again of the connection between the Moon and water, at the moment when she has fallen in love with the ass-headed Bottom: "The *moon*, methinks, looks with a wat'ry eye, / And when she weeps, weeps every little flower, / Lamenting some enforced chastity." (III, i, 179–81)

The next set of characters to appear in the play after Theseus, Hippolyta, and the young lovers are the Athenian workingmen (really English rustics) rehearsing the story of Pyramus and Thisbe that they hope to perform at Theseus' wedding. Once the parts are assigned, Quince the carpenter, who is organizing the group, instructs them to "meet ... in the palace wood a mile without the town by *moonlight*." (I, ii, 82–3)

The fourth and last group to materialize is the faeries. Puck, a "merry wanderer of the *night*" (II, i, 43), and another faery meet in that self-same wood, with the faery regaling Puck with a lovely description of her recent wanderings:

> Over hill, over dale,
>   Thorough bush, thorough brier,

Over park, over pale,
  Thorough *flood*, thorough fire,
I do wander everywhere,
Swifter than the *moon*'s sphere ...

(II, I, 2–7)

Now she is off to "go seek some dewdrops here, / And hang a *pearl* in every cowslip's ear" (II, i, 14–5). Notice the references to the Moon, water as dew, and pearls once again.

Since the faery attends Titania, Puck advises her to warn the faery queen to keep away from the angry faery king. Sure enough, as if on cue, Oberon appears and in his first line reminds us of the night-time setting: "Ill met by *moonlight*, proud Titania" (II, I, 60). Even the faery queen's name, "Titania," ties in with the theme because according to Ovid it is another name for the Moon goddess Diana.[209]

To clinch the argument, Shakespeare does something that definitively reveals his inspiration: he has the workingmen who are rehearsing the play bring the Moon onstage as a character! The Moon becomes a literal participant in the drama, carrying the items conventionally associated with it: a lantern and a little dog.

So, all the various groups—nobles, lovers, workingmen, and faeries—refer to the Moon at their first entrance, and continue to do as the action unfolds. They all encounter each other in the same forest to which the lovers have fled. The main action of the play happens in that specific place, during the night, and under the spell of the Moon. The hints in the title and the many and repeated references to the Moon give us the key to understanding the comedy.

The Many Meanings of the Moon

As Shakespeare's audience would have known, the Moon is the pre-eminent symbol of IMPERMANENCE and continual CHANGE. The most striking fact about the Moon is that unlike the Sun it continually waxes and wanes. First it is invisible at the dark of the new moon, then an increasing crescent, next totally visible at the full moon, and finally decreasing to crescent and invisibility again. Individuals with the Moon prominent in their horoscopes experience their lives going through similar phases of both prominence and obscurity. Both Prince Charles of England and

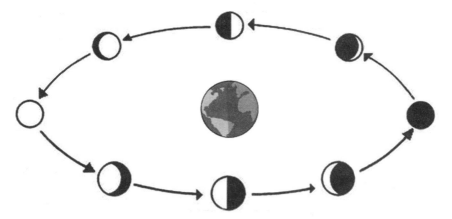

The Moon's shape regularly alters, swelling in light and then shrinking into invisibility through each lunar month, making it the pre-eminent symbol of impermanence and change in the visible world.

former Secretary of State Hillary Rodham Clinton of the USA [in the 8:02 p.m. chart] have the Moon high in their horoscopes, in the very public and visible career sector. Both have been in and out of favor in their respective countries, alternately admired and respected or vilified and rejected—and then admired and respected again.

No wonder Shakespeare has many references to the Moon in his poems and plays with just this connotation. Shakespeare's attitude to the Moon is consistent; in one of his earliest plays, *Love's Labour's Lost*, Rosaline mockingly urges, "Play, music, then. Nay, you must do it soon. / Not yet?—no dance! Thus change I like the *moon*." (V, ii, 210–1) Juliet begs Romeo, "O swear not by the *moon, th' inconstant moon, /* That monthly changes in her circled orb, / Lest that thy love prove likewise variable." (*Romeo and Juliet:* II, i, 153) In one of the last plays, Cleopatra, determined to commit suicide now that Antony is dead, vows, "I have nothing / Of woman in me. Now from head to foot / I am marble-constant. Now the fleeting *moon* / No planet is of mine." (V, ii, 234–7) Since the Moon was thought to rule women in general, Cleopatra renounces her feminine nature to emphasize her firm purpose. The changeability of the Moon is reflected by the metal appropriately associated with it, silver, which darkens as it tarnishes, unlike the metal linked to the Sun, gold, which never loses its luster.[210]

So love begun under the light of the Moon is not to be trusted. When Egeus complains about his daughter Hermia's infatuation with Lysander, he specifically accuses Lysander of wooing her not by clear daylight but by mesmerizing moonlight. In his eyes Lysander has used the notoriously fluctuating lunar light to lure her into his affections, pretending to love her:

> This hath bewitched the bosom of my child.
> Thou, thou, Lysander, thou hast given her rhymes,
> And interchanged love tokens with my child.
> Thou hast by *moonlight* at her window sung
> With feigning voice verses of feigning love,
> And stol'n the impression of her fantasy
> With bracelets of thy hair, rings, gauds, conceits,
> Knacks, trifles, nosegays, sweetmeats—messengers
> Of strong prevailment in unhardened youth.
>
> (I, i, 27–35)

So as far as Egeus is concerned, Lysander's love is untrustworthy.

Demetrius appears to be no more steadfast than Lysander. He is another example of lunar unreliability, since, despite Egeus' preference for him as a son–in–law, Lysander accuses Demetrius of having switched allegiances before the action even began:

> Demetrius—I'll avouch it to his head—
> Made love to Nedar's daughter, Helena,
> And won her soul, and she, sweet lady, dotes,
> Devoutly dotes, dotes in idolatry
> Upon this spotted and inconstant man.
>
> (I, i, 106-10)

Nothing in this play seems fixed, as not only affections but also experiences and appearances transform. Prior to loving Lysander, Hermia equated Athens with paradise; now that she favors him and her life is at stake, love "hath turned a heaven unto a hell" (I, i, 207). Puck, being a faery, has literally the power to shape-shift, for he torments the working-men by changing his appearance and chasing them through the forest.

Bottom, of course, is the one most "translated," sporting an ass's head in place of his own for part of the play due to the merry Puck's prank. Yet when the sound of his singing awakens Titania, she starts up saying, "What angel wakes me from my flowery bed?" (III, i, 132) The power of attraction to transform the loved object into something wondrous is foreshadowed earlier in the play, when the unhappy Helena ponders the power of lovers' vision: "Things base and vile, holding no quantity, / Love can transpose to form and dignity." (I, i, 232–3) So one of the agents of change, under the light of the Moon, is the power of love—even though in this play it is for the most part immature and capricious.

The Moon is the primary symbol of the FEMININE PRINCIPLE. First differentiated in ancient Greece, the three principal phases of the Moon—new, full, and waning—correlate with the three principal stages of a woman's life: maiden, mother, and crone (or wise woman). Matching the Moon phases with these stages allows for contradictory interpretations of females as virginal or maternal, barren or fertile, chaste or seductive. (Theseus mentions the opposite possibilities of either fertility or barrenness when offering Hermia her three options.) No wonder that, with her ever-evolving phases and playful variability, the feminine is thought to be mysterious and unfathomable, irrational and unknowable.

On a literal, physical level the sign Cancer has to do not only with inexperienced youths whose emotions seem to fluctuate like the weather, but also with those even younger—that is, CHILDREN, brought forth by fertile women. This association features prominently in the plot since the conflict between Oberon and Titania is over custody of a changeling child whisked by Titania from the human realm into faeryland. It is significant, given the symbolism of the Moon, that the child is a CHANGEling, transported from one dimension into another and higher one. Titania's attachment to this mortal child is due to her affection for the MOTHER, another association with the Moon, as revealed in these charming images of her while pregnant:

> His *mother* was a vot'ress of my order,
> And in the spiced Indian air by night
> Full often hath she gossiped by my side,
> And sat with me on Neptune's yellow sands,
> Marking th' embarked traders on the flood,

When we have laughed to see the sails *conceive*
And grow big-bellied with the wanton wind,
Which she with pretty and with swimming gait
Following, her *womb* then rich with my young squire,
Would imitate, and sail upon the land ...

                                        (II, i, 123–132)

In the female body, the Moon governs the WOMB as well as breasts that suckle a child, and so it especially symbolizes FERTILITY. In human beings fecundity coordinates with the female's monthly cycle that closely matches the Moon's cycle from new to full and new again, taking about twenty-seven or twenty-eight days. The faeries' blessing at the end of the play singles out the children that will be born to the wedded couples. Oberon's instructions are:

Now until the break of day
Through this house each fairy stray.
To the best bridebed will we,
Which by us shall blessed be,
And the issue there create
Ever shall be fortunate.

                                        (V, ii, 31–6)

Astrological symbols are always double-sided, containing their opposites. In line with her varying phases, the Moon can signify quite the opposite of fertility: BARRENNESS. This is mentioned early in the play as a threat, for if Hermia refuses to obey her father and marry his choice of suitors for her, Theseus decrees that she may withdraw into a nunnery. He presents this as a not terribly attractive option:

Therefore, fair Hermia, question your desires.
Know of your youth, examine well your blood,
Whether, if you yield not to your father's choice,
You can endure the livery of a nun,
For aye to be in shady cloister mewed,
To live a *barren* sister all your life,
Chanting faint hymns to the *cold fruitless moon*.

                                        (I, i, 67–73)

At least Theseus has softened Egeus' demands by offering a third option of "protest[ing] / For aye austerity and single life" on Diana's altar (Diana being the Roman name for the Moon goddess). (I, i, 89–90) Hermia must make her decision, declares Theseus, by the day of his and Hippolyta's anticipated wedding, the day of the apparently approaching new moon.

The Enigma of Time in A Midsummer Night's Dream

The Moon is indispensable to the measurement of TIME. The earliest calendars were based on lunar cycles, marked by notches in bone that apparently tracked new and full moons as well as eclipses.[211] Days and years were established later by the sun's daily rising and setting and by its seasonal variations, but intermediate periods were set by the Moon whose cycle roughly established the length of the weeks and months ("moonths"). Lunar calendars are still used by some cultures and religions, like Judaism and Islam. The Chinese New Year is always the first new moon in the sign of Aquarius; Easter's date is fixed as the first Sunday following the first full moon after the Spring Equinox.[212]

As keeper of time, the Moon relates to mortality. Under the Moon, all visible life is subject to change, as forms materialize, fluctuate in their appearance, and then disappear, like the Moon that dwindles and "dies" each month during its dark phase.[213] It therefore measures human fate. Moon goddesses are often portrayed as spinners or weavers of destiny, like the Norse three Norns or the three Fates of ancient Greece who spun, measured and cut the threads of life on the loom of time.

New moons are especially significant interim time markers. They are moments each month when the Sun and Moon align in the sky as viewed from Earth, inaugurating a new cycle. Theseus specifically wants the old moon to wane as quickly as possible, allowing fresh energy to enter. Astrological tradition generally considers new moons particularly auspicious times for starting new ventures. Thus the setting of Theseus and Hippolyta's wedding date harmonizes with a natural cycle of new beginnings. In addition, the apparent melding of the Sun and Moon represents the union of the male and the female, making a new moon an especially appropriate symbol for a wedding. Any Elizabethan audience would have understood these interpretations.

However, the new moon that Theseus and Hippolyta mention may not be the moment when the two lights actually conjoin. Astrologers these days time each month's new moon with the exact conjunction of the Sun and Moon. This cannot be seen with the naked eye, of course, since the Moon is then invisible. This time is called "the dark of the Moon" and consequently there is *no* moonlight. However, earlier peoples measured the beginning of the month about four days *after* the Sun and Moon aligned, at the point when the first sliver of the Moon became visible. At this time the Moon is "waxing" or growing in size, a time also considered auspicious for a wedding. "Ideally, the moon should be waxing at the time of sexual consummation in order that the woman can partake of its generative power. This is why Theseus and Hippolyta refuse to marry while the old moon is on the wane. For an Elizabethan audience, no explanations were needed: the sympathetic link between humans and planets was self-evident."[214] The first appearance of the thin crescent moon is what Hippolyta describes as "like to a silver bow new bent in heaven." (I, i, 9–10) In that case, we have jumped from the precise moment of the new Moon to a point some days later. So what are the two referring to? The actual new moon or the point at which the Moon first becomes visible?

Whatever moment in time they are alluding to, just how much moonlight would there be? Whether it is the time of the precise new moon or even a few days later, there would be very little light. Yet Lysander seems sure that tomorrow evening, when he and Hermia will elope, the Moon will easily see her "silver visage," suggesting a time of the month closer to a full moon. Oberon announces that he and Titania meet "by moonlight" and the night seems well illuminated for them. When the Athenian artisans arrive in the wood to rehearse their play, the question of how much moonlight will shine on their performance becomes a critical topic of discussion.

> QUINCE: [B]ut there is two hard things: that is, to bring
> the *moonlight* into a chamber—for, you know Pyra-
> mus and Thisbe meet by *moonlight*.
> SNOUT: Doth the *moon* shine that night we play our play?
> BOTTOM: A calendar, a calendar—Look in the almanac,
> find out *moonshine*, find out *moonshine*.
> QUINCE: Yes, it doth shine that night.

BOTTOM: Why, then may you leave a casement of the
great chamber window where we play open, and the
moon may shine in at the casement.

(III, i, 41–50)

Sounds like plenty of light again. Hippolyta's skimpy little "silver bow" would hardly provide enough light for them to rehearse—or for the others to find each other in the woods. So where are we actually in the monthly cycle in this play? Shakespeare deliberately confuses the time of the month to match the chaotic and confused events in the wood and the astrological key to the comedy. He is doing what he so often does in his plays: collapsing time. Perhaps the action of the play, which presumably lasts over four days but seems shorter, expands to encompass the full monthly cycle of the Moon: from dark to full and back to dark again. We end the play in dark night, at midnight, with the nobles and lovers all wending their way to bed.

Not only the time of the <u>month</u> but also the time of the <u>year</u> is equally unclear. Midsummer? For centuries Midsummer Eve was an important annual festival in Europe, especially among the Germanic peoples, and was celebrated the night before June 21st.[215] However, since celebrations around that date were considered pagan, the Catholic Church appropriated the event, renamed it Saint John's Day, and moved it to June 24th.[216] Local traditions continued, though, under the radar of approved custom, still celebrated on the eve of June 20th. Beliefs about this special date match the strange events depicted in Shakespeare's play:

On Midsummer Eve, the invisible beings with whom we share the world are allowed to reveal themselves and roam, unmasked and unashamed, through the pleasant night. Witch, fairy, or walking dead, the creatures of our highest and darkest imaginations crowd the fields, perch on the stiles, rustle in the thick summer trees, meet by moonlight. Under their reign, all magic, white or black, good or evil, petty or terrifying, triples in strength.[217]

An earlier, much more popular holiday was May 1st, called the feast of Beltane in the pagan/Celtic calendar, one of the eight "cross quarter days" midway between the four solstices and equinoxes marking the change of seasons. This day was one of the eight anchoring points of the year, like the stabilizing spokes of a wheel. Festivities for both Belt-ane and the Summer Solstice were similar since at both times the walls between the worlds thinned:

> On this night [May Eve, the night before May 1st] fairies enchanted unwary mortals, but their charms, given the joyful nature of the occasion, were little more than love spells or simple bewilderments. Many reported chasing will-o-the-wisps, or fairy lights, across the countryside, drawn by the beauty of the floating orbs and the unearthly music that accompanied their flight ... [218]

When Theseus and the other nobles arrive early in the morning to hunt in the same woods and see the four sleeping lovers, he comments, "No doubt they rose up early to observe / The rite of May ..." (IV, i, 129–30). And since a play's symbolism is always consistent with the underlying archetype, can it be accidental that Hermia, angry with Helena, calls her a "painted maypole"? (III, ii, 297). [219]

All of this puzzles a modern audience. The title announces "midsummer"; allusions in the play are to May Day. So just where in the yearly calendar are we ... May or Midsummer? [220]

Titania offers a possible explanation for the mix-up in the perception of yearly time. According to her, it is the faeries' dissension that has radically disturbed the order of the seasons as well as our sense of time:

> And thorough this distemperature we see
> The seasons alter: hoary-headed frosts
> Fall in the fresh lap of the crimson rose,
> And on old Hiems' thin and icy crown
> An odorous chaplet of sweet summer buds
> Is, as in mock'ry, set. The spring, the summer,
> The childing autumn, angry winter change
> Their wonted liveries, and the mazed world,
> By their increase now knows not which is which ...
>
>   (II, I, 106–114)

Perhaps the clever dramatist Shakespeare is playing games with us, creating the same disorientation in our minds that the characters in the drama experience. If we try to establish monthly and yearly time under the distorting light of the Moon, we are as confused as they are.

The Moon and the Unconscious

Psychologically, the Moon represents the UNCONSCIOUS, the foundational and largely unknowable part of ourselves, the "night" half of the psyche. Remarkably, because the physical Moon spins on its axis in the identical time that it orbits the Earth, the Moon always has the same face towards Earth: its dark side is never seen. In the same way, the unconscious part of ourselves is never exposed to the light of day, but instead bubbles up through malapropisms, unconscious but revealing actions, and most importantly in our dreams. As Mark Twain said, "Everyone is a moon, and has a dark side which he never shows to anybody."[221] This dark side is often associated with the mysterious feminine.

The modern idea of both a conscious and an unconscious part of the psyche emerged in the late 1800s and early 1900s in the pioneering work of such modern psychologists as Drs. Sigmund Freud and Carl Jung. While Freud reduced the unconscious to a repository of mainly repressed material (especially related to sexuality), Jung expanded the concept to include mind-stuff not necessarily repressed but just forgotten, some of which is actually positive. Both psychologists, along with their followers, believe that all of this material continues to influence our conscious thoughts, attitudes, and behaviors, whether we are aware of this or not.[222]

Jung also added a level beneath the personal unconscious called the collective unconscious, accessible through the personal unconscious. This deeper level is a vast reservoir of the universal and common inheritance of humanity, expressed through varied images and universal symbols found across all cultures and throughout history—especially in artistic works and religious philosophies. All of the astrological symbols are thought to originate here, including the overarching symbol for the play, the Moon.

When the lovers of *A Midsummer Night's Dream* go into the woods, into the realm of uncultivated nature full of dangerous animals, they are symbolically entering the realm of the unconscious.[223] There, under the stress of sudden and inexplicable transferences of affection between them and under the cover of dark night, deeply suppressed emotions and long-buried resentments erupt from the personal unconscious of each. All of them, for one reason or another, become passionately angry and release a volley of invective. It is no longer about love but about hate. The Moon, representative of the feminine, is associated with both positive and negative EMOTIONS, inward tides of feeling that fluctuate from moment to moment and sometimes flood your rational mind against your personal will. If repressed and then suddenly released from the unconscious, as they are in the lovers' nightmarish adventures in the woods, they are explosive and powerful indeed.

First, the previously sweet Hermia, awakening to find Lysander gone, furiously accuses Demetrius of killing him in order to secure her: "Out, dog; out, cur. Thou driv'st me past the bounds / Of maiden's patience. Hast thou slain him, then? / Henceforth be never numbered among men." (III, ii, 65–7) Helena too changes as events take unpredictable turns. From the start she is insecure due to Demetrius' transfer of affections from her to Hermia, so much so that she entreats him to use her as he would use his dog (dogs being associated with the Moon):

> I am your spaniel, and, Demetrius,
> The more you beat me I will fawn on you.
> Use me but as your spaniel: spurn me, strike me,
> Neglect me, lose me; only give me leave,
> Unworthy as I am, to follow you.
>
> (II, i, 203–7)

So self-abasing is she that she cannot believe that anyone (and surely not Lysander who seems devoted to Hermia) could love her. She reacts to Lysander's sudden declaration, "Not Hermia but Helena I love. / Who will not change a raven for a dove?" (II, ii, 119–20) by angrily assuming that he is making fun of her: "Wherefore was I to this keen mockery born? / When at your hands did I deserve this scorn?" (II, ii, 129–30)

When both Lysander and Demetrius protest their love for her, Helena's resentments are even more intensely released. Deeply sure that she is unlovable, she becomes even more wrathful with both of them: "O spite! O hell! I see you all are bent / To set against me for your merriment." (III, ii, 146–7) When Hermia joins them, mystified by Lysander's betrayal, Helena can only think that all three are conspiring to mock her. Typically, she turns on the same-sex person, not either of the men, chastising her former friend by appealing to memories of their earlier closeness:

Injurious Hermia, most ungrateful maid,
Have you conspired, have you with these contrived
To bait me with this foul derision?
Is all the counsel that we two have shared—
The sisters' vows, the hours that we have spent
When we have chid the hasty-footed time
For parting us—O, is all quite forgot?
All schooldays' friendship, childhood innocence?

                                        (III, ii, 196–203)

This is just the build-up to the full-scale emergence of more sub-merged animosities, as the two young men begin to argue about who loves Helena most. When Lysander dismisses the stunned Hermia with "Away, you Ethiope" and "Out, tawny Tartar, out; / Out, loathed medicine; O hated potion, hence . . ." (III, ii, 258, 264–5), the two young women begin to snark at each other. Their speeches reveal previously suppressed feelings, as the more assertive Hermia challenges Helena who takes refuge in wounded innocence and professed honesty and simplicity:

HERMIA: O me, you juggler, you canker-blossom,
        You thief of love—what, have you come by night
        And stol'n my love's heart from him?
HELENA: Fine, i'faith.
        Have you no modesty, no maiden shame,
        No touch of bashfulness? What, will you tear
        Impatient answers from my gentle tongue?
        Fie, fie, you counterfeit, you puppet, you!
HERMIA: Puppet? Why, so? Ay, that way goes the game.
        Now I perceive that she hath made compare
        Between our statures; she hath urged her height,
        And with her personage, her tall personage,
        Her height, forsooth, she hath prevail'd with him—
        And are you grown so high in his esteem,
        Because I am so dwarfish and so low?
        How low am I, thou painted maypole? Speak,
        How low am I? I am not yet so low
        But that my nails can reach unto thine eyes.

                                        (III, ii, 283–99)

Trading more insults, Helena reveals Hermia's underlying choleric nature: "O, when she is angry, she is keen and shrewd [shrewish]. / She was a vixen [a young fox] when she went to school, / And though she be but little, she is fierce." (III, ii, 324–6) The two young men become equally aggressive and, in typical male fashion, more physical than verbal, exit to fight over who has the right to Helena. In line with her vaunted sweet temper, Helena, fearful of Hermia attacking her, declares: "I will not trust you, I, / Nor longer stay in your curst company. / Your hands than mine are quicker for a fray; / My legs are longer, though, to run away." (III, ii, 341–4). At this point the angry spirit of Mars threatens to overcome peace-loving Venus.

The mischievous Puck, enjoying all the confusion and commotion, unrepentantly tells Oberon "their jangling I esteem a sport." (III, ii, 354) The bickering young lovers are only rescued from escalating conflicts catalyzed by the emergence of unconscious feelings when Puck leads them "up and down" until they fall into an exhausted sleep. And their remembrance of the bitter arguments will fade, as Oberon promises that "When they next wake, all this derision / Shall seem a dream and fruitless vision …" (III, ii, 371–2). The upsurging and seething emotions subside back into the unconscious as the young lovers succumb to healing sleep.

To Sleep...

Whatever time of year the play is set, the main action certainly takes place at NIGHT, the half of the day ruled by the Moon. Normally a good portion (on average one-third) of our day is spent in SLEEP. It makes metaphoric sense that as the light fades we go into the dark of our inner selves. While modern scientists have answered many questions puzzling us about human nature and human behavior, they have not fully answered this one: Why do we sleep? As darkness settles, our eyelids droop, and, as Prospero induces Miranda in *The Tempest*, "Thou art inclined to sleep; 'tis a good dullness, / And give it way. I know thou canst not choose." [Miranda sleeps] (I, ii, 186–7)

Circadian neuroscientist Russell Foster goes so far as to say that sleep is the "single most important behavioral experience that we have," and outlines the dangers of lack of sleep: everything from mood changes to increased stress to illnesses like diabetes, high blood pressure and even cancer.[224]

In modern times the attitude to sleep has changed. What used to be welcomed as a period of rest after the day's hustle and bustle is now viewed as time lost that would be better spent being awake and productive. People who sleep little, like Martha Stewart, are admired for pushing back the parameters of the night. Thomas Edison, the inventor of the electric light bulb enabling us to turn night into day, called sleep "a criminal waste of time and a heritage from our cave days." "Sleep," Margaret Thatcher is supposed to have said, "is for wimps."[225]

Shakespeare has an entirely different perspective on sleep. It is the "honey-heavy dew of slumber" that comes easily to those who have "no figures nor no fantasies / Which busy care draws in the brains of men ..." and so they sleep soundly. (*Julius Caesar*: II, i, 229–31) It is the young, the innocent, and the good (like Miranda and Gonzalo in *The Tempest*) who are able to sleep and sleep well in Shakespeare's world. It is only those burdened with cares of state (like Henry IV, sleepless before battle: "O Sleep, O gentle Sleep, / Nature's soft nurse, how have I frighted thee, / That thou no more wilt weigh my eyelids down / And steep my senses in forgetfulness?" [*2 Henry IV*: III, i, 5–8]) or downright villains, suffering from guilty consciences, who do not and cannot sleep. Macbeth, newly embarked on a path of crime, bemoans a dawning awareness that he will sleep no more. He will be deprived of "the innocent sleep, / Sleep that knits up the ravelled sleave of care / ... sore labour's bath, / Balm of hurt minds ... Chief nourisher in life's feast." (*Macbeth*: II, ii, 34–8)

Shakespeare, as always, is uncannily right: sleep is indeed the "balm of hurt minds." We know that after days of sleeplessness, people become irritable and paranoid, subject to hallucinations, long-term memory damage, and even psychosis. But scientists do not yet understand why human beings must sleep...or literally go mad. We might theorize that some of the lovers' increasingly erratic behavior in *A Midsummer Night's Dream* is due to their sleep being interrupted. The lovers, increasingly confused and angry while in the woods overnight, do not get much sleep, but they do in fact finally rest.

The first one to sleep, though, is Titania, lulled by the faeries' incantatory lullaby that chases away the terrors of the night. (This is obviously magical music of the celestial type.) Perhaps one reason we fight sleep is that the night half of day for many is a fearful time. The faeries' song warns away a variety of menacing creatures—"spotted snakes with double tongue, / Thorny hedgehogs ... Newts and blindworms ... weaving spiders ... Beetles black ..." (See II, ii, 9–23)—but even more threatening animals prowl at night. Lysander tries to frighten away the doggedly devoted Helena by saying "wild beasts" may attack her. (II, i, 228) Oberon thinks that Titania may wake to see a lynx, wildcat, bear, leopard—even a "boar with bristled hair." (II, ii, 36–7) Yet the only monstrous creature seen by anyone in the wood is the ass-headed Bottom! As is appropriate in a comedy, potential threats prove to be harmless.

The lovers also sleep, first Demetrius and Hermia, who urges her swain to lie farther off from her. Later, after the confusion of suddenly shifting affections, the surfacing of the women's hidden resentments, and the men's aggressive chasing each other to fight, they all succumb to an exhausted slumber. First Lysander, who cannot seem to catch up to the fleet and fleeing Demetrius, pants, "fallen am I in dark uneven way, / And here will rest me." (III, iii, 5–6) He is followed immediately by Demetrius, and then Helena, who welcomes restorative "sleep, that sometimes shuts up sorrow's eye, / Steal me awhile from mine own company." (III, iii, 23–4) Finally Hermia stumbles into the scene, lamenting her state: "Never so weary, never so in woe, / Bedabbled with the dew, and torn with briers, / I can no further crawl, no further go, / Muy legs can keep no pace with my desires. / Here will I rest me till the break of day." (III, iii, 30–4)

And the "transported" Bottom sleeps, too, in the bower of the faery queen:

> BOTTOM: But I pray you, let none of your people stir me.
> I have an exposition of sleep come upon me.
> TITANIA: Sleep thou, and I will wind thee in my arms.
> Fairies, be gone, and be all ways away.
>
> (IV, i, 34–8)

The sleep of the four lovers and Bottom, in these mysterious woods with faeries present, is no ordinary sleep. Oberon requests that Titania "music call, and strike more dead / Than common sleep of all these five the sense." Titania accedes, calling for special music—celestial music again—"such as charmeth sleep." (IV, i, 78–80) For all of them, sleep is a blessing.

... Perchance to Dream

The eyelids close, the breathing slows, and we sleep ... entering an inner world ruled by the Moon that is often just as vivid, memorable and compelling as the one we experience under the Sun. Human beings have been recording their DREAMS, those inner movies of the night, for over five thousand years, as far back as the Sumerian/Babylonian and Egyptian periods. Dreams feature in both secular and religious writings from the earliest recorded times. In the Bible's Old Testament, Jacob dreams of a ladder on which the angels of God are ascending and descending (Genesis 28); in the New Testament, both the Magi and Joseph are warned in dreams about Herod's evil intentions.[226] Islam celebrates Mohammed's *Lailat al Miraj*, his great dream of initiation into the cosmos, during which he flew on a half-human silver mare to Jerusalem and then upward through the seven celestial spheres. In Hinduism, Vishnu, one of the representations of the divine, sleeps on a great serpent floating on a cosmic ocean, and dreams the world into being.[227]

While everyone dreams (even people who do not think they do or do not remember their dreams), modern scientists have not definitively answered this question either: Why do we dream? Theories about dreams go back to classical times, when philosophers and writers formulated some of the same speculations still current. Some dreams, said the ancients, had physical causes: ill health, poor diet, neurosis, or an imbalance in those bodily fluids mentioned earlier, the humors.[228] Possible types of dreams include not only the materialistic, but also the medical,[229] the psychological, the occult,[230] and the mystical. Many, including ancient Egyptians, followers of the Greek hero Orpheus and the Greek sage Pythagoras, as well as later Neo-Platonists and Renaissance occultists, believed that the soul was freed from the body in sleep and could soar upward to meet and be taught by higher beings. Some dreams might be the residue of such experiences.

Dreams in Shakespeare's plays are always meaningful, never just materialistic or medical. They are most often precognitive, as in *Julius Caesar* where Caesar's wife eerily foresees his murder on the unlucky Ides of March, or psychologically symbolic as when Shylock dreams of money-bags, or occult as when the wicked Richard III dreams during the night before battle of the ghosts of those that he has murdered.

In our time, the interpretation of dreams is heavily psychological.

Freud called dreams "the royal road to the unconscious," and Jung emphasized them even more, seeing them as the principal means by which the
unconscious communicates with the conscious in order to create greater
psychological wholeness. He thought that dreams could correct a conscious imbalance or reveal the inner meaning of an external situation.[231]

The first and most literal dream in *A Midsummer Night's Dream* is
Hermia's, when she has awakened in the wood to find Lysander gone:
"What a dream was here? / Lysander, look how I do quake with fear. /
Methought a serpent ate my heart away, / And you sat smiling at his
cruel prey." (II, ii, 153–6) This is a clear dream with dramatic personal
relevance to her. What she has dreamed perfectly matches what has just
happened externally, as Lysander has just abandoned her for Helena
while she slept. Interpreting Hermia's dream, we might deduce that she
will indeed endure heartache, as painful as if a fanged reptile were cruelly
attacking her breast.

But the snake is also a universal symbol, an image so ubiquitous and
multi-faceted that it must originate in Jung's "collective unconscious."
In the West snakes most often connote evil, like the tempting serpent
in the Garden of Eden. This is how Hermia interprets it. Her terror at
the image in her dream leads her to fear that her lover Demetrius is
dead, and she projects the image of the serpent onto the person she most
suspects of his murder—Lysander: "[H]ast thou killed him sleeping? O
brave touch! / Could not a worm, an adder do so much? / An adder did
it, for with doubler tongue / Than thine, thou *serpent*, never adder stung"
(III, ii, 70–3). In a cruel and ironic twist, under the spell of the flower's
juice, when Hermia finally finds Lysander in the wood and clings to
him, he spurns her, shouting, "Hang off, thou cat, thou burr; vile thing,
let loose, / Or I will shake thee from me like a *serpent*." (III, ii, 261–2)
She has become the serpent! The snake of her dream morphs first into
Lysander and then into Hermia herself. The image migrates from the
insubstantial realm of dream, crystallizes into the "real" world, and then
changes form. All of this is very much in line with the mutability of the
world below the Moon.

But the theme of dreams and dreaming becomes more profound
when the lovers are awakened in the morning by the hunting party. Theseus is surprised to find the four, previously at odds over who marries
whom, sleeping near each other in "gentle concord." Groggy from the

heavy and magical sleep that the faeries have induced, Lysander is confused: "My lord, I shall reply amazedly, / Half sleep, half waking. But as yet, I swear, / I cannot truly say how I came here." (IV, i, 143–5) Now they are unsure of what actually happened and why. Inexplicably, Demetrius' previous love for Hermia has "melted as the snow," gone like a childhood fixation now outgrown. When the nobles and their train depart, the lovers are left bemused, wondering about the reality of what they have experienced.

> DEMETRIUS: These things seem small and undistinguish-
> able,
> Like far-off mountains turned into clouds.
> HERMIA: Methinks I see these things with parted eye,
> When everything seems double ...
> DEMETRIUS: It seems to me
> That yet we *sleep*, we *dream*. Do not you think
> The Duke was here and bid us follow him?
> HERMIA: Yea, and my father.
> HELENA: And Hippolyta.
> LYSANDER: And he did bid us follow to the temple.
> DEMETRIUS: Why then, we are awake. Let's follow him,
> And by the way let us recount our *dreams*.
>   (IV, i, 184–7, 189–95)

For the lovers, the night-time experience has faded as dreams often do in the waking light. But we the audience have witnessed these events and know that they were, in the real-world of the play, no dream.

Immediately after this Bottom wakes. As if no time had passed, he picks up his cue just at the point when the rehearsal was interrupted by Puck's transformation of him. Of all the participants in the adventure in the woods, Bottom is the only one who remembers and believes in the truth of his experience: "I have had a most rare vision. I have had a *dream* past the wit of man to say what *dream* it was. Man is but an ass if he go about t'expound this *dream*." (IV, i, 199–202) Bottom affirms the truth of his irrational experience, beyond the ability of reason to explain it or voice to articulate it. And his vision creatively inspires him: "I will get Peter Quince to write a ballad of this dream. It shall be called 'Bottom's Dream,' because it hath no bottom, and I will sing it in the latter end of a play ..." (IV, i, 207–10). Alone of all the protagonists Bottom keeps the memory of his encounter with the faeries.

The Faeries and the Realm of Faerie

In Shakespeare's time and before, the belief was that the space between the Earth and Moon had to be filled with various entities. Since the Source of all creation is infinite and inexhaustible, no part of creation could possibly be empty; every part of the universe had to be "peopled."[232] Because the realms above the Moon are inhabited by celestial and immortal beings and our earthly regions teem with terrestrial and mortal beings, the intermediate regions between the two (that is, between the Moon and Earth) must be filled as well.[233] The beings that filled this space, being "middle" creatures, are dual in nature: both divine or semi-divine (in that they are either immortal or much longer-lived than mortals) and human (in that they often appear in human-like form).[234]

All the supernatural beings who appear in this play—Oberon and Titania, the nature spirits who tend Bottom, and Puck—are believed to inhabit this intermediate realm between the Moon and Earth, a place of nebulousness and changeability where shadowy forms coalesce and disperse. So these quasi-divine beings could appear in somewhat physical form. Half ethereal and half tangible, they were thought to be a separate but parallel stream to the human one, much longer-lived but capable of interaction with human beings. Oberon and Titania accuse each other of such dallying with mortals. Titania complains that Oberon took the shape of Corin (a shepherd) "playing on pipes of corn, and versing love / To amorous Phillida" (a conventional term for a shepherdess) and also romanced Hippolyta, whom she describes as Oberon's "buskined mistress and your warrior love." (II, i, 67–8, 71) Oberon counters with a charge that he knows her love for Theseus. In fact, their previous involvements with Theseus and Hippolyta are the reason that they have appeared to bless the couple's marriage ceremony.

For such creatures to be both immortal and mortal—which baffles reason—accords with the Moon's variable quality. And when it comes to identifying and classifying them, writers from the classical period through to the Renaissance and even into modern times are confused— also in line with the symbolism of the Moon. Since the Moon is the principal symbol of impermanence and change, continually waxing and waning through its monthly cycle, it makes sense that the creatures that live between the Moon and Earth are various and indeterminate with different names and natures in different cultures and places.

Is it possible to determine what these beings are, what they look like, and what to call them? Since their natures are more "ethereal" than ours and they have the ability to change their form and appearance, the answer must be "no." We cannot pin down their essence or their appear-

QUINCE: *"... here's a marvelous convenient place for our rehearsal. This green plot shall be our stage, this hawthorn brake [thicket] our tiring house [dressing room]..." (III, i, 2-4)*

Even in the smallest detail, Shakespeare is consistent in matching poetic symbols to the play's themes. In Roman times the hawthorn represented chastity (perhaps because its five-petalled flowers are white), though it later changed to a symbol of fertility. Also known as the maytree or maythorn, it blossoms around May 1ˢᵗ and the original maypoles were made of its wood.

Because of its dense growth and prickly thorns, it was used in England to create hedges ("hedgerows") that separated one field from another. Not only a literal boundary, it was also believed to mark the boundary between this world and the faery realm. When Bottom enters the hawthorn brake, he is entering the faery world where Puck can give him an ass's head.

ance. Many labels have been applied to them: spirits, elves, nymphs, ogres, and dwarfs among them.[235]

One of these classifications is "fairies" or "faeries." (I use the word "faery" partly because it connects us to the older meaning of the word and partly because it has fewer associations with the tiny, trivialized "fairies" of the Victorian period.)[236] The faeries of *A Midsummer Night's Dream* do control the fates of the young lovers in the forest, altering their emotions and experience—but it is Shakespeare who truly casts a spell over audience members as they watch the play.

In line with the traditional mixing of their natures and the play's attunement to the Moon, the supernatural beings in *A Midsummer Night's Dream* are actually of different sorts and derive from different historical sources. The first type comes from the classical Greek and Roman tradition. In ancient times, minor gods/goddesses or various spirits accompanied the twelve Olympians (major gods and goddesses such as Jupiter and Venus) like a courtly retinue, reflecting a hierarchy inherent in the Elizabethan worldview explicated earlier. Venus, the goddess of love, was often accompanied by her son Cupid. His arrows, loosed according to Venus' whims, made those struck by them fall madly and hopelessly in love. Neptune, the divinity of the oceans, was surrounded by secondary creatures, sea nymphs and mermaids among them. (Oberon mentions a mermaid he saw while telling Puck how the flower gained its potency.)

Cupid is an important though unseen player in this drama since the effect of the flower's juice drizzled into the lovers' eyes comes from one of his notorious arrows. Oberon tells Puck that he saw Cupid, all armed, "Flying between the cold *moon* and the earth," precisely the middle dimension such creatures normally inhabit. When Cupid let loose an arrow, Oberon saw where it landed:

> It fell upon a little western flower—
> Before, milk-white; now, purple with love's wound—
> And maidens call it love-in-idleness....
> The juice of it on sleeping eyelids laid
> Will make or man or woman madly dote
> Upon the next live creature that it sees.
>
> (II, i, 166–68, 170–2)

In part from the same classical tradition, Oberon and Titania, King and Queen of the faeries, are regal creatures who greatly resemble human beings in their quarrels and discord. Titania's name comes from classical literature, referring to a daughter of the immortal Titans (hence "Titania"), children of Heaven and Earth that were overthrown by Jupiter and his siblings. Oberon's name, however, originates in a thirteenth-century medieval French tale of the adventures of Huon of Bordeaux. In it the faery king Oberon becomes Huon's ally, ultimately saving his life. Shakespeare's Oberon has a similar nobility, and like the Oberon of the medieval story intervenes to help the human characters: he instructs Puck to take actions that sort out the mismatched lovers so that they end up in happy pairs.[237]

A second type of spirit also derives from the classical period but is more attached to Earth than to immortal deities inhabiting the spheres above the Moon. Like all indigenous cultures, the Greeks envisioned spirits linked closely to nature. Usually depicted as beautiful maidens, these beings are generally called "nymphs" and are variously associated with forests, rivers, springs, mountains, and seas. Their tasks are to support the creation and growth of plants, flowers, and trees; to nurture wild birds and animals and protect the places they inhabit; and to watch over all living creatures, including human beings. Early Greeks saw all natural phenomena as full of life, radiating the energy of divinity. Such beings create the "spirit of a place."

When the pagan traditions were suppressed with the rise of Christianity, the nature spirits shrank; they became smaller in size and influence. Their haunts became reduced to rural lands and wild forests where stories about them were preserved as part of local lore. Peaseblossom, Cobweb, Moth, and Mustardseed are the imaginative remnants of that tradition, strongly related to animal and vegetable life. Titania's instructions to them to be "kind and courteous" to Bottom suggest that they are small and innocuous, altogether delightful:

> Hop in his walks and gambol in his eyes.
> Feed him with apricots and dewberries,
> With purple grapes, green figs, and mulberries;
> The honeybags steal from the humble-bees,
> And for night tapers crop their waxen thighs

And light them at the fiery glow-worms' eyes,
To have my love to bed, and to arise;
And pluck the wings from painted butterflies
To fan the *moonbeams* from his sleeping eyes.

(III, i, 147–55)

(A third type of spirit not in this play features in one to be discussed later. This type is associated with the four elements [earth, water, air, and fire] and, logically, are called "elementals." These are like the spiritual essence of the element, the personification of its inner nature. Earth spirits are dubbed "gnomes" [and look much like the dwarves depicted in "Snow White" or the goblins of Gringotts bank in the Harry Potter books], water spirits are called "ondines," air spirits are referred to as "sylphs," and fire spirits are called "salamanders." Shakespeare creates a spirit of air in the character of the appropriately-named Ariel in *The Tempest*.)

Puck seems to be a type apart from these three, a residue of the folkloric, probably Celtic traditions that spoke of a "pook" or "puck." He is a mischief-maker, prone to playing jokes on human beings. While he protests to Oberon that he did not maliciously and intentionally sow confusion among the young lovers, he certainly enjoys the resulting anarchic turmoil: "those things do best please me / That befall prepost'rously." (III, ii, 120–1) And he provides a detached perspective on the silliness of ever-changing human loves and hates when he says, "Lord, what fools these mortals be!" (III, ii, 115)

Puck is an especially deft shape-changer, a mercurial creature of variable form who can even make himself invisible. You cannot imagine Oberon and Titania being other than who they are, but Puck has the ability to transform into other shapes and beings. When the working-men are shocked and terrified by the apparition of Bottom with an ass's head and race away into the forest, Puck plays a practical joke on them:

I'll follow you, I'll lead you about a round,
Through bog, through bush, through brake, through brier.
Sometime a horse I'll be, sometime a hound,
A hog, a headless bear, sometime a fire,
And neigh, and bark, and grunt, and roar, and burn,
Like horse, hound, hog, bear, fire, at every turn.

(III, i, 95–9)

Puck's ability to change shape was not a new idea in Shakespeare's time. We know that he read, was influenced by, and drew plots from the Roman writer Ovid's *Metamorphoses*. True to its title, the stories and myths that Ovid includes in his book all feature transformations.[238] In these tales the boundary between forms in the visible world is a permeable one: human beings can change into trees (as Daphne did when chased by Apollo) or become flowers (as Narcissus did when he fell in love with his own image). Inhabiting the realm beneath the changeable Moon, faeries can both materialize and shape-shift at will. These semi-divinities are not gods and goddesses; they are creatures of spirit intermediate between mortals and immortals and in this play they have physical presence and drive the plot.

Earlier the faeries of folklore emblemized the forces of fate or nature prone to doing active harm or creating chaos (like the disturbances in the weather and the seasons mentioned by Titania) and so had to be placated. But the spirits in *A Midsummer Night's Dream* are mainly beneficent. Indeed, our view of faeries as small and harmless creatures results largely from Shakespeare's depiction of them in this play. Oberon reassures us of their nature: unlike the "ghosts" and "damned spirits" gone to their "wormy beds" at daybreak, Oberon protests that he and his train are "spirits of another sort" (III, ii, 382–89), capable of still being active at dawn. Shakespeare's faery folk may be mischievous but they are not malevolent.

For most Elizabethans, the various non-human spirits inhabiting the space between Earth and Moon were imaginatively real. Either an inborn gift or an enhanced perception, perhaps mediated by a natural substance (like too much wine!), might enable a human being to see these subtle entities—or you might see them by grace, like that shown to Bottom who enjoys a dalliance with the faery Queen. In the modern day, some might be more inclined to think of faeries as the embodiment of an "aliveness" in the plants and flowers of the natural world. Whatever they are, how can we not be charmed by the appearance of these diverse spirits in Shakespeare's play, whether they are sparring over a child or waiting on the phlegmatic Bottom?

Bottom Transformed with an Ass's Head

The changeability of love under the Moon's spell is dramatized by Titania's falling in love with a mortal who has an ass's head, the aptly-named Bottom. (Since another word for one's rear end is "ass," Bottom's fate may have been encoded in his name. In line with the Moon as the dominant symbol of the play, I cannot resist adding that to expose one's bottom is now called "mooning"!)

From classical times on, the ass had mainly negative associations. Followers of the cult of Orpheus, for example, considered this animal to be particularly impure.[239] To this day, it is still an insult to call someone an "ass," suggesting an obvious lack of intelligence. And of course the Elizabethan worldview would have seen any lowering of the human to the animal as a deplorable descent from its natural position in the cosmic hierarchy. The ass was a symbol of the human body with its instincts, sexual drives, and limited five senses, so it is significant that Titania tells Bottom that she will "purge thy mortal grossness so / That thou shalt like an airy spirit go." (III, i, 142–3)[240]

And yet … Jesus rode into Jerusalem on an ass, which is thought to reflect his unpretentiousness as well as the triumph of the spiritual over the physical. Positively, the ass is interpreted as a symbol of humility, patience, and courage. Bottom does indeed show a certain bravery when he is abandoned by his fellows in the forest:

> I see their knavery. This is to make an ass of me, to fright
> me, if they could; but I will not stir from this place, do
> what they can. I will walk up and down here, and I will
> sing, that they shall hear I am not afraid.
>
> (III, i, 106–9)

The ass was associated with the court fool, who sometimes sported a cap with ass's ears. Though onlookers might laugh at the dunce's cap, the fool was often one of the smartest and wittiest members of the court. And Bottom does function as a kind of court jester when he entertains the group of nobles in the last act of the play.[241]

We may initially judge Bottom to be vain (he wants to play all the parts in "Pyramus and Thisbe") and unintelligent (because he mixes up the meaning of words, as when he says he will "aggravate" instead of

The opposite elements of air and earth mingle in the amorous meeting of Titania (Tina Benko) and Bottom (Max Casella). Photo from Julie Taymor's stage production of A Midsummer Night's Dream *at the Polonsky Shakespeare Center in New York, October 30, 2013. (Sara Krulwich/The New York Times/Redux)*

"moderate" his voice to roar as gently as a dove [I, ii, 67]). Yet Bottom is not as much of a clown as it first seems. He is actually a type of Holy Fool, one who has become like a little child and can therefore enter the Kingdom of Heaven. Of all the visitors to the forest, Bottom is the only one to see the faeries and to be loved by their Queen. And "bully Bottom" is completely unfazed by this experience. Not only does he not panic; he is not even startled.

Bottom has a quality of innocence, which results in his relating better to the tiny attendant faeries than to the amorous Titania. As Harold Bloom points out, he acts like a gentleman, a person of a much higher social status in the human world, with courtesy and appreciation for everything the attending faeries do for him.[242] While the lovers are hysterically shouting at each other and chasing phantoms through the woods, Bottom behaves with unusual aplomb in the face of his strange and wondrous elevation into another world.

Bottom's equanimity is in line with his temperament. Each of Shakespeare's plays commonly features a character who is the perfect embodiment of the humor associated with the element of the play's zodiacal sign. Since this play is keyed to the water sign Cancer, Bottom is a classic phlegmatic. This personality type is linked (appropriately for this play) with the Moon and with an excess of the water element. Some of the words in the list provided earlier for this type (in Chapter 2) are "steady," "calm/relaxed," and "tranquil." Bottom's composure and courtesy to the faeries derives from his phlegmatic character. He alone of anyone in the forest keeps his head about him. Titania may rhapsodize seductively about her passion for him, saying,

> I pray thee, gentle mortal, sing again.
> Mine ear is much enamour'd of thy note;
> So is mine eye enthralled to thy shape;
> And thy fair virtue's force perforce doth move me
> On the first view to say, to swear, I love thee.
>
> (III, i, 121–5)

But Bottom has a clear sense of himself and the situation, replying, "Methinks, mistress, you should have little reason for that. And yet, to say the truth, reason and love keep little company together nowadays …" (III, i, 126–8). His comment, in light of what is being enacted on stage, is right on! Consequently, Bottom is a grounding force in the play, the only one (ironically) to "keep his head" when everyone around him is losing theirs. Bottom is a weaver, and, appropriately, Harold Bloom mentions that in that craft's terminology a "bottom" is the center of the skein around which the wool is wound. In a sense, Bottom *is* the stabilizing and unmoving center of the story, and, as Bloom says, "always sound at the core."[243]

Though Shakespeare may have started out portraying the "rude mechanicals" (as Puck dismissively calls them) as lower-class types who mangle language and misunderstand acting, he ends up by creating Bottom as one of the crowning glories of not only this play but also his entire oeuvre. We ultimately view Bottom, with his sincere concern for the affrighting of the ladies, his complete acceptance of his transformation and induction into faeryland, his clear-headedness while transported, and his earnest efforts to perform the story of Pyramus and Thisbe, as one of the most delightful of Shakespeare's characters. Shakespeare has transformed the clown into a comedic yet wise and lovable figure.

Under The Sphere of the Moon

The changeability of the characters, as they transform and are transformed, and our disorientation about the time during which the action occurs is very much in line with beliefs about the Elizabethan cosmos. According to the ancient, medieval, and Renaissance worldview, everything in the realm below the Moon's sphere is characterized by "mutabilitie," so that all created things and all circumstances are inevitably and constantly changing. In part this is due to the continually shifting proportions of the four elements that make up the physical world. Consequently observations and conclusions about material life based on sense impressions cannot be trusted—and might even deliberately, almost mischievously (like Puck), mislead. So it was accepted in Shakespeare's time that under the Moon's rays human beings could easily experience CONFUSION and DELUSION.

The very quality of moonlight harmonizes with the belief in the physical world's fluidity. In moonlight everything loses color, and the world has only shades of gray or black. Things that by day are separate at night merge into one. What has a definite shape in the bright light of day can morph into another form altogether at night. Theseus refers to this when he says, "in the night, imagining some fear, / How easy is a bush suppos'd a bear!" (V, i, 21–2)

In the Moon's sphere, which is the invisible plane immediately above our material one and the first step up on the "ladder" of creation, nothing has a solid form or a permanent boundary. It consists of a sort of "mind-stuff" or floating energy that assumes shapes either randomly or through human intention. Everything flows into everything else.[244]

Some believe that it is possible to rise to this invisible level of the Moon during sleep. Dreams that you might have then while visiting this sphere do not echo the previous day's earthly experiences but reflect contact with more subtle worlds. The quality of such dreams is different, more vivid and more profound than ordinary ones.

Ascending to the sphere of the Moon, or being taken over by lunar energies that descend to the physical level, was thought to be dangerous because you might be driven mad. In particular, people in love were "lunatic," that is, under the spell of the Moon ("luna" is the Latin word for the Moon). We still speak of individuals as "madly" in love, literally "moon-mad," suggesting that love is a form of craziness. This belief was not new even in Shakespeare's time. It appears two thousand years earlier in Plato's dialogues, specifically in the *Phaedrus*. What is different about the philosopher's beliefs to ours, though, is that Socrates speaks quite favorably of this type of madness because the lover may actually be more blessed than someone who is rational:

> 'False is the tale' that when a lover is at hand favor ought rather to be accorded to one who does not love, on the ground that the former is mad, and the latter sound of mind. That would be right if it were an invariable truth that madness is an evil, but in reality, the greatest blessings come by way of madness, indeed of madness that is heaven-sent. It was when they were mad that the prophetess at Delphi and the priestesses at Dodona achieved so much for which both states and individuals in Greece are thankful; when sane they did little or nothing.[245]

The Means of Entering the Moon's Realm: the Faculty of Imagination

When the Moon's rays fall on you, you might behave foolishly or you might have awe-inspiring visions like Bottom's. His experience comes unbidden, as a grace, but philosophers and esotericists believed (and still believe) that it was (and is) possible to climb the rungs of the cosmic ladder through the purposeful use of the imagination. In fact, the sphere of the Moon (as well as the others above it) can <u>only</u> be accessed through the faculty of imagination.

These days we are often told to "dream big" or to "hold on to your dreams." What people mean by this is to hold an image in your mind, charged with purposeful intention and envisioned repeatedly and persistently, of a desired outcome. This is actually a technique used in the practice of magic, defined by Mark Booth as "the application of a scientific way of thinking to the supernatural."[246]

The Elizabethans had two quite opposite views of the imaginative faculty. On the one hand, as "fancy" or ungoverned imagination it could create illusions that would only confuse and delude the experiencer. On the other hand, it might bring the gift of "far-seeing," with the ability to perceive subtle realms with more than earth-dimmed physical sight. Another kind of seeing, a more subtle perception, could overshadow the more circumscribed rational thought. Thus the Moon represents an intuitive and super-sensible way of knowing that is usually opposed to logic.

Theseus' famous speech on the power of the imagination, probably the best known one from the play, picks up on both of these meanings. Theseus is initially a skeptic, dismissive of Hippolyta's observation that the lovers' stories are strange and wonderful, and convinced that they are fabrications of "fancy":

> I never may believe
> These antique fables, nor these fairy toys.
> Lovers and madmen have such seething brains,
> Such shaping fantasies, that apprehend
> More than cool reason ever comprehends.
> The lunatic, the lover, and the poet
> Are of imagination all compact [composed].
> One sees more devils than vast hell can hold:
> That is, the madman. The lover, all as frantic,
> Sees Helen's beauty in a brow of Egypt.
> The poet's eye, in a fine frenzy rolling,
> Doth glance from heaven to earth, from earth to heaven,
> And as imagination bodies forth
> The forms of things unknown, the poet's pen
> Turns them to shapes and gives to airy nothing
> A local habitation and a name.
>
> (V, i, 2–17)

But the tone of Theseus's speech has changed by the end. The poet's ability to spin inspired creations out of his imagination, as a spider spins a web out of its own body, has even in Theseus' thought an overtone of divinity. The poet bridges "from heaven to earth, from earth to heaven," potentially bringing a gift of insight from a higher dimension which others can share. In this view, using the imagination is using the eyes of the mind that are the organs of the soul.[247]

But despite this implied spiritual origin of creativity, for Theseus love and creativity are only the "tricks" of strong imagination. Hippolyta protests: "But all the story of the night told over, / And all their minds transfigured so together, / More witnesseth than fancy's images, / And grows to something of great constancy; / But howsoever, strange and admirable." (V, i, 23–7)

Throughout the drama Shakespeare plays with the tension between imagination's potential either to delude or inspire, as well as with the opposite claims of imagination and reason.[248] The most comic moment comes when he has Lysander suddenly transfer his affection from Hermia to Helena, asserting that he does this for entirely rational reasons. After Puck has squeezed the juice of the purple flower in Lysander's eyes and Helena startles him awake, he jolts from sleep, declaring "And run through fire I will for thy sweet sake. / Transparent Helena ..." (II, ii 109–10). When the bewildered Helena reminds Lysander that he loves Hermia, Lysander attempts to justify his newly-fired feelings for her by saying:

> Not Hermia but Helena I love.
> Who will not change a raven for a dove?
> The will of man is by his reason swayed,
> And reason says you are the worthier maid.
> Things growing are not ripe until their season,
> So I, being young, till now ripe not to reason.
> And, touching now the point of human skill,
> Reason becomes the marshal to my will,
> And leads me to your eyes, where I o'erlook
> Love's stories written in Love's richest book.
>
> (II, ii, 119–28)

Of course, despite Lysander's stress on "reason" as the motivation for his change of heart (he uses the word four times in his justification), reason has nothing to do with his change of heart. Though he believes that he is master of his own feelings and that he has switched love objects through thinking intelligently, Shakespeare clearly shows that we are deluded if we think we are always acting rationally. The real reason Lysander changes is due to the faeries' intervention, symbols of a higher fate.

Under the rays of the Moon, though, nothing is constant. While watching the rustics present their mangled version of the Greek myth, even Theseus and Hippolyta switch perspectives. She criticizes the performance as "the silliest stuff that ever I heard," while Theseus is suddenly more forgiving:

> THESEUS: The best in this kind are but shadows, and the
> worst are no worse if imagination amend them.
> HIPPOLYTA: It must be your imagination, then, and not
> theirs.
> THESEUS: If we imagine no worse of them than they of
> themselves, they may pass for excellent men.
>
> (V, i, 207–12)

Now imagination becomes not just the original inspiration of the poet-playwright, but also a gift offered by the audience to those acting out the poet's vision. The poet's gift is what came from "heaven to earth"; the spectators return it "from earth to heaven."[249]

The Play—and Life?—Is But a Dream

> Row, row, row your boat
> Gently down the stream.
> Merrily, merrily, merrily, merrily,
> Life is but a dream.   —Children's song

Shakespeare pulls off an extraordinary trick in this play: he weaves together the experiences of four entirely different groups of characters into a unified whole through the power of his imagination. So it is deeply meaningful that the most memorable character in the play is Bottom—a weaver! Weaving is the intertwining of many different threads—or in the case of the play, many different levels of being—into a harmonious whole. The spider, as web-weaver, represents another aspect of weaving: the almost magical ability of nature to create something out of apparently nothing, out of its own inner substance. Consequently, weaving is often thought to have been invented by or characteristic of gods or goddesses.[250] It is thus a symbol of inspired creative power. The Moon in particular was thought to be a weaver of destiny, as were the three Fates who were also spinners.[251]

One way in which Shakespeare unifies the play is to ground the action in symbolism related to the Moon, mentioned by each new group—and to bring the Moon onstage as a participant. Another is to have everyone eventually meet in one specific location: the mysterious woods near the Duke's palace. And, of course, whether they know it or not, the various groups all interact with one another—the noble Theseus and Hippolyta with the lovers, the lovers with the faeries, the faeries with the Athenian workingmen—and finally nobles, lovers, and workingmen are together at the wedding celebration watching the working-mens' presentation of their mangled version of "Pyramus and Thisbe." The faeries, who live in the realm between Earth and Moon, lurk in the background there too.

The mixing of entirely different social classes—and entirely different levels of beings—is daring, though entirely appropriate to the mixed world under the influence of the Moon. Theseus' startled response to the description of the laborers' version of "Pyramus and Thisbe" is a question we might ask about the whole play: "How shall we find the concord of this discord?" (V, i, 60) Shakespeare's answer lies in the speeches about dogs and music by both Theseus and Hippolyta as they enter the woods in the morning to hunt. These lines seem like a pointless insertion, irrelevant to what we have previously witnessed, but Shakespeare never includes dialogue unless it has a purpose. The point of this digression is to justify throwing together such disparate people, such different dimensions, in the same play.

> THESEUS: My love shall hear the music of my hounds.
> Uncouple in the western valley; let them go....
> We will, fair Queen, up to the mountain's top,
> And mark the musical confusion
> Of hounds and echo in conjunction.
> HIPPOLYTA: I was with Hercules and Cadmus once,
> When in a wood of Crete they bayed the bear
> With hounds of Sparta. Never did I hear
> Such gallant chiding; for besides the groves,
> The skies, the fountains, every region near
> Seemed all one mutual cry. I never heard
> So musical a discord, such sweet thunder.
>   (IV, i, 103–4, 106–15)

Why the choice of a metaphor involving dogs' barking and baying? One answer may be that a dog was always depicted as accompanying the Moon. So here again, like Helena's describing herself as a "spaniel," is imagery consistent with the astrological symbolism of the play. The realm of the Moon, teeming with vague shapes and unformed creative stuff, seems like a jumbled chaos, like the cacophony of dogs barking, yet out of it can be generated "So musical a discord, such sweet thunder." Dogs are introduced because Theseus and Hippolyta intend to hunt, but the hunt is called off. Hunting would be inappropriate since it is an activity that resonates with Mars, and this play, being a comedy, is assigned to the realm of Venus. Once the lovers are discovered, it is back to Theseus' palace for partying and play-performing—much more in accord with Venus.

And discord is resolved in the end: the human couples are appropriately matched; Oberon and Titania are harmoniously reunited. The play ends with not just one but three weddings, which according to the comic pattern must conclude this type of play. As the festivities come to an end, everyone will head to their chambers. Even the usually ever-rational and highly unimaginative Theseus acknowledges the magical quality of dark night: "The iron tongue of midnight hath told twelve. / Lovers, to bed; 'tis almost fairy time. / I fear we shall out*sleep* the coming morn / As much as we this *night* have overwatched." (V, i, 346–9) In his request, he also reminds us of the principal associations with the Moon: "sleep" and "night."

The faeries appear right on cue after Theseus' lines, the quick Puck first. He slips in, and though he warns of the dangers of night by mentioning the "hungry lion" that roars and the wolf that "behowls the *moon*," Oberon reassures us that the faeries are there to frolic and to bless the bride-beds with song and dance, guaranteeing the couples' fertility (associated with the Moon) and foretelling (a lunar power) the future of both them and their children:

> And the issue there create
> Ever shall be fortunate.
> So shall all the couples three
> Ever true in loving be,
> And the blots of Nature's hand
> Shall not in their issue stand.
> Never mole, harelip, nor scar
> Nor mark prodigious such as are
> Despised in nativity

Shall upon their children be.
… each several chamber bless
Through this palace with sweet peace;
And the owner of it blest
Ever shall in safety rest.

(V, ii, 35–44, 47–50)

Puck was invoked at the beginning of the play when Theseus asked his Master of Revels, Philostrate, to "Awake the pert and nimble spirit of mirth" and so it is fitting that Puck has the last word. Breaking out of his role and speaking directly to the audience, he delivers a common appeal to the audience to forgive the actors' faults and to applaud the performance. But he also offers disappointed play-watchers (if there are any) an astonishing perspective on the performance:

If we shadows have offended,
Think but this, and all is mended:
That you have but *slumbered* here,
While these visions did appear;
And this weak and idle theme,
No more yielding but a *dream* …

(Epilogue, 1–6)

The entire play, Puck suggests, may be only a dream. We have moved from the literal dream of Hermia to the creativity-stimulating vision of Bottom to the startling implication that the entire play may be nothing but a dream. And truthfully it is a "dream" on several levels. It is first of all the "dream" of the playwright, who has conjured out of his own imagination all of the players and their passions and fixed them on the page. It is the actors' "dream" too since it is their imaginations that give life—action and emotion—to the characters on the stage. And it is the audience's "dream" as well. Willingly suspending disbelief, we become enrapt in a dreamlike state as we enter into the fictive reality of the staged dramas, watching imagined events portrayed by actors who are but "shadows." Yet we may respond quite powerfully to this fiction that engages our emotions, our minds, and our hearts.

So whose "dream" really is the "Midsummer Night's Dream"? And where is the boundary between the dream-state and the waking-state?

Shakespeare is only one of a long line of philosophically-inclined minds to contemplate this. The Chinese sage Zhuang Zhou (or alternatively Zhuangzi, alive in the fourth century BCE) raised this question after having a famous dream. He dreamed that he was a butterfly. Upon awakening, he asked himself: "Am I a man dreaming that I am a butterfly? Or am I a butterfly dreaming that I am a man?" The account of Zhuang Zhou's dream ends with his comment that the experience is an illustration of the "transformation of things."[252]

And transformation is the essence of all the characters' experiences in *A Midsummer Night's Dream*. These transformations are mainly due to the power of love, symbolized by the flower's juice, which operates to properly match or harmonize the young lovers to one another. Titania too is changed by her experience of loving Bottom; from angrily refusing to hand over the changeling child to Oberon (who might more appropriately train a boy), she moves to harmonious reconciliation with the faery king. And Titania's adoring acceptance of the transformed Bottom is especially important. Bottom with his ass's head symbolizes the peculiar condition of humanity: half animal in body and instinct and half divine in reason and aspiration, a creature that spans more than one dimension. Yet looking with loving eyes can change our judgment of both Bottom and ourselves, for "Things base and vile, holding no quantity, / Love can transpose to form and dignity." (I, i, 232–3) Titania's love for Bottom is emblematic of the soul's love for the body, despite its imperfections, and for the human, despite its failings.

The restored Bottom is the only one to wake from his dream with his memory intact, though with his expressive ability limited. Since it is impossible to describe a transcendent experience using the language of the five senses, no wonder Bottom confuses them in trying to recount his dream:

> I have had a most rare vision. I have had a dream past
> the wit of man to say what dream it was. Man is but an
> ass if he go about t'expound this dream. Methought I
> was—there is no man can tell what. Methought I was
> and methought I had—but man is but a patched fool if
> he will offer to say what methought I had. The eye of man
> hath not heard, the ear of man hath not seen, man's hand

is not able to taste, his tongue to conceive, nor his heart
to report what my dream was.

(IV, i, 199–207)[253]

Bottom's deeply significant speech exalts imagination over both reason (thought) and the five senses, reminding us how untrustworthy both
are. This provokes yet another important philosophical question: How
do we distinguish between what we think is real and what we think is
illusion in our waking lives? The contrast between appearance and reality
is one of Shakespeare's favorite themes, dramatized by young women in
his plays who disguise themselves as men, by people who only appear
to be dead (like the slandered Hero in *Much Ado about Nothing* or Hermione in *The Winter's Tale*) but come back to life, or, more subtly, by
characters who deliberately dissemble, like Macbeth who vows to "mock
the time with fairest show. / False face must hide what the false heart
doth know." (*Macbeth*: I, vii, 81–2)

Under the sphere of the Moon, distinguishing between what is real
and what is not is difficult if not impossible. The dilemma of discerning
the real as against the illusory is complicated since we have to ask ourselves "How awake are we normally?" We think we are fully conscious
while going through our day's activities, but we are often going through
the motions while "on automatic pilot." And sometimes we are "daydreaming," tuning out space and time during the daylight hours, creating fantastic images analogous to those of our night dreams. And when
today becomes yesterday, the events of today are only memories. And
once they are memories, they become elusive and elastic, like the figures
in our dreams, in that we often cannot remember exactly what happened
or when or even to whom.[254]

Perhaps our experience in the theater is similar to that of the characters we have been watching.[255] We, like the lovers and the Athenian
artisans, have been transported into the realm of the imagination while
we have been absorbed in the play. But when the lights come up, we stir,
like dreamers roused from sleep out of darkness, and the images we have
seen on stage fade … though some like Puck, the spirit of childhood, and
Bottom, the imperturbable man, live in our minds far longer, as we exit
the theater and return to our ordinary lives carrying with us the inspiration for our own potential imaginative creations.

CHAPTER 8

The Hidden Astrological Key to
Romeo and Juliet
Gemini and its Ruler Mercury

Here's much to do with hate, but more with love.
Why, then, *O brawling love, O loving hate* —(*Romeo and Juliet:* I, i, 168–9)

The Story

In Verona, Italy two equally noble families, the Montagues and the Capulets, clash, much to the displeasure of the town's Prince who threatens further fighting with a sentence of death. The lovesick Romeo, a Montague, who has been pining for Rosaline, is persuaded to go in disguise with friends to the Capulets' masked ball where, as fate arranges it, he meets Juliet, the Capulets' only daughter. They instantly fall in love. After the party Romeo sneaks into the Capulets' garden where he sees Juliet on her balcony, and they exchange lovers' vows. Romeo visits Friar Laurence, who agrees to marry them secretly, hoping to heal the two families' enmity.

Immediately after the wedding the angry Tybalt, Juliet's cousin, accosts some Montagues in the street and, trying to keep the peace, Romeo inadvertently allows Tybalt to stab his friend Mercutio to death. Enraged, Romeo fights and kills Tybalt. Instead of condemning him to death, the Prince exiles Romeo to Mantua. To distract the distraught Juliet (who is really grieving for Romeo's banishment and not for Tybalt's death), her parents insist that she marry the Count Paris.

To help Juliet, Friar Laurence gives her an herbal concoction that will make her appear to be dead. The plan is that the Friar will send word to the banished Romeo so that he can rescue her from the family vault, and the two can then escape. But another messenger, who does not know of the ruse, reaches the exiled Romeo first. Romeo speeds to the tomb where he encounters and kills Paris, assumes that Juliet is dead, and swallows poison that he has obtained from an apothecary. Juliet awakes from the plant's spell, sees the dead Romeo, and stabs herself to death. The families, united in grief, vow a new peace.

The Sign Gemini and its Ruler Mercury

Shakespeare, the experienced dramatist, usually grabs the audience's attention in opening scenes by portraying violent acts or visitations from the supernatural—such as the appearance of the Ghost in scene I of *Hamlet* or the three Witches hovering over their cauldron at the opening of *Macbeth*. This tactic is still favored by modern storytellers, novelists, and scriptwriters for television and the movies. After the dramatic opening, Shakespeare then introduces the main characters, gives some necessary back-story, and reveals through language and imagery the thematic basis of the drama.

So *Romeo and Juliet* is unusual in that the play begins with a Prologue that announces both the plot and the point of the story. In the form of a sonnet, a perfectly rhymed fourteen-line poem, the Prologue begins

> Two households, both alike in dignity,
> In fair Verona, where we lay our scene,
> From ancient grudge break to new mutiny,
> Where civil blood makes civil hands unclean.
> From forth the fatal loins of these two foes
> A pair of star-crossed lovers take their life;
> Whose misadventur'd piteous overthrows
> Doth with their death bury their parents' strife.

So we know that we are in Verona, Italy where Mediterranean passions run high and that the play will concern itself with TWO households "both alike in dignity," TWO lovers, and TWO foes, whose bitter hatred of each other has erupted again. Shakespeare strongly emphasizes both the equal status and the bitter opposition of the two enemy families. So when looking for a connection to zodiacal symbolism, we should look for a sign that is "double-figured," with two evenly balanced elements.

Only two signs have balanced doubles in them: Pisces, represented symbolically by two interlinked fish swimming in opposite directions, and Gemini, represented by twins or a glyph of two vertical lines connected by horizontal lines at the top and bottom. As we shall see, a multitude of observations regarding language, characterization, and plot all point to the sign GEMINI as definitely providing the archetypal foundation of the play.

The usual symbol for the sign Gemini shows TWO upright straight lines. The number two has great philosophical and metaphysical significance, for it holds the secret to creation. For centuries questions have been asked: How does the One become the many? How does creation happen? In ancient philosophy, the answer was that it begins with the One appearing to divide itself into two. The resulting polarization is multiplied further into numerous opposites that characterize the visible world and create our experience of it, with all its contrasted dualities.

> Our mind divides the world into heaven and earth, day and night, light and darkness, right and left, man and woman, I and you— and the more strongly we sense the separation between these poles, whatever they may be, the more powerfully do we also sense their unity.[256]

All these polarities desire either a balance, which holds the tension of the opposites in suspension, or a resolution back into unity or harmony (symbolized by the marriage of two human beings, or, on a grander scale,

The symbol for the zodiacal sign Gemini has two upright lines, representing the multiple dualities that characterize the created world. These are either in balance or in conflict, with the potential also for each to turn into its opposite—day into night, summer into winter, peace into war—and back again. The lines at the top and bottom connecting the two pillars signify that the opposites are inextricably linked or contained in the One.

the marriage of heaven and earth). Failing to achieve either of these goals, the opposites may continually wage war with each other. These ideas are embedded in the zodiacal sign of Gemini.

> It was customary among the ancients to regard the Great Spirit under the dual aspect of GEMINI the Twins … In Egypt, as elsewhere, the palpable dualism of Nature—Male and Female, Day and Night, Morning and Evening, Summer and Winter, Sun and Moon, Light and Darkness, Heaven and Earth—was typified as a double Being. "In most of the [Egyptian] hymns," says De Rouge, "we come across this idea of the double Being who engendereth Himself, the Soul in two Twins—to signify two Persons never to be separated."[257]

The polarity of two equal and opposed principles is reflected in the violent antipathy between the Montagues and Capulets, an absolute necessity for this dramatic story. Throughout the play, opposites are starkly contrasted: youth opposed to age, war to peace, happiness to despair, light to dark, and of course love to hate.

The play's connection to the sign Gemini is particularly revealed through the uniqueness of Shakespeare's language in this play.[258] A special hallmark of *Romeo and Juliet* is the number of phrases containing diametrical OPPOSITES, known as "oxymorons" (from the Greek meaning "sharp-dull"), which combine contradictory words in one phrase.[259] The antipathy between the two warring families is thus embedded in the play's very language. When Romeo first hears about the renewed clash between members of the two families in Verona's central square, he protests:

> Here's much to do with hate, but more with love.
> Why then, O brawling love, O loving hate …
> O heavy lightness! Serious vanity …
> Feather of lead, bright smoke, cold fire, sick health,
> Still-waking sleep, that is not what it is!
>
> (I, i, 168–9, 171, 173–4)

Juliet speaks similarly. After meeting Romeo and falling in love with him, she hears from her Nurse who he really is. Shocked, Juliet complains,

My only love sprung from my only hate!
Too early seen unknown, and known too late!
Prodigious birth of love it is to me
That I must love a loathed enemy.

(I, v, 135–8)

Another balanced pair of opposites appears in Romeo and Juliet's families. Rarely in Shakespeare's dramas do we have both parents living and participating in the play's action as prominent authority figures. In most of the plays we see single parents. In *A Midsummer Night's Dream* Hermia's father Egeus alone generates the conflict by insisting that his daughter Hermia marry Demetrius; there is no mother to soften his stubborn will. In *As You Like It* Rosalind's father, the Duke, is the sole parent and his banishment before the play begins is crucial to the action. Again, no maternal figure plays a role in the story. In *King Lear* the father is the sole instigator of the drama, by demanding eloquent (and insincere) declarations of love from his three daughters. Yet in *Romeo and Juliet* Shakespeare gives us two equally balanced couples: Lord and Lady Montague, and Lord and Lady Capulet. In no other play is this so.

The play strongly emphasizes another important correlation with the sign Gemini. In the sequence of the zodiacal signs beginning with Aries and ending with Pisces, Gemini is the first of the AIR signs. The air element has to do with the mental or intellectual level of human beings and is associated with the development of the MIND and the subsequent ability to translate THOUGHTS into WORDS. Shakespeare's audience would have appreciated the fact that the positive manifestation of mental talents is fluent and articulate speech. The downside is being GLIB, talkative without saying anything of substance, SUPERFICIAL, mentally busy but endlessly distracted, ingratiating but "phony"—and "mercurial" in the sense of being vacillating and undependable.

To clinch the play's symbolic resonance with the sign Gemini, the planet associated with Gemini as its "ruler," Mercury, actually shows up as a character in the play! The name of one of the principal characters, Romeo's friend, is an obvious clue. "Mercutio" is the living embodiment of some facets of the symbolic Mercury, as would have been obvious to Shakespeare's audience. Here is a short poem capturing some of Mercury's qualities:

Who's fond of life and jest and pleasure;
Who vacillates and changes ever?
Who loves attention without measure?
Why, Gemini.[260]

This well describes Mercutio, whom we first meet the evening that Romeo and his friends go to the masked ball at the Capulets' home. (Mercury loves disguises.) Mercutio is a talker, someone who loves to hear himself rattle on, a true child of Mercury. He reveals his gift of gab in a very long speech triggered by Romeo's reference to a dream he had that night:

O, then I see Queen Mab hath been with you....
She is the fairies' midwife, and she comes
In shape no bigger than an agate stone
On the fore-finger of an alderman,
Drawn with a team of little atomi
Athwart men's noses as they lie asleep.
Her wagon spokes made of long spinners' legs;
The cover, of the wings of grasshoppers;
Her traces, of the moonshine's wat'ry beams;
Her collars, of the smallest spider web;
Her whip, of cricket's bone, the lash of film;
Her wagoner, a small grey-coated gnat
Not half so big as a round little worm
Pricked from the lazy finger of a maid.
Her chariot is an empty hazelnut
Made by the joiner squirrel or old grub,
Time out o' mind the fairies' coachmakers.
And in this state she gallops night by night
Through lovers' brains, and then they dream of love;
O'er courtiers' knees, that dream on curtsies straight;
O'er ladies' lips, who straight on kisses dream,
Which oft the angry Mab with blisters plagues
Because their breath with sweetmeats tainted are.

(I, iv, 53, 55–76)

Romeo interrupts this extended riff on Queen Mab (which goes on for another eighteen and a half lines!) with the injunction, "Peace, peace, Mercutio, peace! / *Thou talk'st of nothing.*" (I, iv, 95–6)

Mercutio is just having fun here by using Romeo's reference to his dream as a jumping off point to conjure images of the fairy queen, to make up the details of her tiny transport, and to catalogue the dreams she triggers as she gallops through sleepers' brains. It is a long speech with an entirely different quality than, for instance, Hamlet's equally long speech beginning "To be or not to be" that is packed with profound thought. Mercutio's improvisation is only for the purpose of entertainment, which Romeo accurately perceives by saying his friend talks of "nothing." The Gemini type is known to be fond of inducing laughter through JOKES and WIT. Shakespeare's audience, who knew the fundamentals of astrology, would immediately have recognized Mercutio as the type who runs off at the mouth at every opportunity and enjoys the joke himself.

Shakespeare also introduces a feminine version of Mercury in the person of another character who loves to talk. The female counterpart to Mercutio is Juliet's Nurse, whose first appearance on stage noticeably parallels Mercutio's. She dominates the scene in which Lady Capulet meets with Juliet to encourage her to marry her cousin, the "valiant Paris." Taking her cue from Lady Capulet's reference to Juliet's being of a "pretty" (that is marriageable) age, the Nurse reminisces garrulously about Juliet's weaning.

> I remember it well.
> 'Tis since the earthquake now eleven years,
> And she was weaned—I never shall forget it—
> Of all the days of the year upon that day,
> For I had then laid wormwood to my dug,
> Sitting in the sun under the dovehouse wall.
> My lord and you were then at Mantua.
> Nay, I do bear a brain! …
> And since that time it is eleven years,
> For then she could stand high-lone. Nay, by th'rood,
> She could have run and waddled all about,
> For even the day before, she broke her brow,

And then my husband—God be with his soul,
A was a merry man!—took up the child....

(I, iii, 24–31, 37–42)

Lady Capulet breaks in, much as Romeo did, to bid the Nurse stop: "Enough of this. I pray thee, hold thy peace." The Nurse, however, enjoying the sound of her own voice (for all of thirty-three lines) and the joke about Juliet's falling over, continues talking and repeats the joke. At that point even the young Juliet interrupts to stop her, saying, "And stint thou too, I pray thee, Nurse, say I." (I, iii, 51, 60) The Nurse is obviously another example of the connection the play has to the astrological symbolism of Gemini.

The Nurse's reminiscences are especially irritating because, unlike Mercutio's lines, hers are repetitive, true to the automatic nature of memory, as her mind recalls established associations she has with the incident she recounts. Her mind is clearly operating in mental ruts, in marked contrast to Mercutio's brilliant inventiveness. She and Mercutio illustrate yet another polarity, showing two different ways in which the mind can operate. Like Mercutio, though, she ends with the same sexual joke that he uses one scene later. When the toddler Juliet had fallen upon her face, the Nurse's husband had joked, "Thou wilt fall backward when thou hast more wit." (I, iii, 44) Mercutio's is a wittier and more educated version of the same joke because he makes a pun (a play on two meanings of the same word) when he speaks of the fairy queen Mab as one who "when maids lie on their backs, / ... presses them and learns them first to bear, / Making them women of good carriage." (I, iv, 92–4)

So, significantly, we have TWO equally garrulous characters incarnating mercurial tendencies to run off at the mouth.

Mercutio and the Nurse actually meet later in the marketplace, when the Nurse is seeking Romeo. Here she fulfills a most important Mercurial function: being a GO-BETWEEN, in this case transmitting information between Juliet and Romeo. In classical mythology Mercury is the gods' messenger and with winged shoes and hat is capable of speedy travel between heaven and earth. This is Mercury's archetypal role: he is the gods' mouthpiece, a MESSENGER between gods and goddesses, between gods and human beings, or between one human being and another. In this case, Romeo tells the Nurse that Juliet is to go to Friar Laurence's cell that afternoon so that they may be married, happy news that she will relay to Juliet.

Both Mercutio and the Nurse are comedians of a sort, providing comic relief in the drama. Mercutio relies more on witty and sophisticated word-play and the Nurse more on bawdy allusions. Each represents either the higher or lower type of mental functioning. To make this clear, Shakespeare has Mercutio speak most often in poetry while the Nurse speaks most often in prose. Mercutio's wit puts the Nurse at a disadvantage; when they meet in the street, Mercutio makes jokes at the Nurse's expense, singing a brief ditty that puns on "hoar" and "whore." (II, iii, 120–125). Shakespeare emphasizes Mercutio's qualities again when Romeo and the Nurse are at last alone, and the Nurse enquires as to Mercutio's identity:

> NURSE: I pray you, sir, what saucy merchant was this that
> was so full of his ropery [knavery]?
> ROMEO: A gentleman, Nurse, *that loves to hear himself*
> *talk*, and will speak more in a minute than he will
> stand to in a month.
>
> (II, iii, 130–3)

Quick-witted to the end, Mercutio jests even as he is dying, stabbed by Tybalt's sword that passes under Romeo's arm. How many can make a pun as they bleed to death: "Ask for me tomorrow, and you shall find me a grave man"? (III, i, 93–4) Significantly, an ill-aspected Mercury in a horoscope can synchronize with poor hand-arm coordination or mistimed and erratic action that fails to achieve its goal.

Those who reflect the qualities of Mercury are known to be "mercurial" or changeable.[261] This quality is well illustrated by the Nurse who is CAPRICIOUS. For a good part of the play it seems that the Nurse has Juliet's best interest at heart. She even warns Romeo against trifling with her lady's heart:

> [I]f ye should lead her in a fool's paradise, as they say, it were a very
> gross kind of behaviour, as they say, for the gentlewoman is young;
> and therefore if you should *deal double* with her, truly it were an ill
> thing to be offered to any gentlewoman, and very weak dealing.
>
> (II, iii, 147–52)

Yet ironically it is the Nurse herself who later "double deals" (the idea of DOUBLENESS again, associated with Gemini). When Juliet begs her advice after her parents demand that she marry Paris, the Nurse ignores the fact that Juliet is already married to Romeo. She reasons that, "Romeo is banished, and all the world to nothing / … Then, since the case so stands as now it doth, / I think it best you married with the County. / O, he's a lovely gentleman! / Romeo's a dishclout to him." (III, v, 212–13, 216–19)[262] Seeing that the situation has dramatically changed and that events warrant adapting to new circumstances, the Nurse, conscience-free (like Mercury, whose actions—like stealing Apollo's cattle immediately after his birth—are often morally suspect), easily changes sides, even counseling Juliet to become a bigamist! Juliet, of course, is appalled:

> Ancient damnation! O most wicked fiend!
> Is it more sin to wish me thus forsworn,
> Or to dispraise my lord with that same tongue
> Which she hath praised him with above compare
> So many thousand times? Go, counsellor!
> Thou and my bosom henceforth shall be *twain*.
>
> (III, v, 235–40)

["Twain"—notice the allusion to twoness or division again.]

Like the Nurse, Romeo too seems FICKLE at the beginning of the play, going on and on about Rosaline whom he says he loves. But his elaborate protestations of love sound more intellectual than emotional. At this point Romeo is clearly more fixated on the idea of being in love than he is actually feeling love. This is consistent with Gemini's reputation for INCONSTANCY and for talking about emotions rather than experiencing them.

In fact, the Gemini personality may prefer to avoid messy emotions altogether in favor of intellectual gamesmanship. Mercutio, the incarnation of Mercury, certainly recommends this. After exchanging witty banter with Romeo (when he seems to be over his infatuation with Rosaline), Mercutio delightedly advocates mental interchange over emotional turmoil: "Why, is not this better now than groaning for love? Now art thou sociable, now art thou Romeo, now art thou what thou art by art as well as by nature, for this drivelling love is like a great natural [idiot] ..." (II, iii, 76–9).

When Romeo truly falls in love with Juliet, we see a sharp contrast between his superficial preoccupation with Rosaline and his genuinely passionate and intense feelings for Juliet. No wonder, though, that Romeo's friends, seeing such a sudden change, doubt his sincerity. So how do we, the audience, privileged to witness Romeo and Juliet's first encounter, know that the instant mutual recognition of love between them has a completely different quality than Romeo's lovesickness for Rosaline? How do we know that the resolution of the warring opposites may occur through the two coming together? We know because the lines they exchange upon first meeting create a perfect sonnet, each line effortlessly following the previous one in the required rhyme and number of lines. The poetry reveals the meeting not just of their lips but of their souls.

> ROMEO: [*To Juliet, touching her hand*] If I profane with my
> unworthiest hand
> This holy shrine, the gentler sin is this:
> My lips, two blushing pilgrims, ready stand
> To smooth that rough touch with a tender kiss.
> JULIET: Good pilgrim, you do wrong your hand too
> much,
> Which mannerly devotion shows in this.
> For saints have hands that pilgrims' hands do touch,
> And palm to palm is holy palmers' kiss.
> ROMEO: Have not saints lips, and holy palmers, too?
> JULIET: Ay, pilgrim, lips that they must use in prayer.
> ROMEO: O, then, dear saint, let lips do what hands do:
> They pray; grant thou, lest faith turn to despair.
> JULIET: Saints do not move, though grant for prayers'
> sake.
> ROMEO: Then move not while my prayer's effect I take.
> [He kisses her]
>
> (I, v, 90–104)

In an astonishingly short time, Romeo moves from greeting to hand-touching to kissing—typical of speedy Mercury.[263]

What signals the transformation from immature young people to mature courageous lovers is the expressive heights to which their interchanges rise. "Coming back to the effects of love on the two main characters, the most dramatic change is in their command of LANGUAGE," remarks Northrop Frye, one of the twentieth-century's most respected literary critics.[264] Romeo's earlier speeches were self-indulgently rhetorical (like Mercury showing off), well illustrated by these rather forced rhymed lines in which he complains of Rosaline's cool aloofness:

> BENVOLIO: Then she hath sworn that she will still live
>   chaste?
> ROMEO: She hath, and in that sparing makes huge waste;
>   For beauty starved with her severity
>   Cuts beauty off from all posterity.
>   She is too fair, too wise, wisely too fair,
>   To merit bliss by making me despair.
>   She hath forsworn to love, and in that vow
>   Do I live dead, that live to tell it now.
>
> > > > (I, i, 210–17)

(An actor delivering these lines would do well to sound pompous and self-consciously "poetic.") But once he has met Juliet and is driven to lurk unseen in the Capulets' garden hoping to see her, Romeo's language soars:

> > > She speaks.
> O, speak again, bright angel; for thou art
> As glorious to this night, being o'er my head,
> As is a *winged messenger of heaven*
> Unto the white upturned wond'ring eyes
> Of mortals that fall back to gaze on him
> When he bestrides the lazy-passing clouds
> And sails upon the bosom of the air.
>
> > > > (II, i, 67–74)

Notably, Romeo imagines Juliet here as a variant of Mercury, an angelic carrier of messages between mortals and the gods and thus a bridge-being.

Juliet too evolves from the obedient daughter who says practically nothing in her first appearance on stage other than to acknowledge her mother's authority.

> JULIET: How now, who calls?
> NURSE: Your mother.
> JULIET: Madam, I am here. What is your will?
>
> (I, iii, 5–7)

As the drama unfolds, fueled by passion, she speaks much more and speaks more eloquently, rising to poetic heights as when she appeals to the sun to set sooner so that Romeo may come to her:

> Gallop apace, you fiery-footed steeds,
> Towards Phoebus' lodging. Such a waggoner
> As Phaethon would whip you to the west
> And bring in cloudy night immediately.
> Spread thy close curtain, love-performing night,
> That runaways' eyes may wink, and Romeo
> Leap to these arms untalked of and unseen!
>
> (III, ii, 1–7)

The Sign Opposite to Gemini: Sagittarius

Shakespeare often, and more subtly, includes an opposite in another way: he indirectly references the sign that is opposite to the dominant sign for that play. This is the sign that is directly across from it on the zodiacal wheel. In *Romeo and Juliet*, Friar Laurence is the embodiment of the sign Sagittarius, opposite to Gemini and ruled by Jupiter. As the psychologist Jung might have explained, as soon as you have emphasis on one end of a polarity, you automatically constellate its opposite. The opposite is always present, but unseen until it is called into conscious awareness by the stress on the other end of the polarity.

As the opposite and complementary sign to Gemini, Sagittarius represents the higher mind in contrast to the lower or mercurial one. While Gemini focuses on information that is of immediate use but often ephemeral, Sagittarius embraces broader knowledge that has longer term validity and has stood the test of time. Such knowledge has accumulated and been systematized over many hundreds of years. This includes such studies as history, philosophy, religion, metaphysics, and education.

The good friar well embodies many of these associations. He is a member of a religious order, and as such is presumed to be an embodiment of wisdom. The advice he gives at different points in the narrative is both wise and rational. The tragic ending of this play results in part from the lovers' impetuousness, as they rush headlong into love and then into a secret marriage. Friar Laurence, religious advisor to both, admonishes them to "love moderately," to go "wisely and slow. They stumble that run fast"—good advice when trying to restrain Mercury's impulsiveness. (II, ii, 94)

In addition, he is an herbalist. This marks him as a carrier of the ancient wisdom tradition.

Herbalism or the Doctrine of Signatures

[H]e that would know the operation of the Herbs must look up high as the Stars, astrologically ... —Nicholas Culpeper, *The Complete Herbal*

The use of plants and herbs for healing derives from the conceptual model still current in Shakespeare's time, which sees connections between humanity and nature. According to the old traditions, nature provides a cure for every human ill, because the human and natural worlds are part of a greater whole and are resonantly connected.

Herbalism is the science of using the esoteric properties of plants in both medicine and magic. Plant remedies are chosen according to the doctrine of correspondences or sympathies. Plants' virtues are recognized by their "signatures," revealed in their appearance or their taste, all in line with astrological symbolism. Their outward appearances offer clues to their inner properties, and consequently their uses:

A Martial plant is dry and hot, fiery even; a Saturnine plant is dank and cool, perhaps poisonous (though in right doses, poisons can be healing too); a Venusian plant is warm and moist, perhaps softly furred; a Solar plant is golden, probably follows the sun during the day (as does the sunflower), and is good for strengthening the human being; a lunar plant is cool and dry, good perhaps for women's ailments—and so forth. Each plant bears the signature of planetary virtues or qualities, and by these do we know immediately its uses or meanings.[265]

Shakespeare's audience would have been familiar with these associations of planetary qualities with earthly plants. Friar Lawrence, apparently an expert in herbalism (and therefore in astrology), offers an eloquent summary of the philosophy underlying the use of nature's medicinal offerings.

> I must up-fill this osier cage of ours
> With baleful weeds and precious-juiced flowers.
> The earth, that's nature's mother, is her tomb.
> What is her burying grave, that is her womb,
> And from her womb children of divers kind
> We sucking on her natural bosom find,
> Many for many virtues excellent,
> None but for some, and yet all different.
> O mickle is the powerful grace that lies
> In plants, herbs, stones, and their true qualities,
> For naught so vile that on the earth doth live
> But to the earth some special good doth give;
> Nor aught so good but, strained from that fair use,
> Revolts from true birth, stumbling on abuse.
> Virtue itself turns vice being misapplied,
> And vice sometime's by action dignified.
>
> (II, ii, 7–22)

Friar Laurence is such an adept in this art that he seems almost an arbiter of life and death. The potion he concocts to help Juliet escape the unwanted (second) marriage and join Romeo in Mantua will make her appear dead, though she will only be asleep. In line with the astrological symbolism of Gemini, which embraces opposites, the Friar's harmless concoction contrasts to the poison sold to Romeo by the apothecary, an altogether less ethical character than the good friar.

Friar Laurence's last words in the above quotation point to one of the more profound ideas inherent in the symbolism of Gemini. The friar stresses the opposition of weeds and flowers, of earth as both womb and tomb, and of the potential of even the most healing preparation to be harmful or poisonous. This alludes again to the endless polarities of the visible world: day and night, male and female, good and evil. In the visible world things can easily flip into their opposites in ironic reversals ("Virtue itself turns vice being misapplied / And vice sometime's by action dignified"), because the underlying (and esoteric) truth inherent in the sign Gemini is that behind all polarities must be an all-inclusive, undifferentiated One. Ultimately both Romeo's and Juliet's loathing of each other's family is dissolved by their instant liking, and so too the hatred of Capulet for Montague and Montague for Capulet transmutes to love by the end of the play.

The dualities of Gemini are reflected in a modern description of its symbol from an astrological text: the two upright lines are equivalent to "the two temple columns as symbol of the day and night side, as the division of unity, as the differentiation into subject and object, masculine and feminine, the conscious and unconscious, light and dark, heaven and earth, etc."[266] The idea of two pillars fronting a temple is a very ancient one:

> Pillars representing the male and female principles were to be found at temples throughout the East. They were not incorporated in the structure but stood in front of the entrance, the columns forming a symbolic gateway, or door of life.... The two pillars, Jachin and Boaz, which stood before the temple of Solomon, had male and female names."[267]

This same duality characterizes the inner world of the individual as well as the outer world of form, as Friar Laurence cautions:

> Two such opposed kings encamp them still
> In man as well as herbs—grace and rude will;
> And where the worser is predominant,
> Full soon the canker death eats up that plant.
>
> (II, ii, 27–30)

Since poetic language is open-ended and allows for more than one interpretation, the Friar may have in mind a number of inner dualities as the "opposed kings" he refers to: the higher self versus the lower self, one's good angel versus the voice of the tempter, or reason versus passion (a frequent theme in Shakespeare's works).

The Apothecary Shop. Apothecaries, forerunners of modern pharmacists, mixed and sold a variety of items, especially medicinal preparations made from herbs as well as organic (human and animal) and inorganic substances. King Lear begs, "Give me an ounce of civet, good apothecary,/ To sweeten my imagination." (IV, vi, 127-8) Civet is an exotic perfume derived from the sex glands of the civet cat, and still used today as a fixative in perfumes. Apothecaries also sold sweets (sugar being thought to have medicinal properties) and, particularly in Italy, ground pigments for artists' use.

Traditional knowledge of healing with herbs, passed down orally from ancient times, was preserved in monasteries and nunneries during the Middle Ages (so Friar Laurence is appropriately a member of a religious order), but into the Renaissance apothecary shops became independent dispensers of preparations and so freed from church oversight. The more unscrupulous purveyors, like the one Romeo seeks out in Mantua, sold poisons.

The Flaw that Generates the Tragedy: Impulsiveness

We are told in the Prologue that the "star-cross'd lovers" will die at the end, and so we know in advance that the play is a tragedy. For Shakespeare's audience, a tragic outcome implied that the characters have some responsibility for this. This idea goes back at least to ancient Greece where Aristotle suggested in his *Poetics* that doomed heroes had a "tragic flaw" and that this personal flaw was the chief reason for their downfall. For the Elizabethans, these flaws related to the characters' temperament, which revealed the excesses and imbalances of their personalities. So significant were these imbalances that both human beings and fictional creations might suffer—even die—as a result of them.[268]

In *Romeo and Juliet* the character flaw is obviously IMPULSIVENESS, the tendency to act before thinking or to act out of impulse or desire without examining the consequences. This is an exaggerated manifestation of a predominant quality of the planetary ruler of Gemini, Mercury. Positively, Mercury is deemed capable of speedy flight, quick movement, and deft eye-hand coordination, but negatively, when actions are sudden and thoughtless or speed accelerates beyond reasonable limits, the consequences are likely to be unsuccessful outcomes or, at an extreme, life-threatening accidents.

We see this impulsiveness repeatedly in the characters' impatience and their hasty actions.

Even the love-struck Juliet, despite being carried away by emotion, seems to grasp intuitively the wisdom of Friar Laurence's advice: love moderately and take things more slowly. Early in the play, leaning from her balcony as she and Romeo exchange vows of love, she presciently worries:

> Although I joy in thee,
> I have no joy of this contract tonight.
> It is *too rash, too unadvised, too sudden,*
> Too like the lightning which doth cease to be
> Ere one can say it lightens.
>
> (II, i, 158–62)

Yet later, awaiting the slow Nurse's return from her mission to meet with Romeo, she succumbs to impatience:

> Love's heralds should be thoughts,
> Which ten times faster glide than the sun's beams
> Driving back shadows over louring hills.
> Therefore do nimble-pinioned doves draw Love,
> And therefore hath the wind-swift Cupid wings.
> Now is the sun upon the highmost hill
> Of this day's journey, and from nine till twelve
> Is three long hours, yet she is not come.
> Had she affections and warm youthful blood,
> She would be as swift in motion as a ball.
> My words would bandy her to my sweet love,
> And his to me.
> But old folks, many feign as they were dead—
> Unwieldy, slow, heavy and pale as lead.
>
> (II, iv, 4–17)

How much faster are the young than the old! How much faster are thoughts, the products of mercurial activity, than the slow actions of time and time-bound creatures!

In the philosophical model of the time, reason is exalted as the guiding influence within the human being and is seen as a reflection of the Divine. To ignore its influence could generate increasingly unpleasant, even disastrous, consequences. In case the passionate young people missed his earlier counsel, Friar Laurence repeats his advice to moderate passion when Romeo and Juliet arrive at his cell to be married. Despite his willingness to unite them in hopes of creating harmony between the two warring families, he cautions them again (and foreshadows the tragic end to the story):

> These violent delights have violent ends,
> And in their triumph die like fire and powder,
> Which as they kiss consume. The sweetest honey
> Is loathsome in his own deliciousness,
> And in the taste confounds the appetite.
> Therefore love moderately. Long love doth so.
> Too swift arrives as tardy as too slow.
>
> (II, v, 9–15)

Once you grasp the connection between the characters' precipitous actions and the archetypal Gemini/Mercury, correlations leap out from almost every speech. Juliet later voices her excited impatience while awaiting the secret night-time visit of Romeo, the first they will spend as a married couple before he must leave, exiled to Mantua. And she does so in words that both reflect her desire for the speedy arrival of night and describe the opposites inherent in Romeo himself (in italics):

> Gallop apace, you fiery-footed steeds,
> Towards Phoebus' lodging. Such a waggoner
> As Phaethon would whip you to the west
> And bring in cloudy night immediately....
> Come night, come, Romeo; come, *thou day in night,*
> For thou wilt lie upon the wings of night
> *Whiter than new snow on a raven's back.*
> Come, gentle night; come, loving, black-browed night,
> Give me my Romeo ...
>   So tedious is this day
> As is the night before some festival
> To an impatient child that hath new robes
> And may not wear them.
>
>   (III, ii, 1–4, 17–21, 28–31)

Not ony Juliet but other characters also constantly urge each other to speak or to act more quickly. The overwrought Juliet invokes an early coming of night and Romeo. The next morning her father issues excited instructions to the servants before the expected nuptials of Juliet and Paris:

> CAPULET: Come, *stir, stir, stir!* The second cock hath
>   crowed.
>   The curfew bell hath rung. 'Tis three o'clock.
>   Look to the baked meats, good Angelica.
>   Spare not for cost....
>   *Make haste, make haste.* Sirrah, fetch drier logs.
>   Call Peter. He will show thee where they are....
>   The County will be here with music straight,
>   For so he said he would. I hear him near.

> Nurse! Wife! What ho, what, Nurse, I say!
> Go waken Juliet. Go and trim her up.
> I'll go and chat with Paris. *Hie, make haste,*
> *Make haste*, the bridegroom he is come already.
> *Make haste*, I say.
>
> v (IV, iv, 3–6, 14–6, 21–7)

Right after this speech the apparently-dead Juliet is discovered and celebration turns instantly to mourning. Consistent with the mercurial nature of the play, the tone changes immediately to its opposite:

> CAPULET: All things that we ordained festival
> Turn from their office to black funeral.
> Our instruments to melancholy bells,
> Our wedding cheer to a sad burial feast,
> Our solemn hymns to sullen dirges change;
> Our bridal flowers serve for a buried corpse,
> And *all things change them to the contrary.*
>
> (IV, iv, 111–17)

The Idea of Twin Souls and Love at First Sight

The sign Gemini is often represented visually by the figure of TWINS. Sets of double individuals appear in myth, religious iconography, and legend as (among other pairs) the twin brothers Castor and Pollox (one mortal and the other divine), as the siblings Isis and Osiris (who were also husband and wife), and as Tristan and Iseult (unrelated and fated lovers)—and now the literary characters Romeo and Juliet.

The idea of twins and twin souls, a concept that explains love at first sight, first appears in Plato's accounts of Socrates' philosophical teaching in ancient Athens (dating from the fifth century BCE). In one of his dialogues, the *Symposium*, guests at a supper party deliver speeches on the subject of love. One of them, Aristophanes, declares that in the beginning there was a third type of human being, not either male or female but both male *and* female, hermaphrodites descended from the Moon. Since in their strength, energy, and arrogance they tried to scale the heights of heaven and attack the gods, Zeus split them in two. This not only made them weaker, but also

... left each half with a desperate yearning for the other, and they ran together and flung their arms around each other's necks, and asked for nothing better than to be rolled into one.... So you see ... how far back we can trace our innate love for one another, and how this love is always trying to redintegrate our former nature, *to make two into one*, and to bridge the gulf between one human being and another.

... [W]e are all like pieces of the coins that children break in half for keepsakes—making two out of one, like the flatfish—and each of us is forever seeking the half that will tally with himself.[269]

Despite their youth, the instant attraction between Romeo and Juliet is not an attraction between body and body, but soul and soul. Romeo intuits that Juliet is his soul-self when he declares, "It is my soul that calls upon my name. / How silver-sweet sound lovers' tongues by night, / Like softest music to attending ears!" (II, i, 209–11) The concept of a soul is found in almost all cultures and all religions. In the West, the idea of an immaterial aspect of a human being conjoined with a material body during physical life and separated from it at death appears at least as far back as ancient Egypt as well as in Plato's writings in ancient Greece.

This individual soul is thought to be the organ of spiritual perception, a hidden faculty of super-sensing and intuitive knowing. This faculty responds not to the ups and downs of human emotions, but to a higher octave of feeling: the rapture of experiencing higher dimensions, even the Divine. The closest many of us might get to experiencing this, while we are still embodied and relatively unawakened, is the exaltation we feel when attending religious services or when exposed to great art or in the throes of sexual passion or giving birth. This individual soul is thought to retain the wisdom of distilled experience, which carries over into the next life.

Although Romeo and Juliet recognize the soul-filled and hence inevitable nature of their attraction, the rest of the characters in the play (with the exception of Friar Laurence and the Nurse) are completely unaware of their developing relationship. Romeo's friends in particular are quite in the dark. Juliet acknowledges the deep connection she has with Romeo soon after meeting him at the ball. In the famous "balcony scene" Romeo overhears her musing on what constitutes a person's true identity. She is looking beyond his mundane identity to his very essence:

O Romeo, Romeo, wherefore art thou Romeo?
Deny thy father and refuse thy name ...
'Tis but thy name that is my enemy.
Thou art thyself, though not a Montague.
What's Montague? It is nor hand, nor foot,
Nor arm, nor face, nor any other part
Belonging to a man. O be some other name!
What's in a name? That which we call a rose
By any other word would smell as sweet.
So Romeo would, were he not Romeo called ...

(II, i, 74–6, 80–7)

Juliet's ponderings reflect a long-standing philosophical debate about language. Philosophers and linguists ask, Do the words we use to identify things actually reflect the essence of those things? Is it even possible for words to represent the reality of a person or object? Or are they just labels, perhaps contradicting the inner essence?"

We are back to themes associated with Gemini here, about thoughts, words, and language. Glib mercurial types like Mercutio and the Nurse can supply names or labels for everything but often miss the essential meaning. For others, though, the inner essence of a person or thing exists beyond the outer appearance, distinct from personality or character. That is the unrecognized perfection of Being, the true inner Self.

Both Romeo and Juliet use phrases that reflect their mutual recognition of this glorious essence, beyond labels and beyond even physical reality. For Romeo, Juliet is "the sun," the source of light and life, thought in modern astrology to be indicative of your core self. Even though Romeo comprehends how dangerous it will be to trespass in Capulet's orchard, he must do so: "Can I go forward when my *heart* is here? / Turn back, dull earth, and find thy *centre* out" (II, i, 1–2). "Heart" and "centre" are both code words for this essence. One of the indications of a soul-based relationship is this very recognition of the beauty of the other's soul, with the innate understanding that one is recognizing one's own Self.

Individuation and Initiation in Romeo and Juliet

The ancient Greeks said that love ennobles us; a modern psychologist might say that it individuates us—that is, we become more authentically who we are, separate from our parents and capable of acting autonomously, according to our own will and in our own best interests. The youthful Romeo mooning over Rosaline or blubbering on the floor of Friar Laurence's cell evolves into a man who takes direct action in hastening to Verona, fighting with Paris, and dying for love. The immature Juliet, who assured her mother that she would warm to Paris only as far as her mother gave consent, becomes the independent and fearless woman who dares to take Friar Laurence's potion and, like Romeo, to die for love. Psychologically, Romeo and Juliet have "individuated."

Modern psychologists, particularly those in the lineage of Jung, have suggested that aspects of psychological transformation are analogous to aspects of ancient initiatory ceremonies conducted by groups devoted to spiritual pursuits. Such ceremonies developed, it seems, because thoughtful Greeks were dissatisfied with the unseemly antics of Greek gods like Zeus (Jupiter in Rome), busy seducing mortal women and evading his jealous wife. The twelve gods and goddesses who lived on Mount Olympus seemed more like glorified human beings than dignified divinities. Educated Greeks turned to other paths. Both Pythagoras and Plato were reputed to be members of seclusive religio-philosophic schools found in Egypt and elsewhere around the Mediterranean Sea and called "Mysteries." While these groups offered public festivals and open rituals during the day for any adherent, they are better known for the private and closed initiations often celebrated at night.[270]

While these mystery schools operated independently of the state-sanctioned religion, they were well known and accepted in the culture of their day. Dedicated to various deities, both indigenous and imported from abroad—Orpheus in Greece, or Demeter and her daughter Persephone at Eleusis, or Isis and Osiris from Egypt—the secret ceremonies these groups conducted were "initiation rituals of a voluntary, personal and secret character that aimed at a change of mind through experience of the sacred."[271]

We still do not know precisely what occurred in their initiation rites, for, astonishingly, over hundreds of years (between the sixth century BCE and almost 400 CE when imperial decrees prohibited what by then were described as "pagan cults") not a single initiate out of thousands ever divulged the whole of what transpired. A few dropped tantalizing hints: Plato, for one, was severely criticized for revealing some of the secret philosophic principles in his writings. Apuleius also, who was an initiate into the Mysteries of Isis, was chastised for revealing too much in his satiric tale *The Golden Ass.*

We do know that an allegorical drama with profound spiritual import was performed for the assembled initiates, a reminder that theater then was not only esteemed as high art but was originally presented in honor of the gods and goddesses—that is, it had primarily a religious function. Are we surprised that the plays of Shakespeare have imbedded in them some of the same philosophic ideas?

Most of the Mystery schools imparted some special teachings reserved for initiates or those preparing for initiation. One commentator suggests that "Their chief object was to teach the doctrine of one God, the resurrection of man to eternal life, the dignity of the human soul, and to lead the people to see the shadow of the deity in the beauty, magnificence, and splendor of the universe."[272] In particular,

> [T]he Mysteries were devoted to instructing man concerning the operation of divine law in the terrestrial sphere. Few of the early cults actually worshiped anthropomorphic deities, although their symbolism might lead one to believe they did. They were moralistic rather than religionistic; philosophic rather than theologic. They taught man to use his faculties more intelligently, to be patient in the face of adversity, to be courageous when confronted by danger, to be true in the midst of temptation, and, most of all, to view a worthy life as the most acceptable sacrifice to God, and his body as an altar sacred to the Deity.[273]

Watching what happens to Macbeth or Lear is certainly a dramatized lesson about the consequences of one's moral choices in light of a grander philosophic worldview.

Many of the mystery schools not only existed as underground fraternities but also staged their initiations literally underground in caves or structures created beneath the earth. One of the first spiritual heroes, the ancient Persian sage Zarathustra, was said to have "led his followers to secluded grottoes, hidden in the forests. There in underground caverns he initiated them."[274] In several of Shakespeare's plays, like *A Midsummer's Night's Dream* and *As You Like It*, the protagonists escape to a forest where they are in some way transformed.

So there is great significance in the setting of the final stage of *Romeo and Juliet* in a burial crypt, full of decomposing bodies of dead Capulets. From what we know of the later Greek mystery schools, initiations were designed especially to confront the participant with his greatest fear: the fear of death. Tellingly, Mercury, the guiding archetype of the play, was in Greek myth not only a messenger between heaven and earth, but also the psychopomp who guided the dead to and from the underworld.[275]

Shakespeare foreshadows the tragedy and magnifies the threat of death in order to heighten the lovers' heroism and to stress the similarity to an initiation. Juliet is caught in a bind: her father demands that she marry Paris, yet she is already married to Romeo. She goes to Friar Laurence's cell distraught, threatening to kill herself. However, she may escape physical death if she accedes to Friar Laurence's "remedy": a double stratagem that involves her taking the potion that gives only the appearance of death and Romeo rescuing her from the moldy tomb when she wakens. But the good Friar warns that she will still (as in the ancient initiatory rites) have an encounter with Death himself.

> If, rather than to marry County Paris,
> Thou hast the strength of will to slay thyself,
> Then is it likely thou wilt undertake
> *A thing like death* to chide away this shame,
> *That cop'st with Death himself to scape from it*;
> And, if thou dar'st, I'll give thee remedy.
>
> (IV, i, 71–6)

Juliet vows that love will give her the strength to meet whatever initiatory trials she fears, all described as confrontations with death in one form or another:

> O, bid me leap, rather than marry Paris,
> From off the battlements of any tower,
> Or walk in thievish ways, or bid me lurk
> Where serpents are. Chain me with roaring bears,
> Or hide me nightly in a charnel house,

O'ercovered quite with dead men's rattling bones,
With reeky shanks and yellow chapless skulls;
Or bid me go into a new-made grave
And hide me with a dead man in his tomb—
Things that, to hear them told, have made me tremble—
And I will do it without fear or doubt,
To live an unstained wife to my sweet love.

(IV, i, 77–88)

The lovers' final encounter is in a cave-like place. When Romeo comes to the churchyard on this fatal night, he must *go down* into the vault where Juliet's body lies. He instructs his servant Balthasar to "stand all aloof, / And do not interrupt me in my course. Why I *descend* into this *bed of death* / Is partly to behold my lady's face ..." (V, iii, 26–9).[276]

We are prepared for the final scene in the archetypal underworld by the lovers' own premonitions. The very last time that Juliet sees the living Romeo, as he is leaving her bed to flee to Mantua there to endure his banishment, she has a disturbing vision:

O God, I have an ill-divining soul!
Methinks I see thee, now thou art so low,
As one dead in the bottom of a tomb.
Either my eyesight fails, or thou look'st pale.

(III, v, 54–7)

Her physical eyesight has not failed but has been superseded by "second sight," as she foresees the future, the final act of the drama. Romeo too has a prescient vision: "I dreamt my lady came and found me dead— / Strange dream, that gives a dead man leave to think!" Yet Romeo's dream of death has a transcendent finale, for in it Juliet "breathed such life with kisses in my lips/ That I revived and was an emperor." (V, i, 6–9)

Their Final Union and the Mystic Marriage

The astrological sign Gemini contains within it both the mystery of creation, the emergence of two out of One, and its completion, when through the union of two there is a return to the One. The most common image for this is a wedding. This may be the deeper reason that comedies typically end with at least one wedding. With two becoming one symbolically, harmony and unity are restored.

Some of these ideas are found in esoteric tradition, divided into the Lesser and Greater Mysteries. The Lesser Mysteries help you to manage your life successfully in this world, and are symbolized by the physical marriage of a bride and bridegroom (and the sexual secrets accompanying it). The Greater Mysteries prepare you for the transcendent experience of the human soul's joining with the Soul of the World, the Anima Mundi. This conscious union of human and divine is also universally envisioned as a wedding, though on a grander scale. A wedding, whether on a microcosmic or macrocosmic scale, is

> ... an almost universal symbol for the uniting of polar opposites ... which from that point on function no longer antagonistically or competitively but complementarily, forming together a higher unity, a whole that is more than the sum of the parts. For the ancients, the *hieros gamos* ('sacred wedding') was a symbol for the creative uniting of heaven and earth, male and female, god and goddess ... [277]

No wonder that weddings are such charged events, carrying not only the weight of the emotions of the bride and groom, the expectations of the parents, and society's hopes for the continuation of life, but also the deeper symbolism of the resolution of opposites—the Lesser and Greater Mysteries conflated into one celebration.

> Traditional symbols of love always express a duality in which the two antagonistic elements are, nevertheless, reconciled.... They are, in other words, symbols of a conjunction, or the expression of the ultimate goal of true love: the elimination of dualism and separation, uniting them in the mystic 'centre', the 'unvarying mean' of Far Eastern philosophy. The rose, the lotus flower, the heart, the irradiating point—these are the most frequent symbols of this hidden centre; 'hidden' because it does not exist in space, although it is imagined as doing so, but denotes the state achieved through the elimination of separation. The biological act of love itself expresses this desire to die in the object of the desire, to dissolve in that which is already dissolved. [278]

The Ultimate Tragedy

Romeo and Juliet not only complete the "biological act of love," but they also ultimately die, as foretold in the Prologue. We can lay much of the blame for the final tragedy on factors related to Mercury. Consistent with a poorly-functioning (in astrological terms, a badly-aspected) Mercury, MISCOMMUNICATION abounds in the play. In every case, events appear to be fated. If only Capulet's *illiterate* servant had not happened to meet Romeo and Benvolio in the street and asked them to read the party invitation for him; if only Benvolio had not urged Romeo to go to the Capulets' party as a distraction from his mooning over Rosaline; if only Juliet's parents had not decided at the most critical time to arrange a marriage for Juliet (who was already secretly married to Romeo); if only Friar Laurence's *letter* had reached Romeo in Mantua so that he would know that Juliet's appearance of death was false... All of these contribute to the tragic outcome and all seem dramatically necessary, for only with the ultimate sacrifice that both Romeo and Juliet make, to die for love, will the enmity between the two households die too.

Terrible sacrifices are frequently enacted in tragedies. Noted literary critic Northrop Frye makes some cogent observations about these tragic gestures:

> Romeo and Juliet are sacrificial victims, and the ancient rule about sacrifice was that the victim had to be perfect and without blemish. The core of reality in this was the sense that nothing perfect or without blemish can stay that way in this world, and should be offered up to another world before it deteriorates. That principle belongs to a still larger one: nothing that breaks through the barriers of ordinary experience can remain in the world of ordinary experience. One of the first things Romeo says of Juliet is: "Beauty too rich for use, for earth too dear!"[279]

Romeo and Juliet operates on several levels: it is a human tragedy, an acutely observed psychological drama, and a vehicle for spiritual truths. The human tragedy is that youth and beauty are sacrificed to the hardened demands of a city-consciousness that has divided itself into TWO heart-hardened enemy camps. But a psychological transformation has taken place in both of the lovers, as they struggle with their passions,

confront their fears, and mature into young adults. And a spiritual transformation appears to take place at the end of the play as the warring
opposites fuse and become one.

The Prince of Verona chastises both the Montagues and Capulets when he says, "See what a scourge is laid upon your hate, / That
Heaven finds means to kill your joys with love.... All are punished." (V,
iii, 292–3). Old Capulet, Juliet's father, begs his former enemy "O brother
Montague, give me thy hand," and the gesture of hand-clasping signals
the resolution of the conflict of opposites that has driven the conflict
between the two families.

Old Montague, Romeo's father, generously offers to raise a statue of
Juliet in pure gold. In honoring the daughter of his former enemy and
especially in creating a likeness of her in the most valued of all metals—one at the top of the hierarchy of metals—a higher level of peace
and harmony is invoked. That remarkable proposal is echoed by Capulet,
who offers to raise one "as rich" of Romeo to lie by Juliet's. For each of
them dies not just for the other, but for Love. The extraordinary self-
sacrifice of the two young people has in effect transubstantiated them
from flesh to golden Light. The duality of Gemini, so prevalent in the
manifest world with its ever-present clashing opposites, is resolved into
a spiritual unity. With this acknowledgement and in sad recognition
of the foolishness of their quarrel, all the characters make their exit as
the onlookers contemplate the tragic exaltation of the two "star-cross'd
lovers."

CHAPTER 9

The Hidden Astrological Key to

The Merchant of Venice

Taurus and its Ruler Venus
and Libra and its Ruler Venus

All that glisters is not gold. —(*The Merchant of Venice:* II, vii, 65)

Antonio, a Venetian merchant, assures friends that his sadness is not due to worry over the fate of his merchant ships at sea or to a lack of love in his life. One friend, Bassanio, asks Antonio for more money to court the wealthy and beautiful Portia of Belmont. For love of his friend, Antonio agrees, but since Antonio's fortunes are invested in his ships, he suggests that Bassanio obtain a loan using Antonio's credit.

In Belmont, Portia, also melancholic, bemoans the terms of her father's will: suitors for her hand in marriage must choose between chests of gold, silver, and lead. If the chosen casket holds Portia's portrait, he wins her as wife; if not, he must leave Belmont immediately and never marry. None of the numerous current suitors appeal to her, though she and her lady-in-waiting Nerissa favorably recall an earlier visit by Bassanio.

Back in Venice, Bassanio and Antonio petition the Jewish moneylender Shylock for three thousand ducats (gold coins). Although Shylock resents Antonio's anti-Semitism and his criticism of Shylock's usury (lending money at exorbitant interest), he agrees to a loan with no interest, but adds a condition: if Antonio fails to repay the amount in three months, Shylock may claim a pound of his flesh.

In Shylock's household, his servant Launcelot decides to leave Shylock's service and attach himself to Bassanio. Shylock's daughter Jessica too contrives to abandon her father's house, taking his money and jewels, to marry Antonio's friend Lorenzo and become a Christian.

In Belmont, the Prince of Morocco selects the golden casket, and discovers only a death's head. Next, the Prince of Aragon chooses the silver one, but finds only a portrait of a "blinking idiot." Finally, the newly-arrived Bassanio opts for the lead one, and finds Portia's likeness. She immediately gives herself, all her wealth, and a ring to the fortunate Bassanio. Graziano, a friend who accompanies Bassanio, has wooed and won Nerissa, who also gifts him with a ring. Both women declare that the rings affirm their husbands' faithful love and must never be lost or given away. Suddenly news comes that all of Antonio's ventures have failed and that he will be unable to repay Shylock. The men leave immediately for Venice to try and save Antonio's life.

Portia and Nerissa depart for Venice too, disguised as a young lawyer ("Balthasar") and his clerk, and appear in the court where the Duke of Venice is hearing Shylock's suit against Antonio. Shylock, distraught and angry about his daughter's elopement and bent on revenge for Antonio's bullying behavior, spurns offers of three times the loan's value and insists on the fulfillment of the bond. The disguised Portia urges Shylock to have mercy. When he refuses, she appears to find the contract legally binding, but as Shylock is about to stab Antonio, Portia stops him, saying that he is entitled to flesh—and only precisely a pound of that—but no blood. Defeated, Shylock now wants to take the money previously offered, but Portia claims that since he conspired to kill a Venetian citizen, his life is forfeit.

The Duke mercifully spares Shylock, and further mitigates the judgment by vowing that the state will only fine him instead of taking half his property. Antonio, who could claim the other half of Shylock's wealth, is merciful too and refuses it on two conditions: Shylock must convert to Christianity and must will his estate to his runaway daughter and her Christian husband. Sick at heart, Shylock leaves. Both Bassanio and Gratiano are pressured to reward the disguised lawyer and his clerk for their service to Antonio with the rings their wives gave them.

The two women return to Belmont. When Bassanio and Graziano arrive, both women accuse them of false love since they gave away the rings that pledged their devotion. Finally, Portia reveals their role in saving Antonio, she and Nerissa produce the rings, and Portia announces that all three of Antonio's ships have "richly come to harbour." Nerissa produces Shylock's deed promising to leave his wealth to his daughter and her husband. All retire happily to celebrate their various good fortunes.

Determining the Play's Astrological Link

Clues to the ruling planet and the signs involved appear in the questions Antonio's friends ask him in the very first scene. Salerio and Solanio first guess that Antonio's sadness must be due to worry about the potential loss of his ships at sea which are "even now worth this" but might in a moment be "worth nothing" (I, i, 35–6). How variable and unpredictable is the value of anything! Solanio projects himself into Antonio's shoes and says, if I were you, "every object that might make me fear / Misfortune to my ventures out of doubt / Would make me sad." (I, i, 20–22)

Antonio dismisses this possibility, saying: "My ventures are not in one bottom trusted, / Nor to one place; nor is my whole estate / Upon the fortune of this present year: / Therefore my merchandise makes me not sad." (I, i, 42–5) Immediately Solanio leaps in with the only other reasonable possibility: Antonio must be in love. So the themes of the play are instantly framed: money and love. Since most of the interchange between the three concentrates on Antonio's ships and the threat of their loss, the theme of money has more emphasis.

The planet Venus represents both wealth and romance, and points to not one but <u>two</u> signs of the zodiac: Taurus and Libra. Both have been connected to the planet Venus since ancient times, though each represents different facets of the symbol. By drawing on two zodiacal signs, Shakespeare creates a complex interweaving of ideas and themes in this play.

Venus: The Planetary Ruler of Taurus and Libra

> And when love speaks, the voice of all the gods
> Makes Heaven drowsy with the harmony.
> (*Love's Labour's Lost*: IV, iii, 318–9)

Venus to the ancients is the goddess (or principle) of LOVE and BEAUTY, a divinity who wears a magic girdle that magnifies the wearer's charms so much that anyone who approaches her immediately falls in love with her.[280] In Greek and Roman mythology Venus is the eternal and irresistible SHE. To express her essence, flowers spring up where she walks on Earth. No surprise that Brigitte Bardot, a modern-day incarnation of the love goddess, has the Sun in Libra (ruled by Venus) in her horoscope or that Angelina Jolie has Venus rising in hers.

Venus has to do with the POWER OF ATTRACTION, the beauty or charisma that draws you to one special partner. But it correlates not just with the drive to form PERSONAL RELATIONSHIPS but also with the formation of FRIENDSHIPS, the creation of a network of social interconnectedness. This Venus lurks in the background of <u>all</u> Shakespeare's comedies and

Venus as the ruler of two signs, Taurus (lower left circle) and Libra (lower right circle. This vain Venus looks at herself in a mirror. (medieval woodcut)

romances, since the plots generally center on the ultimate joining of one or more couples clearly meant for each other. These plays also often feature close friendships between both females (like Rosalind and Celia in *As You Like It*) and males (like Proteus and Valentine in *The Two Gentlemen of Verona* and in this play, the characters Antonio and Bassanio).

Although her sterling qualities include charm, tact, and diplomacy, Venus most often inspires romantic attraction and stirs sexual desire. This draws men and women into relationships both for personal fulfillment and for greater psychological wholeness. For men, Venus in their horoscopes describes their inner feminine side or *anima*, the ideal woman conceived in their imaginations and shaped by their experiences. Several of the women in Shakespeare's romantic comedies are idealized projections of the men, though at the same time they are genuine catalysts for the their maturation (like the Princess in *Love's Labour's Lost* who unmasks Ferdinand's foolish rejection of pleasure in favor of study) or even their saving grace (like Portia in *The Merchant of Venice* who prevents Antonio's threatened death).

In the philosophical tradition undoubtedly familiar to Shakespeare, however, there are <u>two</u> Venuses: the earthly Venus who is superficial and fickle and the heavenly Venus who is glorious and perfect. Pausanias discourses on these in one of Plato's most famous Socratic dialogues, the *Symposium*, which records a series of speeches delivered at a supper party on the topic of Love. Pausanias declares that "the earthly Aphrodite's Love is a very earthly Love indeed, and ... governs the passions of the vulgar." The follower of earthly Love

> desires the body rather than the soul; his heart is set on what is mutable and must therefore be inconstant. And as soon as the body he loves begins to pass the first flower of its beauty, he 'spreads his wings and flies away,' giving the lie to all his pretty speeches and dishonoring his vows, whereas the lover whose heart is touched by moral beauties is constant all his life, for he has become one with what will never fade. [281]

For both the ancient Greeks and Romans, this earthly and earthy Venus was a lustful and lecherous goddess who led human beings into often disastrous or even degrading associations. [282]

But the Venus of Shakespeare's comedies and romances has little to do with the disruptive force of obsession or lust and more with heartfelt love and genuine friendship—in other words, more with the heavenly and enobling one. The devotee of the heavenly Aphrodite may experience an increase of wisdom along with other virtues, for as another guest at Plato's *Symposium*, Agathon, adds, Love bestows not only an increase of moral excellence, but also such qualities as righteousness, temperance, and tenderness. Love, he asserts, "is never injured by, nor ever injures, either god or man. For, whatever Love may suffer, it cannot be by violence ... nor does he need to go to work by force...." [283] In other words, Venus' nature is the extreme opposite of Mars.

For some ancient Greeks, the tension between qualities inherent in the elements (hot versus cold and wet versus dry) was due to these two fundamental principles of attraction and repulsion that underlie all polarities—symbolized in the astrological alphabet as Venus versus Mars. One of the Greek philosophers, Empedocles, called these principles *philia* (or "love" or "friendship") in contrast to *neikos* ("strife" or "hate"). [284] They are the opposite impulses behind comedy and tragedy, which pulsate with just these powerful emotions.

Besides love and beauty, Venus also has a third symbolic association: that of MONEY. This is not only because the clothes, ornaments, and beautifying items used to enhance your attractive qualities are often expensive, but also that wealth often substitutes for love. Opting for economics over emotion, though, can create problems. We see this in cases in which a moneyed man sports a beautiful woman on his arm as "eye candy," to advertise his worth. Or a beautiful woman may cash in on her attractiveness by attaching herself to a rich man. Such unions come at a price. No wonder that in the divorce courts both men and women in such relationships may seek revenge for a lack of love by compelling the legal system to award them the largest payouts possible. In these cases, Venus can be ruthless. This ruthlessness explains Shylock's psychological motivation for desiring Antonio's flesh as revenge for having been treated badly—for being unloved—by the citizens of Venice.

Venus and Taurus: Issues of Money and Value

Taurus is the second sign of the zodiac and the first of the earth signs. As a fixed sign, it is especially grounded (in both senses), stable, and resistant to change. Venus here often has more earthy, sensual associations. Taurus relates literally to the land, to agriculture, and to fertility and fecundity. Since worth was at one time measured by the amount of land you owned and the value of crops produced on it, Taurus came to be associated with your total WEALTH.[285] The animal symbol for the sign is the bull, a particularly weighty animal, indicative of primal potency and of determined, even stubborn, commitment to success. The symbol or glyph for Taurus is a circle topped with a semicircle representing the horns of a bull. It is meaningfully ironic, then that a flourishing economy is described as a "bull" market.

One correlation with Taurus is POSSESSIONS or PORTABLE PROPERTY. This refers to anything that can be fairly easily moved or carried on your person: coins, gems, or other relatively small and valuable objects that can be easily exchanged for money elsewhere. Called "movables" in Shakespeare's time, portable property features in the play when Shylock's daughter escapes from his house taking with her his golden coins ("ducats") and some gems.

A more abstract association with Taurus is the idea of VALUE. What do we own that we really value? Do these "movables" have intrinsic value? Or are they precious to us because of the emotional associations we attach to them? One way to determine this for yourself is to think about what you would seize if your house were threatened by fire or flood. Or what you could unobtrusively carry on your person if you were fleeing the country. A deeper question related to the sign Taurus is this: which is of more value to you, love or money? If you could have only one, which one would you choose? Each of the principal characters in the play reveals at some point what is of greatest value to him or her.

Every astrological symbol has both a negative and positive side. In the case of Taurus and its ruler Venus, the downside comes into play if you do not "own" your Venus—that is, become conscious of your genuine values, create truly love-based relationships, and invite trustworthy friends into your life. If you do not do this, that energy may be projected onto material objects as compensations.

> [I]f this projection fixes itself on money or possessions, then one becomes a hoarder, obsessed with accumulating money and possessions. This is the dark troll-like side of Taurus, which springs not from real pleasure in beautiful things, but from an identification of those things with one's sense of self-value. This is of course extremely dangerous, because if one loses one's possessions, one loses oneself.[286]

Shylock is thrown into emotional despair when his daughter Jessica abandons him, taking his money and jewels with her. He is clearly in the throes of just such a dilemma. Which is the worse loss, his child or his valuables? Has he invested more in his relationship with Jessica or in the apparent security of his accumulated wealth? Solanio describes Shylock's crying out in the streets:

> I never heard a passion so confused,
> So strange, outrageous, and so variable ...
> "My daughter! O, my ducats! O, my daughter!
> Fled with a Christian! O, my Christian ducats!
> Justice! The law! My ducats and my daughter!
> A sealed bag, two sealed bags of ducats,
> Of double ducats, stol'n from me by my daughter!

And jewels, two stones, two rich and precious stones,
Stol'n by my daughter! Justice! Find the girl!
She hath the stones upon her, and the ducats."

(II, viii, 12–13, 15–22)

Shakespeare colors the story so that we should side with Jessica, rejoicing at her escape. After all, she has left a gloomy household, one in which music was shut out (never a good sign in Shakespeare's world); she is leaving for love of Lorenzo; and she is switching her allegiance to a religion that promises she will be saved. And yet … Jessica appears not to value what she has taken. Tubal reports that she is profligate with the stolen money, spending in Genoa fourscore ducats in one night and trading a valuable ring for a mere monkey. Significantly, "In Christian symbolism, the monkey has a rather unfavorable aspect, representing the idea of man degraded by sin, and therefore reverting to a lower life form."[287] All of this makes us very uncomfortable. In fact, as we shall see, very little in this play can be taken at *face value*.

Venice: the City of Venus

Venice is a remarkably apt setting for exploring issues around money and values since in Shakespeare's time it was the richest city in Renaissance Europe and the pre-eminent city of international trade.[288] Adventurers, merchants, and sailors brought all the treasures of the known world to the port of Venice—among them the silks and spices of the exotic East—and gained immense profits from the exchange of goods for money. From its earliest beginnings, "The Venetians were always known as a mercantile people…." As a city built on water, with no arable land, the Venetians had to earn a living by trade and industry.[289] The City was also unusually cosmopolitan, attracting laborers and artisans, buyers and sellers, of all faiths and nationalities. Antonio alludes to Venice's prominence and reach of business as well as its international populace in saying that "the trade and profit of the city / Consisteth of all nations." (III, iii, 30–1) Fittingly, Venice was also known as a place of beauty, both architectural and human, and its courtesans (ruled by Venus) too were famous. So all the themes of Venus—riches, trade, profits, sex sold for money—are associated with this city.

Also in harmony with the symbolism of both Venus and Taurus, one of the noteworthy developments of the Renaissance is the rise of capitalism. By the fifteenth century, the market had been established as the basic institution of European economic life. One theory (of three) about the growth of capitalism as noted by historian Theodore K. Rabb is that it is marked by a change of attitude on the part of the businessman:

> It is the outlook of the capitalist, rather than the institutions and patterns within which he operated, that is decisive. Unlike the bazaar merchant, who closed his shop as soon as he had earned enough for dinner (to put the distinction in its simplest form), his more disciplined successor stayed on to make a profit that he could reinvest in his business. Sober judgment, long-term planning, careful record keeping, rational pursuit of sustained profit—these are the marks of the capitalist.[290]

The qualities Rabb identifies with the budding capitalist certainly seem to apply to Shylock, who is sober, careful, and rational in his dealings. He says more than once that he will lend Antonio money only because Antonio is "good" for it; clearly, he secures loans only when the risk is minimal. Careful money management is an essential value for Shylock; after telling Antonio the Old Testament story of Jacob and Laban, he concludes, "thrift is blessing" (I, iii, 86). "Thrift" is one of the words that recurs in the play so often (along with others such as "bond") that it rings in the listener's ears like a loud bell. Shylock harps on it: his grudge against Antonio derives in part because Antonio "rails, / Even there where merchants most do congregate,/ On me, my bargains, and my well-won *thrift*—/ Which he calls interest." (I, iii, 43–6) His first reference to his servant Lancelot is as an "*unthrifty* knave" (I, iii, 172). Before Shylock goes to dinner with the Christians, he puts Jessica in charge of his house, instructing her, "Do as I bid you. Shut doors after you. / Fast bind, fast find—/ A proverb never stale in *thrifty* mind" (II, v, 51–2).[291]

Shylock's criticism of Lancelot highlights his own values by contrast. No wonder Shylock seems unaffected by Lancelot's departure from his household, complaining that the servant did "gormandize" (overeat) and did "sleep and snore, and rend apparel out" (wear out the clothes he was given). (II, v, 3, 5) Shylock tells Jessica that

> The patch is kind enough, but a huge feeder,
> Snail-slow in profit, and he sleeps by day

More than the wildcat. Drones hive not with me;
Therefore I part with him, and part with him
To one that I would have him help to waste
His borrowed purse.

(II, v, 44–9)

Described thus, Lancelot fits the description of a negative Taurean type: one who is lazy, averse to work, and overindulgent in food and drink.

To make the connection between VENICE and VENUS more obvious, I cannot resist pointing out the similarity in sound of the two words. As I was completing this chapter, I was abashed to discover that I am not the first to see connections between Venice and Venus:

> The city was invariably represented as a female symbol, whether as the Virgin in majesty or as Venus rising from the sea. It was stated in legend that Venice was founded on 25 March 421, the feast of the Annunciation, and on that same day *Venus was in the ascendant.* [As in Angelina Jolie's horoscope, previously mentioned.]
>
> ... *So Venice was the city of Venus.* The goddess was born from the sea. She was intimately associated with the sea.... The word Venice conjures up Venus within its syllables.[292]

Taurus and the Theme of Money Management

If you decide that you particularly value money, a number of questions arise. How will you obtain it? And what will you do with it once you have it? Hoard it? Save it? Spend it? Overspend it? Lend it out? Obtaining and managing income is as problematic for the characters in this play as it is for us who watch it.

When we look closely at the play, a striking fact emerges: not a single character is completely responsible with money! Even Shylock, who seems the most conservative and most representative of true capitalist values, himself goes into debt to supply Bassanio with the money he requests. "I am debating of my present store, / And, by the near guess of my memory / I cannot instantly raise up the gross / Of full three thousand ducats. What of that? / Tubal, a wealthy Hebrew of my tribe, / Will furnish me" (I, iii, 48–53). His rather cavalier attitude seems at odds with what he declares to be his fundamental values.

Portia, too, on hearing of the loss of Antonio's ships, urges Bassanio to offer Shylock many thousands of ducats more than the bond is worth:

> PORTIA: What sum owes he the Jew?
> BASSANIO: For me, three thousand ducats.
> PORTIA: What, no more?
>   Pay him six thousand and deface the bond.
>   Double six thousand, and then treble that,
>   Before a friend of this description
>   Shall lose a hair through Bassanio's fault.
>
> (III, ii, 296–301)

Portia's response seems extremely and enthusiastically extravagant. Just a few lines earlier she vowed to Bassanio, "Myself and what is mine to you and yours / Is now converted." (III, ii, 166–7) So the money she is so profligately urging Bassanio to spend is technically not even hers anymore!

The one who presents the most glaring evidence of financial mismanagement, though, is Bassanio. First, he quite openly reveals that his lifestyle is leading him more and more into debt: "'Tis not unknown to you, Antonio, / How much I have disabled mine estate / By something showing a more swelling port [extravagant lifestyle] / Than my faint means would grant continuance." (I, i, 122–5) And he does not intend to cut back, either! Even after obtaining additional money from Antonio, Bassanio does not curb his spendthrift ways; he plans a masked entertainment for that same evening, before leaving for Belmont. It is clear that Bassanio values high living and is willing to take risks to continue to live well.

Bassanio's plan to restore his financial health (which includes repaying Antonio for moneys he has already borrowed) can only be described as bizarre:

> In my schooldays, when I had lost one shaft,
> I shot his fellow of the selfsame flight
> The selfsame way with more advised watch,
> To find the other forth; and by adventuring both,
> I oft found both. I urge this childhood proof
> Because what follows is pure innocence.

> I owe you much, and, like a wilful youth,
> That which I owe is lost; but if you please
> To shoot another arrow that self way
> Which you did shoot the first, I do not doubt,
> As I will watch the aim, or to find both
> Or bring your latter hazard back again,
> And thankfully rest debtor for the first.
>
> (I, I, 140–52)

Bassanio's argument is this: I have gone into debt, I do not want to change my ways—and will you lend me even more money? Imagine what a parent, a private lender, or the loan officer of a bank would make of this request! What could be more irresponsible than to increase your indebtedness in the fanciful hope of getting out of debt by marrying an heiress?

Bassanio's strategy could not be riskier: he will court the wealthy Portia in hopes of making an alliance with her, accessing her fortune, and repaying his debts. Bassanio's plan is therefore to borrow money in order to marry money. To put it bluntly, he is a fortune hunter. The language he uses to describe Portia is less romantic than mercenary; in it he employs the vocabulary of economics:

> In Belmont is a lady *richly left*,
> And she is fair, and, fairer than that word,
> Of wondrous virtues. Sometimes from her eyes
> I did receive fair speechless messages.
> Her name is Portia, nothing *undervalued*
> To Cato's daughter, Brutus' Portia;
> Nor is the wide world ignorant of her *worth*,
> For the four winds blow in from every coast
> Renowned suitors; and her sunny locks
> Hang on her temples like a *golden fleece*,
> Which makes her seat of Belmont Colchis' strand,
> And many Jasons come in quest of her.
> O my Antonio, had I but the means
> To hold a rival place with one of them,
> I have a mind presages me such *thrift*
> That I should questionless be *fortun*ate.
>
> (I, i, 161–76)

For Bassanio, Portia is golden in more senses than one. In the structured symbolism of the Elizabethan worldview, gold is the highest of the metals, suggesting that Portia is the most worthy of all women. Equating her with the golden fleece that the mythological Roman hero Jason searched for also exalts her. It is said that Venus "ornaments herself with gold, and is herself 'golden'...."[293] Artists commonly depicted her with golden hair.[294] And yet, Portia is reduced to an object, the "golden fleece," and there is a disturbing undertone of "fleecing"—that is, cheating or swindling someone out of something valuable.

Lest you think that Bassanio is too crass in describing Portia in financial terms, she does the same herself, immediately after Bassanio has chosen the correct casket:

> You see me, Lord Bassanio, where I stand,
> Such as I am.   ... for you
> I would be trebled *twenty* times myself,
> A *thousand* times more fair, *ten thousand times more rich*,
> That only to stand high in your *account*
> I might in virtues, beauties, livings, friends,
> *Exceed account*. But the *full sum* of me
> Is *sum* of something, which, to term in *gross*,
> Is an unlessoned girl, unschooled, unpractised ...
>   (III, ii, 149–50, 152–9)

In the subplot, Jessica is a lesser representation of the golden girl, a parallel to Portia. Jessica absconds with her father's gold coins, throwing them down to the waiting Lorenzo in a casket. Then she goes back into the house to "make fast the doors, and *gild* myself / With some moe ducats, and be with you straight." (II, vi, 49–50) Like Portia—and like the goddess Venus herself—she is associated with gold.

Melancholia and the Wealthy

Venus can certainly bring you wealth, whether through trade, marriage, or inheritance (almost everyone in the play gets rich through one of these three ways), but once you have it, it must be managed and can be all too easily lost or stolen. This can generate a lot of anxiety and worry, as you realize how vulnerable your assets are to misadventure, mismanagement, or thievery. Characters in the play are very aware of this. None of the wealthy in this play—Antonio, Shylock, and Portia— seem very happy.

Since this play is keyed in part to Taurus, an earth sign, we would expect to find at least one classic melancholic type taking center stage. The most obvious one is Antonio, since the play opens with his inexplicable melancholic mood that his friends try to understand and lighten. Though they think that he has become sadder over time, Antonio insists that he has a consistently melancholic temperament: "I hold the world but as the world, Graziano— / A stage where every man must play a part, / And mine a sad one." (I, i, 77–79) Antonio fits the general description of this type, being thoughtful, pessimistic, and depressive. Having wealth does not seem to alleviate his mood or alter his temperament.

Announcing melancholia so early in the play would alert Shakespeare's audience to its resonance with one of the earth signs and its themes. In line with the zodiacal sign of Taurus (concerned with money and its management), Shakespeare reminds us periodically how vulnerable Antonio's possessions are in order to increase suspense and foreshadow their loss, which will enable Shylock to claim his bond.

Shylock, too, is temperamentally melancholic. He runs a "sober" household, one in which music is not welcome and one that is well shut away from the boisterous street life of Venice. Shylock repeatedly orders Jessica to lock up the doors, and though he is leaving her to go and dine with the men he is doing business with, he has no "mind of feasting forth tonight" (II, v, 28–37, esp. 36). Like most melancholics, he is reluctant to socialize unless for a practical purpose. It is hard to imagine Shylock smiling or laughing in any social situation. And like the typical melancholic he is obstinate and persistent in pursuing the bond.

> I'll have my bond. I will not hear thee speak.
> I'll have my bond, and therefore speak no more.
> I'll not be made a soft and dull-eyed fool
> To shake the head, relent, and sigh, and yield
> To Christian intercessors. Follow not.
> I'll have no speaking. I will have my bond.
>
> (III, iii, 12–17)

The principal Venusian figure in the play, the beautiful and wealthy Portia, is also discontented. Her wealth does not bring her happiness either. Her first speeches show her to be in the same sad place as Antonio: "By my troth, Nerissa, my little body is aweary of this great world." (I, ii, 1–2) Nerissa urges her to consider the miseries of those who have less than she does, and makes the astute observation that wealth can both corrupt you and even shorten your life. Nerissa's recommendation is to hold the middle, the "golden mean."

> You would [have reason to be weary], sweet madam, if your miseries were in the same abundance as your good fortunes are; and yet, for aught I see, they are as sick that surfeit with too much as they that starve with nothing. It is no mean happiness, therefore, to be seated in the mean. Superfluity comes sooner by white hairs, but competency [moderate estate] lives longer. (I, ii, 3–8)

But unlike Antonio and Shylock, Portia's melancholy seems more circumstantial than innate. She seems to be both sated by a limited wealthy lifestyle and frustrated by the restrictions of her father's last instructions. Once she is united with Bassanio, her mood changes dramatically and her role in the play also changes, from one of passive observer to active (though disguised) participant. But before that she had little opportunity to exercise her own free will. Her father's will had set up a strange test for any potential suitor for her hand: he had to choose between one of three caskets made of gold, silver, or lead.

The Fairy-Tale Element of the Play: the Three Caskets

Shakespeare, with his usual audacity, introduces a fairy-tale element into a story that is mainly about hard-nosed businessmen making deals.

Like astrology, fairy tales are far from being superficial stories to entertain children or the simple-minded. Modern psychology has plumbed the depths of these deceptively simple tales and unearthed profound psychological and spiritual insights. The figures in the stories (like talking animals or wicked stepmothers) and repeated motifs (like being granted three wishes) all have deep symbolic significance. Fairy tales carry an intuitive wisdom, revealed from a perspective quite opposite to the conventional. They are always thwarting our expectations by inverting commonly accepted *values* and insisting that we look beyond the obvious: ugly frogs may be princes in disguise; ugly hags may be wise women dressed in rags. And golden caskets may not be the right choice.

Here is the primary irony of the entire play: when presented with the choice of the three chests, Bassanio does *not* choose the one that matches his announced intention to gain the "golden" fleece. He does *not* choose the one that aligns with the chief capitalist goal, that of gaining more and more wealth. He does *not* choose the one that has the highest value in the "great chain of being." Instead he picks the one that is the *least* attractive, the *least* valuable, and the *least* desirable: the one of lead (the substance associated with Saturn, the planet governing melancholics).

When the Prince of Morocco selects the golden casket, he finds not the portrait of the living Portia but a Death's head with a written scroll in its empty eye socket. He reads what is written there:

> 'All that glisters is not gold;
> Often have you heard that told.
> Many a man his life hath sold
> But my outside to behold.
> Gilded tombs do worms infold.
> Had you been as wise as bold,
> Young in limbs, in judgement old,
> Your answer had not been inscrolled.
> Fare you well; your suit is cold.'
>
> (II, vii, 65–73)

Money is here explicitly opposed to the positive values of wisdom and good judgment. We are warned in these words, ostensibly from Portia's father from beyond the grave, that one should not "sell his life"— that is his capacity to live life abundantly, joyfully, and expansively—for the sake of success measured by money-making. To do so is to court Death. This gives new meaning to the phrase "your money or your life"!

Obviously, to limit yourself to the negative Venusian interpretation of money as the chief and only value in human life is to limit your experience and deny you things of even greater value. We get a similar message in the subplot when Lancelot leaves "a *rich* Jew's service, to become / The follower of so *poor* a gentleman." (II, ii, 132–3) He believes that the quality of life that he will have will more than make up for his financial loss.

In fairy tales things are never what they seem. The same is true in Shakespeare's works, where a favorite theme is that of appearance contrasted to an underlying truth or an inner reality—a common theme in fairy tales. "All that glisters is not gold" indeed. A significant example of appearing to be something one is not is Bassanio's presentation of himself to Portia. Funded by Antonio's money, he comes to Belmont appearing to be a wealthy gentleman. Though he has told her he is really worth nothing, once he has won her hand, he has to admit the entire truth:

> [D]ear lady,
> Rating myself at nothing, you shall see
> How much I was a braggart. When I told you
> My state was nothing, I should then have told you
> That *I was worse than nothing*; for indeed
> I have engaged myself to a dear friend,
> Engaged my friend to his mere enemy,
> To feed my means.
>
> (III, ii, 255–262)

Taurus and Money-Lending: The Problem of USURY

Taureans are deeply concerned with the problem of managing money. One option is lending it, which has a very complicated religious and legal history. Looking at attitudes toward money-lending and the history of its practice helps to clarify the antipathy between Antonio and Shylock. Many thorny issues arise from the use of minted or printed money. Besides questions about its inherent worth and its management to avoid debt, comes the practical issue of established beliefs, customs, and laws for its circulation.

"Usury" is now generally defined as making loans at excessive or exploitative interest rates, but originally it referred to loaning money and charging *any* interest at all. The earliest references to it in religious writings are uniformly condemnatory; the sacred Vedas of India (2000 to 1400 BCE), both the Old and New Testaments, and the Koran (ca 600 CE) all either criticized, limited, or forbade it. Philosophers were equally critical. Frequently read and quoted during the Middle Ages, Aristotle's view was that money was a good consumed by use and so could not be loaned out at interest, unlike flocks or herds which reproduce and consequently increase in both number and value. (This explains Shylock's telling Antonio the story of Jacob who finds a clever way to get more new-born lambs than his uncle. See I, iii, 67–86).

Yet both religious and secular commentators were inconsistent. Because usury often exploited the poor or unfortunate, it was condemned for moral reasons, as in Exodus 22:25: "If you lend money to any of my people with you who is poor, you shall not be to him as a creditor, and you shall not exact interest from him." But in Deuteronomy 23:20, this directive is altered: "To a foreigner you may lend upon interest, but to your brother you shall not lend upon interest...." Here charging interest is allowed, but not within one's ethnic group. For this reason, Jews did not exact interest when lending to each other, but were allowed to do so when lending to non-Jews. So Shylock could charge Antonio interest on a loan but presumably Tubal will not charge interest on his loan to Shylock.

Christians had an especially complicated response to this issue of money-lending. Early Christian theologians explicitly condemned loans at interest. Echoing the Roman statesmen Cato and Seneca, Saint Jerome even equated it with murder since it consumed the life of the borrower. (This remarkably correlates to Shylock attaching the penalty of a pound of flesh in his agreement with Antonio.) In Dante Alighieri's fourteenth-century epic poem *The Divine Comedy*, usurers are placed in the seventh circle of hell, along with blasphemers and sodomites.[295]

Like the Old Testament, the New Testament conveyed equally mixed messages. On the one hand, Jesus angrily expelled the moneychangers from the temple in Jerusalem and taught, "if you lend to those from whom you hope to receive, what credit is that to you? Even sinners lend to sinners, to receive as much again. But love your enemies, and do good, and lend, expecting nothing in return ..." (Luke 6:34–4). Yet in the parable of the talents (in Matthew 25:14–30, with a slightly different version in Luke 19:11–27) he ostensibly condemned the third servant, the fearful one who buried the one talent he was given, whose punishment was to be cast "into the outer darkness where men will weep and gnash their teeth." The servant is explicitly told that he should have invested the money with lenders so that the returning master would have received his own with "interest"—a word that is translated in earlier Bibles of Shakespeare's time (the King James version as well as the Douay-Rheims) as "usury." So what was a Christian to do?

From the fourth century on, Christian authorities continued to condemn lending with interest as a sin and included this stricture in Canon Law, from which, of course, Jews were exempt, but enterprising merchants and potential lenders came up with creative ways around this. Shortly before Shakespeare's lifetime, with the Reformation underway and capitalism on the rise, attitudes began to shift. Both Catholics and Protestants became more open to considering lending legitimate if the intentions of the lender were non-exploitative and for social good. The emphasis shifted onto the loaner's inner motivations and not the actual practice of lending itself.[296]

The source of the conflicted attitudes and practices (and indeed of the conflict between characters in the play) is the deeper question of the correct attitude toward money—the realm of Taurus. Excessive attachment to money was in the New Testament explicitly linked with sin. Since the love of money was "the root of all evils" (I Timothy 6:10), a stigma was attached to it. In the early days of Christian history the most committed Christians took vows of poverty as a sign of their spiritual devotion. No surprise that those who valued money and accrued interest from lending it were despised, as Antonio despises Shylock.

Yet it is hard *not* to be sympathetic with Shylock for several compelling reasons. The first is that historically Jews had few vocational options. Ostracized from most professions by guilds, local authorities, and the church, they were pushed into marginal or less desirable occupations, money-lending among them. As well, Jews at different times and places were forbidden to own property—which would have been chancy in any case since they could have their property confiscated or be driven out of a city or country. Indeed, in 1290 the Jews were expelled from England and (tellingly, in light of the already-stated association of Taurus with portable property) allowed to take only what they could carry. That they were practicing usury was the official reason for their expulsion, but the Crown wasted no time in taking possession of everything they left behind.

Second, Shylock very surprisingly offers at first to loan Antonio the three thousand ducats *at no interest at all*. Only when Antonio continues to insult Shylock, rejecting his overtures of friendship, does Shylock introduce the "merry sport" of adding the penalty of receiving a pound of Antonio's flesh if the money is not paid.

Third, Shylock suffers the loss of both his daughter and his wealth, both during and at the end of the play. This eats away at him, and contributes greatly to his resentment of Antonio and his unwillingness to be merciful in the courtroom scene.

Lastly, Shylock appeals to our sympathies by asserting his common humanity in what may be the most famous speech in the play:

> [Antonio ...] hath disgraced me, and hindered me half
> a million; laughed at my losses, mocked at my gains,
> scorned my nation, thwarted my bargains, cooled my
> friends, heated mine enemies, and what's his reason?—I
> am a Jew. Hath not a Jew eyes? Hath not a Jew hands,
> organs, dimensions, senses, affections, passions; fed with
> the same food, hurt with the same weapons, subject to
> the same diseases, healed by the same means, warmed and
> cooled by the same winter and summer as a Christian is?
> If you prick us, do we not bleed? If you tickle us, do we
> not laugh? If you poison us, do we not die?
>
> (III, I, 46–55)

So although Shylock seems to be a type of Scrooge, who hoards his golden ducats in his house and uses his resources to increase his wealth, for both historical and personal reasons we can understand why he is a Taurean-type character and why he acts as he does. Shakespeare may have started by basing his character on a stereotypical villain, but ends up inspiring such sympathy for him and his constrained situation that he becomes the most memorable character in the play. Indeed, when we think of "the merchant of Venice" we think first of Shylock.

Venus as the Planetary Ruler of Libra

Venus is also the planet associated with Libra, the seventh sign of the zodiac and the second of the air signs. This sign is prominently associated with cultivating skills that facilitate cooperative and harmonious human relations—such as tact, good manners, politeness, and the rituals of etiquette that arise from an awareness of others' feelings or circumstances. Such qualities, once labeled "good breeding," mark a civilized person, one who has been raised to participate gracefully in the human community.

A good example of the lack of such skills in the play is the garrulous and socially unaware Graziano, who goes on and on giving blunt and unwanted advice to the melancholic Antonio at the very beginning of the play. Lorenzo observes that "Graziano never lets me speak," and once Graziano has exited the scene, Bassanio comments that even when he does, he "speaks an infinite deal of nothing, more than any man in all Venice." (I, i, 107, 114–5) Clearly this quality is an irritant to his friends and puts him at a disadvantage in society.

When Graziano insists on accompanying Bassanio to Belmont, Bassanio has an opportunity to caution his friend to change his behavior to be more in line with the Libran ideal:

> But hear thee, Graziano,
> Thou art too wild, too rude and bold of voice—
> Parts that become thee happily enough,
> And in such eyes as ours appear not faults;
> But where thou art not known, why, there they show
> Something too liberal [unrestrained]. Pray thee, take pain
> To allay with some cold drops of modesty
> Thy skipping spirit, lest through thy wild behaviour
> I be misconstered [misconstrued] in the place I go to,
> And lose my hopes.
>
> (II, ii, 161–9)

Graziano takes this well and immediately acquiesces, using language that any Venusian would recognize:

> Signior Bassanio, hear me.
> If I do not put on a sober habit,
> Talk with respect, and swear but now and then,
> Wear prayer books in my pocket, look demurely—
> Nay more, while grace is saying, hood mine eyes
> Thus with my hat, and sigh, and say 'Amen',
> Use *all the observance of civility,*

Like one well studied in a sad ostent [solemn appearance]
To please his grandam, never trust me more.

(II, ii, 170–8)

Can it be an accident that Graziano's very name recalls the word
"ingratiate," meaning "to bring oneself (purposely) into the favor of
another"? True to his agreement, Graziano has obviously taken Bassanio's advice to be more civilized in Belmont for he says nothing while
Bassanio is choosing a casket and speaks only briefly and graciously at
the end of the scene to reveal his successful courtship of Nerissa.

Another motivation of Libra is the desire to deepen human connections in order to tranform an acquaintance into a close friend, lover, or
ultimately committed partner. The Libran type, as an air sign, thinks and
talks a great deal, especially about LOVE or MARRIAGE, and is fascinated
by the behaviors and compromises that allow close human associations
to flourish. On the plus side, charm, tact, and diplomacy are skills that
the Libran uses to soften the hard edges of human interactions. Librans
can thus be successful negotiators and diplomats, since they have an
exquisite sense of fairness. No wonder that the symbol for the sign is the
scales with two equally weighted pans suspended from a central support.
In a perfect world, each negotiating side or each partner would receive
exactly the same amount of attention, love, or goods from the other.

On the minus side, Librans are criticized for their niceness, their
veneer of Venusian sweetness and docility, which often hides a sharp
mind, an acute perception, and an ability to manipulate others cleverly to
get what they want. For the sake of harmony, Librans may not say what
they really think, but in private or in the long run their true thoughts and
feelings may be subtly implied, blurted out, or stated directly. Librans
can be surprisingly and sharply derisive, often adept at satire or irony.
(Barbara Walters has a Sun in Libra. Adept at harmonizing the varied
viewpoints of the women of "The View," she was also capable of sharp
questioning in the interviews she was famous for.)

Portia is a perfect example of both sides of the Libran personality.
She modestly underrates herself in the typically self-deprecating style of
the Venusian, protesting to the Prince of Aragon that he has come "to
hazard for my worthless self" (II, ix, 17). This is a very pretty but hardly
truthful speech, since she is obviously both beautiful and rich. After

Bassanio has won her in the test of the caskets, she again undervalues herself as:

> [A]n unlessoned girl, unschooled, unpractised,
> ... She is not bred so dull but she can learn;
> Happiest of all is that her gentle spirit
> Commits itself to yours to be directed
> As from her lord, her governor, her king.
>
> (III, ii, 159,162–5)[297]

Yet only a few scenes later we see her confidently disguised as a young man and assertively playing the role of an educated and intelligent lawyer in the Venetian court. In that role it falls to her to make the critical determination of the validity of Shylock's conditions of the bond and deliver a wise and judicious ruling that will determine the lives and fates of both Shylock and Antonio. She is the most powerful character in the play and the one most in control during the crucial courtroom scene.

Portia is like Venus, the ruler of Libra, too in that she is described by others as perfection, the living embodiment of the IDEAL woman. The Prince of Morocco hymns her as the "fair Portia" whom all the world desires, for "From the four corners of the earth they come / To kiss this shrine, this mortal breathing saint." One of the caskets contains her picture: "an angel in a golden bed / Lies all within." (II, vii, 43, 39–40, 58–9) Jessica, who as another woman might be more objective, also finds her to be a nonpareil:

> LORENZO: How dost thou like the Lord Bassanio's wife?
> JESSICA: Past all expressing. It is very meet
>   The Lord Bassanio live an upright life,
>   For, having such a blessing in his lady,
>   He finds the joys of heaven here on earth,
>   ... for the poor rude world
>   Hath not her fellow.
>
> (III, v, 62–6, 72–3)

Yet in private Portia can be quite human and less than perfect, judgmental rather than compassionate in her assessment of others. She is devastatingly and consistently critical of her former suitors, demonstrating the oft-hidden acuteness of the observant Libran:

> NERISSA: First, there is the Neapolitan prince.
> PORTIA: Ay, that's a colt indeed, for he doth nothing but talk of his horse …
> NERISSA: Then is there the County Palatine.
> PORTIA: He doth nothing but frown … He hears merry tales and smiles not. fear he will prove the weeping philosopher when he grows old, being so full of unmannerly sadness in his youth. I had rather be married to a death's-head with a bone in his mouth than to either of these. God defend me from these two!
>
> (I, ii, 34–6, 39–40, 41–5)

Her portraits of the various suitors, partly based on national stereotypes, are sharply satiric. On the one hand you have to admire her wit, while on the other you notice that even she has reservations about making fun of them: "In truth, I know it is a sin to be a mocker …" (I, ii, 47–8), but she goes on to skewer the French lord, the young baron of England, the Scottish lord, as well as the young German who is particularly unlikeable since he is a drunk: "I will do anything, Nerissa, ere I be married to a sponge." (I, ii, 83, but see all of 31–83)

Portia's mocking observations of the suitors are astute. Despite the contrast between her exaltation as goddess-like and her all-too-human judgmentalism, her sharp observations prepare us for her transformation into the wise and judicious legal expert who appears later.

Portia is not the only example of a character praised as ideal but whose words or actions contradict that ideal. Antonio may be "that royal merchant, good Antonio" (III, ii, 238) whom Bassanio praises as

> The dearest friend to me, the kindest man,
> The best-conditioned and unwearied spirit
> In doing courtesies, and one in whom
> The ancient Roman honour more appears
> Than any that draws breath in Italy.
>
> (III, ii, 291–5)

(Note the Venusian word "courtesies.") But he is the same man who spits on Shylock and speaks ill of him to his face throughout the entire play. Why is Shakespeare doing this? No doubt to contrast the ideal, which in part reflects the divinity of our inner nature, with our imperfect and human selves.

Libra and its Associations with the LAW

The sign Libra incorporates ideas that move beyond considerations of fairness and harmony in personal relationships to fairness and equal treatment in society, in courts of law. Libra is the only sign of the zodiac that is represented by an object rather than a living creature. The scales, the symbol of perfect balance, are an appropriate glyph since the moment when the Sun appears to enter the sign Libra is the moment of the autumnal equinox, when light is equally poised with dark, and day and night are the same. Measuring scales, with their two equally balanced pans, have become the symbol of the legal profession, and of the principles of JUSTICE, FAIRNESS, and EQUALITY BEFORE THE LAW that ideally underlie its practice.

The association of the scales and the law is an old one. In Egypt, after death the heart was weighed on scales to determine the balance of good works and evil-doing in its previous life and direct its progress in the afterlife. (That the heart was weighed is notable in light of Shylock's intention to carve his pound of flesh from nearest Antonio's heart.) In Babylonian mythology the scales were considered sacred to the sun god Shamash, who is the god of truth and justice. Justitia, the Roman goddess of Justice, is usually depicted as blindfolded (indicating impartiality in rendering verdicts), carrying a sword in one hand (standing for the sharpness of truth or perhaps warning of possible harsh punishment), and holding scales in the other (representing the potential for balance and fairness in judgments).

More than one character in this play is subject to legal constraints. Portia must abide by the dictates of her father's will with regard to her marrying. The person most bound by legality is, of course, Antonio whose life is literally at stake in the agreement he has signed with Shylock. Hear how the word "bound," only a slight change from "bond," resonates at the moment when Antonio agrees to the deal:

SHYLOCK: Three thousand ducats. Well.

BASSANIO: Ay, sir, for three months.

SHYLOCK: For three months. Well.

BASSANIO: For the which, as I told you, Antonio shall be
    bound.

SHYLOCK: Antonio shall become bound. Well.

BASSANIO: May you stead me? Will you pleasure me?
    Shall I know your answer?

SHYLOCK: Three thousand ducats for three months, and
    Antonio bound.

                                        (I, iii, 1–9)

The only character who sincerely *wants* to be bound by the law is
Shylock:

The pound of flesh which I demand of him,
Is dearly bought. 'Tis mine, and I will have it.
If you deny me, fie upon your *law*:
There is no force in the decrees of Venice.
I stand for *judgement*.

                                        (IV, i, 98–102)

Shakespeare does something extraordinary in creating the character
of Shylock. He uses the stereotype of the Jew as someone focused on
two things: making money and fulfilling the Law. Remarkably he has
conflated in Shylock the negative manifestations of both overarching
archetypes of the play: he is the incarnation of the unevolved Taurean's
narrow focus on money-making and the undeveloped Libran's resort to
literalism and legalism. Yet though he may have envisioned Shylock initially as a comic villain, his creation is a figure with such vitality and
psychic force that he threatens to explode out of the comic framework.
He takes hold of our imaginations and becomes the most memorable
character in the play.

The court scene, when Antonio and Shylock come before the Duke,
in which Shylock demands the fulfillment of the bond, is the climax of
the play, even though it constitutes Act IV and there is another act to
come. In that scene, the words "bond," "law," "judgment," and "justice"
echo like hammer blows in the audience's ears, repeated again and again

to convey both Shylock's obsessiveness and the law's necessity. The tension is increased since we think that Antonio is doomed, for we have heard earlier that "The Duke cannot deny the course of *law* ..." (III, iii, 26).[298]

With the force of established law seeming to support him, Shylock is implacable. In the manner of the stuck and stubborn Taurus (a personality type notorious for its recalcitrance and resistance to coercion), he insists on the fulfillment of the contract. Portia urges him to relent, in a famous speech eloquently comparing the God-like descent of grace to the falling of soft rain:

> The quality of mercy is not strained.
> It droppeth as the gentle rain from heaven
> Upon the place beneath. It is twice blest:
> It blesseth him that gives, and him that takes.
> 'Tis mightiest in the mightiest. It becomes
> The thronèd monarch better than his crown.
> His sceptre shows the force of temporal power,
> The attribute to awe and majesty,
> Wherein doth sit the dread and fear of kings;
> But mercy is above the sceptred sway.
> It is enthronèd in the hearts of kings;
> It is an attribute to God himself,
> And earthly power doth then show likest God's
> When mercy seasons justice.
>
> (IV, i, 179–192)

Shylock's response is brief: "My deeds upon my head! I crave the *law*, / The penalty and forfeit of my bond." (IV, i, 201–2)

To Bassanio's added plea (and repeated offers of more money than was originally part of the agreement) and Portia's continued urgings, Shylock stands by his adherence to the law:

> It doth appear you are a worthy *judge*.
> You know the *law*. Your exposition
> Hath been most sound. I charge you by the *law*
> Whereof you are a well-deserving pillar,
> Proceed to *judgement*. By my soul I swear

There is no power in the tongue of man
To alter me. I stay here on my bond.

(IV, i, 231–37)

Ironically, Shylock gets more from the law's precise enactment than
he had anticipated. The disguised Portia—at the very moment when
Shylock is about to carve the pound of flesh from Antonio's chest—
stops him. He can cut flesh from Antonio's body but must shed no blood.

At this point the exalted ideal of the law, the human reflection of
God's divine justice, descends to nitpicking and quibbling over the precise wording of a contract. We have seen something of this literalism
earlier when Portia advises Shylock to have some surgeon by to stanch
Antonio's wound lest he bleed to death. Shylock's rejoinder is "Is it so
nominated in the bond? … I cannot find it. 'Tis not in the bond." (IV, i,
254, 257) It is true. If you read it carefully, the bond allows for no shedding of blood or stand-by surgeons. In addition, the injunction is to take
a pound of flesh—not one bit more or less—or the contract is invalid.
Here the scales of Libra are physically seen on stage, to weigh the amount
promised by legal agreement to Shylock.

> PORTIA: Therefore prepare thee to cut off the flesh.
> Shed thou no blood, nor cut thou less nor more
> But just a pound of flesh. If thou tak'st more
> Or less than a just pound, be it but so much
> As makes it light or heavy in the substance
> Or the division of the twentieth part
> Of one poor scruple—nay, if the *scale* do turn
> But in the estimation of a hair,
> Thou diest, and all thy goods are confiscate.
>
> (IV, i, 319–27)

The outcome would have been different had Shylock responded to
both the Duke's and the disguised Portia's earlier appeals to drop the
suit. To Shylock's implacable insistence on the fulfillment of the law they
oppose the mitigating force of "mercy," a quality equivalent to compassion and forbearance: "in a legal sense mercy may involve such acts as
pardon, forgiveness, or the mitigation of penalties…. mercy is experienced and exercised by a person who has another person in his power, or

under his authority, or from whom no kindness can be claimed."[299] Ironically, the root of the word "mercy" originates from the Medieval Latin
merced,—merces, "price paid, wages," going back to the Latin *merc-merxi*
meaning "merchandise." *We cannot escape the associations with money and
the sign Taurus!*

The quality of mercy is rooted in the nature of God, as is emphasized
in many of the world's great religions. As Portia stresses in her speech,
there is always an imbalance of power between the one being merciful
and the one being forgiven, whether it be God and human beings, or a
king and his subjects, or a judge and the accused. Therefore, for a human
being to be merciful elevates him or her to a higher status, implying
the possibility of experiencing, even if only momentarily, the divine. By
being merciful, you have an opportunity to climb the ladder of Heaven.

That divine quality of compassion, when it enters into a human
being, is directed into and through the heart. In the bodily symbolism
that is part of the "Great Chain of Being," the heart as the center of the
body was equivalent to the Sun as the center of the solar system or to
God as the center and origin of creation. In line with this, Portia, in the
lovely speech just cited, asserts that mercy "is enthroned in the *hearts* of
kings." These implicit associations, which would be grasped immediately
by Shakespeare's audience, account for the word "heart" occurring frequently in the court scene, balancing the repetition of "law," "justice," and
"bond." The Duke welcomes the young and learned doctor "with all my
heart." Bassanio offers again to pay the bond—even twice the required
amount—by saying: "If that will not suffice, / I will be bound to pay it
ten times o'er, / On forfeit of my hands, my head, my *heart.*" When death
seems inevitable, Antonio assures Bassanio that he loves him sincerely
enough to pay the debt "instantly with all my *heart.*" (IV, i, 146, 205–7,
276) Appropriately, when the Egyptian goddess of Truth Ma'at judged
the soul after death, it was the heart that was put on one side of the
scales, weighed against justice (represented by an ostrich feather) in the
other.[300]

This emphasis on the heart reminds us of the overarching archetype
for this play: Venus, the goddess of love. The heart, one of her symbols (think Valentine's Day), is always pictured as the seat of love in the
body. On a physical level, the heart pumps blood and so the red fluid
that gushes when the body is cut resonates with the heart: it is literally
love in movement. Even though the circulation of the blood, pumped by

the heart, was unknown in Shakespeare's time, it is uncannily right that Shylock is prevented from claiming his pound of flesh because he has no right to blood. Blood connotes spirit as opposed to flesh, the body. Shylock stands for the letter, not the spirit, of the law and so can only hope to demand flesh. This legal quibble that ultimately defeats Shylock and saves Antonio is foreshadowed by Bassanio's passionate assurance to his friend earlier in the scene that: "The Jew shall have my flesh, blood, bones, and all / Ere thou shalt lose for me one drop of *blood*." (IV, i, 111–2)

When Shylock refuses the claims of mercy, another Venetian law comes into play, an impersonal one beyond the personal suit of Shylock, one that puts both his life and his goods at risk. Because Shylock is deemed a foreigner threatening the life of a Venetian citizen, his own life is forfeit. Half his goods will go to the target of his malice and the other half devolve to the city. Now, just after Portia's eloquent speech, when Portia, Antonio, and the others could demonstrate the quality of mercy in action, they turn hard-hearted themselves. The extent to which the key players are unmerciful to Shylock is troubling.

The only truly merciful one here is the Duke, who pardons Shylock before he asks for mercy so at least he will be allowed to live. But when Portia asks Antonio to be merciful, Antonio does not acquiesce in the same spirit as the Duke. He does not refuse the moneys that will come to him, though he says he will leave the gains to Lorenzo upon Shylock's death. Then he imposes a cruel and discomforting condition on Shylock that is not in Shakespeare's sources: Shylock must become a Christian.

What is loving about the forced conversion of Shylock? While Shakespeare's audience may have accepted this as a way to compel the alien to join the dominant community, a modern audience can only read this as damning the Christians as hypocrites, eloquently rhapsodizing about mercy and yet showing none. In Antonio's insisting on Shylock's adoption of Christianity, Shylock will lose his livelihood since as a Christian he can no longer charge interest. It is difficult to see how Shylock will have anything to bequeath Jessica upon his death—especially recalling that he is out the three thousand ducats he borrowed from Tubal. We are confronted again with the discrepancy between the lauded ideal and human behavior.

Venus and the LOVE of FRIENDS

Particularly striking in the court scene is the depth of the friendship between Antonio and Bassanio. It is one thing to loan money to a friend and quite another to be willing to give your life for him. Bassanio, for his part, repeatedly offers money, more and more money, in futile attempts to obtain the release of Antonio. (Here again is the equation of money with the exent of one's love.) The strength of their emotional tie is not surprising, for we have seen at the very beginning of the play Antonio's generosity in hazarding all his wealth to finance Bassanio's courtship of Portia. We might say that, as far as Bassanio is concerned, Antonio is all heart.

The depth and open expression of Antonio's love for Bassanio may seem unusual to us who live in an era when the free expression of emotion between males, whether friendly or sexual, is generally stifled. Inspired by the classical idea that male friendship was purer and more refined than male-female relations, it was not only accepted in Shakespeare's time but also thought preferable by some to liaisons between the opposite sexes. Arguments, temper tantrums, and outbreaks of jealousy, obsession, and—in a classic reversal—downright hatred could all too often disrupt male-female relationships and cloud the mind. All of this impeded rational thought; this was disastrous since for the ancients reason was the evidence of the divine in human beings and so entanglements that obscured reason should be shunned. [301]

Antonio's unstinted generosity and willingness to support his friend, even when the success of Bassanio's adventure might alter their close friendship, ennobles his pure and unselfish love. Antonio is willing to risk all his worldly goods, as well as his very existence, for the sake of this friendship. He also expresses appreciation for his other friends besides Bassanio; when Salerio is about to exit in Scene I, Antonio says with great sincerity, "Your worth is very dear in my regard." (I, i, 62) Yet while he is kind, generous, and helpful to those in his immediate circle of friends, only two scenes later we see both Antonio and Bassanio being extremely unloving and unkind to someone outside their circumscribed group. The difference in their words and behavior to the two social groups is stark. Obviously the ideal of love that Antonio shows to Bassanio has limits, which raises some important questions: Who are we to love? Who are we capable of loving? Only our immediate family and friends? Only our social, ethnic, or religious "in group"? Yet who are we encouraged to love by religion, and moral and ethical philosophy?

Typical for Shakespeare, to more vividly highlight the injunction to love unreservedly, he shows us completely opposite behavior in contrast. The highest ideal inherent in Venus is to love universally, to love those who seem alien: from foreign countries, of a different race or faith, or simply different in appearance or dress. This is certainly a challenge: to love those outside our family, clan, community, or race.[302] The lines are drawn in this play, with certain characters definitely excluded, particularly Shylock and his fellow Jews. By both actions and words, Antonio and his group are repeatedly both physically and emotionally abusive to Shylock. Antonio has spit upon and kicked him, for Shylock tells us that Antonio "did void [his] rheum upon my beard, / And did foot me as you spurn a stranger cur / Over your threshold." (I, iii, 113–15) The blatant and ugly maledictions pronounced on Shylock by both Antonio and Gratiano are shockingly vicious. Even while petitioning Shylock for money, Antonio insults Shylock to his face. After Shylock has recounted a story from the Old Testament, Antonio reviles him:

> The *devil* can cite Scripture for his purpose.
> An *evil* soul producing holy witness
> Is like a *villain* with a smiling cheek,
> A goodly apple *rotten* at the heart.
> O, what a goodly outside *falsehood* hath!
>
> (I, iii, 94–8)

Shylock's servant Lancelot also assures us that "the Jew is the very devil incarnation" (though it is hard to see what Shylock has done to Lancelot to inspire that epithet, except perhaps made him work harder) (II, ii, 21–2). Even Shylock's daughter agrees with Lancelot's description, saying: "Our house is hell, and thou, a merry devil. / Didst rob it of some taste of tediousness" (though it is hard to see what Jessica has to complain about except that Shylock keeps a "sober," cautious household) (II, iii, 2–3).[303]

Repeatedly the Christians call Shylock a dog or a wolf. Describing someone as an animal, of course, in light of the worldview of Shakespeare's time, insists that he has fallen below the human realm and become inferior—a serious insult. Tact and diplomacy, not to mention

This play dramatizes the opposing demands of friendship between men versus love between a man and a woman. Since the latter was thought to afflict reason with disturbing passion, male friendship was valued as ennobling and enriching as depicted in this image of two men embracing. In this play, though, unlike The Two Gentlemen of Verona, *Shakespeare has Antonio acknowledge the newly-married Bassanio's commitment to Portia and voluntarily take second place to her. (from Richard Brathwaite,* The English Gentleman, *2nd ed., 1633)*

the unselfish and unstinted love that is the highest expression of Venus, is sorely missed here. Although Shylock has attempted a friendly overture when Antonio approaches him for a loan, he is rebuffed. How can there be social harmony and cooperation when hate-filled curses are hurled by one side to the other?

In the twenty-first century it is impossible not to read this play, with its virulent sixteenth-century intolerance of Jews, as anti-Semitic. Jew-hating has had a long and bitter history throughout western Europe for many centuries. Just prior to Shakespeare's writing *The Merchant of Venice*, in the early 1590s, Christopher Marlowe had penned *The Jew of Malta*, with its villainous Jewish protagonist Barabbas. Yet in Shakespeare's time Shylock would have been perceived as a comic villain, a stock figure from medieval drama with elements added from Venetian commedia dell'arte, complete with a red wig and shoes with curled-up toes. Viewers of the play had probably never met a Jew, since the Jews had been expelled from England in 1270 and were not re-admitted until the mid-1600s when Oliver Cromwell orchestrated their re-admission because he saw financial benefits for the country. All their information would have been based mainly on a long-existing stereotype, which exaggerated the worst qualities.[304]

Not only is there no love directed toward Shylock by the Christians in the play, but there is also an intense constellation of its opposite, hatred. The stark enactment of cruel words and vicious actions presses the case even more for less rancor and more cooperation between both groups—in other words, more Venus! Antonio may love Bassanio as deeply as possible; yet he hates Shylock bitterly. And Shylock loves his daughter, his dead wife, and members of his tribe; yet he hates Antonio passionately. Hatred enters at Shylock's first appearance. He reveals his animus toward Antonio in an aside, showing that the mutual hatred is well established:

> How like a fawning publican he looks.
> I *hate* him for he is a Christian;
> But more, for that in low simplicity
> He lends out money gratis, and brings down
> The rate of usance here with us in Venice.
> If I can catch him once upon the hip

I will feed fat the ancient grudge I bear him.
He *hates* our sacred nation, and he rails,
Even there where merchants most do congregate,
On me, my bargains, and my well-won thrift—
Which he calls interest. Cursed be my tribe,
If I forgive him.

(I, iii, 36–47)

Both characters are locked in an obsessive relationship with one another, each bent on destroying the other. Their hatred binds them as powerfully as love. In light of the psychology of Jung, both Shylock and Antonio are each other's "shadow." The psychological explanation for this is that each has projected onto the other traits that he desires but must reject consciously. The brilliant poet and novelist Margaret Atwood elucidates their deadly fascination with one another:

> Antonio is usually interpreted as a good guy because he lends money without charging interest, but why give him points on that? As a Christian in the play's pretend "Venice" of that time, he wasn't *allowed* to charge interest! He needn't have lent any money at all, of course. So by lending it he's undercutting Shylock's business, but not as a business rival. He isn't a business rival: he isn't in the *business* of moneylending at all, since he doesn't make anything by it. As far as I can see, he's doing it out of anti-Semitism. From the evidence in the play, he's been acting viciously toward Shylock for some time, both in word and in deed. He has projected onto Shylock—as his Shadow—the malice and the greediness that he himself possesses but can't acknowledge. He's made Shylock his whipping boy. That's why Shylock hates him—not just because he's been bringing down the rate of exchange.[305]

No accident that upon the disguised Portia's entrance to the court, her first query is "Which is the merchant here, and which the Jew?" (IV, i, 174)

All the characters in the play at some point behave unlovingly, even the minor character of the clown Lancelot. He makes fun of his own blind father, telling him first that he is dead and then mocking the old man's blindness by kneeling to present the back of his head to his father to identify himself. The old man gropes Lancelot's head, baffled, and can only say, "Thou has got more hair on thy chin than Dobbin my fill-horse on his tail." (II, ii, 83–4)

The major characters behave even more extremely in ways that exhibit downright prejudice. We have already heard Portia's condemnation of her various suitors based on national stereotypes. When the "noble prince" of Morocco comes to Belmont to court Portia and chooses the wrong casket, she comments after he leaves, "Let all of his complexion choose me so." (II, vii, 79). Antonio's bias is based on difference of religion, hers on difference of race. Here the negative aspects of the two signs, Taurus and Libra, come together in both fixed prejudice and unloving language and behavior. The shadow side of Taurus derives from its fixity, its tendency to stay in a rut, to be resistant to change—and consequently reject the unfamiliar or the unconventional.

> The most typical form is intolerance. Taurus is not known for his easy acceptance of others' viewpoints.... Intolerance has a close relationship with prejudice. And prejudice is one of Taurus' chief difficulties on the shadow side. Once he makes up his mind that a particular ideology, religion, race or type of person is a loss, there his mind stays. There's no moving it, no budging it. And he can be incredibly offensive in his criticism of others' values. For Taurus, his values are the only values. He's not averse to being either rude or insulting if you contradict them.[306]

Venus and Libra: LOVE and MARRIAGE

Libra and its sign ruler Venus are associated not only with friendship but also with the creation of one special relationship usually solemnized in the ritual of marriage. Sometimes a friendship develops into a more intimate loving relationship. Once you are partnered or married, though, friendships may be lost or reduced in importance. So balancing friendship with love can become a challenge.

This is a particular theme in *The Merchant of Venice*, since tensions arise from the opposing claims of Antonio and Portia on Bassanio's affections. That Antonio exemplifies the religious ideal of "Greater love than this no man hath, that a man lay down his life for his friends" seems to put his love above everyone else's, even Portia's. This statement recalls the exalted status of male-male relationships in classical through Renaissance times. Antonio's depth of affection for Bassanio is expressed through his generous offering of money. If we measure love that way, Portia's spontaneous and generous offering on Bassanio's behalf to save Antonio's life by doubling or even trebling the original amount of the loan establishes her as an equal to Antonio in virtually unlimited giving.

As Shakespeare's audience would undoubtedly have known, in the Bible the matured young man is told explicitly that in the course of time he will transfer his affections from parents to a marriage partner: "Wherefore a man shall leave father and mother, and shall cleave to his wife; and they shall be two in one flesh" (Gen. 2:24, repeated in Matt. 19:5 and Mark 10:7). The social expectation is also that the loyalty and brotherly love felt with same-sex friends will also be transferred to your mate.

But Bassanio does not quite get the claims of marriage over friendship. Portia sees this and tests him by giving him a ring, declaring that she and all she owns goes with it. The ring is weighted with even greater significance, for Portia warns Bassanio "when you part from, lose, or give away [this ring], / Let it presage the ruin of your love ..." (III, ii, 172–3). Bassanio swears to keep the ring sacred: "But when this ring / Parts from this finger, then parts life from hence. / O, then be bold to say Bassanio's dead." (III, ii, 183–5) Besides setting up a test of his commitment, the giving of the ring has several symbolic resonances. Since Portia is both the earthly and the heavenly Venus, the ring in part signals not only the transfer of assets from her to Bassanio but also represents the heavenly gift of love bestowed on him. It is significant that *she*, goddess-like, gives *him* a ring rather than him giving one to her.

Rings are multi-faceted symbols, connoting on a mundane level a link or a bond between two people or two entities. But they also have other meanings: they unite a couple within a circumscribed territory as a unit; they are more expansive symbols of continuity and wholeness; in the form of a circle, they indicate transcendent ideas of eternity and unending love. Appropriately, a Grecian fable initiated the custom of wearing a wedding ring on the fourth finger of the left hand because an artery from that finger goes directly to the heart, reminding us once again of the link to Venus.

The tension regarding the giving of the rings has to do with Bassanio's allegiance. During the trial scene, when Antonio is just about to be killed, he delivers an explicit statement of his greater claim on Bassanio:

> Give me your hand, Bassanio; fare you well.
> Grieve not that I am fall'n to this for you …
> Commend me to your honourable wife.
> Tell her the process of Antonio's end;
> Say how I loved you. Speak me fair in death,
> And, when the tale is told, *bid her be judge*
> *Whether Bassanio had not once a love.*
>
> (IV, i, 260–1, 268–72)

Irony of ironies! The disguised Portia *is* present and functioning as a "judge"!

Distressed by Antonio's imminent death (and this eloquent speech), Bassanio blurts out:

> Antonio, I am married to a wife
> Which is as dear to me as life itself,
> But life itself, my wife, and all the world
> Are not with me esteemed above thy life.
> I would lose all, ay, sacrifice them all
> Here to this devil, to deliver you.
>
> (IV, i, 277–82)

So Antonio still comes first. To which the disguised Portia, understandably taken aback by this, comments, "Your wife would give you little thanks for that / If she were by to hear you make the offer." (IV, i, 283–4) To intensify the men's ill-advised relegation of their wives to secondary stature, Graziano follows Bassanio's lead to the extreme of wishing his wife dead!—which wins no points with the disguised Nerissa:

> GRAZIANO: I have a wife who, I protest, I love.
>   I would she were in heaven so she could
>   Entreat some power to change this currish Jew.
> NERISSA: [aside] 'Tis well you offer it behind her back;
>   The wish would make else an unquiet house.
>
> (IV, i, 285–9)

No surprise that Shylock comments sarcastically, "These be the Christian husbands." (IV, i, 290)

Of course, in the manner of fairy tales in which the hero does just what he is warned not to do, Bassanio is persuaded to part with the ring. Though he initially resists, he gives in when urged to do so by Antonio, who again presses the superiority of his claim on Bassanio: "My Lord Bassanio, let him have the ring. / Let his deservings and my love withal / Be valued 'gainst your wife's commandement." (IV, i, 445–7)

But when re-united with Portia in the idealized world of Belmont, the full force of Bassanio's commitment to her and the required transfer of allegiance, symbolized by the ring, comes home to him. This is drama- tized first by Nerissa, who chastises Graziano for giving away his ring. Graziano is dismissive of the literal value of the ring he received from Nerissa, reminding us of some Taurean issues prevalent throughout the play: the value we assign to physical things and their intrinsic versus their emotional worth. What's the big deal?, Graziano protests:

> GRAZIANO: … a hoop of gold, a paltry ring
>   That she did give me, whose posy was
>   For all the world like cutlers' poetry
>   Upon a knife—'Love me, and leave me not.'
> NERISSA: What talk you of the posy or the *value*?
>   You swore to me, when I did give it you
>   That you would wear it till your hour of death,
>   And that it should lie with you in your grave.
>   Though not for me, yet for your vehement oaths
>   You should have been respective and have kept it.
>   (V, i, 146–55)

Portia picks up the theme, playing with Bassanio by vowing that *he* would never have parted with the ring she gave him; no, "he would not leave it, / Nor pluck it from his finger for the *wealth* / That the world masters" (V, i, 171–3). Once again the material value of the ring is contrasted to its immaterial significance. Poor Bassanio also protests in his own defense, but is rebutted by Portia in parallel form to his own, establishing Portia as equally clever and equally capable of intelligent argument:

BASSANIO: Sweet Portia,
        If you did know to whom I gave the ring,
        If you did know for whom I gave the ring,
        And would conceive for what I gave the ring,
        And how unwillingly I left the ring
        When naught would be accepted but the ring,
        You would abate the strength of your displeasure.
PORTIA: If you had known the virtue of the ring,
        Or half her worthiness that gave the ring,
        Or your own honour to contain the ring,
        You would not then have parted with the ring.
                                        (V, i, 191–201)

Both women accuse the men of having given the rings to other women—ironic again because, of course, they *were* given to women. The very serious issue of faithfulness in love—a major issue for the success of many Venusian relationships—is made comic because we, the audience, as well as Portia and Nerissa know that the rings came full circle to the original givers. Still, Portia threatens to "have that doctor for my bedfellow" (V, i, 232), and Nerissa vows the same with regard to the doctor's clerk. For the men to be confronted with the prospect of their wives' brazenly-announced adultery sparks a threat of violence from Graziano: "Well, do you so. Let not me take him then, / For if I do, I'll mar the young clerk's pen." (V, i, 235–6)

At this point the quarrel threatens to disrupt the comic atmosphere, and Antonio intervenes, guiltily admitting that "I am th'unhappy subject of these quarrels." Portia, tellingly, reassures him, saying: "Sir, grieve not you. You are welcome notwithstanding." (V, i, 237–8) She seems to intuit that Antonio urged the rings' surrender. This is a crucial time in Portia's and Bassanio's relationship, but Bassanio reaffirms his faith and the primacy of his bond with her: "Pardon this fault, and by my soul I swear / I never more will break an oath with thee." (V, i, 246–7) Now Antonio steps in, once more vouching for Bassanio—only this time he pledges to assure Bassanio's faithfulness to Portia, thus graciously ceding place to her.

        I once did lend my body for his wealth
        Which, but for him that had your husband's ring,

Had quite miscarried. I dare be bound again,
My soul upon the forfeit, that your lord
Will never more break faith advisedly.

(V, i, 248–252)

Once "body bound," now Antonio is "soul bound," and this time he relinquishes his claim on Bassanio by vouching for Bassanio's love for Portia. Though lesser in intensity, this is a forced "conversion" somewhat similar to Shylock's. We may at first believe that Antonio's victory over Shylock was complete, that he can exult in his revenge since he insisted on Shylock's conversion to Christianity and imposed conditions on the distribution of Shylock's assets upon his death. But in this scene Antonio is "bound" again, forced to withdraw his emotional claim on Bassanio in the light of Bassanio's uniting with Portia in marriage.

It All Ends in Belmont…

Like Shylock, who vanishes from the play at the end of Act IV, Antonio though present is an outsider in the final scene in Belmont, where three happy couples celebrate their good fortune. Though he remains unmated and loveless, he does get his money back. (That trade again, money for lack of love.) Antonio's wealth is magically restored when Portia produces a letter revealing that three of his argosies have "richly come to harbour suddenly." (How Portia came to know this is a mystery; she only hints, "You shall not know by what strange accident / I chanced on this letter.") (V, i, 276–8).

So much seems orchestrated by the goddess-like Portia: the triumph in the courtroom, the giving of the rings with the foreknowledge that they will be relinquished, and the miraculous restoration of Antonio's wealth. Portia's almost-divine status has been earlier implied through the language used by characters such as Bassanio who lauds her as "golden" and the Prince of Morocco who hymns her as a "saint" and an "angel." Venus-like, Portia descends like a goddess from the upper world, disguised, for often divinities appeared on Earth obscured in cloud or mist, or embodied in an object like a burning bush, or pretending to be an ordinary mortal testing human beings.

Belmont, that higher place, has overtones of the ideal world. "Belmont" means "beautiful mountain," and it is indeed a place of music,

moonlight, and celebration above the grubby and imperfect world of
Venice with its manipulative deal-making and implacable law. When we
return to Belmont after Portia's appearance in the Venetian court, it is
nighttime, the feminine half of day. Lorenzo and Jessica are looking up
at the stars and Lorenzo is lauding music (an art favored by Venus and,
as we remember, an echo of celestial harmony). His lovely paean sets the
tone for Portia's reappearance, with earthly gold now translated to stars
studding the floor of heaven and angel-like planets sounding a cosmic
symphony:

> How sweet the moonlight sleeps upon this bank!
> Here will we sit, and let the sounds of music
> Creep in our ears. Soft stillness and the night
> Become the touches of sweet harmony.
> Sit, Jessica. Look how the floor of heaven
> Is thick inlaid with patens of bright gold.
> There's not the smallest orb which thou behold'st
> But in his motion like an angel sings ...
>
> (V, i, 53–60)

These "touches of sweet harmony" have an almost magical ability to
stop wild animals in their tracks, or, like Orpheus, have power over trees,
stones, and floods, or may transform the agitated human soul,

> Since naught so stockish, hard, and full of rage
> But music for the time doth change his nature.
> The man that hath no music in himself,
> Nor is not mov'd with concord of sweet sounds,
> Is fit for treasons, stratagems, and spoils.
> The motions of his spirit are dull as night
> And his affections dark as Erebus [hell].
>
> (V, i, 81–7)

In this play "the man that hath no music in himself" is Shylock, who
shuts the doors and windows of his house against "the drum / And the
vile squealing of the wry-necked fife" lest "the sound of shallow fopp'ry
enter / My sober house." (II, v, 28–9, 34–35) Music, in its sweetness,
melodiousness, and concord, has as its template the cosmic "music of

the spheres." No wonder it introduces the final scene of adjustment and reconciliation.

The two locales of the play, Venice and Belmont, stand for the two signs of the zodiac that inspire the interwoven stories: Venice is a Taurean place of money-making and stubborn prejudice, on both sides; Belmont is the realm of Libra, a place of great wealth, the arts (especially music), and union in marriage. In Belmont the values of Venice—the pursuit of money as primary—are reversed. That is why Bassanio, in Belmont to court Portia, must choose the lead casket and not the golden one. Belmont is the place of the idealized Libra, ruled by Venus in her highest representation as love, compassion, and forgiveness, and far removed from the rough negotiations of the world of trade and time.

So the main themes associated with the planet Venus—LOVE, FRIENDSHIP, and MONEY— that rules over the two zodiacal signs of Taurus and Libra saturate the play, vividly incarnated in the principal players in the drama and in almost all the events in the plot. It is difficult to separate the three, since they are deftly interwoven throughout the drama. From the opening of the play, there is an equivalence of wealth and worth or wealth and beauty or wealth and love. Money and love are frequently conflated. Scene I began with Antonio's friends assuming that the only two possible causes for his sadness are either the fear of losing money or the experience of unrequited love, and with Bassanio's declaration "To you, Antonio, / I owe the most, *in money and in love* …"; and with Antonio equating: "*My purse, my person*" (I, i, 130–1, 138).

The key word in the play, the one word in which are embedded the play's triple themes of money, friendship, and love, is the word "bond." With multiple meanings, this word encompasses all the associations with both Taurus and Libra. In finance it is "an interest-bearing certificate of debt … obligating the issuer to pay the principal at a specified time." In law, it is "an obligation in writing under seal, the simple form being that in which a person or corporation agrees to pay a certain sum at a specified time." And in relationship, it connotes "that which binds or holds together; a bond; tie; a uniting force or influence: *bonds* of friendship," as well as "a substance that cements or unites; also, the union itself." This last meaning is the one referred to when we say, "These are the ties that *bind*." No wonder that the word "bond" is so often repeated in the courtroom scene.

In the ideal world, those who are beautiful are good, those who speak eloquently of their highest values act in accord with them, and those who have wealth also sincerely love. In *The Merchant of Venice*, we are presented with lovely poetry that exalts the ideal human being and the ideal ethic (mercy) for both an individual and a society. Yet we see imperfections and contradictions when human beings fail to live up to those ideals. We see the gap between the inner, original, and perfect human being and the physical, embodied, imperfect creature who stands at the fulcrum of creation. In so witnessing, we as onlookers are put in the same position of honoring the ideal of mercy by forgiving the behaviors and hypocrises of the all-too-human protagonists and antagonists. We may judge Bassanio as foolish and shallow, Portia to be hypocritical, Antonio to be a failed Christian…but the true distillation of the essence of the drama we have witnessed unfolding over several hours will be in our tender response to the imperfections of the characters and our compassionate forgiveness of their human actions in the light of their times and circumstances. We can then rejoice with them as they celebrate their good fortune (in every sense of the word) in the uplifted place of Belmont.

If mapped for a period of eight years, the cycles of Venus and the Earth around the Sun create a five-pointed star or five-petalled flower, so regularly that the pentagram became the symbol of Venus and of perfect beauty and rhythmic harmony. (Image from A Little Book of Coincidence in the Solar System *by John Martineau, Wooden Books, 2006.)*

CHAPTER 10

The Hidden Astrological Key to
Macbeth

Scorpio and its Ruler Mars

Even the evil meet with good fortune as long as their evil has
yet to mature. But when it's matured, that's when they meet with evil.
Even the good meet with bad fortune as long as their good has yet to mature.
But when it's matured, that's when they meet with good fortune.

—Dhammapada 9, translated by Thanissaro Bhikkhu

O, full of scorpions is my mind, dear wife! —Macbeth (III, ii, 37)

The Story

In thunder and lightning, three witches meet on a heath and plan an encounter with Macbeth. In the meantime, King Duncan of Scotland receives reports from a wounded sergeant, a "bloody man," describing how the acclaimed warrior Macbeth, along with his fellow general Banquo, has put down an internal rebellion led by the traitorous thane of Cawdor and has heroically massacred external invaders from Norway. Duncan declares that he will transfer Cawdor's title to Macbeth. The three "weird sisters" do appear suddenly to Macbeth and Banquo as they return from battle and predict that Macbeth, now thane of Glamis, will become thane of Cawdor, and eventually King. When Banquo asks the witches to "look into the seeds of time" for him, he is told that he will beget a line of kings though he will be none. Fueled by the witches' prophecies, Macbeth's imagination as well as his fear is stirred and his ambition grows—especially when Duncan suddenly names his son Malcolm as his successor.

When the King arrives at Macbeth's castle, Macbeth is tempted by his presence and goaded by his wife to assassinate him in order to take the throne. After struggling with his conscience, Macbeth tells his wife that he wants to cancel their plan. But Lady Macbeth needles her husband into proceeding with the plan to murder Duncan, who is drugged by her and stabbed by Macbeth that very night. Once he has killed Duncan, though, Macbeth's mind is disturbed and he regrets his deed. He forgets to leave the bloody weapons at the murder scene, and Lady Macbeth must return to the chamber to plant the gory daggers on Duncan's drugged grooms.

Macduff and Lennox arrive, pounding on the door to awaken a drunken porter, and discover the king's bloodied body. To prevent them from protesting their innocence, Macbeth kills the grooms. Anxious and suspicious, Duncan's sons flee to England and Ireland.

Once invested as King, Macbeth's conscience begins to trouble him even more. Beset by terrible dreams, his fear and insecurity lead him to arrange the killing of his former friend Banquo, who has begun to suspect that Macbeth arranged Duncan's murder. Banquo's ghost appears to disrupt a royal banquet and disturb Macbeth who is also fearful and doubtful because Banquo's son Fleance escaped the hired murderers. Macbeth now actively seeks out the three witches, who promise that he cannot be destroyed until "Birnam wood come to Dunsinane" castle and that he is invincible unless he confronts someone "not of woman born." Reassured, Macbeth proceeds to order the massacre of the family of Macduff, around whom opposition to his rule has begun to coalesce. Scotland is suffering under the tyrant's rule.

Macduff himself has fled to England, where he seeks out Malcolm whose virtues are contrasted with Macbeth's vices. They and the English forces that have gathered there proceed to invade Scotland. Just before the final battle Lady Macbeth, now guilt-ridden, haunted, and sleepwalking at nights, commits suicide. A messenger reports that Birnam wood moves toward the castle and Macbeth realizes that he has been manipulated by "juggling fiends." Disheartened but driven to fight, Macbeth arms and leaves the castle. In a final bloody encounter Macduff reveals that he had a caesarian birth (and thus is not "of woman born"), clashes with the "hell-hound" Macbeth, and beheads him. Duncan's son Malcolm is hailed as king, honors his fellow fighters as newly created "earls," and, promising to "perform in measure, time, and place" whatever else is needful, restores order.

The Key to Macbeth: Mars

Clues to the archetypal symbolism underlying *Macbeth* are dramatically revealed in both the first and second scenes of the play. Scene 1 is unusually brief—only twelve lines—and features three supernatural creatures: the malevolent witches who speak in ambiguities (the battle will be "lost and won") and invoke a clouded and contaminated atmosphere ("fog and filthy air"). We are in the realm of the occult.

Scene ii, however, takes us into the human world, where battles are raging. An alarum sounds, characteristically the noise of war, and the first spoken words are "What bloody man is that?" A Captain reporting to King Duncan paints a picture of the tireless Macbeth's superhuman achievement in slaughtering the rebel leader Macdonwald:

> [B]rave Macbeth—well he deserves that name!—
> Disdaining Fortune, with his brandished steel
> Which smoked with bloody execution,
> Like Valour's minion
> Carved out his passage till he faced the slave,
> *Which ne'er shook hands nor bade farewell to him,*
> Till he unseamed him from the nave to th'chops,
> And fixed his head upon our battlements.
>
> (I, ii, 16–23)

Without the courtesies of Venus mentioned in the previous chapter (like a gentlemanly shaking of hands), Macbeth confronts the head of the rebel forces, the "merciless Macdonwald," and in hand-to-hand combat slices him from nave (navel) to the chops (jaw). This aggression is celebrated as a defense of the state and of established authority. King Duncan, upon hearing the Captain's vivid description of the battle, exclaims, "O valiant cousin! Worthy gentleman!" (I, ii, 24). In line with hierarchical symbolism explored earlier, both Macbeth and Banquo are compared to eagles and the lion, both at the top of their class. So our first impression of the two generals is supremely positive (I, ii, 35).

To reinforce our immediate impression of Macbeth as an undaunted warrior, Shakespeare doubles the battle: not only must Macbeth defeat rebellious forces that threaten the state from within, but he must also take arms against the opportunistic Norwegians who seize the chance to invade from without. The Captain assures the King that neither Macbeth nor Banquo were disheartened by this second threat: "I must report they were / As cannons overcharged with double cracks / So they doubly redoubled strokes upon the foe" (I, i, 36–8). The word "double" will assume a more sinister meaning later when the witches begin their incantation around the cauldron with "Double, double, toil and trouble," recalling this unusual double combat as well as the "double dealing" that is rampant throughout the play.

Many key words in this scene—bloody, revolt, soldier, brave, merciless, valor, quarrel, execution, and, conflict—point inexorably to MARS, the god of WAR. Mars, dubbed "the red planet," has specific rulership over blood. We are unquestionably in the arena of Mars.

Like all astrological symbols, Mars is double-sided, as is illustrated by two quite different classical interpretations. The Greeks' name for their god of war was Ares. They considered him unevolved, a symbol of unthinking brute and blundering force with a low level of conscious development and little self-awareness. This aspect of Mars appears in Shakespeare's *Troilus and Cressida* as the character of Ajax. Thersites, an unpleasant fellow who is always spewing invective, verbally attacks Ajax, calling him a "mongrel beef-witted lord." Thersites vows that Ajax has in his skull "no more brain than I have in mine elbows. An asnico [little ass] may tutor thee." Tellingly, he comments that: "Mars [is] his idiot!" (II, i, 11–2, 42–4, 52) As a follower of this unevolved Mars, Ajax is foolish, uncivilized, and animal-like. Throughout Thersites' denunciation, Ajax can only threaten or repeatedly pummel him—thus proving the truth of Thersites' assessment that Ajax is dull-witted and simply brawn for hire.[327]

By contrast, the Romans exalted Mars as defender of the state, appropriate for an empire that depended on military might for its expansion and consolidation.[308] At the beginning of the play, when he has earned praise and honor as captain of the King's forces, Macbeth is almost the literal incarnation of this more positive Roman Mars. To defend the state, under the direction of a legitimate king, is highly esteemed. Duncan judges that the captain's words and wounds "smack of honour both." This honor applies to Macbeth as well, who has dominated the field. Ross even dubs him "Bellona's bridegroom," married to the Roman goddess of war. (I, ii, 54)[309] Infused with the spirit of Mars, Macbeth is invincible:

[H]e has the light of the Berserker in his eyes, the divine inebria-
tion of war. The Berserker is the Teutonic version of the spirit of
Ares, the warrior who is drunk on the wine of combat. When a
warrior is taken over by this spirit, nothing can harm him; he can go
right through the enemy's battle lines without a scratch.[310]

When Macbeth and Banquo enter in the next scene, they seem perfectly healthy: having been infused with the Martian spirit of war, they
seem untouched, unwounded, and unscarred by their experiences on the
field of battle.

In astrological tradition prior to the modern era Mars had a poor reputation as the "lesser malefic"—not bringing as many difficulties as Saturn,
the "greater malefic," but coinciding with bad luck or ill fortune nonetheless. Consistent with the more reprehensible side of Mars, as the story
progresses Macbeth devolves into a "bloody-sceptered" tyrant instead of
legitimate ruler, a murderer of defenseless women and children instead of a
hero in battle against armed men, and finally a "dead butcher" mated with
a "fiend-like queen" (V, xi, 35). Ironically, just as at the beginning he decapitated the traitorous Macdonwald and mounted his head on the Scottish
battlements, at the end *he* is decapitated and *his* head is displayed as a
trophy of war. Symbolically, since Macbeth has progressively become more
obsessed and less rational, he has "lost his head." (It is also significant that
the head is the part of the body ruled by Mars!)

In keeping with the spirit of Mars (who is too impatient to allow for
lulls in the action), *Macbeth* is the shortest of Shakespeare's plays, and
the action proceeds directly and precipitously (like the Martian arrow
loosed from a bow) once it begins. The pace of the play is relentless,
and Macbeth acts in accord with it. After his second encounter with
the weird sisters, he vows, "From this moment / The very firstlings of
my heart shall be / The firstlings of my hand. And even now, / To crown
my thoughts with acts, be it thought and done." (IV, i, 162–5) Without reflection or hesitation, his intentions will immediately manifest in
direct Mars-like action.

The Zodiacal Sign of Scorpio, Ruled by Mars

Mars is traditionally assigned rulership of SCORPIO, the eighth sign of
the zodiac. As a tragedy and for dramatic purposes, the play concerns

itself with the uglier and more repugnant expressions of the sign Scorpio along with the downsides of its ruler Mars.

Scorpio is probably the most complex and difficult zodiacal symbol to unspool, encompassing profound areas of challenge, mystery, and taboo: the secrets of birth, the fearsomeness of death, and the enigma of an afterlife; the compelling power of sexual desire with all its ecstasies and degradations; the forbidden realm of the occult, both exalting and damning (and damned); the challenge of wielding power in the sphere of politics; and the use of depth psychology to probe the inner psyche. Individuals with strong Scorpio energy in their horoscopes may attain positions of influence without being elected, like Mahatma Gandhi who influenced millions and altered history or Bill Gates who made millions and midwived the transition into the computer age. Other Sun in Scorpio figures, like Teddy Roosevelt, Charles de Gaulle, and Hillary Rodham Clinton, participated dramatically in the political process through conducting conventional campaigns and occupying established offices. Politics and leadership positions offer particular challenges for Scorpios; you may run for office with the most idealistic of motives—to serve the people who elect you and legislate for the good of the state—but all too easily become bogged down in the quagmires of the political process, tempted by money and influence and lured into egotistic displays of bombastic rhetoric.

Because Scorpios often exude a charged energy through a forceful personality as a result of sustained focus, a developed will power, and consistent self-discipline, others often fear them or are in awe of them. It is easy to impute sinister motives to a Scorpio even when the Scorpio person may be working to bring about the greatest good for the greatest number. Whether a force for good or ill, the Scorpio type is magnetically compelling. The challenges for a Scorpio are daunting: coping with physical desires; finding a creative outlet for intense feelings; keeping psychologically healthy; and exerting appropriate influence in a chosen sphere. All of these themes are explored in *Macbeth*.

The Scorpio type is especially driven by strong and passionate DESIRES, usually manifested as a hunger for power, sexual pleasure, or wealth (or all of these). Gaining the fruits of these desires is not necessarily evil, unless you use illegal or immoral means to do so. The first step to a healthy integration of these desires into your life is to acknowledge your lust for power, or the intensity of your sexual drive, or your yearning for money. If you feel GUILT about any of these, the tendency is to SUPPRESS DESIRE, which leads to various personality kinks, perversions, and displacements that can cause you to act out in destructive ways—destructive to yourself and possibly to others around you. GUILT can also trigger an overactive CONSCIENCE, so that regret for past actions haunts you while desires still persist.

For Macbeth, what drives him is the desire for POWER, his AMBITION to be king of Scotland. This is confirmed by both Lady Macbeth who describes her husband as "not without ambition" (I, v, 17) and Macbeth himself who admits that the only spur to his intent is "vaulting ambition"—but adds ominously that it "o'erleaps itself / And falls on th'other—" (I, vii, 25–8). Then begins the terrible struggle within Macbeth between acting on this desire or restraining it.

The struggle is made more complex by the influence of the three witches, who predict his elevation to kingship, and by the persuasion of his wife, who urges him on to greatness by "catching the nearest way." We know he is tormented by their combined influence and by his own lust for power which conflicts with social and cultural inhibitions because he laments, "O, full of scorpions is my mind, dear wife!" (III, ii, 37) The SCORPION, of course, is the creature associated with the sign Scorpio, and the pictograph for the sign includes an upturned stinger that warns of danger and threatens death.[311]

Another animal associated with the sign Scorpio is the SNAKE, a powerful symbol in the West. In the story of Adam and Eve in the Garden of Eden the snake represents the first couple's desire for knowledge and consequently is a personification of temptation and evil. There are many telling references to snakes in *Macbeth*, especially Lady Macbeth's advice to her husband: "To beguile the time, / Look like the time; bear welcome in your eye, / Your hand, your tongue; look like the innocent flower, / But be the *serpent* under 't." (I, v, 61–4) When Macbeth anguishes over the prophecy that Banquo's sons will continue the kingly line, he determines to arrange the deaths of both Banquo and his son Fleance. He tells Lady Macbeth, "We have scorched [slashed] the *snake*, not killed it," implying that the threat now comes from Banquo. (III, ii, 15) After Banquo's murder, Macbeth commends the murderers: "Thanks for that. / There the grown *serpent* lies. The *worm* that's fled [Banquo's son Fleance] / Hath nature that in time will *venom* breed, / No teeth for th' present." (III, iv, 27–30) Psychologically it is revealing that while Lady

Macbeth suggests that Macbeth should be the serpent, by the time he arranges the deaths of Banquo and Fleance, he has projected his own evil onto them: *they* have become the serpents. (This recalls a similar projection of snake imagery in *A Midsummer Night's Dream*, mentioned in Chapter 7.)

The snake is a potent symbol for Scorpio because it is capable of continually renewing itself, periodically shedding an outgrown skin for a new and fresh one. Positively, "Snakes are guardians of the springs of life and of immortality, and also of those superior riches of the spirit that are symbolized by hidden treasure … since its sinuous shape is similar to that of waves, [they] may be a symbol of the wisdom of the deeps and of the great mysteries."[312] Connected not only with water but also with the feminine (Scorpio is a yin or feminine sign), snakes were often depicted in the hands of various Mediterranean goddesses, like Artemis, Persephone, and—tellingly—Hecate (who appears in the play along with the three witches). This probably indicated that these goddesses had power over life and death. Negatively, the image of Medusa as snaky-haired and capable of turning one who looked on her into stone coincides with the propensity of the Scorpio type as a fixed sign to become stuck in repetitive patterns and frozen in inaction—or to freeze you with its fixed stare and root you to the spot in fear.[313]

Other animals associated with the dark side of Scorpio are black birds such as ravens and all creatures of the night such as owls. Owls are mentioned several times during the play, most significantly immediately before Duncan's murder when Lady Macbeth hears it shrieking, and then after the murder when an owl achieves ascendency by killing a noble falcon. Falcons fly at higher altitudes than owls, implying that the higher has been brought down by the lower. Before the banquet and just after Macbeth has enlisted hired assassins to kill Banquo and his son, Macbeth again invokes darkness to hide his deeds and refers to a black bird: "Light thickens, and the *crow* / Makes wing to the rooky wood; / Good things of day begin to droop and drowse, / Whiles night's *black* agents to their preys do rouse." (III, ii, 51–4) As always in Shakespeare's works, dominant images such as these reinforce other clues to the archetypal zodiacal sign to which the play is keyed.

Not just black birds, but all things of the color BLACK are associated with the sign Scorpio, often decorated with splashes of RED. Innumerable references to black night and to blood stud the play from beginning to end. These are the main colors mentioned throughout.

The Water Element and Emotions: Control versus Repression

Scorpio is a WATER sign, the second of three in the zodiacal pantheon. Shakespeare inserts many and significant references to water in the play, like Lady Macbeth's confident assumption that a small amount can wash away their sin: "A little water clears us of this deed." (II, ii, 65) Even more stunning is Macbeth's lament after the murder of King Duncan: not only will "a little water" *not* wash away his crime, but he questions whether "all great Neptune's ocean [can] wash this blood / Clean from my hand? No, this my hand will rather / The multitudinous seas incarnadine, / Making the green one red." (II, ii, 58–61) The power attributed to water, of purification, has been reversed, and Macbeth's dreadful deed corrupts the entire ocean. After Macbeth has added the death of Banquo to his account, Macbeth says, "I am in blood/Stepped in so far that, should I wade no more, / Returning were as tedious as go o'er." (III, iv, 135–7). His previous comment foreshadows a complete transformation of the sea; it no longer consists of water but is now entirely blood, as if Macbeth's blood-letting has flooded the world.

Water symbolizes the emotional level of each human being, and individuals with many water signatures in their horoscopes are motivated primarily by feelings. One of the key challenges for the Scorpio type is dealing with emotions. The archetypal Scorpio is sensitive to emotional undercurrents and may experience more intense and more deeply felt EMOTIONS than most. You must learn to manage these in various ways or they can flood your psyche and destabilize your personality. Ungovernable temper tantrums or weeping fits may be symptoms of this. Deliberately inducing tears periodically by reading books or watching films that trigger emotional responses can help blow off some emotional energy before it becomes overwhelming. You can also exert some CONTROL over feelings by engaging the mind in positive self-talk, writing about emotional responses to situations, or committing yourself to long-term therapy. In each case, the mind, the level above feelings in the Elizabethan worldview and symbolized by the air element, is used as a counter-balance.

Because intense feelings can be overwhelming and not easily integrated, the Scorpio person may opt for EMOTIONAL REPRESSION. This correlates perfectly with the specific manifestation of water associated with Scorpio, its frozen form as ice.[314] The typically repressed Scorpio can become fixated on emotional issues that may either fester openly or be driven below conscious awareness. Buried in the unconscious, these emotional complexes can drive actions compulsively and uncontrollably; in that case, long-term therapy is the best choice.

Good advice for this personality type is to get in touch with these strong feelings gingerly and gradually, to admit deeper feelings (especially the disturbing ones) honestly, and to try and manage them so that they are less overpowering. This may prevent them from becoming so dominant that the entire personality shapes itself around their management or repression. The process of release and relief is difficult because Scorpio types seem fated to deal with the most negative emotions—such as jealousy, envy, resentment, bitterness, hatred, vengefulness, and anger, even escalating to rage. These may also include FEAR and, in the extreme, even paranoia and terror. As we shall see, fear is the emotion that most colors the atmosphere of *Macbeth*. The worldview of Shakespeare's time implicitly encourages individuals to work to transform and purify negatives into positives; Scorpios in particular have the task of transmuting these negative emotions into kindness, compassion, and unselfish love—a very difficult task.

It is emotionally exhausting to keep strong emotions at bay or to keep them below the conscious threshold. One consequence is that you can lose the capacity to feel anything, even the more desirable and socially acceptable emotions.

We see the intensity of Macbeth's emotions from the beginning of the play, when he reacts sensitively and strongly to the witches' declarations by being startled, fearful, and shaken. But by the end of the drama, Macbeth is so out of touch emotionally that he has entirely lost the capacity to respond. When women cry within, mourning the Queen, he who trembled to think of murdering Duncan cannot feel any alarm or disquiet:

> I have almost forgot the taste of fears.
> The time has been, my senses would have cooled
> To hear a night-shriek, and my fell of hair

Would at a dismal treatise rouse and stir
As life were in't. I have supped full with horrors.
Direness, familiar to my slaughterous thoughts,
Cannot once start me.

(V, v, 9–15)

Macbeth is so emotionally dead that when he is told the reason for
the women crying, that the Queen is dead, he can only remark, "She
should have died hereafter …" (V, v, 17). Then comes one of the most
powerful statements of emotional numbness in Western literature:

To-morrow, and to-morrow, and to-morrow
Creeps in this petty pace from day to day
To the last syllable of recorded time,
And all our yesterdays have lighted fools
The way to dusty death. Out, out, brief candle.
Life's but a walking shadow, a poor player
That struts and frets his hour upon the stage,
And then is heard no more. It is a tale
Told by an idiot, full of sound and fury,
Signifying nothing.

(V, v, 18–27)

As a deliberate contrast to Macbeth's managing of his emotions (or
mismanagement since they are ultimately suppressed), Shakespeare presents Macduff as a foil. Macduff is told, shockingly and unexpectedly, that
his castle was surprised and his wife and children savagely slaughtered.
You cannot imagine more horrible news for a husband and father. But
Shakespeare has Macduff respond in ways that outline deliberate strategies to cope with powerful feelings triggered by traumatic events. At this
terrible emotional blow, at first Macduff cannot even speak. When he
tries to, encouraged by Malcolm, his first attempts are in choppy lines as
he reels at the enormity of his loss.

MALCOLM: What, man, ne'er pull your hat upon your
brows.
Give sorrow words. The grief that does not speak
Whispers the o'erfraught heart and bids it break.
MACDUFF: My children too?

ROSS: Wife, children, servants, all
     That could be found.
MACDUFF: And I must be from thence!
     My wife killed too? ...
     He has no children. All my pretty ones?
     Did you say all? O hell-kite! All?
     What, all my pretty chickens and their dam
     At one fell swoop?

                                        (IV, iii, 209–14, 217–20)

When Malcolm urges Macduff to "Dispute it like a man," Macduff delivers this extremely important statement: "I shall do so. / But I must also feel it as a man." Macduff acknowledges the necessity of staying with his feelings, however uncomfortable, and not banishing them from conscious awareness: "I cannot but remember such things were / That were most precious to me." (IV, iii, 221–5) In this brief exchange, we can perceive four stages of handling grief that Shakespeare sequences: initial silence, groping speech, acknowledged deep feeling, and consciously sustained remembrance.

In line with the more positive Mars, Macduff is urged to go one step farther: to convert the emotional energy of the grief he feels at the slaughter of his family into sharp and focused REVENGE on the perpetrator. Macduff does exert *some* emotional control, keeping his feelings under the governance of reason; then he redirects his powerful rage, an accepted masculine response, to justifiable vengeance:

MALCOLM: Be this the whetstone of your sword. *Let grief*
     Convert to anger. blunt not the heart, *enrage it.*
MACDUFF: O, I could play the woman with mine eyes
     And braggart with my tongue! But gentle heavens
     Cut short all intermission. Front to front
     Bring thou this fiend of Scotland and myself.
     Within my sword's length set him ...
MALCOLM: This tune goes *manly.*

                                        (IV, iii, 230–36, 237)

This anoints Macduff as the legitimate executioner of Macbeth, because Macduff has just cause, a personal motive. But eliminating Macbeth satisfies an impersonal goal too, one that is in line with the world-view outlined in Chapter 3: to exorcize the evil that has infected the country and restore the body politic to health.

Water Signs and the Power of the Imagination

All of the water signs (Cancer, Scorpio, and Pisces) have potentially powerful IMAGINATIONS, that is, pictures easily and vividly come before their inner eyes, whether triggered by an interior thought or an external stimulus. No wonder that Albert Einstein (with the Sun in Pisces in his horoscope) famously said, "Imagination is more important than knowledge. For knowledge is limited to all we now know and understand, while imagination embraces the entire world, and all there ever will be to know and understand." We have already encountered Shakespeare's ruminations on imaginative power in *A Midsummer Night's Dream*, when Theseus observes:

> The lunatic, the lover, and the poet
> Are of *imagination* all compact.
> One sees more devils than vast hell can hold;
> That is, the madman. The lover, all as frantic,
> Sees Helen's beauty in a brow of Egypt.
> The poet's eye, in a fine frenzy rolling,
> Doth glance from heaven to earth, from earth to heaven;
> And as *imagination bodies forth*
> *The forms of things unknown, the poet's pen*
> *Turns them to shapes and gives to airy nothing*
> *A local habitation and a name.*
>
> (V, i, 7–17)

An enhanced ability to experience fresh and vibrant images is a gift to the creative artist, but a curse to those whose imagination tends to the morbid as does Macbeth's. He has the most powerful imagination of anyone in the drama, but like many *sensitives*, he is attuned to doom and disaster. King Duncan's observation of Macbeth in the midst of the Norwegian invaders, as reported by Ross, is eerily apt: he is "Nothing afeard of what thyself didst make, / Strange images of death." (I, iii, 94–5)

Almost immediately "strange images of death" do indeed swim into

Macbeth's inner vision. The witches' prophecies stimulate his imagination to produce a "horrid image [that] doth unfix my hair / And make
my seated heart knock at my ribs …" (I, iii, 134–5). He may already be
visualizing the death of Duncan as the route to kingship. So strong is his
imaginative capability that on the night of the assassination a phantom
dagger almost achieves physical form, leading him to Duncan's chamber
to make the "horrid image" a reality. True to the definition of "image,"
this dagger can be seen but not touched, emphasizing the distinction
between the sensible and the insensible. For those with much water
energy in their horoscopes, the boundary between the visible and invisible worlds can be very thin. So real does this image appear to Macbeth
that he tries to seize hold of it:

> Come, let me clutch thee.
> I have thee not, and yet I see thee still.
> Art thou not, fatal vision, sensible
> To feeling as to sight? Or art thou but
> A dagger of the mind, a false creation
> Proceeding from the heat-oppressed brain?
> I see thee yet, in form as palpable
> As this which now I draw....
> Mine eyes are made the fools o' th' other senses,
> Or else worth all the rest. I see thee still,
> And on thy blade and dudgeon gouts of blood,
> Which was not so before. There's no such thing.
> It is the bloody business which informs
> Thus to mine eyes.
>
> (II, i, 34–41, 44–9)

As if he is clairvoyant, Macbeth sees the image morph, jumping
from the present when the dagger is clean to the future when it is daubed
with blood. It seems that through an enhanced faculty of imagination
Macbeth precognitively sees the future. Other characters are contrasted
to him, so that the vitality of his almost psychic imagination is contrasted to their insensitivity. After the murder, Lady Macbeth rebukes
her unnerved husband with "The sleeping and the dead / Are but as
pictures. 'Tis the eye of childhood / That fears a painted devil." For her
"A little water clears us of this deed," while he imagines that the blood on
his hands will flood the entire ocean. (II, ii, 51–3, 65, 58–61)

As the action unfolds, Macbeth creates (or we might say Shakespeare dramatizes) "strange images of death" objectively on the stage, as Macbeth orchestrates more and more killings, first of Banquo and then of Macduff's wife and children. And the initially hardened and insensitive Lady Macbeth entertains images of death subjectively, while sleeping and sleepwalking. The powerful imaginative ability of the water-sign types surfaces, whether the characters want it to or not.

The Need to Protect: Masking and Hiding

You may consciously acknowledge and be in touch with your emotions and intentions, but if they are socially unacceptable or morally questionable, you may be driven to mask them. For that reason Scorpios are often masters of dissimulation. So good are they at "putting on a poker face" that they often appear calm, cool, and in control, though much may be roiling beneath the surface. Early in the action, Macbeth consciously chooses to hide his powerful feelings and intense ambition. Upon hearing Duncan proclaim Malcolm as his heir, Macbeth immediately importunes, "Stars, hide your fires, / Let not light see my black and deep desires ..." (I, iv, 50–1). Lady Macbeth reinforces his determination to conceal his true feelings, observing, "Your face, my thane, is as a book where men / May read strange matters. To beguile the time, / Look like the time; bear welcome in your eye, / Your hand, your tongue; look like the innocent flower, / But be the serpent under't" (I, v, 60–4). Once persuaded to do the murder, Macbeth bids them both be "Away, and mock the time with fairest show. / False face must hide what the false heart doth know." (I, vii, 81–2)

Lady Macbeth does likewise: while conjuring the dark powers to turn her into a hardened and committed plotter, she invokes dark night to come: "And pall thee in the dunnest smoke of hell, / That my keen knife see not the wound it makes, / Nor heaven peep through the blanket of the dark / to cry 'Hold, hold!'" (I, v, 49–52)

Once gaps widen between your inner feelings and your projected image, you face two possible ways of coping with this disjunction: you can either identify yourself with the outward show and suppress your true self or you can sustain a conscious and uncomfortable awareness of the distance between your thoughts and actions while continuing to participate in communal life. This dilemma is especially poignant for leaders and rulers, who are often obliged to represent ideals or institute programs they do not personally espouse. Truthfully, we are all hypocrites to some extent, since we all wear social masks, but acknowledging our hypocrisy is often embarrassing or deeply disturbing.

The most comfortable of all hypocritical rulers in Shakespeare's works (at least initially) is Richard III, who not only knows he is putting on a show but also gleefully reveals his shocking stratagems directly to the audience. Eventually Richard's conscience catches up to him, in the form of ghosts who haunt him on the battlefield. "The ghosts who appear to him at Bosworth suggest to us that in proportion as one conceals oneself from the tragic society one makes oneself visible to the unseen world of the dead, from which revenge so frequently comes."[315] As with Richard so with Macbeth, who from the beginning is less capable of holding the tension between his private and public selves. His hypocrisy eats away at him and feeds an increasing isolation from those around him. As with Richard, it sensitizes his imagination and allows his vision to penetrate the subtle realms. He alone sees Banquo's ghost.

Scorpio and the Will

Whether or not a person gravitates to the dark side often hinges on the influence of others. This introduces yet another key issue for Scorpio, that of the WILL and WILL POWER. What does it mean to have a strong will? What is will *power* exactly? We associate it first with the internal ability to control our own desires and actions, refraining from destructive ones (like risking our resources in gambling or undermining our health by overeating) and opting for ones that improve our physical or mental health (like exercise) or benefit us spiritually (like prayer).

From ancient times and into the Elizabethan period, the will was thought of as uniquely positioned to consider the evidence of the senses, memories of past occurrences, and accumulated knowledge and understanding, and then to decide on the most rational action to take. Both esoteric philosophy and the Christian religion acknowledge that human beings have free will; each assumes that the best use of the will is to choose what is "good." Both religious doctrine and spiritual practice stress the need for using the will to control the appetites—sometimes literally, demanding both fasting and chastity. The challenge is, as it has always been, not to allow imposed control to become excessive, thereby turning our zeal for improvement into an obsessive, almost fanatical self-deprivation.

Another way of exerting the will is to externalize it, using it to influence or control others' behavior to make them do what you want them to do (thereby undermining their own will and integrity). Methods used to subvert another's better intentions may include appeals to baser instincts (like lust, greed, or selfishness) or blatant manipulation using various persuasive techniques.

One of the influences driving Macbeth to his doomed end is his wife. She uses *her* will power to urge her husband along the criminal path to achieving his desire. She ultimately takes CONTROL of the situation herself, advising him to "put / This night's great business into my dispatch." (I, v, 65–6) It is she who devises the plan to drug Duncan's grooms and to leave bloody daggers next to their sleeping bodies so that they will appear to be guilty of the murder. Confidently, she directs him to "Leave all the rest to me." (I, v, 71) Macbeth has entertained doubts about killing Duncan, fearing that others will use similar methods on him: "we but teach / Bloody instructions, which, being taught, return / To plague th'inventor. This even-handed justice / Commends th'ingredients of our poisoned chalice / To our own lips." (I, vii, 8–12) (This is an insightful comment about the workings of karma.) He is also aware that he is Duncan's kinsman, subject, and host, all strong grounds for sparing the King, who is portrayed as a virtuous and capable leader. Macbeth admits that his essential motivation is at root nothing but "vaulting ambition." His wife knows this too, and she becomes a powerful influence directing him to murder the rightful King.

Mars, Masculinity, and the Roots of Violence: Lady Macbeth's Manipulative Technique

Just as Venus is the pre-eminent symbol of the feminine, Mars is the outstanding symbol of the masculine. It is double-sided as all astrological symbols are. The side explored in this play is very much in accord with the Greek Ares instead of the Roman Mars. The unevolved, reductively stereotypical Greek Ares-type male (what we would today call the extreme "macho man") may be body-based and unthinking, brutal and bullying, posturing and swaggering, and at an extreme destructively violent. The Roman Mars-type may be a hero—even superhero—who rescues damsels in distress, finds the hidden treasure, and saves the city. For those who lack confidence in their ability to assert themselves, who have no outlets for constructive activity, and who are not recognized as productive and successful, challenges to their masculinity may tip them into negative Mars (as in the Greek Ares) territory.

An additional problematic element in all of this is that Scorpio, like all the water signs, is considered yin or feminine. It is especially challenging for men born with the Sun or a number of other planets in the sign Scorpio to acknowledge their feminine sides; many over-compensate by becoming bossy and bullying or even villainous and criminal. They may become terrified of their inner sensitivity and vulnerability, which they interpret as weakness.

As a Scorpio type, Macbeth is especially sensitive to challenges to his masculinity. So when he tells his wife that he will go no further with their plans to murder Duncan, she knows just how to get him back on board. As he hesitates, Lady Macbeth needles him by questioning his maleness:

> Art thou afeard
> To be the same in thine own act and valour
> As thou art in desire? Wouldst thou have that
> Which thou esteem'st the ornament of life,
> And live a *coward* in thine own esteem ... ?
>
> (I, vii, 39–43)

Macbeth is well aware of her tactic, and protests, "Prithee, peace. / I dare do all that may become a man; / Who dares do more is none." (I, vii, 45–7) Relentless in pressing the point, Lady Macbeth acidly continues: "What beast was't, then / That made you break this enterprise to me? / When you durst do it, *then you were a man* ..." (I, vii, 47–9). In answer to his feebly expressed fear of failure, she presses him (with an implied sexual taunt) to "screw your courage to the sticking-place, / And we'll not fail." (I, vii, 60–1) She literally shames him into killing the King.

Lady Macbeth thus provokes painful feelings in Macbeth of fearing dishonor or disgrace. What greater humiliation could there be for the heroic Macbeth described in the opening scene of the play than to be accused of being effeminate? Lady Macbeth chastises her husband again immediately following the murder. Macbeth hears a voice cry out that he has murdered sleep, and he refuses to return to the king's chamber with the bloody daggers, saying, "I'll go no more. / *I am afraid to think what I have done,* / Look on't again *I dare not*." (II, ii, 48–50) Lady Macbeth herself must place the weapons by the sleeping grooms. On her return she reproaches Macbeth with "My hands are of your color, but *I shame / To wear a heart so white*." (II, ii, 62–3) Taking charge, it is she who gives him instructions: to retire to their chamber, to put on his nightgown, and not to be lost in regretful thoughts.

Understanding her husband's character, Lady Macbeth employs the same strategy later when Macbeth disrupts the banquet held to consolidate his position with the Scottish lords. Upon seeing the gory locks of the murdered Banquo's ghost, Macbeth appears to be having a fit, and blurts out strange phrases that upset the guests. Attempting to jolt the distraught Macbeth into an awareness of the social occasion, she challenges him with "Are you a man?" Macbeth can only protest:

> MACBETH: Ay, and a bold one, that dare look on that
>   Which might appal the devil.
> LADY MACBETH: O proper stuff!
>   This is the very painting of your fear;
>   This is the air-drawn dagger which you said
>   Led you to Duncan. O, these flaws and starts,
>   Imposters to true fear, *would well become
>   A woman's story* at a winter's fire
>   Authorized by her granddam. *Shame* itself,
>   Why do you make such faces? When all's done
>   You look but on a stool.
>
>   (III, iv, 57, 58–67)

What a spectacular lack of imagination she exhibits! While his vision sees a blood-daubed specter with "twenty mortal murders" on its crown, she looks "but on a stool."

Once the Ghost vanishes, Lady Macbeth resumes her attack: "What, quite *unmann'd* in folly?" (III, iv, 72)

Macbeth is not without self-insight. He realizes that his courage rises in the normal challenge of battle with animal or human enemies, but falters when confronted with the supernatural, precisely because he is so attuned to it through his heightened faculty of perception, the imagination.

What man dare, I dare.
Approach thou like the rugged Russian bear,
The rhinoceros, or th' Hyrcan tiger;
Take any shape but that [Banquo's ghost], and my firm
     nerves
Shall never tremble. Or be alive again,
And dare me to the desert with thy sword.
If trembling I inhabit then, protest me
The baby of a girl.

(III, iv, 98–105)

Once the ghost vanishes, Macbeth can assert "Why so, being gone, / *I am a man again.*" (III, iv, 106–7)

Macbeth has learned from Lady Macbeth's strategy of attacking a man's masculinity, for he uses it himself with the assassins he has hired to kill Banquo and his son. In a previous meeting, he has already planted the seed-idea in the hired killers that Banquo is to blame for their misfortunes. Now he challenges them to do something about it: "Do you find / Your patience so predominant in your nature / That you can let this go?" To which the murderers protest, "*We are men*, my liege." And Macbeth insults them by answering: "Ay, in the catalogue ye go for men, / As hounds and greyhounds, mongrels, spaniels, curs, / Shoughs, water-rugs, and demi-wolves are clept / All by the name of dogs." (III, i, 87–9, 92–6) The second murderer is daunted by this insult, and agrees to whatever Macbeth will suggest, saying, "I am one, my liege, / Whom the vile blows and buffets of the world / Hath so incensed that I am reckless what / I do to spite the world." (III, i, 109–12) Fueled by Scorpionic emotions of both anger and resentment, he is willing to take on the task of murdering the two. Just as Lady Macbeth manipulated Macbeth into murdering Duncan, so Macbeth manipulates the two murderers into killing Banquo and his son. Like Lady Macbeth, too, he has a well-thought-out plan to ensure the crime's success.

Uncannily, Shakespeare has the psychological source of violence, as we now understand it, absolutely right. We should not be surprised at this because if Shakespeare tapped the archetypal level in creating his works (as discussed in Chapter 6), they not only endure over time but can also be interpreted in the vocabulary of any particular era. So contemporary psychology offers some cogent insights into Macbeth's behavior. In a series of books and articles exploring the roots of violence, psychiatrist Dr. James Gilligan concludes, after many years of experience with prisoners and those in prison mental wards, that

> ... the basic psychological motive, or cause, of violent behavior is the wish to ward off or eliminate the feeling of shame and humiliation, a feeling that is painful and can even be intolerable and overwhelming, and replace it with its opposite, the feeling of pride.... But pride must be in much shorter supply than shame, because there are literally dozens of synonyms for the latter feeling, a partial listing of which would include feelings of being slighted, insulted, disrespected, dishonored, disgraced, disdained, demeaned, slandered, treated with contempt, ridiculed, teased, taunted, mocked . ... Envy and jealousy are members of this same family of feelings: people feel inferior to those whom they envy, or of whom they are jealous ... [316]

Why, after being so acclaimed on the battlefield and awarded with land and titles, would Macbeth be vulnerable to shame and humiliation? One reason is that opportunities for glory on the battlefield have passed; he is back in civilian territory. His fixation on becoming king is perhaps a substitute for battlefield glory. It would be a logical step up the ladder, another way to exhibit his power and potency. Macbeth, though, is not a trained or experienced political leader—he is a warrior. This illustrates the danger in attempting to fulfill a role for which you have no experience or talent but only ego motives.

Another reason is King Duncan's abrupt and curiously timed announcement, immediately following Macbeth's great achievement, that the kingdom will pass to his eldest son Malcolm. Rulership of Scotland was established through election by the nobles. It was not hereditary. Surely as the most important of Duncan's supporters and defenders, Macbeth would be the logical choice to take the reins of the kingdom. Perhaps this is precisely why Duncan chooses this moment to decree that the next in line will be his own progeny. Macbeth instantly recognizes this as an obstacle—and an insult. He has been publicly slighted. Lady Macbeth's castigations fall onto a newly-sensitized psyche.

The Banishment of the Feminine (Venus)

Since the astrological symbol Mars provides the archetypal foundation for the play, *Macbeth* focuses predominantly on males and male psychology (Mars)—so much so that there is hardly any room for female (Venus) values and little space on stage for female characters. Lady Macbeth hardly counts as female since she deliberately renounces her sex, invoking the dark powers to perform the unnatural act of transforming her into a male:

> Come, you spirits
> That tend on mortal thoughts, unsex me here,
> And fill me from the crown to the toe top-full
> Of direst cruelty. Make thick my blood;
> Stop up th'access and passage to remorse,
> That no compunctious visitings of nature
> Shake my fell purpose, nor keep peace between
> Th'effect and it. Come to my woman's breasts,
> And take my milk for gall, you murd'ring ministers,
> Wherever in your sightless substances
> You wait on nature's mischief.
>
> (I, v, 38–48)

Lady Macbeth asks for the conversion of her milk, the symbol of femininity, to bitter "gall," an acrid secretion assigned (like all bitter substances) to the masculine symbol of Mars. The one who initially has "milk," the liquid of maternal nurturance, is Macbeth. His wife describes him as "too full o'th' *milk* of human kindness / To catch the nearest way." (I, v, 15–6) In rejecting her womanhood (turning her milk to "gall"), Lady Macbeth reveals that she associates femininity with remorse and masculinity with cruelty—even evil. So close a couple are they that Macbeth absorbs these associations, as she "pours [her] spirits in [his] ear" (I, v, 24) and convinces him to murder his way to the throne.

One of many ironies in the play is that Lady Macbeth, despite her husband's military victories, is initially more masculine in spirit than her husband. The balance in their personalities shifts, however, as the plot progresses to its inevitable conclusion. She weakens and becomes vulnerable, troubled by "thick-coming fancies / That keep her from her rest" (V, iii, 40–1), while Macbeth, initially sensitive and reluctant to do evil, progressively hardens. This reversal of sex and gender qualities accords with the disorder in the country and the upheavals in nature.

The only truly feminine character in the play is Lady Macduff, who as a mother mourns her young son's future without his father who has fled to England. She avows that it is a "womanly defence" to protest her innocence, saying that she has done no harm to anyone and so should fear no danger despite being alone and deserted by her husband. If you think Venus stands a chance in this play, think again. She is promptly murdered! It seems that women cannot survive in Macbeth's world where only the lowest level of Mars progressively dominates. In her care and concern for her child Lady Macduff is a dramatic contrast to Lady Macbeth, who threatens not to protect but to destroy her own child:

> I have given suck, and know
> How tender 'tis to love the babe that milks me.
> I would, while it was smiling in my face,
> Have plucked my nipple from his boneless gums
> And dashed the brains out, had I so sworn
> As you have done to this.
>
> (I, vii, 54–9)

No wonder that Macbeth in admiration of his wife asserts, "Bring forth men-children only, / For thy undaunted mettle should compose / Nothing but males." (I, vii, 72–4) Indeed, the play features almost "nothing but males" (Mars).

We are in a patriarchal world in this medieval Scotland many centuries before Shakespeare's time. As such, the gender roles are tightly scripted. As Dr. James Gilligan observes,

> [I]t is men who are expected to be violent, and who are honored for doing so and dishonored for being unwilling to be violent. A woman's worthiness to be honored or shamed is judged by how well she fills her roles in sexually related activities, especially the roles of actual or potential wife and mother. . . . Women are honored for inactivity or passivity, for not engaging in forbidden activities. They are shamed or dishonored if they are active where they should not be—sexually or in realms that are forbidden (professional ambition, aggressiveness, competitiveness and success; or violent activity, such as warfare or other forms of murder). Lady Macbeth, for example,

realized that to commit murder she would have to be "unsex'd," i.e. freed from the restraints on violence that were imposed on her by virtue of her belonging to the female sex; and even then, she was unable to commit murder herself, but had to shame her husband into committing murder for her, so that she could only participate in violent behavior vicariously.... [317]

As for the other apparently female characters, the witches, they hardly count as women either for their gender is suspect. They look like human inhabitants of the earth yet, as Macbeth protests, "You should be women, / And yet your beards forbid me to interpret / That you are so." (I, iii, 43–5) Whether they are demonic entities who cannot successfully replicate a human body or whether they are authentically androgynous in nature, they have none of the traditional feminine virtues of sensitivity, kindness, and compassion. They amuse themselves by killing swine and tormenting a sailor solely because his wife would not share some chestnuts with one of the witches. (I, iii, 1–24)

The Witches' Persuasive Technique: Equivocation

Lady Macbeth's Scorpionic manipulative technique is that of humiliation, shaming Macbeth by questioning his masculinity in order to override his will. The witches are as adept in Scorpionic-style manipulation as Lady Macbeth, only they use a different strategy. The principal persuasive technique they practice on Macbeth is" equivocation": the use of ambiguous language with intent to mislead or deceive. Since they have none of the esteemed feminine qualities and obviously enjoy bragging about their sadistic treatment of the sailor, we can be sure that they are up to no good in their use of this tactic.

To make Macbeth more confident about the truth of their prophecies, the first two pronouncements they deliver are simple statements that are true or do come true. Macbeth *is* Thane of Glamis. Within minutes of their pronouncement that he will be Thane of Cawdor, Ross arrives to tell Macbeth that Duncan has bestowed this new title on him. So it is logical for him to think that he will become King. And he does become King—though a question nags at us: would this have happened had he not taken criminal action to bring it about? Or do the witches suggest it because they know that impatient ambition will drive him to take immoral steps to *make* it happen?

But the second set of three prophecies, dramatized when Macbeth actively seeks the witches, is delivered partly in statements and partly in riddles, and by apparitions and not the witches themselves. The warning to beware Macduff seems reasonable and resonates with Macbeth's own fear of him. But then he is told to "Be bloody, bold, and resolute. Laugh to scorn / The power of man, for *none of woman born* / Shall harm Macbeth." (IV, i, 95–7) He interprets this to mean that he is invincible, but he is disabused of this when Macduff, with sword in hand, challenges Macbeth to hand-to-hand combat after Macbeth's castle is breached, revealing that Macduff "was from his mother's womb / Untimely ripped" (V, x, 15–6). Since his birth was caesarean, Macduff is technically not "of woman born." The witches have told the precise truth but in such a way as to mislead Macbeth into thinking that he is unkillable.

The third phantom delivers what would seem to be the most improbable possibility:

> Be lion-mettled, proud, and take no care
> Who chafes, who frets, or where conspirers are.
> Macbeth shall never vanquished be until
> Great Birnam Wood to high Dunsinane Hill
> Shall come against him.
>
> (IV, i, 106–10)

Confidently, Macbeth responds, "That will never be. / Who can impress the forest, bid the tree / Unfix his earth-bound root? Sweet bodements, good!" (IV, I, 110–12) So seductive are these assurances that Macbeth mistakes the evil intent behind the prophecies for "good."

Both the second and third pronouncements encourage him to be arrogant, to scorn the threat of the invading English and Scottish forces, and to continue to trust in the witches' words:

> Bring me no more reports. Let them fly all.
> Till Birnam Wood remove to Dunsinane
> I cannot taint with fear. What's the boy Malcolm?
> Was he not born of woman? The spirits that know
> All mortal conseqences have pronounced me thus:

'Fear not, Macbeth. No man that's born of woman
Shall e'er have power upon thee.' Then fly, false thanes,
And mingle with the English epicures.
The mind I sway by and the heart I bear
Shall never sag with doubt nor shake with fear.

(V, iii, 1–10)

But soon Macbeth realizes the extent of the witches' duplicity when a messenger reports that he sees the wood begin to move, and Macbeth's determination weakens: "I pall in resolution, and *begin / To doubt th'equivocation of the fiend, / That lies like truth.*" (V, v, 40–2) The witches have subtly, both at the beginning of the drama and near its end, influenced Macbeth's catastrophic descent into deceit, murder, and ultimately dishonor and despair through leading and misleading words.

This theme of equivocation is introduced earlier and made explicit by the drunken Porter. Unsteady on his feet as he staggers to open the castle gate immediately after Duncan's murder, he delivers a long monologue studded with instances of double-dealing: "Faith, here's an *equivocator,* that could swear in both the scales against either scale, who committed treason enough for God's sake, yet could not equivocate to heaven. O, come in, *equivocator.*" (II, iii, 7–11) He seems to be describing Macbeth as well as the witches.

The drunken porter introduces yet another association with the sign Scorpio. Because of the potential for emotional repression mentioned earlier, the Scorpionic personality may suffer from various ADDICTIONS or COMPULSIONS. Among these is alcoholism. Duncan's guards are vulnerable to Lady Macbeth's plan because they are drugged <u>and</u> made drunk and lie in "swinish sleep." Immediately following the murder, the porter ruminates about the effects of alcohol, especially on sexual performance (also a Scorpionic topic):

Lechery, sir, it provokes, and unprovokes: it provokes the
desire but it takes away the performance. Therefore, much
drink may be said to be an equivocator with lechery: it
makes him and it mars him; it sets him on and it takes
him off; it persuades him and disheartens him, makes
him stand to and not stand to; in conclusion, equivocates
him in a sleep, and, giving him the lie, leaves him.

(II, iii, 26–33)

Embodying the dark side of the occult, the three witches (devolutions of the classic three fates) represent the negative feminine. Creating a vortex of malevolent energy, they enjoy inciting disorder and duping Macbeth, leading him to destruction and death. In this production of Macbeth *at the Park Avenue Armory, the witches were played as young and sexually voracious, an interpretation in line with Mars' rulership of sexuality. (Photo: Stephanie Berger, c2015)*

This eerily describes the witches' effect on Macbeth, from the beginning when he vacillates about killing Duncan through to the end when he at first determines to withstand a siege and then changes his mind, arming and leaving the castle.

Besides alcoholism, another instance of obsessive-compulsive behavior (associated with Scorpio) is Lady Macbeth's repeated washing of her hands in the sleepwalking scene just before she commits suicide. Her repetitive actions are observed covertly both by her gentlewoman and a doctor brought along as a witness.

> DOCTOR: Look, how she rubs her hands.
> GENTLEWOMAN: It is an accustomed action with her,
>   to seem thus washing her hands. I have known her
>   continue in this a quarter of an hour....

LADY MACBETH: Out, damned spot; out, I say....
What, will these hands ne'er be clean? ... Here's the
smell of the blood still. All the perfumes of Arabia
will not sweeten this little hand. O, O, O!

(V, i, 23–6, 30, 37, 42–3)

Scorpio and the Occult

The Scorpio individual is drawn to exploring realms that are hidden or suppressed, that are considered forbidden or dangerous, especially those that society considers taboo. Thus the sign Scorpio has to do with the OCCULT, and with invisible entities that might be either spontaneously experienced or deliberately contacted through a variety of established methods. To be precise, anything "occult" is merely that which is secret or hidden from view, the implication being that "occult" entities are not perceptible through the five senses. In astronomy, an "occultation" of a planet refers to the phenomenon of another planet moving in front of it and blocking it from being seen.

Taking the realm of the occult seriously means that you are willing to explore the possible existence of invisible energies and entities. If so, long-established tradition recommends that you be prepared or initiated before encountering such entities from alternate and immaterial dimensions—or your physical, emotional, and mental health can suffer. It is socially acceptable to have your nervous system titillated by watching horror movies or your imagination stimulated by reading science fiction or fantasy novels, but either passively experiencing or actively contacting mythological figures, ghosts of the departed, or angels or demons is often either denounced or denied. Conventional society generally either ignores or disbelieves in the magical and mystical. You are supposed to get on with your daily life and not pay attention to any eruptions from other dimensions. Scrooge, for example, an archetypal materialist in Dickens' *A Christmas Carol*, dismisses the appearance of his dead partner Marley as due to indigestion; he thinks he sees Marley's ghost because he ate a "fragment of an underdone potato."

The sign Scorpio has particularly to do with pre-birth or after-death states, and so especially with mediumship and the ability to see ghosts of the departed. But the study of the occult embraces more than this. The occult tradition is

> … a coherent intellectual stream that has roots in metaphysics, cosmology and religion and which has tried to bring together widely disparate aspects of God's Creation within a complex structure of connections, sympathies and affinities. Within its realm are numerous sub-systems such as magic, astrology, demonology, Kabbalah, numerology, pyramidism, divination, theurgy and much else. An occult quality is one that is hidden from the senses, as opposed to a manifest quality that is readily apprehended. As such it would come to include the more supernatural elements of normative religion, such as providence, prophecy and millenarianism.[318]

According to this, even entities like angels, archangels, and God Itself would be classed as "occult."

Our culture is just as fascinated by invisible beings as earlier ones. Our books and movies fixate on Harry Potter's education as a wizard at Hogwarts, on Frodo's encounters with elves and orcs, and on ordinary people confronted by sudden intrusions of vampires and zombies into everyday life (or the lives of famous people like Jane Austen or Abraham Lincoln). The people of Shakespeare's time were just as willing to believe in daemons or demons. No surprise then that in many of Shakespeare's plays unearthly beings appear: delightful fairies and the mischievous Puck in *A Midsummer Night's Dream*; elemental spirits of earth and air in *The Tempest*; Greek gods and goddesses in *Cymbeline* and *The Tempest*; and ghosts in *Hamlet*, *Julius Caesar*, and *Richard III*. In Shakespeare's corpus, the antithesis to Macbeth as a tool of black forces is Prospero in *The Tempest*, a practicing white magician who controls both spirits of the light like Ariel and of the dark like Caliban.[319]

And, of course, Shakespeare includes a ghost and witches in *Macbeth*. This is the *only* play of Shakespeare's in which witches appear, the *only* one to feature a human character invoking the dark powers. So dark is the atmosphere of the play that even some virtuous characters take on a dark cast. When Banquo takes his leave of Macbeth before the great feast, he tells Macbeth of plans to take his horse out for a ride that evening: "I must become a borrower of the night / For a dark hour or twain." (III, i, 27–8) Macbeth's response is "Fail not our feast," and Banquo assures him: "My lord, I will not." Ironically Banquo honors Macbeth's instruction when he appears as an ominous ghost that disrupts the celebratory dinner.

Though Banquo is depicted as good when alive, his silent and somber spirit is the very incarnation of retributive justice and seems as menacing to us as it does to Macbeth. Overall, this play is Shakespeare's darkest depiction of the occult realm, focusing exclusively on the dark side and presenting only powers that toy with human beings for their fell purposes, that gleefully instigate violent and evil acts, and that enjoy upsetting order by creating disorder. So successful is Shakespeare in creating a vortex of malevolent forces in this work that many actors have a superstitious fear of even speaking the play's name. They refer to it as "That Play," or "The Scottish Play," or, in the case of a joking Peter O'Toole, "The Harry Lauder Show."[320]

Ominously, many disasters have been recorded that have disrupted its performance. These disasters began with the first performance of the play at Hampton Court on August 7, 1606. According to James Aubrey, the boy actor playing Lady Macbeth was taken ill and died suddenly backstage. Terrible events continued to be associated with the play:

> Before a Manchester opening of the play, two actors died of heart attacks, the Third Witch collapsed whilst dancing around her cauldron, and a month later, as a consequence of laryngitis, flu, sackings and a broken toe, four actors had to play the part of Macbeth in a single week.
>
> When Paul Rogers played the Thane in Moscow in the 1950's, he clashed so violently one afternoon with Macduff that half his claymore [a double-edged broadsword formerly used by Scottish Highlanders] flew across the stage and embedded itself in an empty seat; the very seat that President Khrushchev was to occupy three hours later. In 1954, the company manager of a Dublin production broke both his legs, an electrician electrocuted himself, and Banquo tried to commit suicide....
>
> In 1980, Peter O'Toole played Macbeth at the Old Vic. Two weeks before rehearsals began, while driving to Connemara to meet his Lady M. (Frances Tomelty) O'Toole's car suddenly went out of control, crashing into a stone wall. As he sat stunned at the wheel, the vehicle began to veer slowly towards the cliff edge. It was Friday

the 13th. From then on things began to go steadily down hill for the production, becoming one of the most notorious in recent years.[321]

So many tragic events are connected with performances of *Macbeth* that telling them takes on a tone of gallows humor. Actors are clearly spooked by the play: for instance, when Dame Sybil Thorndike took on the role of Lady Macbeth at the Prince's Theatre in 1926, a string of terrifying events within the acting company drove her to kneel one evening in her dressing room with her husband, Sir Lewis Casson, and together they recited the Ninety-first Psalm.

The atmosphere of evil generated by performances of the play may derive in part from characters in the play deliberately summoning dark forces. One of the established methods for actively contacting occult entities, whether good or evil, is INVOCATION: calling upon a power or various powers to aid you or to perform a certain act. Lady Macbeth becomes a witch-like figure, invoking clearly negative entities when she calls to them: "Come, you spirits that tend on mortal thoughts, unsex me here, / And fill me from the crown to the toe top-full / Of direst cruelty! … Come to my woman's breasts, / And take my milk for gall, you murd'ring ministers…. Come, thick night, /And pall thee in the dunnest smoke of hell…" (I, v, 38–41, 45–6, 48–9). This transforms her into one possessed by the dark entities she has summoned.

On several occasions Macbeth also appeals to the black powers. Soon after hearing of the prophecies and then witnessing Duncan's proclamation of his son as "Prince of Cumberland," next in line to the throne, he demands, "Stars, hide your fires, / Let not light see my black and deep desires; / The eye wink at the hand; yet let that be / Which the eye fears, when it is done, to see." (I, iv, 50–3) Before Banquo's killing, he petitions, "Come, seeling night, / Scarf up the tender eye of pitiful day, / And with thy bloody and invisible hand / Cancel and tear to pieces that great bond / Which keeps me pale." (III, ii, 47–51) Literally calling on blackness and intentionally invoking the dark powers, Macbeth abrogates the "great bond"—his connection to a moral universe in which he is bound by various roles and responsibilities to his fellow human beings in accord with his place in the grand hierarchy.

Entities contacted by means such as invocation are not necessarily evil. Neither, probably, were the historical models for the "weird sisters": likely local wise women, perhaps the village herbalists, who might have had some intuitive ability. "Wyrd" was a Celtic term for oracles inspired by visions and thus capable of prophecy. The Norns of Scandinavian mythology are similar figures. By Shakespeare's era, the chronicler Holinshed (whose work was published in 1577) writes of them: "the common opinion was, that these women were either ... the goddesses of destinie, or else some nymphs or feiries, indued with knowledge of prophesie by their necromanticall science, bicause everie thing came to passe as they had spoken."[322]

Holinshed assumes, as many then and now do, that such foreknowledge more often comes from the use of black magic. But like other figures, such as seers or prophets, the Norns were not of the dark side. Originally only one, they evolved into three, like the Greek fates representing Past, Present, and Future. Following this tradition, in *Macbeth* the first witch delivers a statement that was true in the past: when his father Sinel died, Macbeth became thane of Glamis. The second witch speaks of an event that is accurate in the present: Macbeth is about to be named thane of Cawdor. The third speaks of that which will be true in the future: Macbeth will become king.[323]

Over the centuries Christianity's unrelenting disapproval of pagan traditions, in which women prophetesses figured prominently, led to their demonization. This condemnation of females and their transformation into "witches" came about because of a combination of anti-paganism and anti-feminism. But it is true that the female entities that toy with Macbeth *are* clearly malevolent. This is implied from the opening of the play: they meet in awful weather, "thunder, lightning, or in rain"; the atmosphere around them is one of "fog and filthy air"; and they inhabit a morally questionable universe in which "Fair is foul, and foul is fair." (I, i, 1–11). By Scene iii, when they meet on the heath, they have been "killing swine," and are plotting revenge on a sailor's wife by tormenting her husband at sea.

The witches do influence Macbeth to actively court the dark forces. The first terrible deed that Macbeth commits, the murder of a kinsman, guest, and king, catalyzes a burgeoning career in crime, one that inaugurates his slide into an inner hell. Shakespeare signals this within minutes of the murder of Duncan, for the porter unconsciously and ironically describes himself as the doorman of the doomed, saying: "Here's a knocking indeed! If a man were porter of *hell-gate*, he should have [a grand] old [time] turning the key.... Who's here in the name of Beelzc-bub?" (II, iii, 1–3)[324] It hardly seems accidental that the servant who stays with Macbeth until the calamitous end is named "Seyton," which would probably be pronounced "Satan."

Issues for Scorpio: Temptation, Sin, and Evil

In the Medieval age that preceeded Shakespeare's era, western culture was obsessed with the idea that the forces of good and evil were at war with each other and that the battleground was the human soul. The battle was lost if you succumbed either to inner desires or to outer persuasion to do the forbidden. In either case it was a given that TEMPTATION was constantly present. To be "tempted" is to be enticed into doing something unwise or morally wrong. Issues of succumbing to or resisting desire, of indulging in or refraining from temptation (in all its various forms) have always traditionally been associated with the astrological sign Scorpio.

How do you know which actions are permissible and which are not? You look to established moral and ethical codes to help you differentiate between intentions, decisions, and actions that are "good" or "right" and those that are "bad" or "wrong." In the West you might look first at the Ten Commandments in the Bible's Old Testament, which are described as being written by the finger of God (Exodus 31:18) and thus divinely prescribed. To transgress these directives means that one has fallen into SIN: one has violated divine law. One of these commandments explicitly prohibits murder. Presumably exposure to such established and culturally-sanctioned moral codes, transmitted through parents, the extended family, the educational system, and religious institutions, helps you internalize principles that encourage you to love and to care for yourself and others.

Macbeth definitely knows the codes of his culture: he is expected to serve his sovereign, to honor his guest as a protective host, and to be loyal to a kinsman. He also hints at an awareness of greater consequences to his soul should he do what is proscribed—he fears that ending Duncan's life would imperil "the life to come." (I, vii, 7)

Acting in ways that will have destructive consequences for ourselves or others brings us back to the topic of the will and the strength of our will power. Along with the mental awareness of moral codes and influences, it is necessary to have a strong character, with the ability to self-inhibit in order to resist temptation.

To dramatize the fact that people may be tempted but not necessarily succumb, Shakespeare provides Banquo as a foil to Macbeth. At the first appearance of the three witches, Banquo asks them to give prophecies to him as they have for his fellow thane, but qualifies it by saying, "Speak then to me, who neither beg nor fear / Your favours nor your hate." (I, iii, 58–9) He is careful to distance himself from them and their influence. When Macbeth solicits Banquo's support ("If you shall cleave to my consent when 'tis, / It shall make honour for you." [II, i, 24–5]), Banquo emphasizes his own integrity by saying: "So I lose none / In seeking to augment it, but still keep / My bosom franchised and allegiance clear …" (II, i, 25–7). This reveals an inner commitment to his own principles and a resistance to Macbeth's influence should it lead to a dishonorable action. Banquo opts for a consistency between his internal image of himself and his external behavior.

Banquo has another quality that enables him to resist temptation: the perceptive ability to discern the witches' true nature. When Ross arrives with the news that Macbeth is to be dubbed thane of Cawdor, Banquo speaks (in an aside), "What, can the *devil* speak true?" (I, iii, 105) Noticing that Macbeth is distracted by the witches' prophecies, he presciently warns Macbeth, " 'tis strange, / And oftentimes to win us to our harm / The *instruments of darkness* tell us truths, / Win us with honest trifles, to betray 's / In deepest consequence." (I, iii, 120–4) Later he also intuits that Macbeth has acted criminally to achieve the throne: "Thou hast it now: King, Cawdor, Glamis, all / As the weird women promised; and I fear / Thou played'st most foully for 't." (III, i, 1–3)

How would the audience of Shakespeare's time account for the intrusion of the devil and its agents into the human world? The worldview of his time assumed that resonant bonds of sympathy linked different levels of creation to each other, so that higher levels could influence the lower. We still do this in petitioning the help of God/Goddess, or our "good" or guardian angel, or other helpful spirits. The Elizabethans believed that the lower could also affect the higher. The very lowest level of creation, sometimes thought to be EVIL because it is farthest from God, is personified as the devil or demons or other unnatural creatures like the "weird women." For many, both then and now, this realm and the entities thought to inhabit it are real—and actively malevolent. They tempt us by encouraging us to willfully violate moral principles: to harm ourselves, others, even the Earth itself, as they do.

But here is "the rub"—and the critical issues especially pertinent to the sign Scorpio. Who or what is most responsible for Macbeth's succumbing to the temptation to murder Duncan? The dark powers appearing in the play as the witches and possessing the person of Lady Macbeth? Circumstance? Macbeth himself? Shakespeare's artistic work, as it frequently is, is ambiguous. It is easy for us to interpret the witches psychologically as projections of Macbeth's own thoughts and desires. How else to understand the eerie similarity of his first words to the witches' earlier ones: "fair is foul, and foul is fair"? When he and Banquo enter, Macbeth's opening line is, "So foul and fair a day I have not seen." (I, iii, 36) The day is certainly "foul" in terms of weather and "fair" in terms of the day's great victories. Does the similarity of their words indicate a secret psychic link between Macbeth and actual forces of evil? Does that place more of the responsibility on him or on unseen and malevolent forces?

When first confronting the startled Macbeth, the witches deliver three prophecies: they hail him as "Thane of Glamis," which he already is; as "Thane of Cawdor" (which he protests since he believes that the traitorous Cawdor still lives); and as King hereafter. When Ross enters to tell Macbeth that the King has awarded the title of the now-dead thane of Cawdor to him, thus proving the witches correct, Macbeth spontaneously envisions rising even higher in the ranks—by using foul means to get there. Macbeth's imagination immediately presents horrific pictures to his inner eye. Puzzled, he asks why, if the witches are instruments of "good ... do I yield to that suggestion /Whose horrid image doth unfix my hair / And make my seated heart knock at my ribs? ... My thought, whose murder yet is but fantastical, / Shakes so my single state of man that function / Is smothered in surmise, and nothing is / But what is not." (I, iii, 133–6, 138–41) How extraordinary that immediately after hearing the prophecy of kingship he can envision *only* murder as the path to that goal. Blessed—or cursed—with the imaginative ability ascribed to all the water signs and vulnerable to the dark side of life as represented most especially by Scorpio, Macbeth immediately sees only a negative route to gaining the position of king. The temptation to do evil has begun.

Macbeth does not have to murder in order to get the throne. It is possible to attain a position higher on the hierarchical ladder through hard-won effort or by the decree of a sovereign. But attaining it unlawfully had serious consequences. The Elizabethans believed that seizing such a place illegitimately would not only rebound disastrously on the initiator but also threaten the integrity of the whole system, from bottom to top.

According to the worldview described in Chapter 3, malign influence can also spread horizontally, from one person to another. Temptation has an occult aspect to it, relating to a weaker personality's vulnerability to a stronger one. Individuals on the same level can affect each other through a transfer of energy. We have all had the experience of being in someone's presence and feeling happier or more stimulated or being in the presence of someone who "brings you down." More powerful or charismatic personalities, whether politicians or performers, are like living reverse tuning forks: they have a compelling influence on people around them, especially on those who are like "open strings" and easily take on another's frequency. This theory accounts for the "grace of the guru," the idea that a spiritually advanced being can confer spiritual benefits on those who just sit in his or her presence. This gives added meaning to Lady Macbeth's exhortation that Macbeth must come to her so that she can "pour [her] spirits in [his] ear" (I, v, 24). It seems that she intends to transmit her masculine vitality into him through the power of her words, the force of her personality, and the energy of her male-like spirit once he is with her.

The Consequences of Evil: In Nature, the Human Realm, and the State

The negative Mars (as Ares), ruler of the zodiacal sign Scorpio and often depicted as the savage and uncivilized god of war, often causes chaos when he appears. That chaos easily spreads, since it stirs up long-suppressed grudges and buried feelings. No surprise, then, that the eruption of evil into the human world affects not just Macbeth; it begins to infect even the innocent. Duncan is described as a meek and virtuous king, but even he seems subtly influenced by the presence of the witches. They ambiguously refer to a "battle lost and won." After Cawdor is executed, Duncan decrees, "What he hath lost, noble Macbeth hath won." (I, ii, 67) The resemblance of even the good Duncan's words to the witches' statement implies that the psychic infection is spreading.

With the eruption of evil into the human realm comes a disruption in nature, for these realms are subtly connected. We have already seen an unnatural reversal of sexual identity as Lady Macbeth and Macbeth seem to exchange genders. Once Macbeth upsets the established hierarchy by killing the lawful king, nature itself synchronously reflects the upturned order. Lennox, who has accompanied Macduff to Macbeth's castle to wake Duncan, speaks of this:

> The night has been unruly. Where we lay
> Our chimneys were blown down, and, as they say,
> Lamentings heard i' th' air; strange screams of death,
> And prophesying with accents terrible
> Of dire combustion and confused events
> New-hatched to th' woeful time. The obscure bird [the
>   owl]
> Clamoured the livelong night. Some say the earth
> Was feverous and did shake.
>
> (II, iii, 50–7)

Macbeth concurs in a line reeking with irony: "'Twas a rough night."

Disruption spreads further. Three more strange and unnatural events occur almost immediately after Duncan's death, revealed in the conversation between an old Man and Ross outside Macbeth's castle.

> ROSS: By th' clock 'tis day,
>   And yet dark night strangles the travelling lamp.
>   Is't night's predominance or the day's shame
>   That darkness does the face of earth entomb
>   When living light should kiss it?
> OLD MAN: 'Tis unnatural,
>   Even like the deed that's done. On Tuesday last
>   A falcon, tow'ring in her pride of place,
>   Was by a mousing owl hawked at and kill'd.
> ROSS: And Duncan's horses—a thing most strange and
>   certain—
>   Beauteous and swift, the minions of their race,

Turned wild in nature, broke their stalls, flung out,
Contending 'gainst obedience, as they would
Make war with mankind.

(II, iv, 6–18)

That the owl, normally the prey of the bigger bird, attacks and kills
the falcon is a reversal of the natural way of things. Beautiful things of
nature, like Duncan's horses, turn against each other and against human
beings, violating the harmony of the whole.

As the play progresses, disasters and disruptions overwhelm the
entire country. Macduff, fled to England to persuade Duncan's oldest
son and heir to return and depose the tyrant Macbeth, reports to Malcolm that: "Each new morn / New widows howl, new orphans cry, new
sorrows / Strike heaven on the face, that it resounds / As if it felt with
Scotland …" (IV, iii, 4–7). After the invasion of the combined English
and Scottish forces, the apparent uprooting of Birnam wood and its
eerie movement up Dunsinane Hill seem strangely apt in light of the
accumulating unnatural events in nature. Nature itself is turning against
Macbeth.

The consequences of succumbing to evil are most potently and dramatically depicted through the degeneration of Macbeth himself. We
see how precarious Macbeth's mental state is even before the murder
of Duncan when he sees an imaginary dagger hanging in the air leading him toward Duncan's chamber. But the first significant sign of his
broken bond with the grand design is that immediately after Duncan's
death he cannot pronounce words of benediction. When some sleepers stir—and have psychically perceived that a murder has been committed—Macbeth is unable to join their instant invocation of divine
protection. The sleepers are experiencing "night terrors," a sleep disorder
characterized by an inability to wake to full consciousness accompanied
by extreme fear.

MACBETH: There's one did laugh in 's sleep, and one cried
          'Murder!'
       That they did wake each other. I stood and heard
          them.
       But they did say their prayers and addressed them
       Again to sleep.

"Will all great Neptune's ocean wash the blood clean from my hand?" Macbeth's hands—and soul—are now stained with his sovereign's blood, the fluid of life pumped by the heart. Kenneth Branagh as Macbeth *in the Park Avenue Armory production, 2014. (Photo: Stephanie Berger, c2015)*

> LADY MACBETH: There are two lodged together.
> MACBETH: One cried 'God bless us!' and 'Amen' the
> other,
> As they had seen me with these hangman's hands.
> List'ning their fear, I could not say 'Amen'
> When they did say 'God bless us.'
> LADY MACBETH: Consider it not so deeply.
> MACBETH: But wherefore could not I pronounce
> "Amen"?
> I had most need of blessing, and "Amen"
> Stuck in my throat.
>
> (II, ii, 20–31)

The worldview of Shakespeare's time is theocentric, that is, it originates with God or the Great Creative Power; in violating the ban against murder Macbeth has cut himself off from the Divine. Simultaneously he has cut himself off from himself, that is, from his own higher self: "To know my deed 'twere best not know myself. / Wake Duncan with thy knocking. I would thou couldst." (II, ii, 71–2) He immediately regrets what he has done.

Another indication that outward disorder is more and more internalized within Macbeth is that he is more and more unable to sleep. This too is a symptom of his greater disconnection with the established grand order, as well as the sign of a troubled personal conscience. Macbeth has brought this on himself, for immediately after the murder he hears a voice cry, "Sleep no more, / Macbeth does murder sleep." (II, ii 33–4) He seems to have killed his own capacity to rest, be refreshed, and be restored to health through sleep. Then Macbeth delivers a lovely paean to sleep, as if already mourning its loss:

> —the innocent sleep,
> Sleep that knits up the ravelled sleeve of care,
> The death of each day's life, sore labour's bath,
> Balm of hurt minds, great nature's second course,
> Chief nourisher in life's feast.
>
> (II, ii, 34–8)

Loss of sleep is a significant consequence of the intrusion of the dark forces into the human realm. This is mentioned earlier when Banquo, sensing the swirling currents of evil just before Duncan's murder, says: "A heavy summons likes like lead upon me, / And yet I would not sleep." (II, i, 6–7) After Banquo's death and the disruption of the banquet, Lady Macbeth tries to comfort Macbeth by observing, "You lack the season of all natures, sleep." (III, iv, 140) The inability to sleep spreads from Macbeth to others, for one of the Scottish lords, while revealing that Macduff is fled to England, hopes that, "—with Him above / To ratify the work—we may again / Give to our tables meat, *sleep to our nights* ..." (III, vi, 32–4).

Some symptoms of sleep deprivation are irritability, anxiety, and depression—even paranoia—all of which we see in Macbeth at different points during the play. In the final scenes he is especially vexed by the approach of the invading armies and expresses exasperated annoyance with his servant, exhibiting the ire of an agitated Mars in cursing the poor fellow (abusing him in the same way he impugned the masculinity of the hired assassins):

> MACBETH: The devil damn thee black, thou cream-faced
>   loon!
>   Where gott'st thou that goose look?
> SERVANT: There is ten thousand—
> MACBETH: Geese, villain?
> SERVANT: Soldiers, sir.
> MACBETH: Go prick thy face and over-red thy fear,
>   Thou lily-livered boy. What soldiers, patch?
>   Death of thy soul, those linen cheeks of thine
>   Are counselors to fear. What soldiers, whey-face?
> SERVANT: The English force, so please you.
> MACBETH: Take thy face hence.
>
>   (V, iii, 11–19)

A particular disruption of the night's rest is sleepwalking—and we see vividly the consequences of embarking on a course of evil in the inadvertent revelation of Lady Macbeth's haunted CONSCIENCE while she sleepwalks in the castle late in the play. Macbeth, too, has suffered "terrible dreams that shake [him] nightly." (III, ii, 20–1)

So Macbeth has no rest and no peace. A dominant psychological need for a Scorpio is SECURITY, which drives the Scorpio compulsion to have control (and therefore power) over yourself and your environment. For Macbeth, though, instead of achieving a comfortable situation once he has become king, he becomes more and more *in*secure. "To be thus is nothing / But to be safely thus" (III, i, 49–50), he worries, now transferring his anxieties to Banquo. Lady Macbeth, his feminine Scorpio counterpart, also feels that she is on shaky ground: "Naught's had, all's spent, / Where our desire is got without content. / 'Tis safer to be that which we destroy / Than by destruction dwell in doubtful joy." (III, ii, 6–9)

As he becomes less and less secure, Macbeth is more and more fearful. Of all the emotions that a Scorpio can be subject to, FEAR, the opposite of Martial courage (since every astrological symbol contains its opposite), dominates him. Macbeth's underlying fears—of not being manly enough, of being shamed by his wife, of his crimes being discovered, of Banquo as a living rebuke to his regicide, of being disliked and deposed by his people—more and more obsess him and increase his insecurity. After he has instructed and sent the two murderers to kill Banquo and his son, a third murderer suddenly appears. The second murderer protests, "He needs not our mistrust, since he delivers / Our offices and what we have to do / To the direction just." (III, iii, 3–4) (Literary critics speculate that the third murderer may be Macbeth himself, so unsure about their capabilities as hired assassins that he lurks in the background to monitor their efforts.) When Fleance escapes, Macbeth laments, "But now I am cabined, cribbed, confined, bound in / To saucy doubts and fears." (III, iv, 23–4). Suspicious of the loyalty of his subjects, he reveals that "There's not a one of them but in his house / I keep a servant fee'd." (III, iv, 130–1).

This is a critical point in the play, for now Macbeth determines to seek out the witches being "bent to know / By the worst means the worst." He reduces everything to his own ego's needs, committing himself to complete SELFISHNESS, the bane of Scorpios: "For mine own good / All causes shall give way." Now he consciously acknowledges that there is no turning back, for he is "in blood stepped in so far that, should I wade no more, / Returning were as tedious as go o'er." (III, iv, 131–7)

The steady deterioration of Macbeth coincides with increasing disorder within the ranks of the nobles. The thanes, arriving at Macbeth's castle in Forres to celebrate his new honor, are urged by him to take their seats according to their status: "You know your own degrees; sit down." (III, iv, 1) But by the end of the scene, after Macbeth falls into a fit of passion and seems to lose his reason after seeing Banquo's ghost, Lady Macbeth rebukes him, saying "You have displaced the mirth, broke the good meeting / With most admired disorder," and requests that the thanes "Stand not upon the order of your going, / But go at once." (III, iv, 108–9, 118–9) In Shakespeare's worldview, all levels are connected: when one person admits evil into his being, all of nature, all of the human realms, the great cosmos itself becomes disordered and suffers as a result.

Another of the terrible consequences of embarking on what the Porter describes as "the primrose way to th' ever-lasting bonfire" (II, iii, 17–8) is progressive isolation. Unable to trust anyone (witness the third murderer) or to unburden himself even to Lady Macbeth, Macbeth is more and more removed from human connection. Previously when he writes to her after the battle, he addresses her as "my dearest partner of greatness" (I, v, 9–10); when he arrives at their castle ahead of Duncan

and his retinue, he greets her as "My dearest love" (I, v, 56). They plan
the death of Duncan as a couple, collaborating on the plan and its execution, working together both before and after. But Macbeth arranges
for the death of Banquo without any contribution from her. In fact she
knows nothing about it. And Macbeth does not want her to know anything in advance: "Be innocent of the knowledge, dearest chuck, / Till
thou applaud the deed." (III, ii, 46–7) This suggests that he is looking
to gain points for masculinity by orchestrating something dastardly on
his own.

The deep love Macbeth and Lady Macbeth shared in a close working relationship dissipates under the terrible pressure of their criminal
acts. This is entirely in line with the propensity of Mars, in contrast to
Venus, to separate rather than to bring together. Macbeth now keeps
himself aloof from her. She plaintively asks, "Why do you keep alone, /
Of sorriest fancies your companions making … ?" (III, ii, 10–1) (Scorpios
are notorious loners.) After the banquet scene, when Macbeth basically
loses it, we never see Macbeth and Lady Macbeth together again. She
appears only once more, briefly, at the very end of the play in the sleepwalking scene. In her ramblings, witnessed by the gentlewoman and the
doctor, she reveals that she is lost in an inner underworld. The doctor
reports to Macbeth that she is not physically ill, but "is troubled with
thick-coming fancies / That keep her from her rest." (V, iii, 40–1) The
next we hear of her is that she is dead by her own hand. Embarking on
a career of crime has destroyed their relationship—and ended her life.

Macbeth is more and more removed, too, from his peers. His closest
friend and co-captain in the battles is Banquo. After they both witness
the witches' prognostications, Macbeth invites Banquo to talk with him,
saying, "Think upon what hath chanced, and at more time, / The interim
having weighed it, let us speak / Our free hearts each to other." (I, iii,
152–4) We do not know whether they do converse later, but it is notable
that at this point Macbeth is reaching out to Banquo to help him process
what they have seen. The night of the murder, when Banquo restlessly
walks within Macbeth's castle and encounters a figure he cannot at first
identify, he asks, "Who's there?" That person is Macbeth who responds,
"A friend." (II, i, 9–10). Yet soon Macbeth plots to have him killed.

In the final scenes we see that Macbeth's subjects are alienated from
him too. One of the invading lords, Angus, observes that "Those he
commands move only in command, / Nothing in love." (V, ii, 19–20)

Eventually Macbeth also acknowledges that he has sacrificed the lasting comforts of advanced years for the precarious position of king:

> I have lived long enough. My way of life
> Is fall'n into the sere, the yellow leaf,
> And that which should accompany old age,
> As honour, love, obedience, troops of friends,
> I must not look to have, but in their stead
> Curses, not loud but deep, mouth-honour, breath
> Which the poor heart would fain deny and dare not.
>
> (V, iii, 23–9)

Some hells may be the fate of being trapped with other people, as Jean Paul Sartre dramatizes in his play "Huis Clos" ("No Exit"), but the hells that Macbeth and Lady Macbeth inhabit are lonely and alienated ones.

As Macbeth accumulates more and more murders to his account, he sinks lower and lower in the hierarchy of being, until he is at the animal level: "They have tied me to a stake. I cannot fly, / But *bear-like* I must fight the course" (V, vii, 1–2).[325] "Bear-like," Macbeth knows he is trapped. As the play progresses, darker and darker epithets are applied to him: he is a "tyrant" (III, vi, 25), then "black Macbeth" (IV, iii, 53), "a devil … damn'd in evils" (IV, iii, 57), and lastly, in final hand-to-hand combat, Macduff addresses him as a "hell-hound" (V, x, 3). In the long-awaited confrontation with the avenger "not of woman born," the tyrant is destroyed. He has progressively left the human kingdom, dropped to the animal level, then to the realm of hell, and finally, in ultimate isolation, into nothingness.

Scorpio: From Degeneration to Regeneration

While Scorpio symbolism embraces possible disintegration on the physical, emotional, or mental levels, it also carries the promise of transformation, a restoration not just of the original state but the creation of one that includes a wisdom born of enduring suffering or surviving ordeals. For this to happen, according to the worldview of Shakespeare's time the hero-villain must inevitably die. The realm must be purged of evil; only the death of the scapegoat-hero will allow for a fresh start. In *Macbeth* the new regime will be inaugurated under the leadership of Duncan's previously named heir, Malcolm.

We might expect Malcolm to be a "good guy" because he is the son of a commendable ruler. His father had a generous spirit, praising Macbeth and the other conquering fighters with no signs of envy or resentment for their outstanding achievements. Duncan rewards Macbeth in particular with a new title and sends his wife a diamond. The fact that diamonds are the highest in the category of gems indicates Duncan's inner quality. Significantly, diamonds are under the rulership of Mars, perhaps because of their hardness and ability to cut into other substances while remaining whole—a positive manifestation of Mars.[326] Some of Duncan's innate goodness, along with his mother's, has devolved onto Malcolm. Macduff praises their virtue in saying to Malcolm, "Thy royal father / Was a most sainted king. The queen that bore thee, / Oftener upon her knees than on her feet, / Died every day she lived." (IV, iii, 109–12)

In important ways, though, Malcolm is a vastly better choice of ruler than his father. Duncan was good-hearted but naïve, an innocent too easily taken in by appearances, as many sanguine types are. He knew this about himself, commenting on his mistaken assessment of the traitorous Cawdor that "There's no art / To find the mind's construction in the face. / He was a gentleman in whom I built / An absolute trust." (I, iv, 11–14). Since he immediately greets Macbeth as "worthiest cousin!," he is obviously being taken in again. He pays the price for his too-trusting nature with his life.

Malcolm, on the other hand, has the wit to realize that he and his brother are in danger immediately after his father's murder, sensing that "This murderous shaft that's shot / Hath not yet lighted, and our safest way / Is to avoid the aim." (II, iii, 137–9) So he escapes to England. Later, after Macduff flees to England to urge him to invade Scotland and depose Macbeth, he carefully tests Macduff's sincerity. Initially Malcolm is skeptical: "What I believe I'll wail, / What know believe; and what I can redress, / As I shall find the time to friend, I will. / What you have spoke it may be so, perchance." (IV, iii, 8–11) Suspecting Macduff's motives, since others have petitioned him to arm against Macbeth, Malcolm wonders why Macduff would abandon his family, implying that he must be in Macbeth's service since only then would his family be safe in his absence.

Malcolm then employs a stratagem, a very Scorpionic trick, designed to test Macduff's sincerity: he assures Macduff he is so full of vices that Scotland would be better ruled by "black" Macbeth. He pretends to be the opposite of what he truly is. This, of course, is precisely contrary to the Macbeths' Machiavellian scheme of masking their evil intentions with outward goodness: Malcolm covers his innate goodness with a pretense of evil. He specifies two of the Scorpio vices, LUST and GREED, as his particular flaws. The first he describes as a bottomless sexual appetite:

> I grant [Macbeth] bloody,
> Luxurious, avaricious, false, deceitful,
> Sudden, malicious, smacking of every sin
> That has a name. But there's no bottom, none,
> To my voluptuousness. Your wives, your daughters,
> Your matrons, and your maids could not fill up
> The cistern of my lust ...
>
> (IV, iii, 58–64)

Desperate for a legitimate challenger to Macbeth, Macduff assures him that he can indulge his lusts in secret and that Scotland has "willing dames enough." But Malcolm magnifies his unsuitability for the throne by adding that he has an unappeasable appetite—a rampant desire—for acquiring and hoarding riches:

> With this there grows
> In my most ill-composed affection such
> A staunchless avarice that were I king
> I should cut off the nobles for their lands,
> Desire his jewels and this other's house,
> And my more having would be as a sauce
> To make me hunger more, that I should forge
> Quarrels unjust against the good and loyal,
> Destroying them for wealth.
>
> (IV, iii, 77–84)

The troubled Macduff counters by saying that while this is a more serious trait, Scotland has enough wealth to satisfy him, as long as he has other graces to counterbalance the two vices Malcolm has described. But Malcolm protests:

But I have none. The king-becoming graces,
As justice, verity, temp'rance, stableness,
Bounty, perseverance, mercy, lowliness,
Devotion, patience, courage, fortitude,
I have no relish of them, but abound
In the division of each several crime,
Acting it many ways. Nay, had I power I should
Pour the sweet milk of concord into hell,
Uproar the universal peace, confound
All unity on earth.

(IV, iii, 91–101)

(Notice the reference to maternal "milk" corrupted, similar to Lady Macbeth's wish to convert her milk to "gall.") Pushed beyond patience, Macduff explodes: "Fit to govern? / No, not to live." (IV, iii, 103–4) With Macduff about to depart in disgust, Malcolm accepts that Macduff is genuinely what he presents himself to be and reveals the motivation for his trick:

Macduff, this noble passion,
Child of integrity, hath from my soul
Wiped the black scruples, reconciled my thoughts
To thy good truth and honour. Devilish Macbeth
By many of these trains hath sought to win me
Into his power, and *modest wisdom plucks me*
From over-credulous haste ...

(IV, iii, 115–21)

Malcolm exhibits both the "wisdom of the serpent" and the harmlessness of the dove in testing before trusting Macduff. He recants his former statements and paints a picture of himself almost too good to be true:

[I] here abjure
The taints and blames I laid upon myself,
For strangers to my nature. I am yet
Unknown to woman, never was forsworn,
Scarcely have coveted what was mine own,
At no time broke my faith, would not betray

> The devil to his fellow, and delight
> No less in truth than life. My first false-speaking
> Was this upon myself. What I am truly,
> Is thine and my poor country's to command …
>
> (IV, iii, 124–33)

I have quoted at length because the entire scene is crucial. It establishes Malcolm as an ideal king, a being of light opposed to black Macbeth. While the scene seems static, full of talking heads, it would be a major mistake to cut or omit it altogether. It provides a welcome pause before the final battle and introduces the audience more fully to the praiseworthy Malcolm. Most especially, Malcolm mentions that he is a virgin. It is unusual in a Mars-oriented play for a male to admit chastity, commonly valued in women and not in men, but as we near the end of the play the feminine and the feminine virtues are on the rise. This is essential if peace (associated with Venus) is to come to Scotland. Symbolically, at the end Venus must overcome Mars. Malcolm's strength of will in mastering desire and honoring his values demonstrates a degree of self-control that results from the positive discipline of the Scorpio type.

When Ross arrives later in this key scene and delivers the news of the slaughter of Macduff's wife, children, and servants, Macduff becomes the logical avenger of these brutal killings by dispatching Macbeth. While Scorpio embraces the issue of revenge, the rightful avenger must have justifiable cause and, as much as possible, wreak vengeance as the impersonal tool of fate. The virtuous Malcolm cannot be tainted by killing, and so Macduff is designated as the hero-deliverer of the state in his place.

Scorpio: Wounding and Healing

The Scorpio person can be either a controller and destroyer or a helper and healer (many doctors and nurses have Scorpio emphasis in their horoscopes). Sometimes Scorpio people who spend their early lives oriented to business, amassing a fortune and becoming famous, spend the latter part of their lives giving their wealth away, endowing charities, especially hospitals or medical programs dedicated to eradicating disease. Bill Gates, a Sun in Scorpio, is a perfect example.

This attunement to helping and healing is applicable to Malcolm in two ways. First, while finding asylum in England, Malcolm is allied with its king, Edward (the Confessor). With perfect timing, a doctor enters the scene between Malcolm and Macduff to describe this English king's special talent, the ability to heal through the laying on of hands: "at his touch, / Such sanctity hath Heaven given his hand, / They presently amend." (IV, iii, 144–6) Macduff seems unfamiliar with this:

> MACDUFF: What's the disease he means?
> MALCOLM: 'Tis call'd the evil—
> A most miraculous work in this good King,
> Which often since my here-remain in England
> I have seen him do. How he solicits Heaven,
> Himself best knows, but strangely-visited people,
> All swoll'n and ulcerous, pitiful to the eye,
> The mere despair of surgery, he cures,
> Hanging a golden stamp about their necks,
> Put on with holy prayers ...
>   With this strange virtue,
> He hath a heavenly gift of prophecy,
> And sundry blessings hang about his throne
> That speak him full of grace.
>
>   (IV, iii, 147–55, 157–60)

"Miraculous," "good," "Heaven," "golden stamp," "holy prayers," "heavenly gift," "blessings," "grace"—contrast these to the cluster of words descriptive of Macbeth at the start of the play. By affiliating with Edward, Malcolm becomes associated with the same goodness and heavenly graces. Edward not only has the gift of healing, but also, like the witches, has the gift of prophecy. In this he is their counterpart: his gift is from heaven and engenders good while theirs is demonic and catalyzes evil.

Second, Malcolm himself is in a sense a healer, for when the defecting Scottish nobles march to meet with the invading English force, one of them, Caithness, declares, "Meet we the medicine [Malcolm] of the sickly weal [country], / And with him pour we in our country's purge / Each drop of us." (V, ii, 27–9) Even before Malcolm is hailed as the new ruler, chaos begins to dissipate and order be re-established as Malcolm confidently gives instructions to the nobles accompanying him as they gather before Macbeth's castle: "You, worthy uncle, / Shall with my cousin, your right noble son, / Lead our first battle. Worthy Macduff and we / Shall take upon 's what else remains to do / *According to our order.*" (V, vi, 2–6) The alignment of forces into an arrangement that musters the nobles according to their degree re-establishes an order (disrupted earlier in the banquet scene) that reflects the cosmic hierarchy and re-introduces harmony into the world of the play.

Macbeth—and Evil—Destroyed

Once the hero chooses to obey evil impulses, the classical conventions of tragedy decree an inevitable and ignoble death. His nature is so corrupted that his destiny is inescapably either to self-destruct or to be destroyed by a rightful avenger. Lady Macbeth's suicide illustrates the former. She who willingly—even exultantly—invoked the dark powers, bidding them to fill her "from the crown to the toe top-full / Of direst cruelty" and to "Stop up th' access and passage to remorse" (I, v, 45–7) by the end of the drama sleepwalks, rubs her hands together uselessly to remove not just the physical but the moral stain, and moans "Hell is murky!" (V, i, 31) Ironically, she is overcome with remorse. Finally she "as 'tis thought, by self and violent hands / Took off her life …" (V, xi, 36–7). The dark powers have toyed with her just as they did with Macbeth; her request to feel no guilt or regret for her actions is denied. In this play, as in most of Shakespeare's tragedies, the maxim holds: "evil is self-destroyed or invites its own destruction."

While Macbeth does not technically commit suicide, he goes to certain death. Confronted by the elected avenger Macduff, who is determined to exact satisfaction for the murder of his family, and disheartened by Macduff's revelation that he is not "of woman born," Macbeth knows that he is doomed. He first refuses to fight, until Macduff taunts him:

> Then yield thee, coward,
> And live to be the show and gaze o' th' time.
> We'll have thee as our rarer monsters are,
> Painted upon a pole, and underwrit
> "Here may you see the tyrant."
>
> (V, x, 23–7)

His masculinity stung again (Macduff also knows how to use shaming and humiliation), Macbeth elects not to live as a bound and disgraced
captive but to fight to the end. Now we see a flash of the heroic bravery that he exhibited at the very beginning; we remember the Macbeth
who displayed the positive virtues of Mars and whom Duncan excitedly
acclaimed as "valiant cousin, worthy gentleman!" (I, ii, 24) Macbeth's last
words are

> I will not yield
> To kiss the ground before young Malcolm's feet,
> And to be baited with the rabble's curse.
> Though Birnam Wood be come to Dunsinane,
> And thou opposed being of no woman born.
> Yet I will try the last. Before my body
> I throw my *warlike* shield. Lay on, Macduff,
> And damned be him that first cries, "Hold, enough!"
>
> (V, x, 27–34)

They exit fighting.

This play is a meditation on the Scorpionic topic of evil. It explores
the ways in which evil can enter the human world, ripen, mature, and
ultimately disintegrate in a spectacular and devastating cataclysm. We
see the whole trajectory, from beginning to end. There are other villains
in Shakespeare's oeuvre, Iago for example. Yet Iago, who consciously
and deliberately manipulates Othello's jealousy to drive him to kill Desdemona, is villainous from the very beginning, unlike Macbeth who is
an admirable hero at the start. Iago's evil has coalesced before the play
opens; at the end, he is led away to be tortured, still stubbornly unrepentant. Because he is largely a creature of motiveless malignancy, we cannot
identify as well with him as we can with Macbeth.

Macbeth, on the other hand, is initially the incarnation of positive
Mars: a brave noble, one who courageously defends the kingdom and
so compels our admiration in line with Duncan's praise. But he transforms from a defender of country and King to a destroyer of country and
King. We watch the stages of his gradual descent into evil, as he becomes
trapped in a miasmic hell, unable to get off the path he travels or to
reverse direction. He engages our sympathies and compels our horrified
fascination as no other villain in Shakespeare does, for he is uncomfort-

ably accessible to us. We have accompanied him on his journey, from the moment when he is described as slicing open Macdonwald's body to the moment when he retreats offstage, still fighting.

Perhaps in ripping open the traitorous Macdonwald from the nave to the chops, Macbeth releases a kind of contaminating evil into the air, a psychic infection of disease-producing germs. The infection from the rebellious Macdonwald is breathed in by a vulnerable Macbeth and he in turn becomes the agent of regicide. Unable to fight off the infection or to resist the seductive prophecies of the witches and the manipulation of his determined wife, Macbeth embarks on a career of crime unstopped until the wise and disciplined Malcolm declares his intent to heal the torn country by the "grace of grace" (V, xi, 38).

At the end of the play we are left with ever-recurring questions that are embedded in the zodiacal sign of Scorpio. Is evil real? And if it is, how and to what extent does it affect the human realm? Is there an external and eternal malignant force responsible for human sin and corruption? Can we ascribe much of the blame for Macbeth's tragedy to the demonic "weird sisters"? There are three possible answers: first, that Evil is an independent principle, opposed to and as real as Good; second, that it exists but is subordinate to Good, as depicted in the Bible's Book of Job, where Satan reports to God about his testing of the poor tormented Israelite; or lastly, that it is an illusion, a nothingness that only appears to have power. Shakespeare in his play *Macbeth* does not provide a definitive answer. Though the witches appear first before anyone else in the drama, implying that there are pre-existing evil forces that can work on the human psyche, there is equal emphasis on Macbeth's own desires and drives and on the influence of another powerful human being, his wife. Shakespeare, so often ambiguous, allows us to make up our own minds.

CHAPTER 11

The Hidden Astrological Key to
The Tempest
Pisces and its (traditional) Ruler Jupiter
(and Modern Ruler Neptune)

Now I will believe
That there are unicorns . . .
(*The Tempest*, III, iii, 21–2)

The Story

Twelve years before the opening of the play the scholar and rightful Duke of Milan, Prospero, was deposed by his ambitious brother Antonio with the collaboration of Alonso, King of Naples. Though Prospero and his three-year-old daughter Miranda were placed in a small boat to die on the open sea, Prospero's faithful counselor Gonzalo put supplies (as well as Prospero's beloved books) on board so that they arrived safely on an isolated island.

In the following twelve years there, Prospero becomes an accomplished magician, able to free the airy spirit Ariel from a tree in which he was trapped by the evil witch Sycorax. Ariel now serves him but longs for freedom. Prospero's other servant is the earthy, ugly, and resentful Caliban, son of Sycorax, who complains that he is the rightful master of the island and who wants freedom too. Upon his arrival on the island, Prospero tried to teach Caliban, but after Caliban attempted to rape Miranda, Prospero keeps tight control over him.

As the play opens, Prospero knows that his brother Antonio, along with the King of Naples and their entourage, are in a ship passing near the island. Using Ariel as the instrument of his developed powers, Prospero raises a violent tempest that drives the ship to the island, and separates the ship's passengers into three isolated groups. One, all by himself, is Alonso's son Ferdinand, who encounters the lovely Miranda. The two immediately fall in love, but Prospero, fearing a too-hasty romance, enchants Ferdinand by his magic art. The second group is the nobles.

Antonio, along with Alonso's brother Sebastian, begins plotting the murder of Alonso so that Sebastian can usurp his brother's place. The last is the jester Trinculo and the drunken butler Stephano, who has rescued wine casks from the shipwreck. They encounter Caliban, and the three, more and more intoxicated, plot to destroy Prospero and return the island to Caliban's control.

Prospero's magic thwarts the evil intentions of the nobles, as well as those of the inebriates. He celebrates the impending marriage of Miranda and Ferdinand with a conjured masque, featuring the goddesses Juno and Ceres to bless their union. At the end of the play, Prospero forgives his brother, frees Ariel, guarantees safe voyage back to Italy for all, and renounces his magic art.

Pisces and its (Traditional) Ruler Jupiter

The first clues to the sign associated with the play are its title and its opening with a tremendous storm. Appropriately, since the element of water symbolizes human emotions, the tempest can be interpreted as a manifestation of Prospero's rage at having been ousted by his usurping brother and his co-conspirators. Only now can he direct his anger through the medium of nature to the very persons who betrayed him, since they are sailing nearby.

So a WATER sign is likely to be the key to understanding this play. Pisces, the third of the water signs and the last and twelfth sign of the zodiac, is entirely apt. One of its chief symbols is the OCEAN, ruled by the Greek god NEPTUNE. The ocean is the largest body of water on our planet, filled with sleek swimming FISH as well as other odd-looking creatures. In line with this, references to fish abound within the play. Alonso, grieving for his presumed-drowned son, muses, "O thou mine heir / Of Naples and of Milan, what strange *fish* / Hath made his meal on thee?" (II, i, 111–3) In the droll scene of Trinculo encountering the prone Caliban, Trinculo tries to determine what the bundle on the ground actually is:

> What have we here, a man or a *fish*? Dead or alive?—A
> *fish*, he smells like a *fish*; a very ancient and *fish*-like smell;
> a kind of not-of-the-newest poor-john [dried hake com-
> monly eaten by the poor]. A strange *fish*!
>
> (II, ii, 23–6)

To gain shelter from the returning storm, Trinculo creeps under Caliban's cloak, laying his body next to Caliban's, but facing the opposite direction. This creates a puzzling visual spectacle, unlike anything in any other Shakespearean play. This strange image suddenly reveals its meaning when we note that the primary symbol for the sign Pisces is two fish, connected by a cord, swimming in opposite directions. Trinculo and Caliban literally create this symbol with their bodies, as they lie on the ground facing opposite directions.

That the action transpires on an island, surrounded by water (and thus removed from ordinary life) is significant. Commentators have noticed Ariel's reference to fetching dew from an island in the New World, the "still-vexed [ever-stormy] Bermudas" ("Bermoothes" in some editions) (I, ii, 230). This has led to an interpretation of the play as a commentary on Western Europeans' colonialism. But Ariel establishes the location of Prospero's island as somewhere in the Mediterranean between the coast of northern Africa and Italy. Whatever the precise location, the island on which the action of *The Tempest* takes place has no name and is unidentifiable. This indeterminacy of location accords with the nebulousness of Pisces, associated with places that exist outside of time and space.

> What is most magical about the isle … is that in being many places at once, geographically, culturally, and mythographically hybrid, it eludes location and becomes a space for poetry, and for dream. It is not found on any map. Prospero's enchanted island, while drawn from real explorations and published accounts, is ultimately a country of the mind.[327]

There is a long-established tradition of enchanted islands in Western literature. Some of the most notable are the Isles of the Blessed, the Western Isles to which King Arthur of Celtic legend has gone and from which he is expected to return at some future time (as the "once and future king"). This fits the trajectory of the story: Prospero has vanished from Milan, has sailed away to a mysterious island, and will return at the end of the play to take his place as rightful ruler.

> Of the many universal symbols on which *The Tempest* is erected that of the island is fundamental. An island is a bit of a higher element rising out of a lower—like a fragment of consciousness thrusting

up out of the ocean of unconsciousness. Like a clearing in the wilderness or a walled city, like a temple or a monastery, it is a piece of cosmos set over against chaos and ready to defend itself if chaos, as it will be bound to do, tries to bring it back under its old domination. It is a magic circle, a small area of perfection shutting out all the rest of infinite space. What wonder that an island has come to be a symbol of birth and of rebirth, or that from the fabled Atlantis and that earthly island, the Garden of Eden, to the latest Utopia, an island, literal or metaphorical, is more often than any other the spot the human imagination chooses for a fresh experiment in life![328]

Ferdinand intuitively recognizes that the ideal or mythic has transformed this mundane island: "Let me live here ever! / So rare a wondered father and a wise / Makes this place paradise." (IV, i, 122–4) That an island is shaped like a magic circle and that this particular island is a place of magic and enchantment also directs our attention to the sign Pisces.

Another clue to the associated sign comes from the fact that Prospero and his daughter Miranda have been on this unnamed island for the significant figure of twelve years. The planet Jupiter, traditional ruler of the sign Pisces, has a twelve-year cycle (that is, it takes approximately twelve years for it to appear to circle the Earth, as it travels along the ecliptic, the apparent path of the Sun). Jupiter has been described as the GREATER BENEFIC, the planet of LUCK AND GOOD FORTUNE. Prospero is obviously alluding to Jupiter as "bountiful Fortune" and a "most auspicious star" in a key speech in Act I. As he explains to Miranda:

> By accident most strange, bountiful Fortune,
> Now my dear lady, hath mine enemies
> Brought to this shore; and by my prescience
> I find my zenith doth depend upon
> A *most auspicious star*, whose influence
> If now I court not, but omit, my fortunes
> Will ever after droop.
>
> (I, ii, 179–185)

This same number is mentioned again in the drama, for the spirit Ariel was imprisoned by the witch Sycorax in a cloven pine for twelve years before being released by Prospero. Analogous to Ariel's period of captivity, Prospero and Miranda spend the same amount of time on this isolated isle before themselves being released to go home to Milan. The type of tree in which Ariel was confined is also revealing, for the pine tree and the oak, in which Prospero threatens to re-incarcerate Ariel, are both sacred to Jupiter.

Prospero is obviously the embodiment of certain Jupiterian qualities. Even his name, Prospero, recalls a key idea associated with the planet: it signifies abundance, wealth, and PROSPERITY. Too, Prospero describes himself as "the prime duke—being so reputed / In dignity, and for the LIBERAL ARTS / Without a parallel—those being all my study ..." (I, ii, 72–4). Devoted to these studies, the seven liberal arts,[329] he neglected "worldly ends, all dedicated / To closeness and the bettering of my mind" (I, ii, 89–90). He valued his library above all else and is grateful that, once deposed and set adrift in a small boat on the sea, his trusted counselor Gonzalo provided him with volumes that Prospero prized above his dukedom. (I, ii, 166–9) This study has paid off, since Prospero has become a master of esoteric arts while stranded on this island—an illustration of Jupiter as a kind of GUARDIAN ANGEL bestowing some positive development even in the midst of dark events. The blessing is that Prospero has made good use of his time there.

Astrologers interpret a good Jupiter as a force that prevents the worst from happening. That is definitely so for Prospero, for he acknowledges that a "Providence divine" saved himself and Miranda from death, especially since the small boat he and his infant daughter were placed in was nothing more than "A rotten carcass of a butt, not rigged, / Nor tackle, sail, nor mast—the very rats / Instinctively have quit it." (I, ii, 146–8) It was a miracle that they landed safely on the island. Jupiter was operant first in that the conspirators did not kill Prospero and his daughter outright; instead they set them adrift on the sea. Second, the conspirators' long-term goal, of the two dying at sea, was frustrated by Prospero's and Miranda's survival. Clearly a beneficent force is at work in their lives.

However, the negative side of Jupiter is obvious too: Jupiter's propensity for laziness. Prospero admits that he was not doing the job of Duke, but passed off his responsibilities to his brother while he "to my state grew stranger, being transported / And rapt in secret studies." (I, ii, 76–7) No wonder that the brother, "being thus lorded" (I, ii, 97), receiving the revenues of the state, and "executing th' outward face of royalty / With all prerogative" (I, ii, 104–5), began to believe that he was in fact the Duke. Why not, since he was doing all the work?

Where the brother defied cosmic order and fell morally, of course, was in forcibly removing the rightful ruler from his allotted position. As discussed with regard to *Macbeth*, in the Elizabethans' view of the world this goes against the natural order of the universe and generates unpleasant consequences. The tempest created at the beginning of the play is a symbol not only of Prospero's anger but also of the disorder introduced into both the human and natural worlds by Antonio's usurpation of his brother's rightful place in the hierarchy. As the ship founders, disorder increases as the nobles get in the way of the sailors' efforts to manage the boat while the tempest rages. The Boatswain urges Antonio and his fellow nobles to go below and stay out of the laboring sailors' way: "Keep your cabins; *you do assist the storm.*" (I, i, 12–3) They are doing that in more ways than one!

Prospero's responsibility for his current situation lies in his negligence of duty, his abrogation of the responsibilities associated with his rightful place in the grand scheme of things. The ensuing twelve years of exile stem from this fault. It is the equivalent of the tragic hero's fatal flaw—generating uncomfortable consequences, but of lesser magnitude in a comedy than the tragic hero's error. Fittingly, Prospero lacked the qualities of a positive Saturn: performance of duty, faithful fulfillment of responsibilities, consistent hard work, restriction of pleasure in favor of slow-attained success—characteristics that balance a too-active Jupiter. Jupiter and Saturn represent diametrically opposed qualities: while Jupiter likes the pomp and title of position, Saturn is usually the one getting things done. Ideally, you should balance both.

A lesser Jupiterian figure is the good Gonzalo, who embodies that planet's characteristic OPTIMISM and GOOD HUMOR. Even as the tempest rages, Gonzalo comforts himself with his intuitive perception that the Boatswain has "no drowning mark upon him" (I, i, 26); that is, fate does not intend the fellow to die a watery death—and hopefully that means that Gonzalo will not either. Three times—a significant number in myth and fairy tale as a number of completion—he asserts that the ship's officer is destined to hang.

Gonzalo is the only one to keep his head during the storm, while those higher up in the scale (the nobles Antonio and Sebastian) resort to screaming insults at the sailors ("A pox o' your throat, you bawling, blasphemous, incharitable dog!" is a good example [I, i, 36–7]). When the ship seems to split, Gonzalo assumes a typically Jupiterian religious attitude; though he wishes for a bit of dry land, he gives himself over to the Divine: "Now would I give a thousand furlongs of sea for an acre of barren ground ... The wills above be done ..." (I, i, 58–9, 60). Gonzalo, of course, earlier had the foresight, loyalty, and generosity (all qualities associated with Jupiter) to supply Prospero and his daughter with food, water, and other "necessaries" for their survival in that miserable boat.

Once on land, of all the nobles and their associates who are grouped together in one part of the island, Gonzalo alone strives to be cheerful. He takes the stance of the PHILOSOPHER who reasons that however bad your own situation is, others may have it worse. He attempts to comfort the King of Naples, saying,

> Beseech you, sir, be merry. You have cause,
> So have we all, of joy; for our escape
> Is much beyond our loss. Our hint of woe
> Is common; every day some sailor's wife,
> The masters of some merchant, and the merchant,
> Have just our theme of woe. But for the miracle,
> I mean our preservation, few in millions
> Can speak like us. Then wisely, good sir, weigh
> Our sorrow with our comfort.
>
> (II, i, 1–9)

Since this is a water-sign-themed play, at least one character should embody the attributes of the phlegmatic type, the temperament associated with the water element.[330] Gonzalo is an ideal candidate, for even when threatened by death in the midst of a raging gale, even when marooned on an eerie island, his nerves are steady and he exhibits a calm, relaxed mental state capable of religious and philosophical reflection. This allows him to notice what others do not. He is the only one who observes that miraculously their clothes are not sea-stained: "Methinks our garments are now as fresh as when we put them on first in Afric, at the marriage of the King's fair daughter Claribel to the King of Tunis." (II, i, 68–70). Though he comments on this three times, the others, caught up in their emotional attitudes of either grief (Alonso) or resentment (Antonio and

Sebastian), ignore him. Because they are emotionally upset (and have little "phlegm" in their temperament), they not only do not register the odd state of their clothing but they also seem unable to perceive the physical beauties of the island.

The good and faithful counsellor Gonzalo, who helped save Prospero and Miranda, is in turn "rescued" by Prospero. The conspirators have drawn their swords, intending to stab Gonzalo and the others who are asleep, but Prospero's agent Ariel wakes them with music and song. How appropriate is this karmic turn-about, with the Jupiterian figure of Gonzalo himself rewarded for his loyalty and compassion by being saved by the Jupiterian intervention of Prospero.

So, early in the play many of the customary associations with Jupiter are emphasized: THE HIGHER MIND, LEARNING, BOOKS/LIBRARIES, and even LONG-DISTANCE TRAVEL, especially to exotic or unusual places (in this case Prospero's journey over the sea, his arrival on the island itself with its strange inhabitants, and the nobles' voyage to Africa for Claribel's wedding).

The important theme of EDUCATION, also related to Jupiter, crops up repeatedly in the play. We first see this in the long scene of exposition in which Prospero finally enlightens Miranda as to her real identity. He has for many years been her TEACHER: "here / Have I, thy schoolmaster, made thee more profit / Than other princes can, that have more time / For vainer hours and tutors not so careful." (I, ii, 172–5) She is a most grateful learner. Not so the earthy Caliban; though he admits that Prospero did "teach me how / To name the bigger light, and how the less, / That burn by day and night" (he means, of course, the Sun and Moon) (I, ii, 337–9), he is predominantly resentful. Prospero chastises him:

> I pitied thee,
> Took pains to make thee speak, taught thee each hour
> One thing or other. When thou didst not, savage,
> Know thine own meaning, but wouldst gabble like
> A thing most brutish, I endowed thy purposes
> With *words* that made them known.
>
> (I, ii, 356–61)

Caliban's retort is "You taught me language, and my profit on't / Is I know how to curse. The red plague rid you / For learning me your language!" (I, ii, 366–8) In fact, Caliban's first words upon entering the play are a string of curses! "As wicked dew as e'er my mother brushed / With raven's feather from unwholesome fen / Drop on you both! A southwest blow on ye, / And blister you all o'er!" (I, ii, 324–7) Commentators have mused about the implications of Caliban's resistance to learning. Are some beings truly uneducable? Does Caliban represent a primitive type that simply cannot absorb modern information? Is Shakespeare commenting on experiences Europeans were having as they colonized the New World?

Prospero seems brutal in the way that he addresses Caliban, threatening him with side-stitches and pinches from invisible creatures, but the real reason for his rancor is that Caliban tried to rape his daughter. Unrepentant, the creature simply laughs: "O ho, O ho! Would't had been done! / Thou didst prevent me; I had peopled else / This isle with Calibans." (I, ii, 352–4) Here is another instance of Fortune (or the beneficent Jupiter) averting a terrible fate—in this case Prospero's prevention of a horrible threat to the daughter he deeply loves. Prospero's powerful voice, heard in his occasional intense chiding of Miranda and repeated harsh threats to Caliban, is an expression of his passionate anger at having been deposed, along with his rage at the ungrateful Caliban's desire to violate his daughter, as well as the magical power that has flowed into his personality as a result of his studies.

Jupiter and The Theme of Freedom

The planet Jupiter relates both to the EXPANSION of your mental horizons (as in reading, reflection, or study) and to the literal extension of your borders or boundaries (as in TRAVEL). As well, and more pertinent to *The Tempest*, Jupiter longs for greater possibilities for independent action, self-government, and exercise of your free will, ideally without the restrictions of parents, society, government, or even nature. Of course, complete FREEDOM is impossible in this realm, with human beings apparently limited to three dimensions and five senses—yet most beings, whatever their situations are, long for more.

The two spirits under Prospero's control repeatedly ask for or seek freedom. Ariel, earlier a servant to the witch Sycorax (and further limited by being encased in a pine tree), was initially freed by Prospero but then bound again in service to *him*—but only for a specified time. Ariel's subservient position is clear; Prospero explicitly calls him "my slave" (I, ii, 272). Ariel continually complains about being given more work to do, and reminds Prospero repeatedly of his promised freedom.

> ARIEL: Is there more toil? Since thou dost give me pains,
>   Let me remember thee what thou hast promised
>   Which is not yet performed me.
> PROSPERO: How now? Moody?
>   What is't thou canst demand?
> ARIEL: *My liberty.*
> PROSPERO: Before the time be out? No more!
> ARIEL: ... Thou did promise
>   To bate [remit] me a full year.
>
> (I, ii, 243–7, 250–1)

Though Prospero continues to assert his power over Ariel, their relationship has a tender side. When Ariel suddenly asks Prospero, "Do you love me, master?," the deposed Duke's response is: "Dearly, my delicate Ariel." (IV, i, 48–9) Later, he admits, "I shall miss thee, / But yet thou shalt have *freedom.*" (V, i, 97–8) Throughout the action Prospero has been assuring Ariel that he will be freed and, significantly, the final words of the drama are about Ariel's release: "My Ariel, chick, / That is thy charge. Then to the elements / Be *free*, and fare thou well." (V, I, 320–2) Ariel has achieved the longed-for Jupiterian freedom.

Caliban, the other creature under Prospero's command, also complains about his servitude and demands freedom. Like Ariel, Caliban is Prospero's "slave"; he is compelled to make the fire, fetch wood, and perform other services. He protests that the island is his by rights from his witch-mother and that Prospero (ironically) has deposed him as its rightful overlord: "For I am all the subjects that you have, / Which first was mine own king, and here you sty me / In this hard rock, whiles you do keep from me / The rest o' th' island." (I, ii, 344–7)

In yet another irony in the play, when Caliban drinks the wine proffered by the newly-arrived Stephano, he simply transfers his subservience from one person to another by immediately subjugating himself to the drunken butler. He obsequiously declares, "That's a brave god, and bears celestial liquor. I will kneel to him.... I'll swear upon that bottle to be thy true subject, for the liquor is not earthly.... I'll show thee every

fertile inch o' th' island, / And I will kiss thy foot. I prithee, be my god."
(II, ii, 109–10, 116–7, 140–1) (The foot is the part of the body ruled by
Pisces!) This is likely a repetition of his offer to the newly-arrived Prospero twelve years ago, indicating that Caliban has not learned much in
the interim. The threesome exit the scene with Caliban singing "Ca-Cal-
iban / Has a new master.—Get a new man! / *Freedom*, high-day! High-
day, *freedom*! *Freedom*, high-day, *freedom*!" (II, ii, 175–8) But Caliban is not
at all free. Stefano continually addresses him as "servant monster" and
happily exploits his knowledge of the island and of Prospero's personal
habits. (III, ii, 1–1–7) Instead of obtaining freedom, Caliban succumbs
not only to the influence of the two clowns but also to the addiction of
alcohol.

Yet Caliban *will* have the island restored to him after everyone
departs for Italy at the end of the story. More importantly, he does actually attain a measure of self-awareness: "I'll be *wise* hereafter, / And seek
for grace. What a thrice-double ass / Was I to take this drunkard for a
god, / And worship this dull fool!" (V, i, 298–301) Of greatest importance
for him may be the inner freedom he has gained now that he is aware of
his tendencies to abase himself. In vowing to seek for "grace"—a gift of
Jupiter—he is also acknowledging something higher than himself.

With regard to the human characters, most are restricted or experience some kind of imprisonment. None experiences any sort of freedom
until the end. The sailors are safely stowed under the hatches, charmed
into sleep for the entire play. The nobles and their attendants, reminded
of their guilt by Ariel who appears to them as a harpy, are enrapt by one
of Prospero's spells: "My high charms work, / And these mine enemies
are all knit up / In their distractions. They now are in my power; / And in
these fits I leave them …" (III, iii, 88–91). When Prospero inquires as to
the situation of Alonso and his entourage, Ariel confirms this:

> Confined together
> In the same fashion as you gave in charge,
> Just as you left them; all *prisoners*, sir,
> In the lime-grove which weather-fends your cell;
> They cannot budge till your release.
>
> (V, i, 7–11)

Only in the last scene does Prospero dissolve the charm that has
kept them "spell-stopped," and their awakening senses "Begin to chase

the ignorant fumes that mantle / Their clearer reason." (V, i, 61, 66–8) Since reason is the highest faculty in human beings, Prospero knows that he has to restore it to them: it is a necessary prelude to forgiveness and reconciliation, since they must be fully mentally competent to understand what has happened both before and after their arrival on the island.

Earlier two other human characters experience a lack of freedom in two entirely different ways. The first is more physical. When Ferdinand first encounters Miranda and the two instantly fall in love, Prospero slows the progress of their love by accusing the young man of being a traitor. He threatens to manacle Ferdinand's neck and feet together and sustain him with only sea-water, fresh-brook mussels, withered roots and the husks of acorns. The noble Ferdinand protests and draws his sword, but Prospero charms him so that he cannot move. Poor Ferdinand laments that

> My spirits, as in a dream, are all *bound up*.
> My father's loss, the weakness which I feel,
> The wreck of all my friends, nor this man's threats
> *To whom I am subdu'd*, are but light to me,
> Might I but through my *prison* once a day
> Behold this maid. All corners else o' th' earth
> Let *liberty* make use of; space enough
> Have I in such a *prison*.
>
> (I, ii, 490–7)

Yet Ferdinand's captivity is not as horrible as Prospero threatened; he is simply compelled to do what Caliban does: carry logs from one place to another. This is a physical slavery. But of all those restricted during the course of the play, he is the only one to bear his restraint with grace. Actions that might have been humiliating are ENOBLED by his love for Miranda. Unlike Ariel, he does not plead for release; unlike Caliban, he expresses no resentment in curses.

> There be some sports are painful, and their labour
> Delight in them sets off. Some kinds of baseness
> Are nobly undergone, and most poor matters
> Point to rich ends. This my mean task

Would be as heavy to me as odious, but
The mistress which I serve quickens what's dead,
And makes my labours pleasures.

(III, I, 1–7)

Miranda, witnessing his labors, out of her newly-birthed love for him, volunteers to substitute for him and carry the logs herself—which, of course, no gentleman would permit.

MIRANDA: If you'll sit down
    I'll bear your logs the while. Pray give me that;
    I'll carry it to the pile.
FERDINAND: No, precious creature.
    I had rather crack my sinews, break my back,
    Than you should such dishonour undergo
    While I sit *lazy* by.
MIRANDA: It would become me
    As well as it does you ...

(III, I, 23–9)

Ferdinand does not disdain hard work; he does not succumb to the negative Jupiterian temptation of being idle and sitting "lazy by" while someone else labors.

But how, really, to define freedom? One of the paradoxes of the play is that Ferdinand and Miranda, who gladly accept or even request low service, have an inner freedom—an emotional freedom—of much greater value than the outer kind. They are not stirred up by negative feelings like resentment; no inner tempest disturbs their hearts and minds, for each is content with the loving company of the other. With each offering to be servant to the other, they place themselves at the service of something higher than their lower selves: the redemptive power of Love itself.

FERDINAND: I am in my condition
    A prince, Miranda, I do think, a king—
    I would not so—and would no more endure
    This wooden *slavery* than to suffer
    The flesh-fly blow my mouth. Hear my soul speak.

The very instant that I saw you did
My heart fly to your service; there resides,
To make me *slave* to it. And for your sake
Am I this patient log-man.

(III, I, 59–67)

This is an initiatory test, and both pass it with the highest degree,
as Prospero acknowledges: "All thy vexations / Were but my trials of
thy love, and thou / Hast strangely [wonderfully] stood the test." (IV, i,
5–7) Initiations in organizations as various as college fraternities, military units, and secret societies often involve voluntary abasement as a
preliminary to assuming a new identity. Ferdinand not only happily suffers humiliation despite being a prince, but also aligns himself during the
experience with the higher power of Love. He illustrates the idea that
you can appear to have no freedom, to be outwardly enslaved, and yet be
inwardly—and happily—free.

The young lovers have a second test to pass, though, one that has
to do with the emotional level: to restrain their passions until after
marriage.

PROSPERO: [T]ake my daughter. But
    If thou dost break her virgin-knot before
    All sanctimonious ceremonies may
    With full and holy rite be ministered,
    No sweet aspersion shall the heavens let fall
    To make this contract grow ...
FERDINAND: As I hope
    For quiet days, fair issue, and long life
    With such love as 'tis now, the murkiest den,
    The most opportune place, the strong'st suggestion
    Our worser genius can, shall never melt
    Mine honour into lust ...

(IV, i, 14–19, 23–8)

Is this introduced as a nod to Christian dogma, which exalts the
state of celibacy and virginity above all others? Or praise directed to
the English queen at that time, the "Virgin Queen" as Elizabeth I was
known? Or, in line with the Elizabethan worldview, a recommendation

to overcome passion with reason? It is probably all three. In any case, Prospero advises Ferdinand to sit and talk with Miranda—an occupation engaging the mind—and later we see the two in an inner chamber, of all things playing chess! A more intellectual endeavor could not be imaged on stage. Playing chess requires using the HIGHER MIND, ruled by Jupiter and associated with education and learning. Concentrating on the game helps them to rein in passion.

The Modern Ruler of the Sign Pisces: Neptune

In Shakespeare's time the sign Pisces was associated with the planet Jupiter. In the modern era, it is now more commonly linked to the planet Neptune. Although the Elizabethans would not have known of the *planet* Neptune, through Greek and Roman mythology they would have been familiar with the Roman *god* Neptune, lord of the oceans. Once discovered (in 1846), the planet Neptune had to be placed within the zodiacal circle. The most logical assignment was to the last sign of the zodiac, Pisces, whose symbol is the vast sea. Though Shakespeare was unaware of the later connection between the planet Neptune and the sign Pisces, the many references to the meanings of both in the play is remarkable—or maybe not! If Shakespeare consciously used archetypal symbols as the basis for his plays, then it is entirely right that they can be meaningfully interpreted in the language of any era and not just the one in which they were written.

Shakespeare in fact refers directly to Neptune several times. One reference occurs, appropriately, in Ariel's description of the storm he creates at Prospero's command: "The fire and cracks / Of sulphurous roaring the most mighty *Neptune* / Seem to besiege, and make his bold waves tremble, / Yea, his dread trident shake." (I, ii, 204–7) Near the end of the play Prospero draws a magic circle and conjures the various spirits ("elves" and "demi-puppets") who have aided his magic arts; some are those "that on the sands with printless foot / Do chase the ebbing *Neptune*, and do fly him / When he comes back ..." (V, i, 34–6).

Regardless of rulership, the sign Pisces relates thematically to SENSITIVITIES on several different levels. The first level correlates to a heightened awareness of *physical* things, such as the aromas and flavors of food, the atmospheres of places, and the energetic "vibrations" of people.

The second level enhances *emotional* resonance, which often makes a person capable of being especially deeply feeling, highly sensitive, and not just sympathetic but empathic. Prospero's daughter Miranda displays these attributes. When she beholds the great tempest, it is not just that she feels sorry for the presumed drowned sailors but that she actually experiences what they have experienced, in sympathetic rapport with them: "O, I have suffered / With those that I saw suffer! ... O, the cry did knock / Against my very heart!" (I, ii, 5–6, 8–9) When Prospero has begun to unfold the story of the "foul play" which brought them to the island, the impressionable Miranda exclaims, "O, my heart bleeds / To think o' th' teen [trouble] that I have turned you to" (I, ii, 63–4).

Miranda weeps easily while Prospero recounts the full story of the treachery perpetrated against herself and her father. When he tells her that she cried as a child when they were put into the boat, she vows, "I, not rememb'ring how I cried out then, / Will cry it o'er again. It is a hint / That wrings mine eyes to't." (I, ii, 133–5) Later, the spell-bound Ferdinand, obliged by Prospero to carry logs, reveals that his "sweet mistress / Weeps when she sees me work" (III, i, 11–2). Her tears when Ferdinand declares he loves her, though, are happy ones: "I am a fool / To weep at what I am glad of." (III, ii, 73–4)

In fact, lots of people cry in the play! The "good old lord Gonzalo: / His tears run down his beard like winter's drops / From eaves of reeds." (V, i, 15–7) When Prospero sees him, his eyes too spill over: "Holy Gonzalo, honourable man, / Mine eyes, ev'n sociable to the show of thine, / Fall fellowly drops." (V, i, 62–4) (Notice that it is only the good characters who cry; the conspirators—both the nobles and the trio of drunks— never do.)

A third level of special Piscean sensitivity is on a *spiritual* level: an altered or visionary awareness, in which people lose their perception of the mundane world (as when they sleep and dream), or see images of things that are not "real" (as when the wandering hungry nobles see a rich banquet laid out for them which Ariel then whisks away), or perceive the realities of another dimension momentarily perceptible in this one (like the spirit of Ariel or the goddess figures conjured by Prospero in the masque he creates to celebrate his daughter's impending wedding).

The sleep state, in which one is oblivious to the everyday world and capable of experiencing enchanting dreams, is in the modern age under Neptune's rulership.[331] Characters in this play are frequently put to SLEEP, usually through magic arts (also ruled by Neptune). Prospero makes Miranda sleep just after telling her about their past so that he can summon Ariel: "Here cease more questions. / Thou art inclined to *sleep*; 'tis a good dullness, / And give it way. I know thou canst not choose. [Miranda *sleeps*.]" (I, ii, 185–7) Ariel reports to Prospero that he has safely put the ships and sailors in a protected harbor: "The mariners all under hatches stowed, / Who, with a charm joined to their suffered labour, / I have left *asleep.*" (I, ii, 231–3) Later Ariel puts most of the nobles to sleep, except the treacherous Antonio and corruptible Sebastian, who proceed to plot the murder of Alonso. As Antonio observes, "What a strange drowsiness possesses them! ... They fell together all, as by consent; / They dropped as by a thunderstroke." (II, i, 195, 199–200) Luckily, Prospero detects the two as they plot to murder their sleeping comrades and sends Ariel to wake the threatened lords.

As in *Macbeth*, only the good get to sleep.

In the final scene, the Boatswain and other sailors are brought on stage, and are urged to explain what happened to them:

> ALONZO: These are not natural events; they strengthen
> From strange to stranger. Say, how came you hither?
> BOATSWAIN: If I did think, sir, I were well awake,
> I'd strive to tell you. We were *dead of sleep*,
> And—how, we know not—all clapped under hatches;
> Where but even now, with strange and several noises
> Of roaring, shrieking, howling, jingling chains,
> And more diversity of sounds, all horrible,
> We were *awaked*; straightway at *liberty*;
> Where we in all her trim freshly beheld
> Our royal, good, and gallant ship, our Master
> Cap'ring to eye her. On a trice, so please you,
> Even in a dream, were we divided from them,
> And were brought moping [dazed] hither.
>
> (V, i, 230–43)

Even Prospero sleeps! Much is made of the fact that he takes afternoon naps and that the drunken threesome will take advantage of this to attack him in his cell while he is asleep. But of course, Prospero is in perfect control, and, aware of their plans, he frustrates them.

Dreams, Altered States, and the Perfect World:
Pisces and Neptune

The realm of Pisces is one in which "there are more things in heaven and earth … than are dreamt of in our philosophy" (*Hamlet*: I, v, 168–9). In particular, dreams, those strange and vivid inner playlets enlivening our sleep, may seem nonsensical upon waking but may actually convey deep truths. References to dreams or dream-like states abound in *The Tempest*. Miranda's vague recollection of their departure from Milan seems "far off, / And rather like a *dream* than an assurance / That my remembrance warrants." (I, ii, 44–6) When Ferdinand is en-spelled by Prospero so that he cannot move or use his sword, he muses, "My spirits, as in a *dream*, are all bound up." (I, ii, 490)

Lovely things can be experienced in dreams, even to the coarse Caliban:

> Be not afeard. The isle is full of noises,
> Sounds, and sweet airs, that give delight and hurt not.
> Sometimes a thousand twangling instruments
> Will hum about mine ears, and sometime voices
> That if I then had waked after long sleep,
> Will make me sleep again; and then in dreaming,
> The clouds methought would open and show riches
> Ready to drop upon me, that when I waked,
> I cried to dream again.
>
> (III, ii, 130–38)

The altered states correlative to Pisces are not always trustworthy or desirable, though. They may be illusory or even caused by mental imbalance. The other ships accompanying Alonso's group "are upon the Mediterranean float [sea] / Bound sadly home for Naples, / Supposing that they saw the King's ship wrecked, / And his great person perish"—an illusion created by the ever-busy Ariel. (I, ii, 235–8) While this serves Prospero's purposes, it is entirely untrue.

After Ariel appears to the plotting nobles, the "three men of sin," he confronts them with their misdeeds and drives them mad. The distracted Alonso dashes off, vowing to commit suicide by joining his presumed-drowned son in the sea-depths, while Gonzalo, the only one still in his right mind and ever the phlegmatic, observes,

All three of them are desperate. Their great guilt,
Like poison given to work a great time after,
Now 'gins to bite the spirits. I do beseech you
That are of suppler joints, follow them swiftly,
And hinder them from what this ecstasy [frenzy]
May now provoke them to.

(III, iii, 53, 58, 104–9)

Always associated with Pisces is the problem of staying grounded in this world, honoring its demands, and maintaining an emotional and mental balance. The Pisces personality type is all too vulnerable to the siren call of the fantastic, to the attractions of other worlds, to an escape into the realm of fairy and fable.

Yet sometimes dreams or visions point to the possibility of the miraculous. A whole spectrum of fantastical creatures is spoken of in the play, from the loveliest and most beneficent (Ariel, unicorns, the phoenix) to the ugliest and most threatening (a harpy, goblins, and the "monster" Caliban). It is through the water element that such beings may be imagined or intuited. Under the surface of the ocean, the largest body of water on our planet and thought of as a Piscean realm, the quality of light alters, objects are less clearly discernible, and things—even the bodies of the dead—can morph through a mysterious process of secret transformation into something precious. This best outcome is described in Ariel's delightful song:

Full fathom five thy father lies.
　　Of his bones are coral made;
Those are pearls that were his eyes;
　　Nothing of him that doth fade
But doth suffer a sea-change
Into something rich and strange.
　　Sea-nymphs hourly ring his knell …

(I, ii, 400–5)

No wonder Ferdinand, hearing the unearthly music of the island, is sure that, "This is no mortal business, nor no sound / That the earth owes. I hear it now above me." (I, ii, 410–1) Shakespeare could not be clearer in letting the audience know that this is not human-made but celestial music. Only this higher-level music could accompany such a mysterious transformation.

The great temptation for a sensitive Pisces type is DRUGS OR ALCO-HOL, either as escapes from the hardships of the mundane world or as mistaken means to access the beauties of the invisible ones. Imbibing alcohol does produce an "altered state," though one less likely to inspire visions of other worlds and more likely to make one behave foolishly. No surprise then that the humorous subplot involves drunkenness. The butler Stephano who survived the apparent wreck by sitting on a cask of Spanish wine that the sailors heaved overboard (II, ii, 112–3) first appears staggering on stage with a bottle in his hand. Seeing the strange four-legged, four-armed creature on the ground, he vows to calm it by sharing the wine:

> He shall taste of my bottle. If he have never drunk wine
> afore, it will go near to remove his fit.... Open your
> mouth; here is that *which will give language to you* ... If
> all the wine in my bottle will recover him, I will help his
> ague [fever].
>
> (II, ii, 71–2, 78–9, 86–7)

Caliban immediately converts to Stephano, declaring, "That's a brave god and bears *celestial liquor.* / I will kneel to him.... I'll swear upon that bottle to be thy true subject, for the *liquor is not earthly.*" (II, ii, 109–10, 116–17) In a parody of a religious act (RELIGION is ruled by Jupiter), Stephano urges Caliban to "kiss the book," and Caliban, awed, queries, "Hast thou not dropped from heaven?" Convinced that Stephano is divine, Caliban vows to kiss not the book but Stephano's foot (the part of the body ruled by Pisces) and begs, "I prithee, be my god." (II, ii, 129, 141) Unfamiliar with alcoholic drinks, Caliban immediately succumbs to its powerful allure.

In a dream-like state or an alcoholic haze, people and places may seem beautiful, exalted beyond their mundane appearance. Pisces has the power to envision an IDEAL or perfect place, so that we may see the world as we would like it to be (due to the unreal or fantastic side of Neptune), merely a projection of our hopes and wishes. On the other hand, Pisces may give a glimpse of the world as it truly is (due to the spiritual side of Neptune). Pisces promises that if only the doors of our perception were cleansed or "we saw not through a glass darkly but face to face," we might see both ourselves and creation as they truly are.

Gonzalo vividly creates for us one of these ideal worlds, rhapsodizing about the island as a commonwealth truly characterized by "common wealth":

> All things in common nature should produce
> Without sweat or endeavour. Treason, felony,
> Sword, pike, knife, gun, or need of any engine [weapon],
> Would I not have; but nature should bring forth
> Of it own kind, all foison [plenty], all abundance,
> To feed my innocent people....
> I would with such perfection govern, sir,
> T' excel the Golden Age.
>
> (II, i, 159–164, 167–8)

Gonzalo's description reminds us of the original perfect world: the Garden of Eden.

Piscean "Knowledge" and the Study of Magic

In traditional astrology, the planet Jupiter links with or rules the sign Pisces, but it is also connected to another sign, Sagittarius. The theme of knowledge is common to both signs. The knowledge signified by the Sagittarian Jupiter is a body of traditions and practices passed down through the centuries and preserved as history, legal precedent, religious doctrine or dogma, and educational content. It is extroverted knowledge, the distillation of traditions that guide life in this world. The Piscean Jupiter's knowledge is spiritual (rather than religious); it is an inner knowing, based on esoteric truths of secret mysteries, occult lore, and hidden wisdom that reveals the deepest workings of the universe. It is an interior knowledge, a knowledge of higher worlds and the laws by which they operate.

Obtaining this type of knowledge is the work of a lifetime, gleaned from consistent dedication to certain practices and rituals that lead to mastership. As in many religious, spiritual, and esoteric traditions, these include withdrawal from the world, periods of fasting or abstinence, and the study of sacred texts. Circumstances have created the opportunity for

Prospero to fulfil all these requirements: he has obviously been in seclusion on the island, an enforced solitude that has fortuitously served his spiritual purposes; he has had no personal relationship or sexual contact; and he has spent his time reading the books he loves and, presumably, performing the required rituals.

Shakespeare obviously knows something about traditions associated with magic, which is ruled by Pisces. Critics and scholars—particularly Frances A. Yates—have speculated that Shakespeare's model for Prospero was the eminent Elizabethan Dr. John Dee, whose reputation has undergone its own "sea-change" in the twentieth century.[332] Dee was a talented mathematician (he wrote an introduction to Euclid's *Elements*); skilled in navigation (he studied with the famous geographer Gemma Frisius, became friends with the renowned mapmaker Gerard Mercator, and was consulted by English nobles planning expeditions to the New World); and a tutor to the sons of several noble families (Sir Philip Sidney among them). Before leaving for the Continent in 1583 he was "perhaps *the* major guiding spirit behind the glorious saga of English expansion."[333] His extensive travels in Europe may have been spying missions for Elizabeth's government. Signing some letters sent back to England as "007," Dee may even have inspired the character of James Bond![334]

Shakespeare may have drawn on public information about Dee for his portrait of Prospero as magician or he may have gleaned details of magical practices from a variety of other sources: legends of Biblical figures such as Moses and Solomon, or popular characters such as Merlin and Dr. Faustus, or widespread contemporary folkloric traditions, or earlier Elizabethan plays.[335] Wherever he absorbed the details, Shakespeare equips Prospero with the three required magical accoutrements: a special robe, which Prospero refers to as "my magic garment" and "my art" (I, ii, 24, 25); a staff which seems to function as the wizard's conventional wand; and a book in which recipes and rituals were typically recorded. The ceremonial robe is worn not because it has intrinsic power, but because putting it on (like getting dressed up for the Prom) alters your emotional state, helps focus on the ritual to be performed, and prepares your consciousness for an experience that is out of the ordinary.

A magician typically performs rituals within a magic circle that has an important function: to create a protected and consecrated space within which the mage can safely enact his art. When Ariel brings the entranced noble party to Prospero at the end of the play, "They all enter the circle which Prospero had made, and there stand charmed ..." (V, I, stage directions after line 57). The circle has significance in religious rituals because any representation of the circle is a miniature cosmos. The drawing of one, as some native American shamans and Tibetan monks do in creating sand mandalas, is believed to affect the world positively through resonance between the little microcosm of the circle and the larger macrocosm of the world.

In psychological terms, as Jung notes, "the protective circle, the mandala, is the traditional antidote for chaotic states of mind."[336] In this last scene the most frantic character is Alonso. As he and his fellows enter the magic circle, Prospero calls for music: "A solemn air, and the best comforter / To an unsettled fancy, cure thy brains, / Now useless, boiled within thy skull." (V, i, 57–9) Music adds to the potency of the described circle—music that harmonizes the inner and outer Alonso. We have seen (in Chapter 3 in the section "The 'Music of the Spheres") how important music was to Elizabethan thinkers, since it reflected and revealed cosmic harmony. It was especially important as a healing tool for those whose minds were disturbed, as is Alonso's.

The practice of white magic very much relates to the worldview covered in Chapter 3, the one that saw the universe as a divine unity containing a limitless sympathetic network of interrelated levels with humanity at the balancing point between the levels above and below. A majority of people living during Shakespeare's lifetime considered themselves integrated into this transcendent unity of humanity, nature, and the Divine:

> In essence, white magic reflects this theory of unity, for the white magician assumes that God has concealed within the framework of the universe specific divine powers or virtues available to him through ritual and meditation. Attracting such powers through the celestial aid of angels, spirits, stars, and planets, or through invoking the terrestrial virtues of the four elements, or those of animals, plants, metals, and stones, the magician channels these sources of divine energy through himself to affect the harmonious outcome of his beneficent works. Like the king who as God's deputy also possesses divine powers, the white magician heals those who seek his aid and imposes benevolent order on anarchy.[337]

Prospero's Control of the Four Elements

White magicians might become adept in several specialized studies. They might study alchemy, which involves the use of fire to transform base metals into their perfect inner essence, equivalent to gold. They might also learn to summon spirits and to heal with herbs. But most especially they need to understand astrological symbolism and planetary cycles. Astrology is particularly important because the magician as astrologer believes that "the planets and stars possess both life and intelligence, endowed with divine powers by God, the Prime Mover. Thus, he times his magic to coincide with that particular character of each planet whose special influence changes sublunary events and affects the hidden virtues of plants, animals, and minerals."[338] This is how Prospero knows about and is determined to use Jupiter's auspicious cycle to effect his daughter's happiness and to regain his dukedom.

With a knowledge of astrology, the Shakespearean magus would be familiar with the importance of the four elements. Shakespeare follows esoteric tradition in showing that the white magician is expected to master each of them: earth, water, air, and fire. They are integral to characterizing and understanding the twelve signs of the zodiac, each of which is assigned to one of the four. In line with the importance of these four categories, the magician employs four magical implements: a wand, a cup, a sword, and a pentacle or disk:

> They are associated with the four traditional elements: the wand with fire, the sword with air, the cup with water, and the disk with earth. More importantly, they point to the four basic skills a magician must command: to raise power (symbolized by the wand); contain it (symbolized by the cup); cut away extraneous forces (the sword); and ground the energy on earth (the disk).[339]

The four elements also symbolize the four levels of a human being: earth the physical, water the emotional, air the mental, and fire the spiritual. Controlling them is equivalent to mastery of all levels of one's inner being and is an essential part of the training of the Piscean white magician.

Prospero's dominance over Caliban, an earthy creature, illustrates his mastery of the physical level: Caliban is compelled to obey Prospero's commands to perform mundane-world physical services, like lugging logs, though he does so with curses and complaints. That Prospero prevents Caliban from discharging his lust upon Miranda symbolizes the magician's control of his own desire nature. Prospero's control of Ariel reveals his mastery of the element of air or the mental level. Prospero confirms Ariel's elemental nature since Ariel can be summoned through mental power alone ("Come with a thought!" [IV, i, 164]) and belongs most properly to a single element: "thou, which art but *air* ..." (V, i, 21). Ariel performs to the letter all of Prospero's commands, many of them instructions to conjure illusions literally out of "thin air," like the banquet that torments the party of nobles. Representing the creative power of both thinking and imaging, Ariel's presence is often accompanied by music and song.

Why, we might ask, are only these two representative spirits actors in the play? Why not spirits of fire and water as well? Perhaps for reasons of economy, Shakespeare actually combines in Ariel two of the elements, fire along with air. When Ariel first appears to assure Prospero that he has created the tempest as directed, he describes multiple fiery manifestations:

> I boarded the king's ship. Now on the beak,
> Now in the waist, the deck, in every cabin,
> I *flamed* amazement. Sometime I'd divide,
> And *burn* in many places; on the topmast,
> The yards, and bowsprit, would I *flame* distinctly;
> Then meet and join. Jove's *lightning*, the precursors
> O' th' dreadful thunderclaps, more momentary
> And sight-outrunning were not. The *fire* and cracks
> Of sulphurous roaring the most mighty Neptune
> Seem to besiege, and make his bold waves tremble,
> Yea, his dread trident shake.
>
> (I, ii, 197–207)

In this passage is another reference to Jupiter, by his alternate Roman name Jove, with allusions to his weapons of thunder and lightning.[340]

Caliban also embodies two elements: water as well as earth. He certainly inhabits the earth—directors of the play often have him emerge from a deep hole onto the stage at his first appearance, literally announcing his lower nature—but Caliban is also associated with water in its varied manifestations. In cursing Prospero, Caliban begs that a multitude of contaminants in stagnant water infect Prospero: "All the infections that the sun sucks up / From bogs, fens, flats, on Prosper fall, and make him / By inch-meal a disease." (II, ii, 1–3) He is susceptible to the alcoholic liquid that Stephano offers him. When he accompanies the two drunken clowns on their trek to Prospero's home to attack him while he sleeps, he is led into a "filthy-mantled pool" in which they all lose their precious bottles and emerge smelling "all horse-piss" (IV, i, 182, 198, 207).

Perhaps Shakespeare foregrounds the elements of air and earth because they are the two most representative of human beings: earth, indicative of the body, and air, representing the spirit or the divine animating Breath. We are described as creatures of "body and soul." Without the breath of life, the body disintegrates and its elements return to the earth itself as dust. Antonio alludes to this while seductively tempting Sebastian to kill Alonso: "Here lies your brother, / No better than the earth he lies upon / If he were that which now he's like, that's dead." (II, I, 276–8) The importance of these two particular elements is reinforced by Ferdinand's musing, upon first hearing Ariel's song: "Where should this music be? I' th' air or th' earth?" (I, ii, 391). This implies that control of earth and air are more essential—perhaps because more difficult—attainments for the Piscean white magician.

These two elements also gain emphasis due to the particular divinities that Prospero conjures in the masque to celebrate the impending wedding of Miranda and Ferdinand. Ceres is the goddess of agriculture, of the Earth's bounty produced literally from the ground, and so she corresponds to the element of earth. Juno is Queen of Heaven, always representative in Renaissance symbolism of the element of air.[341]

So by his control of Caliban and Ariel, Prospero displays his already-achieved dominion over the physical (earth) and mental (air) planes. However, gaining control of the emotional (water) level seems much more difficult for him. The tempest he conjures up at the beginning of the play is the externalization of his rage, and his occasional harsh speech to Caliban—and even to Miranda—bespeaks suppressed anger. He is obviously still furious with his brother and his brother's co-conspirator, because even the lovers notice it:

> FERDINAND: This is strange. Your father's in some passion
> That works [agitates] him strongly.

Devoted to his library and esoteric studies, Prospero has mastered the magi-
cal arts, especially the ability to control nature as he does in conjuring the
"tempest" that opens the play. Christopher Plummer as Prospero holds the
magician's staff in the Stratford Festival (Ontario, Canada) production of
2010. (Photo: Andrew Eccles)

> MIRANDA: Never till this day
> Saw I him touched with anger, so *distempered*.
>   (IV, i, 143–5)

Being "distempered" means he is out of balance in the mixture of the four humors, as Shakespeare's audience would have known. Prospero admits that he is "vexed" (IV, i, 158), and tells Ferdinand and Miranda that to calm down, "A turn or two I'll walk / To still my beating mind." (IV, i, 162–3) Ariel even hesitates to tell Prospero about the progress of the drunkards' plot against him, saying, "I feared / Lest I might anger thee." (IV, i, 168–9) Prospero clearly has a temper, suggesting that it is the fire element (or choler) that threatens to destabilize him emotionally. When Ariel reports that the would-be usurpers and murderers are all under his spell, Prospero threatens, "I will plague them all, / Even to roaring." (IV, i, 192–3) It was easier to restrain his feelings during the twelve years of isolation on the island, but now that the men who did him wrong are physically present and in his power, he is maximally tempted to wreak revenge. The delicate Ariel appeals to Prospero's higher side, encouraging reason to overcome passion (in line with the belief that air is a higher level than water):

> ARIEL: Your charm so strongly works 'em
>   That if you now beheld them, your affections
>   Would become tender.
> PROSPERO: Dost thou think so, spirit?
> ARIEL: Mine would, sir, were I human.
> PROSPERO: And mine shall.
>   Hast thou, which art but air, a touch, a feeling
>   Of their afflictions, and shall not myself,
>   One of their kind, that relish all as sharply
>   Passion as they, be kindlier moved than thou art?
>   Though with their high wrongs I am struck to th'
>   quick,
>   *Yet with my nobler reason 'gainst my fury*
>   *Do I take part.* The rarer action is
>   In virtue than in vengeance. They being penitent,
>   The sole drift of my purpose doth extend
>   Not a frown further. Go release them, Ariel.

> My charms I'll break, their senses I'll restore,
> And they shall be themselves.
>
> (V, i, 17–32)

We actually witness Prospero's triumphant mastery of his emotions, as the Christian virtues of compassion and forgiveness (especially associated with the sign Pisces) overpower his rage and vengefulness. It is such a contentious internal struggle that Prospero must declare his forgiveness more than once, in both cases unable to refrain from reminding Antonio of his sins:

> Flesh and blood,
> You, brother mine, that entertained ambition,
> Expelled remorse and nature, who, with Sebastian—
> Whose inward pinches therefore are most strong—
> Would here have killed your king, *I do forgive thee*,
> Unnatural though thou art....
> For you, most wicked sir, whom to call brother
> Would even infect my mouth, *I do forgive*
> Thy rankest fault, all of them, and require
> My dukedom of thee, which perforce I know
> Thou must restore.
>
> (V, i, 74–9, 132–6)

Is Prospero a White Magician?

The practice of magic has often been disparaged throughout history because *all* magical practice has mistakenly been categorized as "black." However, tradition clearly distinguishes between "black" magic and "white":

> The simplest means of differentiating the two is by means of their motivation. White magic is intended to promote some beneficial end, whether it is healing or simply greater cosmic harmony. Black magic involves some harm to someone else—if not directly, then obliquely, say, by disarming his free will.[342]

Black magicians were easy to identify: "With avowedly secular ends in mind, the black magician sought temporal and personal rewards, such as sexual gratification, the location of buried treasure, the control of weather, or the diplomatic secrets and policies of nations."[343] Often unrepentant to the end, like Christopher Marlowe's Dr. Faustus who seeks power, wealth, and fame, they are frequently characterized as stubborn, willful, arrogant, and avowedly atheistic. White magicians, on the other hand, seek to do good to others, have more laudable personal qualities, and acknowledge something greater than themselves. Practitioners of white magic also strive to refine their souls in order to climb the "ladder of heaven" (as described in Chapter 3) and gain direct experience of the Divine. A number of historical personages are reputed to have had special and magical abilities, among them Jesus of Nazareth. His turning water into wine, healing the sick, walking on water (again symbolizing control of the emotions), and even raising the dead all put him in the category of a white magician.[344]

Prospero is obviously not a black magician; the black magician of the drama is Sycorax, Caliban's mother, who imprisoned Ariel in a pine tree. But although Prospero falls into the category of a white one, he does have a bit of gray about the edges.[345] "Grey magic (a less common term) generally applies to magic that is performed with mixed motives. Whatever the practitioners may think they're doing, grey magic probably constitutes the majority of magic performed."[346] This is in keeping with Shakespeare's consistent creation of characters who are not unalloyedly good or unalloyedly bad. All human beings are imperfect creatures, being mixtures of both the celestial and the terrestrial.

Where the gray enters with regard to Prospero is that he does interfere with the free will of others. He puts Miranda to sleep whether she wants to lose consciousness or not. He binds Ariel to his service despite Ariel's pleas for freedom and keeps Caliban enslaved despite his protestations that the island is his by inheritance. Yet these two are not precisely human, but rather elemental spirits or aspects of Prospero's own psyche, and so his control of them can be justified. Caliban especially warrants being restrained since his intentions, as in wanting to rape Miranda, are malevolent.

Prospero's magic seems more gray early on because his motivation at that point is not entirely unselfish; it is tinged with an angry desire to wreak revenge on his duplicitous brother. But his design is not principally selfish (unlike Macbeth, whose ambition spurred him to murder exclusively for his own benefit). Prospero's plan is in part to re-establish himself at the level to which he was born and called. His intention is also to orchestrate his daughter's happiness because of his deep love for her, telling her "I have done nothing but in care of thee, / Of thee, my dear one, thee, my daughter, who / Art ignorant of what thou art ..." (I, ii, 16–8). And he has not killed—not even damaged—his enemies. Despite the terror of the tempest, Prospero assures Miranda that "There's no harm done ... No harm." (I, ii, 15) "No harm": this is the key statement that puts Prospero firmly in the category of a white practitioner.

Prospero gets "whiter" by the end of the play for several reasons. For one, he obeys the New Testament injunction to "forgive seventy times seven," showing mercy to those who have plotted to remove and even murder him. Love, mercy, compassion—these are all virtues particularly associated with Pisces in its highest expression.[347] For another, the tremendous inner struggle to subdue his rage and desire for revenge culminates in the triumphant overcoming of his passion by reason.

For Shakespeare's audience, the final confirmation of Prospero's spiritual quality is his stunning decision to abandon the practice of magic altogether.[348] This is his highest accomplishment as a white magician and accords with the spirit of sacrifice also connected with the sign Pisces. Since his goals have been accomplished, he does not retain special powers that might eventually swell his ego. Before relinquishing them, he describes the extraordinary scope of his art, to emphasize the sacrifice:

> I have bedimmed
> The noontide sun, called forth the mutinous winds,
> And 'twixt the green sea and the azured vault
> Set roaring war—to the dread-rattling thunder
> Have I given fire, and rifted Jove's stout oak
> With his own bolt; the strong-based promontory
> Have I made shake, and by the spurs [roots] plucked up
> The pine and cedar; graves at my command
> Have waked their sleepers, oped, and let 'em forth
> By my so potent art. *But this rough magic*
> *I here abjure.* And when I have required
> Some heavenly music—which even now I do—
> To work mine end upon their senses that

This airy charm is for, I'll break my staff,
Bury it certain fathoms in the earth,
And deeper than did ever plummet sound
I'll drown my book.

(V, i, 41–57)

In line with the play's predominant element, Prospero will not burn his book—that is, consign it to the fire—but drown it, committing it to water. (Notice that he refers to all four of the elements in this speech, affirming his command over them.)

Yet another indication of Prospero's psychological and magical maturity is his declaration, "This thing of darkness I acknowledge mine." (V, i, 278–9) He appears to be referring to Caliban, who immediately responds to this statement by mourning, "I shall be pinched to death." In this one short sentence of Prospero's is a world of psychological truth: Prospero is aware of his terrible rage—an inner "darkness" that incarnated itself as the tempest—and his powerful drive to destroy his enemies. His recognition and admission of his inner dark side, the side that might have indulged the destructive impulse, is testament to his inner integration. Caliban may be the literal manifestation of that spirit of darkness, but he is an essential complement to—even component of—Prospero.

Remarkably, the stubborn Caliban, now freed to take possession of the island once more, has gained some self-awareness. Pardoned by Prospero, he vows, "I'll be wise hereafter, / And seek for grace. What a thrice-double ass / Was I to take this drunkard for a god, / And worship this dull fool!" (V, I, 298–301) Unable to benefit previously from Prospero's attempts to educate him, Caliban has gained some wisdom through being fooled and made to suffer. What he seeks and what he has gained—grace and wisdom—are both associated with the Jupiter- and Neptune-ruled sign of Pisces. Caliban's gaining of some wisdom at the end of the play parallels on a lesser scale Prospero's great achievement of mastering and then wisely abandoning his magical studies.

Shakespeare is making a point later recognized in depth psychology: as Jung advised, the goal of all inner work is not perfection but wholeness: "[I]t is possible for a man to attain totality, to become whole, only with the co-operation of the spirit of darkness, indeed that the latter is actually a *causa instrumentalis* of redemption and individuation."[349] Caliban is that spirit of darkness.

Harmony—and Order—Restored

All of the events and themes of the play are obviously linked to the zodiacal sign Pisces and its traditional and modern rulers, Jupiter and Neptune. The play began with dramatic discord, a raging tempest, as the ship carrying the villainous Antonio and his confederate Alonso apparently splits up in the "wild waters." The Boatswain advises Gonzalo either to work some magic to quell the storm or take to his cabin and be ready for whatever befalls: "[I]f you can command these elements to silence, and work the peace of the present, we will not hand a rope more; use your authority." (I, i, 19–21) It is not Gonzalo, though, but Prospero who has the power both to raise the elements and to command them to be still. By the end of the play it is Prospero who has "worked the peace of the present" and resolved discord into concord both through external magical acts and through internal command of his passions.

All has been orchestrated by Prospero through his magical abilities: the exposure of his brother's treachery, the resumption of his rightful place as Duke, and the happy marriage of his daughter to a noble and loving man. A great feat of magic, though, also embedded in the symbolism of the sign Pisces, is the facilitation of rebirth or resurrection—a miraculous restoration of life. This is dramatically represented in the last scene by the reappearance of the supposed-drowned Ferdinand emerging out of oceanic chaos (or alternatively the waters of life). Sebastian blurts out that it is "A most high miracle!" and Ferdinand, on seeing his father, acknowledges, "Though the seas threaten, they are merciful. / I have cursed them without cause." (V, i, 181–2)

There will be no more tempests, for Prospero assures the travellers "I'll deliver all, / And promise you calm seas, auspicious gales, / And sail so expeditious that shall catch / Your royal fleet far off." (V, i, 317–20) The seas, the water element ruled by Pisces, which roiled in the storm at the beginning of the play will now be still, assuring a peaceful arrival home. Another voyage of long-distance travel awaits them, but luck and good fortune will attend it. With that confirmed, Prospero releases Ariel to the elements and to his promised freedom.

But—that's not the end! In the Epilogue Shakespeare does something unusual: he puts the onlookers in a place of power by having Prospero petition the audience to set *him* free. With his magical abilities gone, his "charms are all o'erthrown, / And what strength I have's mine own, / Which is most faint." He asks the onlookers to release *him* "With the help of your good hands," which on one level is asking for applause. But further, Shakespeare puts the viewers in a similar situation to the one Prospero was in earlier, where granting mercy "frees all faults." And as Prospero he offers the viewers some wise advice: "As you from crimes would pardoned be, / Let your indulgence set me free." To be released from the consequences of your failures and faults, you would be wise to forgive others those same failures and faults. In so doing, everyone becomes free: not only the mistake-makers but also anyone holding on to the need for redress or revenge. And with the audience's applause, the actor too is freed from his role, free to quit the stage, leaving us with the memory of the delightful but "insubstantial pageant" that lives in our imaginations long after the enactors of the drama have disappeared.

CHAPTER 12

The Hidden Astrological Key to

King Lear

The Sign Capricorn and its Ruler Saturn

Come not between the dragon and his wrath.
                    —Lear (*King Lear:* I, i, 122)

These late eclipses in the sun and moon portend no good
    to us."
                    —Gloucester (*King Lear:* I, ii, 96–7)

You do me wrong to take me out o' the grave.
Thou art a soul in bliss; but I am bound
Upon a wheel of fire, that mine own tears
Do scald like molten lead.
                    —Lear (*King Lear:* IV, vii, 45–8)

The Story

In ancient Britain, King Lear plans to abdicate and divide the kingdom among his three daughters, with the largest part going to the one who declares she loves him most. When his youngest and favorite, Cordelia, refuses to flatter him, the enraged Lear disowns her. His trusted advisor the Earl of Kent protests and Lear banishes him (though he returns later in disguise). The King of France eagerly takes the dowerless Cordelia as his Queen. She reluctantly leaves her father in the care of her malicious and greedy sisters, Goneril and Regan, who immediately plot against him.

Meanwhile the Earl of Gloucester's illegitimate son Edmund, resenting his bastardy, schemes to get his legitimate brother Edgar's inheritance. The credulous Gloucester falls for the ruse, and blames recent eclipses believed to cause discord, treason, and disruptions in families. Later Edmund stages a swordfight with his brother, urging him to flee. Eluding a search, Edgar disguises himself as a filthy beggar, the mad "poor Tom o' Bedlam."

At the Duke of Albany's palace, Goneril, exasperated by the rowdy behavior of the King and his hundred knights, instructs her sycophantic servant Oswald and his fellows to treat the King disrespectfully. She asks Lear to reduce his retinue by half. Enraged, he curses her with sterility and leaves for Regan's palace. He finds Regan at Gloucester's home, where Kent has been put in the stocks, and refuses to return to Goneril's castle with a reduced retinue. When he declares he will go to Regan's, she insists that he bring only twenty-five men, and finally, none. More and more enraged, Lear protests. As a storm begins, the increasingly distraught Lear goes out into open country, accompanied by his Fool, who relentlessly mocks Lear's greater foolishness in giving away his titles and lands.

Increasingly mad, Lear encounters the disguised Edgar and continues to rage against his daughters. Gloucester surreptitiously brings Lear, the fool, and the disguised beggar inside to receive warmth and food and arranges for Lear's transfer to Dover where Cordelia and an invading force from France wait. When Edmund reveals his father's treason, Cornwall tears out Gloucester's eyes and thrusts him outside the castle. There he encounters the disguised Edgar who leads him to the coast. Inside the castle Goneril has taken up with Edmund, and the Duke of Cornwall dies, wounded by a servant protesting his cruel treatment of Gloucester.

The English troops march toward Dover, where the King has arrived in Cordelia's camp. On the cliffs of Dover, Gloucester asks his disguised son to lead him to the very top so that he can commit suicide, but Edgar fools him into thinking he has leapt and survived. A newly-patient Gloucester resolves to live. Oswald discovers Gloucester and attempts to kill him, but instead is killed by Edgar.

In the invaders' camp, Lear awakes, a changed man. Acknowledging both his age and folly, he is reconciled with Cordelia, but her forces lose the battle and they are both taken to prison. Now humble and patient, Lear accepts this since he will be with Cordelia. As the victors confer, Regan becomes ill and Albany confronts his wife with her plan to murder him and marry Edmund. Albany invites any comer to challenge Edmund as a traitor. The disguised Edgar comes forward, fights with and stabs Edmund. Edgar reveals that when he unmasked himself to his father, Gloucester's "flawed heart" burst and he died. A messenger reports that Goneril has poisoned her sister and taken her own life.

Dying, Edmund repents his instructions to have Cordelia hanged and Lear killed, but before they can send to the prison, Lear staggers in carrying Cordelia's body. In an extremity of pain, grief, and horror—and believing that he sees something on Cordelia's lips—Lear faints and dies. Albany appoints Edgar ruler of the kingdom, and all depart to the strains of a funeral march.

The Sign Capricorn and its Ruler Saturn

Some critics consider *King Lear* the "crown jewel" of all Shakespeare's works, though there is controversy about a definitive version of the play.[350] While not the longest of his plays (that distinction belongs to *Hamlet*), it is possibly his most profound, and deserves a long and in-depth analysis. This profundity accords with the astrological key to the play. Determining the astrological signature is not difficult since it is the only play in which Shakespeare stresses the age of the title character. Lear is an old man, and the reason he plans to divide his kingdom among his daughters and retire from ruling is that he thinks he cannot do the job anymore: "'tis our fast intent / To shake all cares and business from our *age*, / Conferring them on younger strengths, while we / Unburthened crawl toward death." (I, i, 36–9) The zodiacal sign and planet correlated with the last phases of life—OLD AGE, DEBILITY and ultimately DEATH—are Capricorn and Saturn. At different points in the play, not only Lear but also Gloucester and Kent are referred to as old men.

Shakespeare mocks this stage of life in Jaques' famous speech on the Seven Ages of Man (cited in full in Chapter 3 under "The Number Seven—as in the Seven Classical Planets").

> The sixth age shifts
> Into the lean and slippered pantaloon,
> With spectacles on nose and pouch on side,
> His youthful hose, well saved, a world too wide
> For his shrunk shank, and his big, manly voice,
> Turning again toward childish treble, pipes
> And whistles in his sound. Last scene of all,
> That ends this strange, eventful history,
> In second childishness and mere oblivion,
> Sans teeth, sans eyes, sans taste, sans everything.
> (*As You Like It*: II, vii, 156–65)

"Second childishness" and "sans eyes" assume a terrible and ironic significance in this play as we see Lear become an obedient child and Gloucester lose his eyes.

The sign Capricorn fits the play given its tragic plot, its tone of melancholy, and its darkness (literal in both the storm and Gloucester's blinding). The Sun enters the sign Capricorn at the time of the Winter Solstice, when the Sun reaches the Topic of Capricorn below the Equator. In the northern hemisphere it is the shortest day of the year with the least amount of sunlight. In line with the despairing mood of the play created by Lear's suffering and Cordelia's death, it is the moment of greatest darkness and least hope. We are in the season of winter, of cold weather, of deprivation and scarcity of food, with limited light and little life. Many animals withdraw from activity, hibernating in a death-like sleep. Fittingly the color associated with both Capricorn and its ruling planet Saturn is BLACK.

With Saturn, the planetary ruler of the sign Capricorn, we come to the last of the planets visible to the naked eye, the seventh in the classical pantheon. Saturn takes approximately twenty-nine years to travel around the ecliptic and return to its original position. In Shakespeare's time it would have been the slowest planet with the longest cycle and so an appropriate symbol for old age. Like all astrological symbols, Saturn is double-sided, packed with meanings that are extremely positive as well as meanings that are deeply negative. What tends to get the most emphasis in astrological writings is the darker side. And, of course, because *King Lear* is a tragedy and for dramatic purposes, the play focuses on the terrible and depressing implications of the sign Capricorn along with the most negative associations of its ruler Saturn.

Saturn is known as the "greater malefic"; that is, it correlates with the conditions, challenges, and obstacles that prevent you from achieving your goals and dreams, from most fully expressing your talents and potentials, from being successful in life. In more extreme cases, it bodes EVIL or DISASTER (the root of which is "dis" + "aster," meaning "away from" + "the stars"—that is, deprived of the helpful power of the stars). Of all the letters of the astrological alphabet, Saturn was in Shakespeare's time the symbol most likely to be associated with dark FATE—a meeting with terrible and unavoidable circumstances that bring PAIN, SUFFERING, and finally DEATH.

Before looking in greater detail at the negatives, it is important to remember that there is a positive side to Saturn.

> If its energy is applied as DISCIPLINE, HARD WORK, PATIENCE, sustained effort, and the mature assumption of duties and responsibilities, ... it leads to genuinely earned and long-lasting success. Saturn builds a foundation for achievement in a professional way that lends STABILITY to any endeavor. No surprise that he ruled over the Golden Age, and was Lord of the Seventh Heaven.[351]

A sterling example of the best use of Saturn can be seen in the life of Queen Elizabeth II of England, whose horoscope shows Saturn prominent at the top of the chart (at the "career point") and Capricorn, ruled by Saturn, as the ascending sign. She truly exemplifies the "mature assumption of duties and responsibilities" in fulfilling the role of Queen while exhibiting the serious and sober demeanor synchronous with Capricorn rising. In line with the dominance of Saturn and Capricorn, she demonstrates a modest but regal dignity.[352] Queen Elizabeth II has not abdicated her throne—and with Saturn in such high focus in her horoscope, it is highly unlikely she will.[353]

One reason for the tragic ending of *King Lear* is his deliberate renunciation of his position as King. Given the violent history of battles for the English crown (which Shakespeare depicted in his history plays) and the looming dilemma of who would take the throne after the childless Elizabeth I died, Shakespeare's audience would have been deeply troubled to see a king voluntarily abdicate. More importantly, in the grand scheme of the universe described earlier in this book, for a king to reject his role and responsibilities was sure to invite disorder on all levels: personal, social, and national, as well as in the natural world. (The same was true for the illegitimate usurpation of the status of king, as in *Macbeth*.) No wonder the Fool harps constantly on the folly of Lear's giving away his kingdom: "Thou hadst little wit in thy bald crown, when thou gavest thy golden one away." (I, iv, 141–2)

To the Elizabethans, equivalencies existed on multiple levels, from the higher to the lower:

> In the cosmos: GOD the Father
> In the country: the KING, the Ruler of the State

> In the family unit: the FATHER as Head of the Family
> Within the individual: REASON, the highest of the Faculties

With God, King, and the family's head being analogous symbols equivalent to Saturn and having a similar meaning—authority in each sphere—the play dramatizes tragedy in personal, interfamilial, national, and even cosmic dimensions. This makes Cordelia's especially revealing statement of purpose late in the play resonate on several levels. Returning to England with the invading army intent on rescuing Lear and restoring him to the throne, she says, "O dear *father*, / It is thy business that I go about; / ... No blown ambition doth our arms incite, / But love, dear love, and our aged father's right." (IV, iv, 24–5, 28–9) Her first line echoes Jesus' statement in the New Testament, "I must be about my father's business." (Luke 2:49) Cordelia's reference thus conflates father and Father: her words point to both her physical father and the Divinity that shapes and structures the universe. It affirms that her motives are not egotistic ones, to gain power or wealth—often basic drives for a Capricorn type—but to right a wrong. With the intention of restoring her father to his rightful place in the hierarchy and thus re-establish order on a larger scale, Cordelia is aligned with the more positive function of Saturn.

Of course, it was expected—or at least hoped—that the King would rule over the country and a father would exercise authority within his family in the same way that God was presumed to hold sway over the cosmos: with compassion and mercy, with justice and good judgment. Obviously, this is not always the case. The shadow side, the underbelly of the patriarchal position, whether local or national, is the TYRANT.

> The Father—whether the figure appears in a man's or a woman's psyche—is in his positive form the one who offers support, guidance, wisdom, training in the ways of the world. The Father in his negative form offers support only if you're prepared to take his advice; he offers guidance only if you accept his view *in toto*; he offers wisdom only if you recognize no other source for it; and he trains in the ways of the world according to his own image of the world. This kind of Father withholds if there is no obedience. The root of it is the intense emotional drive which Capricorn so often represses, and which eventually begins to eat away at his usually

reasonable thinking processes, making him blind just when he believes he has got sight.[354]

How apropos this is for this play: Lear is indeed the type of father who withholds love from Cordelia because in his eyes she is disobedient; he is the type of King who silences and banishes those like Kent who contradict him; and he is the type of person whose egotistical reliance on his own image of how the world should operate has created an inner blindness.

In modern democratic states, we forget that divinity was indeed once thought to "hedge a king." In our day, the few remaining kings and queens are eager to exhibit the "common touch," but in previous ages the belief was that the ruler had a direct connection to the Divine and that the manner in which he exercised his authority could have dramatic repercussions on himself as well as others:

> A king's body was often the abode of a god; want of respect would therefore be more than mere impoliteness—it would be impiety.... [I]n the old tales, when a king gave an unjust or incorrect judgment, some untoward and unpleasant incident might take place, show-ing, perhaps, the displeasure of the unknown supernatural powers, the divinities who hedged the King in a very stringent manner. Half of the building in which the wrong judgment was given might slip down the hill on which it was built ... the King's collar might tighten uncomfortably.[355]

King Lear's decision to abandon the throne is definitely "an unjust or incorrect judgment," as subsequent events prove. The reason for his abdication does not actually seem to be that he *cannot* do the job any more. He just does not *want* to. King Lear does not seem to be weak, either physically or mentally, and so the motive for resigning his role is questionable. Once he dispenses with the cares of the kingdom, he spends his time hunting and carousing with the hundred knights still in his service. Goneril's complaints about the behavior of her father and his retinue have some justification: "His knights grow riotous, and himself upbraids us / On every trifle." (I, iii, 6–7) Lear just seems to want to have fun—and if Saturn has arranged for you to be in a position of responsi-bility, it does not allow you a lot of fun!

Told in a prophecy that one of his children would overthrow him, the god Saturn literally ate his offspring as each child was born. Lear embodies the "devouring" parent who uses various strategies (emotional abuse, shaming, and deprivation of inheritance) to disempower his children, especially Cordelia. Peter Paul Rubens, Saturn Devouring his Son, *1636. (Scala/Art Resource, NY)*

Saturn in Classical Mythology

The Elizabethans—including Shakespeare—were quite familiar with Greek and Roman myths, particularly through Ovid's tales of transformations of nature and divinity in his *Metamorphoses*.[356] Greek and Roman mythological tales of the god Saturn support interpretations given to the astrological Saturn and are especially relevant to this play. Saturn (Cronus in Greek) is one of the Elder Gods, a Titan, who seizes rulership of heaven by castrating his father Uranus with a flint sickle.[357] These stories are filled with passion and violence, with horrific details like a son cutting off his own father's testicles—a way of graphically depicting the younger generations' emasculation of their elders by taking over their power and authority. In the subplot of *King Lear*, Edmund the bastard prematurely and inappropriately schemes to usurp his father's position, to be awarded his father's name (Earl of Gloucester) and to receive his property and estates. The tearing out of Gloucester's eyes is analogous to the castration of Uranus, for it renders Gloucester powerless and dependent on others, like his disguised son Edgar. (Shakespeare could hardly have staged a castration of Gloucester.)

So the very first story we have about Saturn tells of a child overthrowing his father in order to take his position. But of course, as is the case with all usurpers, the position once seized is not secure. A prophecy that one of his children would dethrone him drives the mythological Saturn to literally eat his own children as they are born, one by one, of his sister-wife Rhea. At the birth of the last one, his angry and resentful wife hands him a swaddled stone to swallow instead of the live child. That child is Jupiter. After a war in heaven, Saturn is overthrown, is forced to regurgitate the stone as well as the other ingested children, and is exiled from heaven into the underworld.

This myth elaborates what is perhaps the key meaning of Saturn in astrology: it is the symbol of the FATHER, of PATRIARCHY in its most fixed form, resistant to youth and change. In an effort to hold his position, the mythological Saturn will even devour his children.

Lear resembles this Saturn in that he is the epitome of the harsh and demanding father. We have encountered figures of hardhearted patriarchs in other Shakespearean plays, in the persons of Egeus in *A Midsummer Night's Dream*, who insists that his daughter marry the man of his choice or die, and Juliet's father, who demands that she marry

County Paris or be thrown out onto Verona's streets. Like them, Lear is a controlling and demanding father. He has already determined which parts of the divided kingdom will be allotted to his three daughters long before the scene in which he demands ritualized and empty statements of forced love from them. When Cordelia demurs, disrupting the staged show, he becomes angry, revokes her inheritance, and banishes her from the kingdom. In this way he is attempting to destroy her just as Saturn, in a more literal way, tries to destroy his children.

This early myth of violent struggles between generations even in heaven eerily resonates with themes and situations in *King Lear*. In the classical myth a child attacks a parent and then that same being, now a parent himself, literally consumes his own children. Shakespeare subtly alludes to this well-known story in the opening scene. When Cordelia refuses to participate in the charade of flattering declarations of exclusive love to the king and Lear disowns her, he says in this key speech:

> Here I disclaim all my paternal care,
> Propinquity and property of blood,
> And as a stranger to my heart and me
> Hold thee, from this [time], for ever. *The barbarous Scythian,*
> *Or he that makes his generation messes*
> *To gorge his appetite, shall to my bosom*
> *Be as well neighboured, pitied, and relieved,*
> As thou my sometime daughter.
>
> (I, i, 113–20)

The Greeks thought of the Scythians as notoriously savage nomads, whom they believed actually ate their children ("gorged" on their "generations"). Lear is allying himself with a tribe that consumed what they begot, just as Saturn did. He is justifying the right of fathers to have absolute authority—even to the point of death—over their offspring. While Lear does not literally kill Cordelia, he does try to destroy her spirit and reduce her to nothing.

We could say that he eats her in another way. What might it mean psychologically to "eat" your children? A dominant parent, one who controls his children's expression and fate, deprives them of the use of their free will and interferes with the fulfillment of their destiny. He redirects their energy toward himself: they exist only to fulfill *his* purposes, to satisfy *his* needs and desires. In doing so, he prevents the independent use of their highest faculty, reason. In a sense, he *has* "eaten" them.

What Lear has done—and is still doing in the opening scene— his two older daughters will in a way do to him. By gradually reducing his retinue, from one hundred, to fifty, to twenty-five and finally to no knights at all, they exert more and more control over him, reversing his previous control over them. (They are also doing to him what he did to Cordelia: depriving her of her inheritance.) Thrusting him out of doors into a terrible storm is the apex of their revenge on his compulsion of their speech, on his narcissistic need for all their love, and his usurpation of their lives. In a literal way they eat *him* up, reducing his remaining retinue and depriving him of home and status. Like Edmund, they conspire to emasculate their father, just as Saturn castrated his parent.

The Astrological Saturn: Its Qualities and Symbolism

Shakespeare is obviously familiar with the worst possible astrological interpretations of Saturn, in line with its mythological antecedents. In another of his plays, *Titus Andronicus* (a bloody revenge tragedy filled with the horrors of rape, mutilation and cannibalism), he has Aaron the Moor describe to his lover Tamora, Queen of the Goths, Saturn's effects in his character:

> Madam, though Venus govern your desires,
> *Saturn* is dominator over mine.
> What signifies my deadly-standing eye,
> My silence, and my cloudy *melancholy*,
> My fleece of woolly hair that now uncurls
> Even as an adder when she doth unroll
> To do some fatal execution?
> No, madam, these are no venereal [Venusian] signs.
> Vengeance is in my heart, death in my hand,
> Blood and revenge are hammering in my head.
>
> (II, iii, 30–9)

Similarly, the tone of this play is melancholic and King Lear, like Aaron, could equally say, "Vengeance is in my heart, death in my hand, / Blood and revenge are hammering in my head."

Such depressing and horrific associations with Saturn are common from the earliest writings in antiquity through the Renaissance:

> Saturn—coldest, driest, and slowest of planets—was associated with abject poverty, old age, and death, as well as many other negative elements—violence, cruelty, solitude, sadness, desolation. Those born under his influence were gloomy and melancholic, and occupied the lowest levels of society—cripples, *beggars*, criminals, grave diggers and the poorest of peasants.... A Florentine astrological text of the second half of the thirteenth century states that ... [Saturn stands for sadness and melancholy, toil and evil] ... [The property of Saturn is constraint: he is the receptacle and instigator of all evil, wickedness, dangers, and death].[358]

In light of Saturn's connection with beggars, it is symbolically significant that Edgar decides to disguise himself as one.

So Saturn in astrology is associated with RESTRICTIONS, LIMITATIONS, and DISAPPOINTMENTS in life that can foster an attitude of frustration, resentment, bitterness, and COLD-HEARTEDNESS. In classical astrology, Saturn was considered literally to have the quality of COLD, in line with the Sun's transit of the sign Capricorn in the dead of winter. It is remarkable how often characters in *King Lear* refer to being physically cold. At his very first appearance the Fool warns King Lear that by banishing Cordelia and relying on his other two daughters he will "catch *cold* shortly" (I, iv, 86). Such references increase once the storm has begun to rage. "How dost, my boy?" Lear asks the Fool. "Art *cold*? / I am *cold* myself." (III, ii, 66–7) Soon after, the Fool swears "This *cold* night will turn us all to fools and madmen." (III, iv, 75) At Edgar's first appearance, disguised as the mad Tom o' Bedlam, his first lines are "Through the sharp hawthorn blows the *cold* wind. / Humh! Go to thy *cold* bed, and warm thee." (III, iv, 47–8—repeated at l. 91) He repeatedly complains "Tom's a-*cold*"; in the muddle of his pretended mental ramblings it is almost his signature line. (III, iv, 57, 78, 135, 161; IV, i, 53).

Lear, Edgar, and the Fool have suffered cold before this, only on the emotional level. "And let his knights have *colder* looks among you," Goneril instructs Oswald. (I, iii, 22) In a manner the Elizabethans would have understood, coldness filters down from the emotional level into the physical realm. It becomes literally cold as the play progresses because Lear has banished Love in the person of Cordelia (whose name is derived from the Latin "cor, cordis," meaning "heart"). It is entirely apt, then, that his two other daughters become progressively more hard-hearted or stony-hearted in their treatment of both Lear and Gloucester: STONES were also ascribed to Saturn.[359] After Kent helps Lear and the Fool to a hovel on the heath, he intends to return "to this hard house,— / More harder than the *stones* whereof 'tis raised, / Which even but now, demanding after you, / Denied me to come in …" (III, ii, 61–4). This recalls the original myth about Saturn in which he swallowed a stone.

Another detail pointing to Saturn as the dominant archetype for the play is the number of references to knees and kneeling. In no other play of Shakespeare's do characters kneel so often or refer to kneeling so frequently. Saturn rules the KNEES in the physical body, and more significantly, relates to the positive quality that motivates one most often to kneel: HUMILITY. But not everyone who kneels does so in the spirit of being truly "humble": that is, "free from pride or vanity; modest; meek; unassuming; unpretentious;" and "respectful." The first time Lear kneels, it is done in the spirit of mockery, as he demonstrates to Regan how he would kneel to Goneril.

> REGAN: O, sir, you are old;
>   Nature in you stands on the very verge
>   Of her confine. You should be ruled and led
>   By some discretion, that discerns your state
>   Better than you yourself. Therefore, I pray you,
>   That to our sister you do make return;
>   Say you have wronged her, sir.
> LEAR: Ask her forgiveness?
>   Do you but mark how this becomes the house:
>   "Dear daughter, I confess that I am old; *(kneeling)*
>   Age is unnecessary. On my *knees* I beg
>   That you'll vouchsafe me raiment, bed, and food."
>
> (II, iv, 139–49)

Lear refuses to return to Goneril's with a reduced train, and compares the shame of it to bending the knee to "hot-blooded France" now married to Cordelia. "I could as well be brought / To *knee* his throne, and, squire-like, pension beg / To keep base life afoot." (II, iv, 208–10)

But near the end of the play Lear kneels in an entirely different spirit. Having gone mad, railing against the terrible tempest both within his mind and without in the heavens, Lear has been taken to Cordelia's camp, allowed to sleep, and dressed in fresh garments. Awakening, he is disoriented; yet we know that the revived Lear has gained true humility, patience, and clarity of judgment, because he kneels to Cordelia in a spirit of sincerity.

> CORDELIA: Sir, do you know me?
> LEAR: You are a spirit, I know. When did you die?
> CORDELIA: Still, still, far wide!
> DOCTOR: He's scarce awake. Let him alone a while.
> LEAR: Where have I been? Where am I? Fair daylight?
>   ... Would I were assured
> Of my condition!
> CORDELIA: O, look upon me, sir,
> And hold your hand in benediction o'er me.
> No, sir, you must not *kneel*.
>
>   (IV, vii, 48–52, 56–9)

Now Lear evidences a humble acceptance of the restrictions and limitations that Saturn brings.

To reinforce the extraordinary transformation of Lear's temperament, after being taken prisoner by the villainous sisters and the scheming Edmund, Lear does not become angry, does not curse the victors, shows no resentment or resistance, but instead in a spirit of gentle acceptance he envisions imprisonment with Cordelia as a kind of enclosed paradise:

> Come, let's away to prison.
> We two alone will sing like birds i' the cage.
> When thou dost ask me blessing, I'll *kneel down*,
> And ask of thee forgiveness. So we'll live,
> And pray, and sing, and tell old tales, and laugh
> At gilded butterflies ...
> Upon such sacrifices, my Cordelia,
> The gods themselves throw incense.
>
>   (V, iii, 8–13, 20–1)

But before Lear arrives at this peaceful acceptance of fate, he endures terrible trials. To suffer rejection, to be deprived of position and possessions, to lose your faculties and senses, to be imprisoned as a captive of hard-hearted enemies—Saturn offers a bleak vision of a host of tragic possibilities that can befall you in the course of earthly life. Its inherent PESSIMISM is expressed frequently in the play. With his eyes torn out, Gloucester laments, "All dark and comfortless." (III, vii, 88) The melancholic Gloucester sees human beings as victims of a sadistic divinity: "As flies to wanton boys, are we to the gods; / They kill us for their sport." (IV, i, 37–8) His disguised son Edgar, on encountering his disfigured father, offers the observation that no matter how bad things are, they can always become more miserable: "O gods! Who is't can say, 'I am at the worst'?/ I am worse than e'er I was.... / And worse I may be yet; the worst is not / So long as we can say, 'This is the worst'." (IV, i, 26–9)

For the suffering Lear, the physical world and his physical life can only be continuous torture: "I am bound / Upon a wheel of fire, that mine own tears / Do scald like molten lead." (IV, vii, 46–8) Appropriately, the metal associated with Saturn is LEAD. Kent would seem to offer the final judgment in the last scene, as more deaths are announced: "All's cheerless, dark, and deadly. / Your eldest daughters have fordone themselves, / And desperately are dead." (V, iii, 289–91) Edgar's last words in the play carry the same leaden heaviness: "The weight of this sad time we must obey ...," reminding us that DUTY is one of the compulsions of Saturn, though it has rewards in the satisfaction of a job well, efficiently, and consistently done.

Esteemed Virtues of Saturn: Patience, Loyalty, and Honesty

Saturn embraces other positive qualities besides those of discipline, hard work, and the "mature assumption of duties and responsibilities." Along with humility—notable in the repeated symbolism of knees and kneeling—one of the chief virtues of Saturn is PATIENCE. Of course, patience, especially when defined as "quiet, uncomplaining endurance under distress or annoyance" is a virtue that Lear at the beginning does not have. We first see this lack when Goneril chastises Lear about the riotousness of his knights: "Not only, sir, this your all-licensed fool, / But other of your insolent retinue / Do hourly carp and quarrel, breaking forth / In

rank and not-to-be-endured riots." (I, iv, 175–8) Lear's immediate and
unthinking response is to call for his horses, intending to depart immediately for Regan's castle, and to curse Goneril, calling her a "degener-
ate bastard" (I, iv, 229). Her husband Albany, alarmed at the tone of the
confrontation, urges Lear, "Pray, sir, be *patient*." (I, iv, 238)

Albany is not the only one bidding Lear to do this. When Lear
complains to Regan about Goneril's treatment of him, saying that "she
hath tied / Sharp-toothed unkindness, like a vulture, here!" , Regan's
answer is "I pray you, sir, take *patience*." (II, iv, 127–8, 131) It is precisely
this quality that could restrain Lear's increasing agitation. When Regan
insists that he return to Goneril with his train reduced from a hundred
to fifty, he begs, "I prithee, daughter, do not make me mad.... I can be
patient ..." (II, iv, 213, 225). He implores the powers above to bestow this
gift on him: "You heavens, give me that *patience, patience* I need!" (II, iv,
266) But he obviously still does not have it since in the next few lines he
curses his daughters again and swears vengeance:

> No, you unnatural hags,
> I will have such revenges on you both,
> That all the world shall—I shall do such things—
> What they are, yet I know not; but they shall be
> The terrors of the earth!
>
>   (II, iv, 273–7)

Out in the storm and raging at the elements, Lear still has enough
awareness to know that what he lacks is this quality of long-suffering
that would enable him to cease daring the elements. He cries out, "No,
I will be the pattern of all *patience*; I will say nothing" (III, ii, 36), but
he is unable to restrain his passion. Frustrated by his powerlessness and
enraged at what he deems his daughters' ingratitude, Lear realizes that
he is losing his reason. Kent tells Gloucester, "All the power of his wits
have given sway to his *impatience*," and once with Lear, questions him:
"Sir, where is the *patience* now, / That you so oft have boasted to retain?"
(III, vi, 4–5, 53–4). Only at the end, his great rage abated, do we see Lear
both humbly and patiently accepting his fate, envisioning a blissful life
in prison with Cordelia.

The only character in the play to exhibit patience throughout is
Cordelia. As she departs for France, banished and disinherited, she com-

mits the care of her father to her sisters. She tells them to their faces, "I know you what you are, / And like a sister am most loath to call / Your faults as they are named." The sisters naturally deflect this, but Cordelia intuits that "Time shall unfold what pleated cunning hides: / Who cover faults, at last shame them derides." (I, i, 270–2, 281–2) Patient in the sense of being "capable of tranquilly awaiting results or outcomes," she trusts that unfolding events will reveal all. It is appropriate that Saturn is the Lord of TIME. To the ancients "Saturn signifies Time because Time devours temporal events as Saturn did his children."[360]

Saturn stands for LOYALTY, too. This is best exemplified in the noble Earl of Kent's determined attachment to Lear. Kent dares to challenge Lear's casting off Cordelia and his unwise plan to split his time between the two obsequious daughters:

> [B]e Kent unmannerly,
> When Lear is mad. What wilt thou do, old man?
> Think'st thou that *duty* shall have dread to speak,
> When power to flattery bows? To plainness honour's
>   bound
> When majesty stoops to folly....
> I'll tell thee thou dost evil.
>
> (I, i, 145–9, 167)

Small thanks Kent gets for his attempts to get the king to "see better." Lear banishes him too, giving him ten days to leave the country. If he is found after that, he will be killed. Stubbornly, in the hardened manner of Saturn, Lear declares, "This shall not be revoked." (I, i, 180)

Kent proclaims his long-standing devoted service to Lear, saying, "Royal Lear, / Whom I have ever honoured as my king, / Loved as my father, as my master followed,/ As my great patron thought on in my prayers ..." (I, i, 139–42). (Notice that all the roles he mentions are Saturn-ruled: king, father, master, patron.) This is not just excessive praise designed to please Lear or commend himself; its truth is confirmed when Kent, instead of hastening out of the kingdom to save his own life, disguises himself and returns to request a place in Lear's train.

> LEAR: What wouldst thou?
> KENT: Service.

LEAR: Who wouldst thou serve?

KENT: You.

LEAR: Dost thou know me, fellow?

KENT: No, sir; but you have that in your countenance
    which I would fain call master.

LEAR: What's that?

KENT: Authority.

(I, iv, 19–27)

Kent is consistently loyal to the rightful king, even when banished and in disguise.

Kent exemplifies yet another Saturnian virtue: HONESTY. In the speech above, Kent asserts "to plainness honour's bound." Though he is punished for it, Kent's offence is acknowledged by Gloucester to be "honesty" (I, ii, 108). This underlines a central theme in the play, first dramatized by the elder daughters' calculated and exaggerated avowals of love for Lear as opposed to Cordelia's restrained simplicity ("plainness") of speech: the opposition between flattery and sincerity. Lear hears Cordelia's truthful statement of her relationship to her father—according to her "bond" or her duty as a daughter—as stark in the extreme. Yet it is a Saturnian acknowledgement of appropriate behavior in light of the established hierarchy in both the microcosm and the macrocosm. Cordelia's staunch adherence to honest and sincere speech reinforces our perception of her as the incarnation of many virtues. Significantly her name reinforces this particular sterling quality; "cordiality" means "warmth; sincerity of feeling."

Cordelia's reluctance to gush is due in part to her recognizing the difficulty of expressing deep emotion in facile speech. As she says, "my love's / More ponderous than my tongue" and so she cannot "heave / My heart into my mouth" (I, i, 76–7, and 90–1). That is why she will not go along with Lear's staged demonstration of affection. She also refuses to participate because she will not indulge in flattery, which she calls "that glib and oily art, / To speak and purpose not" (I, i, 225–6). Kent's caution to Lear in the first scene that power is bowing to flattery supports the play's criticism of insincere ego-stroking. The principle of Saturn accords with simplicity and sincerity—and silence.

Kent is depicted as compulsively honesty. When he secretly stays in the country, disguises himself, and offers to serve Lear, the king asks him, "What wouldst thou with us?" Kent's answer is "I do profess to be no less than I seem: to serve him truly that will put me in trust; to love him that is *honest*; to converse with him that is wise and says little ..." (I, iv, 11–14). In answer to Lear's query, "What art thou?" Kent responds, "A very *honest*-hearted fellow, and as poor as the King." (I, iv, 17) In case we are not getting the message, Shakespeare hits us over the head with it again. When Lear asks what services Kent can perform, his response is, "I can keep *honest* counsel, ride, run, mar a curious tale in telling it, and *deliver a plain message bluntly.*" (I, iv, 28–30) Unlike many of the characters in the play, everything he says is true. With Kent, another true embodiment of Saturnian virtues, what you see is what you get.

Yet Kent does seem to take plain and honest speaking to an extreme. Arriving at Gloucester's castle, he recognizes the sycophantic servant Oswald and proceeds to berate him mercilessly. His loud and violent condemnation of Oswald seems justified because Kent knows the steward's purpose and has perceived his inner character: "You come with letters against the king, and take Vanity the puppet's part against the royalty of her father." (II, ii, 30–2) Oswald is the extreme opposite type to Kent; as Kent observes, "No contraries hold more antipathy / Than I and such a knave." (II, ii, 79–80) A significant reason for this is that Oswald is a "smiling rogue" who "wears no *honesty*" (II, ii, 65). But Kent's ranting against Oswald does seem excessive: at the end of a long string of insults, he calls Oswald "nothing but the composition [combination] of a knave, beggar, coward, pandar, and the son and heir of a mongrel bitch" (II, ii, 18–19). Questioned by Cornwall, Kent states, "Sir, 'tis my occupation to be plain," but Cornwall dismisses this with

> CORNWALL: This is some fellow,
>   Who, having been praised for bluntness, doth affect
>   A saucy roughness, and constrains the garb
>   Quite from his nature. He cannot flatter, he,
>   An *honest* mind and plain, he must speak truth! ...
> KENT: I am no flatterer. He that beguiled you in a plain
>   accent was a plain knave; which for my part I will not
>   be ...
>   (II, ii, 84, 87–91, 102–3)

(To reinforce Kent's sincerity, he speaks at this point in plain prose, not the fancier poetry of the Duke.) To be sure, Saturn does tend to be blunt and forceful, so much so that its words can be shocking and upsetting to listeners since they lack the veneer of Venus' social graces.

Yet better to be blunt and forceful than to be glib and oily. Flattery is strongly condemned in this play. Though it may seem a minor fault, the tragedy begins because Lear believes his flattering daughters and banishes the one who truly loves him. The last words of the play, uttered by Edgar, reinforce the importance of honesty and sincerity: "The weight of this sad time we must obey; / *Speak what we feel, not what we ought to say.*" (V, iii, 322–3) Altogether, patience, loyalty, and honesty, all commendable Saturnian virtues, are the most praised and valued in the drama.

Disorder—How the Tragedy Begins and Multiplies

In the Elizabethan worldview that included astrology as described earlier in Chapter 3, suffering and tragedy arise—at least in part—from flaws and imbalances in human beings that lead to foolish actions. Disorder then spreads to the world of nature and even the cosmos. (See Chapter 4 for a more complete discussion.) The particular sources of disorder in the world of *King Lear* are suggested in the opening scene of the play, where we should be listening for keys to the underlying symbolism. Kent comments to Gloucester in the very first line, "I thought the King had more affected [favored] the Duke of Albany than Cornwall." Though Gloucester replies that it is hard to tell from the division of the kingdom which noble the king prefers, ideally enlightened rulers were not supposed to have preferences—and if they did, it was wise not to make them obvious. To play favorites was to encourage conflict among their subjects and resentful threats against their own position.

To make matters worse, King Lear is blatant not only about his political preferences but also about his personal ones. Everyone knows which of his three daughters he prefers (and which one he plans to give most to) because he himself announces it: "Now, our joy, / Although our last and least ... what can you say to draw / A third more opulent than your sisters?" (I, i, 81–2, 84–5) The two older sisters have not missed this; as Goneril observes, "He always loved our sister most; and with what poor judgment he hath now cast her off appears too grossly." (I, i, 288–9) While they do not voice their resentment about this as directly as Edmund complains about his bastardy (they seem more annoyed about Lear's "unruly waywardness that infirm and choleric years bring with them"), undoubtedly this blatant preference contributes to their hard-heartedness toward their father. Those who feel unloved (and that includes Edmund as well as the older sisters) are often prone to cruelty.

The subplot too suggests disorder at the beginning of the play, with the failure of Saturnian restraint to control passion. Gloucester introduces his illegitimate son Edmund to Kent rather brazenly, saying that while it used to embarrass him to admit his paternity, now he is comfortable with publicly recognizing him.

> KENT: Is not this your son, my lord?
> GLOUCESTER: His breeding, sir, hath been at my charge. I
>   have so often blushed to acknowledge him, that now
>   I am brazed to't.
> KENT: I cannot conceive you.
> GLOUCESTER: Sir, this young fellow's mother could;
>   whereupon she grew round-wombed, and had,
>   indeed, sir, a son for her cradle ere she had a husband
>   for her bed. Do you smell a fault?
> KENT: I cannot wish the fault undone, the issue of it
>   being so proper.
> GLOUCESTER: But I have, sir, a son by order of law, some
>   year elder than this, who yet is no dearer in my
>   account. Though this knave came something sauc-
>   ily into the world before he was sent for, yet was his
>   mother fair; there was good sport at his making, and
>   the whoreson must be acknowledged.
>
> (I, i, 7–22)

Given the celebration of sexual license in our time, it is difficult for us to reconcile Gloucester's seemingly minor fault with the terrible punishment he endures as a result of siring Edmund and airily downplaying passion. After all, "there was good sport at his making." Yet in the worldview of Shakespeare's time, control and direction of the passions—lust among them—was essential if order was to be maintained not only within the individual but also outwardly in society. This control and direction is the positive application of Saturn:

> Gloucester is proud of his sin and pleased with his own virility, but
> it's precisely lust and pride that lead to his fall: unlawful appetite

breeds unholy offspring, and Gloucester's sexual vanity distorts his vision so that he can see a handsome son only as the living proof of his own physical prowess, not as a reminder of his sin. Edmund must have heard his father's crude boast a thousand times, but to an Elizabethan audience, bastardy was no laughing matter: it always signaled something wayward and unnatural. The illegitimate line of a noble family bore a crest with the bar sinister—"sinister" meaning "left" [in Latin] as opposed to right, but also implying what is morally sinister about bastardy, a violation of the sacred marriage vow.[361]

Gloucester is not the only character in the play who flaunts lustful passion. Both Regan and Goneril are sexually attracted to the opportunistic Edmund, so much so that Goneril plots unrepentantly against her husband's life and poisons her sister. Both pay with their lives. Gloucester too pays dearly for his cavalier admission of indulging in adulterous passion. At the conclusion of the play, as the wronged son Edgar avenges his blinded father by killing Edmund in a duel, Edgar reveals his identity and offers this pronouncement on the cause of Gloucester's suffering:

> The gods are just, and of our pleasant vices
> Make instruments to plague us.
> *The dark and vicious place where thee he got*
> *Cost him his eyes.*
>
> (V, iii, 169–72)

Edmund earlier chafed at his secondary status, being both younger than Edgar and a bastard unable to inherit from his father. Rebelling against custom and rejecting the obedience owed to his father, Edmund takes "Nature" as his goddess. What he means by "Nature" is the animal level of nature, the "Nature, red in tooth and claw,"[362] the nature that justifies predatory selfishness and ambition in rebellion against civility and order. In so doing, Edmund, like Goneril and Regan, becomes a child violating the family hierarchy by overthrowing a parent. He consciously intends to be an agent of disorder:

> Thou, nature, art my goddess; to thy law
> My services are bound. Wherefore should I

Stand in the plague of custom, and permit
The curiosity of nations to deprive me,
For that I am some twelve or fourteen moonshines
Lag of a brother?
                 ... Well, then,
Legitimate Edgar, I must have your land....
Well, my legitimate, if this letter speed,
And my invention thrive, Edmund the base
Shall top the legitimate. I grow; I prosper.
Now, gods, stand up for bastards!

                             (I, ii, 1–6, 15–6, 19–22)

The letter Edmund refers to is the one that he claims was written by Edgar, but it expresses precisely how he, Edmund, feels. He has no respect for age, long life experience, or the wisdom that ideally accompanies old age, the Saturnian stage of life, for he pens, "This policy and *reverence of age* makes the world bitter to the best of our times; keeps our fortunes from us till our *oldness* cannot relish them. I begin to find an idle and fond bondage in the oppression of *aged* tyranny ..." (I, ii, 45–8). Pretending that this is Edgar's opinion, Edmund tells Gloucester that, "sons at perfect age and fathers declining, the father should be as ward to the son, and the son manage his revenue." (I, ii, 68–70) (Lear's two older daughters have the same attitude.) This of course reminds us of the original myth of Saturn in which he emasculates his father and takes over the universe. Edmund seeks to reverse the roles of parent and child, and upend the idea of order within the family. No wonder his father Gloucester is outraged: "O villain, villain! His very opinion in the letter! Abhorred villain! Unnatural, detested, brutish villain! Worse than brutish! Go, sirrah, seek him. I'll apprehend him. Abominable villain!" (I, ii, 71–4) The irony, of course, is that it is Edmund, the one who has taken "Nature" as his goddess, who is really the "unnatural" one.

It is an eerie synchronicity that a poem associated with the sign Capricorn in the *Encyclopedia of Astrology* by Nicholas de Vore describes the very situation depicted in the subplot. With Capricorn being ruled by Saturn, similar themes are embedded in both symbols; they can be understood as equivalent to each other.

Relentless Capricorn

Who climbs and schemes for wealth and place,
And mourns his brother's fall from grace—
But takes what's due in any case?
Safe Capricorn.[363]

According to the viewpoint of Shakespeare's era, it entirely follows that once disorder has entered the kingdom as kings abdicating and children disempowering parents, it must multiply. We hear of Lear's riotous knights, who will not acknowledge Goneril's authority in her own home. Soon the dukes of Albany and Cornwall are rumored to be falling out. According to the courtier Curan, "ear-kissing arguments" are being whispered to that effect: "Have you heard of no likely wars toward, 'twixt the Dukes of Cornwall and Albany? ... You may do, then, in time." (II, i, 10–1, 13) While Lear contends with the wind and the rain, Kent confirms that, "There is division / Although as yet the face of it be covered / With mutual cunning, 'twixt Albany and Cornwall ..." (III, i, 19–21).

Eventually Lear's two older daughters fall out with each other, driven by jealousy since each passionately desires Edmund. Goneril turns against her sister, poisoning Regan and in despair committing suicide. Disorder within the individual has spread to disorder within the family and the kingdom, infecting many. Goneril was vulnerable to becoming imbalanced because, like Lear, she was surrounded by servants who encouraged her excesses. Edgar, after killing Goneril's steward Oswald, recognizes and condemns Oswald's pandering to Goneril (as Kent did earlier): "I know thee well: a serviceable villain, / As duteous to the vices of thy mistress / As badness would desire" (IV, vi, 247–9). We would call Oswald an "enabler." Since he encourages and increases disorder, his death is symbolically necessary since he sides with evil.

The most visible symbol of a magnified disorder, of course, is the violent tempest that Lear endures out on the heath. The heavens, in sympathy with the upsets in the human and political realms, display the same tumult in the turbulent wind and rain that batter Lear. But the storm occurs within Lear as well as without; it is the externalization of his tempestuous and ungoverned thoughts and feelings.

The principal person in the drama who <u>does</u> control passion is Cordelia. She is the primary exemplar of a positive Saturn. After Lear rejects her, she remains calm and still in the face of his rage, asking only that her suitors be informed of the reason for her being disinherited. Later, when her armies have invaded England, she is given letters informing her of the terrible events that have taken place during her absence. A Gentleman reports to Kent on Cordelia's outstanding ability to master her emotions:

> KENT:　Did your letters pierce the queen to any demon-
> 　　stration of grief?
> GENTLEMAN:　Ay, sir. She took them, in my presence,
> 　　And now and then an ample tear trilled down
> 　　Her delicate cheek. *It seemed she was a queen*
> 　　*Over her passion, who, most rebel-like,*
> 　　*Sought to be king o'er her.*
> KENT:　　　　　　　　　　O, then it moved her.
> GENTLEMAN:　*Not to a rage. Patience* and sorrow strove
> 　　Who should express her goodliest. You have seen
> 　　Sunshine and rain at once: her smiles and tears
> 　　Were like a better way. Those happy smilets,
> 　　That played on her ripe lip, seemed not to know
> 　　What guests were in her eyes, which parted thence,
> 　　As pearls from diamonds dropped.
> 　　　　　　　　　　　　　　　　(IV, iii, 9–21)

Eclipses: Portents of Disorder and Disaster

Shakespeare emphasizes in this play, as in no other, eclipses as a symbol of potential and actual disorder.[364] Eclipses are significant astrological factors with a long history of being associated with disruptive events. Shakespeare has Gloucester voice the specifics of this tradition. According to him, the heavens have recently foretold disruption on all levels:

> These late eclipses in the sun and moon portend no good
> to us. Though the wisdom of nature can reason it thus
> and thus, yet nature finds itself scourged by the sequent
> effects. Love cools, friendship falls off, brothers divide: in
> cities, mutinies; in countries, discord; in palaces, treason;
> and the bond cracked twixt son and father. This villain
> of mine comes under the prediction; there's son against
> father. The king falls from bias of nature; there's father

against child. We have seen the best of our time. Machi-
nations, hollowness, treachery, and all ruinous disorders,
follow us disquietly to our graves.

(I, ii, 96–106)

A solar eclipse is a major astronomical/astrological event that typically occurs only twice a year and rarely over a particular geographical
location. It was to the Elizabethans as it was to many other cultures a
terrifying and disturbing event. The disappearance of the primary symbol
of royalty and divinity was thought to threaten the life of the ruler/leader
represented by the Sun. The obscuring of the Sun, on which so much
of human life depends, disturbs the order of the universe by changing
light to dark, with the likelihood of releasing everything associated with
the dark side. In a chapter on "Eclipses in Mythology" in their book
Totality: Eclipses of the Sun, Littmann, Willcox, and Espenak comment,

*Solar eclipses have often been considered omens of disaster and death. Since
the Sun symbolizes the ruler, a solar eclipse was thought to portend the fall
of kings. This interpretation of a solar eclipse figures prominently in* King
Lear.

"Corruption and death are a frequent theme of eclipse myths. Evil spirits descend to Earth or emerge from underground during eclipses."[365] What is unusual in *King Lear* is that in voluntarily renouncing the throne, *the King is eclipsing himself.*[366]

Shakespeare really wants us to get the connection between these eclipses and the tragic events that unfold in the play, so much so that he has Edmund repeat his father's melancholic observations. Ever the opportunist, Edmund sees the usefulness of passing his father's worried comments on to his brother, to upset him and prepare him for a break with his father:

> EDGAR: How now, brother Edmund? What serious con-
> templation are you in?
> EDMUND: I am thinking, brother, of a prediction I read
> the other day, what should follow these *eclipses.*
> EDGAR: Do you busy yourself about that?
> EDMUND: I promise you, the effects he writes of succeed
> unhappily; as of *unnaturalness between the child and*
> *the parent; death, dearth, dissolutions of ancient amities;*
> *divisions in state, menaces and maledictions against king*
> *and nobles; needless diffidences, banishment of friends,*
> *dissipation of cohorts, nuptial breaches,* and I know
> not what,
> EDGAR: How long have you been a sectary astronomical?
> [follower of astrology]
> EDMUND: Come, come! When saw you my father last?
> ... Bethink yourself wherein you may have offended
> him ...
>
> (I, ii, 126–38, 145)

For dramatic purposes Shakespeare emphasizes the worst possible associations with these celestial events. Negative interpretations of eclipses go back many centuries and appear in many civilizations. For instance, in accordance with the theme of parents "eating" children and vice versa in both the original Greek myth and *King Lear*, "The earliest Chinese word for eclipse, *shih*, means 'to eat' and referred to the gradual disappearance of the Sun or Moon as if it were eaten by a celestial dragon."[367] The word "dragon" is relevant to eclipse terminology in the

West too, since eclipses happen when the Sun and Moon are close to points called "the dragon's head" and "the dragon's tail."[368]

Dragons—Symbol of Saturn—and their Fiery Breath

Shakespeare's audience would certainly have been aware of the associations between eclipses and horrible mundane events. Whether or not Shakespeare knew of the connection between eclipses and dragon symbolism, it is poetically and archetypally apt that he has Lear make the astonishing comparison of himself to a dragon. Shocked and angered by Cordelia's refusal to gush about how much she loves him, he warns Kent, "Come not between the *dragon* and his wrath." (I, i, 122) In another archetypically resonant connection between the ruler of the sign Capricorn and this play, the sphere of Saturn "is sometimes symbolized by the image of a dragon ..."[369]

While dragons were sometimes positively associated with the ruler of a kingdom (as in Chinese culture where a five-clawed dragon was the emblem of the Emperor), dragons in Western myth, religion, and literature are almost always frightening and destructive creatures, depicted with the characteristics of many threatening animals combined into one: serpentine tails, armoring scales, sharp talons, and great wings. "The dragon ... stands for 'things animal' *par excellence* ... its symbolic meaning ... [is] related to the Sumerian concept of the animal as the 'adversary,' a concept which later came to be attached to the devil."[370] Dragons are thus representations of evil.

In many myths and legends dragons are a primordial symbol of the enemy that the hero must vanquish in the supreme test of his powers. In Greek mythology the god Zeus destroys the terrible Typhon and buries it under Mt. Etna in Sicily where it continues to rumble and belch fire. In these ancient tales, superheroes, part god and part mortal, like Hercules, Perseus, and Bellerophon, destroy monstrous dragon-like creatures, sometimes to rescue beautiful maidens or to gain hoarded treasure. In religious iconography the Archangel Michael is depicted as the slayer of a (red) dragon,[371] as is St. George who also famously slew a dragon.

Dragons, of course, are known to be voracious, with an unappeasable appetite for both young virgins and/or golden treasure (like Smaug in *The Hobbit*). They are commonly devourers, reminding us of Lear as the devouring parent. The scene in which Lear makes this telling comparison of himself to the dragon is precisely the one in which he "devours" Cordelia by reducing her inheritance and dowry to nothing.

In most of these stories the heroes slay the monsters by running them through with pikes or swords, as St. George does in a story that was as familiar to the Elizabethans as it was in medieval times. But the Greek hero Bellerophon destroys one by flying on the winged horse

"Come not between the dragon and his wrath."—King Lear
The image for the dark and terrifying dangers of both external nature and
the inner psyche. Usually dwelling in the underworld (beneath the earth or
psychologically in the unconscious), the dragon guards a hard-to-attain trea-
sure, whether material or spiritual. Like fire-breathing dragons, Lear spits
the destructive fire of his violent rage. Having confronted his own dark side,
his wrath burns itself out and he attains both humility and a wisdom born of
suffering. (Drawing by Vera Manzi-Schacht, NY)

Pegasus over its head and dropping "*lead,* a proven antidote for dragons, into her gaping fiery mouth."[372] LEAD, of course, is the metal associated with Saturn. Consistent with the symbolism of Capricorn and Saturn, near the end of the play when Lear awakes from restorative sleep, he refers to this metal:

> You do me wrong to take me out o' th' grave.
> Thou art a soul in bliss; but I am bound
> Upon a wheel of fire, that mine own tears
> Do scald like molten *lead.*
>
> (IV, vii, 45–8)

Leaden tears are metaphors for the scalding Saturnian trials Lear has undergone.

Lear is not the only character in the play who associates himself with a dragon. No surprise that Gloucester's bastard son Edmund plots evil against his father and innocent brother, for he reveals that he was born under inauspicious stars: "My father compounded with my mother under the *dragon's tail,* and my nativity was under Ursa Major, so that it follows, I am rough and lecherous." (I, ii, 117–20)[373]

For Lear to equate himself to a dragon is revealing, implying that on some level he is aware of his own tremendous capacity for destructive rage. We see it instantly in the explosion of his wrath directed at both Kent and Cordelia. Dragons are frequently described in myth and literature as breathing fire and having stinking breath. (Saturn, too, was characterized as "cold, moist, heavy, and of stinking wind."[374]) Metaphorically, Lear does indeed "breathe fire" and blow bad breath, for he is a world-class curser. Lear's diatribe against Goneril, after she asks her father to control his "disordered" knights, is malevolent in expression and purpose:

> Darkness and devils! ...
> Degenerate bastard! ...
> Hear, Nature, hear! Dear goddess, hear!
> Suspend thy purpose, if thou didst intend
> To make this creature fruitful!
> Into her womb convey sterility!
> Dry up in her the organs of increase;

And from her derogate body never spring
A babe to honour her! If she must teem,
Create her child of spleen, that it may live
And be a thwart disnatured torment to her!
Let it stamp wrinkles in her brow of youth;
With cadent tears fret channels in her cheeks;
Turn all her mother's pains and benefits
To laughter and contempt, that she may feel
How sharper than a serpent's tooth it is
To have a thankless child!

(I, iv, 227, 229, 252–66)

Dragons had the reputation of burning up crops with their fiery breath and making the land sterile, just as Lear wishes a winter-like sterility on Goneril. "Whole tracts of countryside could be rendered uninhabitable and birds made to fall out of the sky by the very breath of a dragon.... In addition, dragons deliberately ate poisonous herbs" to make their bites more venomous.[375] Lear does seem to feed on poisonous thoughts of hatred and revenge, which empower his curses and rages.

Regan rightly understands that Lear will blast her in the same way if she thwarts him: "[S]o will you wish on me, / When the rash mood is on." (II, iv, 162–3) Once Lear grasps the fact that both daughters intend to deprive him of his men, he opts not to stay with either of them but to go out into the storm where he is drenched by the rain. (Interestingly, Hindus believe that the safest place to be during an eclipse is in water![376]) There his enraged speech invites greater chaos in nature:

Blow, winds, and crack your cheeks! rage! blow!
You cataracts and hurricanoes, spout
Till you have drenched our steeples, drowned the cocks!
You sulphurous and thought-executing fires,
Vaunt-couriers of oak-cleaving thunderbolts,
Singe my white head! And thou, all-shaking thunder,
Strike flat the thick rotundity o' the world!
Crack Nature's molds, all germens spill at once,
That make ingrateful man! ...
Rumble thy bellyful! Spit, fire! spout, rain!

(III, ii, 1–9, 13)

This speech of Lear's alludes to both the traditional associations of dragons and fire as well as dragons and water. Dragons were credited with bringing rain and storms in many cultures, and "The dragon ... plays a vital role in the supply of life-sustaining water; indeed, dragon-serpents, because of their undulating motion, are widely regarded as the traditional symbol of water."[377] But when angry, dragons stir up an excess of water that is overwhelming and frightening. In this play, it seems that Lear's own projected dragon-wrath literally conjures the storm into physical manifestation.

> When rain is to be expected, the dragons scream and their voices are like the sound made by striking copper basins. Their breath becomes clouds, and on the other hand they avail themselves of the clouds in order to cover their bodies. Therefore they are invisible.... there are often heavy rains, and those who speak about these rains say: "Fine moistening rain is heavenly rain; *violent rain is dragon rain*."[378]

Elizabethan Psychology: Saturn, Melancholy, and Madness

[A]ll things under Saturn conduce to sadness, and melancholy....
—Agrippa[379]

The Elizabethans drew on the theory of the humors, a theory derived from astrological symbolism, to understand human personality. Lear's anger, the "wrath of the dragon," suggests that his personality type according to this theory should be choleric. Though he rages through most of the play, the source of his frenzy is more likely to be found in another type: the melancholic.[380] Shakespeare has Edmund point us in this direction when he says, "My cue is villainous *melancholy* ... " (I, ii, 123–4). Edmund is clearly this type since "Melancholic persons, being given to trickery and deceit, were particularly apt at assuming a false appearance; and the humor they often chose was the direct opposite of themselves, the genial, open, sanguine disposition, calculated to allay the suspicions of their dupes ..."[381] Lear is a better example, though, since only melancholics were thought capable of manic behavior, erratic frenzies, and extremes of magnified emotion, all characteristic of Lear. Plato also associated melancholia with tyrants, and Lear's behavior at the start is certainly autocratic. Most convincing of all, melancholia is the appropriate temperament for Lear since it is associated with the earth element and Saturn, which are keys to the play. (See Chapter 2, especially the sub-section "The Melancholic Type: Keyed to Earth and Saturn," for more about this type.)

> Nearly all the writers of the later Middle Ages and the Renaissance considered it an incontestable fact that melancholy, whether morbid or natural, stood in some special relationship to Saturn, and that the latter was really to blame for the melancholic's unfortunate character and destiny.[382]

Why is it important to understand melancholia and its history up to and through the English Renaissance? Because, of all of the temperaments, the Elizabethans (along with others before them) were most fascinated by it[383]—and because Shakespeare based many of his most famous characters on this type. Hamlet is the most famous tragic melancholic in Western literature. Romeo is a romantic melancholic, mooning over Rosaline at the beginning of *Romeo and Juliet*. His excessive and highly stylized dramatizing of his emotion makes it seem more artificial than real. By Shakespeare's time wallowing in sadness at being rejected by the one you love had become an established literary tradition in the form of the lover's lament. And Lear is an outstanding example of a melancholic, in this case a tragic one.

Melancholia intrigued the earliest classical writers many centuries BCE, who laid the foundations for the theory of humors from observations of symptoms of illness. Their descriptions of melancholy do make it sound like a pathology: it might be characterized by rapidly changing mental states, ranging from fear, misanthropy, and depression to madness in its most extreme forms.[384]

But by the fourth century BCE the concept of melancholia had significantly changed. Due to the dramatization of states of madness in the great Greek tragedies as well as the notion of a divine "creative frenzy" in Plato's philosophical circle, melancholia came to be viewed as not merely an illness but as characteristic of great heroes. Not only were heroic figures like Hercules and Ajax melancholics, but all outstanding men, whether in the fields of arts, poetry, philosophy or statesmanship, were also thought to be melancholics. That included Socrates and Plato. And that includes many of the tragic heroes in Shakespeare's plays.

After centuries of neglect, fascination with melancholia surged in the Renaissance due to interest in it by physician/translator/astrologer Marsilio Ficino. Ficino was the head of the Platonic Academy in Florence, Italy, and an especially important figure because he translated Platonic and Hermetic writings from the early centuries CE that may have indirectly influenced Shakespeare. He also had a deep interest in this temperament type since it was his own. Ficino's horoscope has Saturn prominently placed, on the horizon, and so he coped all his life with both depression (the negative side of melancholia) and intellectual brilliance (the positive side).

> He it was who really gave shape to the idea of the melancholy man of genius and revealed it to the rest of Europe—in particular, to the great Englishmen of the sixteenth and seventeenth centuries ... for he himself was a melancholic and a child of Saturn—the latter, indeed, in particularly unfavourable circumstances, for in his horoscope the dark star in whose influence he so unshakably believed stood in the ascendant, and as it did so, moreover, it was in the sign of the Aquarius, Saturn's "night abode."[385]

In his *Liber de Vita*, or *Book of Life*, Ficino advised students and scholars (thought to be particularly influenced by Saturn) on how to live better and longer. As a doctor and astrologer (the two then went together) he had specific recommendations for countering melancholic states, among them suggestions for diet, exercise, and listening to music. "I complain of my melancholy temperament," he wrote, "for to me it seems a very bitter thing, and one that I can only ease and sweeten a little by much lute-playing...."[386]

Ficino understood that melancholia was a type given to extremes. Since black bile, the fluid or humor correlated with melancholia, was powerfully affected by heat and cold, the gifted melancholic was likely to be mentally "abnormal" in one way or another. If the black bile was subjected to cold, the person could be lethargic or dull, but if subjected to heat, the person could be lively, excitable, reckless (think of Hamlet), highly creative, prone to trances and ecstasies, or even mad, experiencing fits of terror.[387] This sounds a lot like an early description of what used to be called manic-depressive illness and is now called bipolar disorder. Now, as then, it is often associated with highly creative people.

While melancholics can experience spiritual exaltation, they can also be subject to uncontrolled fantasies, since mental images were supposed to affect their minds more strongly than for most people. So it is imperative that melancholics, once they understand their type, work diligently to keep a mean or balance.[388] This is difficult since melancholics experience a constant high tension in their lives, are prone to a "fatal lack of moderation," and have an enhanced sensibility of soul which gives them a capacity for greater depth of experience, and "above all, for suffering."[389] All of this seems particularly apt for King Lear.

Most especially, melancholics can tip into madness, losing their rational faculties. Saturn-ruled melancholics might be supremely intellectually gifted, but they can also go to the other extreme and be severely mentally disordered. In accordance with the more negative side of Saturn, the melancholic may be "inclined to devious thinking, to anger, dullness, rage, sadness, and envy, to a deceitful mind, and to cruelty, and at his worst he can be overtaken by bestial raving ..."[390] So Lear's constant use of animal imagery while railing at his ungrateful daughters makes sense in light of his temperament. In one of his most famous rants, their ingratitude is "sharper than a serpent's tooth," but references to savage beasts abound in the play. As Caroline Spurgeon has noticed, "In addition to savage wolves, tigers and other animals, there are *darting* serpents, a *sharp-toothed* vulture and *detested* kite, *stinging* adders and insects, *gnawing* rats, the *baited* bear, as well as *whipped, whining, barking, mad* and *biting* dogs." (Emphasis in the original.)[391]

Melancholia as a key to understanding the conclusion of the play, especially regarding the significance of Lear's final words, will be considered at the end of this chapter.

Given Saturn's rulership over the earth sign Capricorn, we would expect to find at least one character in the play who exemplifies this temperament. King Lear is clearly a melancholic, but he is not the only one. Besides Edmund, mentioned earlier, Lear's Fool is also clearly a melancholic type. When Lear first calls for the Fool, Lear's knight informs him, "Since my young lady's going into France, sir, the fool hath *much pined away*." (I, iv, 62–3) When the Fool does appear, his comments to Lear are all sharp gibes about Lear's foolishness in handing over his power and wealth to his daughters. Lear protests that the Fool's words are "nothing." The Fool's comeback is "you gave me nothing for 't," and he mockingly adds—speaking to Kent but really taking a dig at Lear—"tell

him, so much the rent of his land comes to." No wonder Lear reacts with
"A bitter fool!" (I, iv, 83–117) The *bitter* taste was the one associated with
melancholia. Shakespeare is letting his audience know that the Fool is a
true melancholic.

Edmund is a more negative or villainous type of melancholic, one
who strikingly fits the expected description according to astrological tradition:

> Now Saturn was considered by the astrologers to be the most pow
> erful of the malefic planets. He worked havoc when in dominion
> over any of the other planets, and was on most occasions envi
> ous, covetous, jealous, a malicious dissembler, a servant of anger, a
> begetter of strife, a spreader of incurable diseases, an accomplisher
> of destruction and decay.[392]

Modern Psychology: Saturn and the Breakdown of the Ego

The theory of the humors, based on astrological symbolism, was what
the Elizabethans (and westerners before them) employed to understand
an individual's psychology. The people of Shakespeare's time knew that
the Capricorn personality is often driven by the need for financial and
emotional security. For many the way to achieve this is to acquire material goods and to attain a position of prominence and respect within a
community. Behaving with dignity, having the self-discipline to achieve
these goals, and acquiring a position of authority are important to Capricorns and often define "success" for them. Having had the position of
King and exhibiting the inner quality that Kent recognizes as "authority," as an archetypal Capricorn Lear would seem to be a strong enough
personality to cope with challenges to his status as king and father.

Yet that is not the case.

Since most of us are not familiar with the theory of the humors and
especially Shakespeare's use of it to shape his characters, we are more
likely to look to a modern psychological interpretation of Lear's personality. If Shakespeare did indeed tap the archetypal level in creating his
works (as suggested in Chapter 6), they not only endure over time but
can also be interpreted in the vocabulary of any particular era. So it is not
surprising that a contemporary psychological interpretation of Lear's
personality is startlingly in accord with the symbolism of Saturn and

Capricorn. Looking at the play from a modern psychological perspective not only reinforces the universality of Shakespeare's creations but also offers a different but complementary perspective on Lear's character.

Over time, Lear has identified with the position of King and the patriarchal (that is, Saturnine) role of father to the point that he has become rigidly bound to these functions. Because he feels no genuine emotional connection with his family, his supporters, or common humanity, he is unable to experience authentic relationships. In his eyes Cordelia has no independent existence of her own but exists only to fulfill his needs: "Better thou/ Hadst not been born than not to have pleased me better." (I, i, 234–5) Since he is entirely focused on acting as these positions conventionally dictate—as the final and uncontested authority—he cannot accept advice from others. And because he has been seduced by flatterers and enablers who support his role-playing for their own benefit, he cannot perceive the true nature of those around him. "Identification with one's office or one's title is very attractive indeed, which is precisely why so many men are nothing more than the decorum accorded to them by society.... We all of us know the professor whose whole individuality is exhausted by his professorial role; behind the mask, we find nothing but peevishness and infantilism."[393] Lear's explosive temper is "peevishness and infantilism" writ large.

Lear is very much bound up in his ego. In Jung's psychology the ego is defined as the center of consciousness that gives rise to sense of having an "I" or an identity, a relatively fixed point of awareness that mediates between the greater Self and the world, and between the conscious and unconscious minds.[394] Saturn as the last and farthest out of the known planets is deemed by many modern astrologers to represent the bounds of the individual ego.

Once Lear's ego has attached itself to the idea of King and Father, the challenge to it comes when Cordelia throws a verbal monkey wrench—a single word—into Lear's elaborately staged division of the kingdom. Lear intends to give the largest piece to the daughter who rhapsodizes most eloquently about her love for him. But Cordelia refuses to play the game, refuses to answer the question "Which of you shall we say doth love us most?" (I, i, 49) in the same exaggerated way that her two older sisters do, and replies simply, "Nothing." Lear's first response is revealing. He recognizes that these patterned and formal responses are motivated by material gain: "Nothing will come of nothing.... [M]end your speech

a little, / Lest it may mar your *fortunes....* Thy truth, then, be thy *dower!*"
(I, i, 89, 93–4, 108) (We are back in the world of *The Merchant of Venice*,
where money may be substituted for love.)

Like the unevolved earth-sign Capricorn, who most reductively
measures success in life by physical and external things, Lear continues
to measure regard by numbers. Later, when the sisters collude to reduce
the number of his knights, from a hundred to fifty and then to twenty-
five, Lear reasons, " [To Goneril] I'll go with thee: / Thy fifty yet doth
double five-and-twenty, / *And thou art twice her love.*" (II, iv, 253–5)

You would think Lear would have noticed the different attitudes of
Burgundy and France, both wooers of Cordelia early in the play. Once
Cordelia has no dowry, no inheritance with "shadowy forests and with
champains [en]riched, / With plenteous rivers and wide-skirted meads"
(I, i, 62–3), Burgundy refuses to take her without the promised portion.
But France avows that Cordelia is "most rich, being poor; / Most choice,
forsaken; and most loved, despised!" (I, i, 251–2) and seizes upon her and
her virtues. She becomes Queen of France and more, not less, loved and
respected by him. As often in Shakespeare's works, the truth of a situation is the opposite of what it appears to be on the surface. He often
dramatizes the fact that money or physical possessions in general—so
often valued by earth signs—is no measure of value. This is one of the
lessons that Lear will painfully learn.

When you consistently act out a role, without acknowledging your
true needs and deeper feelings, you lose touch with your authentic inner
self and truly "do not know who you are." Lear's older daughters perceive
this, since Regan observes that her father "hath ever but slenderly known
himself." (I, i, 291–2) This theme of self-knowledge is prominent in the
play. Witness the confrontation between Goneril and Lear, when she
chastises Lear over the behavior of his knights:

> LEAR: Are you our daughter?
> GONERIL: Come, sir.
> I would you would make use of that good wisdom,
> Whereof I know you are fraught, and put away
> These dispositions, that of late transform you
> *From what you rightly are....*
> LEAR: Doth any here know me? This is not Lear.

> Doth Lear walk thus? speak thus? Where are his
>   eyes?
> Either his notion weakens, his discernings
> Are lethargied—Ha! waking? 'Tis not so.
> *Who is it that can tell me who I am?*
>
>   (I, iv, 193–8, 201–5)

The character who repeatedly tells Lear "who he is" is the Fool. Knowing that appearances can be deceiving and people are often opposite to what they seem, the Fool is the wisest one in the play. It is eerily apt that the Fool answers Lear's question of who can tell him who he really is by saying, "Lear's shadow." The Fool accompanies Lear onto the wild heath and is his inseparable companion through the terrible storm. Just as our shadow is always apparently attached to our physical body, so the Fool literally "shadows" Lear. He tells Lear the truth of his situation—that one daughter is like to the other "as a crab's like an apple," that he was foolish to give away his home and property, and that he should not have been old before he was wise—but Lear is so caught up in emotional torment that he cannot hear him.

It is striking that Shakespeare has the Fool use the word "shadow" since it has come to have a deeper psychological meaning in modern times. The concept of a "personal shadow" is an integral element of Jung's psychology. It refers to the area of your psyche that contains parts of your personality that have been suppressed, driven into the personal unconscious, because your ego cannot accept them. Although the shadow can contain both positive and negative traits, in line with the idea that a shadow is "a comparative darkness within an illuminated area," the shadow is more likely to reflect aspects of ourselves that we feel guilty about or are ashamed to admit. Thus as our "dark side" the shadow accords with Saturn whose color is black and whose position in the horoscope often points to a place of particular weakness, vulnerability, or perceived inferiority. So we might expect that facing his shadow would require Lear to become aware of his inflated ego and the degree to which he is dominated by the power motive.

Religious, mythological, and cultural traditions depict images that accord with the shadow, that "stand for the universally human dark side within us, for the tendency toward the dark and inferior that is inherent in every man."[395] These are often imagined as the Devil, demons, or monsters that lurk literally under the earth or in a hellish underworld. The shadow figure has special prominence in literature as such frightening figures as Mary Shelley's Frankenstein, Robert Louis Stevenson's Mr. Hyde, and Shakespeare's own Caliban in *The Tempest*.[396]

Coming to know yourself more fully (which Jung calls the process of "individuation") necessitates facing your shadow. If you have not consciously admitted your weaknesses and failings, then the shadow can erupt in behavior that may surprise others or shock you:

> It is in ourselves that we most frequently and readily perceive shadow qualities, provided we are willing to acknowledge them as belonging to ourselves; for example, when an outburst of rage comes over us, when suddenly we begin to curse or behave crudely, when quite against our will we act antisocially, when we are stingy, petty, or choleric, cowardly, frivolous, or hypocritical, so displaying qualities which under ordinary circumstances we carefully hide or repress and of whose existence we ourselves are unaware. When the emergence of such traits of character can no longer be overlooked, we ask ourselves in amazement: how was it possible? Is it really true that things like this are me?[397]

Unacknowledged unattractive qualities are frequently projected onto others; "they, not me" display these less desirable traits. This is true for Lear since he consistently blames his daughters for being ungrateful and for mistreating him. He refuses to look at his own flaws, convinced that he is "a man more sinned against than sinning." (III, ii, 57–8) Yet we have seen Lear exhibit extremely unattractive behaviors before this. We have witnessed him suddenly and cold-heartedly disinheriting Cordelia, abruptly and rashly banishing his long-trusted advisor Kent, wielding authority with a sense of entitlement and an egotistic vulnerability to flattery, and raining emotional—even physical—abuse on anyone who thwarts him (he not only curses but also strikes Oswald). In many ways his own behavior is reflected in and is taken further by his daughters.

To have your ego challenged and to have to face the shadow is a frightening experience. Your personality may initially resist looking at the darker side and strenuously deny any failings. And it may become enraged, as Lear does, at the thought of being less than perfect, less than admired, less than who it thinks it is. The more defended and pompous the personality is, the greater the rage. The personality feels that if the defenses go, it will be reduced to nothing, that a loss of identity will cause it to fall into an abyss equivalent to death. So defensive are ego-bound persons that they create a "yes" culture around them. No wonder that CEO's, politicians, gurus, and Hollywood stars often end up surrounded by an entourage whose constant feeding of their ego isolates them and reinforces their behavioral excesses.

Here is the intriguing point about the challenge to Lear's ego. Although it seems to be catalyzed by Cordelia's refusal to cater to it, it is really Lear himself who sets the wheel in motion by determining to divide the kingdom and to stage the ritualized love-test. As psychologists of the twentieth century have discovered, sometimes our own unconscious mind causes us to act in ways that upset our tidy lives, that instigate an unpleasant, even agonizing period of suffering, but that take us into new levels of self-awareness. The unconscious thus sometimes drives psychic growth, regardless of what the personality prefers. To evolve, Lear has to lose himself to find himself.

Loss of Identity: Voluntary or Involuntary

In accord with the principle of Saturn, as the story unfolds Lear is progressively stripped of ego-based assumptions about who he is. Saturn may require the development of an ego, but at a certain point that ego must be challenged and made secondary to the Self. Lear's loss of his ego-based identity occurs in stages. First, he voluntarily resigns his kingship ("we will divest us, both of rule, / Interest of territory, cares of state"—I, i, 47–8) though he foolishly expects still to keep the perks of the job ("Only we still retain/ The name, and all the addition to a king;/ The sway, revenue, execution of the rest"—I, i, 135–7). After that *others* progressively strip him of what identifies him both as King and as Lear. His daughters collude to deprive him of the hundred knights he demanded as an entourage, leaving him with no trappings for the role of King. In a fit of pique, he refuses to lodge with either daughter, and so abandons human habitation to live out in the open heath. At this point he has no job, no home, and no supportive family.

This is entirely in line with Saturn, which is the principle of REDUCTION and RESTRICTION. Under Saturn, your assets may shrink, your opportunities dry up, and even your body lose size and weight. Saturn favors asceticism and abstemiousness. What is visually obvious on stage is that Lear's lodging has been radically reduced: once inhabiting a grand palace, he now finds shelter in a small wretched hovel. Once surrounded by gorgeously attired nobles, his companions now are a Fool, a disgraced and disguised servant, and an apparent madman, all meanly dressed. In the extremity of his frenzy, Lear even tears off his clothes, declaring of himself, "Thou art the thing itself; unaccommodated man is no more but such a poor, bare, forked animal as thou art. Off, off, you lendings! come, unbutton here." (III, iv, 98–100) Lear strips to his almost-naked body. At this point he is diminished to almost nothing.[398]

Reminding us that Saturn can reduce us to naught, the word "nothing" resonates ominously throughout the play. Heard first in scene 1 from Cordelia, who can produce "nothing" to overtop her sisters' flattery and who is warned by Lear that "Nothing will come of nothing," this word recurs startlingly often. Cordelia is offered to either of the French suitors as only herself "and nothing more." (I, i, 201) When Burgundy importunes Lear to include the first-promised dowry with her, Lear insists she gets "Nothing! I have sworn; I am firm." (I, i, 246)

In the subplot, when Edmund sets in motion his scheme against his father and brother, he cleverly downplays the importance of the falsified letter he pretends to keep from his father in speeches that emphasize "none," "no," and "nothing":

> GLOUCESTER: Edmund, how now! What news?
> EDMUND: So please your lordship, *none*.
> GLOUCESTER: Why so earnestly seek you to put up that letter?
> EDMUND: I know *no* news, my lord.
> GLOUCESTER: What paper were you reading?
> EDMUND: *Nothing*, my lord
> GLOUCESTER: No? What needed, then, that terrible dispatch of it into your pocket? The quality of *nothing* hath not such need to hide itself. Let's see. Come, if it be *nothing*, I shall not need spectacles.
>
> (I, ii, 26–35)

The Fool, too, again and again uses the word "nothing," relentlessly reminding Lear that since he gave away his territory and its income, now he has nothing:

KENT: [in response to one of the Fool's songs] This is *nothing*, Fool.

FOOL: Then 'tis like the breath of an unfee'd lawyer; you gave me *nothing* for 't. Can you make no use of *nothing*, nuncle?

LEAR: Why, no, boy; *nothing* can be made out of *nothing*.

FOOL: (to Kent) Prithee, tell him, so much the rent of his land comes to. He will not believe a fool.

(I, iv, 111–6)

When Goneril enters in the same scene, annoyed at the disruptions caused by Lear and his knights, the Fool remarks to Lear, "Thou wast a pretty fellow when thou hadst no need to care for her frowning; now thou art an O without a figure. I am better than thou art now; I am a fool, thou art *nothing*." (I, iv, 167–9) Whereas the Fool previously told Lear he *had* nothing, now he tells him he *is* nothing.

The final loss for Lear is his mind—he descends into madness. Returning to a state of childlikeness, fantastically dressed and draped with wild flowers, he runs playfully from Cordelia's gentlemen so that they must chase him. He regresses to a period in his life before his identity was established as imperial monarch in order to reconnect with his deeper self. In a second childhood he has the opportunity to regain the pure and untrammelled innocence characteristic of the young.

Yet even in his ravings there is, as Edgar sees, "matter and impertinency mixed! / Reason in madness!" (IV, vi, 168–9) Lear knows well enough that he is king—"Aye, every inch a king!" (IV, vi, 105)—but he now also recognizes his essential and vulnerable humanity, a core of him deeper than the ego.

> They flattered me like a dog; and told me I had white hairs in my beard ere the black ones were there. To say "aye" and "no" to everything that I said!—"Aye" and "no" too was no good divinity. When the rain came to wet me once, and the wind to make me chatter; when the thunder would not peace at my bidding; there I found 'em, there I smelt 'em out. Go to, they are not men o' their words! They told me I was everything. 'Tis a lie, I am not ague-proof.
>
> (IV, vi, 95–103)

Though he is impoverished in body and mind, having been subjected to terrible Saturnian ordeals and torments, Lear paradoxically recovers his spirit. One of the first signs that his character is transforming as his "wits begin to turn" is his increasing awareness of others' sufferings. He sees that the Fool is cold (the temperature of Saturn), and agrees to follow Kent to the straw-strewn hovel, remarking, "Poor fool and knave, I have one part in my heart/ That's sorry yet for thee." (III, ii, 67, 70–1) This dawning sensitivity is reaffirmed when they arrive at the shed, and Lear urges the Fool to enter before him—unthinkable previously for a man so invested in his role as King. Then, of course, he would have been the first to enter. Now Lear urges the fool to go before him, and even offers a compassionate prayer to other beings lashed by the storm:

> KENT: Good my lord, enter here.
> LEAR: Prithee, go in thyself; seek thine own ease....
> [To the Fool] In boy; go first. You houseless poverty—
> Nay, get thee in. I'll pray, and then I'll sleep.
> [Fool goes in]
> Poor naked wretches, wheresoe'er you are,
> That bide the pelting of this pitiless storm,
> How shall your houseless heads and unfed sides,
> Your looped and windowed raggedness, defend you
> From seasons such as these? O, I have ta'en
> Too little care of this! Take physic, pomp;
> Expose thyself to feel what wretches feel,
> That thou mayst shake the superflux to them,
> And show the heavens more just.
> (III, iv, 23, 26–37)

Lear has endured the archetypal descent into the underworld, the realm originally home to Saturn, as made explicit in his protest to Cordelia, "You do me wrong to take me out o' the grave." (IV, vii, 45) This is an acknowledgement of both his underworld journey and his birth into a new attitude of humility and acceptance: "If you have poison for me, I will drink it." (IV, vii, 73) There is no more talk of being king. Now, accepting his age and his flaws, he simply begs, "Pray you now, forget and forgive. I am old and foolish." (IV, vii, 85) Lear has lost his identity but gained humanity.

Other characters, too, have been stripped of possessions and place. Cordelia, denied her inheritance, is reduced to "little seeming substance." (I, i, 199) Yet she absorbs this blow with equanimity and almost immediately attains an even higher place as Queen of France along with the deeper love of her suitor. Kent too, deprived of office and banished from court, retains his emotional balance and re-dedicates himself to service with Lear. Kent knows his fundamental identity, aside from trappings and rank; when Lear asks who he is, Kent replies simply, "A man, sir." (I, iv, 10) Since both Cordelia and Kent have already attained a degree of wisdom, a deeper confidence in who they are aside from their names and positions, they stay steady and clear-headed when their fortunes decline. Placed in the stocks, Kent calmly assures Gloucester, "Some time I shall sleep out, the rest I'll whistle." (II, ii, 148) Not only do both display a remarkable calm in the face of adversity, but both are gifted with the ability to perceive the true natures of those around them: Cordelia sees through the sisters' obsequious speeches and Kent "gets" the pandering Oswald. (II, ii, 11–28) In handling the reversals of fortune with such grace and poise, they are exemplifying the more positive traits of Saturn.

But it is the character of Edgar who offers the most remarkable response to a fall from place. Very much in line with what Saturn sometimes demands, Edgar understands that he must acquiesce to life-threatening disgrace and opts for voluntary SIMPLICITY, shedding his customary clothing and assuming the identity of the most despised of human beings in Shakespeare's time: a mad beggar from Bedlam.[399] Saturn is associated with people on the very bottom rungs of society, particularly beggars, so Edgar is fully acquiescing to Saturn. By immediately embracing the lowest, he avoids the slow and increasingly painful humiliation that Lear endures. Here is Edgar's plan to ensure his survival:

> ... I will preserve myself, and am bethought
> To take *the basest and most poorest shape*
> That ever penury, in contempt of man,
> Brought near to beast. My face I'll grime with filth,
> Blanket my loins, elf all my hair in knots,
> And with presented nakedness out-face
> The winds and persecutions of thy sky....
>
> (II, iii, 6–12)

He ends this speech describing the abdication of his identity with the startling line, "Edgar I nothing am." (That word "nothing" again!) Yet because his voluntary renunciation of name and status is consciously done, he is able to affirm a rock-solid sense of who he is when he declares to his blind father (who thinks his voice has changed), "Y'are much deceived. In *nothing* am I changed/ But in my garments." (IV, vi, 9–10) When the trumpet sounds three times at the end of the play to invite a challenger against Edmund, Edgar appears in armor, his face obscured. He declares, "Know, my name is lost;/ By treason's tooth bare-gnawn and canker-bit./ Yet am I noble as the adversary/ I come to cope." (V, iii, 120–3) Nameless and identity-less, Edgar still recognizes his essential and noble nature.

Cordelia, Kent, and Edgar do not go mad when they are stripped of name, property, and status. Their characters are already developed, as revealed by their emotional grounding and compassion for others. Their identities are not limited to their egos. In Cordelia's gentle refusal to take revenge on her father ("No cause, no cause"—IV, vii, 76), in Kent's humble acceptance of being placed in the stocks ("Fortune, good-night; smile once more; turn thy wheel!"—II, ii, 165), and Edgar's developed empathy for fellow sufferers ("My tears begin to take his part so much,/ They'll mar my counterfeiting."—III, vi, 55–6) is affirmed their already highly developed humanity, a consciousness expanded beyond the personal to embrace the larger world.

Suffering, the End of Suffering—and the Ending of King Lear

The drastic purgatorial process undergone principally by Lear in the play (but also by Gloucester and Edgar) is a heightened version of the basic pattern of tragic drama and very much in line with the astrological Saturn. Lear's suffering, though, seems beyond that experienced by Hamlet, Macbeth, or Othello. His agony threatens to break through the container of the drama, to burst the bounds of the physical stage. Lear's cataclysmic suffering fractures his fragile ego, pitching him into madness, and pushes up against the Saturnian limits of the created and knowable world, threatening to throw the whole of creation into chaos. The atmosphere created in the play resembles the Apocalypse, the end times when the world is consumed by fire and the great dragon is cast out. Shakespeare suggests this comparison when Lear comes onto the stage carrying the dead body of Cordelia: the shocked Kent protests, "Is this the promised end?" echoed by Edgar, "Or image of that horror?" (V, iii, 262–3)[400] Lear's frenzied apostrophes to nature invite a dramatically imagined general destruction, the much-feared Doomsday:

> Blow, winds, and crack your cheeks! rage! blow!
> You cataracts and hurricanoes, spout
> Till you have drenched our steeples, drowned the cocks!
> You sulphurous and thought-executing fires,
> Vaunt-couriers to oak-cleaving thunderbolts,
> Singe my white head! And thou, all-shaking thunder,
> Strike flat the thick rotundity o' the world!
> Crack Nature's molds, all germens spill at once,
> That make ingrateful man!
>
> (III, ii, 1–9)

This is not just Lear's subjective experience; the cataclysm that the whole world suffers with him is echoed in Kent's description of the objective storm:

> [T]he wrathful skies
> Gallow the very wanderers of the dark,
> And make them keep their caves. Since I was man,
> Such sheets of fire, such bursts of horrid thunder,
> Such groans of roaring wind and rain, I never
> Remember to have heard. Man's nature cannot carry
> The affliction nor the fear.
>
> (III, ii, 41–7)

No wonder that human nature cannot long endure such torment. As human beings suffer along with the world's magnified tribulation, one overpowering image dominates the play. As Caroline Spurgeon has noticed, to heighten the "atmosphere of buffeting, strain and strife, and, at moments, of bodily tension to the point of agony … this sensation in us is increased by the general 'floating' image, kept constantly before us, chiefly by means of the verbs used, but also in metaphor, of a human body in anguished movement, tugged, wrenched, beaten, pierced, stung, scourged, dislocated, flayed, gashed, scalded, tortured and finally broken on the rack."[401] No wonder that at the end of the play Gloucester's "flawed heart— / Alack, too weak the conflict to support!— / 'Twixt two extremes of passion, joy and grief,/ Burst smilingly." (V, iii, 195–8) All of this is very much in tune with the most extreme manifestations of Saturn as externalized suffering in both the natural and human worlds.

All that Lear, Gloucester, and Edgar—as well as Kent and Cordelia—suffer are the worst possible Saturnine experiences in the human realm: restrictions, limitations, and disappointments in the form of slander, rejection, banishment, fall from position and power, poverty, homelessness, loss of identity, physical and emotional torture, and, ultimately, death. Death may be the end of the natural cycle, but it may be hastened because of the overwhelming weight of afflictions endured over a long time. This gloomy (and melancholic) perspective is reflected in Lear's belief that babies cry at birth in protest at entering this Saturnian world: "… we came crying hither;/ Thou know'st, the first time that we smell the air, / We wail and cry. … When we are born, we cry that we are come/ To this great stage of fools." (IV, vi, 172–4, 176–7)

Caught in the maelstrom of extreme emotions over his powerless position and his harsh treatment by the ungrateful daughters, Lear rails at a world that seems dominated by negative Saturn, where such travails are common. A world where manipulative machiavellians like Edmund, Goneril, Regan, Cornwall, and even Oswald commit themselves solely to gaining wealth, power and influence, and the worst sorts rise to the top and abuse their place. A disgusted Lear denounces "how this world goes" in a bitter indictment of the fact that the powerful and wealthy are morally reprehensible and rarely brought to justice:

> LEAR: A man may see how this world goes with no eyes.
>   Look with thine ears. See how yond justice rails upon
>   yond simple thief. Hark, in thine ear. Change places
>   and, handy-dandy, which is the justice, which is the
>   thief? Thou hast seen a farmer's dog bark at a beggar?
> GLOUCESTER: Aye, sir.
> LEAR: And the creature run from the cur? There thou
>   mightst behold the great image of authority: a dog's
>   obeyed in office.
>   Thou rascal beadle, hold thy bloody hand!
>   Why dost thou lash that whore? Strip thy own back;

The nadir of the play, with characters at maximum suffering: the mad Lear (Colm Feore, right) and the blinded Gloucester (Scott Wentworth, left) in the Stratford Festival (Ontario, Canada) production of 2014. (Photo by David Hou)

> Thou hotly lusts to use her in that kind
> For which thou whipp'st her. The usurer hangs the
>   cozener.
> Through tattered clothes great vices do appear;
> Robes and furred gowns hide all. Plate sin with gold,
> And the strong lance of justice hurtless breaks;
> Arm it in rags, a pigmy's straw does pierce it.
>   (IV, vi, 146–161)

Lear is also repulsed by uncontrolled sexual indulgence (reminding us of Gloucester's flaw), not only in the person of the beadle who lusts after the whore, but generally.

> The wren goes to 't, and the small gilded fly
> Does lecher in my sight.
> Let copulation thrive ...
>   To 't, luxury, pell-mell!
> For I lack soldiers. Behold yond simp'ring dame,
> Whose face between her forks presages snow;
> That minces virtue, and does shake the head
> To hear of pleasure's name;
> The fitchew nor the soiled horse, goes to 't
> With a more riotous appetite.
> Down from the waist they are Centaurs,
> Though women all above.
> But to the girdle do the gods inherit.
> Beneath is all the fiends'; there's hell, there's darkness,
> There's the sulphurous pit, burning, scalding,
> Stench, consumption! Fie, fie, fie! pah! pah!
>   (IV, vi, 110–2, 114–26)

Since evil and injustice seem to dominate in this world (the physical world ruled by Saturn), we can only, along with Edgar, "pray that the right may thrive." (V, ii, 2) Yet Cordelia's armies lose. We might adjust to this setback partly because we see the wisdom of the stalwart Edgar's Saturnian advice, offered immediately after the news of the defeat arrives: "Men must endure / Their going hence, even as their coming hither; / Ripeness is all." (V, ii, 9–11) We might accept the outcome even more because of Lear's newly-acquired humble and patient attitude: he says that he and Cordelia "will "take upon 's the mystery of things, / As if we were Gods' spies; and we'll wear out, / In a walled prison, packs and sects of great ones, / That ebb and flow by the moon." (V, iii, 16–19) His immediate accommodation to the new circumstances somewhat alleviates the pessimistic mood of the play.

But others are not as able to adapt. Gloucester, his eyes ripped out by Cornwall and his body thrust out of his own home to "smell his way to Dover," determines to commit suicide—and indeed, in the face of the grinding pressure and multiple disappointments consistent with Saturn, a discouraged person might wish to opt out of human life altogether. How can one continue to live in a world of ungrateful and cruel daughters? In which the cunning and power-hungry reach the top? In which the hard-hearted inflict torture on the compassionate? But Shakespeare presses the view that suicide is not the right choice. He enacts one of the most amazing scenes in his canon when he has Gloucester's disguised son Edgar convince his father that he has actually leapt off the white cliffs of Dover and survived. It is, as Harold C. Goddard remarks, "a scene whose theme is the supremacy of the imagination over the senses!"[402]

Edgar's determination to help his father echoes in the subplot the ability of the rejected child to be the means of the parent's redemption. Edgar announces his purpose: "Why I do trifle thus with his despair/ Is done to cure it." (IV, vi, 33–4) Gloucester kneels (in yet another instance of the emphasis on knees as the part of the body ruled by Saturn) to say his final prayer: "O you mighty gods!/ This world I do renounce, and in your sights,/ Shake patiently my great affliction off." (IV, vi, 34–6) At this point Gloucester "falls," and is persuaded by Edgar that he has descended "many fathom down" and that he left above on the cliff's edge some "fiend"—suggesting that the "fiend" left behind is an externalized form of Gloucester's self-destructive thoughts. Edgar assures his father that "Thy life's a miracle" (IV, vi, 55) and sees his father's attitude radically change:

> EDGAR: Therefore, thou happy father,
> 　　　Think that the clearest gods, who make them hon-
> 　　　　ours
> 　　　Of men's impossibilities, have preserved thee.
> GLOUCESTER: I do remember now. Henceforth I'll bear
> 　　　Affliction till it do cry out itself

"Enough, enough," and die....
EDGAR: Bear free and patient thoughts.

(IV, vi, 72–7, 80)

Gloucester has evolved; he has gained the Saturnian virtue of patience. Outwardly he kneels, and inwardly he "kneels" as well, submitting to a higher authority or an overriding fate that he trusts will determine the appropriate moment for his death. Like Lear, he has a newly-acquired humble and patient attitude.

The Death of Cordelia—and What Does Lear See?

The unpalatable but inescapable Saturnian fact that we are forced to accept is that pain, suffering and ultimately death are inevitable experiences in human life. As Marjorie Garber comments, "Retreat from the public arena, from governance and power, for this King is tantamount to a symbolic death, and ... in many ways *King Lear* is a play about the acceptance of death."[403] In tragic dramas, we know in advance that the hero will die. We are not surprised, when we see performances of *Macbeth*, *Othello*, and *King Lear*, that the stage is littered with bodies at the end of the play or that many have died even before the final scene. In the case of *King Lear*, we can see justice in the deaths of Cornwall (stabbed by a servant avenging the plucking out of Gloucester's eyes), of Oswald (killed by Edgar as Oswald attempted to murder Gloucester), of Goneril and Regan (both dead by Goneril's hand due to jealousy over Edmund), and of Edmund (killed in an honorable duel by the brother he plotted to destroy).

The crowning horror of *King Lear*, though, is the death of Cordelia—so revolting to audiences that for many years the play's ending was changed with Cordelia surviving to marry Edgar and eventually rule over England.[404] Her death particularly affects and offends our sensibilities, in part because of her goodness and innocence. We protest with Lear, "Why should a dog, a horse, a rat, have life, / And thou no breath at all?" (V, iii, 305–6) We are left in a mood deeper than melancholia, one of tragic despair.

Or are we? Most literary critics assume that Lear, still not completely in his right mind, hopes in vain that Cordelia was cut down in time. He calls, confusingly, for a mirror to see if her breath will mist it and then a feather to see if her breath will stir it. His last lines, "Do you see this? Look on her, look, her lips, / Look there, look there!" (V, iii, 309–10) are interpreted as delusional. Yet we should not so quickly dismiss the possibility that Lear sees something that we do not. There are a number of compelling reasons why we might rather think that Lear sees with more than physical eyes.

To begin, Lear, at the Saturn stage of life, is a dying man. Recent events—their capture by the English forces still led by the vicious Goneril, Edmund, and Regan; the expense of physical energy needed for Lear to kill the slave that was hanging Cordelia; his staggering onstage with the burden of Cordelia's dead body in his arms—have exhausted him. Those on the verge of quitting the material plane have ever been thought to have enhanced sight. Shakespeare has had his characters refer to eyes and seeing constantly in this play,[405] emphasizing over and over again that physical sight, in the normal course of life, is often untrustworthy. Gloucester had to lose his eyes in order to grasp the true nature of his sons; only then does he realize, "I stumbled when I saw." (IV, i, 20) Now that Lear is on the verge of quitting this world, his physical sight is diminished ("Mine eyes are not o' th' best" [V, iii, 278]) while his intuitive sight may be augmented. So we should trust what he says in his last lines.

As well, Lear has at last attained wisdom, the crown jewel of the Saturnian virtues, a quality that he notably lacked at the beginning of the play. Wisdom is defined as "the power of true and right discernment"; to be wise is "to see clearly what is right and just," hence to see through hypocrisy, through false shows, to the truth behind myriad appearances. So we should be paying attention when Lear urges us to "Look there, look there!"

We know Lear was deficient in wisdom at the beginning of the play, not only from his own actions but also from others' comments, especially the Fool's. Without wisdom, Lear was more foolish than the professional Fool, who actually has more wisdom than any other character except Cordelia. He who was utterly taken in by his two older daughters' insincere protestations of love now knows that he is not "ague-proof," that his true identity is based not on the role he fulfilled but on his essential humanness: "unaccommodated man," stripped of all pretension and artifice. He has also gained the patience and humility that shows a kind of wisdom in accommodating to life's circumstances, no matter what they are. Now, finally, he has the wisdom (as well as the other virtues) traditionally thought to attend old age, the Saturn stage of life.[406]

Many have commented on the fact that the Fool disappears after Act III. His disappearance reinforces the idea that Lear has gained the profound Saturnian gift of wisdom. If we interpret the Fool symbolically, it is as if Lear has integrated the Fool into himself now that he has become wise. Paradoxically, he gains wisdom once he accepts that he was a fool! Lear comments on the cutting quality of the Fool's foolery: when the Fool needles Lear for giving his daughters his lands and income, Lear's reply is: "A bitter fool!" Jung throws some light on the opposition between wisdom and bitterness: "Tears, sorrow, and disappointment are bitter, but wisdom is the comforter in all psychic suffering. Indeed, bitterness and wisdom form a pair of alternatives: where there is bitterness wisdom is lacking, and where wisdom is there can be no bitterness."[407] So the "bitter" fool dematerializes as Lear's wisdom grows. Both the quality of bitterness and the characteristic of wisdom are considered attributes of Saturn.

Most especially, we should trust Lear's final vision as he looks on Cordelia's lips because he is a true melancholic, ruled by Saturn. Only melancholics were reputed to have the capacity for the highest spiritual exaltation,[408] be prone to trances and visions,[409] and, according to Plato, experience "an otherworldly realm of supracelestial light" in moments of ecstasy.[410] Even Christian writers thought a melancholy disposition, glorified by Aristotle, was preferable because "it withdrew men from physical pleasures and worldly turmoil, prepared the mind for the direct influx of divine grace, and elevated it, in cases of special holiness, to mystic and prophetic visions."[411] During Shakespeare's lifetime this belief was still current: the Italian astrologer Jerome Cardan (Girolamo Cardanus, 1501–1576) expressed the idea that "certain men, especially those of a melancholy temperament, exceed others in clairvoyancy and occult sense."[412] Shakespeare has carefully foreshadowed certain important events of the play, particularly Lear's madness and Gloucester's blinding, by both hints and direct statements long before they occur. He has done the same with Lear's last words. After being restored to consciousness following a period of sleep and entertainment with music (a classic antidote for melancholia), Lear earlier recognized Cordelia by saying, "You're a *spirit*, I know. Where did you die?" (IV, vi, 49) At the moment of Lear's physical death Kent urges, "O vex not his *ghost*. O let him pass!" (V, iii, 312), reminding us of the belief in the immortality of the soul. Albany reflects this in his request to Kent and Edgar, "Friends of my *soul*, you twain / Rule in this realm, and the gored state sustain." (V, iii, 318–9) So for all these reasons—Lear's sufferings, his age, his ultimate gaining of wisdom, and his melancholic temperament—we might easily interpret his last words as an indication that he sees her spirit newly departed from her body. His recently awakened perceptive ability along with the enhanced faculties of a melancholic disposition lend weight to interpreting "Do you see this? Look on her, look, her lips, / Look there, look there!" as a final ecstatic vision. (V, iii 309–10)

Like Cordelia's mixed "smiles and tears" and Gloucester's death as his heart "burst smilingly," Lear dies experiencing a mixture of both grief and joy. In line with the opposites juxtaposed so strikingly throughout the play—of parent/child, old/young, speech/silence, wisdom/folly, sight/blindness—we are invited at the end of the play to see both the black and the white together, both grieving with Lear at Cordelia's death and rejoicing at his release. How significant that, according to classical astrological tradition, 0° of the sign Cancer was thought to be the soul's doorway into incarnation, while 0° degree of the sign of Capricorn, the sign to which this play is keyed, was the gate of its exit and symbolic of rebirth into spirit.

There is no escape from the Saturnian fact that whatever "gate" by which we enter or exit, we are passing through mortality into Eternity. In light of this, the ending of *King Lear* is truly like the conclusion of all of human life—both tragic and transcendent. Lear, who sets the wheel in motion himself by dividing the kingdom and banishing Cordelia, descends into a kind of hell but emerges transformed, reborn into a heaven of reunion with Cordelia. Although much is lost, much has been gained. On a human and mundane level, the consequences are physical disaster; on a soul level, the consequences are spiritual triumph. Lear is spiritually transformed at both his own instigation and by Cordelia's grace. If we take this view of the play, we, the audience, are left with the same mixed and opposite emotions that infused Cordelia, Gloucester, and Lear, all experiencing both "sunshine and rain at once," while the characters who remain exit the stage affirming that life will go on, duty will be fulfilled and the "gored state" sustained.

Summing Up:
Celestial Design Then and Now

> "[I]t is a recognized . . . function of great poets . . . that they
> should gather up the threads of the centuries, and weave them into
> a pattern in which the old wisdom shines anew."—John Vyvyan[413]

Now we can look back on what has been presented in this book. Section II, just concluded, looks at some of Shakespeare's greatest plays through the lens of the celestial philosophy that includes astrology. It begins with the Moon, the lowest sphere of the heavens, and ends with Saturn, the hard crystalline crown jewel at its apex. Now we return to the crucial questions that inspired this exploration: "Does astrological symbolism provide the conceptual framework for Shakespeare's works?" And "Does a knowledge of such symbolism help to better understand and appreciate the plays?" Without question, knowing the astrological correlates of each work sheds light on the characters and their motivations, provides a rationale for the plays' overarching themes, and offers a vaster—that is to say, cosmic— context from which to interpret the action and the outcome of the dramas.

Section I prepares for such an exploration by giving the background necessary to understand this perspective on the plays. It first uncovers Shakespeare's use of astrological symbolism to establish time and mood (through references to the daily and seasonal cycles of the Sun) and to create characters (based on the theory of humors that correlates elements and planets with recognizable "temperaments"). These are keys to understanding Shakespeare's characters who are, unusually, at the same time entirely individual and yet true to their type.

Section I further explores the overarching worldview integrating the celestial and the terrestrial, one which not only underpins the creation of Shakespeare's characters but also provides a unique multi-leveled and multi-faceted vocabulary for a poet to convey deeper truths common to human experience.

435

Great literature is at work to interweave temporal and transient subtleties with eternal verities: the swing of the seasons, storm-wrack, sun, stars, comets; and with universal principles, of life, death, resurrection.[414]

Embedded in this worldview are ideas about mathematics and music that translate into artistic choices harmonizing with the higher purposes of such art. Shakespeare elects to use an iambic foot (with its short-long stress replicating the heart's rhythm) and to write in lines with five such poetic feet. He also specifies the type of music (Venusian or Martian) to accompany the action in particular scenes. Thus the "magic" of Shakespeare is created in part by a unique marriage of content and form: substantive wisdom conveyed by powerfully rhythmic poetry whose imagery reflects consistent comparisons between all levels of creation, with background sounds harmonizing with the overall conception.

With these hidden keys to the enduring appeal of Shakespeare's work now exposed, we might ask if another Shakespeare could appear in our time. At first glance this seems unlikely because of the difference in worldviews between Shakespeare's time and our own. Artists generally create art which accords with the commonly-held cosmological view of their historical era. Both artists and audience tend to share a view of the world that influences the artists' creation of works of art and the audience's expectations of them. Are they merely decorative, filling a space on a wall or in a museum? Are they expected to make a statement about the social or political circumstances of their time? Are they credited with the power to affect onlookers by lifting them emotionally, or inspiring them intellectually, or even transporting them momentarily to a higher reality?

In the Classical and Romantic periods, art imitated nature, attempting to reflect exactly what we see, but by the early twentieth century artists like Picasso, along with the Dadaists and Surrealists, created art that was chaotic, broken into jagged lines and distorted bodies, reflecting the breakdown of a common outlook and the rejection of a transcendent reality. Salvador Dali's melting pocket watches, for example, conveyed the idea that even time was unreliable, being fluid and unfixed. Influenced by the prevailing cultural belief that the visible world has no pattern or meaning, some artists in our time fling paint onto canvas in random patterns or create performance or visual art based solely on their personal experience and their own psychology.

Elizabethan cosmology (explored in Chapter 3) presents a different perspective. Often using religious or mythological imagery, much Renaissance art and architecture gains its power from seeing the individual human being at the center of a great linked chain of interrelationships originating in the Divine and encompassing all of creation. Humanity is thus at the crucial intersection of both nature and the cosmos, and human lives have a meaning and purpose in relationship to all levels of being both above and below them. Shakespeare's dramas may teem with a multitude of inexhaustibly varied characters who voice multiple perspectives, but they all interact within a context of a coherent framework of internally consistent meaning— the original unified field theory, if you like. One of the secrets to his art is this very internal consistency, with all aspects of the drama part of an integrated perspective that includes heaven and earth, the invisible as well as the visible realms.

The current mainstream paradigm in Western culture is radically different—entirely opposite—to the one dominant in Shakespeare's time. Modern Western culture currently foregrounds the conventional scientific worldview, which says that the only reality is physical and that higher spheres do not exist. In *The Tao of Physics: An Exploration of the Parallels between Modern Physics and Eastern Mysticism* Fritjof Capra describes this worldview, which has dominated the West for several centuries and is influencing cultures around the world:

> This paradigm consists of a number of ideas and values among them the view of the universe as a mechanical system composed of elementary building blocks, the view of the human body as a machine, the view of life as a competitive struggle for existence, the belief in unlimited material progress to be achieved through economic and technological growth, and—last, but not least—the belief that a society in which the female is everywhere subsumed under the male is one that is "natural."[415]

But according to Capra and other writers this paradigm is proving inadequate and unsatisfying to many in our time. Malcolm Hollick, for instance, exposes materialistic science's so-called dark side:

> Perhaps the most deep-rooted harm comes from the bleak classical vision of a lifeless, uncaring, mechanistic universe at the mercy of blind forces; of a world of separation and alienation of mind from body, person from person, and human from nature; and of a world of unbridled, ruthless competition that lacks consciousness, spirit

or love. Is it any wonder that it has given birth to a society of alienated, despairing, lonely, powerless people?[416]

The underlying assumptions of this extremely reductive and conventional scientific view are being challenged and are changing due partly
to the evolving theories of modern physics, especially quantum physics.
This is why another Shakespeare *could* potentially appear in our time.
Some of these theories are startlingly similar to ideas that are part of the
"Elizabethan worldview" underlying Shakespeare's art. The shift in modern times began most obviously with Albert Einstein. His insight that
mass is a form of energy invalidates the belief that solid matter is the
fundamental building block of reality since matter sometimes behaves
like a particle but at other times like a wave. With the development of
quantum physics by such brilliant thinkers as Niels Bohr (1885–1962),[417]
Werner Heisenberg (1901–1976), and John Bell (1928–1990), it became
obvious that the universe does not work in a simple cause-and-effect
way:

> The laws of atomic physics are statistical laws, according to which
> the probabilities for atomic events are determined by the dynamics
> of the whole system. Whereas in classical physics the properties
> and behaviour of the parts determine those of the whole, the situ-
> ation is reversed in quantum physics: *it is the whole that determines
> the behavior of the parts....* Whereas the hidden variables in classical
> physics are local mechanisms, those in quantum physics are nonlo-
> cal; *they are instantaneous connections to the universe as a whole.*[418]

This is remarkably like the foundational idea behind astrology as well
as the Elizabethan world picture: "interconnectedness" or "correspondence." As I previously wrote, according to the astrological worldview,
"The entire universe is envisioned as a single conscious and intelligent
entity, with each of the unfolded parts corresponding in design to levels above it and in sympathetic resonance with *all* levels both above
and below it. That means that everything has a secret sympathy with
everything else, and every level is connected to every other level."
For the Elizabethans (and astrologers), the universe operates not as a
"bottom-up" model but a "top-down" one (so that consciousness gives
rise to matter and not the other way around)—or, to be more accurate,
as a fully integrated and interconnected system so that all parts can

affect or be affected by all other parts. The modern re-statement of this is in accord with this: Bell's famous theorem convincingly "demonstrates that the universe is fundamentally interconnected, interdependent, and inseparable."[419]

Another intriguing development, this one in the field of particle physics and called the "bootstrap theory," places a significant emphasis on the idea of order. "Order" here means an order operative in the interconnectedness of subatomic processes arising from self-consistency within subatomic structures.

> At present, the significance of order in subatomic physics is still somewhat mysterious and not yet fully explored. However, it is intriguing to note that ... *the notion of order plays a very basic role in the scientific approach to reality* and is a crucial aspect of our methods of observation. The ability to recognize order seems to be an essential aspect of the rational mind; every perception of a pattern is, in a sense, a perception of order. The clarification of the concept of order in a field of research where *patterns of matter and patterns of mind are increasingly being recognized as reflections of one another* promises thus to open fascinating frontiers of knowledge.[420]

Any Elizabethan would immediately respond to the emphasis on order, applicable to an individual's inner psychic state as well as to the social and political spheres. Could the people of Shakespeare's time—and before— have intuited that it operates even in the invisible sub-atomic one? For Bohm in particular, order (which he describes as "implicate" or enfolded) is inherent within a cosmic web of relations at a deep and unseen level. He uses the analogy of a hologram (a three-dimensional free-standing image created by photographic projection) since each of its parts contains in some mysterious way the whole. As Capra notes, "In Bohm's view, the real world is structured according to the same general principles, with the whole being enfolded in each of its parts."[421] The Elizabethans would have wholeheartedly agreed.[422]

Bohm's observation highlights an important difference of interpretation and emphasis between the conceptual view of the Elizabethans and the new physicists. The hierarchical model of the Elizabethans implies a judgment of value: things at the top of the chain or at the top of their classification are "better" than things below. (This distinction is inherent in most religions and philosophies from ancient times even to the present: up is good and down is bad.) From the perspective of the New Physics, though, since the whole can be understood through *any one* of its parts, all parts are theoretically equivalent to each other since each mysteriously contains the whole.

So given the similarities between the Elizabethan worldview and recent scientific theories, can we expect sometime, perhaps sometime soon, another Shakespeare, inspired by and speaking in some amalgam of the earlier worldview and the terminology of modern physics? *Great and lasting literature must reflect a grand and meaningful paradigm, one that emerges from the archetypal dimension and is garmented in contemporary terminology.* The language of our time is the language of science; the language of meaning derives from religion, philosophy, and myth. A new Shakespeare would likely draw on and blend both.

While we wait and see, we can continue to delight in Shakespeare's works and celebrate his ability to entertain and enlighten us. Their power to affect us derives from their all-inclusive and essentially optimistic vision. The ancient holistic worldview, affirming the innate spiritual nature of human beings and the possibility of their spiritual evolution, infuses Shakespeare's work and accounts for his enduring popularity and the flourishing of many theatrical organizations devoted to performing his plays.

Unquestionably experiencing a live performance makes the plays more accessible and more powerful than reading them. Seeing the plays enacted allows the ancient archetypes to speak directly to both the conscious and unconscious parts of the psyche. From ancient times, theater had a religious or spiritual purpose: the familiar stories of human beings and their relationship to the Divine taught powerful lessons. Being dramatized, their essential meanings were absorbed subliminally, conveyed in words but mediated by the imagination. In this way dramatic performance was like repeated religious ritual and had an initiatory function, uniquely capable of conveying spiritual ideas and revealing knowledge of the inner workings of the universe. Onlookers might leave the theater at the very least profoundly moved, but also potentially more philosophically aware and better able to apply a greater wisdom to their own lives. Having momentarily transcended themselves, they might even be transformed.

For Shakespeare's works to affect us so profoundly and to have such universal appeal they must be based on an archetypal foundation, something we sense in them but may have difficulty seeing and articulating.

> As our knowledge of a Shakespearian play increases we become more and more intensely aware of a certain quality peculiar to it. This can be held in the mind after the events which help to build it are forgotten; indeed, the ability to leave such an impression is the distinguishing mark of high imaginative literature.... [W]e must intuitively recognize a central principle of some kind and call on quotations only as evidence.... From this central principle we can begin to understand the work in its wholeness.[423]

The "peculiar quality," the "central principle," the blend of the temporal and eternal is characteristic of artistic works based on fundamental Ideas or Forms.

The questions posed in the Introduction —"Why Shakespeare?" And "How did he do it?"—are answered in realizing that his expanded (or "capacious") consciousness, combined with literary craft, midwived a unique body of work that could only have been produced in a particular time period by a unique individual having an unusual combination of literary artistry, astute perception, and vivid imagination, along with a profound understanding of philosophical, esoteric, and spiritual wisdom. The originality of his language, the musicality of his poetry, the vitality of his characters, and the depth and profundity of the truths he expresses about human nature and human experience impress us more and more with repeated engagement, so that he is truly, in Ben Jonson's words, "not of an age but for all time."

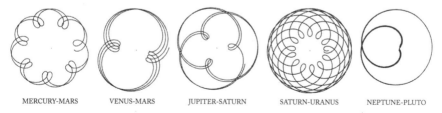

MERCURY-MARS VENUS-MARS JUPITER-SATURN SATURN-URANUS NEPTUNE-PLUTO

Every set of planets (not just Venus and Earth, as depicted in the image at the end of Chapter 9) creates patterns together if their orbits are mapped heliocentrically, suggesting a hidden and mathematical beauty in the cosmos. (Images from John Martineau, A Little Book of Coincidence in the Solar System, *Wooden Books, 2006.)*

Is Alchemy also a Key
to Understanding King Lear?

The Play as an Allegory of Alchemy: The Dragon Transformed

It may seem unusual to introduce the third of the major esoteric studies (besides astrology and magic) into a discussion of *King Lear*. Yet the transformation of Lear from patriarchal monster to humble father has some remarkable analogies to alchemical processes, which draw heavily on the symbolism of Saturn. Alchemy provides the imagery of extreme suffering that matches that of Lear and accords with the atmosphere of the play. Such symbolism would have been familiar to many in Shakespeare's audience.[424]

In a book entitled *The Chemical Theatre*, British writer Charles Nicholl examines alchemical texts in circulation in the sixteenth and seventeenth centuries and discovers that alchemy as a philosophy underpins the writings of many famous figures of the time, Sir George Ripley, Dr. John Dee, Paracelsus, and Basil Valentine among them. Alchemical symbols and themes also surface in the artistic works of Shakespeare's contemporaries, like playwright Ben Jonson and poet John Donne, and most especially, according to Nicholl, in Shakespeare's own *King Lear*.[425] Many in Shakespeare's audience, particularly the educated, would have recognized its symbolism. So is alchemy another esoteric key to understanding this play?

To appreciate this interpretation and before looking at some of Nicholl's points, it is necessary to have some knowledge of the fundamental principles of alchemy. What motivated its secretive adherents, busy conducting strange experiments in their hidden laboratories?

Modern physics concerns itself with two vast and intractable questions: the fundamental nature of matter and the workings of the universe. Centuries have not much altered these concerns: in the Middle Ages and even earlier, the same two questions also attracted many of the most subtle minds of the day to the related studies of alchemy and astrology. *Basically, alchemy was the investigation of the properties of matter and astrology those of the universe.*[426]

While astrologers were more focused on the heavens, alchemists were working with elements of the earth. Alchemy likely developed as an offshoot of astrology, starting with the associations of the seven classical planets with specific metals:

Sun	gold
Moon	silver
Mercury	quicksilver or electrum
	(an amalgam of gold and silver)
Venus	copper
Mars	iron
Jupiter	tin
Saturn	lead

Alchemy is essentially a development of astrological principles, especially the Hermetic maxim, "As above, so below," applied to physical experiments. The descriptions and fantastic pictures of alchemical processes that represent changes in metals and other substances contain astrological references, particularly to the planet Mercury. Astrology also had practical value for the alchemist because laboratory operations were to be performed when celestial influences were most auspicious. It was best to begin the whole process when the Sun was in Aries, in the spring of the year, and culminate when the Sun and Moon were aligned in the sign of Leo, at the end of summer.[427]

Most discussions of alchemy focus on the concrete efforts of these experimenters, hopeful of transforming lead (at the bottom of the above list) into gold (at the top of the list) and discovering the elixir of life to cure all disease. However, there are actually three levels of alchemical work: physical alchemy, which manipulated substances to transmute one form of matter into another;[428] psychological alchemy, which aimed to catalyze changes in the consciousness of the alchemists themselves;[429] and spiritual alchemy, which sought to tap into the source of life itself, equivalent to having a mystical experience of union with God. To the alchemists of Shakespeare's time the psychological and spiritual goals of alchemical research were as important as the physical.[430] So we should not be surprised that some of the best "scientific" minds of the time were explorers of alchemy. Isaac Newton (1642-1727) wrote over a million words on the topic, a study that inspired his discoveries of the laws of light and theory of gravity. He was deeply interested in religion, magic, and alchemical transformations in the laboratory.

While physical alchemy was marginalized with the rise of the mechanistic-materialistic paradigm in the eighteenth century, the psychological approach to it has flowered in the past hundred years. The insightful psychologist C. G. Jung became fascinated with alchemy and its symbolism, due to the appearance of alchemical symbols in his own dreams and those of his patients.

> From the vantage point of modern psychiatric and psychological observation, the core of [the alchemists'] endeavor has come to reveal itself as a search for the wholeness of the personality and for the indestructible essence of the soul which they expressed in countless images and symbols ranging from the elixir of life and the philosopher's stone to the image of the hermaphrodite. Even the transmutation of base metals into gold, which is commonly assumed to have been the object of their practical labors, had its transcendent counterpart, for the gold itself became a symbol of the pure indestructible essence whose sun-like color reflected the immortal quality of the psyche.[431]

Alchemists of Shakespeare's time worked on all three levels simultaneously because according to the worldview then, spirit and matter were part of a continuum. All of creation flowed from the Divine, in a series of emanations, like water down the steps of a rock wall. The last and apparently lowest level of creation, our mundane world, whose varieties of human, animal, and vegetable life resulted from combinations of the four elements (fire, air, water, and earth), was imperfect and always changing. The alchemists endeavored to manipulate the inner structure of physical substances in order to "perfect" them, to restore them to their original state, and in so doing to release the "spirit" in matter. Brian Cotnoir succinctly sums up the essence of their art: "The central concept in alchemy is transmutation: the fundamental change of one thing into another, from a grosser, impure state to a more refined, balanced, and pure state. This is to be understood on multiple levels—physically, spiritually, and symbolically."[432]

This process was presented in diverse ways, depicted in strange images and told in stories of perilous sea journeys, of descents into underground caves, of dangerous animals (lions, wolves, serpents, and dragons) trapped and tortured inside alchemical containers, and of Kings and Queens mating. But writers of alchemical manuscripts from many times (especially the early centuries CE and the Renaissance) and places (China, India, Egypt, the Middle East, and Europe) depicted their experiments with universally recognizable stages. They began by identifying the base matter to be worked on in the laboratory, dark and chaotic "stuff" needed to start the process. The initial phase was called the *nigredo*, or blackening, and may be the reason that alchemy was in some places called the "Black Art."[433] All of the experimenters started with "black stuff"—black being the color of Saturn.

This *prima materia* or primal black substance is often directly "referred to as Saturn, or as lead, or both. The implication is that lead, being the manifestation of the Great Malefic, is the basest substance in the universe."[434] Sometimes—and this is especially relevant to *King Lear*--this Prime Matter is equated with a dragon.[435] On the psychological level, this dark stuff or *prima materia* is the problem that drives you into therapy and is usually "found in the shadow, that part of the personality that is considered most despicable. Those aspects of ourselves most painful and most humiliating are the very ones to be brought forward and worked on."[436] The emphasis on blackness, on lead as the physical substance for the alchemist to work on, and the shadow as the psychological weakness to be faced, all link alchemical and astrological (Saturn) symbolism to *King Lear*.

Of the eight stages of alchemical transformation the one most applicable to Lear's journey is called the "calcinatio." Though the sequence of the stages varies with different writers, most accounts of alchemical operations start with this one. Many alchemical processes involve either heating a substance (applying fire) or dissolving it (adding water)—two techniques that attempt to manipulate its elemental structure in order to change its form. The physical process of *calcinatio* starts by subjecting the primal material to intense heat in order to drive off water or other constituents, leaving a fine dry powder. Imaginatively, the alchemical books describe this as burning a ravening wolf, cutting off the paws of a fierce lion, or trapping a roaring dragon in a stoppered flask. Lear's comparison of himself to a "dragon" immediately suggests a connection to this alchemical symbolism.

Psychologically, the fire kindled in this stage comes from stifled desires—hunger, lust, greed, longing for power--whose frustration erupts in rage and violence. "As a rule, life … provides plenty of occasions for the *calcinatio* of frustrated desirousness. The primitive, undifferentiated desire that says 'I want' operates on the implicit assumption that it is entitled to have what it wants. When denied, it becomes enraged."[437] This happens in *King Lear* at the moment when Cordelia says "Nothing," refusing her father's demand to express profusions of love. At this point is unleashed the primitive destructive force of desire denied.[438]

> One of the most characteristic areas of life in which the stage of the calcinatio occurs is the area of frustrated love. This experience burns away a great deal of dross, if it is entered into with some consciousness. Normally if a person cannot have the object of his or her desire, there is great anger, and the other person or some outer circumstance is blamed; or there is a kind of sodden self-pity and self-denigration. … Passion is a great catalyst, perhaps the greatest

The alchemist points to the stars, specifying the auspicious time to begin the Great Work: when the Sun is in Aries, as revealed by the symbol of the ram in the small upper square. The beginning of the seasonal year (spring) is appropriate for the first stage of the process, the calcinatio, *represented as the fiery furnace emitting smoke and funneling a dried powder into the waiting flask in the lower left.*

we have, and frustration of passion is the essence of this stage of the opus.[439]

Disrespected and stripped of his entourage, the infuriated Lear castigates his two eldest daughters, cursing Goneril with sterility and blasting her as a disease within his "corrupted blood" (II, iv, 220) and vowing revenges on them both that "shall be/ The terrors of the earth" (II, iv, 276-7). Later on the heath, in his maddened imagination he subjects both Goneril and Regan to a trial; after "arraigning" Goneril, he begs the court to "anatomize Regan; see what breeds about her heart. Is there any cause in nature that make these hard hearts?" (III, vi, 70-2) Lear's purgatorial sufferings persist as long as he burns with the desire for revenge, until finally passion consumes itself; as the doctor confirms: "the great rage,/ You see, is kill'd in him" (IV, vii, 79-80). This signals that order is restored within (and will subsequently be without).[440]

What is gained at the end of the *calcinatio*? For the alchemists, it is the successful completion of one stage of their work, a sign of progress on the way to the greater experience of the ultimate mastery of matter and release of spirit from earthly limitations. Psychologically, it is the development of a solid sense of identity based on both a recognition of oneness with all humanity and an identification with an authentic spiritual Self that transcends the body and the ego. This is relevant to the ending of *King Lear*, as Lear's identity has been re-focused and expanded and he is released from the limitations and sufferings of this world.

This abbreviated comparison of Lear's purgatorial journey and its analogies to the alchemical stage of the *calcinatio* is much enlarged in Nicholl's *The Chemical Theatre*. In an extensive and extremely persuasive exploration, Nicholl builds an impressive case for the resemblance of the enacted drama of *King Lear* to detailed descriptions of alchemical processes. His thesis is this:

> What Lear undergoes is something very like an alchemical transmutation. I shall try to show this by a series of parallels between the plot and imagery of the play and the patterns and symbols of alchemy, drawn almost exclusively from contemporary alchemical texts which Shakespeare could have read.[441]

To give one example, he explores the relevance of the central image of the wheel to both the play and alchemy: as the turning Wheel of

Fortune which Kent in the stocks petitions to "Smile once more; turn thy wheel!" (II, ii, 165); as the cyclic Wheel of Generations on which "the younger rises when the old doth fall" (III, iii, 22); and as the refining Wheel of Fire on which Lear is bound so that his tears do "scald like molten lead" (IV, vii, 48). The turning wheel "is clearly comparable to the alchemists' emphasis on circulation as the pattern of the *opus* ... and provides the concrete link between *King Lear* and contemporary alchemy."[442]

He also compares the rage that erupts from within Lear to the dragon, a complex figure in alchemy. Alchemically the dragon is both the "chaos of unredeemed nature" (and as such "related to other reptilian or bestial emblems for the Raw Stuff—serpent, toad, salamander, green lion")[443] and the secret inner fire that consumes that chaos. So it literally devours itself, as suggested by the often-depicted dragon/snake eating its own tail, the Ourobouros. "The sick King announces himself as the Dragon and begins to devour himself . . . the Dragon and the true object of its wrath are one thing: Lear himself. . . . And beyond the wrath, beyond the total eclipse of Lear now beginning, lies the promise of transformation."[444] Lear protests the rising of that base element within himself: "O, how this mother swells up toward my heart!/ Hysterica passio, down, thou climbing sorrow,/ Thy element's below!" (II, iv, 54-6) Yet the lower element rises, spreads its cursing poison, and at last consumes itself. Lear is purged and reborn.[445]

Nicholl makes the especially important point that the stories of the symbolic characters in the alchemical dramas resemble all the stories of the rise, fall, and restoration of tragic heroes in the world's mythologies:

> These alchemical parables depict alchemy in emblematic but *human* terms, and the pattern which emerges in those terms is this. The beginning is grossness, infertility, ailment, poverty, incompleteness. The middle, or 'action' of the narrative, entails a submission to some drastic, mysterious and overwhelming process ... which leads to imprisonment and death. The end, as a result of this purgatorial process, is exultant.... The dangerous but ultimately healing journey through darkness and ruin is ... the human pattern which corresponds to the alchemical process. And this journey or pattern is one we know well, in a form more familiar to our ears than alchemical allegory. It is the basic pattern of tragic drama.[446]

Acknowledgments

A book like this is a long time in the writing (almost eight years) and a long time in the making (over thirty). It is the result of years of reading and reflection, frequent viewing of performances of Shakespeare's plays, rich and varied life experiences, and a variety of influences and encounters with many people.

It would not exist, however, without the participation of four people in particular who each played a major role in its creation. The first is Aaron Milrad, a friend who is a lawyer extraordinaire in the field of arts, entertainment, and the media. We were having lunch one day, catching up on our mutual activities, and I happened to mention that I was giving talks on Shakespeare's plays and taking groups to see performances at the Stratford (Ontario) Festival. He said the magic words: "I think there's a book in that." Well, there was—and here it is, Aaron! You gave me the idea; it would never have occurred to me to write a book without your vision.

The second person is my brilliant, funny, insightful, and red-pen-wielding friend Paul Craig, Ph.D. (history) who volunteered to edit every section as I proceeded to write them over many months and years. Thank you, Paul, for quizzing me on the ideas and questioning their expression, and for saving me from many an awkward or unclear phrase or downright inaccuracy. Alternately criticizing and praising, he kept me going when the writing process seemed interminable and explaining sophisticated ideas clearly seemed impossible. His encouragement (and many delicious lunches) helped support—in fact, midwife—the project. In the process my karma came home to roost; after years of red-penning students' writing, I was on the receiving end of critiques by an editor who loved challenging every phrase and every point. I could not have had a better friend or coach through the years of writing this book.

The third person is the publisher of this book, Yvonne Paglia (and her husband Donald Weiser). They kindly opened their home to me and offered support over the years while I was transitioning to my semi-American life; their friends became my friends; and they made me feel a part of their personal, professional, and literary worlds. And finally,

Yvonne offered to have Ibis Press publish this book and even provided the excellent title. And she and her husband were the connecting link to the fourth significant participant.

The fourth person is a long-time friend and associate of Yvonne and Donald: Jim Wasserman, the General Editor and graphic designer who turned my manuscript into a real book. With a determined focus on what would work on the page, he created its elegant design, all the while coaching me through the process of polishing a manuscript, creating a cover, incorporating illustrations, and including captions. He also linked me to one of his associates, a gifted professional editor, Lisa Wagner, who made many helpful suggestions and asked many thought-provoking questions. This is a much better and much more coherent book as a result of her involvement.

A number of others supported this project in various ways: Christeen Skinner, English astrologer extraordinaire, invited me to contribute two articles on the topic of Shakespeare and astrology for the Urania Trust web site; Mimi Alonzo photo-shopped the cover illustration; Michael Barwick contributed his time and expertise in designing a publicity flyer; and many read and critiqued parts of the manuscript or advised on questions that arose during its creation: Matt Armstrong, Barbara Craig, Ami Ronnberg, Carol Kay, Janet Markham, Bill Christie, Nancy Needham, Simon Barker-Benfield, Mary Wiens, and Peter Pringle. Their friendship, support, and interest during the ongoing creation of this book are much appreciated.

I am particularly grateful to have had the opportunity to spend several weeks doing research at the Warburg Institute (part of the University of London) in London, England. With its specialization in the influence of classical Mediterranean traditions on European culture from the Middle Ages to the modern period, especially in the Renaissance, its open-access library was the ideal place providing endless opportunities to explore ideas relevant to this project. I spent many happy hours there. My thanks go both to the patient assistants who helped me collect information and to Dorian Gieseler Greenbaum, who facilitated my admission and my stay in London.

In the field of Shakespearean scholarship, I have been most impressed and inspired over the years by the writings of G. Wilson Knight, Dame Frances Yates, John Vyvyan, Harold C. Goddard, S.K. Heninger, Jr., E.M.W. Tillyard, Northrop Frye, and Marjorie Garber.

And finally, I am deeply appreciative of being associated with a community of brilliant thinkers and fellow enthusiasts in the fields of astrology, philosophy, and cultural history, in particular Robert Hand, Ph.D., Richard Tarnas, Ph. D., Nicholas Campion, Ph.D., Robert Zoller, M.A., Dorian Gieseler Greenbaum, Ph. D., and Liz Greene, Ph.D., from whom I have learned much over the years. The National Council for Geocosmic Research, one of the foremost international astrological organizations in the world, has been a particular home. It has been an honor to have attended and spoken at many of their conferences, contributed to their newsletters and journals, and served in various capacities on their Boards. Astrology is flourishing in the twentieth and twentieth-first centuries and having a Renaissance of its own, as this community can attest.

BIBLIOGRAPHY

Note: I have included many books consulted while writing this one, although they may not be cited in the text.

Ackroyd, Peter. *Venice: Pure City*. New York, NY: Doubleday, 2009.

Addey, John. "Shakespeare's Attitude to Astrology." In *An Astrological Anthology: Essays and Excerpts from the Journal of the Astrological Association*. Vol. I, 1959-70. Selected and Arranged by Zach Matthews. London, England: The Astrological Association, 1995.

Agrippa of Nettesheim, Henry Cornelius. *Three Books of Occult Philosophy*. Completely Annotated with Modern Commentary. Trans. James Freake, Ed. and Annotated by Donald Tyson. St. Paul, MN: Llewellyn Publications, 1995.

Allen, Don Cameron. *The Star-Crossed Renaissance: The Quarrel about Astrology and Its Influence in England*. New York, NY: Octagon Books, Inc, 1966.

Anderson, Ruth Leila. *Elizabethan Psychology and Shakespeare's Plays*. University of Iowa Humanistic Studies, Franklin H. Potter, Ed. Vol. III, No. 4. Iowa City, Iowa: U. of Iowa, 1927.

Andreasen, Nancy C. "Secrets of the Creative Brain". *The Atlantic* magazine, Vol. 314, No. 1, pp. 62-75.

Andrews, Ted. *Enchantment of the Faerie Realm*. Woodbury, MN: Llewellyn, 1993 and 2006.

Anonymous. *The Deeper Truths of Shakespeare*. Compiled by a Student of The Rosicrucian Fellowship Teachings. 1st ed. Oceanside, CA: Rosicrucian Fellowship, 1980.

Apuleius, Lucius. *The Golden Ass*. Trans. William Adlington (1566). New York, NY: Collier Books, 1962.

The Archive for Research in Archetypal Symbolism. *The Book of Symbols*. Ed.-in-Chief Ami Ronnberg. Cologne, Germany: Taschen, 2010.

The Archive for Research in Archetypal Symbolism. *An Encyclopedia of Archetypal Symbolism*. Ed. Beverly Moon. Boston, MA and London, England: Shambhala, 1991.

Arikha, Noga. *Passions and Tempers: A History of the Humours*. New York, NY: HarperCollins, 2007.

Arroyo, Stephen. *The Practice and Profession of Astrology: Rebuilding Our Lost Connections With The Cosmos*. Reno, Nevada: CRCS Publications, 1984.

Asimov, Isaac. *Asimov's Guide to Shakespeare*. Avenel, NJ: Wings (Random), 1970.

Atwood, Margaret. *Payback: Debt and the Shadow Side of Wealth*. Toronto, Canada: House of Anansi Press, 2008.

Baigent, Michael, Nicholas Campion, and Charles Harvey. *Mundane Astrology*. Wellingborough, Northamptonshire, England: The Aquarian Press, 1984.

Bamford, Christopher. "The Magic of Romance" in *Alexandria 2: The Journal of the Western Cosmological Tradition*. Ed. by David Fideler. Grand Rapids, MI: Phanes Press, 1993.

Banzhaf, Hajo, and Anna Haebler. *Key Words for Astrology*. York Beach, ME: Samuel Weiser, Inc., 1996.

Barber, C. L. *Shakespeare's Festive Comedy: A Study of Dramatic Form and its Relation to Social Custom*. Princeton, NJ: Princeton U. Press, 1959.

Barnet, Sylvan, Morton Berman, William Burto, eds. *An Introduction to Literature: Fiction, Poetry, Drama*. 2nd ed. Boston, MA: Little, Brown and Company, 1963.

Bate, Jonathan. *Shakespeare and Ovid*. Oxford, UK: Clarendon Press, 1993.

Begg, Ean. *Myth and Today's Consciousness*. London, England: Coventure Ltd., 1984.

Biedermann, Hans. *Dictionary of Symbolism: Cultural Icons and the Meanings Behind Them*. Trans. James Hulbert. New York, NY: Penguin Books (Meridian), 1994.

Bloom, Harold. *Genius: A Mosaic of One Hundred Exemplary Creative Minds*. New York, NY: Warner, 2002.

Bloom, Harold. *Shakespeare: The Invention of the Human*. New York, NY: Riverhead Books (Penguin Putnam), 1998.

Bodkin, Maud. *Archetypal Patterns in Poetry: Psychological Studies of Imagination*. London, UK: Oxford U. Press, 1963.

Bonatti, Guido. *Liber Astronomiae, Part II*. Trans. Robert Zoller, ed. Robert Hand. Project Hindsight, Latin Track, Volume VIII. Berkeley Springs, WVa: 1994.

Booth, Mark. *The Secret History of the World*. New York, NY: The Overlook Press, 2010.

Brady, Bernadette. *Astrology, A Place in Chaos*. Bournemouth, England: The Wessex Astrologer, 2006.

Brau, Jean-Louis, Helen Weaver, and Allan Edmands. *Larousse Encyclopedia of Astrology*. Ed. and with a preface by Helen Weaver. Consulting and contributing editors: Robert Hand, Charles Harvey, and Charles Jayne. New York, NY: McGraw-Hill Book Company, 1980.

Brown, Philip. "Shakespeare, Astrology, and Alchemy." *Mountain Astrologer* magazine, Feb/Mar. 2004, pp. 78-87.

Bulfinch, Thomas. *Mythology.* New York, NY: Dell Publishing, 1959.

Burckhardt, Titus. *Alchemy: Science of the Cosmos, Science of the Soul.* Baltimore, MD: Penguin Books Inc., 1967, 1971.

Burkert, Walter. *Ancient Mystery Cults.* Cambridge, MA: Harvard U. Press, 1987.

Busenbark, Ernest. *Symbols, Sex, and the Stars In Popular Beliefs: An Outline of the Origins of Moon and Sun Worship, Astrology, Sex Symbolism, Mystic Meaning of Numbers, the Cabala, and Many Popular Customs, Myths, Superstitions and Religious Beliefs.* Escondido, CA: The Book Tree, 1997.

Butler, D. M. *The Myth of the Magus.* Cambridge, England: Cambridge U. Press, 1948.

Camden, Carroll, Jr. "Astrology in Shakespeare's Day." *Isis,* Vol. 19, No. 1 (Apr., 1933), pp. 26-73. Published by the U. of Chicago Press on behalf of the History of Science Society.

Campbell, Joseph. *The Hero with a Thousand Faces.* Cleveland, OH: The World Publishing Company, 1949, 1956.

Campbell, Joseph. *The Masks of God: Primitive Mythology.* New York, NY: The Viking Press, 1970.

Campbell, Lily B. *Shakespeare's Tragic Heroes: Slaves of Passion.* New York, NY: Barnes and Noble, 1930.

Campion, Nicholas. *The Dawn of Astrology: A Cultural History of Western Astrology, Vol. I: The Ancient and Classical Worlds.* London, England: Continuum, 2008.

Campion, Nicholas. *A History of Western Astrology, Vol. II, The Medieval and Modern Worlds.* London, England: Continuum UK, 2009.

Campion, Nicholas. "Is Astrology a Symbolic Language?" In *Sky and Symbol: The Proceedings of the Ninth Annual Conference of the Sophia Centre for the Study of Cosmology in Culture, University of Wales, Trinity Saint David, 4-5 June 2011.* Ed. Nicholas Campion and Liz Greene. Ceredigion, Wales: Sophia Centre Press, 2013, pp. 9-46.

Capra, Fritjof. *The Tao of Physics: An Exploration of the Parallels between Modern Physics and Eastern Mysticism.* Fourth ed., updated. Boston, MA: Shambhala, 2000.

Chevalier, Jean and Alain Gheerbrant. *A Dictionary of Symbols.* Trans. from the French by John

Buchanan-Brown. London, England: Penguin, 1994/1996.

Ciavolella, Massimo and Amilcare A. Iannucci, eds. *Saturn from Antiquity to the Renaissance*. Ottawa, Canada: Dovehouse editions (U. of Toronto Italian Studies, 8), 1992.

Cirlot, J.E. *A Dictionary of Symbols*. Trans. from Spanish by Jack Sage. New York, NY: Philosophical Library, 1962.

Clark, Cumberland. *Astronomy in the Poets*. Bournemouth, England: Sydenham & Co., no date.

Clark, Cumberland. *Shakespeare and Science*. Birmingham, England: Cornish Brothers Ltd., 1929.

Cooper, J. C. *An Illustrated Encyclopaedia of Traditional Symbols*. London, England: Thames and Hudson, 1978.

Cooper, J.C. *Symbolism: The Universal Language*. Wellingborough, Northamptonshire: The Aquarian Press, 1982.

Copenhaver, Brian P. *Hermetica: The Greek Corpus Hermeticum and the Latin Asclepius in a new English translation, with notes and introduction*. Cambridge, England: Cambridge U. Press, 1992.

Costello, Priscilla. "Astrology and Shakespeare, Part I." www.uraniatrust.org/articles.

Costello, Priscilla. "Astrology and Shakespeare, Part II." www.uraniatrust.org/articles.

Costello, Priscilla. "From Ladder to Labyrinth: the Spiritual and Psychological Dimensions of Astrology". Published in *Gnosis* 38 (winter 1996) and reprinted in *The Inner West: An Introduction to the Hidden Wisdom of the West*. Ed. and Intro. by Jay Kinney. New York, NY: Jeremy P. Tarcher/Penguin, 2004.

Costello, Priscilla. *The Weiser Concise Guide to Practical Astrology*. York Beach, ME: Red Wheel/Weiser, 2008.

Couliano, Ioan P. *Eros and Magic in the Renaissance*. Trans. Margaret Cook. With a Foreword by Mircea Eliade. Chicago, IL: U. of Chicago Press, 1987.

Coxhead, David and Susan Hiller. *Dreams: Visions of the Night*. New York, NY: Thames and Hudson, 1976.

Davies, Paul. *God and the New Physics*. New York, NY: Simon & Schuster, 1983.

de Rougemont, Denis. *Love in the Western World*. Trans. Montgomery Belgion, rev. and augmented ed. Greenwich, Conn.: Fawcett Publications, 1956.

de Vore, Nicolas. *Encyclopedia of Astrology*. New York, NY: Philosophical Library, 1947.

Denning, Melita & Osborne Phillips. *Planetary Magic: A Complete System for Knowledge and Attainment*. St. Paul, MN.: Llewellyn Publications, 1992.

Draper, John W. *The Humors & Shakespeare's Characters*. Durham, NC: Duke U, Press, 1945.

Dunn, Catherine M. "The Function of Music in Shakespeare's Romances". Folger Shakespeare Library, *Shakespeare Quarterly*, Vol. 20, No. 14 (Autumn, 1969).

Dyer, Rev. T. F. Thiselton. *Folklore of Shakespeare*. London, England: Griffith & Farran, 1883.

Epstein, Joseph, ed. *Literary Genius: 25 Classic Writers Who Define English & American Literature*. London, England: Haus Books, 2007.

Epstein, Norrie. *The Friendly Shakespeare: A Thoroughly Painless Guide to the Best of the Bard*. New York, NY: Penguin, 1993.

Evans, Bertrand. *Shakespeare's Comedies*. London, England: Oxford U. Press, 1961, 1967.

Fabricius, Johannes. *Alchemy: The Medieval Alchemists and their Royal Art*. Wellingborough, England: The Aquarian Press (Thorsons), 1976.

Faivre, Antoine and Jacob Needleman, eds. Assoc. ed: Karen Voss. *Modern Esoteric Spirituality*. Vol. 21 of World Spirituality: An Encyclopedic History of the Religious Quest. New York, NY: Crossroad, 1992.

Ferguson, George. *Signs & Symbols in Christian Art*. New York, NY: Oxford University Press, 1966.

Ferguson, Kitty. *The Music of Pythagoras: How an Ancient Brotherhood Cracked the Code of the Universe and Lit the Path from Antiquity to Outer Space*. New York, NY: Walker & Company, 2008.

Ficino, Marsilio. *The Book of Life*. Trans. Charles Boer. Dallas, Texas: Spring Publications, 1980.

Filbey, John D. F. Astrol. S., and Peter Filbey, B. Sc. *Astronomy for Astrologers*. Wellingborough, Northamptonshire, England: The Aquarian Press, no date.

Foster, Russell. www.ted.com/talks/russell_foster_why_do_we_sleep.html. TED talk, filmed June, 2013.

Fowler, Alastair. *Time's Purpled Masquers: Stars and the Afterlife in Renaissance English Literature*. Oxford, England: Clarendon Press [Oxford U. Press], 1996.

Francis, Clive (compiler and illustrator*). There is Nothing Like a Thane!: The Lighter Side of Macbeth*. New York, NY: St. Martin's Press (Thomas Dunne Books), 2001.

French, Peter J. *John Dee: The World of an Elizabethan Magus*. London, England: Routledge & Kegan Paul, 1972.

Frye, Northrop. *Anatomy of Criticism: Four Essays*. Princeton, NJ: Princeton U. Press, 1957.

Frye, Northrop. *Fools of Time: Studies in Shakespearean Tragedy*. Toronto, Canada: U. of Toronto Press, 1967.

Frye, Northop. *A Natural Perspective: The Development of Shakespearean Comedy and Romance*. New York, NY: Harcourt, Brace & World, Inc., 1965.

Frye, Northrop. *Northrop Frye on Shakespeare*. Ed. by Robert Sandler. Markham, Ontario: Fitzhenry & Whiteside, 1986.

Frye, Roland Mushat. *Shakespeare and Christian Doctrine*. Princeton, NJ: Princeton U. Press, 1963.

Garai, Jana. *The Book of Symbols*. London, England: Lorrimer Publishing, 1973.

Garber, Marjorie. *Dream in Shakespeare: From Metaphor to Metamorphosis*. With a New Prologue by the Author. New Haven, Conn. & London, England: Yale U. Press, 1974/2013.

Garber, Marjorie. *Shakespeare After All*. New York, NY: Random House (Anchor), 2004.

Garin, Eugenio. *Astrology in the Renaissance: The Zodiac of Life*. Trans. by Carolyn Jackson and June Allen. Trans rev. in conjunction with the author by Clare Robertson. London, England: Arkana, 1983.

Gettings, Fred. *The Arkana Dictionary of Astrology*. London, England: Arkana (Penguin Group), 1990.

Gilligan, James. *Violence: Our Deadly Epidemic and Its Causes*. New York, NY: Putnam's, 1996.

Goddard, Harold C. *The Meaning of Shakespeare*. Vols. I and II. Chicago, IL: The U. of Chicago Press, 1951.

Godwin, Joscelyn. *The Golden Thread: The Ageless Wisdom of the Western Mystery Tradition*. Wheaton, IL: Theosophical Publishing House (Quest Books), 2007.

Godwin, Joscelyn. *Robert Fludd: Hermetic Philosopher and Surveyor of Two Worlds*. London, England: Thames and Hudson Ltd., 1979.

Godwin, Joscelyn. *Harmonies of Heaven and Earth: Mysticism in Music from Antiquity to the Avant-Garde*. Rochester, VT: Inner Traditions International, 1995.

Godwin, Joscelyn. "Kepler and Kircher on the Harmony of the Spheres." Talk presented at the Giorgio Cini Foundation, Oct. 29-30. 2007. See www.hermetic.com/godwin/kepler-and-kircher-on-the-harmony-of-the-spheres.html.

Goodrick-Clarke, Nicholas. *The Western Esoteric Traditions: A Historical Introduction*. New York, NY: Oxford U. Press, 2008.

Grasse, Ray. "The Songs of Dismembered Gods: Exploring the Archetypal Roots of Astrology". *The Mountain Astrologer* magazine. Feb./Mar. 2011, pp. 34-42.

Graves, Robert. *The Greek Myths*, Vols. 1 and 2. Rev. ed. London, England: Penguin, 1960.

Greenbaum, Dorian Gieseler. *Temperament: Astrology's Forgotten Key*. Bournemouth, England: The Wessex Astrologer, 2005.

Greenblatt, Stephen. *Shakespeare's Freedom*. Chicago, IL: U. of Chicago Press, 2010.

Greene, Liz and Howard Sasportas. *Dynamics of the Unconscious: Seminars in Psychological Astrology*. Vol. 2. York Beach, ME: Samuel Weiser, 1988.

Greene, Liz and Howard Sasportas. *The Inner Planets: Building Blocks of Personal Reality*. Seminars in Psychological Astrology. Vol. 4 [on Mercury, Venus, and Mars]. York Beach, ME: Samuel Weiser, Inc., 1993.

Greene, Liz. *Star Signs for Lovers*. New York, NY: Stein and Day, 1980.

Grose, K. H. and B.T. Oxley. *Shakespeare*. New York, NY: Arco Publishing Company, Inc., 1969.

Hall, Manly P. *Lectures on Ancient Philosophy: Companion to The Secret Teachings of All Ages*. New York, NY: Tarcher/Penguin, 2005.

Hall, Manly P. *The Secret Teachings of All Ages: an Encyclopedic Outline of Masonic, Hermetic, Qabbalistic and Rosicrucian Symbolical Philosophy*. Los Angeles, CA: The Philosophical Research Society, Inc., 1978.

Hamilton, Edith and Huntington Cairns, eds. *The Collected Dialogues of Plato, Including the Letters*. With Introduction and Prefatory Notes. New York, NY: Bollingen Foundation, 1961.

Hamilton, Edith. *Mythology*. New York, NY: Little, Brown, and Company, 1940, 1942.

Harpur, Patrick. *The Secret Tradition of the Soul*. Berkeley, CA: Evolver Editions, 2011.

Harwood, A. C. *Shakespeare's Prophetic Mind*. Great Britain: Rudolf Steiner Press, 1964.

Heninger, S. K., Jr. *Touches of Sweet Harmony: Pythagorean Cosmology and Renaissance Poetics*. San Marino, CA: The Huntington Library, 1974.

Hill, Wayne F. and Cynthia J. Ottchen. *Shakespeare's Insults: Educating Your Wit*. Cambridge, England: MainSail Press, 1991.

Hogarth, Peter with Val Clery. *Dragons*. Middlesex, England: Penguin Books, 1980.

Hollick, Malcolm. *The Science of Oneness: A Worldview for the Twenty-First Century*. Hants., U.K.: O Books, 2006.

Holman, C. Hugh. *A Handbook to Literature*. Based on the Original by William Flint Thrall and Addison Hibbard. 3rd ed. Indianapolis, IN: Bobbs-Merrill (Odyssey Press), 1972.

Holman, C. Hugh and William Harmon. *A Handbook to Literature*. 6th ed. Based on the Original Edition by William Flint Thrall and Addison Hibbard. New York, NY: Macmillan Publishing Company, 1992.

Houlding, Deborah. "Hippocrates, Humours & Temperament-Theory in the Traditional Teachings of Astrology and Medicine." www.skyscript.co.uk/humours.html.

Hughes, Ted, ed. *Essential Shakespeare: Selected and with an Introduction by Ted Hughes*. New York, NY: HarperCollins (Essential Poets series), 1991.

Hughes, Ted. *Shakespeare and the Goddess of Complete Being*. New York, NY: Barnes & Noble, [1992], 2009.

Huxley, Francis. *the dragon: nature of spirit, spirit of nature*. New York, NY: Collier Books (Macmillan), 1979.

The I Ching or Book of Changes. The Richard Wilhelm Translation rendered into English by Cary F. Baynes. (Bollingen Series XIX) 3rd ed. Princeton, NJ: Princeton U. Press, 1950/1967.

Jacobi, Jolande. *The Psychology of C. G. Jung: An Introduction with Illustrations*. New Haven Conn. and London, England: Yale U. Press, 1962, 1973.

Jansky, Robert Carl. *Interpreting the Eclipses*. San Diego, CA: Astro Computing Services, 1977.

Jayne, Sears. *Plato in Tudor England*. Unpublished work, 1993. On microfilm at The Warburg Institute, London, England.

Johnson, Robert A. *We: Understanding the Psychology of Romantic Love*. San Francisco, CA: Harper & Row, 1983.

Judge, Michael. *The Dance of Time: The Origins of the Calendar: A Miscellany of History and Myth, Religion and Astronomy, Festivals and Feast Days*. New York, NY: MJF Books, 2004.

Jung, C. G. *Archetypes and the Collective Unconscious*. 2nd ed. Trans. R.F.C. Hull. Bollingen Series XX. The Collected Works of C. G. Jung, Vol. 9, Part 1. Princeton, NJ: Princeton U. Press, 1959, 1969.

Jung, Carl G. and M.-L. von Franz, Joseph L. Henderson, Jolande Jacobi, Aniela Jaffe. *Man and his Symbols*. New York, NY: Dell Publishing Co. (Laurel), 1964.

Jung, C. G. Appendix in *The Secret of the Golden Flower: A Chinese Book of Life*. Trans. from the Chinese by Richard Wilhelm. Trans. from the German by Cary F. Baynes. New York, NY: Harcourt, Brace & World, Inc., 1931, 1969.

Jung, C. G. *The Spirit in Man, Art, and Literature*. Trans. R.F.C. Hull. New York, NY: Bollingen (Random House), 1966.

Katz, David S. *The Occult Tradition: From the Renaissance to the Present Day*. London, England: Pimlico, 2007.

Kelly, Robert. "The Music of the Spheres, or the Metaphysics of Music." www.aetherforce.com/the-music-of-the-spheres-or-the-metaphysics-of-music/.

Kermode, Frank, ed. *The Tempest*. (The Arden Shakespeare) Cambridge, MA: Harvard University Press, 1958.

King, Walter N. "Shakespeare and Parmenides: The Metaphysics of Twelfth Night." *Studies in English Literature, 1500-1900.* Vol. 8, No. 2: Elizabethan and Jacobean Drama. Spring, 1968, pp. 283-306.

Kinney, Jay, ed. *The Inner West: An Introduction to the Hidden Wisdom of the West.* New York, NY: Jeremy P. Tarcher/Penguin, 2004.

Klibansky, Raymond, Erwin Panofsky, and Fritz Saxl. *Saturn and Melancholy.* Studies in the History of Natural Philosophy, Religion, and Art. London, England: Nelson, 1964.

Knight, G. Wilson. *The Christian Renaissance: with Interpretations of Dante, Shakespeare and Goethe and New Discussions of Oscar Wilde and the Gospel of Thomas.* London, England: Methuen & Co., 1962.

Knight, G. Wilson. *The Crown of Life: Essays in Interpretation of Shakespeare's Final Plays.* London, England: Methuen (University Paperbacks), 1947.

Knight, G. Wilson. *The Imperial Theme.* London, England: Methuen & Co. Ltd, 1965.

Knight, G. Wilson. *Shakespearian Production: with especial reference to the Tragedies.* London, England: Routledge & Kegan Paul Ltd., 1968.

Knight, G. Wilson. *The Wheel of Fire: Interpretations of Shakespearian Tragedy with Three New Essays.* London, England: Methuen & Co. Ltd., 1967.

Lepage, John L. *The Revival of Antique Philosophy in the Renaissance.* New York, NY: Palgrave (Macmillan), 2012.

Levenda, Peter. *Stairway to Heaven.* New York, NY: Continuum, 2008.

Lewis, C. S. *The Discarded Image: An Introduction to Medieval and Renaissance Literature.* Cambridge, England: Cambridge U. Press, 1964.

Line, Jill. *Shakespeare and the Ideal of Love.* Rochester, VT: Inner Traditions, 2004/2006.

Lings, Martin. *The Secret of Shakespeare.* New York, NY: Inner Traditions International, 1984.

Littmann, Mark, Ken Willcox, and Fred Espenak. *Totality: Eclipses of the Sun.* 2nd ed. New York, NY: Oxford U. Press, 1999.

Lovejoy, Arthur O. *The Great Chain of Being: A Study of the History of an Idea.* Cambridge, MA: Harvard U. Press, 1936/1964.

Maguire, Laurie and Emma Smith. *30 Great Myths About Shakespeare.* West Sussex, England: Wiley-Blackwell, 2013.

Matthews, John and Caitlin, eds. *A Fairy Tale Reader: A Collection of Story, Lore and Vision.* Foreword by R. J. Stewart. London, England: Aquarian/Thorsons (HarperCollins), 1993.

Matthews, Caitlin and John. *The Western Way Omnibus: Vol. 1, The Native Tradition; Vol. 2, The Hermetic Tradition.* London, England: Penguin Books (Arkana), 1985/1994.

Maxwell-Stuart, P.G. *Astrology: From Ancient Babylon to the Present.* Stroud, England: Amberley, 2010.

McGinn, Colin. *Shakespeare's Philosophy: Discovering the Meaning Behind the Plays.* New York, NY: Harper Perennial, 2006.

Meyer, Marvin W., ed. *The Ancient Mysteries, A Sourcebook: Sacred Texts of the Mystery Religions of the Ancient Mediterranean World.* San Francisco, CA: Harper & Row, 1987.

Milward, Peter. *Shakespeare's Other Dimension.* Ren. Monographs: 15. Tokyo, Japan: The Renaissance Institute, Sophia U., 1987.

Moore, Thomas. *The Planets Within: The Astrological Psychology of Marsilio Ficino.* Great Barrington, MA: Lindisfarne Press, 1990.

Naylor, Edward W. *Shakespeare and Music: with Illustrations from the Music of the 16th and 17th Centuries.* London, England: J.M. Dent & Co., 1896. Now posted on the internet by Project Gutenberg: www.gutenberg.org/files/19676/19676-h/19676-h.htm.

Nicholl, Charles. *The Chemical Theatre.* London, England: Routledge & Kegan Paul, 1980.

Norton, Andre. *Huon of the Horn.* New York, NY: Fawcett Crest, 1951, 1979.

Nozedar, Adele. *The Illustrated Signs and Symbols Sourcebook: An A to Z Compendium of Over 1000 Designs.* New York, NY: Metro Books, 2008.

Nuttall, A.D. *Shakespeare the Thinker.* New Haven, Conn. & London, England: Yale U. Press, 2007.

Oken, Alan. *Alan Oken's Complete Astrology.* Rev. ed. New York, NY: Bantam Books, 1988.

Olson, Donald W., Marilyn S. Olson, and Russell L. Doescher. "The Stars of Hamlet". *Sky & Telescope* 96.5, pp. 67-73.

Parr, Johnstone. *Tamburlaine's Malady and Other Essays on Astrology in Elizabethan Drama.* U. of Alabama Press, 1953.

Partridge, Eric. *Shakespeare's Bawdy: A Literary & Psychological Essay and a Comprehensive Glossary.* New York, NY: E. P. Dutton & Co., 1960.

Perera, Sylvia Brinton. *Descent to the Goddess: A Way of Initiation for Women.* Toronto, Canada: Inner City Books, 1981.

Perry, Glenn, Ph.D. "The New Paradigm and Post-Modern Astrology". NCGR memberletter, Vol. IX No. 3, March 1992.

Perry, Glenn. "Science and Astrology: A False Dichotomy". NCGR memberletter, Vol. VI No. 4, April 1989.

Rabb, Theodore K. *The Last Days of the Renaissance: The March to Modernity.* New York, NY: Basic Books, 2006.

Rosenbaum, Ron. *The Shakespeare Wars: Clashing Scholars, Public Fiascoes, Palace Coups.* New York, NY: Random House, 2006.

Roud, Steve. *The English Year: A month-by-month guide to the nation's customs and festivals, from May Day to Mischief Night.* London, England: Penguin, 2006.

Ruperti, Alexander. *Cycles of Becoming: The Planetary Pattern of Growth.* Davis, CA: CCRS Publications, 1978.

Schneider, Michael S. *A Beginner's Guide to Constructing the Universe: The Mathematical Archetypes of Nature, Art, and Science.* New York, NY: HarperCollins, 1994.

Scott, Walter. *Hermetica: The Ancient Greek and Latin Writings which Contain Religious or Philosophic Teachings Ascribed to Hermes Trismegistus.* Eng. trans., Intro. and Appendix by Walter Scott. Great Britain: Solos Press, no date.

Seay, Albert. *Music in the Medieval World.* NJ: Prentice-Hall, 1965.

Shakespeare, William. *The Complete Plays and Poems of William Shakespeare.* William Allan Neilson, and Charles Jarvis Hill, eds. Cambridge, MA: Houghton Mifflin Company, 1942.

Shakespeare, William. *The Norton Shakespeare: Based on the Oxford Edition.* 2nd ed. Greenblatt, Stephen, ed. New York, NY: W.W. Norton & Company, 2008.

Shesso, Renna. *Math for Mystics: From the Fibonacci Sequence to Luna's Labyrinth to the Golden Section and Other Secrets of Sacred Geometry.* San Francisco, CA: Weiser (Red Wheel/Weiser), 2007.

Shumaker, Wayne. *The Occult Sciences iin the Renaissance.* Berkeley, CA: U. of California Press, 1972.

Smoley, Richard and Jay Kinney. *Hidden Wisdom: A Guide to the Western Inner Traditions.* New York, NY: Penguin/Arkana, 1999.

Sondheim, Moriz. "Shakespeare and the Astrology of his Time." *Journal of the Warburg Institute.* 2. 1938/39.

Spencer, Theodore. *Shakespeare and the Nature of Man.* Cambridge, England: Cambridge U. Press, 1943/2009.

Spurgeon, Caroline. *Shakespeare's Imagery: and What it Tells Us.* Cambridge, U.K.: Cambridge U. Press, 1935,1966.

Tarnas, Richard. *Cosmos & Psyche: Intimations of a New World View.* New York, NY: Viking (Penguin Group), 2006.

Tarnas, Richard. *The Passion of the Western Mind: Understanding the Ideas That Have Shaped Our World View.* New York, NY: Ballantine Books, 1991.

Tarnas, Richard. "The Role of Astrology in a Civilization in Crisis." The Carter Memorial

Lecture. Astrological Association Conference 2013. www.astro.com/astrology/ aa_article140203_e.htm.

Thorndike, Lynn. *A History of Magic and Experimental Science.* Vols. V and VI: The Sixteenth Century. New York, NY: Columbia U. Press, 1941.

Thorndike, Lynn. "The True Place of Astrology in the History of Science." Reprinted in *An Astrological Anthology: Essays and Excerpts from the Journal of the Astrological Association*. Vol. I, 1959-70. Selected and Arranged by Zach Matthews. London, England: The Astrological Association, 1995.

Tillyard, E.M.W. *The Elizabethan World Picture*. New York, NY: Vintage/Random, 1942.

Tindall, William York. *The Literary Symbol*. Bloomington, IN: Indiana U. Press, 1955/1965.

Usher, Peter D. "Kepler's Supernova and Shakespeare's *All's Well*". *JRASC*, June 2013, pp. 103-5.

Versluis, Arthur. *Shakespeare the Magus*. St. Paul, MN: Grail Publishing, 2001.

Voss, Angela. "The Power of a Melancholy Humour: Divination and Divine Tears."   www.academia.edu/472454/Divination and Divine Tears the power of a melancholic humour

Vyvyan, John. *Shakespeare and Platonic Beauty*. London, England: Shepheard-Walwyn, (1961) 2013.

Vyvyan, John. *Shakespeare and the Rose of Love*. London, England: Shepheard-Walwyn, (1960) 2013.

Vyvyan, John. *The Shakespearean Ethic*. London, England: Shepheard-Walwyn, (1959) 2013.

Walker, D. P. "Esoteric Symbolism." Originally in *Poetry and Poetics From Ancient Greece to the Renaissance: Studies in Honor of James Hutton*. Ithaca, NY" Cornell U. Press, 1975. Reprinted in *Music, Spirit and Language in the Renaissance*. London, England: Variorum Reprints, 1985.

Walker, D. P. *Spiritual & Demonic Magic: from Ficino to Campanella*. University Park, PA: The Pennsylvania State U. Press, 2000.

Wasserman, James. *The Mystery Traditions: Secret Symbols and Sacred Art*. Rochester, VT: Destiny Books, 2005.

Whitfield, Peter. *Astrology: A History*. New York, NY: Harry N. Abrams, Inc., 2001.

Whitney, John O. and Tina Packer. *Power Plays: Shakespeare's Lessons in Leadership and Management*. New York, NY: Simon and Schuster, 2000.

Wiles, David. *Shakespeare's Almanac: A Midsummer Night's Dream, Marriage and the Elizabethan Calendar*. Cambridge, England: D. S. Brewer, 1993.

Woodman, David. *White Magic and English Renaissance Drama*. Cranbury, NJ: Associated U. Presses, Inc. [Fairleigh Dickinson U. Press], 1973.

Wooley, Benjamin. *The Queen's Conjurer: The Science and Magic of Dr. John Dee, Adviser to Queen Elizabeth I*. New York, NY: Henry Holt and Co., 2001.

Wright, M.R. *Cosmology in Antiquity*. London, England and New York, NY: Routledge, 1995.

Yates, Frances A. *The Art of Memory*. Chicago, IL: The U. of Chicago Press, 1966.

Yates, Dame Frances. "Chapman and Durer on Inspired Melancholy." Text of a speech given at the U. of Rochester on Sept. 18, 1980. Printed in The U. of Rochester Library Bulletin, Vol. xxxiv, 1981.

Yates, Frances. "Elizabethan Neoplatonism Reconsidered: Spenser and Francesco Giorgi." Annual Lecture of the Society for Renaissance Studies delivered at University College, London on 14 January 1977.

Yates Frances A. *Giordano Bruno and the Hermetic Tradition*. Chicago, IL: U. of Chicago Press, 1964.

Yates, Frances A. "The Hermetic Tradition in Renaissance Science". Reprinted from *Art, Science, and History in the Renaissance*. Ed. Charles S. Singleton. Baltimore, MD: Johns Hopkins Press, 1968.

Yates, Frances A. *The Occult Philosophy in the Elizabethan Age*. London, England: Ark Paperbacks (Routledge & Kegan Paul), 1979/1983.

Yates, Frances. "Renaissance Philosophers in Elizabethan England: John Dee and Giordano Bruno." In *History & Imagination: Essays in honour of H. R. Trevor-Roper*. London, England: Duckworth, 1981.

Yates, Frances A. "Shakespeare and the Platonic Tradition." Reprinted from the U. of Edinburgh Journal, Autumn, 1942.

Yates, Frances A. *Shakespeare's Last Plays: A New Approach*. London, England: Routledge & Kegan Paul, 1975.

Yates, Frances A. *Theatre of the World*. New York, NY: Barnes & Noble, [1969] 2009.

Endnotes

Introduction

1 Adam Kirsch, in Bookends: "Should an author's intentions matter?," New York Times Book Review, March 15, 2015, p. 31.

2 Cumberland Clark, *Shakespeare and Science*, Birmingham, England: Cornish Brothers Ltd., 1929, p. 27.

3 British writer Patrick Curry distinguishes between the different levels of astrology, which roughly correlate with the three social strata of lower, middle, and upper class. The lower form of astrology is that of the itinerant fortuneteller, of modern almanacs, and those ubiquitous sun-sign columns (which professional astrologers disparage because of their over-simplification). The middle variety involves casting and interpreting horoscopes, tasks that require lengthy study, mathematical ability, and interpretive skills. These can provide astute psychological analysis of your character and information about cycles of challenge and opportunity as your life unfolds. "High" astrology is more abstract and considers profound religious and spiritual questions about the nature of the universe, the place of the individual in it, and the extent to which we are fated versus free. See Patrick Curry, *Prophecy and Power: Astrology in Early Modern England*, Oxford: Polity Press, 1989. Cited in Nicholas Campion, *A History of Western Astrology, Vol. II, The Medieval and Modern Worlds*, London: Continuum UK, 2009, p. xii. Both the middle and higher forms of astrology feature in this book and are the levels that Shakespeare's work reflects.

4 Johnstone Parr shows (in *Tamburlaine's Malady and Other Essays on Astrology in Elizabethan Drama*, University of Alabama Press, 1953) that George Chapman included the Duke of Byron's horoscope in one of his plays and that Christopher Marlowe did the same for Tamburlaine.

5 "The idea of Western character, of the self as a moral agent, has many sources: Homer and Plato, Aristotle and Sophocles, the Bible and St. Augustine, Dante and Kant, and all you might care to add. Personality, in our sense, is a Shakespearean invention, and is not only Shakespeare's greatest originality but also the authentic cause of his perpetual pervasiveness." He adds, "Falstaff and Hamlet are the invention of the human, the inauguration of personality as we have come to recognize it." Harold Bloom, *Shakespeare: The Invention of the Human*, NY: Riverhead Books (Penguin Putnam), 1998, p. 4. The quotation comes from the chapter entitled "Shakespeare's Universalism." Bloom's answer to "Why Shakespeare?" is "Who else is there?" Ibid., p. 1.

6 "We know what Milton thought about many things. He didn't believe in the doctrine of the Trinity; he thought the execution of Charles I was morally

right; he believed that married couples who didn't get on should be allowed to divorce. But we have no idea what Shakespeare thought, finally, about any major question. The man is elusive—we might almost say, systematically elusive. There is something eerie about a figure that can write so much and give so little away." A.D. Nuttall, *Shakespeare the Thinker*, New Haven & London: Yale University Press, 2007, p. 1.

7 Nuttall observes, "He can hardly have failed to notice what was happening around him ... Yet his plays are eloquent of nothing so much as a rosy unconsciousness of division. Neither the Reformation nor the shock waves it produced in the counter-culture of Catholicism—the Council of Trent— make any palpable impression on the plays." Ibid., p. 17.

8 Roland Mushat Frye also tries to verify Shakespeare's religious beliefs. Was he a believing Christian? Frye's conclusion is this:

> ... the mirror of Shakespearean drama was held up to nature, and not to saving grace. With Milton and Bunyan, literary creation was closely geared to theological ideas, and indeed was often structured by those ideas. In their works, both literary character and literary action were explicitly presented in terms of Christian doctrine, and the reader was explicitly informed of the Christian purposes which the authors sought to achieve. Even if there were no overt assertions of theological intent in *Paradise Lost* and in *Pilgrim's Progress*, however, critics would find pervasive and indeed inescapable evidences of such intent throughout both works. The same may be said of the works of Dante, Langland, and Spenser. *Nothing of the kind can justifiably be said of Shakespeare.* [Emphasis added.] Roland Mushat Frye, *Shakespeare and Christian Doctrine*, Princeton, N.J., Princeton U. Press, 1963, p. 267.

9 Nuttall, p. 5.

10 Harold C. Goddard comments in another way on the difference between drama and poetry.

> Drama is the most democratic of the arts in the sense that a play must have a wide and almost immediate appeal to a large number of people of ordinary intelligence if it is to have success enough in the theater to permit the author to go on writing plays.... he must keep no secrets if he is to feed that specifically theatrical emotion which resides in the sense of omniscience....
>
> Poetry, on the contrary, is an aristocratic art. The poet is bound to please himself and the gods rather than the public—to tell the truth regardless of its popularity, to seek the buried treasure of life itself. In that sense he cannot help hav-

ing a secret, and, even if he would, he cannot share it with the populace. When the moment of inspiration passes, he may not even comprehend it fully himself.

What wonder, if this is so, that, among innumerable playwrights and many poets, there have been so few poet-playwrights. The poet-playwright is a contradiction in terms. Yet a poet-playwright is exactly what the young Shakespeare was.

Harold C. Goddard, *The Meaning of Shakespeare, Vol. I,* Chicago: The University of Chicago Press, 1951, p. 61. Goddard goes on to say that consequently the poet-playwright must practice some deception, not only to fool the audience but also to placate the powers-that-be. He must sometimes speak a language not generally understood. Shakespeare may have done that not only to obscure his social and political views but also to embed some esoteric truths.

11 Letter to Sir William Young, 10 January 1773.

12 Harvard-educated cultural historian Richard Tarnas was intrigued by astrology precisely for these reasons: that it flourished during eras of intellectual and cultural creativity when science and culture were at their height; that it provided the foundation for the earliest development of science; that philosophers, scientists, and writers who espoused the astrological thesis were of high intellectual caliber: ... to my surprise ... [they included] many of the greatest figures of Western thought: Plato and Aristotle, Hipparchus and Ptolemy, Plotinus and Proclus, Albertus Magnus and Thomas Aquinas, Dante, Ficino, Kepler, Goethe, Yeats, Jung." Richard Tarnas, *Cosmos & Psyche: Intimations of a New World View,* NY: Viking (Penguin Group), 2006, pp. 62–3.

13 A well-known astrologer of the twentieth-century expands on this: ... modern astrology can be, in the words of Marc [Edmund] Jones, a *science of the relationship of all things to all other things in the space-time continuum."* Alexander Ruperti, *Cycles of Becoming: The Planetary Pattern of Growth,* Davis, CA: CCRS Publications, 1978, p. 54. Emphasis added.

14 C. G. Jung, Appendix to *The Secret of the Golden Flower: A Chinese Book of Life,* translated from the Chinese by Richard Wilhelm, translated from the German by Cary F. Baynes, NY: Harcourt, Brace & World, Inc., 1931, 1969.

15 Noga Arikha, *Passions and Tempers: A History of the Humours,* New York: HarperCollins, 2007, pp. 130, 133.

16 Cumberland Clark, *Astronomy in the Poets,* Bournemouth: Sydenham & Co., no date, pp. 59, 60.

17 Parr, p. 59.

18 Ibid.

19 This play, filled with horrors—like Titus vengefully killing one of Tamora's children and surreptitiously feeding it to her in a pie— is doubtless entirely keyed to the planet Saturn, associated with the troubles and travails of life. Another clue to this correlation is that one of the main characters is named "Saturninus." For more about Saturn, see Chapter 12.

20 Parr, p. 64.

21 S. K. Heninger, Jr., *Touches of Sweet Harmony: Pythagorean Cosmology and Renaissance Poetics*, San Marino, CA: The Huntington Library, 1974, p. xii.

22 Ibid.

23 Parr, pp. 67–8.

24 The debate about the extent to which human beings are fated or free has raged for centuries and is too complicated to address in detail here. However, for hundreds of years philosophers and theologians distinguished between "natural astrology" which allowed for planetary influence over nature (including weather and agriculture) and "judicial astrology" which applied astrology to human life, character, and destiny. Through the Medieval and Renaissance periods the for-mer was permitted and the latter denounced by the religiously orthodox. In *Cymbeline* Shakespeare has Imogen receive a letter from her husband Leonatus and exclaim, "O learned indeed were that astronomer [astrologer]/ That knew the *stars* as I his characters [handwriting]— / He'd lay the future open." (III, ii, 27–9) This certainly suggests that Shakespeare knew the difference between the two since he has Imogen express belief in the accuracy of judicial astrology.

25 Parr, p. 61, n. 39.

26 Donald W. Olson, Marilyn S. Olson, and Russell L. Doescher, "The Stars of Hamlet," *Sky & Telescope 96.5*, 67–73.

27 Peter D. Usher, "Kepler's Supernova and Shakespeare's *All's Well*," JRASC, June 2013, 103–5.

28 Shakespeare is certainly not the only writer to reference astrology, to use it as a literary device to describe characters, or to allude to the philosophical/ spiritual worldview that encompasses it. Long before Shakespeare, astrology features in the works of Chaucer, who used astrology for plot development and character depiction in *The Canterbury Tales*. One of the pilgrims travelling from London to Thomas a Becket's shrine, the memorable Wife of Bath, tells us that she was born with Mercury and Venus weakly positioned in her horoscope, "indicating a lecherous, lusty and ignorant character, driven mainly by instinct, rarely by intelligent thought. Chaucer gambled on his audience being suffi-ciently versed in the arts of the stars to understand this." Campion, *A History of Western Astrology, Vol. II*, p. 69. The celebrated Italian poet Dante too used the model of the seven planetary spheres for the seven circles of hell and heaven, mirror reflections of each other, in *The Divine Comedy*. In Shakespeare's own time, Edmund Spenser's works, especially *The Faerie Queene*, reflect the belief

in an orderly cosmos that contains the planetary spheres. Frances A. Yates, *The Occult Philosophy in the Elizabethan Age*, London: Ark Paperbacks (Routledge and Kegan Paul), 1983, p.147.

Writers today still draw on astrological principles for creative inspiration. It is rumored that Margaret Mitchell based both characters and places on astrological archetypes in her sweeping novel of the American Civil War *Gone with the Wind*. Scarlett is presumed to be an Aries (a fire sign, whose color is red—scarlet), Rhett Butler is a typical Leo, and the Wilkes' plantation is called, significantly, Twelve Oaks, possibly an allusion to the twelve signs of the zodiac. The principal characters do exhibit the personality traits associated with those signs: Scarlett, for instance, is extroverted, strong-willed, and self-ishly determined to survive. Another author, J. K. Rowling, created the Harry Potter saga to unfold in seven books, each one darker than the last, culminating in the most Saturn-like (Saturn being the last of the seven classical planets) in which the final battle takes place between good and evil. British astrologer Robert Currey believes that "Astrology provides the structure and basis of the characterization for the Harry Potter series. One of the first clues is that the author provides every major character in the books with a birth date." Notably, Harry Potter himself is given the same birth date as his creator, J. K. Rowling: July 31st. Rowling is evidently knowledgeable about astrology. In mid-2010 a woman submitted to the BBC TV series "Antiques Roadshow" a twelve-page handwritten horoscope prepared by Rowling in 1994 for a friend's child. This rare unpublished work was being offered for sale for 25,000 pounds. Notice of this was originally published on the internet site www.astrology.co.uk/news/jkrowlingastrology.html.

More recently, the 2013 Man Booker Prize was awarded to Eleanor Catton, whose novel *The Luminaries* is set in a New Zealand mining town in the mid-1860's and is explicitly astrological in conception and construction. A Character Chart provided at the beginning of the book lists twenty characters who represent the twelve signs, seven planets, and Earth itself. Each Part is prefaced with an astrological chart set for a specific date; the events in that Part occur on that day. Separate chapters within each Part have headings that allude to a planetary placement in that chart; what occurs in the chapter correlates with the meaning of the astrological placement. Chapter one of Part One, for example is headed "Mercury in Sagittarius," and the events are summarized as "In which a stranger arrives in Hokitika; a secret council is disturbed; Water Moody conceals his most recent memory; and Thomas Balfour begins to tell a story." All of these events are symbolically related to Mercury, which is associated with journeys, meetings, mental processes, and the act and art of communicating.

29 A complete text was published in Venice in 1497; later editions were issued in 1544 and 1551—but only in Latin.

30 First published in 1491, other editions of Bonatti's work appeared as late as 1581.

31 Ganivet's book was written in 1431 but re-printed numerous times, one edition appearing in 1596.

32 Parr, p. 120. I am indebted to Parr's thorough and detailed survey of astrological writings available between 1473 and 1625. See Parr, "Sources of the Renaissance Englishman's Knowledge of Astrology: A Bibliographical Survey and a Bibliography," pp. 112–50. Despite the fact that Parr's book has eighteen pages of printed works on astrology available during Shakespeare's time, he comments, "a complete bibliography of works concerned in any way with astrology is virtually impossible to compile. The subject, with all of its ramifications, is too large." Ibid., p. 130.

33 See Caroline Spurgeon, *Shakespeare's Imagery: and What it Tells Us*, Cambridge, U.K.: Cambridge University Press, 1935,1966; Bloom, *Shakespeare: The Invention of the Human*; Bertrand Evans, *Shakespeare's Comedies*, London: Oxford University Press, 1961/1967; Eric Partridge, *Shakespeare's Bawdy: A Literary & Psychological Essay and a Comprehensive Glossary*, New York: E. P. Dutton & Co., 1960.

34 Jonathan Bate, *Shakespeare and Ovid*, Oxford, Clarendon Press, 1993.

35 Roland Mushat Frye, *Shakespeare and Christian Doctrine*.

36 Colin McGinn, *Shakespeare's Philosophy: Discovering the Meaning Behind the Plays*, New York: Harper Perennial, 2006.

37 John O. Whitney and Tina Packer, *Power Plays: Shakespeare's Lessons in Leadership and Management*, New York: Simon and Schuster, 2000.

38 David Wiles, *Shakespeare's Almanac: A Midsummer Night's Dream, Marriage and the Elizabethan Calendar*, Cambridge: D. S. Brewer, 1993, pp. 129–30. This bias was particularly strong in academic communities in the early twentieth century. The century's leading figure in the study of ancient astronomy, Otto Neugebauer, a committed astrophobe (someone with an irrational fear of astrology), openly condemned astrology as the study of "wretched subjects" and then had to work hard to explain why anyone in academia would bother to write about them. See Otto Neugebauer, "The Study of Wretched Subjects," in the journal *Isis*, vol. 42, June 1951. This attitude has changed and is still changing, spurred by the research and writings of Dame Frances A. Yates, a British historian working out of the Warburg Institute in London whose works, particularly *The Occult Philosophy in the Elizabethan Age* and *Giordano Bruno and the Hermetic Tradition*, stimulated academic interest and strongly influenced my research and writing. Yates' argument, much debated since her statement of it, is "that the dominant philosophy of the Elizabethan age was precisely the occult philosophy ..." Frances A. Yates, *The Occult Philosophy in the Elizabethan Age*, London, England: Ark Paperbacks (Routledge & Kegan Paul), 1979/1983, p. 75.

Chapter 1

Shakespeare's Use of Daily and Seasonal Cycles to Establish Time and Set the Mood: Astrology in Essence

39 Nicholas Campion, *The Dawn of Astrology: A Cultural History of Western Astrology, Vol. I: The Ancient and Classical Worlds*, London: Continuum, 2008, p. 3. Campion adds: "As soon as human beings realized that sunrise, the most dramatic event of the day, was necessarily connected to the experience of heat and light, they were doing astronomy, in the modern sense of the word. And, the moment they attached meaning to this phenomenon, they were well on the way to becoming astrologers. They may have been aware of the equation of light, the presence of the sun, with good; and darkness, the sun's absence, with hidden dangers.... They may have made symbolic correspondences, perhaps between the sun's heat and fire, its colour and objects and red or gold colouring. Just when this happened is a matter of wild conjecture." Ibid., pp. 2–3.

40 "In Babylon the divine ruler, at least from the early second millennium onwards, was Marduk, the god connected to the planet Jupiter. In the Enuma Elish he was the son of Ea, but in another suggested etymology, the name Marduk is derived from the Sumerian Amar-Utu, meaning 'calf of Utu', the sun; literally, the presiding god of Babylon was the son of the sun god. And so, a tradition in which the sun and kingship were identified with each other began." Emphasis added. Campion, *Dawn of Astrology*, p. 39.

41 "The sun was universally recognized in medieval thought as the living, celestial symbol of kingship." Campion, *A History of Western Astrology, Vol. II*, p. 110.

42 David Woodman, *White Magic and English Renaissance Drama*, Cranbury, NJ: Associated U. Presses, Inc. [Fairleigh Dickinson U. Press], 1973, p. 100.

43 Quotation is from the Houghton Mifflin edition of Shakespeare's plays.

44 Heninger, p. 351.

45 Stephen Arroyo, *The Practice and Profession of Astrology: Rebuilding Our Lost Connections With The Cosmos*, Reno, Nevada: CRCS Publications, 1984, p. 2.

46 Clark, *Shakespeare and Science*, p. 6.

Chapter 2

The Planets, the Elements, and the "Humors": Why Shakespeare's Characters Are The Way They Are

47 Shakespeare knows his Greek mythology: Autolycus was a son of Mercury, and therefore of a similar quality. The examples mentioned are cited in Arthur Versluis, *Shakespeare the Magus*, St. Paul, MN: Grail Publishing, 2001, pp. 32–3.

48 Priscilla Costello, *The Weiser Concise Guide to Practical Astrology*, York Beach, ME: Red Wheel/Weiser, 2008, p. 19. See also Howard Sasportas, "Tricksters,

Thieves, and Magicians: the Many Faces of Mercury in Mythology," in Liz Greene and Howard Sasportas, *The Inner Planets: Building Blocks of Personal Reality*, Seminars in Psychological Astrology, Vol. 4 [on Mercury, Venus, and Mars], York Beach, ME: Samuel Weiser, Inc., 1993, p. 26.

49 See Hamlet's letter to Ophelia that begins "Doubt thou the stars are *fire*" (II, ii, 116), or Julius Caesar's rhapsodizing on the heavens: "The skies are painted with unnumbered sparks; / They are all *fire*, and every one doth shine ..." (III, i, 63–4).

50 Michael S. Schneider, *A Beginner's Guide to Constructing the Universe: The Mathematical Archetypes of Nature, Art, and Science*, New York, HarperCollins, 1994, p. 66. Schneider adds this important comment about the four elements: "These elements provided the mythopoeic way of referring to the modern scientific four states of matter: solids, liquids, gases, and plasma or electronic incandescence. The three denser states are familiar to everyone as ice, water, and steam. The fourth state, which the ancients called 'fire,' is known today as 'plasma,' the glowing electrified gases that 'burn' in the sun and stars and cause the fiery glow within fluorescent lights and neon signs. We laugh at the simplicity of the ancient concept of just four 'elements' comprising the world when today we recognize over one hundred varieties of atom. But no matter who looks at the world or when, we can find only four *phases* of *mater* [matter as represented by the ancient Earth Mother goddess], four clothings of nature." Ibid., p. 67.

51 Here is a more detailed version of the debate about the primal element and the subsequent development of the theory of the humors. Thales of Miletus (sixth century BCE) was one of the Pre-Socratic thinkers who avowed that it was water, while Heraclitus of Ephesus said that only capricious fire could account for the constant changes in all created things. Whichever element they favored, most early speculators, probably observing variations between heat and cold, humidity and dryness in the cycle of the seasons, added four categories to their theories: hot, cold, wet, and dry. These categories are obviously still fundamental to our experience of the days, months, and seasons of the year. We still talk obsessively about the weather, and in terms reminiscent of these early thinkers: it is either too hot or too rainy, for example, or so dry that there is an increased risk of fire.

The Greek philosopher Alcmaeon of Crotona (fifth-century BCE) was apparently the first who not only saw existence as embodying a tension between opposite pairs but also proposed that human health was a result of a balance between them. Thus he applied the theory of the qualities on a grander scale to the condition of a body on a smaller scale.

Another Greek philosopher who lived around the same time, Empedocles, established a school of medicine, setting out four "roots"— earth, water, air, and fire—rather than favoring just one. He theorized that everything in the visible world was made up of combinations of these four factors in fixed proportions.

In his thought we find the first fully-developed theory of four specific factors that are the building blocks of matter.

After him, the famous Greek physician Hippocrates (fifth to fourth century BCE) connected these "roots" with four main fluids in the human body: blood, yellow bile, black bile, and phlegm. He also correlated the qualities of these substances with the seasons: blood surges in spring, yellow bile dominates in summer, black bile is strongest in autumn, and phlegm flourishes in winter. In line with the famous Greek maxim, "All things in moderation," Hippocrates asserted that health could be defined as a balance between these four bodily substances or "humors ."

52 For an excellent history of the development of humoral theory in relation to astrology, see Dorian Gieseler Greenbaum, *Temperament: Astrology's Forgotten Key*, Bournemouth, England: The Wessex Astrologer, 2005. I am indebted to her for many details provided here.

53 Ibid., p. 19.

54 Ibid., p. 24.

55 Cleopatra is about to commit suicide, and her speech is in part an acknowledgement that she will soon drop the two heavier elements: her earthly body and its watery parts. However, "fire and air" well describe her temperament throughout the play, since she has both the powerful charisma and perceptive intelligence to attract great men like Antony and Caesar.

56 See, for example, *A Handbook to Literature*, p. 260, as well as Greenbaum.

57 Arikha, p. 55. Arikha's book is a delightfully written and comprehensive history of humoral theory, interweaving medicine, science, psychology, and philosophy.

58 Guido Bonatti, *Liber Astronomiae, Part II*, trans. Robert Zoller, ed. Robert Hand, Project Hindsight, Latin Track, Volume VIII, Berkeley Springs, WV, 1994, pp. 1–2. Cited in Greenbaum, p. 27.

59 Arikha, p. xx.

60 Cited in full in the section headed "The Number Seven" in Chapter 3.

61 Using some of the traditional formulae, Greenbaum analyzes charts of famous modern personalities to determine their temperament. Her example of a modern-day melancholic type is Paul Simon, whose song titles and lyrics resonate with decidedly melancholic feeling: "The Sound of Silence," "Bridge over Troubled Water," and "Think Too Much" are examples. Other melancholics she lists are Carrie Fisher, Matt Damon, and Elizabeth I. Greenbaum, pp. 97–100.

62 John W. Draper, *The Humors & Shakespeare's Characters*, Durham, NC: Duke University Press, 1945, p. 44.

63 Greenbaum's example of a choleric type is George W. Bush, with his horoscope revealing the "choleric's burning ambition and steadfastness of purpose."

She also remarks, "For cholerics especially it is easy to see the world as black and white, and a can-do attitude combined with activity (without thinking necessarily about the consequences of that activity) is embraced as the solution to any problem." She also notes that "hyperarrogance" may characterize the choleric type. Other cholerics she lists are Martha Stewart, Barbra Streisand, and Donald Trump. Ibid., pp. 91–4.

64 Greenbaum's choice of a well-known phlegmatic type is Beatle George Harrison. Known as "The Quiet Beatle," Harrison stayed in the background, "playing his guitar with a slowly and continuously refined skill, seemingly unperturbed at not being in the spotlight ... He spent several years slowly developing his style by listening to other guitarists ...—a true phlegmatic's approach to learning (imitation and slow deliberation brings you where you want to be)." Other phlegmatics she mentions are Nathan Lane, Liza Minnelli, Jerry Lewis, Johnny Cash, and Joni Mitchell. Ibid., pp. 100–3.

65 Raymond Klibansky, Erwin Panofsky, and Fritz Saxl, *Saturn and Melancholy, Studies in the History of Natural Philosophy, Religion, and Art*, London: Nelson, 1964, p. 105.

66 Ibid., p. 11.

67 Greenbaum's choice to illustrate the sanguine type is former British Prime Minister Tony Blair. Describing him as "sociable" and "affable," Greenbaum marvels at Blair's ability to keep his allies even when they disagreed with him. "Articulate, intelligent, sincere and genuinely interested in consensus ... it remains difficult not to like him—perhaps the mark of a true sanguine." Other sanguines she points out are Cary Grant, Venus Williams, Pope John Paul II, and Britney Spears. Greenbaum, pp. 94–7.

68 Determining your own type requires evaluating your entire horoscope, but your basic type might be hinted at by the element of your Sun sign. If you are born with the Sun in a water sign (Cancer, Scorpio, or Pisces), for instance, consider the degree to which you relate to qualities listed for the phlegmatic type. In the medieval and early Renaissance periods, however, more complicated formulae were used to determine the basic orientation of the personality, putting special emphasis on the Ascendant sign and its ruler and on the Moon. See Greenbaum, pp. 141–6, for the seven different methods used by astrologers to determine temperament between Ptolemy (first century CE) and astrologer John Partridge (1644–1715) along with her application of these methods to a research study.

Chapter 3

The "Elizabethan World Picture":
The Framework for Shakespeare's Plays

69 The I Ching or Book of Changes, The Richard Wilhelm Translation rendered into English by Cary F. Baynes, (Bollingen Series XIX), 3rd ed., Princeton: Princeton University Press, 1950/1967, p. 91.

70 Shakespeare's worldview is based on what is called the "Ptolemaic model," that is, the picture of the universe described by Claudius Ptolemy (late first century to second century CE), the most significant transmitter of astrological/astronomical ideas for many hundreds of years after him. Ptolemy was a Greco-Roman writer living in Alexandria, Egypt, the most intellectually alive city of his day, where the great Library of Alexandria was located. He was interested in everything and gathered material on astrology/astronomy, mathematics, optics, and geography.

Ptolemy's main work on astrology was his popular *Tetrabiblos*, a thirteen-book compendium of 800 years of astronomical/astrological information that included a version of Hipparchus' catalogue of fixed stars as well as a mathematical model of the universe that explained the motion of the Sun, Moon, and planets against the background of the "fixed" stars. Despite the fact that Ptolemy was not a practicing astrologer, his collected materials about astrology not only summarized the findings of Greek science of hundreds of years before him, but also influenced science, philosophy, and astrology for nearly 1,500 years after him.

Ptolemy's model represents what the universe looks like after the unfolding of the realms of the fixed stars, planetary spheres, and mundane world—in other words, after creation. While you can envision the unfolded cosmos vertically (looking both up to heaven, through all the intervening spheres, and down to Earth), Ptolemy's model is oriented to the horizontal, looking laterally from an Earth fixed in the center of the solar system, with five planets plus the Sun and Moon revolving around it in concentric crystalline spheres.

Although this view was being challenged during Shakespeare's time by Copernicus' heliocentric theory (with the Sun replacing the Earth as the center of our solar system), the heliocentric theory only gradually replaced the geocentric one in the century after Shakespeare. Writers in Shakespeare's era were still inspired by the Ptolemaic view, and nothing in Shakespeare's writings reveals that he knew about or shifted allegiance to the Copernican model. (See Parr, who shows that references to astrology and to the Ptolemaic worldview are common in the plays of Christopher Marlowe, John Lyly, Robert Greene, George Chapman, John Webster, and Ben Jonson, as well as William Shakespeare.) Rather, Shakespeare and his fellow playwrights "continually refer to the power of the stars; and there is no other single topic referred to in Elizabethan drama more often—unless it be mythology." Emphasis added. Parr, p. x.

This geocentric model reflects our experience of life on this planet. Though astronomers tell us that Earth is hurtling through space at the speed of 67,062 miles an hour, it does—weirdly—seem to be fixed and stable. Though it is Earth that moves, we experience the Sun rising above the horizon every morning. Though we ooh and aah over a lovely "sunrise" or "sunset," we should more accurately be saying "I saw a lovely earthturn this morning" or "this evening." So we continue to speak in the language of the Ptolemaic model— as does Shakespeare. In his works "The old ideas of the Ptolemaic astronomy ... occur repeatedly, though in a poetic and metaphorical sense, and not in a descriptive and scientific sense." Clark, *Shakespeare and Science*, p. 32.

71 See E. M. W. Tillyard, *The Elizabethan World Picture*, NY: Vintage/Random, 1942, p. 26 for a brief discussion of the transmission of these ideas. For a more detailed description, see Priscilla Costello, "Astrology and Shakespeare, Part II," at www.uraniatrust.org/articles.

72 Campion, *A History of Western Astrology Vol. 2*, p. 95.

73 In the first text of the Hermetic collection (the Corpus Hermeticum), the author has a vision during which an entity called Poimandres explains how the planets came to be. The creative power, "as god of fire and spirit, crafted seven governors; they encompass the sensible world in circles, and their government is called fate." Brian P. Copenhaver, *Hermetica: The Greek Corpus Hermeticum and the Latin Asclepius in a new English translation, with notes and introduction*, Cambridge: Cambridge University Press, 1992, p. 2.

74 Heninger, pp. 6–7.

75 The "emanationist" theory of creation was elaborated particularly by a group of philosophers dubbed the "Neo"-Platonists, especially Plotinus (third century CE), who built on Plato's ideas. Here is a clear account of their version of creation:

> The Neoplatonic cosmos is the result of a divine emanation from the supreme One, which is infinite in being and beyond all description or categories. The One ... in an overflow of sheer perfection produces the 'other'—the created cosmos in all its variety— in a hierarchical series of gradations ... The first creative act is the issuing forth ... of the divine Intellect or Nous, the pervasive wisdom of the universe, within which are contained the archetypal Forms or Ideas that cause and order the world. From the Nous comes the World Soul, which contains and animates the world, [and] is the source for the souls of all living beings ... The entire universe exists in a continual outflow from the One into created multiplicity, which is then drawn back to the One—a process of emanation and return .... Richard Tarnas, *The Passion of the Western Mind: Under-*

standing the Ideas That Have Shaped Our World View, New York: Ballantine Books, 1991, pp. 84–5, 86.

76 Mark Booth, *The Secret History of the World*, N.Y: The Overlook Press, 2010, pp. 37, 39.

77 The basic framework is derived from Tillyard's *The Elizabethan World Picture* as well as Arthur O. Lovejoy's classic work, *The Great Chain of Being*. See Lovejoy, *The Great Chain of Being: A Study of the History of an Idea*, Cambridge, MA: Harvard University Press, 1936/1964.

78 Tillyard summarizes a popular account of each level of "the Great Chain of Being," beginning with the lowest, from a shortened version of the *Natural Theology* of Raymond de Sebonde, originally in Latin and translated into French in 1550. Using Sebonde's work as an example of what must have been the common belief, Tillyard writes,

> First there is mere existence, the inanimate class: the elements, liquids, and metals. But in spite of this common lack of life there is vast difference of virtue; water is nobler than earth, the ruby than the topaz, gold than brass: the links in the chain are there. Next there is existence and life, the vegetative class, where again the oak is nobler than the bramble. Next there is existence life and feeling, the sensitive class. In it there are three grades. First the creatures having touch but not hearing memory or movement. Such are shellfish and parasites on the base of trees. Then there are animals having touch memory and movement but not hearing, for instance ants. And finally there are the higher animals, horses and dogs etc., that have all these faculties. The three classes lead up to man, who has not only existence life and feeling, but understanding. Tillyard, pp. 27–8.

79 Ibid., pp. 30–31.

80 Edith Hamilton and Huntington Cairns, eds., *The Collected Dialogues of Plato, Including the Letters*, With Introduction and Prefatory Notes, Symposium, NY: Bollingen Foundation, 1961, p. 555. Emphasis added.

81 Priscilla Costello, "From Ladder to Labyrinth: the Spiritual and Psychological Dimensions of Astrology," published in *Gnosis* magazine, #38 (winter 1996), p. 25. Reprinted in *The Inner West: An Introduction to the Hidden Wisdom of the West*, ed. and Intro. by Jay Kinney, New York: Jeremy P. Tarcher/Penguin, 2004. Though these "fixed" stars appear to be unmoving, they actually do drift very slowly—one degree of the zodiac every 72 years.

82 You can now find lists of this sort in books on Kabbalah (Jewish mysticism), in magical texts, in pagan and Wiccan writings, and in herbals. A comprehensive list can be found, for example, in a book by Melita Denning and Osborne

Phillips: *Planetary Magic: A Complete System for Knowledge and Attainment*, St. Paul, Minn.: Llewellyn Publications, 1992. This book includes visual representations of the seven main Greek and Roman gods and goddesses, along with equivalents from other cultures (Etruscan, Babylonian, Hindu and Egyptian). In Shakespeare's time an important source of elaborate lists of such correspondences was *The Three Books of Occult Philosophy* by Henry Cornelius Agrippa. See Henry Cornelius Agrippa of Nettesheim, *Three Books of Occult Philosophy*, Completely Annotated with Modern Commentary, Trans. James Freake, Ed. and Annotated by Donald Tyson, St. Paul, MN: Llewellyn Publications, 1995.

83 Klibansky et al, p. 165.

84 *Collected Dialogues of Plato*, "Symposium," pp. 562, 563.

85 Epist. ad Horontianum, 44, 3, cited in Klibansky et al, p. 164.

86 Cited in Klibansky et al, p. 165.

87 "Arguably the oldest civilization with a recorded history and a recorded religion is that of ancient Sumer. Our best estimates give us a date somewhere in the fourth millennium BCE for the appearance of the Sumerian city-states in what is now Iraq. There are votive inscriptions on cuneiform clay tablets that date to the third millennium BCE, which is the same era as that of the oldest Egyptian Books of the Dead. It is generally accepted that Sumer is the oldest known civilization in the Middle East, if not the oldest in the world ...." Peter Levenda, *Stairway to Heaven*, N.Y.: Continuum, 2008, p. 24.

88 Ibid., p. 25.

89 Ibid., pp. 25–6. Schneider expands on the "otherness" of the number seven:

> "The ancients referred to seven as the 'virgin' number. It is untouched by other numbers in the sense that no number less than seven divides or enters into it, as two divides four, six, eight, and ten, three divides six and nine, four divides eight, and five divides ten. Seven was also considered childless since it produces no other number (by multiplication) within the ten, as two produces four, six, and so forth." In line with this symbolism, certain ancient temples sacred to the virgin goddesses "were designed and constructed around the number seven. This tradition continued in Renaissance music, which called for seven voices when singing of the Virgin Mary." Schneider, pp. 224, 226.

90 Levenda, pp. 26–7.

91 Matt. 14: 1–12.

92 Manly P. Hall interprets this same story, only the goddess' name is given as Ishtar (or Astarte): "The story deals particularly with the descent of Ishtar through the seven worlds into hades, the inferior sphere. The allegory simply

signifies the incarnation of the rational soul in the substances of the irrational world. The irrational world is divided into seven strata by the rings of the planets upon which sit, according to the Mysteries, the Seven Governors of the World, each of whom bestows upon the incarnating soul one of the seven limitations of matter called veils by Hermes." Manly P. Hall, *Lectures on Ancient Philosophy: Companion to The Secret Teachings of All Ages*, NY: Tarcher/Penguin, p. 77.

93 See Levenda, pp. 12–16.

94 Schneider, p. 222. See all of Chapter Seven: "Heptad, or Enchanting Virgin" on the number seven.

95 Sunday for the Sun, Monday for the Moon, Tuesday for Tiu (the Germanic god of war equivalent to Mars), Wednesday for Woden (the chief Anglo-Saxon Teutonic god similar to Mercury), Thursday for Thor (the Norse god of thunder, akin to Jupiter, the principal Roman god of the sky and thunder), Friday for Freya (the Teutonic goddess of love, beauty, and fertility, like the Roman goddess Venus), and Saturday for Saturn. The day chosen by each of the three main Western religions as sacred (Islam: Friday, Judaism: Saturday, and Christianity: Sunday) is presumed to have symbolic significance related to each religion.

96 In ancient Greece recommended studies included grammar, rhetoric, and logic (or dialectic), later called collectively "the Trivium" for the three subjects. In the fifth century CE Martianus Capella writes *De Nuptiis*, a book of decisive importance to the history of education; he includes four other areas of study: arithmetic, geometry, music, and astrology/astronomy (the two being the same at that time). These additions were called "the Quadrivium," and the seven (the "Trivium" and the "Quadrivium" together) became the basis for the curriculum of medieval universities. They were still considered essential studies in Shakespeare's day.

97 Klibansky et al refer to Victorinus of Pettau (ca 250–305 CE) who "distributed the seven gifts of the Holy Spirit among the seven heavenly spheres." Saint Ambrose (fourth century CE) also writes, "According to this sevenfold circle of spiritual virtues we see created a sevenfold ministration of the planets, by which this world is illumined." Berthold von Regensburg (ca 1220–72 CE) many centuries later is still asserting, "There are seven stars in the sky. Thereby shall ye read and learn virtue, for if ye have not virtue ye shall never enter into the promised land, and therefore God hath shown forth the seven virtues in the seven planets, so that they shall show you the way to heaven." Klibansky et al. pp. 164, 166. Berthold was a popular preacher deeply interested in exhorting his listeners to higher moral ground.

98 In Ptolemy's compendium of astrology, the *Tetrabiblos*, he presents the idea that every person's life unfolds in seven ages, each one ruled by a planet in a sequence from the fastest to the slowest. The Moon rules the first 4 years of life, Mercury governs the next 10, then Venus the next 8, the Sun for 19 more, Mars for 15 years, Jupiter for the following 12, and Saturn for however many years are

left. See Peter Whitfield, *Astrology: A History*, New York: Harry N. Abrams, Inc., 2001, p. 64.

99 In the modern age, the "music of the spheres" has become more than a poetic metaphor, for the "idea of heavenly harmonics is making a comeback among astronomers." Kitty Ferguson, *The Music of Pythagoras: How an Ancient Brotherhood Cracked the Code of the Universe and Lit the Path from Antiquity to Outer Space*, NY: Walker & Company, 2008, p. 324. Starting in 1962, astronomers discovered that the Sun is like a ringing bell, with millions of different overtones. One astronomer created a tape reproducing the power spectrum of the Cosmic Background Radiation as an audible sound, covering the first million years of the cosmos in 10 seconds! So the idea that the universe is a cosmic symphony and that such sound has an order and pattern seems to be a constant in human speculation. Ibid., p. 325.

100 Music "held an essential position in the philosophy and theology of the period. Not only was it considered as the appropriate medium for addressing God, but it was also understood as a tool by which God and his works could be comprehended and interpreted. Music was thus unique among the arts, for it served as a requisite stage in medieval education, utilizing its physical manifestations as the basis of metaphysical extensions." Albert Seay, *Music in the Medieval World*, New Jersey: Prentice-Hall, 1965, p. 16. While Seay is referring to the esteemed place of music in the Middle Ages, the same view was held through the Renaissance.

101 If you pluck a string, it sounds a certain pitch. If you divide the string in half and pluck it again, the note that sounds will be exactly one octave higher and consonant with the first: it is the same note at a higher pitch. If you pluck the string at two-thirds of its original length, the sound produced is a perfect fifth in the ratio of 3:2. If you pluck a string at three-quarters the length of the original, the sound is a perfect fourth in the ratio of 4:3—and so on. This was a momentous discovery, and led Pythagoras to conclude that if music is expressed in precise numerical ratios of whole numbers, it must be the ordering principle of the world. See "The Music of the Spheres, or the Metaphysics of Music" by Robert Kelly, http://aetherforce.com/the-music-of-the-spheres-or-the-metaphysics-of-music/ pp. 5–6.

102 Even earlier, the Sumerians were creating music in harmony with the gods. The research of Professor Richard Dumbrill, a leading expert on the archaeomusicology of the Ancient Near East, shows that the Sumerians chose tones and their ratios to correspond to their divinities: "the cosmology of the gods is present in the notes and they define the fundamental structure of the scale...." See www.ancientlyre.com/historical_research for links to five videos in which Dumbrill discusses ancient music.

103 The cosmos may indeed be a gigantic musical instrument. In 1772 astronomers Titius and Bode discovered a rational mathematical pattern behind

planetary distances, now called "Bode's Law." Starting with a unit related to Mercury's distance from the Sun and adding to that value, you obtain numbers that approximate the actual mean distances of the other planets from the Sun. The pattern held with the discovery of the modern planets except for Neptune. More recently researchers have attempted to discover a harmony in planetary distance and "whenever the astronomical data are investigated with a Pythago rean attitude, cosmic harmony never fails to manifest." Joscelyn Godwin, *Harmonies of Heaven and Earth: Mysticism in Music from Antiquity to the Avant-Garde*, Rochester, VT: Inner Traditions International, 1995, p. 117. See pp. 112–40 for an overview of various approaches to discovering cosmic harmony (not only using planetary distances but also divisions of the circle and planetary orbits) from Pythagoras through Kepler and into the modern period.

104 Cited in Edward W. Naylor, *Shakespeare and Music: with Illustrations from the Music of the 16th and 17th Centuries*, London: J.M. Dent & Co., 1896. Emphasis in the original. Now posted on the internet as part of Project Gutenberg; the quotation is on p. 70 in that version. See *www.gutenberg.org/files/19676/19676-h/19676-h.htm*.

105 Instruments had symbolic significance in the Elizabethan age. While viols were praised, hautboys (or oboes) were literally "ill winds that blew no good; their sounds presaged doom or disaster." *www.britannica.com/EBchecked/topic/1369568/Music-in-Shakespeares-Plays/248487/Instrumental-music*, p. 1. Appropriately they sound in Macbeth at the opening of Act 1, scene vi just before Duncan enters Macbeth's castle where he will be murdered.

106 Noted in Catherine M. Dunn, "The Function of Music in Shakespeare's Romances," Folger Shakespeare Library, *Shakespeare Quarterly*, Vol. 20, No. 14 (Autumn, 1969), p. 394.

107 Seay, p. 20. Seay also refers to music as "the knowledge of numbers related to sound." Ibid., p. 3.

108 Shakespeare through Lorenzo is alluding to the Neo-Platonic idea that the body shrouds the soul, making it difficult to remember and reconnect with its original source and so be deaf to celestial music. Only advanced souls who discipline their desires and devote their energies to climbing the cosmic ladder are able to hear it. The "patens of bright gold" that Lorenzo mentions are the fixed stars, the backdrop to the wandering planets. The audience may also have remembered Job 38:7, which tells of a time "when the morning stars sang together."

109 Music "accompanies resurrection and reunion. This music may seem to perform a dual function: first, to suggest, as a symbol of pure aesthetic delight, the mystic nature of the act being performed; second, to anaesthetize the critical faculty, as does the overture in a theatre, and prepare the mind for some extra-ordinary event. But these are in reality twin aspects of the same function: for music, like erotic sight, raises the consciousness until it is in tune with a real-

ity beyond the reach of wisdom." G. Wilson Knight, *The Crown of Life: Essays in Interpretation of Shakespeare's Final Plays*, London: Methuen (University Paperbacks), 1947, p. 18.

110 The music of the spheres or celestial music (*musica mundana* or *musica caelestica*) is only one of three types of music alluded to by Shakespeare in his plays. In line with Renaissance theories about different types of music and their influence, first classified by the Roman writer Boethius (ca 480–524 CE), there were two other types. The Elizabethans, being fond of hierarchies, thought of these as high, middle and low. Celestial music is the highest, of course, reflected in our earthly world by the regular cycle of the seasons and the harmony of the elements.

While precise meanings of these types vary, the lowest type (*musica instrumentalis*) refers to what we generally deem "music" these days: the physical production of vocal or instrumental sounds arranged in time to produce a continuous piece that may exhibit rhythm, harmony, and melody. In Shakespeare's time this included knowing the mathematical basis of music theory (the ratios and relationships between different tones) and the practicalities of learning to play or sing well. Since music was one of the seven liberal arts, every gentleman was instructed in both its theories and the essentials of making music.

Musica instrumentalis is not "low" because it has no value. It is foundational, a necessary basic skill. An instance of *musica instrumentalis* shows up in *The Taming of the Shrew* when Hortensio woos Bianca by disguising himself as her music teacher and instructing her in the diatonic scale: "Madam, before you touch the instrument/ To learn the order of my fingering,/ I must begin with rudiments of art,/ To teach you gamut [a musical scale] in a briefer sort ..." (III, i, 62–5)

The second type of music, the middle type (*musica humana*), has the greatest potential impact on human beings since it functions at the level where the immaterial soul penetrates the material body. "For by imitating in the *musica instrumentalis* the ideal order of the *musica [caelestis]*, man might again achieve the perfection of *musica humana* which had been impaired by the Fall." Dunn, p. 392.

111 We seem to be rediscovering this in the modern age with the development of music therapy. "All sorts of studies verify the power of music to boost the well-being of medical patients.... Researchers have seen the stress hormone, cortisol, drop in brains that have been exposed to relaxing songs.... It has also been shown to decrease chemotherapy-induced nausea, vomiting and anxiety." Dr. James Aw, "Medicine to our ears," article in the National Post, July 2, 2013. Dr. Aw talks about professor Daniel Levitin's research at McGill University in Montreal demonstrating that music can do "everything from regulate one's mood to enhance concentration, stamina and motivation." Levitin and his colleague Mona Lisa Chandra have determined that "brainstem neurons tend to

fire in sync with a song's tempo, alternately raising or lowering body responses like heartbeat." See Daniel J. Levitin, *This is Your Brain on Music: The Science of a Human Obsession*, Penguin, 2006. All of the modern work in this area validates the Elizabethans' perspective on the power of music to affect every level of a human being.

112 The belief in the power of music to heal a disturbed psyche is not new in Shakespeare's time. In the Old Testament of the Bible, when King Saul's spirit is troubled, David is brought to him to cure his distemper by playing sweet music. "And so when the evil spirit of God came upon Saul, David took an harp and played with his hand, and Saul was refreshed, and was eased: for the evil spirit departed from him." I Samuel: 23.

113 Dunn, pp. 395, 398.

114 "The 'disorder'd string' is himself, who has been playing his part 'out of time ... and this has resulted in breaking the 'concord'—i.e., the harmony of the various parts which compose the state." Naylor, p. 33 in original, p. 17 on the internet.

115 *Collected Dialogues of Plato*, The Republic III, 398 (e, f), 399 (a, b), pp. 643–4.

116 G. Wilson Knight, *The Shakespearian Tempest*, London: Methuen & Co., Ltd., 1932. See pp. xiv–xx for a more thorough and nuanced explanation of his approach. Knight dogmatically asserts, "Tempests are thus all-important. Taken in opposition with music they form the only principle of unity in Shakespeare.... all may be shown to revolve on this one axis." Ibid., p. 6.

117 Cited in Heninger, p. 3. Spelling modernized.

118 Ibid., pp. 3–4.

119 It was more likely conscious than unconscious since "Renaissance thinkers made much of the correspondences between the systole and diastole of the human heartbeat and the alternation of upbeat and downbeat in musical rhythm." Dunn, p. 396.

120 From his commentary on Dante's *Divina commedia*, cited in Heninger, p. 292.

121 See Heninger, p. 10.

122 Ibid., p. 15.

123 Ibid., pp. 338, 340.

124 C. Hugh Holman and William Harmon, *A Handbook to Literature*, 6th ed., Based on the Original Edition by William Flint Thrall and Addison Hibbard, New York: Macmillan Publishing Company, 1992, Entry on "Image," p. 240.

125 Harvard professor Marjorie Garber mentions in her readable and insightful *Shakespeare After All* that this is one of her favorite images in Shakespeare's works, and observes that it points "forward to a moment when the two Macbeths, likewise '[d]oubtful' and exhausted, doom each other and pull each other

down." Marjorie Garber, *Shakespeare After All*, NY: Random House (Anchor), 2004, p. 701. I highly recommend this brilliant and comprehensive collection of essays on thirty-eight of Shakespeare's plays, the fruit of thirty years of teaching at Yale and Harvard. The Miami Herald called it "The best one-volume critical guide to the plays." Two other excellent literary critical commentaries on Shakespeare's plays are Harold C. Goddard's two-volume set of intelligent and provocative writing and the introductions to each of the plays in the Norton collection.

126 Spurgeon, p. 6.

127 "An item on one level of existence is described by comparing it with its correspondent item on another level of existence known to the reader. By this transfer of information from one level to another the poet explains the unknown by means of the known and fulfills the purpose of metaphor. Poets frequently employ a partial metaphor of this sort within the totality of God's inclusive metaphor. Often by this part, a poet implies the whole, so that by a single metaphor he activates the entire system of cosmic correspondences ..." Heninger, p. 341. Emphasis added.

128 J. E. Cirlot, *A Dictionary of Symbols*, trans. from the Spanish by Jack Sage, New York: Philosophical Library, 1962, p. 81.

Chapter 4

If All is Order and Harmony,
How Do Disorder and Disharmony (Evil) Enter?

129 Tillyard, pp. vii, 14. G. Wilson Knight agrees: "Kingship must be related closely to 'order'; and this concept is of profound importance in Shakespeare. Most of the history plays and many of the tragedies present a plot of conflict and disorder. Disorder in man, party, or state is a recurring theme. It is often related to images of 'disease' ... the king is himself an order-symbol, being both heart and head of the organic body of the state. So a close attention to the exceeding importance of Shakespeare's 'order' and 'disorder' thought will explain the almost superhuman importance of his kings, the continued emphasis on fidelity and allegiance as the purest forms of 'honour', and the consequent hatred of treachery, seen in an extreme instance in the plot against Henry V, where it is shown to merit sixty-five lines of vigorous and withering reproof prior to the offenders' execution. By viewing the king as a symbol of order we may often focus in the individual speech, act, or play a more than local and individual significance." G. Wilson Knight, *The Imperial Theme*, London: Methuen & Co. Ltd, 1965, pp. 6–7.

130 Knight, *The Shakespearian Tempest*, p. 23.

131 Costello, "From Ladder to Labyrinth ...," p. 25.

132 Several different explanations have been offered over the centuries for the world's and humanity's imperfection. Is it simply due to the downward pressure of creation whose energies are so powerful that they create ruptures at various levels (called the "breaking of the shells" in Jewish mysticism)? Or is it humanity's responsibility, an "original sin" due to disobedience at the very beginning of the creative unfolding? Or is it, as suggested in Platonic, Neo-Platonic, and Gnostic thought in the West, because the material world is an inferior copy of the higher one? Or is it due not to sin but to ignorance of humanity's true nature and origin, as implicit in some Asian religions and philosophies?

133 Many writers through history, though, argued against blaming the planets. The Neo-Platonists, theorizing in the early centuries CE, saw the heavenly bodies as exclusively benevolent. One of them, Iamblichus, wrote "For, in truth, all the astral divinities are good and are the cause of good, since they all equally gaze upon the good and complete their courses according to the good and the beautiful alone." Cited in Klibansky et al, p. 152. Later, William of Auvergne (ca 1180/1190–1249), a medieval philosopher and theologian who served as Bishop of Paris, was still arguing that the influence of the stars could only be good; this influence only turned to its opposite due to humanity's misuse of the planets' gifts. Klibansky et al, pp. 169–70.

134 Northrop Frye, *Fools of Time: Studies in Shakespearean Tragedy*. Toronto: U. of Toronto Press, 1967, p. 24.

135 It was Plato in the sixth and fifth centuries BCE who first dramatically opposed the two worlds: the above world of being, in which the ideal Forms exist in sublime perfection and never change, with the world of becoming, which is imperfect and is always changing. To the later Neo-Platonists the worlds are not quite so separate, but the good influence of the higher one is not easily received by the lower. According to the later Neo-Platonist Iamblichus, (ca 245–ca 325 CE), "The world of becoming, however, since it is itself multiform and composed of different parts, can because of its own inconsistency and fragmentation, absorb these uniform and homogeneous forces only in a contradictory and fragmentary way." Cited in Klibansky et al, p. 152.

136 Tarnas, *Passion*, pp. 44–5.

137 Cited in Klibansky, p. 184.

138 A concept in Jewish mysticism (emphasized by Isaac Luria in the 1500's), "tikkun ha-olam," is similar. It is the job of humanity to repair and restore a broken and fallen world, in part by rejoining the opposites divided in the act of creation.

139 Northrop Frye, *Fools of Time*, p. 1.

140 Tillyard, p. 76.

141 Cited in Campbell, p. 7. Spelling modernized.

142 Ibid. Spelling modernized. The other classical virtues besides Temperance were Prudence (or wisdom), Justice (or fairness), and Fortitude (or courage).] These four noble virtues were originally specified by Plato and Aristotle many centuries before Plotinus and later joined to the three theological virtues (faith, hope, and charity) by Christian theologians to create a total of "seven virtues."

143 Stanford Encyclopedia of Philosophy, http://stanford.edu/entries/cardano, p. 22.

144 Arikha, p. 121.

145 Antony Munday, from *The Mirror of Magistrates* printed in 1579 and cited in Campbell, p. 10. Again, spelling modernized.

146 Tillyard, p. 71. For a more detailed explanation of both physical and mental anatomy, see Tillyard, pp. 69–72 and Campbell, pp. 65–8 in Chapter VI, "The Anatomy of the Soul. The Anatomy of the Passions."

147 Arikha, p. 121.

148 See the section on "The Choleric Type: Keyed to Fire and Mars" in Chapter 2.

149 Arikha, p. 35.

150 Ficino, influenced by Galen and also a practicing astrologer and doctor, based his system on a synthesis of both pagan and Christian thought. Since he held the ancient view that "out there" and "in here" were one, he is "not only the man who set the philosophical course for much of the Italian Renaissance, but its great psychologist as well. He may be the first psychologist of the modern world." *Marsilio Ficino: The Book of Life*, A translation by Charles Boer of Liber de Vita (or De Vita Triplici), Dallas, Texas: Spring Publications, 1980, p. xviii.

151 Arikha, p. 18.

152 Ibid., pp. 58–9.

Chapter 5

Archetypes and Symbols: Exploring the Language of Astrology

153 Tarnas, *Passion*, p. 6.

154 Ibid., pp. 3–4.

155 Ibid., p. 10. Emphasis added.

156 Jewish mysticism or Kabbalah considers the 22 letters of the Hebrew alphabet as the sacred principles on which the universe is constructed.

157 For a clear and elegantly-written introduction to archetypes that explores some of these analogies in relation to astrological thought, see Ray Grasse, "The Songs of Dismembered Gods: Exploring the Archetypal Roots of Astrology," in *The Mountain Astrologer* magazine, Feb./Mar. 2011, pp. 34–42.

158 Tarnas, *Passion*, p. 8. I cite Tarnas frequently because he writes clearly, eloquently, and elegantly about Greek philosophy and the archetypes both in *The Passion of the Western Mind* and in *Cosmos and Psyche*. See especially pp. 3–15 in the former for a fuller and extremely nuanced discussion of archetypes in Greek thought.

159 Ibid., p. 10. Emphasis added.

160 Tarnas, *Cosmos*, p. 57.

161 John Vyvyan, *The Shakespearean Ethic*, London, England: Shepheard-Walwyn, (1959) 2013, p. 88.

162 Ibid., pp. 32–3. Vyvyan's three books are thought-provoking discussions of the influence of Platonic thought on Shakespeare's plays in which he consistently interprets the plays—very convincingly— as allegories. He also perceives a repeated structural pattern in Shakespeare's tragedies according to which the tragic hero is subjected to several temptations, one of which is either to accept or reject love. See especially *The Shakespearean Ethic*, pp. 5–6.

163 Ibid., p. 89.

164 John Vyvyan considers that ... the figures of the drama are not unlike transformation symbols between the conscious mind and the unconscious." Vyvyan, *Ethic*, p. 2. In other words not only analyzing your dreams but also seeing a Shakespearean play performed can facilitate a more harmonious relationship between different levels of your psyche and make you psychologically healthier.

165 J. C. Cooper, *Symbolism: The Universal Language*, Wellingborough, Northamptonshire: The Aquarian Press, 1982, p. 9. Emphasis added.

166 Cited in Hans Biedermann, *Dictionary of Symbolism: Cultural Icons and the Meanings Behind Them*, trans. James Hulbert, New York, NY: Meridian (Penguin), 1989, p. ix.

167 Some recommended symbol dictionaries are not only J. E. Cirlot, *A Dictionary of Symbols*, trans. from the Spanish by Jack Sage, New York: Philosophical Library, 1962, but also J. C. Cooper, *An Illustrated Encyclopaedia of Traditional Symbols*, London, England: Thames and Hudson, 1978; J.C. Cooper, *Symbolism: The Universal Language*, Wellingborough, Northamptonshire: The Aquarian Press, 1982; Hans Biedermann, *Dictionary of Symbolism: Cultural Icons and the Meanings Behind Them*, trans. James Hulbert, New York, NY: Meridian (Penguin), 1989; *An Encyclopedia of Archetypal Symbolism*, The Archive for Research in Archetypal Symbolism, ed. Beverly Moon, Boston and London: Shambhala, 1991; and *The Book of Symbols*, The Archive for Research in Archetypal Symbolism, Ed.-in-Chief Ami Ronnberg, Cologne, Germany: Taschen, 2010.

168 C. G. Jung in Carl G. Jung, M.-L. von Franz, Joseph L. Henderson, Jolande Jacobi, Aniela Jaffe, *Man and his Symbols*, N.Y.: Dell Publishing Co. (Laurel), 1964, p. 3.

169 Jung, ibid., p. 4. Emphasis added.

170 Ibid.

171 Cirlot, p. xxxi.

172 Ibid. The introduction to J. E. Cirlot's *A Dictionary of Symbols* is an excellent and wide-ranging discussion of the interpretation of symbols, covering among other topics the origin and definitions of symbols and their appearance in dreams and alchemy.

173 Titus Burckhardt, *Alchemy: Science of the Cosmos, Science of the Soul*, Baltimore: MD: Penguin Books Inc., 1967, 1971, pp. 11–2. Cited in James Wasserman, *The Mystery Traditions*, Rochester, VT: Destiny Books, 2005, p. 1.

174 Jung, *Man and his Symbols*, p. 90.

175 Knight, *The Shakespearian Tempest*, p. 14.

176 Vyvyan, *Ethic*, pp. 38, 14–5, 14.

177 Tarnas, *Cosmos*, p. 67.

178 Ibid.

179 For a wide-ranging exploration of the various meanings of Venus as well as other planets see Costello, *Weiser Concise Guide*, pp. 13–33.

Chapter 6

The Mystery of Artistic Creation and the Genius of Shakespeare — and Did He Create Consciously?

180 Nancy C. Andreasen, "Secrets of the Creative Brain," *The Atlantic* magazine, Vol. 314 No. 1, pp. 68–9.

181 Vyvyan, *Ethic*, p. 2.

182 A similar statement is made by Sir Philip Sidney, that the poet inspired by the philosopher "coupleth the general notion with the particular example." Cited in Peter J. French, *John Dee: The World of an Elizabethan Magus*, London, England: Routledge & Kegan Paul, 1972, p. 150.

183 L. A. Post gives details about how Metrodorus' memory system works: "I suspect that Metrodorus was versed in astrology, for astrologers divided the zodiac not only into 12 signs, but also into 36 decans, each covering ten degrees; for each decan there was an associated decan-figure. Metrodorus probably grouped ten artificial backgrounds (loci) under each decan figure. He would thus have a series of loci numbered 1 to 360, which he could use in his operations. With a little calculation he could find any background (locus) by its number, and he was insured against missing a background, since all were arranged in numerical order. His system was therefore well designed for the performance

of striking feats of memory." L. A. Post, "Ancient Memory Systems," *Classical Weekly*, New York, XV (1932), p. 109. Cited in Frances A. Yates, *The Art of Memory*, Chicago: The University of Chicago Press, 1966. Yates' book is a comprehensive and definitive history of the development of the art of memory from classical times through the Renaissance.

184 French, p. 148.

185 Ibid. Giordano Bruno, who visited England in the 1580's, may have brought information about the esoteric use of memory theaters into England.

186 Yates, *Art of Memory*, pp. 344–5. Emphasis added.

187 Ibid., p. 355. Yates mentions that the layout of the Roman theater as described by Vitruvius (first century BCE to first century CE) was constructed by using four equilateral triangles inscribed within a circle. She adds, "Vitruvius likens these four triangles to the triangles inscribed by astrologers within the zodiac to form the *trigona* of the signs (triangles connecting related signs of the zodiac with one another). The classical stage was thus planned in accordance with the *fabrica mundi*, to reflect the proportions of the world. May we not assume that the Globe theatre, with its 'heavens' over part of the stage, would also have been planned in accordance with the *fabrica mundi*, as was the classical stage, and that the four triangles inscribed within a circle would have played a part in determining its *frons scaenae* and gangways?" Ibid., p. 356. Emphasis added.

188 G. Wilson Knight, *The Christian Renaissance: with Interpretations of Dante, Shakespeare and Goethe and New Discussions of Oscar Wilde and the Gospel of Thomas*, London: Methuen & Co., 1962, p. 6.

189 Ibid., p. 7.

190 Ibid.

191 Ibid., p. 13.

192 Jung, "On The Relation of Analytical Psychology to Poetry," in *The Spirit in Man, Art, and Literature*, Trans. R. F. C. Hull, New York: Bollingen (Random House), 1966, p. 82. Emphasis added.

193 Introduction to *The Tragedy of Romeo and Juliet*, in *The Complete Plays and Poems of William Shakespeare*, William Allan Neilson and Charles Jarvis Hill, eds., Cambridge, MA: Houghton Mifflin Company, 1942, p. 975.

194 Ibid., pp. 1136, 1137.

195 Jung, *The Spirit in Man, Art, and Literature*, p. 82.

196 Knight, *The Imperial Theme*, p. xi.

197 Jung, *Man and his Symbols*, p. 25. Emphasis added.

Introduction to Section II:

The Plays

198 Astrology and contemporary psychology still mesh well. In the 1900's the eminent psychologist C. G. Jung investigated astrology, found correlations between horoscopes and his clients' psychic states, and referred them for astrological consultations. He wrote confidently that "Astrology is assured recognition from psychology, without further restriction, because astrology represents the summation of all psychological knowledge of antiquity." Emphasis added. Jung, from the Commentary on "The Secret of the Golden Flower." Jung's psychology correlates especially well with astrology because it focuses on the dynamic role of images and symbols both within a culture and within the individual psyche. These images and symbols carry a variety of meanings, just as they do in the astrological language.

199 Northrop Frye, *A Natural Perspective: The Development of Shakespearean Comedy and Romance*, New York: Harcourt, Brace & World, Inc., 1965, p. 72.

200 Hamartia is "sometimes literally translated as 'missing the target,' sometimes as 'vice' or 'flaw' or 'weakness', but perhaps best translated as 'mistake.' Aristotle seems to imply that the hero is undone because of some mistake he commits, but this mistake need not be the result of a moral fault; it may be simply a miscalculation—for example, failure to foresee the consequences of a deed. Brutus makes a strategic mistake when he lets Marc Antony speak at Caesar's funeral, but we can hardly call it a vice." *An Introduction to Literature: Fiction, Poetry, Drama*, 2nd ed., Sylvan Barnet, Morton Berman, William Burto, Boston: Little, Brown and Company, 1963, p. 459.

201 Hajo Banzhaf and Anna Haebler, *Key Words for Astrology*, York Beach, ME: Samuel Weiser, Inc., 1996.

202 Ibid.

203 Ibid.

204 C. Hugh Holman, *A Handbook to Literature*, Based on the Original by William Flint Thrall and Addison Hibbard, 3rd ed., Indianapolis, Bobbs-Merrill (Odyssey Press), 1972, p. 533.

Chapter 7

The Hidden Astrological Key to A Midsummer Night's Dream:
Cancer and its Ruler the Moon

205 In ancient, medieval, and Renaissance astrology, charts were interpreted differently according to whether the horoscope was for a day ("diurnal") or night ("nocturnal") birth, and so the word "night" in the title would have had a special meaning to anyone familiar with astrology. It would point to the importance of the Moon, since nocturnal horoscopes give the Moon precedence over the Sun.

206 Spurgeon, p. 260.

207 Robert Graves, *The Greek Myths, Vol. 1*, NY: Penguin, 1960, p. 355. Most mythologists, though, trace the word to the Greek a meaning "not" and "mazos" meaning "breast" in line with the belief that Amazons cut off their right breasts so that they could loose arrows from their bows more freely. The breast is a part of the body ruled by the Moon, though, so the connection to Moon symbolism still holds.

208 David Wiles, *Shakespeare's Almanac: A Midsummer Night's Dream, Marriage and the Elizabethan Calendar*, Cambridge: D. S. Brewer, 1993, p. 49.

209 Introduction to *A Midsummer Night's Dream* in the Houghton Mifflin Shakespeare, p. 89.

210 Shakespeare elaborates on Moon symbolism at great length in *I Henry IV*, where Falstaff and the young Hal, Prince of Wales, banter about the Moon:

> FALSTAFF: ... we that take purses go by the moon and the seven stars, and not 'By Phoebus [the sun] ...' when thou art king let not us that are squires of the night's body be called thieves of the day's beauty. Let us be 'Diana's foresters,' 'gentlemen of the shade', 'minions of the moon', and let men say we be men of good government, being governed, as the sea is, by our noble and chaste mistress the moon, under whose countenance we steal.
>
> PRINCE: Thou sayst well, and it holds well too, for the fortune of us that are the moon's men doth ebb and flow like the sea, being governed as the sea is by the moon.

(I, ii, 11–13, 20–9

This is a revealing speech for several reasons. Since Prince Hal is hanging out with the fat and frivolous Falstaff and his rowdy associates at nights, drinking, carousing, and apparently thieving— much to his father's dismay— he is indeed a man of the night or the dark side of life. To be under the dominance of the Moon, though, is inappropriate for him as heir to the throne, for kings should be bright and shining leaders of the day, unchanging in their quality, and therefore governed by the Sun. To fulfill the image of a king, eventually Hal must cast off Falstaff and take up his assigned role.

211 See Alexander Marshack, *The Roots of Civilization*, Mt. Kisco, NY and London: Moyer Bell Ltd., 1991.

212 Both secular and religious calendars combine solar and lunar cycles. "Within the half-year period from Christmas to Corpus Christi (or ... from the winter solstice to the summer solstice), two festive cycles were mapped out. The nativity cycle, incorporating the twelve days of Christmas, the feast of the Purification (or Candlemas) and the Annunciation (Lady Day, start of the calendar

year) was related to the solar cycle, and thus those feasts enjoyed fixed dates. The Passion cycle, incorporating Shrovetide, Lent, Easter and Corpus Christi, was related to the lunar cycle, and enjoyed movable dates." Wiles, p. xv. Emphasis added.

213 "The moon not only measures and determines terrestrial phases but also unifies them through its activity: it unifies, that is, the waters and rain, the fecundity of women and of animals, and the fertility of vegetation. But above all it is the being which does not keep its identity but suffers 'painful' modifications to its shape as a clear and entirely visible circle.... This accounts for the mythic belief that the moon's invisible phase corresponds to death in man, and in consequence, the idea that the dead go to the moon (and return from it—according to those traditions which accept reincarnation). 'Death', observes Eliade, 'is not therefore an extinction, but a temporal modification of the plan of life. For three nights the moon disappears from heaven, but on the fourth day it is reborn....'" Emphasis added. Eliade's comment adds a deeper significance to the timing of Theseus' and Hippolyta's wedding in four days, which now takes on the meaning of a collective rebirth. Cirlot, pp. 204–5.

214 Wiles, p. 73.

215 This date marks the maximum point of the Sun's apparent movement 23° north of the Equator to the Tropic of Cancer at the summer solstice. In Latin, "Sol" plus "sistere" means "the Sun stands." So the "solstice" was the moment when the Sun appeared to stand still for several days before appearing to turn south again.

216 This date was picked because the Bible mentioned that John the Baptist was born six months before Jesus, hence June 25th.

217 Michael Judge, *The Dance of Time: The Origins of the Calendar: A Miscellany of History and Myth, Religion and Astronomy, Festivals and Feast Days*, NY: MJF Books, 2004, p. 156.

218 14 Ibid., p. 143.

219 British folklore researcher Steve Roud agrees that, despite the title of the play, its events are more appropriate to May than to June: "Midsummer was undoubtedly one of the high spots of the festival year in medieval times, but ... the text makes clear that the play's action takes place on May Day Eve, which in European folklore is certainly the time when fairy and mortal worlds were believed to intermingle." Steve Roud, *The English Year: A month-by-month guide to the nation's customs and festivals, from May Day to Mischief Night*, London: Penguin, 2006, p. 297.

220 C. L. Barber thinks Shakespeare has meshed the seasons together, with Oberon resembling the May King and Titania the Summer Lady (since she says "I am a spirit of no common rate:/ The summer still doth tend upon my state . . . " [III, i, 136–7]). He also believes that "Shakespeare does not make

himself accountable for exact chronological inferences; the moon that will be new according to Hippolyta will shine according to Bottom's almanac. And in any case, people went Maying at various times . . . This Maying can be thought of as happening on a midsummer night, even on Midsummer Eve itself, so that its accidents are complicated by the delusions of a magic time. The point of the allusions is not the date, but the kind of holiday occasion." C. L. Barber, *Shakespeare's Festive Comedy: A Study of Dramatic Form and its Relation to Social Custom*, Princeton, NJ: Princeton U. Press, 1959, p. 120. Harold Bloom refers to Barber's observations, adding: " . . . the young went Maying when the impulse moved them. We are neither at May Day nor at Midsummer Eve, and so the title probably should be read as any night at all in midsummer. There is a casual, throwaway gesture in the title: this could be anyone's dream or any night in midsummer, when the world is largest." *Shakespeare's A Midsummer Night's Dream*, with an essay by Harold Bloom [from *The Invention of the Human*] New York: Riverhead Books, 2004, p. 4. The indeterminacy of the time is very much in line with blurred and indistinct perception below the sphere of the Moon.

221 Cited in *The Book of Symbols*, entry on "The Moon," Ed.-in Chief Ami Ronnberg, Taschen, 2010, p. 28.

222 According to Jung, part of the personal unconscious: ." . . consists of a multitude of temporarily obscured thoughts, impressions, and images that, in spite of being lost, continue to influence our conscious minds." Jung, *Man and his Symbols*, p. 18.

223 "Forest-symbolism is . . . connected at all levels with the symbolism of the female principle . . . The forest is the place where vegetable life thrives and luxuriates, free from any control or cultivation. And since its foliage obscures the light of the sun, it is therefore regarded as opposed to the sun's power . . . Since the female principle is identified with the unconscious in Man, it follows that the forest is also a symbol of the unconscious." Cirlot, p. 107.

224 Foster's TED talk, filmed in June of 2013, is an excellent introduction to the importance of sleep, noting theories about what happens in the body and brain while we sleep and exploring ways in which neuroscience is discovering connections between sleep and mental health. See www.ted.com/talks/russell_foster_why_do_we_sleep.html.

225 Cited by Foster, ibid.

226 Altogether there are 121 references to dreams in the Bible. See www.dream-interpretation.org.uk/christian-dream-symbols/biblical— dreams.html for a partial list.

227 For a fine discussion of the history and role of dreams in a variety of cultures—Greek, Biblical, Islamic, Aboriginal/indigenous, Indian—and information on lucid dreaming, as well as modern theories about dreams and dreaming, see the richly-illustrated book by David Coxhead and Susan Hiller, *Dreams: Visions of the Night*, NY: Thames and Hudson, 1976. The writers mention the

well-known dream of the German chemist F. A. Kekule that led to his discovery of the benzene molecule's formula, showing the practical value of dreams. Indigenous cultures, though, were more interested in dreams that were creatively inspiring. They hoped that the dreamer would return from the dream world with "a song, a dance, a cure, with information about the future, information about a distant place or with a new idea of some kind." Ibid., p. 16. Bottom's wish that Peter Quince write a ballad of his dream accords with this.

228 Skeptics try to explain all irrational or supernatural experiences along these lines. Charles Dickens' famous miser Scrooge in *A Christmas Carol*, upon first seeing the ghost of his former partner Marley, refuses to believe the evidence of his own senses, dismissing Marley's ghost as "an undigested bit of beef, a blot of mustard, a crumb of cheese, a fragment of an underdone potato."

229 The famous Greek physician Hippocrates, for whom doctors' Hippocratic oath is named, believed that dreams could reveal malfunctioning organs or causes of illness. Coxhead and Hiller, p. 6.

230 This refers to telepathic or predictive dreams, or visitations by the ghosts of the departed.

231 "To Jungians the dream is . . . an integral, important, and personal expression of the individual unconscious. It is just as 'real' as any other phenomenon attaching to the individual. The dreamer's individual unconscious is communicating with the dreamer alone and is selecting symbols for its purpose that have meaning to the dreamer and to nobody else." Jung, *Man and His Symbols*, p. x.

232 This idea, developed during the Greek and medieval period, is called the "Principle of Plenitude."

233 See C. S. Lewis, *The Discarded Image: An Introduction to Medieval and Renaissance Literature*, Cambridge, U.K.: Cambridge U. Press, 1964, pp. 40–44, 56. Lewis, in discussing the writers contributing to the development of this idea, starts by referring to Plato. In his *Apology*, Plato speaks of a voice, both divine and daemoniac, that guides his actions. In the *Symposium* he identifies these daemons as "creatures of a middle nature between gods and men." Lewis, p. 40. Lewis adds that they are "like Milton's 'Middle spirits—Betwixt the angelical and human kind'. Through these intermediaries, and through them alone, we mortals have any intercourse with the gods." Ibid., p. 41. In his essay *On the God of Socrates* the Latin writer Apuleius (ca 125–180 CE) (whose *The Golden Ass* is relevant to *A Midsummer Night's Dream* and will be mentioned below) elaborates on Plato by asserting that there are "middle spirits" with bodies of finer consistency than clouds so that they are not normally visible to us. They inhabit this region between the Earth and the Moon, the realm of air. Lewis next cites Chalcidius (fourth century CE), whose translation of and commentary on the first part of Plato's *Timaeus* from Greek into Latin around 325 CE was the only extensive Latin translation of a Platonic dialogue known to scholars in the West for almost 800 years. This work transmitted the worldview of the

Greeks into the medieval and Renaissance periods. According to Chalcidius, the space between Earth and Moon must be populated "lest any region be left void." Ibid., p. 56.

234 The space between Earth and Moon was divided into a lower region, the realm of air, and a higher one, the realm of "aether" or the fifth element or "quintessence." Beings that inhabited the higher one, closer to the Moon, might be immortal whereas beings that inhabited the lower one, closer to Earth, might be long-lived but still mortal.

235 One writer of Shakespeare's time, Reginald Scot, offers a hodge-podge listing of strange entities that adults have used to frighten children: "Our mothers' maids have so terrified us with bull-beggars [bogies], spirits, witches, urchins, elves, hags, fairies, satyrs, pans, faunes, sylens, tritons, centaurs, dwarfs, giants, nymphes, Incubus, Robin good fellow, the spoom, the man in the oke, the fire-drake, the puckle, Tom Thombe, Tom tumbler boneles, and such other bugs." Cited in Lewis, ibid., p. 125. Lewis is quoting from Scot's *Discouerie of Witchcraft* of 1584.

236 The word "faery" first occurs in English in John Gower's *Confessio Amantis* (ca 1450) in which the hero is described as being "as if he were of Faerie." See the Introduction to *A Fairy Tale Reader: A Collection of Story, Lore and Vision*, Chosen and edited by John and Caitlin Matthews, Foreword by R. J. Stewart, London, U.K.: Aquarian/Thorsons (HarperCollins), 1993, p. 10. The word derives from the earlier Old French "faerie" referring to the realm and activity of legendary beings featured in French epics and romances and called "faie" or "fee." Morgan le Fay, Merlin's enchantress in the Arthurian legends, is thus "Morgan of Fee or Faerie," a supernatural being with supernatural powers. Going back even farther, the word may derive "from the Latin 'fatum', or 'fate,' in recognition of the skill faeries had in predicting and even controlling human destiny. In France, *feer* referred to the faeries' ability to alter the world that humans saw—to cast a spell over human vision." Ted Andrews, *Enchantment of the Faerie Realm*, Woodbury, MN, 1993 and 2006, p. 12.

237 In an interesting detail that ties in with *A Midsummer Night's Dream*, in *Huon of the Horn* Oberon so favors Huon that he gives him a cup of pearl and silver (both associated with the Moon) that brims with fine wine if held by an honest man. *Huon of the Horn*, retold by Andre Norton, New York: Fawcett Crest, 1951, 1979, p. 50.

Shakespeare could have known the story of Huon since the medieval epic/romance was translated into English around the mid-1500's by John Bourchier, Lord Berners, and became very popular. Norton's retelling is based upon Bourchier's *Boke of Duke Huon of Burdeux* as it appears in the publications of the Early English Text Society. A play based on it, entitled *Hewen of Burdocize*, was performed in London in December of 1593. Shakespeare may have lifted the name of the faery king from either the translation or the play. As well, C. L.

Barber mentions that an "Auberon" was husband to a faery queen in a pageant performed for Elizabeth I at Elvetham in 1591. Barber, pp. 121–2.

In keeping with the tendency to lump a host of supernatural creatures into the middle realm, at the end of Huon's tale when Oberon withdraws from Elf-land and appoints Huon and his wife Claramonde as the new King and Queen of that realm, he summons all the creatures in his dominion: ."... there gathered from the four corners of that land a diverse and wondrous company. From the mountains came dwarfs and kobolds, goblins and air sprites. From out of the streams sprang merpeople and nixies and the green kelpies. From the fire darted forth the glowing salamanders and dragons, and out of the green earth came the elves and will-o'-the-wisps, nymphs and fauns." *Huon of the Horn*, pp. 189–90.

238 This characteristic particularly applies to faeries. In *A Dictionary of Symbols*, Cirlot writes that "Fairies probably symbolize the supra-normal powers of the human soul ... Their nature is contradictory: they fulfill humble tasks, yet possess extraordinary powers. They bestow gifts upon the newly born; they can cause people, palaces and wonderful things to appear out of thin air; they dispense riches (as a symbol of wisdom). Their powers, however, are not simply magical, but are rather the sudden revelation of latent possibilities.... *They are prone to sudden and complete transformations* ..." Cirlot, p. 96. Emphasis added.

239 Jana Garai, *The Book of Symbols*, London: Lorrimer Publishing, 1973, p. 53.

240 The spirit Titania embraces the earthy Bottom, winding him in her arms as "doth the woodbine the sweet honeysuckle/ Gently entwist; the female ivy so/ Enrings the barky fingers of the elm." (IV, i, 39–41) This poetic image is reminiscent of a detail from the creation story told in the collected Egyptian wisdom teachings, the *Corpus Hermeticum*, attributed to the ancient sage Hermes Trismegistus. In the first book, *Poimandres*, the cosmic Man breaks through the boundary of the planets' orbits, looks down on Nature, who falls in love with his image, and wills to dwell with her. "And the deed followed close on the design; and he took up his abode in matter devoid of reason. And Nature, when she had got him with whom she was in love, wrapped him in her clasp, and they were mingled in one; for they were in love with one another.

"And that is why man, unlike all other living creatures upon the earth, is twofold. He is mortal by reason of his body; he is immortal by reason of the Man of eternal substance." *Hermetica: The Ancient Greek and Latin Writings which Contain Religious or Philosophic Teachings Ascribed to Hermes Trismegistus*, Eng. trans., Intro. and Appendix by Walter Scott, Great Britain, Solos Press, no date, p. 50. Since these writings had been re-introduced into the West by Marsilio Ficino's translations in fifteenth-century Florence, it is possible Shakespeare may have encountered them.

241 Where might Shakespeare have found the inspiration for Bottom's transformation into a human being with an ass's head? One possible source is the Greek myth of King Midas, who most unwisely preferred music played by the minor god Pan piping on his rustic panpipes over that of the major god Apollo

strumming his lyre, and was punished for his foolish judgment. "Apollo would not suffer such a depraved pair of ears any longer to wear the human form, but caused them to increase in length, grow hairy, within and without, and movable on their roots; in short, to be on the perfect pattern of those of an ass." Thomas Bulfinch, *Mythology,* New York: Dell Publishing, 1959, p. 47.

Shakespeare may also have been familiar with a popular satire written many centuries before by Apuleius of Madeira entitled *The Golden Ass,* in which the main character through experimenting with magic is turned completely into one. Frances Yates describes Apuleius as "a striking example of one of those men, highly educated in the general culture of the Graeco-Roman world who, weary of the stale teachings of the schools, sought for salvation in the occult, and particularly in the Egyptian type of the occult. Born circa A.D. 123, Apuleius was educated at Carthage and at Athens and later travelled to Egypt ... He is famous for his wonderful novel, popularly known as *The Golden Ass,* the hero of which is transformed by witches into an ass, and after many sufferings in his animal form, is transformed back into human shape after an ecstatic vision of the goddess Isis, which comes to him on a lonely seashore whither he has wandered in despair. Eventually he becomes a priest of Isis in an Egyptian temple. The whole mood of this novel, with its ethical theme (for the animal form is a punishment for transgression), its ecstatic initiation or illumination, its Egyptian colouring, is like the mood of the Hermetic writings." Frances A. Yates, *Giordano Bruno and the Hermetic Tradition,* Chicago: U. of Chicago Press, 1964, 9–10. While having the shape of an ass, the poor hero endures many adventures during which he is beaten, mistreated, and forced to carry heavy burdens, before he regains his human shape through the grace of the goddess Isis.

The centerpiece of Apuleius' work is a retelling of the Greek myth of Cupid and Psyche. Psyche is a beautiful mortal woman, so beautiful in fact that the goddess Venus becomes jealous and determines to make her life miserable. She sends her winged son Cupid to "revenge fully the injury which is done to thy mother upon the false and disobedient beauty of a mortal maiden ... that she may fall in desperate love with the most miserable creature living, the most poor, the most crooked, and the most vile, that there may be none found in all the world of like wretchedness." Lucius Apuleius, *The Golden Ass,* trans. William Adlington (1566), New York: Collier Books, 1962, p. 110. Of course, this backfires, since as soon as Cupid looks upon the lovely Psyche, he falls in love with her himself, and whisks her away to his secret abode.

Venus' instructions sound remarkably like the punishment that Oberon intends to inflict on Titania. Once he has the flower that Puck will fetch for him,

> I'll watch Titania when she is asleep,
> And drop the liquor of it in her eyes.
> The next thing then she waking looks upon—
> Be it on lion, bear, or wolf, or bull,
> On meddling monkey, or on busy ape—

> She shall pursue it with the soul of love.
> (II, i, 177–82)

However, Shakespeare creatively changes both of these stories: while Midas only endures the addition of ass's *ears* to his human head and the narrator of *The Golden Ass* is transformed completely into an ass in form, Bottom gets only an ass's *head* grafted onto his human body. And Bottom, unlike Midas and Apuleius' narrator who are embarrassed and humiliated by their transformation, takes the change quite in stride. In fact, he seems rather oblivious of his sudden transformation, other than to marvel that ." . . methinks I am marvelous hairy about the face; and I am such a tender ass, if my hair do but tickle me I must scratch." (IV, i, 23–4)

242 Bloom, p. 4.

243 Ibid., p. 6.

244 The best description of this level of creation is found in Kabbalah or Jewish mysticism. This first invisible rung of the ladder of heaven above the visible Earth (on the "Tree of Life") is called Yesod, "the treasurehouse of Images." If you are able to rise to this level, you may have a vision of the workings of the universe. You might also gain the ability to perceive the shapes of things before they coalesce and appear in physical form—in other words, the ability to foresee the future. Modern esotericists have given different names to the substance of this dimension. One, Eliphas Levi, dubbed it "astral light," a watery stuff so fluid that it has no shape of its own but can take on any shape imagined or imaginable. See Richard Smoley, "Hermes and Alchemy: the Winged God and the Golden Word" in *The Inner West: An Introduction to the Hidden Wisdom of the West*, New York: Jeremy P. Tarcher/Penguin, 2004, p. 23. Interested readers may wish to look into several fine books on Jewish mysticism, among them ones by Warren Kenton (aka Zev Ben Shimon Halevi), or on Christian Kabbalah, among them *The Mystical Qabalah* by Dion Fortune.

245 *Collected Dialogues of Plato, Phaedrus*, p. 491.

246 Booth, p. 152.

247 Socrates anticipates Shakespeare again by describing the relationship between madness and artistic creation.

> There is a third form of possession or madness, of which the Muses are the source. This seizes a tender, virgin soul and stimulates it to rapt passionate expression, especially in lyric poetry, glorifying the countless mighty deeds of ancient times for the instruction of posterity. But if any man come to the gates of poetry without the madness of the Muses, persuaded that skill alone will make him a good poet, then shall he and his works of sanity with him be brought to nought by the

poetry of madness, and behold, their place is nowhere to be found. *Collected Dialogues of Plato, Phaedrus*, p. 492.

248 Another gifted writer of Shakespeare's time also plays with the effect of the imagination. Its power to alter appearances is a theme of *Don Quixote*, Miguel Cervantes' great novel written during Shakespeare's lifetime. (Cervantes died on April 23, 1616, the same day as William Shakespeare). Mark Booth's interpretation of the book highlights imagination's secret power:

> The whole novel is a play on enchantment, illusion, disillusion—and a deeper level of enchantment. . . . But the deepest level of meaning has to do with the role of imagination in forming the world. Don Quixote . . . is being shown that material reality is just one of many layers of illusions, and that it is our deepest imaginings that form them. The implication is that if we can locate the secret source of our imaginings, we can control the flow of nature. By the end of the novel, the Don *has* subtlely changed his surroundings. Booth, pp. 392–3.

249 In a later play, *Henry V*, Shakespeare plays with this interaction between the author's imagination and the audience's in speeches delivered by a Chorus who continually urges onlookers to envision a larger world than that contained on the circumscribed stage of the theater, one that posts from small palace rooms to vast battlefields, from England to France and back again:

> Can this cock-pit hold
> The vasty fields of France? Or may we cram
> Within this wooden O the very casques
> That did affright the air at Agincourt? . . .
> *And let us . . .*
> *On your imaginary forces work.*
> Suppose within the girdle of these walls
> Are now confin'd two mighty monarchies . . .
> *Piece out our imperfections with your thoughts*:
> Into a thousand parts divide one man,
> And make *imaginary* puissance.
> Think, when we talk of horses, that you see them,
> Printing their proud hoofs i'th'receiving earth;
> For '*tis your thoughts that now must deck our kings* . . .
> (Prologue, 11–4, 17, 18–20, 23–8)

The Chorus' speeches at the beginning of each Act continue to petition the audience's participation in the creation of the drama. So Act III begins, "Thus with *imagined* wing our swift scene flies/ In motion of no less celerity/ Than that of thought" and ends "Still be kind,/ And *eke out our performance with your mind*." (III, 0, 1–3, 34–5)

250 In India, "in the Upanishads, the Supreme Brahma is designated 'He upon whom the worlds are woven as warp and woof'. At the same time, the alternation of life and death, condensation and dissolution, the predominance of Yang or of Yin, are, for the Taoists, like the alternating 'waves' of thread in the weave of the fabric." Cirlot, p. 359. The very motion and framework of the loom replicated the structure of the universe, since it had four parts: the two rollers, one upper and one lower, symbolizing heaven and earth and the two uprights symbolizing the supports of the cosmos. The weaver's cutting the thread of the finished fabric is like the midwife's cutting of the umbilical cord, so "Weaving is a work of creation and of bringing to birth." Jean Chevalier and Alain Gheerbrant, *A Dictionary of Symbols*, Trans. from the French by John Buchanan-Brown, London: Penguin, 1994/1996, p. 1093.

251 Significantly the three Fates were sometimes described as the daughters of Night, perhaps hinting at our inability to see into our future. Clotho spun the thread of life, Lachesis held it and determined its length, and Atropos cut it at the point of death.

252 Zhuang Zhou is considered the greatest Taoist philosopher in ancient China. Here is Lin Yutang's translation of this dream: "Once upon a time, I, Zhuangzi, dreamt I was a butterfly, fluttering hither and thither, to all intents and purposes a butterfly. I was conscious only of my happiness as a butterfly, unaware that I was Zhuangzi. Soon I awakened, and there I was, veritably myself again. Now I do not know whether I was then a man dreaming I was a butterfly, or whether I am now a butterfly, dreaming I am a man. Between a man and a butterfly there is necessarily a distinction. The transition is called the transformation of material things."

253 This is an audacious scrambling of I Corinthians 2:9–10 from the Biblical New Testament, which cautions us that it is difficult to grasp what "God has prepared for those who love him" because they must be spiritually discerned. (I Cor. 2:14.)

254 In Western philosophy, several thousand years before Shakespeare's time, this same issue comes alive in Socrates' famous allegory of the cave, used to argue for the importance of an education in philosophy. Plato records Socrates describing human beings living in a cave with their legs and necks fettered, watching shadows projected on a blank wall and mistaking the shadows for reality. When one of them is freed and leaves the cave, ascending to the upper world, his vision adjusts itself so that he can see not only shadows and reflections, but "things themselves, and from these he would go on to contemplate the appearances in the heavens and heaven itself . . . the ascent and the contemplation of the things above is the soul's ascension to the intelligible region . . . ," where it gazes on the eternal and unchanging Forms or Ideas. *Collected Dialogues of Plato*, *The Republic*, Book VII, 514a–520a, pp. 747–752. In the Mystery religions of antiquity, in the mystical side of orthodox religions, and in various

secret societies, adherents were given knowledge or experiences presumed to awaken them to the realities of other dimensions. Even in the twentieth century, teachers like Gurdjieff and Ouspensky challenged their followers to become more awake. Coming to such an awareness or expanding one's consciousness is frequently compared to waking from a dream.

255 Shakespeare is eloquent elsewhere on the similarity of the theater and the theater of life. It is a theme he returns to in *The Tempest*, when Prospero dismisses the spirits he conjured in the masque with these words:

> Our revels now are ended. These our actors,
> As I foretold you, were all spirits, and
> Are melted into air, into thin air;
> And like the baseless fabric of this vision,
> The cloud-capped towers, the gorgeous palaces,
> The solemn temples, the great *globe* itself,
> [with a pun on both worldly life and the Globe Theater]
> Yea, all which it inherit, shall dissolve;
> And, like this insubstantial pageant faded,
> Leave not a rack behind. We are such stuff
> As dreams are made on, and our little life
> Is rounded with a sleep.
> (IV, i, 148–58)

Chapter 8

The Hidden Astrological Key to Romeo and Juliet: Gemini and its Ruler Mercury

256 Karl Menninger, cited in Schneider, p. 21.

257 Harold Bayley, *The Lost Language of Symbolism, Vol. II: The Origins of Symbols, Mythologies & Folklore*, London: Bracken Books, 1996 (1912), p. 1. Bayley's book is a quirky compendium of lore from many different cultures. Chapter 1 of his second volume (Chapter XIV in the two-volume set) is on "The Heavenly Twins."

258 "*Romeo and Juliet* is saturated with language games: paradoxes, oxymorons, double entendres, rhythmic tricks, verbal echoings, multiple puns." Introduction to *Romeo and Juliet*, *The Norton Shakespeare*, Based on the Oxford Edition, 2nd ed., New York: W.W. Norton & Company, 2008, p. 898.

259 Holman and Harmon, *Handbook to Literature*, 6th ed., p. 338.

260 Nicolas de Vore, *Encyclopedia of Astrology*, NY: Philosophical Library, 1947, p. 364.

261 "Mercurial" figures can often contain or switch to opposites. In alchemical representations of Mercury, the figure is represented as a hermaphrodite—that is, a being who is both male and female in one body (a blend of both the male

Hermes and the female Aphrodite). Possibly aware of this, Baz Luhrmann has the character of Mercutio portrayed as a cross-dresser in his 1996 film version of *Romeo and Juliet*. In line with Mercury's curious fluidity of essence, his character in Shakespeare's play belongs neither to the Capulet nor the Montague households; as a kinsman of the Prince, he enjoys access to both families.

262 To impress Juliet with the County Paris' worth, she compares him to an eagle, the king of birds which is at the highest level within the avian kingdom, as mentioned in Chapter 3. (III, v, 219)

263 Shakespeare here follows the classic tradition of the five stages of love, four of which are accomplished within minutes of Romeo and Juliet's first meeting. Acknowledged by Denis de Rougemont in his classic *Love in the Western World*, this sequence was first recorded by Aelius Donatus (fourth century CE) in his Commentary on Terence. As de Rougement comments, "The theme of the five lines of love can be traced right through the Latin poetry of the Middle Ages down to the Renaissance, where it reappears in Clemont Marot and Ronsard. . . . in 1510 Jean Lemaire de Belges wrote in his *Illustrations de Gaule*: 'The noble poets say that five lines there are in loves . . . gazing, speaking, touching, kissing, and the last [sexual congress].'" Shakespeare, of course, shows in Act III, scene v that the two have consummated their love, spending the night together in Juliet's bed, completing the fifth stage. Denis de Rougemont, *Love in the Western World*, trans. Montgomery Belgion, rev. and augmented ed., Greenwich, Conn.: Fawcett Publications, 1956, p. 126, n. 1.

264 Northrop Frye, *Northrop Frye on Shakespeare*, Ed. Robert Sandler, Markham, Ontario: Fitzhenry & Whiteside, 1986, p. 24. Emphasis added.

265 Arthur Versluis, *Shakespeare the Magus*, Grail Publishing, St. Paul: MN, 2001, p. 42. On the same page Versluis also quotes from the famous Renaissance herbalist Nicholas Culpeper's classic *The Complete Herball*, a portion of which was cited at the beginning of this section: "I knew these various affections of man, in respect of sickness and health, were caused naturally . . . by the various operations of the Microcosm . . . as the cause is, so must the cure be; and therefore he that would know the operation of the Herbs, must look up high as the Stars, astrologically . . . ." Emphasis added. See all of Chapter IV, "The Sacred Lore of Plants." This passage is also cited in Woodman, p. 51. See his entire chapter on "Healers in Shakespeare," pp. 50–63.

266 Banzhaf and Haebler, p. 28. This pictograph also symbolizes the "dual character of the creative forces which were thought to be responsible for life on earth." Ernest Busenbark, *Symbols, Sex, and the Stars In Popular Beliefs*, Escondido, California: The Book Tree, 1997, p. 202.

267 Busenbark, ibid.

268 Of the four temperament types, both Romeo and Juliet are obviously sanguine. This means that they exhibit a dominance of the air element, and so can be described as "hot and moist" as well as "joyful and amorous."

269 *Collected Dialogues of Plato*, *Symposium*, pp. 543, 544, sections 191a, 191d, 191e. Emphasis added.

270 Walter Burkert, *Ancient Mystery Cults*, Cambridge, MA: Harvard U. Press, 1987, p. 10.

271 Ibid., p. 11. Marvin W. Meyer describes their appeal: "The mysteries were secret religious groups composed of individuals who decided through personal choice to be initiated into the profound realities of one deity or another. Unlike the official religions, in which a person was expected to show outward, public allegiance to the local gods of the polis or the state, the mysteries emphasized an inwardness and privacy of worship within closed groups." Marvin W. Meyer, ed., *The Ancient Mysteries, A Sourcebook: Sacred Texts of the Mystery Religions of the Ancient Mediterranean World*, San Francisco: Harper & Row, 1987, p. 4.

272 Robert Macoy, from the *General History of Freemasonry*, cited in Manley P. Hall, *The Secret Teachings of All Ages: an Encyclopedic Outline of Masonic, Hermetic, Qabbalistic and Rosicrucian Symbolical Philosophy*, Los Angeles, CA: The Philosophical Research Society, Inc., 1978, p. xxi. See the entire chapter on "The Ancient Mysteries and Secret Societies."

273 Hall, ibid.

274 Booth, p. 184. The mystery schools dedicated to Mithras, which came to Rome by way of Phoenician pirates during the first century BCE and were especially popular with Roman soldiers, also conducted their initiations in "Mithraea," designed like caves. Strongly influenced by the Persian god Mithra, these mysteries were open only to men. Aspirants suffered ordeals, and then were purified, initiated, and feasted. Significantly, they were taught that it was possible to climb an upward way: "There is a ladder with seven gates and at its top an eighth gate. . . ." Origen, quoting the pagan writer Celsus in *Contra Celsum*, cited in Meyer, p. 209. Celsus' description is supported by archaeological evidence. At one Mithraeum in Ostia, Italy, the floor is laid out with seven stations decorated with appropriate symbols. These represented seven grades of initiation, beginning with Corax ("Raven") and ending with Pater ("Father"). Given the emphasis on the number seven, they are obviously mundane counterparts to the planetary or heavenly spheres.

275 See, for example, Joseph L. Henderson, "Ancient Myths and Modern Man," in *Man and his Symbols*, NY: Dell Publishing, 1964, pp. 154, 155.

276 Shakespeare is not the only creative artist to use the archetypal pattern of the "love-death" that takes place in a location analogous to the underworld. Verdi's great operatic masterpiece "Aida" sets its final scene in an underground vault in the Temple of Vulcan in which Radames, captain of the Egyptian army, has been walled up as a traitor. He betrayed the route of his army's attack for love of Aida, daughter of the Ethiopian king, so that she could escape. Instead, unknown to anyone, she hides in the underground chamber to end her life with him. They sing a duet, "To die! So pure and lovely," bidding farewell to earthly

griefs and sorrows. Above them the jealous and defeated Amneris, daughter of the Egyptian king and in love with Radames too, weeps in frustration at Radames' fate, while below in the crypt Aida dies ecstatically in Radames' arms.

277 Biedermann, pp. 216–7.

278 Cirlot, p. 185.

279 Northrop Frye, *Northrop Frye on Shakespeare*, p. 32.

Chapter 9

The Hidden Astrological Key to The Merchant of Venice: Taurus and its Ruler Venus and Libra and its Ruler Venus

280 Thomas Bulfinch, *Mythology*, New York: Dell Publishing, 1959, p. 17.

281 *Collected Dialogues of Plato, Symposium*, pp. 535, 537.

282 One version of her creation story was that she was generated after Saturn castrated his father. The drops of Cronus' sperm falling into the ocean birthed her, hence her Greek name Aphrodite (the "foam born"). This level of Venus rarely figures into Shakespeare's comedies and romances, though lust-driven characters do show up in several of the "problem plays." In *Measure for Measure*, Angelo, the temporary ruler of Vienna, attempts to blackmail a young novice by promising to spare her brother's life in exchange for bedding her. In *Troilus and Cressida*, the lovely Cressida, after swearing faithfulness to Troilus, is handed over to the Greeks in a prisoner exchange and allows herself to be seduced by Diomedes. Characters in that play rail that it is all "Lechery, lechery; still wars and lechery; nothing else holds fashion" (V, ii, 196–7) "Wars and lechery" refer to the most debased and negative interpretations of Mars ("wars") and Venus ("lechery").

283 *Collected Dialogues of Plato, Symposium*, p. 548.

284 M. R. Wright, *Cosmology in Antiquity*, London and NY: Routledge, 1995, p. 99.

285 This was increasingly true in Shakespeare's time. Stephen Greenblatt expands on this: "The source of wealth for most of the ruling class, and the essential measure of social status, was landownership, and changes to the social structure in the sixteenth and seventeenth centuries were largely driven by the land market." He adds that in the fifteenth century merchants, manufacturers, and urban professionals owned perhaps a quarter of the land, and by the late seventeenth century they had purchased almost half. Stephen Greenblatt, General Introduction, *The Norton Shakespeare*, p. 7.

286 Liz Greene, "The Great Harlot: The Mythology and Psychology of Venus" in *The Inner Planets: Building Blocks of Personal Reality*, by Liz Greene and Howard Sasportas, Seminars in Psychological Astrology, Volume 4, York Beach, Maine: Samuel Weiser, Inc., 1993, p. 89.

287 Adele Nozedar, *The Illustrated Signs & Symbols Sourcebook: An A to Z Compendium of Over 1000 Designs*, New York: Metro Books (Sterling), 2008, p. 240.

288 Peter Ackroyd notes that "There are forty references by Shakespeare to Venice and its dominions, not all of them complimentary. Two of his plays, *The Merchant of Venice* (1598) and *Othello* (1602), are set wholly or partly in that city. The first act of *Othello*, with its dark street and its shuttered house, well captures the imaginative ambience of the place." Peter Ackroyd, *Venice: Pure City*, New York: Doubleday, 2009, p. 237.

289 Ibid., pp. 4, 14. See particularly chapter 13, "The Merchants of Venice."

290 Rabb defines a capitalist system as one in which "transactions became monetarized, the marketplace controlled economic behavior, supply and demand rather than the 'just price' determined wages and prices, and goods and services were exchanged relatively freely." Theodore K. Rabb, *The Last Days of the Renaissance: The March to Modernity*, New York: Basic Books, 2006, p. 64–5.

291 Whether or not you agree with the idea that capitalism's ascendency is principally due to the increased emphasis on qualities that Rabb mentions ("sober judgment, long-term planning, careful record keeping, rational pursuit of sustained profit") as he says, "the inescapable conclusion is that it came into being during the Renaissance, and that it is one of the defining characteristics of the age. Nor is there any doubt that contemporaries noticed what was happening. Since Shakespeare commented on just about every major issue that his society confronted, it is no surprise that, despite the word not having been invented, he wrote a play (*The Merchant of Venice*) about capitalism and set it in *Venice, capitalism's quintessential home*." Emphasis added. Ibid., pp. 66–7.

292 Ackroyd, p. 268.

293 Greene, *The Inner Planets*, p. 75.

294 Gold not only represents the highest in the West, but also in the East. "Gold is a symbol of purity and is considered sacred, but also signals prosperity. . . . Gold has a rich tradition in the Hindu epics, the Ramayana and the Mahabharata," writes Ganesh Rathnam. "It was associated with the pomp and splendor of the gods and kings who appear in these mythological stories." E-newsletter: *Laissez Faire Today*, Jan. 8, 2013.

295 Dante's guide Virgil justifies the placement of sinners at the various levels of hell by also referring to the works of Aristotle. Usurers belong there because there are only two legitimate sources of wealth: natural resources ("nature") and human activity ("art"); usury is neither and is therefore unacceptable.

296 For a clear and concise overview of the history of usury, see an article by Norman Jones of Utah State University posted on the Economic History Services web site: http://eh.net/encyclopedia/article/jones.usury

297 This is reminiscent of Katharine's long speech to Petruccio and others at the end of *The Taming of the Shrew* when she waxes eloquent about a woman's subservient status relative to her husband—a speech which modern audiences find hard to believe. Both Katharine and Portia are expounding "the party line" that accords with social customs and religious exhortations, though not necessarily with human experience. And not with the character of either one of them.

298 Inflexible law complicates the plot in other Shakespearean plays: in *A Midsummer Night's Dream* in which Egeus demands that if his daughter continues to flout his will, she be executed; in *The Comedy of Errors*, in which Egeon is condemned to death by an inflexible law that even a sympathetic Duke presumably cannot soften; and here in *The Merchant of Venice* in which Antonio's contract with Shylock must be honored since Venetian law cannot be revoked. When Bassanio urges the disguised Portia to "wrest once the law to your authority./ To do a great right, do a little wrong," she refuses, avowing that "There is no power in Venice/ Can alter a decree established. 'Twill be recorded for a precedent,/ And many an error by the same example/ Will rush into the state." (IV, i, 210–11, 213–17)

299 "Mercy," from *Theopedia: an Encyclopedia of Biblical Christianity*, www.theopedia.com/mercy.

300 Nozedar, p. 133.

301 As far back as the Greek philosopher Plato, thinkers debated the nature of love and its expression in friendship. One of the guests at a banquet in Athens, as described in the *Symposium*, avows that there are two kinds of love, one earthy (Aphrodite Pandemus) and one heavenly (Aphrodite Urania). The earthly Aphrodite (or Venus) "governs the passions of the vulgar," for she inspires love of the body rather than of the soul and inspires liaisons with the shallowest sorts. Pausanius, the speaker at the supper party, implies that this characterizes heterosexual relationships. The heavenly Aphrodite, on the other hand, ." . . springs from a goddess whose attributes have nothing of the female, but are altogether male, and who is also the elder of the two, and innocent of any hint of lewdness. And so those who are inspired by this other Love turn rather to the male, preferring the more vigorous and intellectual bent." *Collected Dialogues of Plato, Symposium*, p. 535.

Later in European history, especially in the twelfth and thirteenth centuries, the same idea, that love between males was superior to love between the sexes, recurs in the troubadour poetry and the culture of the south of France. The courtly love ideal, which spread beyond France, conveyed the message that "friendship between men usually rank[ed] higher than love for a mistress, being more disinterested and less of a slavery to passion or an imperious love god." Frye, *A Natural Perspective*, p. 85. This belief was stated through the medieval period and was still current in Shakespeare's time.

302 For a particularly fine and extensive treatment of the problem of the outsider, see Stephen Greenblatt, *Shakespeare's Freedom*, Chicago: U. of Chicago Press, 2010, Chapter 3: "The Limits of Hatred," especially pp. 49–52.

303 That Jessica is instructed to stay indoors has to do with Venetian customs: "Who is the woman on the balcony? It is a familiar Venetian motif. . . . The window is an opportunity for sexual display. It is the way of showing off the goods." Ackroyd, p. 267. Shylock's instructing Jessica to shut the window is done to protect her from lascivious gazes and from appearing to seek sexual contact.

304 The one public case involving a (converted) Jew was that of Roderigo Lopez, a Portuguese physician to Queen Elizabeth I. Becoming involved with court intrigues related to Spain's designs on England and a failed invasion of Portugal, Lopez was accused of trying to poison the Queen, charged with treason, and executed. Some believe him to be a prototype for Shylock. See www. jewishencyclopedia.com/articles/10109-lopez-rodrigo for more on Lopez. One similarity between Lopez and Shylock is that Lopez had been forced to convert. "Furthermore, in the play, the character Gratiano describes Shylock as being possessed by the spirit of a wolf that was 'hanged for human slaughter'. This is significant because the surname Lopez originally means Son of Lope and Lope is derived from Latin meaning 'wolf'." See www.digitalbard.lmc.gatech.edu/wiki/index.php/Doctor_Rodrigo_Lopez.

305 Margaret Atwood, *Payback: Debt and the Shadow Side of Wealth*, Toronto, Canada: House of Anansi Press, 2008, pp. 154–5. This is a brilliant, wide-ranging, and entertaining rumination on all aspects of money and debt. For a brief but well-researched discussion of Libra and its symbol the scales, see pp. 24–5.

306 Liz Greene, *Star Signs for Lovers*, New York: Stein and Day, 1981, pp. 219–20.

Chapter 10

The Hidden Astrological Key to Macbeth: Scorpio and its Ruler Mars

307 This passage came to my attention in Versluis, p. 32.

308 Fittingly, the emperor Augustus Caesar built a large temple to Mars that was similar in design but larger by half than the Temple of Venus in the Forum of Julius: "On my own ground I built the temple of Mars Ultor and the Augustan Forum from the spoils of war." Augustus, Res Gestae (XXI).

309 Alternatively depicted as the sister, daughter, or companion of Mars, Bellona was popular with Roman soldiers. At a temple dedicated to her on the Campus Martius, Rome officially declared war when a spear was hurled over one of its columns, appropriately named the Column of War. The Roman writer Virgil describes her as carrying a bloodstained scourge or whip. Her name derives from the Latin "bellum," meaning war. See www.thaliatook.com that archives "The Obscure Goddess Online Directory" for a detailed description.

310 Greene, *The Inner Planets*, p. 185.

311 "There is a fascinating legend about the scorpion. If you corner him, and give him no avenue for escape, he will sting himself to death. This sounds a little apocryphal. But I have seen it happen. Once in the south of France I watched a group of children surround a small brown scorpion with sticks, so that it was completely trapped. It committed suicide. The message here is that Scorpio would rather destroy himself, and go down in flames by his own hand—literally or psychologically—than submit to another's ultimatum or control. 'Better to reign in hell,' as Lucifer says in Milton's *Paradise Lost* (Milton had Scorpio rising), 'than to serve in heaven.'" Greene, *Star Signs for Lovers*, pp. 426–7. Significantly, Lady Macbeth does commit suicide at the end of the play and Macbeth goes to certain death rather than submit to being displayed in defeat before the conquering troops.

312 Cirlot, p. 272.

313 Ibid., p. 273.

314 The first water sign, Cancer, is correlated with flowing water, while the second water sign, Scorpio, is imaged as ice, and the third water sign, Pisces, is represented by mist and fog as well as the ocean.

315 Frye, *Fools of Time*, p. 85.

316 http://internationalpsychoanalysis.net/wp-content/uploads/2009/02/shamegilligan.pdf, p. 3. His biography on apbsspeakers.com notes that his "theory is able to explain the whole range of violent behaviors, from individual (homicide and suicide) to collective (war, terrorism and genocide), and enables doctors to devise and test practical methods for the prevention of violence. Through his work preventing violence among the most violent people our society produces, in prisons and prison mental hospitals, he has become one of the leading exponents of shifting our emphasis from punishing violence after it occurs to preventing it before it happens."

317 James Gilligan, *Violence: Our Deadly Epidemic and Its Causes*, New York: Putnam's, 1996, pp. 231–2.

318 David S. Katz, *The Occult Tradition: From the Renaissance to the Present Day*, London: Pimlico, 2007, pp. 1–2.

319 Magic is often divided into two types, white and black, but defining each is highly contentious and varies with location, time period, and personal interpretation. White magic is presumed to be that which operates for the good of the practitioner and others, as in healing or prophecy, and that which furthers your spiritual evolution. Some would consider Jesus a white magician since he performed such miracles as turning water into wine, healing the blind, walking on water, and bringing the dead back to life. Black magic, on the other hand, is thought to be that which harms others, by for instance invoking curses, or operates only selfishly to advance your own interests or increase your power

over others. Contemporary popular culture has distorted our understanding of magic, concentrating more on the black side than the white.

320 *There is Nothing Like a Thane!: The Lighter Side of Macbeth*, Compiled and illustrated by Clive Francis, New York: St. Martin's Press (Thomas Dunne Books), 2001, p. 9.

321 Ibid., p. 40.

322 *The Complete Plays and Poems of William Shakespeare*, ed. Neilson and Hill, commentary, p. 1181.

323 Isaac Asimov, *Asimov's Guide to Shakespeare*, New Jersey: Wings (Random), 1970, Volume 2, pp. 160, 161. Asimov highlights the historical version of the story of Macbeth and Shakespeare's changes to it. Another instance of the use of this same classical tradition occurs in Charles Dickens' *A Christmas Carol*, when he creates three spirits to reform Scrooge: the spirit of Christmas Past, of Christmas Present, and Christmas to come.

324 Beelzebub, sometimes translated as "lord of the flies," was variously described as a rebel angel, a leading demon of Hell, or Lucifer itself.

325 Bear-baiting was a popular entertainment in Shakespeare's day; a bear would be chained to a post in the center of a pit and dogs would be released to attack it. Bets were placed on whether the bear or the dogs would survive the fight. Both Henry VIII and Queen Elizabeth I were fans of the sport.

326 Henry Cornelius Agrippa of Nettesheim, *Three Books of Occult Philosophy*, Completely Annotated with Modern Commentary, trans. James Freake, Ed. and Annotated by Donald Tyson, St. Paul, MN: Llewellyn Publications, 1995. See Book I, Chapter XXVII (27), "What things are under the power of Mars, and are called martial," p. 89.

Chapter 11

The Hidden Astrological Key to The Tempest:
Pisces and its (traditional) Ruler Jupiter (and Modern Ruler Neptune)

327 Garber, *Shakespeare After All*, p. 856.

328 Goddard, Vol. II, p. 287.

329 See "The Number Seven—as in the Seven Classical Planets" in Chapter 3.

330 See Chapter 2, the section on "The Phlegmatic Type: Keyed to Water and the Moon." Such a character would be "patient," "easy-going," and "placid."

331 In Shakespeare's time, sleep and dream states were correlated with the Moon; that is why they feature so prominently in *A Midsummer Night's Dream*, a play keyed to the Moon. But they are archetypally relevant to *The Tempest* too since Neptune rules altered states of consciousness.

332 Yates was one of the first in modern times to suggest that Shakespeare was inspired by the brilliant Dee: "It is inevitable and unavoidable in thinking of Prospero to bring in the name of John Dee, the great mathematical magus of whom Shakespeare must have known, the teacher of Philip Sidney, and deeply in the confidence of Queen Elizabeth I." Yates, *Shakespeare's Last Plays*, p. 95. Yates mentions points raised by an Italian scholar, Furio Jesi, in support of this: "[Jesi] notes that Prospero, like Dee, had a library and was a bibliophile, and that, like Dee, he produced a theatrical performance using mechanical contrivances, the masque in *The Tempest* being compared with Dee's production of a performance at Trinity College, Cambridge, involving use of a flying machine on account of which he was accused of magic. Prospero, like Dee, was a magus ..." Ibid., p. 117.

Dee's library was the finest in England, even better than the university libraries, reminding us how much Prospero prizes his library.

333 French, p. 177.

334 Dee was also an astrologer (he set the time for Elizabeth I's coronation) and a spiritual philosopher who wished to learn the language of the angels. His association with the disreputable Edward Kelly, a charlatan, blackened his reputation, making the suspicious think that Dee was a "black magician." Only in the past one hundred years have his intellectual talents and contributions to English society been recognized.

335 See the chapter on "Antecedents of The Tempest" in Woodman, pp. 64–72, which concentrates on figures similar to Prospero in contemporary Renaissance drama.

336 Jung, *Archetypes and the Collective Unconscious*, p. 10.

337 Woodman, pp. 11–2.

338 Ibid., p. 12–3.

339 Richard Smoley and Jay Kinney, *Hidden Wisdom: A Guide to the Western Inner Traditions*, NY: Penguin/Arkana, 1999, p. 112.

340 Because air and fire are elements of the "upper world," higher in the hierarchy than heavier earth and water, they are often more exalted. As G. Wilson Knight discerns,

> ... Shakespeare's imagery of those excelling qualities in men,
> his aspiring pride, his soldiership, his love, his athletic grace,
> beauty of form, [references] all that is "air and fire" rather than
> sluggish "earth and water.".. In *The Tempest*, this facet of the
> Shakespearian imagination clearly receives a final impress in
> Ariel. Ariel, too, is a spirit of air and fire, of fire and music;
> yet able to penetrate the earth itself and dive within the sea.
> He is a spirit of beauty and active grace. He is aptly set beside

Caliban. In Ariel we find the consummation of this Shake-spearian intuition of winged beauty, air, fire, and music.

Knight, *Shakespearian Tempest*, p. 319.

341 The Oxford World's Classics edition of *The Tempest* cites Vincenzo Cartari in a Venetian manuscript dated 1571: "those who say that the ancients worshipped the elements under the names of various gods call Juno the air." *The Tempest*, The Oxford Shakespeare, edited by Stephen Orgel, 1987, p. 48, n. 1.

342 Smoley and Kinney, p. 118.

343 Woodman, pp. 28–9.

344 "Through his wonder-working and healing, the figure of Christ appears as the legendary white magician par excellence. . . . The New Testament shows Christ curing the blind and the dumb and casting out devils. He miraculously creates an abundance of food from very little, transforms water into wine, and produces a gigantic haul of fish, all actions reminiscent of the tribal magician figure who ensured his people of a continued supply of food. Incidentally, the Apocrypha contains episodes in the childhood of Christ that also involved His use of magic." Ibid., p. 43.

345 See Woodman, Chapter 5 on "Prospero as the White Magician," pp. 73–86.

346 Smoley and Kinney, p. 118.

347 Mercy, compassion, and forgiveness are very highly valued qualities in the Christian religion, dominant in the West during the "Age of Pisces" or the constellation of the two fish. Though there is some controversy about the beginning and ending dates for this approximately 2,125-year time period, it is thought to span the past 2,000 years or so starting around the time that Christianity emerged. Christianity is characterized by Piscean symbolism, obvious examples being the disciples' description as fishermen, the miracle of the loaves and fishes, and Jesus walking on water.

348 Having Prospero cease his magical practices might also have enabled Shakespeare to escape condemnation from the orthodoxly religious and the Puritans of his time.

349 Jung, *Archetypes and the Collective Unconscious*, pp. 251–2.

Chapter 12

The Hidden Astrological Key to King Lear: the Sign Capricorn and its Ruler Saturn

350 Note on the Text of *King Lear*: Of all Shakespeare's plays, *King Lear* presents the most challenges in establishing an "authentic" text. All of the plays present problems, but most are of minor significance. Not so with *King Lear*. Knowing about printing practices in Shakespeare's time in general and about

the history of this play's printing in particular reveals why. Surprising to us, "There was in the sixteenth and early seventeenth centuries a social stigma attached to print. Far from celebrating publication, authors . . . often apologized for exposing themselves to the public gaze." Stephen Greenblatt, General Introduction, *The Norton Shakespeare*, p. 12. When Ben Jonson oversaw publication of all his collected works in 1616, he was mocked partly for his vanity and partly because he published them as a folio, a larger form reserved for serious publications like the Bible.

Writers of plays in particular were disparaged. Christopher Marlowe, creator of such popular dramas as *Tamburlaine the Great*, *The Jew of Malta*, and *The Tragicall History of the Life and Death of Doctor Faustus*, was described as a "poet and a filthy playmaker." Laurie Maguire and Emma Smith, *30 Great Myths About Shakespeare*, West Sussex, Wiley-Blackwell, 2013, p. 27. Poetry, on the other hand, had a much higher reputation. It was written by gentlemen, who circulated their writings in manuscript to be read privately by their friends at court, unlike plays that were performed by profit-making companies for viewing by a vulgar public.

Only half of the plays attributed to Shakespeare were published during his lifetime and the earliest of them do not have his name attached as author. See Maguire and Smith, "Myth 1: Shakespeare was the most popular writer of his time," p. 8 and "Myth 4: Shakespeare was not interested in having his plays printed," p. 28–9. Once dramatists sold a play to a theater company, the shareholders owned it and could do whatever they pleased with it. If it was printed, as Maguire and Smith comment, "The selling point of a play was its theater company: the marketing point that promised success for a printed play was the stage on which it had been successful." Ibid., p. 29. Since copyright laws did not exist until the eighteenth century, playwrights of Shakespeare's time knew that once their work was released into the wider world, they had lost any right to it.

Shakespeare himself does not seem to have had any interest in publishing his plays: he left no copies of them, does not mention them in his will, and there is no verifiable record of him supervising the publication of any of them while he was alive. For a more detailed discussion of the status of dramatists and the history of play-printing in Shakespeare's time, see Maguire and Smith, "Myth 4: Shakespeare was not interested in having his plays printed," pp. 26–33.

Printed plays might have been circulated because they were not being performed any longer and so it did not matter if rival companies got hold of them. Or the theater company might have needed money and printing plays provided an additional source of income. Or plays got into print because actors secretly sold their copies to printers. Variations in the different printings (some minor but others quite dramatic) might occur because plays were shortened for performance or because actors wrote the lines down incorrectly. We do not know which of the variants was the original or who might have cut or expanded the plays since they were published over a period of years. It all increases the mystery surrounding this extraordinary body of work and adds to the miracle that it has survived at all.

Determining the "right" text of *King Lear* is a particular problem because two rather different versions exist. *King Lear* was one of Shakespeare's plays that was published, first in 1608 in a Quarto edition entitled *M. William Shakspeare: His True Chronicle Historie of the life and death of King Lear.* Quartos were smaller books, with each sheet folded twice, making four leaves or eight pages so that each page is the size of one-fourth of the sheet. ("Quarto" means "fourth" in Latin; in the imperial measuring system for liquids, a "quart" is one-fourth of a gallon.) The second version of *King Lear* appeared when John Heminges and Henry Condell, Shakespeare's fellow actors, collected the plays attributed to him and published them in a folio edition in 1623. Folios were created by folding a printing sheet only once, forming four pages or two leaves. Since folios used more paper and were bigger and more expensive to print than Quartos, publishing a folio announced a work's value and importance.

In the First Folio, though, the version of *King Lear* (there entitled *The Tragedie of King Lear*) has some striking differences from the Quarto. The earlier edition has approximately three hundred lines that do not appear in the later Folio, and the later Folio has about a hundred lines that are not printed in the Quarto. As well, there are dozens of differences in phrasing and stage directions. Some are unimportant, but others drastically shape our interpretation of and response to the play. Once the differences were noticed during the eighteenth century, editors assumed that the two versions were variants of an original play that contained all the lines and put them together into one play—a "conflated" text that until recently was the accepted one. Only in the last twenty years or so have scholars agitated for separate printings of the two. *The Norton Shakespeare* (based on the Oxford edition) publishes not only the Quarto and Folio renditions separately but also a new amalgamation by Barbara K. Lewalski. All of the quotations I cite from *King Lear* are from the conflated text in that edition.

To make the challenge of determining a definitive text even more complicated, the surviving twelve copies of *King Lear* in earlier Quarto form all have differences in phrasing and punctuation. For more information on the history of *King Lear*'s publication, see *The Norton Shakespeare*, "Textual Note" to *King Lear*, pp. 2332–3.

The First Folio of 1623 is certainly a more polished text. It makes clear distinctions between prose and poetry, has more consistent spelling, and more specific stage directions. It also divides the play into acts and scenes. But the inclusion of the extra lines (and omission of lines from the Quarto) has created heated debate among scholars.

In *The Shakespeare Wars: Clashing Scholars, Public Fiascoes, Palace Coups*, Ron Rosenbaum, a journalist and writer for the *New Yorker* magazine, has written passionately and entertainingly about the violent debates over Shakespeare's writing and his intentions. One of the most contentious issues is the ending of *King Lear*. Lear is given words to speak in the Folio that are not in the Quarto, and the last line given to him in the Quarto is allotted to Kent in the Folio. So here is the dilemma. Are both versions by Shakespeare? If so, why the differences? Is the later Folio version really a rewrite by him? Or could the differences in wording be due to changes or choices made by a theater manager, an editor, a playwright-in-training, or one of Shakespeare's collaborators—not by Shakespeare himself? This raises some interesting questions about what is considered "Shakespearean" and what an author's intentions might be in a particular work.

Steven Urkowitz, a CCNY professor and professional theater director, commented to Rosenbaum that when a director is confronted with the choice of which of the two *King Lear*'s to present on stage, "in each case it's a choice that requires an esthetic strategy or theory about why one includes and omits what one does." Ron Rosenbaum, *The Shakespeare Wars: Clashing Scholars, Public Fiascoes, Palace Coups*, NY, Random House, 2006, p. 144. Maintaining the approach taken in this book, I have chosen to draw on whatever in each version is consistent with the archetypal pattern that I believe to be the underlying foundation for the play.

351 Costello, *Weiser Concise Guide*, p. 24. Emphasis added.

352 "Capricorn's soaring ambitions, shrewd mind, and ways of understanding the true value of objects and services usually bring him to some seat of authority during his lifetime. He is often the director, the president, the manager, the boss. More presidents of the United States have been born with their Sun or Moon in Capricorn than in any other sign.

"The personal goal of the Capricorn leader is most important. If he uses his power for self-aggrandizement at the expense of others, he can be a force of great destruction. (Stalin and Goring had their Sun in Capricorn while Hitler and Goebbels had Capricorn Moons.) If he is a true humanitarian, he sees himself as the vehicle through which a higher power flows and he then directs that flow to aid mankind with his leadership. Such great beings as Joan of Arc, Benjamin Franklin, Martin Luther King, Albert Schweitzer, and Swami Satchidananda were born under the sign of the Sea-Goat." Alan Oken, *Alan Oken's Complete Astrology*, rev. ed., New York: Bantam Books, 1988, p. 147. Oken accurately captures the potential extremes embedded in the sign.

353 Queen Elizabeth exhibited Saturnine traits even at an early age. "She has an air of authority and reflectiveness astonishing in an infant," Winston Churchill said after meeting the two-year-old princess.

354 Liz Greene, *Star Signs for Lovers*, p. 270.

355 J. G. McKay, "The Language of Birds," in *A Fairy Tale Reader: A Collection of Story, Lore and Vision*, Chosen and edited by John and Caitlin Matthews, Forward by R. J. Stewart, London: Aquarian Press (HarperCollins), 1993, p. 137.

356 See Jonathan Bate, *Shakespeare and Ovid*, Oxford, Clarendon Press, 1993.

357 This story is told by Hesiod in his *Works and Days*, and recounted by Robert Graves in *The Greek Myths: Volume 1*, London: Penguin, 1960 (rev. ed.), section 6, "The Castration of Uranus," pp. 17–9.

358 Amilcare A. Iannucci, "Saturn in Dante," in *Saturn from Antiquity to the Renaissance*, Massimo Ciavolella and Amilcare A. Iannucci, eds., Ottawa, Canada: Dovehouse editions (U. of Toronto Italian Studies, 8), 1992, p. 53.

359 Agrippa, p. 96.

360 Klibansky et al, p. 142.

361 Norrie Epstein, *The Friendly Shakespeare: A Thoroughly Painless Guide to the Best of the Bard*, New York: Penguin, 1993, p. 399.

362 This phrase comes from a poem by Alfred, Lord Tennyson, *In Memoriam A. H. H.*, Canto 56, written in 1850.

363 de Vore, p. 371.

364 Eclipses are mentioned in other plays, particularly at a crucial moment in *Othello*. Only seconds after smothering his wife Desdemona, the tragic enormity of his action falls upon Othello: "O, insupportable! O heavy hour!/ Methinks it should be now a huge eclipse/ Of sun and moon, and that th' affrighted globe/ Did yawn at alteration." (V, ii, 98–101) Since Heaven and Earth are connected, there must be disorder in the heavens at the moment of the innocent Desdemona's murder on Earth.

365 Mark Littmann, Ken Willcox, and Fred Espenak, *Totality: Eclipses of the Sun*, 2nd ed., New York: Oxford University Press, 1999, p. 44.

366 "What makes eclipses particularly noticeable is that they often presage the 'eclipse' of those in power. This is particularly the case with solar eclipses where we are, as it were, seeing the solar, authority, principle being cut off by the Moon, the regulator of earthly activities." Michael Baigent, Nicholas Campion, and Charles Harvey, *Mundane Astrology*, Wellingborough, Northamptonshire: The Aquarian Press, 1984, p. 267. The authors give the example of an inauspicious eclipse in the horoscope of U.S. President John F. Kennedy: "Taking the case of Kennedy's assassination, is it simply coincidence that on 20 July 1963 at 20.43 GMT there was a total solar eclipse at 27 CN (Cancer) 24 exactly conjunct Kennedy's natal SA (Saturn) 27 CN 09 in his tenth house? This is the classic picture of a 'fall from power.'"

367 Littmann et al, p. 35.

368 Eclipses occur at the time of a lunation when the Moon and Sun align. Lunations happen once a month, but an eclipse occurs only when the Sun, Moon, and Earth are aligned, an event dependent on where the Moon is in its orbit. The lunar orbit is inclined to the plane of the ecliptic (the apparent path of the Sun around the Earth) by 5°, which is why we do not have eclipses every month.

The two opposite points where the lunar orbit intersects the plane of the ecliptic are called the lunar nodes. The point where the Moon's orbit is moving from south of the ecliptic to north of it is called, naturally enough, "the ascending node." It is also dubbed "the dragon's head" or Caput Draconis, "draco" meaning "dragon" in Latin. (In *Harry Potter and the Philosopher's Stone*, J.K. Rowling makes "Caput Draconis" the password enabling first-year Gryffindor students to get into their dorm. She also chooses an apt first name for the villain of the story, Draco Malfoy.) The descending node, where the Moon's orbit is moving from north of the ecliptic to the south of it is called, logically, "the dragon's tail" or Cauda Draconis. Eclipses can only happen when the Moon is close to one or the other of these points. See the entry on "Eclipse" in the *Larousse Encyclopedia of Astrology*, pp. 99–102. See also John Filbey, D. F. Astrol. S. and Peter Filbey, B. Sc., *Astronomy for Astrologers*, Wellingborough, Northamptonshire: The Aquarian Press, p. 112–114, 190–1. No matter whether an eclipse happens near the ascending or descending node, the belief was that people's lives, especially those of rulers or prominent people, could be adversely affected or "eaten up" by the energy of an eclipse.

Robert Carl Jansky, who was a biochemistry and bacteriological researcher and involved with the Mercury and Apollo space programs from 1961 to 1965, offers a theory that explains the effect of eclipses: "Magnetic energy is just one form of a vast spectrum of energy which we call electromagnetic energy. Other forms of electromagnetic energy include infra-red, ultra-violet, x-rays, light rays, radio waves and so on. . . . We live constantly in a vast sea of electromagnetic energy every minute of our lives, the constitution of which varies from place to place. . . .

"Where does all of this electromagnetic energy originate? Much of it is of course produced by the Sun . . . A substantial proportion also originates from within our own galaxy of stars, the Milky Way . . . This energy is loosely referred to as either 'galactic' or 'cosmic' energy.

"The composition of this field changes from moment to moment due to the movement of all of the planetary and cosmic bodies in our universe. . . . We've also observed that sunspots radically alter the character of the Earth's ionosphere and magnetic field in measurable ways and affect radio transmission. And in the 1930's Takata in Japan demonstrated that the state of the Earth's electromagnetic field also influences the properties of the only substance capable of life, of which we are all composed, protein. . . .

"If the weather can influence our personality and behavior, as we've all observed that it does, it is no strain at all on the credulity and logic to understand that a cause and effect relationship exists between the status of our galaxy and solar system and our human behavior. Or, if not a direct cause and effect relationship, at least a correspondence exists between what goes on out in space and what is happening down here on the surface of the Earth.

"Whereas many of the changes in the electromagnetic field about the Earth are rather subtle from minute to minute, to have the major source of electromagnetic energy to the Earth suddenly blocked off, either partially or completely, for a short time is anything but subtle. It is drastic indeed, and for the ancients who did not understand what was happening it was traumatic and awe-inspiring. With today's advanced technology we are able to measure some rather vast changes in the character of the Earth's electromagnetic field during this blocking off of the Sun during an eclipse." Robert Carl Jansky, *Interpreting the Eclipses*, San Diego, CA: Astro Computing Services, 1977, pp. 3–5.

369 Fred Gettings, *The Arkana Dictionary of Astrology*, London, England: Arkana (Penguin Group), 1990, p. p 483.

370 Cirlot, entry on "Dragon," p. 82.

371 In the last book of the New Testament, in Revelation 12:7–9, Michael and his angels fight against the dragon. In Rev. 20:1–3 an angel descends from heaven, lays hold of the dragon, "that old serpent, who is the Devil and Satan," and binds him a thousand years, casting him into a bottomless pit.

372 Peter Hogarth with Val Clery, *Dragons*, Middlesex, England: Penguin Books, 1980, p. 72.

373 Whether Edmund has in mind the Moon's south node, identified with the tail of the dragon, or the constellation Draco, the symbolism is consistent. According to Agrippa, who gathered all sorts of esoteric lore in his compendious *Three Books of Occult Philosophy*, the astrological dragon's tail introduced "anguish, infirmity and misfortune; and [the Egyptians and Phoenicians] called it the evil genius." Agrippa considered Saturn, the dragon, and the northern constellation Draco to be symbolically linked, so that associations with any of them are negative. Agrippa, p. 99 and p. 101, n. 56. See also Chapter XLV in Book Two entitled "Of the images of the Head and Tail of the Dragon of the Moon," pp. 390–1.

374 Klibansky et al, p. 130.

375 Hogarth and Clery, p. 117.

376 Littmann et al, p. 44.

377 Hogarth and Clery, p. 45.

378 Ibid., p. 61. The authors do not identify the source of this or the culture from which it comes, but this same quotation is cited in Francis Huxley, *the dragon: nature of spirit, spirit of nature*, New York: Collier Books (Macmillan), 1979, p. 59 and is credited to Wang Fu.

379 Agrippa, p. 73.

380 Citing Elizabethan moral theorists, Lily B. Campbell makes a persuasive case for *King Lear* being a "Tragedy of Wrath in Old Age." But Elizabethan thinkers believed that an "unnatural" humor could be created from any one of them. As Tillyard explains, "There was also the terrible possibility of a humor not merely existing to excess, as in a perfectly sane man with some marked

idiosyncrasy, but going bad. A humor could both putrefy or be burnt with excessive heat. The most famous kind of corrupt humor was the burnt or adust; and *melancholy adust* was the name usually given to it even if it was one of the other humors that had been impaired." Tillyard, p. 70–1. Campbell cites Sir Thomas Elyot's *Castle of Health*: ". . . that melancholy is worst, which is engendered of choler . . . For when that humour is hot, it makes men mad . . ." Campbell, p. 75. I have modernized the spelling. I believe that Lear is displaying choler transformed into "melancholy adust." This accords with Aristotle's distinction between "hot (or sanguine) melancholy, which sometimes causes madness, and cold melancholy, which causes 'torpidity and despondency.'" Cited in John L. Lepage, *The Revival of Antique Philosophy in the Renaissance*, New York, NY: Palgrave [Macmillan], 2012, p. 96. Lear's melancholy is obviously of the "hot" type.

381 Draper, p. 95.

382 Klibansky et al., p. 127. I have drawn on this ground-breaking work for much of this section. It is amusingly apt, as Klibansky reveals in his Preface, that in line with Saturn's associations with obstacles and difficulties the preparation of their book was "beset by delay and adversity" at every stage. I had a similar experience with this chapter.

383 Timothy Bright's *Treatise of Melancholy* published in London in 1586 fueled Elizabethan interest in this temperament. Some scholars theorize that Shakespeare read Bright's book and that it influenced his creation of the character of Hamlet. The publication of Richard Burton's *The Anatomy of Melancholy* in 1621 attests to the fact that ideas about melancholia were circulating around that time. Tillyard notes that Burton's treatise actually focuses not on the normal melancholy but on melancholy adust. Tillyard, p. 71.

384 Klibansky, et al., p. 14.

385 Ibid., pp. 255, 256.

386 Ibid., p. 258. The word "bitter" is noteworthy for Lear complains that his jester is a "bitter" Fool, as would be appropriate in a Saturn-dominated play. Cordelia's calling for music at the moment of Lear's awakening is also telling, since this was a standard antidote to melancholia as Shakespeare's audience would have known.

387 "Because [as mentioned in the early Aristotelian text Problemata XXX] . . . the melancholic humour was at once hot and cold, and thus inconstant, its effects included a wide range of disturbances, ranging from apoplexy to torpor if the subject had a generally cold temperament, and from elation to singing, excessive enthusiasm, and even madness if the subject had a generally hot temperament." Arikha, p. 120.

388 Ibid., pp. 31–5.

389 Ibid., 41.

390 Ibid., p. 252.

391 Spurgeon, p. 342.

392 Parr, pp. 26–7. Parr is referring to astrological tradition as found in the writings of Claudius Ptolemy, several Arabic astrologers, and Guido Bonatti, a fifteenth-century astrologer.

393 Jolande Jacobi, *The Psychology of C. G. Jung: An Introduction with Illustrations*, New Haven and London: Yale U. Press, 1962, 1973, p. 29.

394 For a comprehensive alphabetical list of terms from Jung's psychology, see www.terrapsych.com/jungdefs.html. On this list, the ego is defined as "the conscious self; the 'I'; the central, experience-filtering complex of consciousness (in contrast to the Self, the central complex of the collective unconscious)—and the most stable complex because it is grounded in the body sensations. A relatively permanent personification. The most individual part of the person." Terms in italics are defined elsewhere on that list.

395 Jacobi, p. 112.

396 Ibid., p. 110.

397 Ibid., p. 111.

398 This initiatory pattern of progressive stripping away of one's possessions and powers is similar to a myth told about the Sumerian goddess Inanna, the most prominent female deity of ancient Mesopotamia. Wanting to descend to the underworld where her enemy and sister-goddess Ereshkigal is queen, the goddess adorns herself with garments and jewels. Once below, at each of seven gates she is divested of each of them, until she stands naked before her sister who turns her into a corpse and hangs her from a hook. She is ultimately rescued and revived by being sprinkled with the food and water of life.

As Joseph Campbell comments, "The hero, whether god or goddess, man or woman, the figure in a myth or the dreamer of a dream, discovers and assimilates his opposite (his own unsuspected self) either by swallowing it or by being swallowed. One by one the resistances are broken. He must put aside his pride, his virtue, beauty, and life, and bow or submit to the absolutely intolerable . . . . The original departure into the land of trials represented only the beginning of the long and really perilous path of initiatory conquests and moments of illumination. *Dragons* have now to be slain and surprising barriers passed—again, again, and again." Emphasis added. Joseph Campbell, *The Hero with a Thousand Faces*, Cleveland: The World Publishing Company 1949, 1956, p. 108–9. Campbell discusses the story of Inanna's descent on pp. 105–9. See also Sylvia Brinton Perera, *Descent to the Goddess: A Way of Initiation for Women*, Toronto, Canada: Inner City Books, 1981. Her book concentrates exclusively on the Inanna myth, interpreted in light of contemporary psychology and addressed specifically to women.

399 "Bedlam" refers to the hospital of St. Mary at Bethlehem for the insane in London. "Bethlehem" was shortened to "bedlam" which not only refers to a madhouse but is also metaphorically any place or experience of noisy confusion and chaos.

400 A description of the Apocalypse with all its dramatic imagery constitutes the final book of the Bible, the Revelation of St. John. "1 And I saw an angel come down from heaven, having the key of the bottomless pit and a great chain in his hand. 2 And he laid hold on the dragon, that old serpent, who is the Devil and Satan, and bound him a thousand years . . . " Rev. 20, 1–2. KJV. A similar motif occurs in the Norse account of Ragnarok, the twilight of the gods and the end of the world. The great serpent of Midgard, long ago thrown into the depths of the ocean, begins to lash about, flooding the land and blowing clouds of poison that spatter the earth and sky. Though it is finally slain by Thor, son of the chief god Odin, Thor is overcome by the serpent's toxic breath and falls dead. Earth and Heaven are consumed by fire, but after a time "the earth will rise again, green and fair, from the sea. A few gods will have survived, or will be raised from the dead, and will return to the heaven of Asgard. A man and a woman, too, will have escaped oblivion. And so the universe can begin again." Hogarth and Clery, p. 93.

401 Spurgeon, pp. 338–9. Pp. 339–43 give many examples. She also notes the prevalence of animal images, suggesting that humanity is " 'reeling back into the beast' ," as well as images describing the fury of the elements. This accords with the worldview espoused by Shakespeare that sees unrestrained indulgence of the passions as a retrogression to the more primitive level of animals and likely to be reflected in upheavals in nature.

402 Goddard, Vol. 2, p. 151.

403 Garber, *Shakespeare After All*, p. 691.

404 In the Restoration period Irish playwright and adapter Nahum Tate (1652–1715) drastically changed Shakespeare's story, omitting the Fool and the King of France, reinstating Lear on his throne, and allowing Cordelia to live at the end to marry Edgar. Tate's revision of *King Lear*, first performed in 1681, was the version staged for over a hundred and fifty years.

405 Goneril swears at the very start of the play that she loves her father "Dearer than eye-sight" (I, i, 54). Kent urges Lear to "See better, Lear; and let me still remain/ The true blank of thine eye." (I, i, 158–9) Lear protests Goneril's criticism of his unruly knights by asking, "Doth any here know me? This is not Lear./ Doth Lear walk thus? speak thus? Where are his eyes?" (I, iv, 201–2). As the source of tears, Lear rebukes his eyes for revealing that Goneril has "shaken his manhood," vowing, "Old fond eyes,/ Beweep this cause again, I'll pluck ye out . . ." (I, iv, 278–9)—an easily unnoticed yet terrible anticipation of what happens to Gloucester. References to eyes, sight, and blindness are heaped up

in this play, not only to eyes as tear-shedders that express grief but as organs of perception that see beyond the physical.

406 Goddard expands on these ideas, giving five reasons why we should see Lear's final words as evidence of a higher state of consciousness and not as delusional. Lear is an old man. He has suffered terribly, so that "To the vision and wisdom of old age are added the vision and wisdom of misery." Next, he is dying. He has also gone mad. And finally, he has been reborn into a second childhood, gifted with the simplicity and directness of perception characteristic of an innocent child. See Goddard, vol. 2, pp. 163–7. The quotation is on p. 164.

407 From C. G. Jung, *Mysterium Coniunctionis*, CW 14, paragraph 330, cited in Edinger, p. 42.

408 Gellius, cited in Klibansky et al, p. 8.

409 Ibid., p. 32.

410 Ibid., p. 41.

411 Ibid., p. 73. The writer cited is William of Auvergne, Bishop of Paris from 1228 to 1249. William was one of the first in the Latin West to read and respond to the philosophical writings of Greek, Islamic, and Jewish thinkers translated during the "twelfth-century Renaissance."

412 From Cardan's *De rerum varietate*, IX, 84. Mentioned in Lynn Thorndike, *A History of Magic and Experimental Science*. Vol. V: The Sixteenth Century. NY: Columbia U. Press, 1941, p. 575.

Summing Up: Celestial Design Then and Now

413 John Vyvyan, *Shakespeare and the Rose of Love: A Study of the Early Plays in Relation to the Medieval Philosophy of Love*, London, England: Shepheard-Walwyn Ltd., (1960), 2013, p. 176.

414 G. Wilson Knight, *Shakespearian Production: with especial reference to the Tragedies*, London: Routledge & Kegan Paul Ltd., 1968, p 40.

415 Fritjof Capra, *The Tao of Physics: An Exploration of the Parallels between Modern Physics and Eastern Mysticism*, Fourth ed., updated, Boston: Shambhala, 2000, p. 325.

416 Malcolm Hollick, *The Science of Oneness: A Worldview for the Twenty-First Century*, Hants., U.K.: O Books, 2006, p. 55.

417 It is fascinating to note that when Bohr was awarded the Order of the Elephant by the Danish king in 1947, he designed his own coat of arms featuring the motto "contraria sunt complementa," or "opposites are complementary"—a fundamental principle of the astrological worldview.

418 Capra, p. 310. Emphasis added.

419 Ibid., p. 313.

420 Ibid., pp. 318–9. Emphasis added.

421 Ibid., p. 320.

422 Bernadette Brady in *Astrology, A Place in Chaos* explores the similarities between concepts in modern physics and astrological theory. Fractals, for example, which are repeating patterns and shapes of nature that are the building blocks of life and landscape, are analogous to patterns within a horoscope. See Bernadette Brady, *Astrology, A Place in Chaos*, Bournemouth, England: The Wessex Astrologer, 2006 for an extensive discussion of the relevance of fractals, phase portraits, and the concepts of self-similarity and scale invariance (among others) to astrological theory.

423 G. Wilson Knight, *Shakespearian Production with especial reference to the Tragedies*, London: Routledge & Kegan Paul Ltd., 1968, p. 35.

Alchemy Appendix

424 Since it was especially magnified during the Middle Ages, Elizabethans would have been familiar with the sadistic and horrifying imagery of sinners being tortured in Hell: drenched in rivers of fire or ice, weeping and gnashing their teeth, writhing in agony as their entrails are pierced by iron hooks or their lips cut off with red-hot razors or their bodies eaten from the inside out by worms. But there are some significant differences between alchemical and religious traditions. For one, adherents to the alchemical path engage in its practices *voluntarily* while sinners are subject *involuntarily* to a higher judgment and the consequent punishments imposed by an angry God. Consequently, the purgatorial experiences of the alchemical stages have little connection to morality; they are undergone not as a punishment for sins but as a process consciously engaged in to effect change in oneself and in the world. The alchemists' goals were not only to transform themselves but also to perfect nature itself and to create a universal panacea that was a "heal-all." Such practices have impersonal as well as personal goals. Too, the wicked are damned to eternal torment in Hell while the sufferer in the alchemical process eventually progresses through the various stages to be released and reborn in a purified and higher state of being.

425 Nicholl elaborates on alchemy's pervasiveness: "Whether conceived of as a magic, a science, a folly or a crime, it cannot be denied that alchemy was a forceful presence in Shakespearean England. . . . It was a phenomenon of the age, pursued not only by the doughty alchemist *per se*, but by a host of enthusiastic amateurs that included some of the most famous names of the day." Nicholl's list includes Dr. John Dee and Dr. Robert Fludd, as well as astrologer Simon Forman, who prepared medicines using alchemical formulae. Sir Walter Raleigh's interest in alchemy was also for preparation of medicinal distillates, which he

may have taken with him on his voyages. Other "famous dabblers" include poet Sir Philip Sidney and poet and diplomat Edward Dyer, both closely associated with John Dee. Other nobles in Queen Elizabeth's court were also intrigued: Sidney's uncle, the Earl of Leicester; Sidney's sister Mary Herbert, Countess of Pembroke who employed Raleigh's half brother in her home-based laboratory; and Henry Percy, the "Wizard Earl" of Northumberland. Charles Nicholl, *The Chemical Theatre*, London: Routledge & Kegan Paul, 1980, pp. 14–5, 16. Queen Elizabeth herself is rumored to have kept a personal alchemist: according to Edward Dyer, around 1566 the Queen's private alchemist was Cornelius de Lannoy. Nicoll, p. 18. Royal interest in alchemy is understandable if the alchemists could in fact produce gold, since royals always seemed to be cash-strapped.

426 Hogarth and Clery, p. 127. Emphasis added.

427 Johannes Fabricius, *Alchemy: The Medieval Alchemists and their Royal Art*, Wellingborough, England: The Aquarian Press (Thorsons), 1976, p. 26.

428 For a fine introduction to physical alchemy, still practiced today, see Brian Cotnoir, *Alchemy*, part of The Weiser Concise Guide Series, edited and introduced by James Wasserman, San Francisco, CA: Weiser Books, 2006.

429 Psychologist Carl Jung wrote extensively on alchemy, especially in *Psychology and Alchemy* (Volume 12 of his Collected Works), *Alchemical Studies* (Volume 13 of his CW), which has sections on the physician-alchemist Paracelsus and "The Spirit Mercurius," and in *Mysterium Coniunctionis: An Inquiry into the Separation and Synthesis of Psychic Opposites in Alchemy* (Volume 14 of his CW). For more readable explorations of psychological alchemy in light of Jungian psychology, see Edward F. Edinger, *Anatomy of the Psyche: Alchemical Symbolism in Psychotherapy*, La Salle, Illinois: Open Court, 1985, and Marie-Louise von Franz, *Alchemy: An Introduction to the Symbolism and the Psychology*, Toronto, Canada: Inner City Books, 1980.

430 For a good general introduction to the complex topic of alchemy, see Stanislas Klossowski de Rola, *Alchemy: The Secret Art*, London: Thames and Hudson, 1973; for one geared to the popular market, see Francis Melville, *The Book of Alchemy*, Hauppauge, N.Y.: Barron's, 2002. Both of these books are extensively illustrated.

431 Violet Staub de Laszlo, Introduction to *Psyche and Symbol: A Selection from the Writings of C. G. Jung*, edited by Violet S. de Laszlo, Garden City, N.Y.: Doubleday (Anchor), 1958, p. xxvi.

432 Cotnoir, p. 11. Inescapably, they were also working on themselves.

433 Alternatively, this epithet may derive from the ancient name given to Egypt, *Khem*, meaning "black," which referred to the dark silt deposited on the land each year by the Nile River. This is apropos since Egypt was thought to be the place where alchemy originated. See (no author given) *Alchemy: The Art of Knowing*, San Francisco: Chronicle Books, 1994, p. 18.

434 Liz Greene, "Alchemical Symbolism in the Horoscope," in Liz Greene and Howard Sasportas, *Dynamics of the Unconscious: Seminars in Psychological Astrology*, Vol. 2, York Beach, Maine: Samuel Weiser, 1988, p. 263. This essay, a transcript of a workshop, is an excellent introduction to psychological alchemy; it relates alchemy to astrology, and enlarges on the meaning of four particular states of the "Great Work": Calcinatio, Solutio, Coagulatio, and Sublimatio.

435 Francis Huxley, *The Dragon: Nature of Spirit, Spirit of Nature*, New York: Collier, 1979.

436 Edinger, p. 14.

437 Ibid., p 43.

438 Lear's tantrums that begin at this point resemble a two-year-old's. Age two just happens to be the time of the astrological phenomenon known as the first "Mars return," when the planet Mars, having apparently circled the zodiac in its approximate two-year cycle, comes back to the natal degree. This time period usually coincides with an eruption of the child's need for independence and autonomy, a stage known as the "terrible twos" when the child discovers the power of saying "no."

The Introduction to Section II discussed Mars as a constant secondary ruler of all the tragedies. In this particular tragedy Lear exhibits the explosive rage of Mars in the infantile form of petulant demands and violent resistances. His rage is exacerbated by the impotency of old age that is circling back to childhood, and so resembles this early stage.

439 Greene, pp. 279, 283.

440 Edinger compares the *calcinatio* experience to that of the metaphoric "refiners' fire" or baptism by fire, spoken of so frequently in the Bible. An instance is "But he knoweth the way that I take; when he hath tried me, I shall come forth as gold." (Job 23:10. See also Zechariah 13:9, Malachi 3:1–18, Isaiah 48:10, 1Peter 1:7, among others.) This certainly reminds us of the alchemists' goal of transforming lead to gold. In religious tradition, Edinger says, "Everywhere fire is associated with God." Edinger, p. 33.

A related story is told in the Bible's Book of Daniel, in the account of Babylonian King Nebuchadnezzar's burning fiery furnace. When the king sets up an image of gold and Daniel's three friends, Shadrach, Meshach, and Abednego, refuses to bow down and worship it, Nebuchadnezzar is so "full of fury" that he has them thrown into the furnace heated seven times hotter than normal. Yet against them "the fire had no power, nor was an hair of their head singed, neither were their coats changed" because they were protected by an angel who appeared in the furnace with them. (Daniel 3:19, 27) See Edinger's discussion of this account in which he identifies the king with "the power motive, the arbitrary authority of the inflated ego that undergoes *calcinatio* when its overwhelming pretensions are frustrated by the presence of the transpersonal authority (the God of Shadrach, Meshach, and Abednego)." Edinger suggests that the three survive because they are not acting on ego motives or identifying with their own or others' emotional reactions. Edinger, p. 23–5.

441 Nicholl, p. 152.

442 Ibid., p. 149.

443 Ibid., p. 163.

444 Ibid., p. 165.

445 Another observation made by Nicholl may also support an alchemical interpretation of the play. Lear refers to his "pelican daughters" (III, iv, 72), a reference to the belief at the time that mother pelicans wounded their own breasts in order to feed their brood on their own blood. Lear implies by this that his daughters have wounded him, cut him to the heart, and are bleeding the life from him. But "pelican" also refers to a type of alchemical vessel, whose delivery spouts lead back into the vessel itself, permitting a continuous process of evaporation and condensation, thus keeping the process "circulating." Nicholl, p. 148.

446 Nicholl, p. 141. This recalls the three steps of "the hero's journey": separation, initiation, and return, as explored exhaustively in Joseph Campbell's *The Hero with a Thousand Faces*, Cleveland, Ohio: The World Publishing Company, 1949, 1965.

INDEX

Page numbers in **bold type** indicate main discussion of an idea, topic, or characters. Illustrations are noted in italics. Characters are listed under the name of the play in which they appear unless they appear in more than one play.